CONFLICT IN THE CLASSROOM:

The Education of Emotionally Disturbed Children

Edited by

NICHOLAS J. LONG

Hillcrest Children's Center
Washington, D.C.

WILLIAM C. MORSE

University of Michigan

RUTH G. NEWMAN

School Research Project
Washington School of Psychiatry
Washington, D.C.

Wadsworth Publishing Company, Inc.
Belmont, California

L. C. Cat. Card No.: 65–23546

Printed in the United States of America

Third printing: July 1966

FOREWORD

Fritz Redl, Ph.D.

Emotional disturbance is a portfolio term that has come to cover a multitude of traits, behavior, and personality patterns. For instance, two types of children now included under this label don't belong there. Never mind how much they irritate or puzzle a teacher. Calling them "emotionally disturbed children" is inaccurate. Of course, in practice, they are probably among those most frequently so labeled. For, whenever a new diagnostic entity hits the terminological market, it is most tempting indeed, after wanting none of it for three decades, to start flinging it around and overusing it for the next two. Luckily, the term emotional disturbance is just about approaching the end phase of these "next two decades." This book, I think, is good evidence for this.

Back to our two types of children who must *not* have the label "emotionally disturbed child" wasted upon them. They form the end points of a continuum within which the term seems quite appropriate.

End-point 1: mental illness and characterological malformation of the extreme type. There are children about whom the diagnosis autism, childhood schizophrenia, psychosis—or whatever nomenclature a given clinic may be addicted to—leaves no doubts. There are others whose characterological malformation is by now so clear and well ingrained that the term "delinquent" is much too loose for them. What we deal with are premature schizophrenics or underage crooks. School professionals have a penchant for being polite and evasive and for playing it safe by subsuming them under the term "emotionally disturbed." For those cases, the term is a *euphemism*. Not that those children don't show behavior which fits the label well. But then, who would be surprised that schizophrenics act crazy, that crooks do delinquent things? To carry those children under the category "emotionally disturbed" is a disservice to them. It enables parents to fool themselves just a little longer about the severity of the state of affairs and the complexity of steps and facilities that are needed for their children's treatment and care. It allows the community to delude itself into the thought that these children have been taken care of by being put into a smaller class, another child-guidance clinic, or a playground or two. Worse, labeling them under this term discourages the classroom teacher, who begins to think that techniques perfectly suited for the emotionally disturbed children of the other types are perhaps no good at all, because they obviously are not enough or don't work with the ones I am now referring to. In short, if we deal with schizophrenic, psychotic, autistic children on the one hand and with severe character malformations on the other, *let's say so.* It is no help to talk about cancer in its later stages by politely mentioning that the "patient's health seems to be somewhat disturbed. . . ."

End-point 2: the hyperresilient ones. On the other end of the line of children who should not be labeled "emotionally disturbed" are the youngsters for whom we don't even have a name—so eager are we to fool ourselves about the real facts of life. I could call them, for lack of an accepted name, *the hyperresilient ones.*

While apologizing for introducing a new term when we are already flooded with an abundance of technical jargon, let me say which children I have in mind. A classroom teacher will recognize them at once. They are perfectly healthy—as normal, clinically speaking, as anyone might wish a youngster to be. In fact, besides being normal and healthy, they have a sharp nose for situations that are putrid, for life experiences that are sickening, for teacher or parent behavior that is downright impossible on any count. In short, these children quickly "smell" situations that are designed to make them nasty or sick. Their behavior is their means of preventing themselves from being either. They defend themselves against threats to their own inner balance. Let us assume somebody tries to push safety pins, or anything that the organism happens to know is poisonous, down a person's throat. What will the first reaction be? The person thus treated will gag; the organism invaded will regurgitate. In such a case we are not dealing with a sick stomach. We are dealing with a perfectly healthy one that is only defending itself against being made sick. The situation, however, isn't quite so simple as it sounds, for it confronts us with a puzzling problem. Haven't we learned that gagging and regurgitating is *also* symptomatic of disease? It certainly is—but not with these children. In their case, it is the opposite. It is the sign that the organism grasps for *desperate means to ward off danger from without.*

Confronted with a severe threat to their internal balance and organic integrity, some children ward off the dangerous stimulus in a desperate and forceful way. The reason I call these children "hyperresilient" is that the form and intensity of their ward-off maneuvers become vehement to the point of exaggeration. There are two ways in which a healthy child defends himself against what would make him sick and in which a nice child defends himself against being turned into a spiteful or characterologically disorganized brat:

a. He makes frantic ward-off gestures and, in the process, naturally produces behavior which, for all practical purposes, looks like disease or delinquency itself. Thus, the youngster who is scared stiff by a tough subgroup in his classroom, or by the sadistic antics of a desperate and clumsy adult, will defend himself against the fear from within by lashing out wildly against the world around him. In the process of protecting his health, he may easily produce behavior which, by textbook rules, should be displayed only by the "severely disturbed."

b. The child may close out the dangerous stimulus by noninvolvement, by "escape" into the world of fantasy, or just by nonparticipation, motivational fade-out, passivity—in short, by the usual *withdrawal symptoms* so well described in literature. Thus, one may find the same behavior, which is otherwise symptomatic of rather severe pathology, as a signal of *healthy protection against damage from without.*

If one has any idea of what a "snakepit" is like and wishes to transpose that concept from the usual mental-hospital setting, consider the family breakfast table or some scene in a woodshed or a family tantrum over homework. What *would* a healthy person thrown into an inescapable snakepit finally do? He might very well end up screaming furiously or pounding the door while the real catatonics in the locked ward were placid—unaware of what was going on around them. Would you call the screaming person sick? On the other hand, if a man happened to be thrown into a cage full of frantically gesticulating and foaming psychotics experiencing blowups of mass proportion, it would not be surprising if he crawled into a corner and tried to shut this scene of madness out of his awareness. Should such a man be classified as catatonic, because his *behavior* looks catatonic?

In short, it is normal for normal children to defend themselves against damage. Some do it so effectively that one doesn't know what is going on. Some are "hyperresilient"—that is, in the frantic attempt to ward off damage to themselves, they produce behavior that is hard to recognize for what it is; it looks too much like a legitimate piece of madness described in textbooks devoted to severe psychopathology. Yet, these children are not emotionally sick. They are in a state of emotional disturbance, but this disturbance is produced in defense of their character and health. The causes of such "hyperresilient" behavior are basically of three kinds: cruel and irrational behavior by adults charged with their care; an entirely "wrong" environment, which lacks what any child needs for normal home or school life; or blows of destiny which, through nobody's fault, expose a child to conflict or challenge way beyond what his organism is prepared to cope with.

To present one out of dozens of illustrations for each: (1) the panicked child within a sneering group under furious attack by a frightened or sadistic teacher; (2) the originally "interested" youngster exposed to a disorganized learning situation or bored stiff under the impact of poor teaching or wrong grouping with disinterested and learning-hostile peers; (3) the child suddenly faced with the awareness of the impending birth of a sibling for which he was poorly prepared or the youngster moving from a small rural village into the slum classroom of a large industrial city, where the need to adapt to the new way of teaching, as well as to the strange peer group, may crowd out all other learning concerns and throw him into frantic gestures designed to make him acceptable to the new group. An equally wide range of illustrations could be listed for overresilience that is related to or produced by the home situation.

The gist of the matter—the main point that needs to be made as an introductory statement to help put this book into focus—remains: Whatever we say in the excitement and rush of the moment about "emotional disturbances," it makes a great difference whether we talk about *the emotionally disturbed child* or about behavior which obviously indicates a *state of emotional disturbance*. Such behavior may be the clear indication that we have to deal with a youngster whose emotional health or characterological development is in some jeopardy. However, it may also be an indication that we have a youngster before us who is certainly in conflict, but in a conflict that does not come entirely from within and is attributable to a world which does something to him that shouldn't happen—a world wherein the life of the child is set awry and to which he responds by trying to fend off the pathogenic impact.

School people, of necessity, are confronted with both types of children. Therefore, I am happy that this book does not confine itself to the usual clinical or educational speculations on the treatment and rearing of the "emotionally disturbed child," but that it takes the wider view, which includes the handling of all "children in conflict."

The range of those youngsters who fall legitimately within the concept of children with emotional disturbances is wide, indeed. Even after clarifying the two end-types mentioned earlier, we are still faced with confusion and a challenge for sharper delineation of the many kinds of emotional disturbance and how we might deal with them. The needs of the classroom teacher and other school staff who are confronted with live representatives of any one diagnostic category, or with their myriad mixtures, go in three directions, all of which are somewhere woven into this book:

There is no substitute for getting a "feel" of what it is like to be an emotionally disturbed child or to be in a "state of conflict." No accumulation of research data or diagnostic techniques can produce that "imaginative awareness from within." It usually comes through a combination of one's own childhood recollections and the accumulation of just plain "experience, post-situationally thought through." Since anybody's own childhood recollection is, of course, narrower in spread than the actual range of disturbance in the children we teach and since experience carefully thought through takes a long time and a lot of living and teaching, this book attempts to lend you the experience of what it feels like from within in the first, diagnostic section. To my knowledge, this is a unique attempt to bring the impact of internal states of mind close to the classroom teacher's empathy, thus building a bridge between what clinical science can tell us in its textbooks and what we otherwise might experience occasionally here and there.

Classroom teachers and all interested professionals need to know just what concepts and techniques the clinical sciences have developed to try to get a grip on the phenomena of emotional disturbances and childhood conflicts; and, of course, they need to get a picture of what all this looks like when it is condensed into a given moment at a given time in a given classroom with a given teacher. The other sections of the book tell you what has been thought and done in schools, in the community, in treatment, in research. They attempt to show different points of view toward the emotionally disturbed child as represented by a variety of experts. It tries to help you see how the child functions like other children and how he may, because of his difficulties, function differently. Techniques may be suggested by reading; understanding is harder to come by. But it is hoped that this sampler will help the reader deepen his understanding, a necessary step if this child is to be helped through the school.

The three editors are well equipped to set out this smorgasbord for you to savor on their subject. I have known each of them well, and I have respect for their professional taste and judgment. The variety of their experience and thinking that has been brought together in this collection should serve well those with an essential purpose of learning about and helping the emotionally disturbed child in school and out of it. There is so much to be done that a sound over-all beginning, such as this book represents, is an important guideline.

It is clear that everything said in the following pages will have to be translated by the reader into the "reality" he has to deal with in the immediate here and now. It is hoped that the book may help you to live more comfortably with (and, therefore, be more helpful to) those who have to survive with you in your classroom, having a broader and deeper understanding of the total field of emotional disturbances among children, in and out of school.

PREFACE

Within the last decade, the public schools have initiated many experimental studies, demonstration projects, and training programs to bridge the gap between sound mental-health principles and classroom practices. As teachers have become convinced of the importance of their role in mental health, their cry for help has become more vocal and has found more receptive ears. The classroom teachers' *number one* problem has been, is now, and probably will continue to be, the need for mental-health consultation in conjunction with special school programs for the emotionally disturbed children in their classrooms.

The enormity of this problem is shocking and overwhelming. A recent national survey reported by Eli Bower, Consultant to the National Institute of Mental Health, revealed that only ten thousand of our nation's half-million *severely* disturbed children are receiving psychotherapeutic treatment. If we add to this figure the number of children who are beset with affectional, physical, social, and adult-model deprivations, children who are victims of unrealistic standards and expectations, and those resorting to an antisocial code of life, it becomes easier, though still abhorrent, to accept the interpretation that one out of every five children in the public schools has an identifiable learning and/or emotional disability.

In view of these alarming figures, it is no wonder that a new wave of interest in the education and treatment of emotionally disturbed children has arisen on the national, state, and local levels. Probably the major support for this renewed interest has been the enactment of public laws by the United States Congress providing extensive appropriations for research, demonstrations, and training programs for special teachers. With this impetus, the status of our field is changing radically. For example, in March 1964 the Council for Exceptional Children officially approved the establishment of a sixth division, entitled *Children with Behavioral Disorders.* At its official christening, this youngest division in the council became the largest. The rapid enrollment of teachers, psychologists, and administrators dramatically reflects their readiness and enthusiasm to develop a professional national identity as a step toward improving educational programs for these children.

This trend can also be observed at other levels. Ten years ago only five universities offered graduate courses that were designed specifically to educate teachers of emotionally disturbed children. During the summer session of 1965, sixty-eight colleges and universities offered courses in this area. We believe that in ten years, it will be just as common for universities to certify special teachers for children with behavioral problems as it is now for them to certify teachers for the mentally retarded.

This same trend is also observed as we examine the enrollment in special classes for emotionally disturbed children in public schools throughout the nation. From 1948 to 1958 the enrollment in these classes doubled. By 1970, we predict, the enrollment will triple. With the development and expansion of special classes, many important questions will be raised: What type of child should be admitted to these classes? What type of training does the teacher need? What type of supervision should he receive? What type of curriculum is needed? What should be the role of therapy?

We foresee that these new programs will not be as committed to psychiatric formulations as those of the past. At best, psychiatric consultation may be available; but in the majority of programs, educators (including special teachers), school psychologists, visiting teachers, and social workers will assume the significant responsibility. Also, the search for a simple, economical approach to the complex task of re-educating disturbed children will continue.

As in any new field, the teacher in need of direction is faced with conflicting opinions and theories in practically all areas. This book was organized to stem the resulting feelings of confusion by presenting what we consider a positive, though perhaps more difficult, approach to the education of emotionally disturbed children. Particularly on the subject of re-education, our professional bias is evident. We believe in the psychoeducational approach. Briefly, this approach requires a teacher to be aware of basic growth and development principles, as well as the role of a group teacher, the dynamics of group forces, and psychodynamics of the individual. In addition, the teacher must possess remedial skills, and know how to manage surface behavior of children realistically, rather than permissively. However, a well-trained teacher is not the only necessary condition. The teacher needs adequate psychological supervision and ample administrative support. If it seems that we are recommending *ideal* conditions, a comparison of our recommendations with the complex job that must be done will show them to be *minimum requirements*.

Each chapter of the book is organized as a unit of study posing a fundamental question regarding the diagnosis, treatment, and education of emotionally disturbed children. Although we have expressed reaction to the material in such a way that our orientation becomes apparent, by no sense of the imagination do we believe that we have all the answers for this growing and ever changing field. Nor do we believe in any one-track solution to the multiple problems that children bring to school with them. Our intent here is to offer practical suggestions to today's classroom teacher as well as critical, provocative material for tomorrow's teachers who deliberately select to teach emotionally disturbed children.

We wish to acknowledge the invaluable services of Ruth Rosenberg, for her generous assistance in typing; Joan Tilly, for her untiring efforts in acquiring permission approvals; and Marjorie Keith and Joan Long for their skillful assistance in editing and proofreading. Finally, we want to express our personal appreciation to Dr. Eli Bower, who reviewed the manuscript and provided many insightful suggestions. His continued support enabled us to bring our views into focus for the critical task of selecting the readings for this book.

N. J. L.
W. C. M.
R. G. N.

CONTENTS

8   How Is Research Helping?   467

Bibliography   509

1

How Does It Feel to Be Emotionally Disturbed?

Emotional disturbance in childhood is not a new problem, but only recently has it been recognized as a condition that can be corrected through early diagnosis and careful treatment. Although scientists battle over the causes of emotional disturbance and the relative importance of genetic, constitutional, and environmental factors, everyone agrees that its form is in some degree dependent on the cultural and social values of the times.

Each of us contains the whole range of emotional health and disease within himself. Our nightmares, if they serve no other purpose, enable us to share the ways in which many psychotics experience life. If our legs "go to sleep" and refuse to behave as they should, we can briefly experience the helpless and often outraged feelings of the organic spastic. The sudden loss of temper nearly all of us have experienced gives a momentary empathy with the feelings of uncontrollable rage, helplessness, confusion, guilt and self-hate felt by the child with no impulse control. Most of us have shared a variety of neurotic symptoms: the terrifying fear of something that we know rationally should not in itself cause fear; the magical, protective cloak of knocking on wood, crossing fingers, counting to ten, holding our breath; the compulsive need to get one thing done, no matter how inane or how inconvenient, before we can do something else; the piece of work that can never be finished because it is never good enough; the headaches, stomach pains, or shortness of breath (unexplainable in the doctor's office) that often occur at a family reunion, at exam time, or at the appearance of a certain individual; the need to eat greedily though one is not hungry, or the reverse—being unable to swallow a mouthful; the uncontrollable blush or stutter; the immobilizing lapse of memory; the urge to take something, to break something, to say the very thing that will get us into trouble, or the urge to be silent when speaking up might simplify our lives.

Such illogical behavior does not mean that most of us are neurotic—only that some emotional disorder is as much a part of everyone's life as the common cold. It is not surprising, therefore, that emotional disturbance should play so great a role in childhood—a period of dependency and change, in which the world and its demands are new and often confusing, conflicting, and frustrating. When the case histories of severely disturbed children are examined, we often are amazed that more disturbance has not occurred.

Many literary artists have chronicled the actions of disturbed children or of adults with disturbances rooted in the past. Writers were describing these people long before Freud; and, since good writers are skilled in conveying pictures and feelings, their descriptions often have greater impact on us than the clinical descriptions in textbooks. For this reason, in the following section we present excerpts from a variety of fictional works to illustrate the kinds of mental illness that beset children. Mostly, the stories are about children of various ages, but there are also some descriptions of adult behavior that show clearly the final development of a childhood disturbance. There are examples of behavior problems and of delinquency in various forms and degrees. There are accounts of trauma, anxiety, and panic. There are descriptions of the workings of several kinds of neuroses, from mild to severe, as well as some psychotic behavior. You will find here the withdrawn child and the acting-out child; the culturally or emotionally disadvantaged and the physically or mentally handicapped; the social rebel and the autistic child, who lives in a world of his own making; and even the child murderer and the child suicide. You will at the very end be rewarded by a vignette of a normal little boy's after-school activities.

In each case (except where the author does this task for us) we give a description of how a teacher might recognize such a child in the classroom. Also, to familiarize the teacher with those labels of illness found in psychiatric or psychological reports, we give the psychiatric or clinical term used in diagnosing the child. These labels are a short-cut to imply a pattern of personality or behavior.

The fundamental purpose of this section, however, is to offer the reader an intense experience of *how it feels* to be emotionally disturbed and thus a victim of psychological forces which control and even choke off one's sense of acceptance, adequacy, and love.

The Use of Force

William Carlos Williams

They were new patients to me, all I had was the name, Olson. Please come down as soon as you can, my daughter's very sick.

When I arrived I was met by the mother, a big startled looking woman, very clean and apologetic who merely said, Is this the doctor? and let me in. In the back, she added, You must excuse us, doctor, we have her in the kitchen where it is warm. It is very damp here sometimes.

The child was fully dressed and sitting on her father's lap near the kitchen table. He tried to get up, but I motioned for him not to bother, took off my overcoat and started to look things over. I could see

From *The Farmers' Daughters and Other Stories* by William Carlos Williams. © 1961 by New Directions. Reprinted by permission of New Directions, Publishers.

that they were all very nervous, eyeing me up and down distrustfully. As often, in such cases, they weren't telling me more than they had to, it was up to me to tell them; that's why they were spending three dollars on me.

The child was fairly eating me up with her cold, steady eyes, and no expression to her face whatever. She did not move and seemed, inwardly, quiet; an unusually attractive little thing, and as strong as a heifer in appearance. But her face was flushed, she was breathing rapidly, and I realized that she had a high fever. She had magnificent blonde hair, in profusion. One of those picture children often reproduced in advertising leaflets and the photogravure sections of the Sunday papers.

She's had a fever for three days,

began the father and we don't know what it comes from. My wife has given her things, you know, like people do, but it don't do no good. And there's been a lot of sickness around. So we tho't you'd better look her over and tell us what is the matter.

As doctors often do I took a trial shot at it as a point of departure. Has she had a sore throat?

Both parents answered me together, No . . . No, she says her throat don't hurt her.

Does your throat hurt you? added the mother to the child. But the little girl's expression didn't change nor did she move her eyes from my face.

Have you looked?

I tried to, said the mother, but I couldn't see.

As it happens we had been having a number of cases of diphtheria in the school to which this child went during that month and we were all, quite apparently, thinking of that, though no one had as yet spoken of the thing.

Well, I said, suppose we take a look at the throat first. I smiled in my best professional manner and asking for the child's first name I said, come on, Mathilda, open your mouth and let's take a look at your throat.

Nothing doing.

Aw, come on, I coaxed, just open your mouth wide and let me take a look. Look, I said opening both hands wide, I haven't anything in my hands. Just open up and let me see.

Such a nice man, put in the mother. Look how kind he is to you. Come on, do what he tells you to. He won't hurt you.

At that I ground my teeth in disgust. If only they wouldn't use the word "hurt" I might be able to get somewhere. But I did not allow myself to be hurried or disturbed but speaking quietly and slowly I approached the child again.

As I moved my chair a little nearer suddenly with one cat-like movement both her hands clawed instinctively for my eyes and she almost reached them too. In fact she knocked my glasses flying and they fell, though unbroken, several feet away from me on the kitchen floor.

Both the mother and father almost turned themselves inside out in embarrassment and apology. You bad girl, said the mother, taking her and shaking her by one arm. Look what you've done. The nice man . . .

For heaven's sake, I broke in. Don't call me a nice man to her. I'm here to look at her throat on the chance that she might have diphtheria and possibly die of it. But that's nothing to her. Look here, I said to the child, we're going to look at your throat. You're old enough to understand what I'm saying. Will you open it now by yourself or shall we have to open it for you?

Not a move. Even her expression hadn't changed. Her breaths however were coming faster and faster. Then the battle began. I had to do it. I had to have a throat culture for her own protection. But first I told the parents that it was entirely up to them. I explained the danger but said that I would not insist on a throat examination so long as they would take the responsibility.

If you don't do what the doctor says you'll have to go to the hospital, the mother admonished her severely.

Oh yeah? I had to smile to myself. After all, I had already fallen in love with the savage brat, the parents were contemptible to me. In the ensuing struggle they grew more and more abject, crushed, exhausted while she surely rose to magnificent heights of insane fury of effort bred of her terror of me.

The father tried his best, and he was a big man but the fact that she was his daughter, his shame at her behavior and his dread of hurting her made him release her just at the critical moment several times when I had almost achieved success, till I wanted to kill him. But his dread also that she might have diphtheria made him tell me to go on, go on though he himself was almost fainting, while the mother moved back and forth behind us raising and lowering her hands in an agony of apprehension.

Put her in front of you on your lap, I ordered, and hold both her wrists.

But as soon as he did the child let out a scream. Don't you're hurting me. Let go of my hands. Let them go I tell you. She shrieked terrifyingly, hysterically. Stop it! Stop it! You're killing me!

Do you think she can stand it, doctor? said the mother.

You get out, said the husband to his wife. Do you want her to die of diphtheria?

Come on now, hold her, I said.

Then I grasped the child's head with my left hand and tried to get the wooden tongue depressor between her teeth. She fought, with clenched teeth, desperately! But now I also had grown furious—at a child. I tried to hold myself down but I couldn't. I know how to expose a throat for inspection. And I did my best. When finally I got the wooden spatula behind the last teeth and just the point of it into the mouth cavity, she opened up for an instant but before I could see anything she came down again and gripping the wooden blade between her molars she reduced it to splinters before I could get it out again.

Aren't you ashamed, the mother yelled at her. Aren't you ashamed to act like that in front of the doctor?

Get me a smooth-handled spoon of some sort, I told the mother. We're going through with this. The child's mouth was already bleeding. Her tongue was cut and she was screaming in wild hysterical shrieks. Perhaps I should have desisted and come back in an hour or more. No doubt it would have been better. But I have seen at least two children lying dead in bed of neglect in such cases, and feeling that I must get a diagnosis now or never I went at it again. But the worst of it was that I too had got beyond reason. I could have torn the child apart in my own fury and enjoyed it. It was a pleasure to attack her. My face was burning with it.

The damned little brat must be protected against her own idiocy, one says to one's self at such times. Others must be protected against her. It is social necessity. And all these things are true. But a blind fury, a feeling of adult shame, bred of a longing for muscular release are the operatives. One goes on to the end.

In a final unreasoning assault I overpowered the child's neck and jaws. I forced the heavy silver spoon back of her teeth and down her throat till she gagged. And there it was—both tonsils covered with membrane. She had fought valiantly to keep me from knowing her secret. She had been hiding that sore throat for three days at least and lying to her parents in order to escape just such an outcome as this.

Now truly she *was* furious. She had been on the defensive before but now she attacked. Tried to get off her father's lap and fly at me while tears of defeat blinded her eyes.

DIAGNOSIS: *Behavior problem—resistance to adult authority, hostility, aggressiveness—leading to character neurosis.*

This child has had many such a struggle with her parents. Clearly, she has immobilized and terrorized them. In struggles with her parents, she has been the unhappy victor—unhappy because, although momentarily such a child has all her fund of energy concentrated in defeating the adults, she would be greatly relieved to know she was not all-powerful. She would be relieved to know that the adults on whom she *must* depend *can* be depended on to make and carry out decisions that she cannot make. A child feels helpless at best in the adult world, and when parents—and teachers and doctors—are rendered "abject" and impotent, fearful and ineffective, the result is increased anxiety, increased panic, and increased rage. This rage often comes out in a defiant, aggressive onslaught.

It results in making the adults more fearful or angry, in further isolating the child and making her feel more unloved. Thus, she is led into a circle of helplessness, panic, and anger, which also includes the adults in her life. For the child, this circle spirals into misery, isolation, and trouble with the world.

The parents, as Williams describes, are incompetent; their words are ill-chosen, frightening, threatening, and shaming—effective only in arousing fear, not compliance. Even in a matter of life and death such as this, they are so defeated by the child that they are unable to facilitate the throat examination.

William Carlos Williams' reaction to the child is particularly apt in demonstrating what such parental behavior arouses in other adults. He secretly admires the courage and determination of the little girl. At the same time, her defiance evokes counterattack, rage, and a need for "muscular release." He is shamed that such a little child can make him lose control and poise. Though he *has* to complete the throat examination for the sake of the child's very life, he is aware that his excuses to himself for the way he accomplishes the task are rationalizations to cover up his own primitive rage. The girl's behavior is calculated to bring about helplessness, rage, and guilt in the adult and to make herself feel rejected, alone, and unloved. Her strength and independence have been put to the service of making her life (and the lives of those about her) miserable. Education and psychotherapy for the parents and guidance for all other adults who deal with her, such as teachers and doctors, are in order. Possibly the girl herself may need some psychotherapy. Any teacher can recognize such a child in her class.

To Sir, with Love
E. R. Braithwaite

Just about this time a new supply teacher, Mr. Bell, was sent to our school as supernumerary to the Staff for a few weeks. He was about forty years old, a tall, wiry man, who had had some previous experience with the Army Education Service. It was arranged that he should act as relief teacher for some lessons, including two periods of P.T. with the senior boys. One of Mr. Bell's hobbies was fencing: he was something of a perfectionist and impatient of anyone whose co-ordination was not as smooth and controlled as his own. He would repeat a P.T. movement or exercise over and over again until it was executed with clockwise precision, and though the boys grumbled against his discipline they

From the book *To Sir, with Love* by E. R. Braithwaite. © 1959 by E. R. Braithwaite, published by Prentice-Hall, Inc. Used by permission.

seemed eager to prove to him that they were quite capable of doing any exercise he could devise, and with a skill that very nearly matched his own.

This was especially true in the cases of Ingham, Fernman and Seales, who would always place themselves at the head of the line as an example and encouragement to the others. The least athletic of these was Richard Buckley, a short, fat boy, amiable and rather dim, who could read and write after a fashion, and could never be provoked to any semblance of anger or heat. He was pleasant and jolly and a favorite with the others, who, though they themselves chivvied him unmercifully, were ever ready in his defense against outsiders.

Buckley was no good at P.T. or games; he just was not built for such pursuits. Yet, such is the perversity of human nature, he strenuously resisted any efforts to leave him out or overlook him when games were being arranged. His attempts at accomplishing such simple gymnastic performances as the "forward roll" and "star jump" reduced the rest of the P.T. class to helpless hilarity, but he persisted with a singleness of purpose, which though unproductive, was nothing short of heroic.

Buckley was Bell's special whipping boy. Fully aware of the lad's physical limitations, he would encourage him to try other and more difficult exercises, with apparently the sole purpose of obtaining some amusement from the pitiably ridiculous results. Sometimes the rest of the class would protest; and then Bell would turn on them the full flood of his invective. The boys mentioned this in their "Weekly Review," and Mr. Florian decided to discuss it at a Staff Meeting.

"The boys seem to be a bit bothered by remarks you make to them during P.T., Mr. Bell."

"To which remarks do you refer, Mr. Florian?" Bell never used the term "Sir," seeming to think it "infra dig." Even when he granted him the "Mr. Florian," he gave to this form of address the suggestion of a sneer.

"From their review it would seem that you are unnecessarily critical of their persons."

"Do you mean their smell?"

"Well, yes, that and the state of their clothing."

"I've advised them to wash."

"These are the words which appear in one review." The Headmaster produced a notebook, Fernman's, and read:

"'Some of you stink like old garbage.'"

His tone was cool, detached, judicial. "I was referring to their feet. Many of them never seem to wash their feet, and when they take their shoes off the stink is dreadful."

"Many of them live in homes where there are very few facilities for washing, Mr. Bell."

"Surely enough water is available for washing their feet if they really wanted to."

"Then they'd put on the same smelly socks and shoes to which you also object."

"I've got to be in contact with them and it isn't very pleasant."

"Have you ever lived in this area, Mr. Bell?"

"No fear."

"Then you know nothing about the conditions prevailing. The water you so casually speak of is more often to be found in the walls and on the floors than in the convenient wash basin or bath to which you are accustomed. I've visited homes of some of these children where water for a family in an upstairs flat had to be fetched by bucket or pail from the single back-yard tap which served five or six families. You may see, therefore, that so elementary a function as washing the feet might present many difficulties."

Bell was silent at this.

"I've no wish to interfere, or tell you how to do your work; you're an experienced teacher and know more about P.T. than I ever will,"—the Old Man was again patient, encouraging—"but try to be a little more understanding about their difficulties." He then turned to other matters, but it was clear that Bell was considerably put out by the rebuke.

Matters came to a head that Monday afternoon. I was not present in the gym, but was able to reconstruct the sequence of events with reasonable accuracy from the boys' reports and Bell's subsequent admissions.

During the P.T. session he had been putting them through their paces in the "astride vault" over the buck, all except Buckley, who was somewhat under the weather and wisely stood down from attempting the rather difficult jump, but without reference to or permission from Bell, who was not long in discovering the absence of his favorite diversion.

"Buckley," he roared.

"Yes, Sir."

"Come on, boy, I'm waiting." He was standing in his usual position beside the buck in readiness to arrest the fall of any lad who might be thrown off balance by an awkward approach or incorrect execution of the movement. But the boy did not move, and the master stared at him amazed and angry at this unexpected show of defiance by the one generally considered to be the most timid and tractable in the whole class.

"Fatty can't do it, Sir, it's too high for him," Denham interposed.

"Shut up, Denham," Bell roared. "If I want your opinion I will ask for it." He left his station by the buck and walked to where Buckley was standing. The boy watched his threatening approach, fear apparent in his eyes.

"Well, Buckley," Bell towered over the unhappy youth, "are you going to do as you're told?"

"Yes, Sir," Buckley's capitulation was as sudden as his refusal.

The others stopped to watch as he stood looking at the buck, licking his lips nervously while waiting for the instructor to resume his position. It may have been fear or determination or a combination of both, but Buckley launched himself at the buck in furious assault, and in spite of Bell's restraining arms, boy and buck crashed on the floor with a sickening sound as one leg of the buck snapped off with the sound of a pistol shot. The class stood in shocked silence watching Buckley, who remained as he fell, inert and pale; then they rushed to his assistance. All except Potter; big, good-natured Potter seemed to have lost his reason. He snatched up the broken metal-bound leg and advanced on Bell, screaming:

"You bloody bastard, you f—ing bloody bastard."

"Put that thing down, Potter, don't be a fool," Bell spluttered, backing away from the hysterical boy.

"You made him do it; he didn't want to and you made him," Potter yelled.

"Don't be a fool, Potter, put it down," Bell appealed.

"I'll do you in, you bloody murderer." Bell was big, but in his anger Potter seemed bigger, his improvised club a fearsome extension of his thick forearm.

That was where I rushed in. Tich Jackson, frightened by the sight of Buckley, limp and white on the floor, and the enraged Potter, slobbering at the instructor in murderous fury, had dashed upstairs to my classroom shouting: "Sir, quick, they're fighting in the gym." I followed his disappearing figure in time to see Bell backed against a wall, with Potter advancing on him.

"Hold it, Potter," I called. He turned at the sound of my voice and I quickly placed myself between them. "Let's have that, Potter." I held out my hand towards the boy, but he stared past me at Bell, whimpering in his emotion. Anger had completely taken hold of him, and he looked very dangerous.

"Come on, Potter," I repeated, "hand it over and go lend a hand with Buckley."

He turned to look towards his prostrate friend and I quickly moved up to him and seized the improvised club; he released it to me without any resistance and went back to join the group around Buckley. Bell then walked away and out of the room, and I went up to the boys. Denham rose and faced me, his face white with rage.

"Potts should have done the bastard like he did Fatty, just 'cos he wouldn't do the bloody jump."

I let that pass; they were angry and at such times quickly reverted to the old things, the words, the discourtesies. I stooped down beside Buckley, who was now sitting weakly on the floor, supported by Sapiano and Seales, and smiling up at them as if ashamed of himself for having been the cause of so much fuss.

"How do you feel, old man?" I inquired.

"Cor, Sir," he cried, smiling, "me tum does hurt."

"He fell on the buck. You should have seen 'im, Sir."

"Gosh, you should've heard the noise when the leg smashed."

"Mr. Bell couldn't catch Fatty, Sir, you should've seen him."

Most of them were trying to talk all at once, eager to give me all the details.

"Bleeding bully, always picking on Fats." This from Sapiano, whose volatile Maltese temperament was inclined to flare up very easily.

"If I'd had the wood I'd have done the f—er in and no bleeding body would have stopped me." Denham was aching for trouble and didn't care who knew it. Bell had slipped away unharmed after hurting his friend, and Denham wanted a substitute. But I would not look at him, or even hear the things he said. Besides, I liked Denham; in spite of his rough manner and speech he was an honest, dependable person with a strong sense of independence.

"Can you stand up, Buckley?"

With some assistance from Seales and Sapiano the boy got to his feet; he looked very pale and unsteady. I turned to Denham: "Will you help the others take Buckley up to Mrs. Dale-Evans and ask her to give him some sweet tea; leave him there and I'll meet you all in the classroom in a few minutes."

Without waiting for his reply I hurried off to the staffroom in search of Bell.

I was in something of a quandry. I knew that it was quite possible Buckley was all right, but there was no knowing whether he had sustained any internal injury not yet apparent. The Council's rules required that all accidents be reported and logged; the Headmaster should be informed forthwith, and in the light of what he had said to Bell so very recently, there would most certainly be a row.

I went up to the staffroom and found Bell washing his face at the sink.

"I've sent Buckley upstairs for a cup

of tea," I said. "I suppose he'll be all right, anyway he was walking under his own steam."

"What happens now?" His voice was querulous.

"You should know as well as I do," I replied. "Shouldn't you see the Old Man and make some kind of report?"

"Yes, I suppose I'd better get over to his office right away. I should have attended to the Buckley boy, but the other one rushed me. Thanks for helping out."

"Oh, that's all right," I replied. "But why did you insist on the boy doing the vault?"

"I had to, don't you see; he just stood there refusing to obey and the others were watching me; I just had to do something." His whole attitude now was defensive.

"I'm not criticizing you, Mr. Bell, just asking. Buckley's a bit of a mascot with the others, you know, and I suppose that is why Potter got out of hand."

"I guess it was the way he jumped or something, but I couldn't grab him. He hit the buck too low and sent it flying."

"He's a bit awkward, isn't he; anyway I'm sure the Old Man will understand how it happened."

"He might be a bit difficult, especially after what he said the other day."

"Not necessarily. After all, it was an accident and thank Heaven it's not very serious."

He dried his hands and moved towards the door. "I suppose they'll really go to town on this in their weekly reviews," he remarked.

"I'll ask the boys to say nothing about it. I don't suppose Potter is now feeling any too pleased with himself at his conduct."

As he left Clinty came into the staffroom.

"What's happening, Rick?" she asked. "I just saw some of your boys taking Fatty Buckley upstairs. What's happened to him?"

I told her about the incident and added: "Bell has just gone to the Old Man's office to report the matter."

"Well, what do you know?" she chuckled. "Fancy Potter going for Bell like that. I always thought that boy a bit of a softie, but you never know with those quiet ones, do you?"

"He was not the only one. Sapiano and Denham were just as wild, I think, but they were too busy fussing over Buckley to bother with Bell."

"He is a bit of a tyro, isn't he. This might make him take it a bit easier."

"I don't think the boys mind his being strict during P.T. It's just that Buckley's a bit of a fool and they resented his being hurt. If it had been Denham or someone like that, I'm sure they would have done nothing."

"Yes, I guess you're right. Bell is a good teacher. I wonder how long the Divisional Office will let him stay here. I hope he hasn't had too much of a fright."

"Oh, he'll get over that. Now I must go and have a word with my boys."

I left her. For some inexplicable reason I felt nervous about being alone with Clinty; I felt that there was something she wanted to say to me, and for my part I did not want to hear it.

In the classroom the boys were sitting closely grouped together, looking rather sheepish. I knew they were feeling aggrieved and, according to their lights, justifiably so; but nevertheless the matter of Potter's behavior had to be dealt with.

"How's Buckley?" I asked.

"We left him upstairs with Mrs. Dale-Evans, Sir. He didn't want to stay, he kept saying he was all right. But she told him if he wasn't quiet she'd give him some castor oil, Sir. Ugh!" They all managed a smile at Seales' remark.

"Good," I replied, "I expect he'll be quite all right. But there is something I want to say to you about this unfortunate incident." I sat down on the edge of Fernman's desk.

"Potter, there is nothing I can think of which can excuse your shocking conduct in the gym."

Potter's mouth fell open; he looked at me in surprise, gulped a few times and stammered:

"But it was him, Sir, Mr. Bell, making Fatty fall and that." His voice was shrill with outrage at my remark.

"Mr. Bell was the master there, Potter, and anything that happened in the gym was his responsibility. Buckley's mishap was no excuse for you to make such an attack on your teacher."

"But Fatty told him he couldn't do it, Sir, and he made him, he made him, Sir."

Potter was very near tears. His distress was greater because of what he believed was the further injustice of my censure. The others, too, were looking at me with the same expression.

"That may be, Potter. I am not now concerned with Mr. Bell's conduct, but with yours. You came very near to getting yourself into very serious trouble because you were unable to control your temper. Not only was your language foul and disgusting, but you armed yourself with a weapon big enough and heavy enough to cause very serious harm. What do you think would have happened if everyone had behaved like you and had all turned on Mr. Bell like a pack of mad wolves?" I waited for this to sink in a bit, but Potter interjected:

"I thought he had done Fatty in, Sir, he looked all huddled up like, Sir."

"I see. So you didn't wait to find out but rushed in with your club like a hoodlum to smash and kill, is that it? Your friend was hurt and you wanted to hurt back; suppose instead of a piece of wood it had been a knife, or a gun, what then?" Potter was pale, and he was not the only one.

"Potts didn't think. He was narked, we was all narked, seeing Fatty on the deck. I wasn't half bleeding wild myself."

"You're missing the point, Denham. I think you're all missing the point. We sit in this classroom day after day and talk of things, and you all know what's expected of you; but at the first sign of bother you forget it all. In two weeks you'll all be at work and lots of things will happen which will annoy you, make you wild. Are you going to resort to clubs and knives every time you're upset or angered?" I stood up. "You'll meet foremen or supervisors or workmates who'll do things to upset you, sometimes deliberately. What then, Denham? What about that, Potter?" Your Headmaster is under fire from many quarters because he believes in you—because he really believes that by the time you leave here you will have learned to exercise a little self-control at the times when it is most needed. His success or failure will be reflected in the way you conduct yourselves after you leave him. If today's effort is an example of your future behavior I hold out very little hope for you."

At this moment Buckley walked in, smiling broadly and seemingly none the worse for wear. I waited until he was seated then went on:

"I've no wish to belabor this matter, but it cannot be left like this. Potter, you were very discourteous to your P.T. instructor, and it is my opinion that you owe him an apology." Potter stared at me, his mouth open in amazement at my remark; but before he could speak Denham leapt to his feet.

"Apologize?" His voice was loud in anger. "Why should Potts apologize? He didn't do him any harm. Why should he apologize to him just because he's a bleeding teacher?" He stood there, legs slightly apart, heavy-shouldered and truculent, glaring at me. The others were watching us, but agreeing with him; I could feel their resentment hardening.

"Please sit down Denham, and remember that in this class we are always able to discuss things, no matter how difficult or unpleasant, without shouting at each other."

I waited, fearful of this unexpected threat to our pleasant relationship; he looked around at his colleagues indecisively, then abruptly sat down. I continued, in a very friendly tone:

"That was a fair question, Denham,

although you will agree it was put a little, shall we say, indelicately?"

I smiled as I said this, and, in spite of his anger, Denham smiled briefly too. I went on:

"Potter, are you quite pleased and satisfied with the way you behaved to your P.T. teacher?"

Potter looked at me for a moment, then murmured, "No, Sir."

"But he couldn't help it," Denham interjected.

"That may be so, Denham, but Potter agrees that his own actions were unsatisfactory; upon reflection he himself is not pleased with what he did."

"How's about Mr. Bell then: How's about him apologizing to Buckley?" Denham was not to be dissuaded from his attitude.

"Yes, how about him?" echoed Sapiano.

"My business is with you, not with Mr. Bell," I replied.

This was not going to be easy, I thought. Denham was getting a bit nasty; the usual "Sir" had disappeared from his remarks, and Sapiano was following suit.

"It's easy for you to talk, Sir, nobody tries to push you around." Seales' voice was clear and calm, and the others turned to look at him, to support him. His question touched something deep inside of me, something which had been dormant for months, but now awoke to quick, painful remembering. Without realizing what I was doing I got up and walked to where he sat and stood beside his desk.

"I've been pushed around, Seales," I said quietly, "in a way I cannot explain to you. I've been pushed around until I began to hate people so much that I wanted to hurt them, really hurt them. I know how it feels, believe me, and one thing I learned, Seales, is to try always to be a bit bigger than the people who hurt me. It is easy to reach for a knife or a gun; but then you become merely a tool and the knife or gun takes over, thereby creating new and bigger problems without solving a thing. So what happens when there is no weapon handy?"

I felt suddenly annoyed with myself for giving way to my emotion, and abruptly walked back to my desk. The class seemed to feel that something had touched me deeply and were immediately sympathetic in their manner.

"The point I want to make, Potter," I continued, "is whether you are really growing up and learning to stand squarely on your own feet. When you begin work at Covent Garden you might some day have cause to be very angry; what will you do then? The whole idea of this school is to teach you to discipline yourself. In this instance you lost your temper and behaved badly to your teacher. Do you think you are big enough to make an apology to him?"

Potter fidgeted in his seat and looked uncertainly at me, then replied: "Yes, Sir."

"It's always difficult to apologize, Potter, especially to someone you feel justified in disliking. But remember that you are not doing it for Mr. Bell's sake, but your own."

I sat down. They were silent, but I realized that they understood what I meant. Potter stood up:

"Is he in the staffroom, Sir?"

"I think he should be there now, Potter."

Denham and Seales stood and joined Potter and together they went to find Bell. I called Buckley.

"How are you feeling, Buckley?"

"Okay, Sir," he replied, as jovial as ever.

"What will your parents say about all this, Buckley?" I was being devious but, I thought, necessarily so.

"I shan't tell 'em, Sir. Must I, Sir?"

"It's up to you, Buckley. If you feel fine there's no need to bother; but if in the next few days or weeks you feel any pain, it would be best to mention it so that they'd know what to do."

In a few minutes the boys were back, Potter looking red and embarrassed; behind them came Mr. Bell.

"May I speak to your boys for a moment, Mr. Braithwaite?" He came in and stood beside my desk and I nodded to him.

"I want to say to all of you," he began, "that I'm sorry about what happened in the gym a little while ago. I think that one way or another we were all a bit silly, but the sooner we forget the whole thing, the better.

"How're you feeling now, boy?" He addressed himself to Buckley.

"Okay, Sir," the boy replied.

"Fine. Well, I suppose we'll see each other as usual next week." And with that he was gone, having made as friendly a gesture as his evident nervousness would allow.

The boys seemed not unwilling to let the matter drop, so we turned our attention to the discussion of other things.

DIAGNOSIS: *Impulse breakthrough—acting-out children—the syndrome of the socially and economically deprived child.*

This book concerns the experiences of a highly educated, Oxford-trained Negro engineer, who, being unable to find a job consonant with his talents, experience, and training, takes a teaching job at an experimental day school in the poorest slums of London. The school, run by an inspired educator, takes on the obstreperous rejects from other schools. The entire story should be a *must* for anyone working with disturbed or deprived children.

In this case the behavior of Potter was clearly provoked. However, the cause of losing control, as Potter did, frequently is neither so visible nor so apparently justified to the outsider. In very disturbed cases the provocation may come from inner fantasies, from distorted images of the people around the child, which evoke tortured memories or half-memories. It may come from a tone of voice, a seemingly harmless phrase, a frustration that makes the child feel foolish, helpless, inept. Here, Potter's anger was aroused by injustice; and children, even disturbed ones, are happily committed to justice—even though their definitions may not coincide with society's. The crucial factor in Potter's case was not his anger but the way he handled it. Rage is an overwhelming experience. Inability to handle it in an acceptable fashion leads to tragedy.

Braithwaite is careful to make this point to the boys themselves as he details the precarious life ahead for one who is at the mercy of rage instead of its master. His handling of the problem in the group of children, where all could hear and express themselves, displays the kind of skill that comes from human understanding.

This selection also highlights the contagion of rage among children. It indicates, too, that the teacher's revelation of his personal deep feeling communicated real, emotional understanding far more powerfully than intellectual reasoning. This, more than the proper words, got across to the boys. Children, even badly disturbed ones, respond to genuineness. In many cases the more troubled the child, the more therapeutic can a teacher's genuine feelings be, provided they are not overexploited or used to gain sympathy for the teacher.

Breakfast at Tiffany's

Truman Capote

Passing a Woolworth's, she gripped my arm: "Let's steal something," she said, pulling me into the store, where at once there seemed a pressure of eyes, as though we were already under suspicion. "Come on. Don't be chicken." She scouted a counter piled with paper pumpkins and Halloween masks. The saleslady was occupied with a group of nuns who were trying on masks. Holly picked up a mask and slipped it over her face; she chose another and put it on mine; then she took my hand and we walked away. It was as simple as that. Outside, we ran a few blocks, I think to make it more dramatic; but also because, as I'd discovered, successful theft exhilarates. I wondered if she'd often stolen. "I used to," she said. "I mean I had to. If I wanted anything. But I still do it every now and then, sort of to keep my hand in."

DIAGNOSIS: *Psychopathic pattern—the delinquent thrill—stealing.*

The thrill of success is more important psychodynamically than the actual theft. It fills an emptiness that the delinquent feels; it gives him a false sense of power, a momentary feeling of omnipotence. This delusion is directly in contrast to the pervasive underlying sense of helplessness and lostness such children feel in the face of inconsistent and ambiguous communications with the people they depend on. The thrill is an essential aspect of delinquency. It is a complicated emotion, which, in addition to temporarily filling emptiness, may contain hostility, boredom, or sexual displacement.

Member of the Wedding

Carson McCullers

It happened that green and crazy summer when Frankie was twelve years old. This was the summer when for a long time she had not been a member. She belonged to no club and was a member of nothing in the world. Frankie had become an unjoined person who hung around in doorways, and she was afraid. In June the trees were bright dizzy green, but later the leaves darkened, and the town turned black and shrunken under the glare of the sun. At first Frankie walked around doing one thing and another. The sidewalks of the town were gray in the early morning and at night, but the noon sun put a glaze on them, so that the cement burned and glittered like glass. The sidewalks finally became too hot for Frankie's feet, and also she got herself in trouble. She was in so much secret trouble that she thought it was better to stay at home—and at home there was only Berenice Sadie Brown and John Henry West. The three of them sat at the kitchen table, saying the same things over and over, so that by August the words began to rhyme with each other and sound strange. The world seemed to die each afternoon and nothing moved any longer. At last the summer was like a green sick dream, or like a silent crazy jungle under glass. And then, on the last Friday of August, all this was changed: it was so sudden that Frankie puzzled the whole blank afternoon, and still she did not understand.

"It is so very queer," she said. "The way it all just happened."

"Happened? Happened?" said Berenice.

John Henry listened and watched them quietly.

"I have never been so puzzled."

From *Member of the Wedding* by Carson McCullers (Boston: Houghton Mifflin Co., 1946).

"But puzzled about what?"

"The whole thing," Frankie said.

And Berenice remarked: "I believe the sun has fried your brains."

"Me too," John Henry whispered.

Frankie herself almost admitted maybe so. It was four o'clock in the afternoon and the kitchen was square and gray and quiet. Frankie sat at the table with her eyes half closed, and she thought about a wedding. She saw a silent church, a strange snow slanting down against the colored windows. The groom in this wedding was her brother, and there was a brightness where his face should be. The bride was there in a long white train, and the bride also was faceless. There was something about this wedding that gave Frankie a feeling she could not name.

"Look here at me," said Berenice. "You jealous?"

"Jealous?"

"Jealous because your brother going to be married?"

"No," said Frankie. "I just never saw any two people like them. When they walked in the house today it was so queer."

"You jealous," said Berenice. "Go and behold yourself in the mirror. I can see from the color in your eye."

There was a watery kitchen mirror hanging above the sink. Frankie looked, but her eyes were gray as they always were. This summer she was grown so tall that she was almost a big freak, and her shoulders were narrow, her legs too long. She wore a pair of blue black shorts, a B.V.D. undervest, and she was barefooted. Her hair had been cut like a boy's, but it had not been cut for a long time and was now not even parted. The reflection in the glass was warped and crooked, but Frankie knew well what she looked like; she drew up her left shoulder and turned her head aside.

"Oh," she said. "They were the two prettiest people I ever saw. I just can't understand how it happened."

"But what, Foolish?" said Berenice. "Your brother come home with the girl he means to marry and took dinner today with you and your Daddy. They intend to marry at her home in Winter Hill this coming Sunday. You and your Daddy are going to the wedding. And that is the A and the Z of the matter. So whatever ails you?"

"I don't know," said Frankie. "I bet they have a good time every minute of the day."

"Less us have a good time," John Henry said.

"Us have a good time?" Frankie asked. "Us?"

.   .   .

"I'm going to Winter Hill," she said. "I'm going to the wedding."

She waited, to give him a chance to say: "I already knew that, anyhow." Then finally she spoke the sudden truth aloud. "I'm going with them. After the wedding at Winter Hill, I'm going off with the two of them to whatever place that they will ever go. I'm going with them."

He did not answer.

"I love the two of them so much. We'll go to every place together. It's like I've known it all my life, that I belong to be with them. I love the two of them so much."

And having said this, she did not need to wonder and puzzle any more. She opened her eyes, and it was night. The lavender sky had at last grown dark and there was slanted starlight and twisted shade. Her heart had divided like two wings and she had never seen a night so beautiful.

Frankie stood looking into the sky. For when the old question came to her— the who she was and what she would be in the world, and why she was standing there that minute—when the old question came to her, she did not feel hurt and un-

answered. At last she knew just who she was and understood where she was going. She loved her brother and the bride and she was a member of the wedding. The three of them would go into the world and they would always be together. And finally, after the scared spring and the crazy summer, she was no more afraid.

.   .   .

The wedding was all wrong, although she could not point out single faults. The house was a neat brick house out near the limits of the small, baked town, and when she first put foot inside, it was as though her eyeballs had been slightly stirred; there were mixed impressions of pink roses, the smell of floor wax, mints and nuts in silver trays. Everybody was lovely to her. Mrs. Williams wore a lace dress, and she asked F. Jasmine two times what grade she was in at school. But she asked, also, if she would like to play out on the swing before the wedding, in the tone grown people use when speaking to a child. Mr. Williams was nice to her, too. He was a sallow man with folds in his cheeks and the skin beneath his eyes was the grain and color of an old apple core. Mr. Williams also asked her what grade she was in at school; in fact, that was the main question asked her at the wedding.

She wanted to speak to her brother and the bride, to talk to them and tell them of her plans, the three of them alone together. But they were never once alone; Jarvis was out checking the car someone was lending for the honeymoon, while Janice dressed in the front bedroom among a crowd of beautiful grown girls. She wandered from one to the other of them, unable to explain. And once Janice put her arms around her, and said she was so glad to have a little sister—and when Janice kissed her, F. Jasmine felt an aching in her throat and could not speak. Jarvis, when she went to find him in the yard, lifted her up in a roughhouse way and said: Frankie the lankie the alaga fankie, the tee-legged, toe-legged bow-legged Frankie. And he gave her a dollar.

She stood in the corner of the bride's room, wanting to say: I love the two of you so much and you are the we of me. Please take me with you from the wedding, for we belong to be together. Or even if she could have said: May I trouble you to step into the next room, as I have something to reveal to you and Jarvis? And get the three of them in a room alone together and somehow manage to explain. If only she had written it down on the typewriter in advance, so that she could hand it to them and they would read! But this she had not thought to do, and her tongue was heavy in her mouth and dumb. She could only speak in a voice that shook a little—to ask where was the veil?

.   .   .

She watched them with her heart, but all the time she was only thinking: I have not told them and they don't know. And knowing this was heavy as a swallowed stone. And afterward, during the kissing of the bride, refreshments served in the dining room, the stir and party bustle— she hovered close to the two of them, but words would not come. They are not going to take me, she was thinking, and this was the one thought she could not bear.

When Mr. Williams brought their bags, she hastened after with her own suitcase. The rest was like some nightmare show in which a wild girl in the audience breaks onto the stage to take upon herself an unplanned part that was never written or meant to be. You are the we of me, her heart was saying, but she could only say aloud: "Take me!" And they pleaded and begged with her, but she was already in the car. At the last she clung to the steering wheel until her father and somebody else had hauled and dragged her from the car, and even then she could only cry in the dust of the empty road: "Take me! Take me!" But there was only the wedding company to hear, for the bride and her brother had driven away. . . .

DIAGNOSIS: *Identity problem—adolescent pattern.*

The quest for identity is not a disease in itself, but a major part of human growth. However, there are times in life when defining one's identity means leaving behind a part of one's self, taking on a new self, and integrating the past and present selves—a task so difficult that Erik Erikson calls it an "identity crisis."[1] The attempts to resolve the conflicting parts display all the earmarks of neurosis. Indeed, if a person is unable to resolve his identity conflict, whether by repression or acting out or both, he may suffer long-term, intense personality damage. Of all periods, adolescence is the one most clearly marked by identity crisis—so much so that a stormy adolescence often takes on the appearance of mental illness and needs to be handled as tenderly and insightfully. Physical, sexual, emotional, and social growth all flood the individual at different rates and with varying pressure, so the child-turning-youth often feels as if he were caught and churned by a tidal wave—unable to plant either his childish feet or his new adolescent feet on the ground.

Adolescence comes earlier to girls; and, when it is marked by rapid physical growth, as in the case of Frankie-Frances-Jasmine Adams, it is apt to be startling—especially for a motherless girl, whose deepest female attachment is to the warm Negro cook and friend, Berenice. Berenice loves Frankie and comforts her but does not understand what is happening to her and cannot, by virtue of her own society and education, mark out an adequate identification for the

[1] Erik Erikson, *Childhood and Society* (New York: Norton, 1964) and *Young Man Luther* (New York: Norton, 1958).

child. Frankie's father is preoccupied and unaware of anything about the child's growth save the physical and sexual signs. Frankie looks upon her brother's wedding as a rebirth for herself into a family, a belonging, and a pattern of possible identification. She is convinced that the wedding and her participation in it will solve her identity problem and imagines she can go off with the wedding couple. Her sense of distress and loss when she finds she cannot is poignant, indicating that no one can do the job for her and that she must find her own slow way to growth.

Any teacher in a junior high or high school class will recognize Frankie Adams. She is the imaginative, sensitive child who is either lost in daydreams or frantically, restlessly active. A little girl one day and a grown-up the next, she seeks by frantic activity and preposterous (from an adult's point of view) imaginings, to find a self. To help such a child, a teacher needs imagination, empathy, and a sense of humor. He must never ridicule, though he may need to set clearly defined limits in order to clarify for the child what is dream and what is real— what can be and what cannot. It is at this searching time that inspired teachers of art, literature, drama, and music can exploit and channel this boiling imagination by indicating ways for the child to find a self that may prove satisfying.

An Incident

Anton Chekhov

Morning. Brilliant sunshine is piercing through the frozen lacework on the window-panes into the nursery. Vanya, a boy of six, with a cropped head and a nose like a button, and his sister Nina, a short, chubby, curly-headed girl of four, wake up and look crossly at each other through the bars of their cots.

"Oo-oo-oo! naughty children!" grumbles their nurse. "Good people have had their breakfast already, while you can't get your eyes open."

The sunbeams frolic over the rugs, the walls, and nurse's skirts, and seem inviting the children to join in their play, but they take no notice. They have woken up in a bad humour. Nina pouts, makes a grimace, and begins to whine:

"Brea-eakfast, nurse, breakfast!"

Vanya knits his brows and ponders what to pitch upon to howl over. He has

From *The Cook's Wedding and Other Stories,* by Anton Chekhov, translated by Constance Garnett. Reprinted by permission of the Macmillan Company, New York, and Chatto & Windus, Ltd., London.

already begun screwing up his eyes and opening his mouth, but at that instant the voice of mamma reaches them from the drawing-room, saying: "Don't forget to give the cat her milk, she has a family now!"

The children's puckered countenances grow smooth again as they look at each other in astonishment. Then both at once begin shouting, jump out of their cots, and filling the air with piercing shrieks, run barefoot, in their nightgowns, to the kitchen.

"The cat has puppies!" they cry. "The cat has got puppies!"

Under the bench in the kitchen there stands a small box, the one in which Stepan brings coal when he lights the fire. The cat is peeping out of the box. There is an expression of extreme exhaustion on her grey face; her green eyes, with their narrow black pupils, have a languid, sentimental look. . . . From her face it is clear that the only thing lacking to complete her happiness is the presence in the box of "him," the father of her children, to whom she had abandoned herself so recklessly!

She wants to mew, and opens her mouth wide, but nothing but a hiss comes from her throat; the squealing of the kittens is audible.

The children squat on their heels before the box, and, motionless, holding their breath, gaze at the cat. . . . They are surprised, impressed, and do not hear nurse grumbling as she pursues them. The most genuine delight shines in the eyes of both.

Domestic animals play a scarcely noticed but undoubtedly beneficial part in the education and life of children. Which of us does not remember powerful but magnanimous dogs, lazy lapdogs, birds dying in captivity, dull-witted but haughty turkeys, mild old tabby cats, who forgave us when we trod on their tails for fun and caused them agonising pain? I even fancy, sometimes, that the patience, the fidelity, the readiness to forgive, and the sincerity which are characteristic of our domestic animals have a far stronger and more definite effect on the mind of a child than the long exhortations of some dry, pale Karl Karlovitch, or the misty expositions of a governess, trying to prove to children that water is made up of hydrogen and oxygen.

"What little things!" says Nina, opening her eyes wide and going off into a joyous laugh. "They are like mice!"

"One, two, three," Vanya counts. "Three kittens. So there is one for you, one for me, and one for somebody else, too."

"Murrm . . . murrm . . ." purrs the mother, flattered by their attention. "Murrm."

After gazing at the kittens, the children take them from under the cat, and begin squeezing them in their hands, then, not satisfied with this, they put them in the skirts of their nightgowns, and run into the other rooms.

"Mamma, the cat has got pups!" they shout.

Mamma is sitting in the drawing-room with some unknown gentleman. Seeing the children unwashed, undressed, with their nightgowns held up high, she is embarrassed, and looks at them severely.

"Let your nightgowns down, disgrace-ful children," she says. "Go out of the room, or I will punish you."

But the children do not notice either mamma's threats or the presence of a stranger. They put the kittens down on the carpet, and go off into deafening squeals. The mother walks round them, mewing imploringly. When, a little afterwards, the children are dragged off to the nursery, dressed, made to say their prayers, and given their breakfast, they are full of a passionate desire to get away from these prosaic duties as quickly as possible, and to run to the kitchen again.

Their habitual pursuits and games are thrown completely into the background.

The kittens throw everything into the shade by making their appearance in the world, and supply the great sensation of the day. If Nina or Vanya had been offered forty pounds of sweets or ten thousand kopecks for each kitten, they would have rejected such a barter without the slightest hesitation. In spite of the heated protests of the nurse and the cook, the children persist in sitting by the cat's box in the kitchen, busy with the kittens till dinner-time. Their faces are earnest and concentrated and express anxiety. They are worried not so much by the present as by the future of the kittens. They decide that one kitten shall remain at home with the old cat to be a comfort to her mother, while the second shall go to their summer villa, and the third shall live in the cellar, where there are ever so many rats.

"But why don't they look at us?" Nina wondered. "Their eyes are blind like the beggars'."

Vanya, too, is perturbed by this question. He tries to open one kitten's eyes, and spends a long time puffing and breathing hard over it, but his operation is unsuccessful. They are a good deal troubled, too, by the circumstance that the kittens obstinately refuse the milk and the meat that is offered to them. Everything that is put before their little noses is eaten by their grey mamma.

"Let's build the kittens little houses," Vanya suggests. "They shall live in different houses, and the cat shall come and pay them visits. . . ."

Cardboard hat-boxes are put in the different corners of the kitchen and the kittens are installed in them. But this division turns out to be premature; the cat, still wearing an imploring and sentimental expression on her face, goes the round of all the hat-boxes, and carries off her children to their original position.

"The cat's their mother," observed Vanya, "but who is their father?"

"Yes, who is their father?" repeats Nina.

"They must have a father."

Vanya and Nina are a long time deciding who is to be the kittens' father, and, in the end, their choice falls on a big dark-red horse without a tail, which is lying in the store-cupboard under the stairs, together with other relics of toys that have outlived their day. They drag him up out of the store-cupboard and stand him by the box.

"Mind now!" they admonish him, "stand here and see they behave themselves properly."

All this is said and done in the gravest way, with an expression of anxiety on their faces. Vanya and Nina refuse to recognise the existence of any world but the box of kittens. Their joy knows no bounds. But they have to pass through bitter, agonising moments, too.

Just before dinner, Vanya is sitting in his father's study, gazing dreamily at the table. A kitten is moving about by the lamp, on stamped note paper. Vanya is watching its movements, and thrusting first a pencil, then a match into its little mouth. . . . All at once, as though he has sprung out of the floor, his father is beside the table.

"What's this?" Vanya hears, in an angry voice.

"It's . . . it's the kitty, papa. . . ."

"I'll give it you; look what you have done, you naughty boy! You've dirtied all my paper!"

To Vanya's great surprise his papa does not share his partiality for the kittens, and, instead of being moved to enthusiasm and delight, he pulls Vanya's ear and shouts:

"Stepan, take away this horrid thing."

At dinner, too, there is a scene. . . . During the second course there is suddenly the sound of a shrill mew. They begin to investigate its origin, and discover a kitten under Nina's pinafore.

"Nina, leave the table!" cries her father angrily. "Throw the kittens in the cesspool! I won't have the nasty things in the house! . . ."

Vanya and Nina are horrified. Death in the cesspool, apart from its cruelty, threatens to rob the cat and the wooden horse of their children, to lay waste the cat's box, to destroy their plans for the future, that fair future in which one cat will be a comfort to its old mother, another will live in the country, while the third will catch rats in the cellar. The children begin to cry and entreat that the kittens may be spared. Their father consents, but on the condition that the children do not go into the kitchen and touch the kittens.

After dinner Vanya and Nina slouch about the rooms, feeling depressed. The prohibition of visits to the kitchen has reduced them to dejection. They refuse sweets, are naughty, and are rude to their mother. When their uncle Petrusha comes in the evening, they draw him aside, and complain to him of their father, who wanted to throw the kittens into the cesspool.

"Uncle Petrusha, tell mamma to have the kittens taken to the nursery," the children beg their uncle, "do-o tell her."

"There, there . . . very well," says their uncle, waving them off. "All right."

Uncle Petrusha does not usually come alone. He is accompanied by Nero, a big black dog of Danish breed, with drooping ears, and a tail as hard as a stick. The dog is silent, morose, and full of a sense of his own dignity. He takes not the slightest notice of the children, and when he passes them hits them with his tail as though they were chairs. The children hate him from the bottom of their hearts, but on this occasion, practical considerations override sentiment.

"I say, Nina," says Vanya, opening his eyes wide. "Let Nero be their father, instead of the horse! The horse is dead and he is alive, you see."

They are waiting the whole evening for the moment when papa will sit down to his cards and it will be possible to take Nero to the kitchen without being observed. . . . At last, papa sits down to cards, mamma is busy with the samovar and not noticing the children. . . .

The happy moment arrives.

"Come along!" Vanya whispers to his sister.

But, at that moment, Stepan comes in and, with a snigger, announces:

"Nero has eaten the kittens, madam."

Nina and Vanya turn pale and look at Stepan with horror.

"He really has . . ." laughs the footman, "he went to the box and gobbled them up."

The children expect that all the people in the house will be aghast and fall upon the miscreant Nero. But they all sit calmly in their seats, and only express surprise at the appetite of the huge dog. Papa and mamma laugh. Nero walks about by the table, wags his tail, and licks his lips complacently . . . the cat is the only one who is uneasy. With her tail in the air she walks about the rooms, looking suspiciously at people and mewing plaintively.

"Children, it's past nine," cries mamma, "it's bedtime."

Vanya and Nina go to bed, shed tears, and spend a long time thinking about the injured cat, and the cruel, insolent, and unpunished Nero.

DIAGNOSIS: *Childhood trauma caused by parental insensitivity to children's feelings, identifications, and projections.*

Sometimes this story is entitled "A Trivial Incident." On the continuum of disturbance, these two children as we see them are quite normal: fighting with each other, irritable when thwarted, quickly diverted, and deeply involved when the matter at hand (the kittens) interests them. From such a trivial incident, however, the children can grasp, sometimes with only half-awareness, the real attitudes of the significant adults in their world. The parents' callousness and lack of concern for important issues of life, death, or designs for the future shake the very foundations of the children's belief in adults. These two children have had the door opened on adult cruelty, evil, and unconcern; on the lack of imagination or ability to project feelings, characteristic of self-centered people. The children's natural sympathies have been shocked by recognition that others feel, see, and act in quite a different way. From such an event defenses are built. Whether these take the form of hiding vulnerability, of cloaking feelings with cruelty, or of rebellion against the world, will depend on the children's own genetic constitutions and the amount of love they have already received, as well as on the strength and humanness they are able to feed each other.

Children can be shocked into disillusion by crudity and lack of concern from teachers as well as from parents. Since school is the child's initial major sojourn into the world at large, teachers represent the world he is to cope with for good or ill. If both home and teachers affirm the evil and carelessness in the world, the problem of adjustment to injustice, or rebellion against injustice, can become major and provide the soil in which pathology can grow.

A Classical Student

Anton Chekhov

Before setting off for his examination in Greek, Vanya kissed all the holy images. His stomach felt as though it were upside down; there was a chill at his heart, while the heart itself throbbed and stood still with terror before the unknown. What would he get that day? A three or a two? Six times he went to his mother for her blessing, and, as he went out, asked his aunt to pray for him. On the way to school he gave a beggar two kopecks, in the hope that those two kopecks would atone for his ignorance, and that, please God, he would not get the numerals with those awful forties and eighties.

He came back from the high school late, between four and five. He came in, and noiselessly lay down on his bed. His thin face was pale. There were dark rings round his red eyes.

"Well, how did you get on? How were you marked?" asked his mother, going to his bedside.

Vanya blinked, twisted his mouth, and burst into tears. His mother turned pale, let her mouth fall open, and clasped her hands. The breeches she was mending dropped out of her hands.

"What are you crying for? You've failed, then?" she asked.

"I am plucked. . . . I got a two."

"I knew it would be so! I had a presentiment of it," said his mother. "Merciful God! How is it you have not passed? What is the reason of it? What subject have you failed in?"

"In Greek. . . . Mother, I . . . They asked me the future of *phero,* and I . . . instead of saying *oisomai* said *opsomai.* Then . . . then there isn't an accent, if the last syllable is long, and I . . . I got flus-

tered. . . . I forgot that the alpha was long in it. . . . I went and put in the accent. Then Artaxerxov told me to give the list of the enclitic particles. . . . I did, and I accidentally mixed in a pronoun . . . and made a mistake . . . and so he gave me a two. . . . I am a miserable . . . person. . . . I was working all night. . . . I've been getting up at four o'clock all this week . . ."

"No, it's not you but I who am miserable, you wretched boy! It's I that am miserable! You've worn me to a threadpaper, you Herod, you torment, you bane of my life! I pay for you, you good-for-nothing rubbish; I've bent my back toiling for you, I'm worried to death, and, I may say, I am unhappy, and what do you care? How do you work?"

"I . . . I do work. All night. . . . You've seen it yourself."

"I prayed to God to take me, but He won't take me, a sinful woman. . . . You torment! Other people have children like everyone else, and I've one only and no sense, no comfort out of him. Beat you? I'd beat you, but where am I to find the strength? Mother of God, where am I to find the strength?"

The mamma hid her face in the folds of her blouse and broke into sobs. Vanya wriggled with anguish and pressed his forehead against the wall. The aunt came in.

"So that's how it is. . . . Just what I expected," she said, at once guessing what was wrong, turning pale and clasping her hands. "I've been depressed all the morning. . . . There's trouble coming, I thought . . . and here it's come. . . ."

"The villain, the torment!"

"Why are you swearing at him?" cried the aunt, nervously pulling her coffee-coloured kerchief off her head and turning upon the mother. "It's not his fault! It's your fault! You are to blame! Why did you send him to that high school? You are a fine

From *The Cook's Wedding and Other Stories,* by Anton Chekhov, translated by Constance Garnett. Reprinted by permission of The Macmillan Company, New York, and Chatto & Windus, Ltd., London.

lady! You want to be a lady? A-a-ah! I dare say, as though you'll turn into gentry! But if you had sent him, as I told you, into business . . . to an office, like my Kuzya . . . here is Kuzya getting five hundred a year. . . . Five hundred roubles is worth having, isn't it? And you are wearing yourself out, and wearing the boy out with this studying, plague take it! He is thin, he coughs . . . just look at him! He's thirteen, and he looks no more than ten."

"No, Nastenka, no, my dear! I haven't thrashed him enough, the torment! He ought to have been thrashed, that's what it is! Ugh . . . Jesuit, Mahomet, torment!" she shook her fist at her son. "You want a flogging, but I haven't the strength. They told me years ago when he was little, 'Whip him, whip him!' I didn't heed them, sinful woman as I am. And now I am suffering for it. You wait a bit! I'll flay you! Wait a bit . . ."

The mamma shook her wet fist, and went weeping into her lodger's room. The lodger, Yevtihy Kuzmitch Kuporossov, was sitting at his table, reading "Dancing Self-taught." Yevtihy Kuzmitch was a man of intelligence and education. He spoke through his nose, washed with a soap the smell of which made everyone in the house sneeze, ate meat on fast days, and was on the look-out for a bride of refined education, and so was considered the cleverest of the lodgers. He sang tenor.

"My good friend," began the mamma, dissolving into tears. "If you would have the generosity—thrash my boy for me. . . . Do me the favour! He's failed in his examination, the nuisance of a boy! Would you believe it, he's failed! I can't punish him, through the weakness of my ill-health. . . . Thrash him for me, if you would be so obliging and considerate, Yevtihy Kuzmitch! Have regard for a sick woman!"

Kuporossov frowned and heaved a deep sigh through his nose. He thought a little, drummed on the table with his fingers, and sighing once more, went to Vanya.

"You are being taught, so to say," he began, "being educated, being given a chance, you revolting young person! Why have you done it?"

He talked for a long time, made a regular speech. He alluded to science, to light, and to darkness.

"Yes, young person."

When he had finished his speech, he took off his belt and took Vanya by the hand.

"It's the only way to deal with you," he said. Vanya knelt down submissively and thrust his head between the lodger's knees. His prominent pink ears moved up and down against the lodger's new serge trousers, with brown stripes on the outer seams.

Vanya did not utter a single sound. At the family council in the evening, it was decided to send him into business.

DIAGNOSIS: *School anxiety—examination panic.*

The story itself presents a perfect case. In this instance the examination anxiety was brought about by an overambitious mother, who fails to recognize the boy's needs and suffering. When he fails, she is miserable only for herself, and quite unaware of the blow to the child's self-esteem. The child is willing, almost relieved, to be whipped for his failure. He regards the punishment as an end to his misery, but his sense of failure will live within him.

Similar examination or school panic may arise in a child who feels he cannot compete with a successful sibling or a too-successful parent. It may arise, too, from an unconscious fear that if he succeeds too well, he will have beaten one of his parents and in so doing bring about that parent's unconscious hatred or resentment. To be hated for a little while, or to disappoint, seems better to the child than to belittle or win out over a parent whom one wants to respect and whose strength one depends on. This is particularly true in the case of gifted children who "underachieve" when their parents lodge much of their own security in "intelligence." School or examination anxiety also arises when a child unconsciously feels (and usually there is an undercurrent of truth in such feelings) that to succeed will bring more demands from home or school and more burdens than he can handle. Often it is not the academic achievement itself that brings burdens but rather what this achievement symbolizes—growing up (reading disabilities frequently are attributable to such an etiology); figuring out things that may seem best left mysterious (often arithmetic failures are caused by this); understanding the past, even one's own past (history failures can be understood in this light); catching on to what might perhaps more safely remain not understood (often foreign languages fall by the wayside in such cases).

In another, extreme form, the panic becomes school phobia. The child literally panics at the sight of school or the thought of going to school. Almost invariably, such a child has strongly ambivalent feelings toward his parents and fears that the home will "fall apart" while he is at school. Often the parents don't get along with each other, or divorce or death has occurred. Sometimes the mother has a greater attachment to her own mother than to her husband and children. Although the child believes that he fears school, he actually fears being away from home. Treatment requires tremendous understanding and teamwork by home and school (and clinic) to reinforce the parents' efforts, even in the face of hysterical outbursts, to help the child go to school and stay there. Upsetting factors in the home must be ameliorated in a way that reassures the child. School phobia more frequently affects girls than boys. The victims seldom have real academic problems. Both teacher and principal must understand and accept the panic, and help the child stay in school at all costs.

The Runaway

Anton Chekhov

The doctor began seeing the patients. He sat in his little room, and called up the patients in turn. Sounds were continually coming from the little room, piercing wails, a child's crying, or the doctor's angry words:

"Come, why are you bawling? Am I murdering you, or what? Sit quiet!"

Pashka's turn came.

"Pavel Galaktionov!" shouted the doctor.

His mother was aghast, as though she had not expected this summons, and taking

From *The Cook's Wedding and Other Stories*, by Anton Chekhov, translated by Constance Garnett. Reprinted by permission of The Macmillan Company, New York, and Chatto & Windus, Ltd., London.

Pashka by the hand, she led him into the room.

The doctor was sitting at the table, mechanically tapping on a thick book with a little hammer.

"What's wrong?" he asked, without looking at them.

"The little lad has an ulcer on his elbow, sir," answered his mother, and her face assumed an expression as though she really were terribly grieved at Pashka's ulcer.

"Undress him!"

Pashka, panting, unwound the kerchief from his neck, then wiped his nose on his sleeve, and began deliberately pulling off his sheepskin.

"Woman, you have not come here on

a visit!" said the doctor angrily. "Why are you dawdling? You are not the only one here."

Pashka hurriedly flung the sheepskin on the floor, and with his mother's help took off his shirt. . . . The doctor looked at him lazily, and patted him on his bare stomach.

"You have grown quite a respectable corporation, brother Pashka," he said, and heaved a sigh. "Come, show me your elbow."

Pashka looked sideways at the basin full of bloodstained slops, looked at the doctor's apron, and began to cry.

"May-ay!" the doctor mimicked him. "Nearly old enough to be married, spoilt boy, and here he is blubbering! For shame!"

Pashka, trying not to cry, looked at his mother, and in that look could be read the entreaty: "Don't tell them at home that I cried at the hospital."

The doctor examined his elbow, pressed it, heaved a sigh, clicked with his lips, then pressed it again.

"You ought to be beaten, woman, but there is no one to do it," he said. "Why didn't you bring him before? Why, the whole arm is done for. Look, foolish woman. You see, the joint is diseased!"

"You know best, kind sir . . ." sighed the woman.

"Kind sir. . . . She's let the boy's arm rot, and now it is 'kind sir.' What kind of workman will he be without an arm? You'll be nursing him and looking after him for ages. I bet if you had had a pimple on your nose, you'd have run to the hospital quick enough, but you have left your boy to rot for six months. You are all like that."

The doctor lighted a cigarette. While the cigarette smoked, he scolded the woman, and shook his head in time to the song he was humming inwardly, while he thought of something else. Pashka stood naked before him, listening and looking at the smoke. When the cigarette went out, the doctor started, and said in a lower tone:

"Well, listen, woman. You can do nothing with ointments and drops in this case. You must leave him in the hospital."

"If necessary, sir, why not?"

"We must operate on him. You stop with me, Pashka," said the doctor, slapping Pashka on the shoulder. "Let mother go home, and you and I will stop here, old man. It's nice with me, old boy, it's first-rate here. I'll tell you what we'll do, Pashka, we will go catching finches together. I will show you a fox! We will go visiting together! Shall we? And mother will come for you tomorrow! Eh?"

Pashka looked inquiringly at his mother.

"You stay, child!" she said.

"He'll stay, he'll stay!" cried the doctor gleefully. "And there is no need to discuss it. I'll show him a live fox! We will go to the fair together to buy candy! Marya Denisovna, take him upstairs!"

The doctor, apparently a light-hearted and friendly fellow, seemed glad to have company; Pashka wanted to oblige him, especially as he had never in his life been to a fair, and would have been glad to have a look at a live fox, but how could he do without his mother?

•   •   •

A long time passed, but the doctor still did not appear. The nurse brought in tea, and scolded Pashka for not having saved any bread for his tea; the assistant came once more and set to work to wake Mihailo. It turned blue outside the windows, the wards were lighted up, but the doctor did not appear. It was too late now to go to the fair and catch finches; Pashka stretched himself on his bed and began thinking. He remembered the candy promised him by the doctor, the face and voice of his mother, the darkness in his hut at home, the stove, peevish granny Yegorovna . . . and he suddenly felt sad and dreary. He remembered that his mother was coming for him next day, smiled, and shut his eyes.

He was awakened by a rustling. In

the next ward someone was stepping about and speaking in a whisper. Three figures were moving about Mihailo's bed in the dim light of the night-light and the ikon lamp.

"Shall we take him, bed and all, or without?" asked one of them.

"Without. You won't get through the door with the bed."

"He's died at the wrong time, the Kingdom of Heaven be his!"

One took Mihailo by his shoulders, another by his legs and lifted him up: Mihailo's arms and the skirt of his dressing-gown hung limply to the ground. A third— it was the peasant who looked like a woman —crossed himself, and all three tramping clumsily with their feet and stepping on Mihailo's skirts, went out of the ward.

There came the whistle and humming on different notes from the chest of the old man who was asleep. Pashka listened, peeped at the dark windows, and jumped out of bed in terror.

"Ma-a-mka!" he moaned in a deep bass.

And without waiting for an answer, he rushed into the next ward. There the darkness was dimly lighted up by a night-light and the ikon lamp; the patients, upset by the death of Mihailo, were sitting on their bedsteads: their dishevelled figures, mixed up with the shadows, looked broader, taller, and seemed to be growing bigger and bigger; on the furthest bedstead in the corner, where it was darkest, there sat the peasant moving his head and his hand.

Pashka, without noticing the doors, rushed into the smallpox ward, from there into the corridor, from the corridor he flew into a big room where monsters, with long hair and the faces of old women, were lying and sitting on the beds. Running through the women's wing he found himself again in the corridor, saw the banisters of the stair-

case he knew already, and ran downstairs. There he recognised the waiting-room in which he had sat that morning, and began looking for the door into the open air.

The latch creaked, there was a whiff of cold wind, and Pashka, stumbling, ran out into the yard. He had only one thought —to run, to run! He did not know the way, but felt convinced that if he ran he would be sure to find himself at home with his mother. The sky was overcast, but there was a moon behind the clouds. Pashka ran from the steps straight forward, went round the barn and stumbled into some thick bushes; after stopping for a minute and thinking, he dashed back again to the hospital, ran round it, and stopped again undecided; behind the hospital there were white crosses.

"Ma-a-mka!" he cried, and dashed back.

Running by the dark sinister buildings, he saw one lighted window.

The bright red patch looked dreadful in the darkness, but Pashka, frantic with terror, not knowing where to run, turned towards it. Beside the window was a porch with steps, and a front door with a white board on it; Pashka ran up the steps, looked in at the window, and was at once possessed by intense overwhelming joy. Through the window he saw the merry affable doctor sitting at the table reading a book. Laughing with happiness, Pashka stretched out his hands to the person he knew and tried to call out, but some unseen force choked him and struck at his legs; he staggered and fell down on the steps unconscious.

When he came to himself it was daylight, and a voice he knew very well, that had promised him a fair, finches, and a fox, was saying beside him:

"Well, you are an idiot, Pashka! Aren't you an idiot? You ought to be beaten, but there's no one to do it."

DIAGNOSIS: *Panic—anxiety caused by adults' lies to avoid child's tears or anger.*

This is the story of terror in a child, induced by adult mishandling. The child, ignorant and afraid, is brought by his ignorant mother to a clinic-hospital, where she, his protector, is cowed, scolded, and dominated by the doctor, who treats his cases in an utterly routine, unindividualized manner. The child is left to the doctor and the hospital. He has never been left before, and the circumstances are not explained to him. Moreover, the doctor lies to him, promises him candy and a jaunt to a fair. He is put in a room with adults who are sick and in pain. His bewilderment increased by the terrifying atmosphere, he seeks out his "friend," the lying doctor, only to find himself once again helpless in the hands of adults, betrayed by the doctor, deserted by his helpless mother, and living in a nightmare of pain and uncertainty.

Thus are sown the seeds of distrust, suspicion, and the pervasive terror of helplessness. Chekhov, who himself was a doctor, understood how the bewilderment and helplessness of children could lead to cruelty in adults or to ineffective, cowed adults. Here is a traumatic incident that could well affect a child's entire life, for his trust in his mother, and other adults who were supposed to take care of him, was shattered.

Such adult lack of understanding happens daily, and not only in hospitals, clinics, and doctor's offices—though a child's physical helplessness in the hands of doctors and nurses makes him particularly vulnerable. It also happens the first day of school in a classroom, or whenever a ridiculing or sarcastic teacher holds a child up for shame or makes a false promise to the child simply to get himself over a potentially unpleasant situation.

The Day of the Last Rock Fight

Joseph Whitehill

Fallbrook Academy

May 16, 195–

Dear Dad,

I expect this will be a very long letter, so I am sending it to your office marked *Personal*. I know you don't like to do family business at the office, but I wanted you to have a chance to read this all by yourself, and I didn't want Mother or Sue reading it before you did.

Thank you for sending my allowance, and also for the subscription to the home paper. Thank you also for the nice new wallet for my birthday. I really needed it, as my old one was afflicted with rot and falling apart.

I apologize for not having written sooner. As you said in your last letter, "*Something* must have happened in the last

From *Able Baker and Others* by Joseph Whitehill (Boston: Little, Brown and Co., 1957). Reprinted by permission of the author.

two months worth writing down." I have been very busy with things here at school, but mainly I haven't written because I didn't know how to say what I wanted to say. I hope this letter will make up for the long delay.

You keep asking me what I think of Fallbrook Academy and if I'm happy here, and so on. Well, I don't like it here, and I want to come home. That's what this letter is for—to tell you that now it's all right for me to come back home. I guess I know why you sent me here, and I admit that I wanted very much to come when I did. It's not that the people here aren't nice or anything. They are. They're so nice it's phony. In all the catalogues of the school they call it a *Special School*, but the boys here call it *Goodbar*. (Mr. Goodbar is a chocolate bar full of nuts.) They all kid about it, and pretend they don't care about being put in a school for misfits and boys with emotional problems. I guess most of them like it here. Most of them say they hate their parents, one or both, and are really glad to get away from them. All the faculty are so sweet and kind and sympathetic that a lot of the boys get away with murder. (That last word was sort of a poor choice, I suppose, but I'll leave it there anyway.) But I don't feel like I belong here any more.

It is going to be very complicated to explain everything in just one letter, because there are lots of different ways of looking at that mess that happened there at home, and I suppose I am the only one who knows the whole story. I guess you sent me here because you thought I was terribly upset by Gene Hanlon getting killed out there at Manning Day School at home, and seeing his body lying in the creek, and so on. Well, that was part of it, but only a little part. The rest of it I couldn't tell anybody until Detective Sergeant Gorman put the story in the paper last week. I got that paper in the mail yesterday and I have been reading the story over and over, and feeling relieved and awful at the same time.

I'm sure you read the same story, so you already know that Gene Hanlon was murdered, instead of getting killed accidentally as they said at first. But neither you nor anybody else knows that I saw the murder done, and knew all the time who did it. I guess if I acted upset afterwards it was from knowing all this and not being able to tell anyone about it. I'm going to work on this letter all night, if it takes that long, because I have to get all this out of my system. (When you stay up after curfew around here they don't actually *make* you go to bed, but the doctor who is on duty looks in on you every half hour or so to see what you're doing, and to try to make you *want* to go to bed.)

I suppose the beginning is the best place to start, so I will tell you first about Gene Hanlon, the boy who got killed. He came to Manning Day School last fall as a senior. They said he was fired from his last school, but I don't know about that. I didn't like him just from looking at him.

I know you hate judgments that way on first impressions, but I couldn't help it. I wouldn't ever bring him over to our house, but if I had, you might have seen what I was talking about. He was big and beefy, and he played on the first string last fall. He was also blond, and the girls thought he was cute and from what I heard they fought over him for dates. But he was a bully, and he cheated in the classroom and he borrowed your stuff without asking you and then left it some place where you had to go hunt it up for yourself.

In a school like Manning Day there are always a number of tight little groups—cliques, I guess you call them—that move around independently and generally stay out of the way of the others. I mean there is a football group, and a group of boys who drink beer, and a group who studies hard, and a group who loafs and tries to avoid everything that looks like work, and a group that meets in the locker room to talk about sex and tell dirty jokes. It was probably the same way when you yourself went to school, but you may have forgotten. When you go to a school like that, you pretty soon find the group that suits you best, and you stay there and don't try to mix with any of the others, because if you do you won't be let in.

What I am getting at in this long explanation is that Gene Hanlon was the Big Man in all the groups I wouldn't be seen dead in. He was tops among the football players and their fans. He could tell filthier stories and, he said, hold more liquor than anybody else. And he told stories about the things he had done to girls that you wouldn't believe if anybody else had told them, but with him telling them, you knew they were all possible. I guess he was feared more than he was liked, but one thing sure, he never went anywhere alone. There was always a loud bunch along with him horse-laughing and beating him on the shoulders.

I stayed out of his way. There is something about me that brings out the worst in bullies. That's what Peter Irish used to say. I guess it's because I'm slightly built, and because of those glasses I have to wear. Once, I was going upstairs to lab, and Gene Hanlon was coming down and we met halfway, and for no reason I could see, he belted me as hard as he could on my shoulder. My glasses flew off and bounced halfway down the stairs along with a whole armload of books and papers. I had to grab the bannister to keep from following them down myself. Two other guys with him saw him do it and didn't say anything at first, but then they looked at Gene and knew they'd better laugh, so they did. So I sat there on the stairs all confused inside, holding my shoulder to make it stop hurting. Gene Hanlon and the others went on down the stairs laughing to beat all at how I looked there with everything scattered around me. On the way down, Gene kicked my physics book ahead of him, bouncing it all the way to the bottom. When I could stand up all right I went down and got it. When I picked it up it fell apart in my hands with its binding broken and I guess I started to cry. I hate to see books treated that way.

When I had about got everything picked up, Peter Irish came up to where I was and wanted to know what had happened. Peter being my best friend, I told him all about it. Probably there were still tears in my eyes about the physics book because Peter said, "Do you want me to get him for you?"

I thought for a minute how swell that would be, but then I said no. It was almost yes because Peter was the only one in school who could have whipped Gene under any rules, and it was a very satisfying thing to think about. But then I thought about afterwards, when Gene would have gotten over his beating and would begin to wonder why Peter had done it, and he would remember that Peter was my best friend. Then he would put one and one together and start out after me seriously. So I said no.

Peter Irish was a good friend to have. I suppose he was the strongest kid in school, but he didn't ever use his strength to bully people, but just for things that were fun, like squashing a beer can in one hand. You knew him pretty well because of all the times he came over to the house to study with me. I remember the time he beat you at Indian hand wrestling on the dining-room table, and you were a real good sport about it because Mother was watching and laughing at your expression. But anyway, you know how strong Peter was, and you can feature what he would have done to Gene if I'd told him to. Peter always stayed out of fights unless they were for fun, and if they ever got serious he'd quit because he didn't want to hurt anybody. But he would have torn Gene Hanlon apart if I had asked him to.

That was something I don't think you understood—Peter and me, I mean, and why we hung around together. The simplest way to say it is that we swapped talents. I used to write a lot of his themes for him, and help him in labs so he'd finish when the rest of us did, and he'd show me judo holds and how to skin a squirrel, and such things. You would call it a good working agreement.

Now, there are just two more things you have to know about to see the whole picture. The first one is Peter Irish and Angela Pine. Peter and Angela went together all last year and the year before, and neither of them wanted anybody else. Both their folks made them date other kids because they didn't like to see them going steady, but everybody knew that Angela belonged to Peter, and Peter belonged to Angela, and that's all there was to it. He used to talk to me a lot about her, and how they were going to get married and run a riding stable together. And he told me that he would never touch her that way until they were married. They used to kiss good night and that was all, because Peter said that when the great thing happened, he wanted it to happen just right, and it could never be really right while they were both kids in high school. A lot of the fellows thought that more went on between them than I know did, but that's because they didn't understand Peter really. He had a simple set of rules he operated under, and they suited him very well. He was good to Angela and good to animals, and all he asked was to be let alone to do things his own way.

The other thing you have to know about is the noontime rock fights. From the papers and the inquest and all, you know something about them, but not everything. I guess most of the parents were pretty shocked to learn that their little Johnny was in a mob rock fight every day at school, but that's the way it was. The fights started over a year ago, as near as I can recollect, and went on all that time without the faculty ever finding out. The papers made a big scandal out of them and conducted what they called an "exposé of vicious practices at select Manning Day School." It was comical, actually, the way everybody got all steamed up over the things we knew went on all the time, not only at Manning but in all the other schools in town. Of course, we all knew the rock fights were wrong, but they were more fun than they seemed wrong, so we kept them up. (That time I came home with the mouse under my eye, I didn't get it by falling in the locker room. I just forgot to duck.)

We had a strict set of rules in the fights so that nobody would really get hurt or anything, and so the little guys could get into them too without fear of being killed. All sixty of us, the whole school, were divided into two teams, the Union Army and the Confederates, and after lunch in the cafeteria we'd all get our blue or gray caps and head out into the woods behind the school. The faculty thought we played Kick the Can and never followed us out to check up on us.

Each team had a fort we'd built out of sapling logs—really just pens about waist high. The forts were about two hundred yards apart, invisible to each other through the trees and scrub. You weren't allowed to use rocks any bigger than a hazelnut, and

before you pegged one at a guy in the opposite army, you had to go *chk, chk* with your mouth so the guy would have a chance to find where it was coming from and duck in time. We had scouting parties and assault teams and patrols, and all the rest of the military things we could think up. The object was to storm the enemy's fort and take it before recess was up and we had to quit.

These rock fights weren't like the papers said at all. I remember the *Morning Star* called them "pitched battles of unrelenting fury, where injuries were frequent." That was silly. If the injuries had been frequent, it wouldn't have been fun any more, and nobody would have wanted to keep doing it. You *could* get hurt, of course, but you could get hurt a lot worse in a football game with the grandstand full of newspaper reporters and faculty and parents all cheering you on.

Now I guess you know everything that was important before the day Gene Hanlon got killed, and I can tell you how it happened so that you'll know why.

After our last morning class, Peter Irish and I went down to the washroom in the basement to clean up for lunch. All morning Peter had acted funny—silent and sort of tied up inside—and it was worrying me some. At first I thought I had done something he didn't like, but if I had, he'd have told me. He'd hardly said two words all morning, and he had missed two recitations in English that I had coached him on myself. But you couldn't pry trouble out of Peter, so I just kept quiet and waited for him to let me in on it.

While he was washing his hands I had to go into one of the stalls. I went in and shut the door and was hanging up my jacket when I heard somebody else come into the washroom. I don't know why, but I sat down—being real careful not to make any noise.

Somebody said, "Hi, Pete, boy." It was Gene Hanlon, and he was alone for once.

"Hi, Gene." That was Peter. (I am

trying to put this down as near as I can just the way they said it.)

"Oh, man!" Gene said. "Today I am exhaust pipe!"

"Tired?"

"You said the word, man. Real beat under."

"Why so?"

"Big date last night. Friend of yours, Angela Pine." Just as if that stall door hadn't been there, I could see Gene grinning at Peter and waiting for a rise out of him. Peter didn't say anything, so Gene tried again. "You're pretty sly, Pete."

"What do you mean?"

"I mean about Angela. You've done a real fine job of keeping her in drydock all this time."

"She dates other guys," Peter said, sounding like he ought to clear his throat.

"Aaaah. She goes out with those meatballs and then comes home and shakes hands at the door. What kind of a date is that?"

"Well, that's *her* business."

Gene said, giggling, "I don't know what her business is, but I got a few suggestions for her if she ever asks me."

"What are you getting at?"

"Real coy, boy. She's crazy for it. Just crazy. Real crazy hungry chick, yeah."

"Are you through?"

"What? . . . Oh, sure. *Hey!* You sore or something?"

Peter said, "It's time for you to go eat lunch."

"All right already. Jesus! You don't have to get *that* way about it. A guy gives you a compliment and you go and get sore. You *are* an odd ball. You and your screwy horses too. See you around." And Gene went out scuffing his feet along the floor.

When I came out of the stall Peter was hunched stiff-armed over the washbasin. He didn't even know I was around. I wished right then that I could have gone back and unlived the last five minutes. I wished they had never happened, and that everything was back just the way it was

before. I was hurt and mad, and my mind was whirling around full of all the stuff Gene Hanlon had said. Just to be doing something, I got busy combing my hair, wetting and shaking the comb and all, trying to find a way to say what I was feeling. Peter was very busy turning both faucets on and off again in a kind of splashy rhythm.

Finally I said, "If you believe all that crap, you're pretty silly. That guy's a bragging liar and you know it."

Peter looked up at me as though he had just noticed I was there. "I've got to believe it," he said.

I jumped on him for that. "Oh, come on," I said. "Give Angela a little credit. She wouldn't give that pile of you-know-what the right time."

Peter was looking down the basin drain. "I called her this morning to say hello. She wouldn't talk to me, Ronnie. She wouldn't even come to the phone."

Now I knew what had been eating him all morning. There wasn't any more a friend could say to Peter, so I made him let go of the faucets and come with me to eat lunch in the cafeteria. All through lunch he just pushed dishes around on his tray and didn't say anything. As we scraped our plates I asked him if he was going out to the fight in the woods, and he surprised me by saying yes, so we got our caps and hiked out to the Confederate fort.

Almost everybody, Gene Hanlon too, was there before us, and they'd already chosen today's generals. Smitty Rice was General of the Armies of the Confederacy, and Gene Hanlon was the Union Commander. Gene took all his boys off to the Union fort to wait for the starting whistle, and Smitty outlined his strategy to us.

There was to be a feint at the south side of the Union fort, and then a noisy second feint from the north to pull the defenders out of position. Then Smitty and Peter Irish were to lead the real massed assault from the south, under the lip of the hill where the first feint had come from. When five minutes had gone by on my watch, we all got up and Smitty blew the starting whistle and we piled out of the fort, leaving only five inside as a garrison, and a couple of alarm guards a little way out on each side of the fort.

I got the job I usually got—advance observation post. I was to note enemy movements and remember concentrations and directions and elapsed times between sightings. Even though you couldn't see more than a hundred feet through the woods, you could always get a fair idea of the enemy strategy by the way they moved their troops around. So all I had to do was stay in one place and watch and listen and remember, and every so often Smitty would send a runner over from field headquarters to check up on what had happened lately. I had three or four good posts picked out where I could hide and not be seen, and I never used the same one twice running.

Today's was my favorite—Baker Post, we called it. It was a dense thicket of young blackjack oak on a low hill on the inside of a bend in the creek, and because nothing grew on the gravel bars of the creek, you could see a long way to each side. The creek ran generally south, cutting the fighting area between the forts right in two, and it made a good defense line because there were only a few places you could cross it in one jump and not get your shoes wet. The east bank of the creek, directly across from Baker Post, is a vertical bluff about ten feet high so that the ground up there is right on eye level with Baker, and the creek and the gravel bars are spread out between you and the bluff bank. I always knew that Baker Post was good, because every time I took it up I had to flush out a covey of quail or a cottontail.

It was always quiet in the woods during the first few minutes of those fights. Even the birds shut up, it seemed like, waiting for the first troop contacts. Out of the corner of my eye I saw somebody jump the creek at the North Ford, and I rolled over to watch. Because of the brush up there I couldn't see who it was, but I knew

he was there because once in a while a bush would stir, or his foot would slide a little on the gravel. Pretty soon he came out to the edge of the underbrush and crouched there looking around and listening. It was Gene Hanlon. His eyes crossed right over me, without finding me, and after a minute he came out and ran low along the creek. When he got even with Baker Post, he went down to his knees and began filling his cap with rocks. I had to laugh to myself at how stupid that was. He should have collected his ammunition earlier, when he and his army were on their way over to their fort. He was wasting maneuvering time and exposing himself for no good reason. It makes you feel good when a guy you hate does something dumb like that.

I got ready to go *chk, chk* with my mouth just to scare him and see him run. But then I looked up at the bluff above him and my heart flopped over inside me. Peter Irish was there, down on one knee, looking over at Gene Hanlon. Gene never looked up. Peter moves like that—floating in and out of the brush as quietly as if he didn't weigh anything. Peter was a good woods fighter.

So instead of going *chk, chk* I hunkered down lower in my thicket and thought to myself that now it wasn't a game any more. Peter looked a long time over at where I was hiding, then he looked up and down the creek bed, and then he moved back a little from the edge of the bluff. He put all his weight pulling on a half-buried boulder beside him until it turned over in its socket and he could get a good grip on it. Even from where I was I could see the cords come out in his neck when he raised it up in his arms and stood up. I hadn't heard a sound except the creek gurgling a little, and Gene Hanlon scratching around in the gravel. And also the blood roaring in my own ears. Watching this was like being in a movie and seeing the story happen on the screen. Nothing you can do or say will change what is going to happen because it's all there in the unwinding reel.

Peter held the heavy stone like a medicine ball and walked to the edge of the bluff and looked down at Gene Hanlon. Gene had moved a few feet south along the creek, so Peter above him moved south too, until he was even with Gene. Peter made a little grunt when he pushed the rock out and away and it fell. Gene heard the grunt and lifted his head to look up, and the rock hit him full in the face and bent his head away back and made his arms fly out. He sat right down in the water with his red and dirty face turned up to the sky and his hands holding him up behind. Then he got himself up with his head still twisted back like that, so he was looking straight up, and he wandered a little way downstream with the water up to his knees, and then he fell out on a gravel bar on his stomach. His legs and arms spread out like he was asleep, but his head was up rigid and his mouth was open. I couldn't look any more.

Peter hadn't made a sound leaving, but when I looked up, the bluff above was empty. As soon as I could move without getting sick I faded out of there and went up north a ways to Able Post and lay down in the foxhole there and held myself around the knees and just shook. I couldn't have felt more upset if I had dropped that rock myself. Just like a movie reel had the ends tied together, the whole scene kept rolling over and over in front of my eyes, and I couldn't stop the film or even turn off the light in the projector.

I lay there with my head down waiting for someone to find the body and start hollering. It was little Marvin Herold, Smitty's courier, who started screaming in his high voice, "Safety! . . . Oh, God! . . . Safetysafetysafety! . . . Help! . . . Help!" "Safety" was the call we used to stop the fights if anyone saw a master coming or somebody got hurt. I lay there for several minutes listening to guys running past me through the brush heading for Baker Post, then I got up and followed them. I couldn't move very fast because my knees kept trying to bend the wrong way.

When I came out of the brush onto the gravel bank, I was surprised that everything looked so different. When I had left just five minutes before, the whole clearing and the creek were empty and lying bright in the sun, and Gene Hanlon was there all alone on the gravel bar. Now, with all the guys standing around and talking at once with their backs to the body, the whole place was different, and it wasn't so bad being there. I saw little Marvin Herold go over and try to take the pulse of Gene Hanlon's body. Marvin is a Boy Scout with lots of merit badges, and I expected him to try artificial respiration or a tourniquet, but he didn't find any pulse so he stood up and shook his head and wobbled over to where we were. He looked terribly blank, as though the *Scout Manual* had let him down.

The assumption going around was that Gene had run off the bluff and landed on his head and broken his neck. I couldn't see Peter anywhere, so I finally had to ask Smitty where he was. Smitty said he had sent Peter in to the school to tell somebody what had happened, and to get the ambulance. Smitty was still being the General, I guess, because there was nothing less for him to do. I tried to think to myself what Peter must be feeling like now, sent off to do an errand like that, but I couldn't get anywhere. My head was too full of what *I* was feeling like, standing with the fellows on the gravel bar looking at Gene Hanlon spread out half in the water like a dropped doll, knowing just how he had gotten there, and not being able to say anything.

Then Smitty got an idea, and he said, "Ronnie, weren't you here at Baker Post all the time?"

I made myself look at him, and then I said, "No, damn it. I got to thinking their army might try a crossing up by Able Post, so I went up there instead."

He said, "Oh," and forgot it.

Not long after, we heard a siren. We all knew what it was, and everybody stopped talking to listen to it as it got nearer. It was the first time I ever heard a siren and knew while hearing it why it had been called, and where it was going. It was sort of creepy, like it was saying to us over the trees, "Wait right there, boys. Don't anybody leave. I'll be there in a minute, and then we'll see just what's going on." I wanted to run and keep on running, until I got away from all the things swarming around inside me. You always wish afterward you had never joggled the wasp ball.

Pretty soon we heard somebody moving in the woods on the bluff and then two big men in white pants, carrying a folded-up stretcher, and another man in a suit, carrying a black bag, came out to the lip of the bluff. They stood there looking at us a minute without saying anything until one of the stretcher-bearers saw Gene Hanlon lying there all alone on the gravel bar. The man said something to the other two, and they all three looked where he pointed. Then the doctor looked at us all bunched up where we were and said, "Well, how do we get down?" He sounded sore. None of us moved or said anything, and in a minute the doctor got tired of waiting and blasted us. "Wake up over there! How do we go to get down?" Smitty came unstuck and gave them directions, and they went back into the brush heading north.

From then on things got pretty crowded in the woods. Two uniformed policemen and a photographer and a plain-clothes man showed up, and then Peter Irish came back leading almost the whole school faculty, and later a reporter and another photographer arrived. Nobody paid any attention to us for a while, so we just sat there in a clump, not moving or saying much. I managed to get right in the middle, and I kept down, hiding behind the guys around me and looking between them to see what was going on. After the police photographer was through taking pictures of Gene Hanlon from all sides, the two ambulance men raised him onto the stretcher and covered him with a piece of canvas or something and carried him away. The photographer took pictures all around by the creek and then went up onto the bluff and took pictures of the ground up there too. The plain-clothes man poking around on the gravel bar found Gene Hanlon's blue cap half full of rocks and gave it, with the rocks still in it, to one of the policemen to save.

I finally got up nerve enough to look for Peter Irish. He was standing with Smitty and Mr. Kelly, the math teacher, and they were talking. Peter didn't look any different. I didn't see how he could do it. I mean, stand right out there in plain sight of everyone, looking natural, with all that in his head. He looked around slowly as though he felt me watching him, and he found me there in the middle of the bunch. I couldn't have looked away if I had tried. He gave me a little smile, and I nodded my head to show him I'd seen it, then he went back to his talking with the other two.

Then the plain-clothes man went over to the three of them, and I got all wild inside and wanted to jump up and say that Peter couldn't possibly have done it, so please go away and let him alone. I could see the plain-clothes man doing most of the talking, and Peter and Smitty saying something once in a while, as though they were answering questions. After a little the plain-clothes man stopped talking and nodded, and the other three nodded back, and then he led them over to where the rest of us were. Smitty and Peter sat down with us and Mr. Kelly collected all the other faculty men and brought them over.

The plain-clothes man tipped his hat back and put his hands in his pockets and said, "My name is Gorman. Sergeant Gorman. We know all about the rock fight now, so don't get nervous that you'll let on something that'll get you into trouble. You're already *in* trouble, but that's not my business. You can settle that with your instructors and your parents. Uh . . . you might think some about this, though. It's my feeling that every one of you here has a share in the responsibility for this boy's death. You all know rock fighting is dangerous, but you went ahead and did it anyway. But that's not what I'm after right now. I want to know if any of you boys actually saw this (what's his name?), this Hanlon boy run over the bluff." I was looking straight at Sergeant Gorman, but in the side of my eye I saw Peter Irish turn his head around and look at me. I didn't peep.

Then Sergeant Gorman said, "Which one of you is Ronnie Quiller?"

I almost fainted.

Somebody poked me and I said, "Me." It didn't sound like my voice at all.

Sergeant Gorman said, "Which?"

I said, "Me," again.

This time he found me and said, "Weren't you supposed to be lying there in this thicket all the time?"

"Yes," I said. All the kids were looking at me. "But there wasn't anything doing here so I moved up there a ways."

"I see," he said. "Do you always disobey orders?"

"No," I said, "but after all, it was only a game."

"Some game," said Sergeant Gorman. "Good clean fun."

Then he let me alone. There was only one person there who knew I would never have deserted the post assigned to me. That was Peter Irish. I guess, Dad, that's when I began to get really scared. The worst of it was not knowing how much Peter knew, and not daring to ask. He might have been waiting out of sight in the brush after he dropped that rock, and seen me take out for Able Post. I had always been his friend, but what was I now to him? I wanted to tell him everything was okay and I wouldn't for the world squeal on him, but that would have told him I knew he did it. Maybe he knew without my telling him. I didn't know what to do.

Sergeant Gorman finished up, "Let's all go back to the school now. I want to talk to each of you alone." We all got up and started back through the woods in a bunch. I figured Peter would think it was funny if I avoided him, so I walked with him.

I said, "Lousy damn day."

He said, "Real lousy."

I said, "It seems like a hundred years since lunch."

We didn't say any more all the way back.

It took all afternoon to get the individual interviews over. They took us from Assembly Hall in alphabetical order, and we had to go in and sit across from Sergeant Gorman while he asked the questions. He must have asked us all the same questions because by the time he got to me he was saying the words like they were tired. A girl stenographer sat by him and took down the answers.

"Name?"

"Ronnie Quiller." I had to spell it.

"Were you at the rock fight this afternoon?"

"Yes, I was."

"What side were you on?"

"The Confederates."

"What were you supposed to do?"

"Watch the guys on the other side."

"After this whistle, did you see anyone?"

"No."

"You sure?"

"No, I didn't. That's why I moved from Baker Post up to Able Post. There wasn't anything doing where I was hiding."

"In rock fights before, have you ever changed position without telling somebody?"

"Sure, I guess. You can't run clear back to the field headquarters to tell anyone anything. It's up to them to find *you.*"

Sergeant Gorman squinted at me with his eyebrows pulled down. "You know that if you had stayed where you were supposed to be you would have seen him fall over that bluff there?"

"Yes," I said.

"I wish you had."

Afterwards I ran into Smitty out in the hall and I asked him why all this fuss with the police and all. I asked him who called them.

"It was Peter, I think. He told Mr. Kelly to, and Mr. Kelly did."

"What do you suppose they're after?" I asked Smitty.

"Oh, I guess they're trying to get a straight story to tell Gene's parents and the newspapers. From what I get from Mr. Kelly, the school is all for it. They want everybody to know they weren't responsible."

"Do *you* think Gene fell over that bluff?" I couldn't help asking that one.

"I don't know. I suppose so." He cocked his head to one side and grinned a little at me. "Like they say in the papers, 'fell or was pushed,' huh?"

I said, "I guess nobody'd have nerve enough to do that to Gene—push him, I mean." All of a sudden I was thinking about something I had seen. Going back in my mind I remembered seeing Sergeant Gorman pick up Gene's cap half full of rocks. Gravel rocks taken from the low bank of the creek. Now, I figured that Sergeant Gorman wouldn't have been a sergeant if he was stupid, and unless he was stupid he wouldn't go on for long thinking that Gene had fallen from above—*when the cap half full of rocks said he'd been down below all the time!*

I got my bike and rode home the long way to give me time to think about Peter and what he had done, and what I should do. You were real swell that night, and I guess I should have told you the whole story right then, but I just couldn't. I put myself in Peter's place, and I knew he would never have told on me. That's the way he was. He hated squealers. I couldn't think about his ever learning I had squealed on him. That would put me right alongside Angela Pine in his book. To him, I would have been the second person he trusted who let him down.

I felt like a rat in a cage with no place to go and no way out. When you kept me home nights after that, I didn't mind, because I wouldn't have gone out after dark if I'd been paid to. I don't blame you and Mother for thinking I had gone loony over the whole thing. Every noon recess for two whole weeks they pulled us into Assembly Hall and one of the masters would give a speech about group responsibility or pub-

lic conscience or something awful like that, and then, worst of all, they made us bow our heads for five minutes in memory of Gene Hanlon. And there I'd be, sitting next to Peter Irish on the Assembly Hall bench, thinking back to the day of the last rock fight, and how Peter had looked up there on the bluff with the cords of his neck pulled tight, holding that big rock like it was a medicine ball. I had the crawliest feeling that if anybody in the hall had raised up his head and looked over at us together there on the bench, he would have seen two great fiery arrows pointing down at us. I was always afraid even to look up myself for fear I would have seen my own arrow and passed out on the spot.

It was my nightmares that got you worried, I guess. They always started out with Peter and me on a hike on a dusty country road. It was so hot you could hardly breathe. We would walk along without saying anything, with me lagging a little behind Peter so I could always keep an eye on him. And then the road would come out on the football field there at school, and he would go over to the woodpile and pick up a thin log and hold it in one hand, beckoning to me with the other and smiling. "Let's go over to the drugstore," he'd say, and then I'd start running.

I would follow the quarter-mile track around the football field and I'd know that everything would be all right if I could only get around it four times for a full mile. Every time I turned around to look, there he'd be right behind me, carrying that log and running easily, just like he used to pace me when I was out for the 880. I would make the first quarter mile all right, but then my wind would give out and my throat would dry up and my legs would get heavy, and I'd know that Peter was about to catch me, and I'd never make that full mile.

Then I would jar awake and be sweating and hanging on tight to the mattress, and in a minute you'd come in to see why I'd screamed. Your face was always kind of sad over me, and there in my bed in the dark, with you standing beside, I would *almost* let go and tell you why things were so bad with me. But then as I'd come awake, and the hammering in my heart would slow up, and the sweat would begin to dry, all the things I owed Peter Irish would stand out again and look at me, and I would know that I could never tell you about it until my telling could no longer get Peter Irish into trouble.

I'm tired now, Dad—tired in so many ways and in so many places that I don't know where to begin resting. This letter took all night, as I thought it would. It's beginning to get light outside and the birds are starting up. I just reread the story in the paper where it says that Sergeant Gorman knew all along that Gene Hanlon had been murdered. I told you he wasn't stupid. He knew what that cap half full of rocks meant, and he knew what it meant to find a big damp socket in the earth on top of the bluff, and the rock which had been *in* the socket down below in the creek. And after he had talked to each of us alphabetically there in the school office, he knew the name of the only boy in school strong enough to lift up a seventy-pound rock and throw it like a medicine ball. He knew all of these things before the sun went down on the day of the last rock fight, but he was two months putting the rest of the story together so he could use it in his business.

As I read it in the paper, Sergeant Gorman went over to Peter's house last Monday night and talked to him about the things he had learned, and Peter listened respectfully, and then, when Sergeant Gorman was through and was ready to take Peter along with him, Peter excused himself to go upstairs and get his toilet articles. He got his four-ten shotgun instead and shot himself. I suppose it was the same four-ten he and I hunted squirrels with.

There's only one good thing about this whole stinking lousy mess, Dad. Because Sergeant Gorman talked to Peter and Peter listened, there in the living room; when Peter Irish climbed up those stairs he did it knowing that I, Ronnie Quiller, had not squealed on him. That may have made it easier. I don't know.

Now please, Dad—please may I come home again?

RONNIE

DIAGNOSIS: *Traumatic or situational neurosis—severe anxiety reaction.*

This story deals with a neurosis brought about by conflict between guilt and loyalty. Ronnie was fully aware of the guilt he shared with Peter by concealment. His conscience or superego immobilized him. He was torn between society's demand to report homicide to the authorities and his own love for and loyalty to his friend. Peter had so many times protected Ronnie from the cruelty or bullying of other boys, particularly the star bully, Gene Hanlon. Ronnie's guilt was not only that of concealment but also that of shared hostility. He too hated Gene Hanlon and at times may have fantasied the aggression that Peter acted out.

In the adolescent struggle for identity, Peter and Ronnie made up one whole person, each compensating for the other's weaknesses and using the other's strength. "We swapped talents," Ronnie says—Ronnie being the intellectual performer. His self-knowledge of being a natural scapegoat led him to regard Peter, the physical performer, with gratitude and respect. Ronnie sensed he must not under any circumstance betray his friend. His emotions were complicated by partial hostility toward Angela (he also had trouble with trust of his own mother, as indicated in the first paragraph of his letter); but, as the physically more passive of the two boys, he was taking the feminine role, which made him feel superior to Angela.

As a sensitive boy, Ronnie was aware that Peter must be protected not only from the police or another betrayer, but even from knowing that he, Ronnie, knew of the crime. Thus, Ronnie felt trapped—"like a rat in a cage"—by the necessity for silence and the projection of guilt. His overt symptoms were deep depression, nightmares, sweat, and inability to be with his friends.

The *fact* of his letter, written to a trusted parent as soon as the crime was exposed, without his having participated in its exposure, released him from his anxiety reaction. He was able to see his own part in the drama and also to evaluate realistically and without blame the part of the adults. His trust in his father's ability to listen to him sympathetically indicates he had a basically sound relationship and therefore the capacity to grow out of this incident.

If father listens, good! Ronnie should come home, resume normal life, and receive individual psychotherapy for catharsis of trauma, for his identity problems (including sexual identity), and for his scapegoat problems. Obviously the boy has great capacity for awareness, introspection, and meaningful relationships.

In the classroom Ronnie would be the good student, on time with assignments. He would be a verbal boy, good at written expression, probably shy in class, fearful of ridicule. He would be hesitant on the playing field and would avoid physical tussles and contacts with his stronger, more aggressive classmates. His close relationship with one other boy would be recognized by a sensitive teacher as possibly restricting and as a defense against taking on aggression himself.

Paul's Case

Willa Cather

It was Paul's afternoon to appear before the faculty of the Pittsburgh High School to account for his various misdemeanors. He had been suspended a week ago, and his father had called at the Principal's office and confessed his perplexity about his son. Paul entered the faculty room suave and smiling. His clothes were a trifle outgrown, and the tan velvet on the collar of his open overcoat was frayed and worn; but for all that there was something of the dandy about him, and he wore an opal pin in his neatly knotted black four-in-hand, and a red carnation in his buttonhole. This latter adornment the faculty somehow felt was not properly significant of the contrite spirit befitting a boy under the ban of suspension.

Reprinted from *Youth and the Bright Medusa* by Willa Cather, by permission of Alfred A. Knopf, Inc. Copyright 1932 by Willa Cather.

Paul was tall for his age and very thin, with high, cramped shoulders and a narrow chest. His eyes were remarkable for a certain hysterical brilliancy, and he continually used them in a conscious, theatrical sort of way, peculiarly offensive in a boy. The pupils were abnormally large, as though he were addicted to belladonna, but there was a glassy glitter about them which that drug does not produce.

When questioned by the Principal as to why he was there, Paul stated, politely enough, that he wanted to come back to school. This was a lie, but Paul was quite accustomed to lying; found it, indeed, indispensable for overcoming friction. His teachers were asked to state their respective charges against him, which they did with such a rancor and aggrievedness as evinced that this was not a usual case. Disorder and impertinence were among the offenses named, yet each of his instructors felt that it was scarcely possible to put into words the real cause of the trouble, which lay in a sort of hysterically defiant manner of the boy's; in the contempt which they all knew he felt for them, and which he seemingly made not the least effort to conceal. Once, when he had been making a synopsis of a paragraph at the blackboard, his English teacher had stepped to his side and attempted to guide his hand. Paul had started back with a shudder and thrust his hands violently behind him. The astonished woman could scarcely have been more hurt and embarrassed had he struck at her. The insult was so involuntary and definitely personal as to be unforgettable. In one way and another, he had made all his teachers, men and women alike, conscious of the same feeling of physical aversion. In one class he habitually sat with his hand shading his eyes; in another he always looked out of the window during the recitation; in another he made a running commentary on the lecture, with humorous intent.

His teachers felt this afternoon that his whole attitude was symbolized by his shrug and his flippantly red carnation flower, and they fell upon him without mercy, his English teacher leading the pack. He stood through it smiling, his pale lips parted over his white teeth. (His lips were continually twitching, and he had a habit of raising his eyebrows that was contemptuous and irritating to the last degree.) Older boys than Paul had broken down and shed tears under that ordeal, but his set smile did not once desert him, and his only sign of discomfort was the nervous trembling of the fingers that toyed with the buttons of his overcoat, and an occasional jerking of the other hand which held his hat. Paul was always smiling, always glancing about him, seeming to feel that people might be watching him and trying to detect something. This conscious expression, since it was as far as possible from boyish mirthfulness, was usually attributed to insolence or "smartness."

As the inquisition proceeded, one of his instructors repeated an impertinent remark of the boy's, and the Principal asked him whether he thought that a courteous speech to make to a woman. Paul shrugged his shoulders slightly and his eyebrows twitched.

"I don't know," he replied. "I didn't mean to be polite or impolite, either. I guess it's a sort of way I have, of saying things regardless."

The Principal asked him whether he didn't think that a way it would be well to get rid of. Paul grinned and said he guessed so. When he was told that he could go, he bowed gracefully and went out. His bow was like a repetition of the scandalous red carnation.

His teachers were in despair, and his drawing master voiced the feeling of them all when he declared there was something about the boy which none of them understood. He added: "I don't really believe that smile of his comes altogether from insolence; there's something sort of haunted about it. The boy is not strong, for one thing. There is something wrong about the fellow."

The drawing master had come to realize that, in looking at Paul, one saw only his white teeth and the forced animation of his eyes. One warm afternoon the boy had gone to sleep at his drawing board, and his master had noted with amazement what a white, blue-veined face it was; drawn and wrinkled like an old man's about the eyes, the lips twitching even in his sleep.

His teachers left the building dissatisfied and unhappy; humiliated to have felt so vindictive toward a mere boy, to have uttered this feeling in cutting terms, and to have set each other on, as it were, in the gruesome game of intemperate reproach. One of them remembered having seen a miserable street cat set at bay by a ring of tormentors.

As for Paul, he ran down the hill whistling the Soldiers' Chorus from *Faust*, looking wildly behind him now and then to see whether some of his teachers were not there to witness his light-heartedness. As it was now late in the afternoon and Paul was on duty that evening as usher at Carnegie Hall, he decided that he would not go home to supper. . . .

After a concert was over, Paul was often irritable and wretched until he got to sleep,—and tonight he was even more than usually restless. He had the feeling of not being able to let down; of its being impossible to give up this delicious excitement which was the only thing that could be called living at all. During the last number he withdrew and, after hastily changing his clothes in the dressing-room, slipped out to the side door where the singer's carriage stood. Here he began pacing rapidly up and down the walk, waiting to see her come out.

Over yonder the Schenley, in its vacant stretch, loomed big and square through the fine rain, the windows of its twelve stories glowing like those of a lighted cardboard house under a Christmas tree. All the actors and singers of any importance stayed there when they were in the city, and a number of the big manufacturers of the place lived there in the winter. Paul had often hung about the hotel, watching the people go in and out, longing to enter and leave schoolmasters and dull care behind him forever.

At last the singer came out, accompanied by the conductor, who helped her into her carriage and closed the door with a cordial *auf wiedersehen,*—which set Paul to wondering whether she were not an old sweetheart of his. Paul followed the carriage over to the hotel, walking so rapidly as not to be far from the entrance when the singer alighted and disappeared behind the swinging glass doors which were opened by a Negro in a tall hat and a long coat. In the moment that the door was ajar, it seemed to Paul that he, too, entered. He seemed to feel himself go after her up the steps, into the warm, lighted building, into an exotic, a tropical world of shiny, glistening surfaces and basking ease. He reflected upon the

mysterious dishes that were brought into the dining-room, the green bottles in buckets of ice, as he had seen them in the supper party pictures of the Sunday supplement. A quick gust of wind brought the rain down with sudden vehemence, and Paul was startled to find that he was still outside in the slush of the gravel driveway; that his boots were letting in the water and his scanty overcoat was clinging wet about him; that the lights in front of the concert hall were out, and that the rain was driving in sheets between him and the orange glow of the windows above him. There it was, what he wanted—tangibly before him, like the fairy world of a Christmas pantomime; as the rain beat in his face, Paul wondered whether he were destined always to shiver in the black night outside, looking up at it.

He turned and walked reluctantly toward the car tracks. The end had to come some time; his father in his night-clothes at the top of the stairs, explanations that did not explain, hastily improvised fictions that were forever tripping him up, his upstairs room and its horrible yellow wall paper, the creaking bureau with the greasy plush collar-box, and over his painted wooden bed the pictures of George Washington and John Calvin, and the framed motto, "Feed my Lambs," which had been worked in red worsted by his mother, whom Paul could not remember.

•   •   •

The leading juvenile of the permanent stock company which played at one of the downtown theaters was an acquaintance of Paul's, and the boy had been invited to drop in at the Sunday night rehearsals whenever he could. For more than a year Paul had spent every available moment loitering about Charley Edwards's dressing-room. He had won a place among Edwards's following not only because the young actor, who could not afford to employ a dresser, often found him useful, but because he recognized in Paul something akin to what churchmen term "vocation."

It was at the theater and at Carnegie

Hall that Paul really lived; the rest was but a sleep and a forgetting. This was Paul's fairy tale, and it had for him all the allurement of a secret love. The moment he inhaled the gassy, painty, dusty odor behind the scenes, he breathed like a prisoner set free, and felt within him the possibility of doing or saying splendid, brilliant things. The moment the cracked orchestra beat out the overture from *Martha*, or jerked at the serenade from *Rigoletto*, all stupid and ugly things slid from him, and his senses were deliciously, yet delicately fired.

Perhaps it was because, in Paul's world, the natural nearly always wore the guise of ugliness, that a certain element of artificiality seemed to him necessary in beauty. Perhaps it was because his experience of life elsewhere was so full of Sabbath-school picnics, petty economies, wholesome advice as to how to succeed in life, and the unescapable odors of cooking, that he found this existence so alluring, these smartly-clad men and women so attractive, that he was so moved by these starry apple orchards that bloomed perennially under the limelight.

It would be difficult to put it strongly enough how convincingly the stage entrance of that theater was for Paul the actual portal of Romance. Certainly none of the company ever suspected it, least of all Charley Edwards. It was very like the old stories that used to float about London of fabulously rich Jews, who had subterranean halls, with palms, and fountains, and soft lamps and richly apparelled women who never saw the disenchanting light of London day. So, in the midst of that smoke-palled city, enamored of figures and grimy toil, Paul had his secret temple, his wishing-carpet, his bit of blue-and-white Mediterranean shore bathed in perpetual sunshine.

Several of Paul's teachers had a theory that his imagination had been perverted by garish fiction; but the truth was, he scarcely ever read at all. The books at home were not such as would either tempt or corrupt a youthful mind, and as for reading the novels that some of his friends urged upon him—well, he got what he wanted much more quickly from music; any sort of music, from an orchestra to a barrel organ. He needed only the spark, the indescribable thrill that made his imagination master of his senses, and he could make plots and pictures enough of his own. It was equally true that he was not stage-struck—not, at any rate, in the usual acceptation of that expression. He had no desire to become an actor, any more than he had to become a musician. He felt no necessity to do any of these things; what he wanted was to see, to be in the atmosphere, float on the wave of it, to be carried out, blue league after blue league, away from everything.

After a night behind the scenes, Paul found the school-room more than ever repulsive; the bare floors and naked walls; the prosy men who never wore frock coats, or violets in their buttonholes; the women with their dull gowns, shrill voices, and pitiful seriousness about prepositions that govern the dative. He could not bear to have the other pupils think, for a moment, that he took these people seriously; he must convey to them that he considered it all trivial, and was there only by way of a joke, anyway. He had autograph pictures of all the members of the stock company which he showed his classmates, telling them the most incredible stories of his familiarity with these people, of his acquaintance with the soloists who came to Carnegie Hall, his suppers with them and the flowers he sent them. When these stories lost their effect, and his audience grew listless, he would bid all the boys good-by, announcing that he was going to travel for a while; going to Naples, to California, to Egypt. Then, next Monday, he would slip back, conscious and nervously smiling; his sister was ill, and he would have to defer his voyage until spring.

Matters went steadily worse with Paul at school. In the itch to let his instructors know how heartily he despised them, and how thoroughly he was appreciated elsewhere, he mentioned once or twice that he had no time to fool with theorems; adding —with a twitch of the eyebrows and a touch of that nervous bravado which so perplexed them—that he was helping the people down at the stock company; they were old friends of his.

The upshot of the matter was, that the Principal went to Paul's father, and Paul was taken out of school and put to work. The manager at Carnegie Hall was told to get another usher in his stead; the door-keeper at the theater was warned not to admit him to the house; and Charley Edwards remorsefully promised the boy's father not to see him again.

The members of the stock company were vastly amused when some of Paul's stories reached them—especially the women. They were hard-working women, most of them supporting indolent husbands or brothers, and they laughed rather bitterly at having stirred the boy to such fervid and florid inventions. They agreed with the faculty and with his father, that Paul's was a bad case.

•　　•　　•

On the part of the hotel management, Paul excited no suspicion. There was this to be said for him, that he wore his spoils with dignity and in no way made himself conspicuous. His chief greediness lay in his ears and eyes, and his excesses were not offensive ones. His dearest pleasures were the gray winter twilights in his sitting room; his quiet enjoyment of his flowers, his clothes, his wide divan, his cigarette and his sense of power. He could not remember a time when he had felt so at peace with himself. The mere release from the necessity of petty lying, lying every day and every day, restored his self-respect. He had never lied for pleasure, even at school; but to make himself noticed and admired, to assert his difference from other Cordelia Street boys; and he felt a good deal more manly, more honest, even, now that he had no need for boastful pretensions, now that he could, as his actor friends used to say, "dress the

part." It was characteristic that remorse did not occur to him. His golden days went by without a shadow, and he made each as perfect as he could.

•　　•　　•

He rose and moved about with a painful effort, succumbing now and again to attacks of nausea. It was the old depression exaggerated; all the world had become Cordelia Street. Yet somehow he was not afraid of anything, was absolutely calm; perhaps because he had looked into the dark corner at last, and knew. It was bad enough, what he saw there; but somehow not so bad as his long fear of it had been. He saw everything clearly now. He had a feeling that he had made the best of it, that he had lived the sort of life he was meant to live, and for half an hour he sat staring at the revolver. But he told himself that was not the way, so he went downstairs and took a cab to the ferry.

When Paul arrived at Newark, he got off the train and took another cab, directing the driver to follow the Pennsylvania tracks out of the town. The snow lay heavy on the roadways and had drifted deep in the open fields. Only here and there the dead grass or dried weed stalks projected, singularly black, above it. Once well into the country, Paul dismissed the carriage and walked, floundering along the tracks, his mind a medley of irrelevant things. He seemed to hold in his brain an actual picture of everything he had seen that morning. He remembered every feature of both his drivers, the toothless old woman from whom he had bought the red flowers in his coat, the agent from whom he had got his ticket, and all of his fellow-passengers on the ferry. His mind, unable to cope with vital matters near at hand, worked feverishly and deftly at sorting and grouping these images. They made for him a part of the ugliness of the world, of the ache in his head, and the bitter burning on his tongue. He stooped and put a handful of snow into his mouth as he walked, but that, too, seemed hot.

When he reached a little hillside, where the tracks ran through a cut some twenty feet below him, he stopped and sat down.

The carnations in his coat were drooping with the cold, he noticed; all their red glory over. It occurred to him that all the flowers he had seen in the show windows that first night must have gone the same way, long before this. It was only one splendid breath they had, in spite of their brave mockery at the winter outside the glass. It was a losing game in the end, it seemed, this revolt against the homilies by which the world is run. Paul took one of the blossoms carefully from his coat and scooped a little hole in the snow, where he covered it up. Then he dozed a while, from his weak condition, seeming insensible to the cold.

The sound of an approaching train woke him, and he started to his feet, re-membering only his resolution, and afraid lest he should be too late. He stood watching the approaching locomotive, his teeth chattering, his lips drawn away from them in a frightened smile; once or twice he glanced nervously sidewise, as though he were being watched. When the right moment came, he jumped. As he fell, the folly of his haste occurred to him with merciless clearness, the vastness of what he had left undone. There flashed through his brain, clearer than ever before, the blue of Adriatic water, the yellow of Algerian sands.

He felt something strike his chest,—his body was being thrown swiftly through the air, on and on, immeasurably far and fast, while his limbs gently relaxed. Then, because the picture-making mechanism was crushed, the disturbing visions flashed into black, and Paul dropped back into the immense design of things.

DIAGNOSIS: *Severe neurosis bordering on psychosis—hysteria, narcissism—leading to suicide out of desperation.*

It is recognized that the number of youth suicides has been increasing. This story illustrates beautifully one of the syndromes leading to such an end.

The faculty meeting, which is held to rule on Paul's dismissal from school, demonstrates the amount of anxiety, hostility, and aggression such a child evokes. Paul's arrogance—his contempt for the mundane world and its mundane teachers, values, and subjects—so enrages those who must try to teach him that they react punitively and hostilely (see "The Use of Force"). They become ashamed of themselves for allowing a child to get under their skin and build up guilt, which, when they meet with no success in their future encounters, spirals to further anger and guilt and so on.

The child, meanwhile, has developed a poor opinion of the people about him and covers over a lack of trust by a strong wall of contempt. His suspicious or contemptuous ways bring out the worst reactions of people, thus alienating them still further.

Paul, in his hatred for his real life, his home, neighborhood, school, and teachers, takes refuge in a made-up world of theater, glamour, and make-believe. Only this world of showmanship has any meaning to him. He seeks beauty from outside, smooth and unruffled by reality, to make up for the lack of beauty and warmth inside him. Love and understanding have been so far lost in his young life that these values seem to exist only in the wealthy, the glamorous, the dramatic life. His hysterical nature arises from the theory that if one poses enough, the pose may become reality. He steals money, not as a delinquent, but to buy himself the adornment he lacks inside. When the money runs out, the meaning of life runs out for him and he commits suicide.

To handle and reach such a child would require a great deal of security and self-esteem on the teacher's part—so that he would not be thrown by the child's false wall of arrogance and contempt, or repelled by the child's narcissistic or vaguely homosexual manner. He would have to share some of this child's love of the unreal world, encouraging his taste for the drama in a useful way, offering him esthetic outlets and reward for honest work. Suicide might be avoided in such a case if the child were given psychotherapeutic treatment and a sympathetic school atmosphere, especially if he were allowed to work out his feelings of emptiness and despair by identifying with someone of his own sex. The child who cannot care deeply (not necessarily sexually) for someone of his own sex is unlikely to move on to loving someone of the opposite sex. Ergo, the necessary pre-adolescent stage of development where girls are interested only in girls, and boys in boys—the clique, the group, the gang, the pal, the chum.

Lie Down in Darkness
William Styron

[*The family members: Helen, the mother; Milton or Loftis, the father, whom the daughter, Peyton, calls Bunny.*]

. . . He heard Edward's laughter somewhere, Edward who was already tight, with whom he had, for Helen's sake, enacted the most strained and touchy friendship, and for some reason the desire for a drink became hot and powerful. There were other footsteps in the hall, and he started, but they faded away; how silly to have this nervous, quarrelsome conscience, that resentment—yes, he had had it, just for a moment, at Edward's laughter which, in turn, had made him think of Helen and of the ridiculousness of her demands on him, demands he had paradoxically brought on himself—all in all, how silly to have to pussyfoot about like this on Peyton's wedding day, dredging up such ugly conflicts. Or was it silly? Well, my God, just one. He found two glasses, got the bottle out of the dresser and went back to Peyton's room, closing the door behind him.

"Oh, Bunny, you're so clever," she said, "all in such a cunning little bottle."

Loftis looked at her sharply. "Baby,"

he murmured, sitting down beside her, "do you really want a drink? Why don't we wait until afterwards? There's champagne——"

"Don't be a spoilsport. Make me a drink. This is just for my nerves." Obediently he poured an ounce or so into a glass.

"Aren't you going to have one?" she asked.

Why had he suddenly become so depressed? It was unfair of Peyton to seduce him like this, and he found himself saying, "You know, baby, I've found that when everything is going along all right you don't need anything to drink. When you're happy——"

But she broke in with a laugh, her face rosy with some sudden excitement, "Don't be so solemn, Bunny, this is for my nerves, buck up, sweetie. . . ."

He poured himself a drink and with the first swallow, his dark mood fading, he gazed at her, then past her—avoiding those eyes—to say, while the whisky taste began to seem unfamiliarly sweet and strong, "So anyway, honey, you're here and you're going to get married to a swell guy and that's all that counts. Isn't it wonderful?"

"Yes. I'm here. Thanks to you."

"It's not my doing," he said, "thank your mother."

"I've thanked her," she said wryly, looking away.

"Now don't——" he began, for it was wrong, unbearably wrong for her to bring up, on this day of all, the faintest suggestion of regrettable memories; those memories had indeed made this day poignantly perfect, childish in its brazen delight, like the day long ago of the circus or the fair, sweet from its apocalyptic dawning to the last, exhausted, bedtime end; all the near-ruined moments in the family had made this particular day even sweeter, but it was absolutely unfair of Peyton to suggest now that anything had ever been wrong one bit. The illusion of serenity would be swept away like so many dew-drenched spider webs leaving only the unsightly façade, the dusty plaster and all the bricks with their weathered holes. So *quit, quit* it, he was trying to say, softly but forcibly. . . .

"Don't you see, Bunny, I've got my own reasons for coming home. I've wanted to be normal. I've wanted to be like everybody else. These old folks wouldn't believe that there are children who'd just throw back their heads and howl, who'd just *die*, to be able to say, 'Well now my rebellion's over, home is where I want to be, home is where Daddy and Mother want me.' Not with a sort of take-me-back-I've-been-so-wrong attitude—because, Bunny, you can believe me, most kids these days are not wrong or wrongdoers, they're just aimless and lost, more aimless than you all ever thought of being—not with that attitude, but just with the kind of momentary, brief love recognizing those who fed your little baby mouth and changed your didy and paid your fare all the way. Does that sound silly, Bunny? That's all they want to do, that's what I've wanted to do and I've tried, but somehow today it all seems phony. I don't know why. I lied. I'm really not excited at all. Maybe I've got too many sour memories." She paused and looked at him, her eyes enormously sad, and he approached her, with the day in its crumbling promise going before his vision, tried to put his arms around her. "Baby——"

"Don't," she said, "don't, Bunny. I'm sorry." She held him off without even a look, for she was gazing down at the lawn, at the guests moving toward the house, all together, silent, but with a sort of giddy haste, like picnickers before the storm—holding him off as much by her silence as if she had finished erecting between them a curtain of stone, then said gently: "I'm sorry, Bunny." She looked up at him. "I can't figure where the trouble starts. Mother. She's such a faker. Look at this circus. Flaunting the blissful family. Oh, I feel so sorry for us all. If just she'd had a soul and you'd had some guts . . . Come on now," she said, grabbing his sleeve, "let's go downstairs, sweetie. I'll put up a real good front for you."

He stood rooted to the rug, wishing to faint there forever. He had been bludgeoned half to death, not so much by these truths, he told himself while he drained the sedative glass, as by necessity.

"O.K., baby," he said.

.   .   .

And this day had really been a triumph for her. No one would ever know. No one would ever know what electric fulfillment she felt, beneath the soft, tender dignity of her manner, behind the wrinkled, rather sad, but gracefully aging serenity of her brow. No one would ever know the struggle, either. The struggle to accomplish just this casual, collected air of the proud mother: the woman who has sacrificed, whose suffering is known to the community, but who, on the day of her daughter's marriage, presents only the face of humility and courage and gentle good will. It had been cruelly difficult to put on this act, and how she had connived, how she had falsified her true feelings! But she knew that any means justified *this* end, *this* day, and after she had murmured into Milton's ear, "Oh, darling, I do want Peyton to come home," she had rejoiced at the sincere and grateful look in his eyes; she could tell he didn't doubt her honesty.

Her honesty. Oh, what was honesty, anyway? After so much suffering, did a woman really have to be honest to fulfill herself? She felt that her marriage had been such a nightmare, she had endured so many insults—the weight of so many outrages had pressed so heavily upon her spirit—that she could discard honest intentions in order to make this one day come true. *Anything, anything,* she had said to herself these past months, *anything at all.* Anything that Peyton should come home. Anything that people should know Helen Loftis was a good mother, a successful mother. Anything that people should know: it was Helen Loftis, that suffering woman, who had brought together the broken family.

Now, in sheer, rash courtliness, Carey bent down and kissed her hand. She knew how Carey saw her: poised, gentle, smiling brightly. Who could tell, she asked herself —and certainly it wasn't Carey who could tell, in his dense, well-meaning charity— that this genteel sprightliness masked the most villainous intentions? Well they *were* villainous. Here a shadow passed over her mind, just briefly, but long enough for Carey to murmur, "What's wrong, Helen?"

"Why, nothing, Carey!"

They were cruel intentions, cruel feelings, and perhaps unnatural, but what could she do? She had suffered too much and too long not to feel them. Or it. This profound and unalterable *loathing* of Peyton. Poor Peyton. Dishonorable, sinful. Her own flesh and blood.

· · ·

Loftis was aware of the noise but for a solitary instant he felt—looking at Peyton and Helen and Harry—islanded in silence. And during this moment he again tried vainly to recall what he had said or done to bring on such a tense and obvious, such a mutual sense of uneasiness. *Ah, those smiles, those smiles.* Was it the kiss he gave Peyton?

Then all at once he had a flicker of insight and during this moment—so brief that it lasted, literally, one blink of Peyton's eyes—he knew what the smiles were about and he had a crushing, chilling premonition of disaster. Harry smiled politely, but he faded before his sight, for Loftis was

watching Peyton. She held her glass in the air, touched it to her lips. But along with her smile there was something else he was conscious of, too: she had already drunk too much. Her face rubbed pink as if by a scrubbing brush, she glowed with a fever, and in the way her eyes sparkled, her lips moist and parted, he knew somehow, with a plummeting heart, that she was beyond recovery. It was a moment of understanding that came sharp and terrible. He felt that he had waited all of his life for this moment, this flash of insight to come about. He had just said crazy, unthinking, harmless words, but he had said words like "fickle" and "love" and "death," and they, in their various ways, had sent a secret corrosion through these two women's hearts. God help him, hadn't he known all along that they hated and despised each other? Had he had to spend twenty years deceiving himself, piling false hope upon false hope—only to discover on this day, of all days, the shattering, unadorned, bitter truth? Those smiles . . . of course . . . how Peyton and Helen had always smiled at each other like that! There had been words, too, attitudes, small female gestures which it had been beyond him to divine, or even faintly to understand.

And he had gone on for years deceiving himself—too proud, too self-conscious, maybe just too stupid to realize that it had always been he himself who had been at the focus of these appalling, baffling female emotions. Not anything he had done or had failed to do had made them hate each other. Not even Dolly. None of his actions, whether right or wrong, had caused this tragedy, so much as the pure fact of himself, his very existence, interposed weaponless and defenseless in a no-man's-land between two desperate, warring female machines. Now he had kissed Peyton, said the wrong words, and he had somehow hurt her. And the smile she wore concealed her hurt—to everyone else, at least—just as Helen's smile, echoing Peyton's, concealed only the wild, envenomed jealousy which stirred at her breast. What had she done? Why had

Helen deceived him like this? Those smiles. He was chilled with a sudden horror. Those smiles. They had fluttered across the web of his life like deceptive, lovely butterflies, always leading him on, always making him believe that, in spite of everything, these two women really did love each other. That, deep down, there was motherly, daughterly affection. But no. Now he saw the smiles in a split moment for what they were: women smiles—Great God, so treacherous, so false, displayed here—himself between them—like the hateful wings of bats.

. . .

"You just go straight to hell, Edward," Loftis muttered, shoving him away. He plodded on upstairs. In the hallway it was dark and silent. The sounds from below came up muted and indistinct. For a moment he stood at the head of the stairs with his nose in the air, sniffing, reconnoitering. He couldn't see a thing but in the darkness shapes and shadows reeled indiscriminately, and he had to steady himself against the wall. He felt his heart pounding, and a cold dread. He pulled himself together some and moved down the hall on precarious tiptoe, trying to avoid knocking things over. Finally from Helen's room he heard voices. A voice, rather: Helen's. He stole near the door. It was closed but not locked, and a thin wedge of light fell onto the hallway floor. He heard Peyton say, "Words, words, words—why don't you get to the point?" Later he was unable to recollect, because of the fog in his mind, just what came next, but it went something like this:

Helen's voice, unemotional, polite, but direct: "That's what I'm trying to tell *you*, my dear. No, I didn't expect you not to drink some. Do you think I'm a member of the W.C.T.U.? Certainly not. But my dear girl, it's this other thing that matters to me. Really, Peyton, after all we've done to plan this affair for you, do you think——"

Peyton's voice cut in angrily: "Do I think what? What? Will you please explain?"

"This business with your father. Do you really think you have any right to treat him like you have? After all he's done for

you? I saw what happened just now. Really, Peyton, you needn't pretend that it didn't happen or no one saw it. Because I saw it. I *saw* it, I tell you."

"*What?*"

"Just this." Her tone grew short and harsh. "Just this. Lashing out at him like that. In front of everybody. I wasn't the only one who saw it. Chess Hegerty saw it, and the Braunsteins. Everybody. After all I've planned. After everything I've tried—not tried but *had* to forget about you, in order to make this whole affair come off right. I said to myself, 'Well, I'll forget everything that she's done.' For the sake of morality, for the sake of Christian principles. For the sake of everything decent I'll overlook the things you've done——"

"What things?"

"Never mind. I said I'd overlook them for the sake of everything decent. So you could be married properly, in your own home. The home you forsook easily, too. That was the irony. Anyway, for all these decent things, for their sake, I said I'd make this wedding a success. If it killed me. For your father's sake, too. Now see what you've done. Everyone knows you hate me. That doesn't matter. But for them to know you hate him, too! After all these years of your faking and your flattery and your seductions——"

There was a sudden thump, a creak of springs, as if someone had fallen abruptly back upon a bed. There was laughter, too, Peyton's, tense and somewhat hysterical but also muffled, the laughter of someone lying horizontal: "Oh, God, really. If that isn't the limit. Poor Helen, you've really suffered, haven't you? Poor Helen. You're a sad case, you know, and I really shouldn't be talking like this. I really should be silent and forbearing, charitable, really, but I just can't. You're such a wretched case I can't even feel pity——"

"You shut up. You respect your elders. Your parents who——"

"You can't even suffer properly," Peyton broke in, her voice solemn now; "You're like all the rest of the sad neurotics everywhere who huddle over their misery and take their vile, mean little hatreds out on anybody they envy. You know, I suspect you've always hated me for one thing or another, but lately I've become a symbol to you you couldn't stand. Do you think I'm stupid or something, that I haven't got you figured out? You hate men, you've hated Daddy for years, and the sad thing is that he hasn't known it. And the terrible thing is that you hate yourself so much that you just don't hate men or Daddy but you hate everything, animal, vegetable and mineral. Especially you hate me. Because I've become that symbol. I *know* I'm not perfect but I'm free and young and if I'm not happy I at least know that someday I *can* be happy if I work at it long enough. I'm free. If I'd hung around in Port Warwick and married some simple-minded little boy who worked in the shipyard and lived in a little bungalow somewhere and came to see you and Daddy every Sunday, you'd be perfectly content. You'd have your claws in me then. I'd be obeying your precious code of Christian morality, which is phony anyway. But it's not that way. I'm free and you can't stand it——"

"You hate——"

Peyton's feet hit the floor; Loftis could hear them, the snapping, outraged heels. "I know what you're going to say! You're going to say I hate Port Warwick, Daddy, everything. Well, it's not true! I don't hate anything that you haven't forced me to hate and, damn you, you've forced me to hate you——"

Helen's voice rose on a high, hyster-ical wail. "You *tell* me these things and you don't know . . . you don't *know*," she cried wildly, "and you come here and make a mockery—with your—airs . . . and after all your sleeping around . . . you don't know . . . and your filthy little Jew . . ."

Loftis moved toward the door, but it was too late. The moment of silence which lasted between Helen's final word and what came next seemed to possess at once brevity and infinite length; this silence, so brief and so timeless, had, in its sense of awfulness, all the quality of a loud noise. Then Loftis heard it, a scuffling sound and a single, agonized moan, but he was still too late; he threw open the door. Peyton rushed sobbing past him into the hallway, down the stairs. He reached out for her, but she had gone like air, and he stood wobbling in the doorway, watching Helen. With her hands at her face she was moaning, but through her fingers ran trickles of blood and he looked at these, with a sort of remote and objective fascination, and paid no attention to her moans. He never remembered how long he stood there—perhaps half a minute, perhaps more—but when, sensing his presence, she removed her hands and looked at him, her lips moving soundlessly and her cheeks so dead and white beneath the raw, deep slits gouged out by Peyton's fingernails, he only said—making a bad job of it because of his perverse, whisky-thick tongue: "God help you, you monshter."

Then he went downstairs.

DIAGNOSIS: *Family neurosis—alcoholic father, with poorly repressed incestuous feelings toward daughter, embittered mother completely involved with severely handicapped older sister—guilt on both sides and increasingly destructive family relationships.*

This long novel should be read in its entirety. One learns in the first chapter that the focal character, Peyton, committed suicide at the age of 22. Her father is a weak, kind, charming alcoholic, deeply involved and overidentified with his daughter. Her mother, Helen, a borderline psychotic, is deeply resentful and jealous of the relationship of these two. She had given all her attention and affection to the older daughter, Maudie—a feeble-minded cripple who died before Peyton's suicide. Time and again in the novel the author demonstrates how the beautiful, bright, and miserable Peyton is caught in the crossfire of the parents, and is used as a weapon to fight their fight. Finally she learns how to use their hatred and hostile dependency, as a way of turning them further against each other.

Family neurosis is a phenomenon too often seen today. Indeed, most neurosis can be said to be a "family" illness. This story illustrates the common tragedy of an interwoven misery, where the illness of one member causes the illnesses of the other family members and, in turn, is fed by their sickness. No one can seem to disengage himself. Each one chooses an escape that is no escape: the father, alcohol; the mother, withdrawn, delusionary brooding; the daughter, suicide; even the feeble-minded sister found comfort in her helplessness and, finally, in death.

This is not so unusual a history as one would like to think. You will see Peytons in your classroom. They will be bright, pretty, social successes, sporadically brilliant and careless. They will demand special privileges, special hours, turn in overdue reports and superficial papers. They frequently flunk out but more often get by through charm, manipulation, and cleverness.

You will see the father in the classroom as a charming boy—easily led, kindly, weak, unable to stick the hard subjects out, good at those one can bluff at, glib, seductive with his teachers and often successful in his seduction, infantile, passive, too eager to please without a center of gravity of self.

You can also see Helens in your classroom, strong-willed, stubborn, aggressive, dominating the other girls and belittling the weak members of the class, pointing out the worst side of any event or person.

For the Peytons and the Loftis-Miltons, the teacher must set firm limits. He must show full and hearty acceptance of their warmth and responsiveness but refuse to be manipulated or fooled by them. He must show them that they are acceptable and worthy, that bluff and pretense are unnecessary and unrewarding.

The Helens need more love and lower standards of perfection. Their standards for themselves are inhumanly rigid and high. They need to learn to accept their own fallibility and, thus, make room for the human foibles of others. Above all, they should not be allowed to cultivate their own sufferings or use them as a weapon against classmates or teachers.

In the case of Peyton's family, all of them needed treatment of a well-designed sort. Perhaps everybody would not have been cured, or even reached. But some members of the family might have been. At least, Peyton's fate might well have been avoided.

Notes from Underground
Fyodor Dostoyevsky

But, in the beginning, what agonies I went through in this inner struggle! I didn't

From *Notes from Underground* by Fyodor Dostoyevsky, trans. Andrew R. MacAndrew (New York: New American Library of World Literature, Inc., Signet Classics, 1961).

believe that there were others who went through all that, so I've kept it a secret all my life. I was ashamed (perhaps, even now, I am still ashamed). I reached a point where I felt a secret, unhealthy, base little pleasure in creeping back into my hole after some disgusting night in Petersburg and forcing myself to think that I had again done something filthy, that what was done couldn't be undone. And I inwardly gnawed at myself for it, tore at myself and ate myself away, until the bitterness turned into some shameful, accursed sweetishness and, finally, into a great, unquestionable pleasure. Yes, yes, definitely a pleasure! I mean it! . . .

I, for instance, am horribly sensitive. I'm suspicious and easily offended, like a dwarf or a hunchback. But I believe there have been moments when I'd have liked to have my face slapped. I say that in all seriousness—I'd have derived pleasure from this too. Naturally it would be the pleasure of despair. But then, it is in despair that we find the most acute pleasure, especially when we are aware of the hopelessness of the situation. And when one's face is slapped—why, one is bound to be crushed by one's awareness of the pulp into which one has been ground. But the main point is that, whichever way you look at it, I was always guilty in the first place, and what is most vexing is that I was guilty without guilt, by virtue of the laws of nature. Thus, to start with, I'm guilty of being more intelligent than all those around me. (I've always felt that and, believe me, it's weighed on my conscience sometimes. All my life, I have never been able to look people straight in the eye—I always feel a need to avert my face.) And then, I'm also guilty because, even if there had been any forgiveness in me, it would only have increased my torment, because I would have been conscious of its uselessness. I surely would have been unable to do anything with my forgiveness: I wouldn't have been able to forgive because the offender would simply have been obeying the laws of nature in slapping me, and it makes no sense to forgive the laws of nature—but neither could I have forgotten it, because it is humiliating, after all. Finally, even if I hadn't wanted to be forgiving at all, but on the contrary, had wished to avenge myself on the offender, I couldn't have done it, for

the chances are I'd never have dared to do anything about it even if there had been something I could do. Why wouldn't I have dared? Well, I'd especially like to say a few words about that.

. . .

And there, in its repulsive, evil-smelling nest, the downtrodden, ridiculed mouse plunges immediately into a cold, poisonous, and—most important—never-ending hatred. For forty years, it will remember the humiliation in all its ignominious details, each time adding some new point, more abject still, endlessly taunting and tormenting itself. Although ashamed of its own thoughts, the mouse will remember everything, go over it again and again, then think up possible additional humiliations. It may even try to avenge itself, but then it will do so in spurts, pettily, from behind the stove, anonymously, doubting that its vengeance is right, that it will succeed, and feeling that, as a result, it will hurt itself a hundred times more than it will hurt the one against whom its revenge is directed, who probably won't even feel enough of an itch to scratch himself.

. . .

How can one, after all, have the slightest respect for a man who tries to find pleasure in the feeling of humiliation itself? I'm not saying that out of any mawkish sense of repentance. In general, I couldn't stand saying "Sorry, Papa, I'll never do it again."

And it wasn't at all because I was incapable of saying it. On the contrary, perhaps it was just because I was only too prone to say it. And you should've seen under what circumstances too! *I'd get myself blamed, almost purposely, for something with which I'd had nothing to do even in thought or dream.*[1] That's what was most disgusting. But, even so, I was always deeply moved, repented my wickedness, and cried; in this, of course, I was deceiving myself, although I never did so deliberately. It was my heart that let me down

[1] Italics ours—Eds.

here. In this case, I can't even blame the laws of nature, although those laws have oppressed me all my life. It makes me sick to remember all this, but then I was sick at the time too. It took me only a minute or so to recognize that it was all a pack of lies; all that repentance, those emotional outbursts and promises of reform—nothing but pretentious, nauseating lies. I was furious. And if you ask me now why I tortured and tormented myself like that, I'll tell you: I was bored just sitting with my arms folded, so I went in for all those tricks. Believe me, it's true. Just watch yourself carefully and you'll understand that that's the way it works. I made up whole stories about myself and put myself through all sorts of adventures to satisfy, at any price, my need to live. How many times did I convince myself that I was offended, just like that, for no reason at all. And although I knew that I had nothing to be offended about, that I was putting it all on, I'd put myself into such a state that in the end I'd really feel terribly offended. I was so strongly tempted to play tricks of this sort that, in the end, I lost all restraint. . . .

But I can't see any justice or virtue in vengeance, so if I indulge in it, it is only out of spite and anger. Anger, of course, overcomes all hesitations and can thus replace the primary reason precisely because it is no reason at all. But what can I do if I don't even have anger (that's where I started from, remember)? In me, anger disintegrates chemically like everything else, because of those damned laws of nature. As I think, the anger vanishes, the reasons for it evaporate, the responsible person is never found, the insult becomes an insult no longer but a stroke of fate, just like a toothache, for which no one can be held responsible. And so I find that all I can do is take another whack at the stone wall, then shrug the whole thing off because of my failure to find the primary cause of the evil.

• • •

[*Behind the veil of masochism and anger are dreams of glory and grandiose fantasies—Eds.*]

But how much love—ah, how much—I experienced in my dreams, when I escaped to "the sublime and the beautiful." Perhaps it was an imaginary love and maybe it was never directed toward another human being, but it was such an overflowing love that there was no need to direct it—that would've been an unnecessary luxury. Everything always ended safely in a leisurely, rapturous sliding into the domain of art, that is, into the beautiful lives of heroes stolen from the authors of novels and poems and adapted to the demands of the moment, whatever they might be. I, for instance, triumph over everyone, and they, of course, are strewn in the dust, acknowledging my superiority; I'm all-forgiving; I'm a great poet and court chamberlain; I fall in love; I inherit millions and donate them to human causes and take advantage of this opportunity to publicly confess my backslidings and disgrace which, of course, is no ordinary disgrace but contains much that is "sublime and beautiful" in it, something in the Manfred style. Everyone is weeping and kissing me (they could hardly be so thick-skinned as not to); then I leave, hungry and barefoot, to preach new ideas and rout the reactionaries at Austerlitz. Then, a triumphal march is played, an amnesty is declared, the Pope agrees to leave Rome for Brazil, there's a ball for all of Italy at the Villa Borghese on the shores of Lake Como, which lake, for this occasion, is moved to the vicinity of Rome. Then there's a scene in the bushes, and so on and so forth; see what I mean? . . .

DIAGNOSIS: *Masochist solution—repressed or concealed rage, impotent anger covering fantasies of grandeur, glory and supremacy, which are never risked by acting upon.*

These "notes from underground" reflect the very core of the masochistic solution, demonstrating great self-imposed suffering. They indicate the unending hostility and rage behind the abject *mea culpa* attitudes; anger which can never be expressed directly—for, if it is, the masochistic structure falls. Should the structure fall, the lurking, secret contempt and grandiose fantasies would have to be tested in the light of the real world, where they are bound to fail. Failure, though devastating, is less upsetting to the masochist than success. Strange? Think of the children who continually get hurt, always appear put upon, are always the scapegoats. At first one sides with them. Later, one observes, it is always the same little Johnny or Jane who gets in the way of the flung ball or book or rock; who sometimes by his very posture provokes Bill to bullying. It is the same Johnny or Jane whose paper gets torn just as it is to be passed in, or who always has obstacles in the way of completing the assignment that would assure the expected A or B. This Johnny or Jane always—whether academically, physically, or socially—messes up and looks sad and beaten.

Why? There are many possible causes. The answer may lie in a mother who "suffers" all the time, so that joy is not in the child's perception of life and seems somehow wrong. A too-successful and proud parent or sibling may leave no room for Johnny or Jane to be anything special except a special failure. His parents may transmit to him, consciously or unconsciously, a feeling that he is alive only for the purpose of erasing their troubles or complementing their lives. These being impossible, there is nothing left for Johnny or Jane but to live out an apology; to say, "I can't, I can't, I can't, I'm sorry, I'm sorry, I'm sorry." And "I hate you for asking this of me, for then I feel I must but it is too much for me." This last is never said aloud and is often not consciously felt, but it is at the root of many a miserable life dedicated to masochistic suffering and failure.

Melanctha
Gertrude Stein

. . . Melanctha Herbert was always losing what she had in wanting all the things she saw. Melanctha was always being left when she was not leaving others.

Melanctha Herbert always loved too hard and much too often. She was always full with mystery and subtle movements and denials and vague distrusts and complicated disillusions. Then Melanctha would be sudden and impulsive and unbounded in some faith, and then she would suffer and be strong in her repression.

Melanctha Herbert was always seeking rest and quiet, and always she could only find new ways to be in trouble.

Melanctha wondered often how it was

Condensed from "Melanctha: Each One as She May," Copyright 1909 and renewed 1936 by Gertrude Stein. Reprinted from *Three Lives*, by Gertrude Stein, by permission of Random House, Inc.

she did not kill herself when she was so blue. Often she thought this would be really the best way for her to do.

Melanctha Herbert had been raised to be religious, by her mother. Melanctha had not liked her mother very well. This mother, 'Mis' Herbert, as her neighbors called her, had been a sweet-appearing and dignified and pleasant, pale yellow, colored woman. 'Mis' Herbert had always been a little wandering and mysterious and uncertain in her ways.

Melanctha was pale yellow and mysterious and a little pleasant like her mother, but the real power in Melanctha's nature came through her robust and unpleasant and very unendurable black father.

Melanctha's father only used to come to where Melanctha and her mother lived, once in a while.

It was many years now that Melanctha had not heard or seen or known of anything her father did.

Melanctha Herbert almost always hated her black father, but she loved very well the power in herself that came through him. And so her feeling was really closer to her black coarse father, than her feeling had ever been toward her pale yellow, sweet-appearing mother. The things she had in her of her mother never made her feel respect.

Melanctha Herbert had not loved herself in childhood. All of her youth was bitter to remember. . . .

Melanctha Herbert had always been old in all her ways and she knew very early how to use her power as a woman, and yet Melanctha with all her inborn intense wisdom was really very ignorant of evil. Melanctha had not yet come to understand what they meant, the things she so often heard around her, and which were just beginning to stir strongly in her.

Now when her father began fiercely to assail her, she did not really know what it was that he was so furious to force from her. In every way that he could think of in his anger, he tried to make her say a thing she did not really know. She held out and never answered anything he asked her, for Melanctha had a breakneck courage and she just then badly hated her black father.

When the excitement was all over, Melanctha began to know her power, the power she had so often felt stirring within her and which she now knew she could use to make her stronger.

James Herbert did not win this fight with his daughter. After awhile he forgot it as he soon forgot John and the cut of his sharp razor.

Melanctha almost forgot to hate her father, in her strong interest in the power she now knew she had within her.

Melanctha did not care much now, any longer, to see John or his wife or even the fine horses. This life was too quiet and accustomed and no longer stirred her to any interest or excitement.

Melanctha now really was beginning as a woman. She was ready, and she began to search in the streets and in dark corners to discover men and to learn their natures and their various ways of working.

In these next years Melanctha learned many ways that lead to wisdom. She learned the ways, and dimly in the distance she saw wisdom. These years of learning led very straight to trouble for Melanctha, though in these years Melanctha never did or meant anything that was really wrong.

Girls who are brought up with care and watching can always find moments to escape into the world, where they may learn the ways that lead to wisdom. For a girl raised like Melanctha Herbert, such escape was always very simple. Often she was alone, sometimes she was with a fellow seeker, and she strayed and stood, sometimes by railroad yards, sometimes on the docks or around new buildings where many men were working. Then when the darkness covered everything all over, she would begin to learn to know this man or that. She would advance, they would respond, and then she would withdraw a little, dimly, and always she did not know what it was that really held her. Sometimes she would almost go over, and then the strength in her of not really knowing, would stop the average man in his endeavor. It was a strange experience of ignorance and power and desire. Melanctha did not know what it was that she so badly wanted. She was afraid, and yet she did not understand that here she really was a coward.

Boys had never meant much to Melanctha. They had always been too young to content her. Melanctha had a strong respect for any kind of successful power. It was this that always kept Melanctha nearer, in her feeling toward her virile and unendurable black father, than she ever was in her feeling for her pale yellow, sweet-appearing mother. The things she had in her of her mother, never made her feel respect. . . .

James Herbert did not fight things out

now any more with his daughter. He feared her tongue, and her school learning, and the way she had of saying things that were very nasty to a brutal black man who knew nothing. And Melanctha just then hated him very badly in her suffering.

And so this was the way Melanctha

lived the four years of her beginning as a woman. And many things happened to Melanctha, but she knew very well that none of them had led her on to the right way, that certain way that was to lead her to world wisdom.

DIAGNOSIS: *Acting-out girl—racial problems.*

This mulatto girl, whose life of searching ends in a life of being eternally lost, is bright and quiet, with an intellectual and emotional potential that is never realized. Somehow she knew life had more to offer than she could grasp, and in her desire to find herself and a place for herself, she explored the limited pathways open to her. The barrenness of early affectional life is the force that pushes someone like Melanctha into acting out the search sexually. Sex, more often than not, has little to do with lust. So with Melanctha, it was a seeking for love, wisdom, meaning, and power—for answers that actually lie inside the self. When there has been no nourishment from parents or teachers to feed the self, the search takes place through other people and experiences. The sensation achieved, whether through sex or power, momentarily conceals the emptiness within. The excitement of a delinquent act—with girls it most often occurs in sex or in thieving—gives a false meaning, a sense of being alive, since at other times life is depressing and empty.

Melanctha could be found in the classroom. Behind her veiled eyes is the intelligence that only a patient, lovingly firm, genuinely interested teacher can feel. She is the child one hopes to reach but cannot; the reasonably good girl at school who does minimally. With time and consistent effort, her energy and imagination may be tapped. In the light of her racial problem, it will also take some luck.

Doctor Jack-O'-Lantern

Richard Yates

All Miss Price had been told about the new boy was that he'd spent most of his life in some kind of orphanage, and that the gray-haired "aunt and uncle" with whom he now lived were really foster parents, paid by the Welfare Department of the City of New York. A less dedicated or less imaginative teacher might have pressed for more details, but Miss Price was content with the rough outline. It was enough, in fact, to fill her with a sense of mission that

shone from her eyes, as plain as love, from the first morning he joined the fourth grade.

He arrived early and sat in the back row—his spine very straight, his ankles crossed precisely under the desk and his hands folded on the very center of its top, as if symmetry might make him less conspicuous—and while the other children were filing in and settling down, he received a long, expressionless stare from each of them.

"We have a new classmate this morning," Miss Price said, laboring the obvious in a way that made everybody want to giggle. "His name is Vincent Sabella and

From *Eleven Kinds of Loneliness* by Richard Yates, by permission of Little, Brown and Co.– Atlantic Monthly Press and Andre Deutsch Ltd. Copyright © 1961 by Richard Yates.

he comes from New York City. I know we'll all do our best to make him feel at home."

This time they all swung around to stare at once, which caused him to duck his head slightly and shift his weight from one buttock to the other. Ordinarily, the fact of someone's coming from New York might have held a certain prestige, for to most of the children the city was an awesome, adult place that swallowed up their fathers every day, and which they themselves were permitted to visit only rarely, in their best clothes, as a treat. But anyone could see at a glance that Vincent Sabella had nothing whatever to do with skyscrapers. Even if you could ignore his tangled black hair and gray skin, his clothes would have given him away: absurdly new corduroys, absurdly old sneakers and a yellow sweatshirt, much too small, with the shredded remains of a Mickey Mouse design stamped on its chest. Clearly, he was from the part of New York that you had to pass through on the train to Grand Central—the part where people hung bedding over their windowsills and leaned out on it all day in a trance of boredom, and where you got vistas of straight, deep streets, one after another, all alike in the clutter of their sidewalks and all swarming with gray boys at play in some desperate kind of ball game.

The girls decided that he wasn't very nice and turned away, but the boys lingered in their scrutiny, looking him up and down with faint smiles. This was the kind of kid they were accustomed to thinking of as "tough," the kind whose stares had made all of them uncomfortable at one time or another in unfamiliar neighborhoods; here was a unique chance for retaliation.

"What would you like us to call you, Vincent?" Miss Price inquired. "I mean, do you prefer Vincent, or Vince, or—or what?" (It was purely an academic question; even Miss Price knew that the boys would call him "Sabella" and that the girls wouldn't call him anything at all.)

"Vinny's okay," he said in a strange, croaking voice that had evidently yelled it-

self hoarse down the ugly streets of his home.

"I'm afraid I didn't hear you," she said, craning her pretty head forward and to one side so that a heavy lock of hair swung free of one shoulder. "Did you say 'Vince'?"

"Vinny, I said," he said again, squirming.

"Vincent, is it? All right, then, Vincent." A few of the class giggled, but nobody bothered to correct her; it would be more fun to let the mistake continue.

"I won't take time to introduce you to everyone by name, Vincent," Miss Price went on, "because I think it would be simpler just to let you learn the names as we go along, don't you? Now, we won't expect you to take any real part in the work for the first day or so; just take your time, and if there's anything you don't understand, why, don't be afraid to ask."

He made an unintelligible croak and smiled fleetingly, just enough to show that the roots of his teeth were green.

"Now then," Miss Price said, getting down to business. "This is Monday morning, and so the first thing on the program is reports. Who'd like to start off?"

Vincent Sabella was momentarily forgotten as six or seven hands went up, and Miss Price drew back in mock confusion. "Goodness, we do have a lot of reports this morning," she said. The idea of the reports —a fifteen-minute period every Monday in which the children were encouraged to relate their experiences over the weekend— was Miss Price's own, and she took a pardonable pride in it. The principal had commended her on it at a recent staff meeting, pointing out that it made a splendid bridge between the worlds of school and home, and that it was a fine way for children to learn poise and assurance. It called for intelligent supervision—the shy children had to be drawn out and the show-offs curbed—but in general, as Miss Price had assured the principal, it was fun for everyone. She particularly hoped it would be fun today, to help put Vincent Sabella at ease, and that was why she chose Nancy Parker to start off; there was nobody like Nancy for holding an audience.

The others fell silent as Nancy moved gracefully to the head of the room; even the two or three girls who secretly despised her had to feign enthrallment when she spoke (she was that popular), and every boy in the class, who at recess liked nothing better than to push her shrieking into the mud, was unable to watch her without an idiotically tremulous smile.

"Well—" she began, and then she clapped a hand over her mouth while everyone laughed.

"Oh, *Nancy*," Miss Price said. "You *know* the rule about starting a report with 'well.'"

Nancy knew the rule; she had only broken it to get the laugh. Now she let her fit of giggles subside, ran her fragile forefingers down the side seams of her skirt, and began again in the proper way. "On Friday my whole family went for a ride in my brother's new car. My brother bought this new Pontiac last week, and he wanted to take us all for a ride—you know, to try it out and everything? So we went into White Plains and had dinner in a restaurant there, and then we all wanted to go see this movie, 'Doctor Jekyll and Mr. Hyde,' but my brother said it was too horrible and everything, and I wasn't old enough to enjoy it—oh, he made me so mad! And then, let's see. On Saturday I stayed home all day and helped my mother make my sister's wedding dress. My sister's engaged to be married, you see, and my mother's making this wedding dress for her? So we did that, and then on Sunday this friend of my brother's came over for dinner, and then they both had to get back to college that night, and I was allowed to stay up late and say goodbye to them and everything, and I guess that's all." She always had a sure instinct for keeping her performance brief—or rather, for making it seem briefer than it really was.

"Very good, Nancy," Miss Price said. "Now, who's next?"

Warren Berg was next, elaborately hitching up his pants as he made his way down the aisle. "On Saturday I went over to Bill Stringer's house for lunch," he began in his direct, man-to-man style, and Bill Stringer wriggled bashfully in the front row. Warren Berg and Bill Stringer were great friends, and their reports often overlapped. "And then after lunch we went into White Plains, on our bikes. Only we *saw* 'Doctor Jekyll and Mr. Hyde.'" Here he nodded his head in Nancy's direction, and Nancy got another laugh by making a little whimper of envy. "It was real good, too," he went on, with mounting excitement. "It's all about this guy who—"

"About *a man who*," Miss Price corrected.

"About a man who mixes up this chemical, like, that he drinks? And whenever he drinks this chemical, he changes into this real monster, like? You see him drink this chemical, and then you see his hands start to get all scales all over them, like a reptile and everything, and then you see his face start to change into this real horrible-looking face—with fangs and all? Sticking out of his mouth?"

All the girls shuddered in pleasure. "Well," Miss Price said, "I think Nancy's brother was probably wise in not wanting her to see it. What did you do *after* the movie, Warren?"

There was a general "*Aw-w-w!*" of disappointment—everyone wanted to hear more about the scales and fangs—but Miss Price never liked to let the reports degenerate into accounts of movies. Warren continued without much enthusiasm: all they had done after the movie was fool around Bill Stringer's yard until suppertime. "And then on Sunday," he said, brightening again, "Bill Stringer came over to *my* house, and my dad helped us rig up this old tire on this long rope? From a tree? There's this steep hill down behind my house, you see—this ravine, like?—and we hung this tire so that what you do is, you take the tire and run a little ways and then lift your feet, and you go swinging way, way out over the ravine and back again."

"That sounds like fun," Miss Price said, glancing at her watch.

"Oh, it's *fun,* all right," Warren conceded. But then he hitched up his pants again and added, with a puckering of his forehead, " 'Course, it's pretty dangerous. You let go of that tire or anything, you'd get a bad fall. Hit a rock or anything, you'd probably break your leg, or your spine. But my dad said he trusted us both to look out for our own safety."

"Well, I'm afraid that's all we'll have time for, Warren," Miss Price said. "Now, there's just time for one more report. Who's ready? Arthur Cross?"

There was a soft groan, because Arthur Cross was the biggest dope in class and his reports were always a bore. This time it turned out to be something tedious about going to visit his uncle on Long Island. At one point he made a slip—he said "botormoat" instead of "motorboat"—and everyone laughed with the particular edge of scorn they reserved for Arthur Cross. But the laughter died abruptly when it was joined by a harsh, dry croaking from the back of the room. Vincent Sabella was laughing too, green teeth and all, and they all had to glare at him until he stopped.

When the reports were over, everyone settled down for school. It was recess time before any of the children thought much about Vincent Sabella again, and then they thought of him only to make sure he was left out of everything. He wasn't in the group of boys that clustered around the horizontal bar to take turns at skinning-the-cat, or the group that whispered in a far corner of the playground, hatching a plot to push Nancy Parker in the mud. Nor was he in the larger group, of which even Arthur Cross was a member, that chased itself in circles in a frantic variation of the game of tag. He couldn't join the girls, of course, or the boys from other classes, and so he joined nobody. He stayed on the apron of the playground, close to school, and for the first part of the recess he pretended to be very busy with the laces of his sneakers. He would squat to undo and retie them, straighten up and take a few

experimental steps in a springy, athletic way, and then get down and go to work on them again. After five minutes of this he gave it up, picked up a handful of pebbles and began shying them at an invisible target several yards away. That was good for another five minutes, but then there were still five minutes left, and he could think of nothing to do but stand there, first with his hands in his pockets, then with his hands on his hips, and then with his arms folded in a manly way across his chest.

Miss Price stood watching all this from the doorway, and she spent the full recess wondering if she ought to go out and do something about it. She guessed it would be better not to.

She managed to control the same impulse at recess the next day, and every other day that week, though every day it grew more difficult. But one thing she could not control was a tendency to let her anxiety show in class. All Vincent Sabella's errors in schoolwork were publicly excused, even those having nothing to do with his newness, and all his accomplishments were singled out for special mention. Her campaign to build him up was painfully obvious, and never more so than when she tried to make it subtle; once, for instance, in explaining an arithmetic problem, she said, "Now, suppose Warren Berg and Vincent Sabella went to the store with fifteen cents each, and candy bars cost ten cents. How many candy bars would each boy have?" By the end of the week he was well on the way to becoming the worst possible kind of teacher's pet, a victim of the teacher's pity.

On Friday she decided the best thing to do would be to speak to him privately, and try to draw him out. She could say something about the pictures he had painted in art class—that would do for an opening—and she decided to do it at lunchtime.

The only trouble was that lunchtime, next to recess, was the most trying part of Vincent Sabella's day. Instead of going home for an hour as the other children did, he brought his lunch to school in a wrinkled paper bag and ate it in the classroom, which always made for a certain amount of awkwardness. The last children to leave would see him still seated apologetically at his desk, holding his paper bag, and anyone who happened to straggle back later for a forgotten hat or sweater would surprise him in the middle of his meal—perhaps shielding a hard-boiled egg from view or wiping mayonnaise from his mouth with a furtive hand. It was a situation that Miss Price did not improve by walking up to him while the room was still half full of children and sitting prettily on the edge of the desk beside his, making it clear that she was cutting her own lunch hour short in order to be with him.

"Vincent," she began, "I've been meaning to tell you how much I enjoyed those pictures of yours. They're really very good."

He mumbled something and shifted his eyes to the cluster of departing children at the door. She went right on talking and smiling, elaborating on her praise of the pictures; and finally, after the door had closed behind the last child, he was able to give her his attention. He did so tentatively at first; but the more she talked, the more he seemed to relax, until she realized she was putting him at ease. It was as simple and as gratifying as stroking a cat. She had finished with the pictures now and moved on, triumphantly, to broader fields of praise. "It's never easy," she was saying, "to come to a new school and adjust yourself to the—well, the new work, and new working methods, and I think you've done a splendid job so far. I really do. But tell me, do you think you're going to like it here?"

He looked at the floor just long enough to make his reply—"It's awright"— and then his eyes stared into hers again.

"I'm so glad. Please don't let me interfere with your lunch, Vincent. Do go ahead and eat, that is, if you don't mind my sitting here with you." But it was now abundantly clear that he didn't mind at all,

and he began to unwrap a bologna sandwich with what she felt sure was the best appetite he'd had all week. It wouldn't even have mattered very much now if someone from the class had come in and watched, though it was probably just as well that no one did.

Miss Price sat back more comfortably on the desk top, crossed her legs and allowed one slim stockinged foot to slip part of the way out of its moccasin. "Of course," she went on, "it always does take a little time to sort of get your bearings in a new school. For one thing, well, it's never too easy for the new member of the class to make friends with the other members. What I mean is, you mustn't mind if the others seem a little rude to you at first. Actually, they're just as anxious to make friends as you are, but they're shy. All it takes is a little time, and a little effort on your part as well as theirs. Not too much, of course, but a little. Now for instance, these reports we have Monday mornings— they're a fine way for people to get to know one another. A person never feels he has to make a report; it's just a thing he can do if he wants to. And that's only one way of helping others to know the kind of person you are; there are lots and lots of ways. The main thing to remember is that making friends is the most natural thing in the world, and it's only a question of time until you have all the friends you want. And in the meantime, Vincent, I hope you'll consider *me* your friend, and feel free to call on me for whatever advice or anything you might need. Will you do that?"

He nodded, swallowing.

"Good." She stood up and smoothed her skirt over her long thighs. "Now I must go or I'll be late for *my* lunch. But I'm glad we had this little talk, Vincent, and I hope we'll have others."

It was probably a lucky thing that she stood up when she did, for if she'd stayed on that desk a minute longer Vincent Sabella would have thrown his arms around her and buried his face in the warm gray flannel of her lap, and that might have been enough to confuse the most dedicated and imaginative of teachers.

At report time on Monday morning, nobody was more surprised than Miss Price when Vincent Sabella's smudged hand was among the first and most eager to rise. Apprehensively she considered letting someone else start off, but then, for fear of hurting his feelings, she said, "All right, Vincent," in as matter-of-fact a way as she could manage.

There was a suggestion of muffled titters from the class as he walked confidently to the head of the room and turned to face his audience. He looked, if anything, too confident: there were signs, in the way he held his shoulders and the way his eyes shone, of the terrible poise of panic.

"Saturday I seen that pitcha," he announced.

"Saw, Vincent," Miss Price corrected gently.

"That's what I mean," he said; "I sore that pitcha. 'Doctor Jack-o'-lantern and Mr. Hide.' "

There was a burst of wild, delighted laughter and a chorus of correction: "Doctor *Jekyll!*"

He was unable to speak over the noise. Miss Price was on her feet, furious. "It's a *perfectly natural mistake!*" she was saying. "There's no reason for any of you to be so rude. Go on, Vincent, and please excuse this very silly interruption." The laughter subsided, but the class continued to shake their heads derisively from side to side. It hadn't, of course, been a perfectly natural mistake at all; for one thing it proved that he was a hopeless dope, and for another it proved that he was lying.

"That's what I mean," he continued. " 'Doctor Jackal and Mr. Hide.' I got it a little mixed up. Anyways, I seen all about where his teet' start comin' outa his mout' and all like that, and I thought it was very good. And then on Sunday my mudda and fodda come out to see me in this car they got. This Buick. My fodda siz, 'Vinny,

wanna go for a little ride?' I siz, 'Sure, where yiz goin'?' He siz, 'Anyplace ya like.' So I siz, 'Let's go out in the country a ways, get on one of them big roads and make some time.' So we go out—oh, I guess fifty, sixty miles—and we're cruisin' along this highway, when this cop starts tailin' us? My fodda siz, 'Don't worry, we'll shake him,' and he steps on it, see? My mudda's gettin' pretty scared, but my fodda siz, 'Don't worry, dear.' He's tryin' to make this turn, see, so he can get off the highway and shake the cop? But just when he's makin' the turn, the cop opens up and starts shootin', see?"

By this time the few members of the class who could bear to look at him at all were doing so with heads on one side and mouths partly open, the way you look at a broken arm or a circus freak.

"We just barely made it," Vincent went on, his eyes gleaming, "and this one bullet got my fodda in the shoulder. Didn't hurt him bad—just grazed him, like—so my mudda bandaged it up for him and all, but he couldn't do no more drivin' after that, and we had to get him to a doctor, see? So my fodda siz, 'Vinny, think you can drive a ways?' I siz, 'Sure, if you show me how.' So he showed me how to work the gas and the brake, and all like that, and I drove to the doctor. My mudda siz, 'I'm prouda you, Vinny, drivin' all by yourself.' So anyways, we got to the doctor, got my fodda fixed up and all, and then he drove us back home." He was breathless. After an uncertain pause he said, "And that's all." Then he walked quickly back to his desk, his stiff new corduroy pants whistling faintly with each step.

"Well, that was very—entertaining, Vincent," Miss Price said, trying to act as if nothing had happened. "Now, who's next?" But nobody raised a hand.

Recess was worse than usual for him that day; at least it was until he found a place to hide—a narrow concrete alley, blind except for several closed fire-exit doors, that cut between two sections of the school building. It was reassuringly dismal and cool in there—he could stand with his back to the wall and his eyes guarding the entrance, and the noises of recess were as remote as the sunshine. But when the bell rang he had to go back to class, and in another hour it was lunchtime.

Miss Price left him alone until her own meal was finished. Then, after standing with one hand on the doorknob for a full minute to gather courage, she went in and sat beside him for another little talk, just as he was trying to swallow the last of a pimento-cheese sandwich.

"Vincent," she began, "we all enjoyed your report this morning, but I think we would have enjoyed it more—a great deal more—if you'd told us something about your real life instead. I mean," she hurried on, "for instance, I noticed you were wearing a nice new windbreaker this morning. It *is* new, isn't it? And did your aunt buy it for you over the weekend?"

He did not deny it.

"Well then, why couldn't you have told us about going to the store with your aunt, and buying the windbreaker, and whatever you did afterwards. That would have made a perfectly good report." She paused, and for the first time looked steadily into his eyes. "You do understand what I'm trying to say, don't you, Vincent?"

He wiped crumbs of bread from his lips, looked at the floor, and nodded.

"And you'll remember next time, won't you?"

He nodded again. "Please may I be excused, Miss Price?"

"Of course you may."

He went to the boys' lavatory and vomited. Afterwards he washed his face and drank a little water, and then he returned to the classroom. Miss Price was busy at her desk now, and didn't look up. To avoid getting involved with her again, he wandered out to the cloakroom and sat on one of the long benches, where he picked up someone's discarded overshoe and turned it over and over in his hands. In a little while he heard the chatter of returning children, and to avoid being dis-

covered there, he got up and went to the fire-exit door. Pushing it open, he found that it gave onto the alley he had hidden in that morning, and he slipped outside. For a minute or two he just stood there, looking at the blankness of the concrete wall: then he found a piece of chalk in his pocket and wrote out all the dirty words he could think of, in block letters a foot high. He had put down four words and was trying to remember a fifth when he heard a shuffling at the door behind him. Arthur Cross was there, holding the door open and reading the words with wide eyes. "Boy," he said in an awed half-whisper. "Boy, you're gonna get it. You're really gonna *get* it."

Startled, and then suddenly calm, Vincent Sabella palmed his chalk, hooked his thumbs in his belt and turned on Arthur Cross with a menacing look. "Yeah?" he inquired. "Who's gonna squeal on me?"

"Well, nobody's gonna *squeal* on you," Arthur Cross said uneasily, "but you shouldn't go around writing—"

"Arright," Vincent said, advancing a step. His shoulders were slumped, his head thrust forward and his eyes narrowed, like Edward G. Robinson. "Arright. That's all I wanna know. I don't like squealers, unnastand?"

While he was saying this, Warren Berg and Bill Stringer appeared in the doorway—just in time to hear it and to see the words on the wall before Vincent turned on them. "And that goes fa you too, unnastand?" he said. "Both a yiz."

And the remarkable thing was that both their faces fell into the same foolish, defensive smile that Arthur Cross was wearing. It wasn't until they had glanced at each other that they were able to meet his eyes with the proper degree of contempt, and by then it was too late. "Think you're pretty smart, don'tcha, Sabella?" Bill Stringer said.

"Never mind what I think," Vincent told him. "You heard what I said. Now let's get back inside."

And they could do nothing but move

aside to make way for him, and follow him dumfounded into the cloakroom.

It was Nancy Parker who squealed— although, of course, with someone like Nancy Parker you didn't think of it as squealing. She had heard everything from the cloakroom; as soon as the boys came in she peeked into the alley, saw the words and, setting her face in a prim frown, went straight to Miss Price. Miss Price was just about to call the class to order for the afternoon when Nancy came up and whispered in her ear. They both disappeared into the cloakroom—from which, after a moment, came the sound of the fire-exit door being abruptly slammed—and when they returned to class Nancy was flushed with righteousness, Miss Price very pale. No announcement was made. Classes proceeded in the ordinary way all afternoon, though it was clear that Miss Price was upset, and it wasn't until she was dismissing the children at three o'clock that she brought the thing into the open. "Will Vincent Sabella please remain seated?" She nodded at the rest of the class. "That's all."

While the room was clearing out she sat at her desk, closed her eyes and massaged the frail bridge of her nose with thumb and forefinger, sorting out half-remembered fragments of a book she had once read on the subject of seriously disturbed children. Perhaps, after all, she should never have undertaken the responsibility of Vincent Sabella's loneliness. Perhaps the whole thing called for the attention of a specialist. She took a deep breath.

"Come over here and sit beside me, Vincent," she said, and when he had settled himself, she looked at him. "I want you to tell me the truth. Did you write those words on the wall outside?"

He stared at the floor.

"Look at me," she said, and he looked at her. She had never looked prettier: her cheeks slightly flushed, her eyes shining and her sweet mouth pressed into a self-conscious frown. "First of all," she said, handing him a small enameled basin

streaked with poster paint, "I want you to take this to the boys' room and fill it with hot water and soap."

He did as he was told, and when he came back, carrying the basin carefully to keep the suds from spilling, she was sorting out some old rags in the bottom drawer of her desk. "Here," she said, selecting one and shutting the drawer in a businesslike way. "This will do. Soak this up." She led him back to the fire exit and stood in the alley watching him, silently, while he washed off all the words.

When the job had been done, and the rag and basin put away, they sat down at Miss Price's desk again. "I suppose you think I'm angry with you, Vincent," she said. "Well, I'm not. I almost wish I could be angry—that would make it much easier —but instead I'm hurt. I've tried to be a good friend to you, and I thought you wanted to be my friend too. But this kind of thing—well, it's very hard to be friendly with a person who'd do a thing like that."

She saw, gratefully, that there were tears in his eyes. "Vincent, perhaps I understand some things better than you think. Perhaps I understand that sometimes, when a person does a thing like that, it isn't really because he wants to hurt anyone, but only because he's unhappy. He knows it isn't a good thing to do, and he even knows it isn't going to make him any happier afterwards, but he goes ahead and does it anyway. Then when he finds he's lost a friend, he's terribly sorry, but it's too late. The thing is done."

She allowed this somber note to reverberate in the silence of the room for a little while before she spoke again. "I won't be able to forget this, Vincent. But perhaps, just this once, we can still be friends—as long as I understand that you didn't mean to hurt me. But you must promise me that you won't forget it either. Never forget that when you do a thing like that, you're going to hurt people who want very much to like you, and in that way you're going to hurt yourself. Will you promise me to remember that, dear?"

The "dear" was as involuntary as the slender hand that reached out and held the shoulder of his sweatshirt; both made his head hang lower than before.

"All right," she said. "You may go now."

He got his windbreaker out of the cloakroom and left, avoiding the tired uncertainty of her eyes. The corridors were deserted, and dead silent except for the hollow, rhythmic knocking of a janitor's push-broom against some distant wall. His own rubber-soled tread only added to the silence; so did the lonely little noise made by the zipping-up of his windbreaker, and so did the faint mechanical sigh of the heavy front door. The silence made it all the more startling when he found, several yards down the concrete walk outside, that two boys were walking beside him: Warren Berg and Bill Stringer. They were both smiling at him in an eager, almost friendly way.

"What'd she do to ya, anyway?" Bill Stringer asked.

Caught off guard, Vincent barely managed to put on his Edward G. Robinson face in time. "Nunnya business," he said, and walked faster.

"No, listen—wait up, hey," Warren Berg said, as they trotted to keep up with him. "What'd she do, anyway? She bawl ya out, or what? Wait up, hey, Vinny."

The name made him tremble all over. He had to jam his hands in his windbreaker pockets and force himself to keep on walking; he had to force his voice to be steady when he said "Nunnya *business*, I told ya. Lea' me alone."

But they were right in step with him now. "Boy, she must of given you the works," Warren Berg persisted. "What'd she say, anyway? C'mon, tell us, Vinny."

This time the name was too much for him. It overwhelmed his resistance and made his softening knees slow down to a slack, conversational stroll. "She din say nothin'" he said at last; and then after a dramatic pause he added, "She let the ruler do her talkin' for her."

"The *ruler?* Ya mean she used a *ruler* on ya?" Their faces were stunned, either with disbelief or admiration, and it began to look more and more like admiration as they listened.

"On the knuckles," Vincent said through tightening lips. "Five times on each hand. She siz, 'Make a fist. Lay it out here on the desk.' Then she takes the ruler and *Whop! Whop! Whop!* Five times. Ya think that don't hurt, you're crazy."

Miss Price, buttoning her polo coat as the front door whispered shut behind her, could scarcely believe her eyes. This couldn't be Vincent Sabella—this perfectly normal, perfectly happy boy on the sidewalk ahead of her, flanked by attentive friends. But it was, and the scene made her want to laugh aloud with pleasure and relief. He was going to be all right, after all. For all her well-intentioned groping in the shadows she could never have predicted a scene like this, and certainly could never have caused it to happen. But it was happening, and it just proved, once again, that she would never understand the ways of children.

She quickened her graceful stride and overtook them, turning to smile down at them as she passed. "Goodnight, boys," she called, intending it as a kind of cheerful benediction; and then, embarrassed by their three startled faces, she smiled even wider and said, "Goodness, it *is* getting colder, isn't it? That windbreaker of yours looks nice and warm, Vincent. I envy you." Finally they nodded bashfully at her; she called goodnight again, turned, and continued on her way to the bus stop.

She left a profound silence in her wake. Staring after her, Warren Berg and Bill Stringer waited until she had disappeared around the corner before they turned on Vincent Sabella.

"Ruler, my eye!" Bill Stringer said. "Ruler, my eye!" He gave Vincent a disgusted shove that sent him stumbling against Warren Berg, who shoved him back.

"Jeez, you lie about *everything*, don'tcha, Sabella? You lie about *everything!*"

Jostled off balance, keeping his hands

tight in the windbreaker pockets, Vincent tried in vain to retain his dignity. "Think *I* care if yiz believe me?" he said, and then because he couldn't think of anything else to say, he said it again. "Think *I* care if yiz believe me?"

But he was walking alone. Warren Berg and Bill Stringer were drifting away across the street, walking backwards in order to look back on him with furious contempt. "Just like the lies you told about the policeman shooting your father," Bill Stringer called.

"Even *movies* he lies about," Warren Berg put in; and suddenly doubling up with artificial laughter he cupped both hands to his mouth and yelled, "Hey, Doctor Jack-o'-lantern!"

It wasn't a very good nickname, but it had an authentic ring to it—the kind of a name that might spread around, catch on quickly, and stick. Nudging each other, they both took up the cry:

"What's the matter, Doctor Jack-o'-lantern?"

"Why don'tcha run on home with Miss Price, Doctor Jack-o'-lantern?"

"So long, Doctor Jack-o'-lantern!"

Vincent Sabella went on walking, ignoring them, waiting until they were out of sight. Then he turned and retraced his steps all the way back to school, around through the playground and back to the alley, where the wall was still dark in spots from the circular scrubbing of his wet rag.

Choosing a dry place, he got out his chalk and began to draw a head with great care, in profile, making the hair long and rich and taking his time over the face, erasing it with moist fingers and reworking it until it was the most beautiful face he had ever drawn: a delicate nose, slightly parted lips, an eye with lashes that curved as gracefully as a bird's wing. He paused to admire it with a lover's solemnity; then from the lips he drew a line that connected with a big speech balloon, and in the balloon he wrote, so angrily that the chalk kept breaking in his fingers, every one of the words he had written that noon. Returning to the head, he gave it a slender neck and gently sloping shoulders, and then, with bold strikes, he gave it the body of a naked woman: great breasts with hard little nipples, a trim waist, a dot for a navel, wide hips and thighs that flared around a triangle of fiercely scribbled pubic hair. Beneath the picture he printed its title: "Miss Price."

He stood there looking at it for a little while, breathing hard, and then he went home.

DIAGNOSIS: *Culturally and affectionally deprived child in a middle-class environment.*

The story is a realistic description of how a new child in a strange environment tries to find his way. His clothes, manner, and speech make him a stranger. His difference is felt keenly by classmates, the teacher, and himself. His attempt to be like the others by lying or make-believe is understandable enough. Equally understandable is his well-intentioned teacher's overinvolvement with him. Her behavior, although well-meaning and sympathetic, singles him out and further alienates him from the class. Teacher's pet is at best a hard role, particularly when a child is starving for attention and expression.

Vincent's reaction to the teacher's moralistic, middle-class approach to him was confused. In despair, anger, loneliness, and sense of isolation, he used the very tools that shock middle-class society most—bad language and lewd pictures.

Overinvolvement often results in a teacher's withdrawal and disappointment. The danger of the teacher's pet role is clear. A gradual welcome giving the little boy a chance to be different, an understanding that a weekend report from him would be a fiasco, one way or another, is what was needed.

The Long Distance Runner
Alan Sillitoe

I don't say to myself: "You shouldn't have done the job and then you'd have stayed away from Borstal"; no, what I ram into my runner-brain is that my luck had no right to scram just when I was on my way to making the coppers think I hadn't done the job after all. The time was autumn and the night foggy enough to set me and my mate Mike roaming the streets when we should have been rooted in front of the telly or stuck into a plush posh seat at the pictures, but I was restless after six weeks away from any sort of work, and well you might ask me why I'd been bone-idle for so long because normally I sweated my thin guts out on a milling-machine with the rest of them, but you see, my dad died from cancer of the throat, and mam collected a cool five hundred in insurance and benefits from the factory where he'd worked, "for your bereavement," they said, or words like that.

Now I believe, and my mam must have thought the same, that a wad of crisp blue-back fivers ain't a sight of good to a living soul unless they're flying out of your hand into some shopkeeper's till, and the shopkeeper is passing you tip-top things in exchange over the counter, so as soon as she got the money, mam took me and my five brothers and sisters out to town and got us dolled-up in new clothes. Then she ordered a twenty-one-inch telly, a new carpet because the old one was covered with blood from dad's dying and wouldn't wash out, and took a taxi home with bags of grub and a new fur coat. And do you know—you wain't believe me when I tell you—she'd still near three hundred left in her bulging handbag the next day, so how could any of us go to work after that? Poor

old dad, he didn't get a look in, and he was the one who'd done the suffering and dying for such a lot of lolly.

Night after night we sat in front of the telly with a ham sandwich in one hand, a bar of chocolate in the other, and a bottle of lemonade between our boots, while mam was with some fancy-man upstairs on the new bed she'd ordered, and I'd never known a family as happy as ours was in that couple of months when we'd got all the money we needed. And when the dough ran out I didn't think about anything much, but just roamed the streets—looking for another job, I told mam—hoping I suppose to get my hands on another five hundred nicker so's the nice life we'd got used to could go on and on for ever.

·   ·   ·

The pop-eyed potbellied governor said to a pop-eyed potbellied Member of Parliament who sat next to his pop-eyed potbellied whore of a wife that I was his only hope for getting the Borstal Blue Ribbon Prize Cup For Long-Distance Cross-Country Running (all England), which I was, and it set me laughing to myself inside, and I didn't say a word to any potbellied pop-eyed bastard that might give them real hope, though I knew the governor anyway took my quietness to mean he'd got that cup already stuck on the bookshelf in his office among the few other mildewed trophies.

"He might take up running in a sort of professional way when he gets out," and it wasn't until he'd said this and I'd heard it with my own flap-tabs that I realized it might be possible to do such a thing, run for money, trot for wages on piece work at a bob a puff rising bit by bit to a guinea a gasp and retiring through old age at thirty-two because of lace-curtain lungs, a football heart, and legs like varicose beanstalks.

But I'd have a wife and car and get my grinning long-distance clock in the papers and have a smashing secretary to answer piles of letters sent by tarts who'd mob me when they saw who I was as I pushed my way into Woolworth's for a packet of razor blades and a cup of tea. It was something to think about all right, and sure enough the governor knew he'd got me when he said, turning to me as if I would at any rate have to be consulted about it all: "How does this matter strike you, then, Smith, my lad?"

A line of potbellied pop-eyes gleamed at me and a row of goldfish mouths opened and wiggled gold teeth at me, so I gave them the answer they wanted because I'd hold my trump card until later. "It'd suit me fine, sir," I said.

"Good lad. Good show. Right spirit. Splendid."

"Well," the governor said, "get that cup for us today and I'll do all I can for you. I'll get you trained so that you whack every man in the Free World." And I had a picture in my brain of me running and beating everybody in the world, leaving them all behind until only I was trot-trotting across a big wide moor alone, doing a marvellous speed as I ripped between boulders and reed-clumps, when suddenly: CRACK! CRACK!—bullets that can go faster than any man running, coming from a copper's rifle planted in a tree, winged me and split my gizzard in spite of my perfect running, and down I fell.

The potbellies expected me to say something else. "Thank you, sir," I said.

．　　．　　．

It was hard to understand, and all I knew was that you had to run, run, run, without knowing why you were running, but on you went through fields you didn't understand and into woods that made you afraid, over hills without knowing you'd been up and down, and shooting across streams that would have cut the heart out of you had you fallen into them. And the winning post was no end to it, even though crowds might be cheering you in, because on you had to go before you got your breath back, and the only time you stopped really was when you tripped over a tree trunk and broke your neck or fell into a disused well and stayed dead in the darkness forever. So I thought: they aren't going to get me on this racing lark, this running and trying to win, this jog-trotting for a bit of blue ribbon, because it's not the way to go on at all, though they swear blind that it is. You should think about nobody and go your own way, not on a course marked out for you by people holding mugs of water and bottles of iodine in case you fall and cut yourself so that they can pick you up—even if you want to stay where you are —and get you moving again.

．　　．　　．

And down the drive I went, carrying a heart blocked up like Boulder Dam across my arteries, the nail-bag clamped down tighter and tighter as though in a wood-work vice, yet with my feet like birdwings and arms like talons ready to fly across the field except that I didn't want to give anybody that much of a show, or win the race by accident. I smell the hot dry day now as I run towards the end, passing a mountain-heap of grass emptied from cans hooked on to the fronts of lawnmowers pushed by my pals; I rip a piece of tree-bark with my fingers and stuff it in my mouth, chewing wood and dust and maybe maggots as I run until I'm nearly sick, yet swallowing what I can of it just the same because a little birdie whistled to me that I've got to go on living for at least a bloody sight longer yet but that for six months I'm not going to smell that grass or taste that dusty bark or trot this lovely path. I hate to have to say this but something bloody-well made me cry, and crying is a thing I haven't bloody-well done since I was a kid of two or three. Because I'm slowing down now for Gunthorpe to catch me up, and I'm doing it in a place just where the drive turns in to the sportsfield—where they can see what I'm doing, especially the governor and his gang from the grandstand, and I'm going so slow I'm almost marking time. Those on the nearest seats haven't caught on yet to what's happening and are still cheering like mad ready for when I make that mark, and I keep on wondering when the bleeding hell Gunthorpe behind me is going to nip by on to the field because I can't hold this up all day, and I think Oh Christ it's just my rotten luck that Gunthorpe's dropped out and that I'll be here for half an hour before the next bloke comes up, but even so, I say, I won't budge, I won't go for that last hundred yards if I have to sit down cross-legged on the grass and have the governor and his chinless wonders pick me up and carry me there, which is against their rules so you can bet they'd never do it because they're not clever enough to break the rules—like I would be in their place—even though they are their own. No, I'll show him what honesty means if it's the last thing I do, though I'm sure he'll never understand because if he and all them like him did it'd mean they'd be on my side which is impossible. By God I'll stick this out like my dad stuck out his pain and kicked them doctors down the stairs: if he had guts for that then I've got guts for this and here I stay waiting for Gunthorpe or Aylesham to bash that turf and go right slap-up against that bit of clothes-line stretched across the winning post. As for me, the only time I'll hit that clothes-line will be when I'm dead and a comfortable coffin's been got ready on the other side. Until then I'm a long-distance runner, crossing country all on my own no matter how bad it feels.

DIAGNOSIS: *Delinquent social rebel—self-destructive through hostility; deprivations of all kinds: economic, cultural, social, affectional.*

A borstal is the English version of our reform school for delinquents. This borstal is progressive; the "I" of the story has won school privileges by being a good runner and, therefore, is being trained for the long-distance race between borstals.

He has been taught to hate everybody who stands for law, order, and values. His survival has rested on an aggressive, devious, lick-them-or-they'll-lick-you policy. He cannot trust anyone with a background or position different from his. Not only do things come out as he expects them to, but he creates situations where they will have to come out this way. For hate is his way of life; and if he should be proved wrong—if he should see love and benevolence where he sees hate and malevolence—the structure of his view of life would crumble, and he would be left more alone and more afraid than ever. Therefore, the delinquent structure of hostility and need for immediate gain is the essence of his life. (Recall the section describing how the family lived when they had a few dollars.)

To deal with this boy, we have to recognize the depths of his hostility and his need to maintain it, his kind of honesty, and his perception of society and authority. Without awareness of all these factors, teachers find delinquents frustrating and hopeless to deal with. With awareness, a teacher or therapist *gradually* can attack the basis for hostility, leaving the delinquent something to lean on as change occurs.

In class such a student is unreachable. To replace hate with trust, is a task requiring insight, talent, and endless patience. The teacher needs to be a mental trapeze artist to gain an insight on life as this boy sees it.

Ciske, the Rat

Piet Bakker

Thus the talk with Ciske's father produced no practical results and I was too busy to let it worry me too much. For twenty-six hours in the week I had Ciske under my care, but in a week there are 168 hours altogether, and during school time I had forty-seven other children who needed looking after. Moreover, what was involved was not only Ciske's soul but his mind, which had to be trained and stuffed with fractions and historical dates. Ciske's acquired knowledge seemed to be nil. Even Betty Van Gemert, the stupidest child in my class, did not make such fantastic spelling mistakes. It obviously wouldn't be easy to push him into the fifth form. But I wanted to achieve this at all cost, otherwise he would fall the following year into the hands of Maatsuyker. And one thing was quite clear: it would be easier for a hippopotamus to repair a wrist watch than for that professional lion tamer Maatsuyker to tame the Rat!

Ciske was not stupid, but his education had been completely neglected. The red-haired schoolmistress at his old school had probably never given him a chance to learn, because she had not liked him. This was a great pity, because Ciske was not slow-witted. His math, for instance, was quite good by then. It seemed that he should be quite capable of competing with the best boy, Gerard Jonker, in this field.

While the others were trying to solve simple equations, I used to squat beside Ciske and try to explain fractions to him. He made quite good progress. At first he was anything but pleased, and would slowly edge his way to the other end of the bench, as if he thought that there was really no need for such close contact between us. Also, he seemed to take the view

From *Ciske, the Rat* by Piet Bakker (New York: Doubleday & Company, Inc., 1958). Reprinted by permission of Mrs. H. Bakker-Prager.

that one can sail quite happily through life without being able to add one-half and three-fourths.

I resorted to an undignified trick in order to get the Rat to cooperate. For quite a long time I had had the suspicion that Johnny Verkerk was Ciske's confirmed adversary, that there had been a mutual enmity at first sight. Johnny was of course jealous because he noticed that I gave more of my time to Ciske than to him.

"Well, Ciske," I said one day, "we will now wring the necks of these fractions. If you really try, you will soon know as much as Verkerk."

The Rat did not seem particularly interested, but Johnny himself proved to be of great assistance to me in my plan, as that was too much for his pride. "He will never do that!" he said. "He is much too stupid."

I should of course have rebuked him, but instead I turned to the Rat. "Did you hear that? Will you stand for it? Come and sit next to me and we'll show Verkerk how wrong he is!"

Grimly he slid closer to me, and we began diligently to cut apples in four and cakes into three parts. The Rat was a picture of concentration. After fifteen minutes, I left him to himself, but he continued to work away like mad, while I went around the class, praising the industrious and scolding the others.

Five minutes later, Ciske sat back—I thought he had given up already. "What now," I asked him, "are you taking a rest?"

He pushed his exercise book toward me without a word. He had finished!

"You see; it was quite simple really, Ciske."

"They weren't very difficult," said Johnny contemptuously, but I could see that he was mortified.

From then on the Rat worked

doggedly at his fractions. I couldn't boast that I had solved the problem with any particular intelligence, but the result was satisfactory, and this seemed to me to be the important thing.

When it came to singing, the Rat was a dead loss. I could imagine the boy as almost anything—as the strangler of Johnny, as a burglar, as the best at math in the class—but not as somebody who could intone with feeling, "Softly rustles the wind . . ." When the class sang sentimental part songs, Ciske sat there with tightly compressed lips. He hardly ever spoke, so how could one expect him to sing? But I felt I must make him do it. Only when I'd got him to open his mouth and start singing with the others, no matter how badly he did it, would I have reached my second objective. Only then would he really become a boy like the others, an integral part of the class.

Once, before class began, I saw him staring, mouth wide open, at the goldfish bowl on the window sill, quite engrossed in the small world of water plants and goldfish and sticklebacks swimming here and there. He drew back as if he had been caught misbehaving when I came up beside him.

"You could clean the bowl if you felt like it," I said.

He looked at me with astonishment, then laughed rather shame-facedly. If I dared, I would stroke your fat head, I thought to myself. A child that could laugh so naturally could not be unreceptive to a little happiness. This miserable little Rat, who was kicked around by everybody, was capable of deriving pleasure from something beautiful. My God! How many blighted and crippled lives there are around us which can be made happy by some small trifle! Short moments of happiness can mean so much to a human being. Why must one always pursue some big goal, out of one's reach?

• • •

When the long vacation rolls around, the children are happy. When it is over,

they are also happy. This used to strike me forcibly every year. When you asked them, "Are you pleased to be back at school?" they would exclaim in chorus, "Oh, yes!" and "No-oo." They feel somehow obliged to find school horrible and vacation wonderful. But how can one explain that most of them, on the first day of school, run, smiling and happy, to their teacher, as soon as they see him coming around the corner? Why is it always just the first school day that is so particularly nice and happy? And why is one personally so displeased? When everything is back to normal again, with the children sitting at their desks, the geraniums again on the window sill, and the fish in their aquarium, back in place, there is no class and no teacher who are not longing for the Christmas break.

When I looked at my class on that first morning of the new term, I could not discover much evidence of blooming health. Indeed the schools had been closed for a few weeks, but who cared whether the children really enjoyed their vacation or not? Sip Eisma was one of the very few who looked better than they did a month before. He had been staying with his uncle in Ernewouden, on the most lovely part of the coast in Friesland. Full of pride he showed his arms and legs. None of the others was as brown as he. Even Cornel Verstaveren, whose parents had a summer bungalow, seemed pale beside him.

And the Rat?

I didn't like the look of the Rat. It seemed to me that he was even grayer than before. He seemed somehow distrait. During the reading class he could not even find the place.

What could be the matter? Were things going wrong at home?

No, the vacation had done the child no good. When his eyes began to roam aimlessly around the class and I could at last catch his eye, he smiled shyly at me. For a whole five minutes after that the Rat concentrated gallantly, but then his thoughts again escaped somewhere else.

At four o'clock I kept the Rat in as

he had to correct a few sums. "Why were you so inattentive today?" I asked him. "Is there anything the matter with you?"

"No, sir."

"How did you enjoy your vacation?"

"Very much, sir."

"So you had a nice time?"

"Yes, sir."

He answered all my questions mechanically. It was quite obvious that he was putting on an act. Children do it frequently without being conscious of it. Even if Ciske had wanted to tell the truth, he would not have been able to. Grownups and children often speak a different language. A child who does not tell the truth is not necessarily always lying!

Only when I asked the Rat whether he was pleased to be back at school did he say with real conviction, "Oh, yes, sir!"

That was genuine enough. School was Ciske's refuge, the place where he felt safe. The Rat, I was sure, had not had any pleasure during the vacation.

The class was set to write an essay about their vacation, and I read in the Rat's book, "And then I was asked to run a few errands for our neighbor. She gave me five cents, and I bought myself some candy. That was lovely!"

Apart from this, there was nothing "lovely" to be found in Ciske's essay. Only at the end he wrote again, "And then we went back to school, which is lovely!"

That afternoon I went again to visit Mrs. Freimuth. In the "best room" there was a smell of cigars. In the ash tray lay a heap of ashes. This did not necessarily mean anything, but in this case I had a definite feeling that when I appeared a man had been hastily shoved into the kitchen. The lady had obviously had a visitor.

She pretended to be extremely pleased to see me and she even congratulated me belatedly on my marriage. Nothing further had happened about the divorce. Her lawyer had advised her to insist on getting forty guilders a month at any rate.

"Then indeed nothing will come of it,"

I said. "It is rather silly, really, because not only do you lose twenty guilders, but you must also look after Ciske." I had to suppress a desire to comment on the cigar ashes and hint at the possibility of a new life for Mrs. Freimuth, but I was too shy to be so outspoken. "How did Ciske behave during his vacation?" I asked instead.

She shrugged her shoulders. "How should he behave?" she answered harshly. "He has been around the place pestering his mother. One should thank God when children go back to school."

The boy had not been at home much, she continued. Mostly just for his meals and at night. He had sat a lot with Dorus at his house and had, whenever possible, slipped off in the evenings to see his father's woman.

"What, don't you know? His father has got himself a mistress. Too funny for words—a common washerwoman. And after that he wants to tell me what to do! He should be pleased that I don't divorce him for adultery. Then he would have to pay up! Pay through the nose until the day of his death!"

One thing Ciske's mother made quite clear: Ciske would never be able to see that sluttish woman with her blessing—"Auntie Jane," as Ciske called her. (He called her that, of course, only to irritate his mother.) But she knew perfectly well that he was visiting her behind her back. She couldn't keep an eye on such a boy all the time, especially as she was so busy herself. Once she had followed him when he had said he was going to Dorus. But where did he go? Straight to the washerwoman! Well, she had shown him then where he got off. And at night she had been locking him in.

Now I could see quite clearly why the Rat had been so pleased to see the end of the vacation.

Something was in the air. I could not explain why I felt it, but I did. I was worried that the Rat fell silent whenever I mentioned home to him.

Maatsuyker asked me during the

break one day, "How are things going with the Rat now?"

"Excellent! He is a changed boy, quite different from the child who came here some months ago"—I did not need to exaggerate.

"True enough," admitted Maatsuyker, "we have not had any trouble with him for quite some time. But let's wait and see if things remain that way. I don't trust the boy an inch."

Earlier I would have been very angry at this lack of confidence. Now I felt that the doubts expressed by my headmaster were not quite so unjustified. Just because I was so pleased with the Rat, I could not suppress a certain fear of the future. Why did the child stare so grimly into space when the moment before he had been so gay? Why was he suddenly, in the middle of an arithmetic problem, so far away in his thoughts? Why did he start when I called his name? What was going on in his mind?

For Dorus, Ciske would still walk through fire and for Betty and Sip he would run until his feet bled if necessary. I also knew that he was fond of animals. He was even fond of the fish in the tank and was very unhappy whenever one of them died a peaceful death.

If the Rat had only been my pupil and nothing more, I could have been reassured in every respect. But fate had decreed that I be concerned with his welfare outside school. How could I, though, be responsible for a child who spent a great part of his day outside my field of vision?

It became quite obvious to me that the Rat was hiding something from me. Something new and unknown had crept into our relationship. This did not mean that we didn't understand each other any more—quite the contrary. Only recently I had chased Ciske around the desks after class and shoved his head into a wastepaper basket. He had stuck out his tongue at me in reply. A boy does not do that when he does not like you. When he does it, as a

joke and not to be naughty, it proves a certain inner bond. If Johnny had done it, he would have been sharply rebuked. The fact that I was prepared to take it from Ciske proved that our relationship was now capable of withstanding a knock or two.

Ciske was never resentful when sometimes he had to be punished, but he could not bear to be humiliated. In that case he was quickly offended and ready to seek revenge.

Piet Steeman, who sat just behind him, could best testify to this. One day during class I saw Ciske turn suddenly and give Piet a well-aimed blow in the eye. I took him by the collar and put him in the corner. Piet sat in his place with the face of a martyr.

"Piet shouldn't tease him," said Sip, springing to his defense. "Piet said that the Rat has to eat from the garbage pail at his mother's."

Ciske was very good at binding books, and did it very willingly. With Piet and Johnny I asked him once to stay on a little after school break. Piet wanted to go home after a little while because he had been asked to a birthday party, and Johnny went too because he wanted to meet his father's train. I stayed on alone with the Rat and we had a little chat.

"And when is your father coming back?" I asked.

Without looking at me, Ciske answered, "He went yesterday to Aalborg and Stettin, to the Baltic."

"Oh, dear." I was most surprised. "And how long was he here then?"

"Five days."

"Did your mother object to your going to see him?"

"I didn't ask her; I just left her," said Ciske and again he did not look at me.

"And have you since then been to see . . . ?" I wondered how I should refer to "Aunt Jane."

No reaction at all from the Rat!

Something was wrong. I had a definite

impression of this. Was it normal for Freimuth not to have come to see me when he was in town for five days? Or was I imagining things?

I felt at times that the Rat was now playing an active part in the Freimuth marriage tragedy. Ciske's temperament did not allow him to be a silent witness of the horrible quarrel between his parents. He would intervene—and leave nothing undone to help his father. When it came to the point, he would again be the old fighting Rat! And I racked my brains to think how to cope with the dangerous traits in the boy, the cold cruelty which could suddenly swamp all his good qualities.

It seemed to me as if invisible demons were hovering around the child but I could not let myself become a prey to my imagination. Was Maatsuyker by any chance right when he spoke about the "critical clash of personalities"?

Good God, how difficult it all was!

•   •   •

"The father!" exclaimed Mrs. Freimuth in a fury. "The father! He doesn't give a damn for his children. He doesn't even want to support them."

"He wants to, but you prevent him from doing it," I put in. "You should not make these exaggerated claims."

"It's all quite clear," continued the headmaster. "When we get a written request from Ciske's father, the child can be taken away from this school, but not before. And if he does not come to school this afternoon, you will have the police at your house, do you understand?"

Mrs. Freimuth behaved like an offended queen. She cast a poisonous glance at me. "This is just in your line, isn't it?" she shouted. "Two men against a defenseless woman! You bastards!"

"Please get out of here," ordered Maatsuyker. "You can open your mouth as wide as you like at home but not here."

"I believe that you have been handling the lady with kid gloves, Bruis," said Maatsuyker after she had gone. "She is the one who must be treated rough. . . ."

In the afternoon the Rat was back in school. He looked pale and tired.

"So here you are again," I greeted him. "Are you pleased?"

He nodded vigorously. I noticed that his eyes were sad. What must the poor child have suffered when his mother forbade him to go to school! Kept away from Dorus, from Betty and Sip! Ciske must have been dragged straight down from seventh heaven when he got home yesterday, overjoyed about *Pieter Marits,* proud of the trust shown by Dorus in lending him his most wonderful book.

"Tell me what happened," I said gently. God, how sorry I was for my little Rat!

"Well, yesterday Mother told me I could not go to school any more. When I wanted to run here in the morning, she locked me up in the attic. I hammered on the door so hard that she came back and dragged me into the coal cellar. And then today at midday she said suddenly, 'Go to school now!' "

That was Ciske's unadorned report. The boy told his story without emphasis. His fingers drummed nervously on the desk. Something had again been broken in the Rat.

The other children obviously felt that something out of the ordinary was going on. This was not their normal Ciske! It was a quiet, sad little boy who could only understand with difficulty that he was again sitting in his old place.

I purposely didn't call on him. He must first find his feet again. He was staring at his reading book, but his thoughts were goodness knows where. From time to time I gave him a wink, but the Rat behaved like a sick person for whom normal life had become strange.

The last lesson of the day should have been singing, but I didn't feel up to it. "Drawing instead," I ordered, and there were several shouts of "Wonderful!"

The Rat remained apathetic. He tried to draw a horse, but it turned into a dog. I was glad when the bell rang and the class could be dismissed. I would like to have given Ciske a word of encouragement on his way home, but thought better of it. What was the use of words? The child surely felt anyway that I was on his side.

"Go on reading your *Pieter Marits*," was all I said to him. He nodded, and Dorus smiled at him from his chair.

That evening I was more uneasy than ever before. I had not liked the Rat's manner that day at all. What should I do? In despair I paced up and down my room. Susan looked at me quizzically but did not ask me any questions. Ciske, now you are between the four walls which are called your home! Ciske, boy, don't hang your head! Hold out! Ciske, Ciske, Ciske! The thoughts were running around and around in my head. I had to keep wiping the perspiration from my forehead.

At half-past nine, Muysken of the juvenile police knocked at my front door. I let him in. He told me that Ciske had killed his mother. Ciske! My Rat!

I felt the ground slipping away from under my feet. I was so shaken that I could only stare at Muysken without saying a word.

He nodded gravely. Yes, Mrs. Freimuth had ordered Ciske to bed early and tried to take his book away from him, the book he had borrowed from Dorus. She had torn it out of his hand, thrown it on the floor, and, in a senseless rage, trampled it under her feet. The Rat had become mad with rage. He had grabbed a knife which was lying on the table and had thrown it blindly in his mother's direction. It had penetrated Mrs. Freimuth's jugular vein; she had died within a few minutes.

"And the child?"

Ciske had fled instinctively to his Aunt Jane. She had taken him to the police.

•   •   •

When I entered the quiet building of the psychiatric department at the remand school (the detention home where Ciske was being held until his trial), I was overcome by a feeling of uneasiness. From the street the noise of everyday activities penetrated into the prison, the sounds of life itself. Had the Rat irrevocably forfeited this life? Would he never be able to return to the company of happy children?

The head of the department showed me a door, and looking through the small window in it I saw Ciske sitting on a wooden bench. He was swinging his legs, exactly like a boy who is momentarily bored during vacation. Here he was, the Rat, my pupil. I had given my whole heart to the boy and yet I had been unable to prevent fate from striking him down.

Ciske jumped when I went into the cell. So, he was not as unconcerned as he had appeared. At once he hung his head and began to bite his knuckles nervously. He wouldn't look at me.

I couldn't feel anything but a deep, painful sympathy for the cowering child, for this sad little bundle of humanity which —without understanding it completely—had taken upon his conscience a mortal sin.

I felt, not for the first time, how relative guilt can be. A fraction further to the right or to the left and the knife would not have killed the woman, only wounded her. In Ciske's defense, mitigating circumstances would certainly have been found. But because Ciske happened to hit precisely the fatal place, he would be stigmatized for the rest of his life.

I put my hand on his head and stroked his hair. I could find no words. The boy was trembling like a captive, frightened bird. All of a sudden he began to cry, although he tried to keep back his tears. But when I pressed his head lovingly against me, he broke down completely— Ciske was now no more than an unhappy child.

If only I could have taken him home with me! But I had to leave him here, in this bare cheerless building, in which the Rat was a serious, perhaps even an interesting, case. What could I do to lighten for the child the burden of his tragic fate?

"Dorus sends his love," I said finally. "He wants me to tell you that he does not mind at all about the book. He will always remain your friend, he has assured me. Isn't that wonderful?"

The Rat continued to sob.

"Betty and Sip also send their love," I lied.

The boy pressed his wet face against my hand. Wordlessly he begged for my protection, which I was unable to extend to him any more.

Through the little window in the door, the head of the department made a sign that my time was up.

"Listen, my dear boy," I said to the Rat, "we won't discuss now what you have done. It was a terrible misfortune. But you must remember that I won't abandon you because of this—all right? Nor will the others, Ciske!" After a moment I said quietly, "And now I must go, Ciske."

He clung desperately to my arm with both hands. I could feel his loneliness, his utter misery. Gently I freed my arms, and

Ciske lifted his pale face to me. The Rat's eyes imploring me to help him were the last thing I saw as I left.

. . .

Meerstra reflectively chewed on the butt of his cigar. "I would like for five minutes to borrow the robes of the judge of the juvenile court," he said slowly, "and sentence the boy to be taken into a decent family, to people who have some love to spare for such a little fellow and who would not continuously talk of 'guilt and expiation.' I hate all this useless, juristic mumbo-jumbo. Why complicate matters so? It is a lot of dangerous twaddle; to repay evil with evil. Under certain circumstances one can do this with an adult, with a thoroughly depraved character, but not with a child. If you pronounce a vindictive sentence on the boy, you lightly commit spiritual infanticide in the name of the law, too. . . . Do you understand?"

DIAGNOSIS: *Affectional and cultural deprivation—learning difficulties.*

This is a story of a Dutch teacher and a child of spirit whose experience of the world has been altogether negative up to the time he arrived in this class. The teacher is skillful and sensitive—skillful enough to keep from becoming over-involved, sensitive enough to care, and perceptive enough to group his class in such a way that Ciske, the Rat, begins to find areas of success, joy, a sense of beauty, friendship, and relatedness. School becomes Ciske's haven. At home is a hating, complaining mother and a weak, amoral father. Necessities are minimal, and Ciske gets less than minimum love, understanding, or privacy. At school he finds a dying, crippled child whom he protects and who gives him love and value. He becomes part of a group and finds a reliable adult and a world of intellect. When thwarted from reaching toward these values, he loses control of his impulses and fights back.

This story shows the buildup of tension. The teacher, social worker, and police officer admire Ciske's rebellion and spirit. The teacher turns this energy to useful channels. After the murder, however, he recognizes defeat in the trap that Ciske's life has set for him.

Unloved, spunky fighters and despairing, silent haters often sit in classrooms with much reason to hate and little to love, much reason to fight. Some, like Ciske, learn the meaning of love and beauty through a teacher with love and humor in his heart and skillful teaching techniques. Often, as in Ciske's case, there is little we can do to give lasting help.

Of Human Bondage

W. Somerset Maugham

. . . But meanwhile he had grown horribly sensitive. He never ran if he could help it, because he knew it made his limp more conspicuous, and he adopted a peculiar walk. He stood still as much as he could, with his club-foot behind the other, so that it should not attract notice, and he was constantly on the lookout for any reference to it. Because he could not join in the games which other boys played, their life remained strange to him; he only interested himself from the outside in their doings; and it seemed to him that there was a barrier between them and him. Sometimes they seemed to think that it was his fault if he could not play football, and he was unable to make them understand. He was left a good deal to himself. He had been inclined to talkativeness, but gradually he became silent. He began to think of the difference between himself and others.

Two years passed, and Philip was nearly twelve. He was in the first form, within two or three places of the top, and after Christmas when several boys would be leaving for the senior school he would be head boy. He had already quite a collection of prizes, worthless books on bad paper, but in gorgeous bindings decorated with the arms of the school: his position had freed him from bullying, and he was not unhappy. His fellows forgave him his success because of his deformity.

"After all, it's jolly easy for him to get prizes," they said, "there's nothing he *can* do but swat."

He had lost his early terror of Mr. Watson. He had grown used to the loud voice, and when the headmaster's heavy hand was laid on his shoulder Philip discerned vaguely the intention of a caress.

He had the good memory which is more useful for scholastic achievements than mental power, and he knew Mr. Watson expected him to leave the preparatory school with a scholarship.

But he had grown very self-conscious. The new-born child does not realise that his body is more a part of himself than surrounding objects, and will play with his toes without any feeling that they belong to him more than the rattle by his side; and it is only by degrees, through pain, that he understands the fact of the body. And experiences of the same kind are necessary for the individual to become conscious of himself; but here there is the difference that, although everyone becomes equally conscious of his body as a separate and complete organism, everyone does not become equally conscious of himself as a complete and separate personality. The feeling of apartness from others comes to most with puberty, but it is not always developed to such a degree as to make the difference between the individual and his fellows noticeable to the individual. It is such as he, as little conscious of himself as the bee in a hive, who are the lucky in life, for they have the best chance of happiness: their activities are shared by all, and their pleasures are only pleasures because they are enjoyed in common; you will see them on Whit-Monday dancing on Hampstead Heath, shouting at a football match, or from club windows in Pall Mall cheering a royal procession. It is because of them that man has been called a social animal.

Philip passed from the innocence of childhood to bitter consciousness of himself by the ridicule which his club-foot had excited. The circumstances of his case were so peculiar that he could not apply to them the ready-made rules which acted well enough in ordinary affairs, and he was forced to think for himself. The many books he had read filled his mind with ideas which, because he only half understood them, gave more scope to his imagination. Beneath his painful shyness something was growing up within him, and obscurely he realised his personality. But at times it gave him odd surprises; he did things, he knew not why, and afterwards when he thought of them found himself all at sea.

Then a wave of religiosity passed through the school. Bad language was no longer heard, and the little nastinesses of small boys were looked upon with hostility; the bigger boys, like the lords temporal of the Middle Ages, used the strength of their arms to persuade those weaker than themselves to virtuous courses.

Philip, his restless mind avid for new things, became very devout. He heard soon that it was possible to join a Bible League, and wrote to London for particulars. These consisted in a form to be filled up with applicant's name, age, and school; a solemn declaration to be signed that he would read a set portion of Holy Scripture every night for a year; and a request for half a crown; this, it was explained, was demanded partly to prove the earnestness of the applicant's desire to become a member of the League, and partly to cover clerical expenses. Philip duly sent the papers and the money, and in return received a calendar worth about a penny, on which was set down the appointed passage to be read each day, and a sheet of paper on one side of which was a picture of the Good Shepherd and a lamb, and on the other, decoratively framed in red lines, a short prayer which had to be said before beginning to read.

Every evening he undressed as quickly as possible in order to have time for his task before the gas was put out. He read industriously, as he read always, without criticism, stories of cruelty, deceit, ingratitude, dishonesty, and low cunning. Actions which would have excited his horror in the life about him, in the reading passed through his mind without comment, because they were committed under direct

inspiration of God. The method of the League was to alternate a book of the Old Testament with a book of the New, and one night Philip came across these words of Jesus Christ:

If ye have faith, and doubt not, ye shall not only do this which is done to the fig-tree, but also if ye shall say unto this mountain, Be thou removed, and be thou cast into the sea; it shall be done.
And all this, whatsoever ye shall ask in prayer, believing, ye shall receive.

They made no particular impression on him, but it happened that two or three days later, being Sunday, the Canon in residence chose them for the text of his sermon. Even if Philip had wanted to hear this it would have been impossible, for the boys of King's School sit in the choir, and the pulpit stands at the corner of the transept so that the preacher's back is almost turned to them. The distance also is so great that it needs a man with a fine voice and a knowledge of elocution to make himself heard in the choir; and according to long usage the Canons of Tercanbury are chosen for their learning rather than for any qualities which might be of use in a cathedral church. But the words of the text, perhaps because he had read them so short a while before, came clearly enough to Philip's ears, and they seemed of a sudden to have a personal application. He thought about them through most of the sermon, and that night, on getting into bed, he turned over the pages of the Gospel and found once more the passage. Though he believed implicitly everything he saw in print, he had learned already that in the Bible things that said one thing quite clearly often mysteriously meant another. There was no one he liked to ask at school, so he kept the question he had in mind till the Christmas holidays, and then one day he made an opportunity. It was after supper and prayers were just finished. Mrs. Carey was counting the eggs that Mary Ann had brought in as usual and writing on each one the date. Philip stood at the table and pretended to turn listlessly the pages of the Bible.

"I say, Uncle William, this passage here, does it really mean that?"

He put his finger against it as though he had come across it accidentally.

Mr. Carey looked up over his spectacles. He was holding *The Blackstable Times* in front of the fire. It had come in that evening damp from the press, and the Vicar always aired it for ten minutes before he began to read.

"What passage is that?" he asked.

"Why, this about if you have faith you can remove mountains."

"If it says so in the Bible it is so, Philip," said Mrs. Carey gently, taking up the plate-basket.

Philip looked at his uncle for an answer.

"It's a matter of faith."

"D'you mean to say that if you really believed you could move mountains you could?"

"By the grace of God," said the Vicar.

"Now, say good-night to your uncle, Philip," said Aunt Louisa. "You're not wanting to move a mountain tonight, are you?"

Philip allowed himself to be kissed on the forehead by his uncle and preceded Mrs. Carey upstairs. He had got the information he wanted. His little room was icy, and he shivered when he put on his nightgown. But he always felt that his prayers were more pleasing to God when he said them under conditions of discomfort. The coldness of his hands and feet were an offering to the Almighty. And tonight he sank on his knees, buried his face in his hands, and prayed to God with all his might that He would make his club-foot whole. It was a very small thing beside the moving of mountains. He knew that God could do it if He wished, and his own faith was complete. Next morning, finishing his prayers with the same request, he fixed a date for the miracle.

"Oh, God, in Thy loving mercy and goodness, if it be Thy will, please make my foot all right on the night before I go back to school."

He was glad to get his petition into a formula, and he repeated it later in the dining-room during the short pause which the Vicar always made after prayers, before he rose from his knees. He said it again in the evening and again, shivering in his nightshirt, before he got into bed. And he believed. For once he looked forward with eagerness to the end of the holidays. He laughed to himself as he thought of his uncle's astonishment when he ran down the stairs three at a time; and after breakfast he and Aunt Louisa would have to hurry out and buy a new pair of boots. At school they would be astounded.

"Hulloa, Carey, what have you done with your foot?"

"Oh, it's all right now," he would answer casually, as though it were the most natural thing in the world.

He would be able to play football. His heart leaped as he saw himself running, running, faster than any of the other boys. At the end of the Easter term there were the sports, and he would be able to go in for the races; he rather fancied himself over the hurdles. It would be splendid to be like everyone else, not to be stared at curiously by new boys who did not know about his deformity, nor at the baths in summer to need incredible precautions, while he was undressing, before he could hide his foot in the water.

He prayed with all the power of his soul. No doubts assailed him. He was confident in the word of God. And the night before he was to go back to school he went up to bed tremulous with excitement. There was snow on the ground, and Aunt Louisa had allowed herself the unaccustomed luxury of a fire in her bed-room; but in Philip's little room it was so cold that his fingers were numb, and he had great difficulty in undoing his collar. His teeth chattered. The idea came to him that he must do something more than usual to attract the attention of God, and he turned back the rug which was in front of his bed so that he could kneel on the bare boards; and then it struck him that his nightshirt was a softness that might displease his Maker, so he took it off and said his prayers naked. When he got into bed he was so cold that for some time he could not sleep, but when he did, it was so soundly that Mary Ann had to shake him when she brought in his hot water next morning. She talked to him while she drew the curtains, but he did not answer; he had remembered at once that this was the morning for the miracle. His heart was filled with joy and gratitude. His first instinct was to put down his hand and feel the foot which was whole now, but to do this seemed to doubt the goodness of God. He knew that his foot was well. But at last he made up his mind, and with the toes of his right foot he just touched his left. Then he passed his hand over it.

He limped downstairs just as Mary Ann was going into the dining-room for prayers, and then he sat down to breakfast.

"You're very quiet this morning, Philip," said Aunt Louisa presently.

"He's thinking of the good breakfast he'll have at school tomorrow," said the Vicar.

When Philip answered, it was in a way that always irritated his uncle, with something that had nothing to do with the matter in hand. He called it a bad habit of wool-gathering.

"Supposing you'd asked God to do something," said Philip, "and really believed it was going to happen, like moving a mountain, I mean, and you had faith, and it didn't happen, what would it mean?"

"What a funny boy you are!" said Aunt Louisa. "You asked about moving mountains two or three weeks ago."

"It would just mean that you hadn't got faith," answered Uncle William.

Philip accepted the explanation. If God had not cured him, it was because he did not really believe. And yet he did not see how he could believe more than he did. But perhaps he had not given God enough time. He had only asked Him for nineteen days. In a day or two he began his prayer again, and this time he fixed upon Easter. That was the day of His Son's glorious resurrection, and God in His happiness might be mercifully inclined. But now Philip added other means of attaining his desire: he began to wish, when he saw a new moon or a dappled horse, and he looked out for shooting stars; during exeat they had a chicken at the vicarage, and he broke the lucky bone with Aunt Louisa and wished again, each time that his foot might be made whole. He was appealing unconsciously to gods older to his race than the God of Israel. And he bombarded the Almighty with his prayer, at odd times of the day, whenever it occurred to him, in identical words always, for it seemed to him important to make his request in the same terms. But presently the feeling came to him that this time also his faith would not be great enough. He could not resist the doubt that assailed him. He made his own experience into a general rule.

"I suppose no one ever has faith enough," he said.

It was like the salt which his nurse used to tell him about: you could catch any bird by putting salt on his tail; and once he had taken a little bag of it into Kensington Gardens. But he could never get near enough to put the salt on a bird's tail. Before Easter he had given up the struggle. He felt a dull resentment against his uncle for taking him in. The text which spoke of the moving of mountains was just one of those that said one thing and meant another. He thought his uncle had been playing a practical joke on him.

The King's School at Tercanbury, to which Philip went when he was thirteen, prided itself on its antiquity. The masters had no patience with modern ideas of education, which they read of sometimes in *The Times* or *The Guardian,* and hoped fervently that King's School would remain true to its old traditions. The dead languages were taught with such thoroughness that an old boy seldom thought of Homer or Virgil in after life without a qualm of boredom; and though in the common room at dinner one or two bolder spirits suggested that mathematics were of increasing importance, the general feeling was that they were a less noble study than the classics. Neither German nor chemistry was taught, and French only by the form-masters; they could keep order better than a foreigner, and, since they knew the grammar as well as any Frenchman, it seemed unimportant that none of them could have got a cup of coffee in the restaurant at Boulogne unless the waiter had known a little English. Geography was taught chiefly by making boys draw maps, and this was a favourite occupation, especially when the country dealt with was mountainous: it was possible to waste a great deal of time in drawing the Andes or the Apennines.

But a year before Philip entered the school a great change had come over it. It had been obvious for some time that Dr. Fleming, who had been headmaster for the quarter of a century, was become too deaf to continue his work to the greater glory of God.

It became necessary to find a successor. It was contrary to the traditions of the school that one of the lower-masters should be chosen. The common-room was unanimous in desiring the election of Mr. Watson, headmaster of the preparatory school; he could hardly be described as already a master of King's School, they had all known him for twenty years, and there was no danger that he would make a nuisance of himself. But the Chapter sprang a surprise on them. It chose a man called Perkins. At first nobody knew who Perkins was, and the name favourably impressed no one; but before the shock of it had passed away, it was realised that Perkins was the son of Perkins the linendraper. Dr. Fleming informed the masters just before dinner, and his manner showed his consternation. Such of them as were dining in, ate their meal almost in silence, and no reference was made to the matter till the servants had left the room. Then they set to. The names of those present on this occasion are unimportant, but they had been known to generations of school-boys as Sigh, Tar, Winks, Squirts, and Pat.

They all knew Tom Perkins. The first

thing about him was that he was not a gentleman. They remembered him quite well. He was a small, dark boy, with untidy black hair and large eyes. He looked like a gipsy. He had come to the school as a day-boy, with the best scholarship on their endowment, so that his education had cost him nothing. Of course he was brilliant. At every Speech-Day he was loaded with prizes. He was their show-boy, and they remembered now bitterly their fear that he would try to get some scholarship at one of the larger public schools and so pass out of their hands. Dr. Fleming had gone to the linendraper his father—they all remembered the shop, Perkins and Cooper, in St. Catherine's Street—and said he hoped Tom would remain with them till he went to Oxford. The school was Perkins and Cooper's best customer, and Mr. Perkins was only too glad to give the required assurance. Tom Perkins continued to triumph, he was the finest classical scholar that Dr. Fleming remembered, and on leaving the school took with him the most valuable scholarship they had to offer. He got another at Magdalen and settled down to a brilliant career at the University.

The school magazine recorded the distinctions he achieved year after year, and when he got his double first Dr. Fleming himself wrote a few words of eulogy on the front page. It was with greater satisfaction that they welcomed his success, since Perkins and Cooper had fallen upon evil days: Cooper drank like a fish, and just before Tom Perkins took his degree the linendrapers filed their petition in bankruptcy.

In due course Tom Perkins took Holy Orders and entered upon the profession for which he was so admirably suited. He had been an assistant master at Wellington and then at Rugby.

But there was quite a difference between welcoming his success at other schools and serving under his leadership in their own. Tar had frequently given him lines, and Squirts had boxed his ears. They could not imagine how the Chapter had made such a mistake. No one could be expected to forget that he was the son of a bankrupt linendraper, and the alcoholism of Cooper seemed to increase the disgrace. It was understood that the Dean had supported his candidature with zeal, so the Dean would probably ask him to dinner; but would the pleasant little dinners in the precincts ever be the same when Tom Perkins sat at the table? And what about the dépôt? He really could not expect officers and gentlemen to receive him as one of themselves. It would do the school incalculable harm. Parents would be dissatisfied, and no one could be surprised if there were wholesale withdrawals. And then the indignity of calling him Mr. Perkins! The masters thought by way of protest of sending in their resignations in a body, but the uneasy fear that they would be accepted with equanimity restrained them.

"The only thing is to prepare ourselves for changes," said Sighs, who had conducted the fifth form for five and twenty years with unparalleled incompetence.

A year passed, and when Philip came to the school the old masters were all in their places; but a good many changes had taken place notwithstanding their stubborn resistance, none the less formidable because it was concealed under an apparent desire to fall in with the new head's ideas. Though the form-masters still taught French to the lower school, another master had come, with a degree of doctor of philology from the University of Heidelberg and a record of three years spent in a French lycée, to teach French to the upper forms and German to anyone who cared to take it up instead of Greek. Another master was engaged to teach mathematics more systematically than had been found necessary hitherto. Neither of these was ordained. This was a real revolution, and when the pair arrived the older masters received them with distrust. A laboratory had been fitted up, army classes were instituted; they all said the character of the school was changing. And heaven only knew what further projects Mr. Perkins turned in that untidy head of his. The

school was small as public schools go, there were not more than two hundred boarders; and it was difficult for it to grow larger, for it was huddled up against the Cathedral; the precincts, with the exception of a house in which some of the masters lodged, were occupied by the cathedral clergy; and there was no more room for building. But Mr. Perkins devised an elaborate scheme by which he might obtain sufficient space to make the school double its present size. He wanted to attract boys from London. He thought it would be good for them to be thrown in contact with the Kentish lads, and it would sharpen the country wits of these.

"It's against all our traditions," said Sighs, when Mr. Perkins made the suggestion to him. "We've rather gone out of our way to avoid the contamination of boys from London."

"Oh, what nonsense!" said Mr. Perkins.

But Mr. Perkins' most unpopular innovation was his system of taking occasionally another man's form. He asked it as a favour, but after all it was a favour which could not be refused, and as Tar, otherwise Mr. Turner, said, it was undignified for all parties. He gave no warning, but after morning prayers would say to one of the masters:

"I wonder if you'd mind taking the Sixth today at eleven. We'll change over, shall we?"

They did not know whether this was usual at other schools, but certainly it had never been done at Tercanbury. The results were curious. Mr. Turner, who was the first victim, broke the news to his form that the headmaster would take them for Latin that day, and on the pretence that they might like to ask him a question or two so that they should not make perfect fools of themselves, spent the last quarter of an hour of the history lesson in construing for them the passage of Livy which had been set for the day; but when he rejoined his class and looked at the paper on which Mr. Perkins had written the marks, a surprise awaited him; for the two boys at the top of the form seemed to have done very ill, while others who had never distinguished themselves before were given full marks. When he asked Eldridge, his cleverest boy, what was the meaning of this the answer came sullenly:

"Mr. Perkins never gave us any construing to do. He asked me what I knew about General Gordon."

Mr. Turner looked at him in astonishment. The boys evidently felt they had been hardly used, and he could not help agreeing with their silent dissatisfaction. He could not see either what General Gordon had to do with Livy. He hazarded an enquiry afterwards.

"Eldridge was dreadfully put out because you asked him what he knew about General Gordon," he said to the headmaster, with an attempt at a chuckle.

Mr. Perkins laughed.

"I saw they'd got to the agrarian laws of Caius Gracchus, and I wondered if they knew anything about the agrarian troubles in Ireland. But all they knew about Ireland was that Dublin was on the Liffey. So I wondered if they'd ever heard of General Gordon."

Then the horrid fact was disclosed that the new head had a mania for general information. He had doubts about the utility of examinations on subjects which had been crammed for the occasion. He wanted common sense.

Sighs grew more worried every month; and he hated the attitude the head adopted towards classical literature. And Squirts, the master of the middle-third, grew more ill-tempered every day.

It was in his form that Philip was put on entering the school. The Rev. B. B. Gordon was a man by nature ill-suited to be a schoolmaster: he was impatient and choleric. No master could have been more unfitted to teach things to so shy a boy as Philip. He had come to the school with fewer terrors than he had when first he went to Mr. Watson's. He knew a good

many boys who had been with him at the preparatory school. He felt more grown-up, and instinctively realised that among the larger numbers his deformity would be less noticeable. But from the first day Mr. Gordon struck terror in his heart; and the master, quick to discern the boys who were frightened of him, seemed on that account to take a peculiar dislike to him. Philip had enjoyed his work, but now he began to look upon the hours passed in school with horror. Rather than risk an answer which might be wrong and excite a storm of abuse from the master, he would sit stupidly silent, and when it came towards his turn to stand up and construe he grew sick and white with apprehension. His happy moments were those when Mr. Perkins took the form. He was able to gratify the passion for general knowledge which beset the headmaster; he had read all sorts of strange books beyond his years, and often Mr. Perkins, when a question was going round the room, would stop at Philip with a smile that filled the boy with rapture, and say:

"Now, Carey, you tell them."

The good marks he got on these occasions increased Mr. Gordon's indignation. One day it came to Philip's turn to translate, and the master sat there glaring at him and furiously biting his thumb. He was in a ferocious mood. Philip began to speak in a low voice.

"Don't mumble," shouted the master.

Something seemed to stick in Philip's throat.

"Go on. Go on. Go on."

Each time the words were screamed more loudly. The effect was to drive all he knew out of Philip's head, and he looked at the printed page vacantly. Mr. Gordon began to breathe heavily.

"If you don't know why don't you say so? Do you know it or not? Did you hear all this construed last time or not? Why don't you speak? Speak, you blockhead, speak!"

The master seized the arms of his chair and grasped them as though to prevent himself from falling upon Philip. They knew that in past days he often used to seize boys by the throat till they almost choked. The veins in his forehead stood out and his face grew dark and threatening. He was a man insane.

Philip had known the passage perfectly the day before, but now he could remember nothing.

"I don't know it," he gasped.

"Why don't you know it? Let's take the words one by one. We'll soon see if you don't know it."

Philip stood silent, very white, trembling a little, with his head bent down on the book. The master's breathing grew almost stertorous.

"The headmaster says you're clever. I don't know how he sees it. General information." He laughed savagely. "I don't know what they put you in his form for. Blockhead."

He was pleased with the word, and he repeated it at the top of his voice.

"Blockhead! Blockhead! Club-footed blockhead!"

That relieved him a little. He saw Philip redden suddenly. He told him to fetch the Black Book. Philip put down his Caesar and went silently out. The Black Book was a sombre volume in which the names of boys were written with their misdeeds, and when a name was down three times it meant a caning. Philip went to the headmaster's house and knocked at his study-door. Mr. Perkins was seated at his table.

"May I have the Black Book, please, sir?"

"There it is," answered Mr. Perkins, indicating its place by a nod of his head.

"What have you been doing that you shouldn't?"

"I don't know, sir."

Mr. Perkins gave him a quick look, but without answering went on with his work. Philip took the book and went out. When the hour was up, a few minutes later, he brought it back.

"Let me have a look at it," said the headmaster. "I see Mr. Gordon has blackbooked you for 'gross impertinence.' What was it?"

"I don't know, sir. Mr. Gordon said I was a club-footed blockhead."

Mr. Perkins looked at him again. He wondered whether there was sarcasm behind the boy's reply, but he was still much too shaken. His face was white and his eyes had a look of terrified distress. Mr. Perkins got up and put the book down. As he did so he took up some photographs.

"A friend of mine sent me some pictures of Athens this morning," he said casually. "Look here, there's the Akropolis."

He began explaining to Philip what he saw. The ruin grew vivid with his words. He showed him the theatre of Dionysus and explained in what order the people sat, and how beyond they could see the blue Aegean. And then suddenly he said:

"I remember Mr. Gordon used to call me a gipsy counter-jumper when I was in his form."

And before Philip, his mind fixed on the photographs, had time to gather the meaning of the remark, Mr. Perkins was showing him a picture of Salamis, and with his finger, a finger of which the nail had a little black edge to it, was pointing out how the Greek ships were placed and how the Persian. . . .

DIAGNOSIS: *Withdrawal because of physical handicap—use of handicap to foster neurosis, masochism.*

The question of emotional disturbance of children with physical handicaps is the problem of which came first, the chicken or the egg. There is no question that some children with severe, even with multiple physical handicaps have no more than an ordinary dose of emotional problems. These children generally have excellent physical health along with their disability and have warm, accepting, unpitying relationships at home, and reasonable expectations are blended with acceptance of limitations.

It is equally certain that many children who have physical handicaps also suffer from emotional disorders. Being different is hard for children; restriction by edict of fate breeds resentment and is hard on the ego. When parents cannot accept the disability, or when they use it as a means of tying their children to them, damage ensues. When, further, schoolmates and teachers ridicule or set the child apart by too little or too much sympathy, difficulties mount.

Philip's case is a good example. A lonely child, bereft of warmth and understanding, he feels different and unaccepted by his peers. He turns inward to reading and fantasy and removes himself from friendship. Here good teachers could come to the rescue. He looks toward religion—or, in his adolescent view, magic or miracle—to solve his problem. When this fails, he turns more inward and escapes to compulsive reading. Bad teachers underline his troubles. His school work falls off, and a pattern of failure follows through early manhood until he finds a way out for himself via projection, or identity with the sufferings of others.

You have seen this child—whether he be a Philip with a club foot, a stutterer like Maugham himself, or a child with an eye-hand disability that makes it impossible for him to read. He needs careful watching, sympathy but not pity, understanding without overindulgence, acceptance but not resignation. At a further extreme, the brain-damaged child, the epileptic, the blind, and the deaf child (who feels the most isolated) bear similar marks. Special skills and teaching techniques are needed for various severely handicapped children; for the severer the handicap and the greater the "difference" between this child and others, the greater the chance for emotional disturbance.

My Child-Wife

Charles Dickens

. . . "Will you call me a name I want you to call me?" inquired Dora, without moving.

"What is it?" I asked with a smile.

"It's a stupid name," she said, shaking her curls for a moment. "Child-wife."

I laughingly asked my child-wife what her fancy was in desiring to be so called. She answered without moving, otherwise than as the arm I twined about her may have brought her blue eyes nearer to me:

"I don't mean, you silly fellow, that you should use the name instead of Dora. I only mean that you should think of me that way. When you are going to be angry with me, say to yourself, 'it's only my child-wife!'

From *David Copperfield* by Charles Dickens, 1850.

When I am very disappointing, say, 'I knew, a long time ago, that she would make but a child-wife!' When you miss what I should like to be, and I think can never be, say, 'still my foolish child-wife loves me!' For indeed I do."

I had not been serious with her; having no idea, until now, that she was serious herself. But her affectionate nature was so happy in what I now said to her with my whole heart, that her face became a laughing one before her glittering eyes were dry. She was soon my child-wife indeed; sitting down on the floor outside the Chinese House, ringing all the little bells one after another, to punish Jip for his recent bad behaviour; while Jip lay blinking in the doorway with his head out, even too lazy to be teased.

This appeal of Dora's made a strong impression on me. I look back on the time I write of; I invoke the innocent figure that I dearly loved, to come out from the mists and shadows of the past, and turn its gentle head towards me once again; and I can still declare that this one little speech was constantly in my memory. I may not have used it to the best account; I was young and inexperienced; but I never turned a deaf ear to its artless pleading.

Dora told me, shortly afterwards, that she was going to be a wonderful house-keeper. Accordingly, she polished the tab-lets, pointed the pencil, bought an immense account-book, carefully stitched up with a needle and thread all the leaves of the Cookery Book which Jip had torn, and made quite a desperate little attempt "to be good," as she called it. But the figures had the old obstinate propensity—they *would not* add up. When she had entered two or three laborious items in the account-book, Jip would walk over the page, wagging his tail, and smear them all out. Her own little right-hand middle finger got steeped to the very bone in ink; and I think that was the only decided result obtained.

Sometimes, of an evening, when I was at home and at work—for I wrote a good deal now, and was beginning in a small way to be known as a writer—I would lay down my pen, and watch my child-wife trying to be good. First of all, she would bring out the immense account-book, and lay it down upon the table with a deep sigh. Then she would open it at the place where Jip had made it illegible last night, and call Jip up to look at his misdeeds. This would occasion a diversion in Jip's favour, and some inking of his nose, per-haps, as a penalty. Then she would tell Jip to lie down on the table instantly, "like a lion"—which was one of his tricks, though I cannot say the likeness was striking—and, if he were in an obedient humour, he would obey. Then she would take up a pen, and begin to write, and find a hair in it. Then she would take up another pen, and begin to write, and find that it splut-tered. Then she would take up another pen, begin to write, and say in a low voice, "Oh, it's a talking pen, and will disturb Doady!" And then she would give it up as a bad job, and put the account-book away, after pre-tending to crush the lion with it.

Or, if she were in a very sedate and serious state of mind, she would sit down with the tablets, and a little basket of bills and other documents, which looked more like curl-papers than anything else, and endeavour to get some result out of them. After severely comparing one with an-other, and making entries on the tablets, and blotting them out, and counting all the fingers of her left hand over and over again, backwards and forwards, she would be so vexed and discouraged, and would look so unhappy, that it gave me pain to see her bright face clouded—and for me!—and I would go softly to her, and say:

"What's the matter, Dora?"

Dora would look up hopelessly, and reply, "They won't come right. They make my head ache so. And they won't do any-thing I want!"

Then I would say, "Now let us try to-gether. Let me show you, Dora."

Then I would commence a practical demonstration, to which Dora would pay profound attention, perhaps for five min-utes; when she would begin to be dread-fully tired, and would lighten the subject by curling my hair, or trying the effect of my face with my shirt-collar turned down. If I tacitly checked this playfulness, and persisted, she would look so scared and dis-consolate, as she became more and more bewildered, that the remembrance of her natural gaiety when I first strayed into her path, and of her being my child-wife, would come reproachfully upon me; and I would lay the pencil down, and call for the guitar. . . .

What other course was left to take? To "form her mind?" This was a common phrase of words which had a fair and prom-ising sound, and I resolved to form Dora's mind.

I began immediately. When Dora was

very childish, and I would have infinitely preferred to humour her, I tried to be grave—and disconcerted her, and myself too. I talked to her on the subjects which occupied my thoughts; and I read Shakespeare to her—and fatigued her to the last degree. I accustomed myself to giving her, as it were quite casually, little scraps of useful information, or sound opinion—and she started from them when I let them off, as if they had been crackers. No matter how incidentally or naturally I endeavoured to form my little wife's mind, I could not help seeing that she always had an instinctive perception of what I was about, and became prey to the keenest apprehensions. In particular, it was clear to me, that she thought Shakespeare a terrible fellow. The formation went on very slowly.

I pressed Traddles into the service without his knowledge; and whenever he came to see us, exploded my mines upon him for the edification of Dora at second hand. The amount of practical wisdom I bestowed upon Traddles in this manner was immense, and of the best quality; but it had no other effect upon Dora than to depress her spirits, and make her always nervous with the dread that it would be her turn next. I found myself in the condition of a schoolmaster, a trap, a pitfall; of always playing spider to Dora's fly, and always pouncing out of my hole to her infinite disturbance.

Still, looking forward through this intermediate stage, to the time when there should be a perfect sympathy between Dora and me, and when I should have "formed her mind" to my entire satisfaction, I persevered, even for months. Finding at last, however, that, although I had been all this time a very porcupine or hedgehog, bristling all over with determination, I had effected nothing, it began to occur to me that perhaps Dora's mind was already formed.

On further consideration this appeared so likely, that I abandoned my scheme, which had had a more promising appearance in words than in action; resolving henceforth to be satisfied with my child-wife, and to try to change her into nothing else by any process. I was heartily tired of being sagacious and prudent by myself, and of seeing my darling under restraint; so I bought a pretty pair of earrings for her, and a collar for Jip, and went home one day to make myself agreeable.

Dora was delighted with the little presents, and kissed me joyfully; but there was a shadow between us, however slight, and I had made up my mind that it should not be there. If there must be such a shadow anywhere, I would keep it for the future in my own breast.

I sat down by my wife on the sofa, and put the ear-rings in her ears; and then I told her that I feared we had not been quite as good company lately, as we used to be, and that the fault was mine. Which I sincerely felt, and which indeed it was.

"The truth is, Dora, my life," I said, "I have been trying to be wise."

"And to make me wise too," said Dora, timidly. "Haven't you, Doady?"

I nodded assent to the pretty inquiry of the raised eyebrows, and kissed the parted lips.

"It's of not a bit of use," said Dora, shaking her head, until the ear-rings rang again. "You know what a little thing I am, and what I wanted you to call me from the first. If you can't do so, I am afraid you'll never like me. Are you sure you don't think, sometimes, it would have been better to have—"

"Done what, my dear?" For she made no effort to proceed.

"Nothing!" said Dora.

"Nothing?" I repeated.

She put her arms round my neck, and laughed, and called herself by her favourite name of a goose, and hid her face on my shoulder in such a profusion of curls that it was quite a task to clear them away and see it.

"Don't I think it would have been better to have done nothing, than to have tried to form my little wife's mind?" said I, laughing at myself. "Is that the question? Yes, indeed, I do."

"Is that what you have been trying?" cried Dora. "Oh what a shocking boy!"

"But I shall never try any more," said I. "For I love her dearly as she is."

"Without a story—really?" inquired Dora, creeping closer to me.

"Why should I seek to change," said I, "what has been so precious to me for so long? You never can show better than as your own natural self, my sweet Dora; and we'll try no conceited experiments, but go back to our old way, and be happy."

"And be happy!" returned Dora. "Yes! All day! And you won't mind things going a tiny morsel wrong, sometimes?"

"No, no," said I. "We must do the best we can."

"And you won't tell me any more, that we make other people bad," coaxed Dora, "will you? Because you know it's so dreadfully cross!"

"No, no," said I.

"It's better for me to be stupid than uncomfortable, isn't it?" said Dora.

DIAGNOSIS: *Mild mental retardation—ability to function with minimal pressure and limited tasks.*

This is a realistic account of mental retardation or deficiency of a mild variety. If Dora had been exposed to a Binet or a Wechsler, her tests probably would have indicated an I.Q. of 60 to 70. In other words, she would have been placed in the "educable" class. When she is accepted for what she is and the demands upon her do not exceed her capacities, she is cheerful, good-humored, and as pleasant to have around as a good child of 6 or 7 might be. When life's tasks—such as keeping budgets, planning meals, dealing with trades people or servants—are imposed upon her, she becomes confused, miserable, and less able to manage. Worse, when someone she loves and depends on indicates anger, disapproval, or dismay, her confusion and misery contain panic, self-hate, and a sense of being rejected for something she can't help. Unlike most retarded people, Dora is aware of her own difficulties. She tries to warn David, to prepare him, to urge him to accept her limitations. She is resentful and despairing in the face of his attempts to impose standards she cannot meet.

David, like many a parent, tries to deny her limitations, to turn the child wife she tells him she is into the adult wife he longs for. He considers it his duty to educate her out of her own nature. David himself finally recognizes that his path leads only to disaster for their relationship and for their respective self-esteem. When he releases the pressure, he can be more content with her despite the loneliness and sadness he feels. They are able to love and respect each other. This is a rare outcome and requires sensitivity, awareness, and self-containment that are hard to achieve.

Any teacher who has dealt with the retarded will recognize Dora and her problem. It is invariably easier for the Doras who come from unsophisticated environments than for those who are born into intellectual or socially ambitious homes. For this kind of retardation, which is not by nature explosive or difficult to deal with, appropriate standards and acceptance can make the difference between mental health and mental disease—an agreeable, cooperative child or a self-rejecting child who, through despair, functions even worse than her capacities allow.

The Mongoloids and simple retarded tend to be good-natured and easy to live with. The brain-damaged retarded, whose difficulty arose at birth, or by encephalitis, tend to be extraordinarily difficult to live with or manage. Special talents, skills, and personalities are needed to teach both the happy and the unhappy retarded.

Why I Live at the P.O.

Eudora Welty

I

I was getting along fine with Mama, Papa-Daddy, and Uncle Rondo till my sister Stella-Rondo just separated from her husband came back home again. Mr. Whitaker! Of course I went with Mr. Whitaker first, when he first appeared here in China Grove, taking Pose-Yourself photos; and Stella-Rondo broke us up. Told him I was one-sided—bigger on one side than the other, which is a deliberate, calculated falsehood: I'm the same. Stella-Rondo is exactly twelve months to the day younger than I am, and for that reason she's spoiled.

She's always had anything in the world she wanted, and then she'd throw it away. Papa-Daddy gave her this gorgeous Add-a-Pearl necklace when she was eight years old and she threw it away playing baseball when she was nine, with only two pearls.

So as soon as she got married and moved away from home, the first thing she did was separate! From Mr. Whitaker—this photographer with the pop-eyes she said she trusted! Came home from one of those towns up in Illinois, and to our complete surprise brought this child of two.

Mama said she liked to made her drop dead for a second. "Here you had this marvelous blonde child and never so much as wrote your mother a word about it," says Mama. "I'm thoroughly ashamed of you." But of course she wasn't.

Stella-Rondo just calmly takes off this

hat with a snood. She says, "Why, Mama, Shirley-T.'s adopted—I can prove it."

"How?" says Mama, but all I says was, "H'm!"

There I was over the hot stove trying to stretch two chickens over five people and a completely unexpected child into the bargain, without one moment's notice.

"What do you mean—'H'm!'" says Stella-Rondo, and Mama says, "I heard that, Sister."

I said that oh I didn't mean a thing, only that whoever Shirley-T. was she was the spit-image of Papa-Daddy if he'd cut off his beard, which of course he'd never do in the world. Papa-Daddy is Mama's papa and sulks.

Stella-Rondo got furious! She said, "Sister, I don't need to tell you you got a lot of nerve and always did have, and I'll thank you to make no future reference to my adopted child whatsoever."

"Very well," I said, "very well, very well. Of course I noticed at once she looks like Mr. Whitaker's side too. That frown. She looks like a cross between Mr. Whitaker and Papa-Daddy."

"Well, all I can say is she isn't."

"She looks exactly like Shirley Temple to me," says Mama, but Shirley-T. just ran away from her.

So the first thing Stella-Rondo did at the table was turn Papa-Daddy against me.

"Papa-Daddy," she says. (He was trying to cut up his meat.) "Papa-Daddy!" (I was taken completely by surprise. Papa-Daddy is about a million years old and's got this long-long beard.) "Papa-Daddy, Sister says she fails to understand why you don't cut off your beard."

So Papa-Daddy lays down his knife and fork! He's real rich. Mamma says he is; he says he isn't. So he says, "So you don't understand why I don't cut off my beard."

"Why," I says, "Papa-Daddy, of course I understand. I did not say any such of a thing—the idea!"

He says, "Hussy!"

I says, "Why, Papa-Daddy; you know I wouldn't any more want you to cut off your beard than the man in the moon. It was the farthest thing from my mind! Stella-Rondo sat there and made that up while she was eating breast of chicken."

But he says, "So the postmistress fails to understand why I don't cut off my beard. Which job I got you through my influence with the government. Maybe you think it's a bird's nest. Is that it?"

Not that it isn't the next-to-smallest P.O. in the entire state of Mississippi.

I says, "Oh, Papa-Daddy." I says, "I didn't say any such of a thing. I never dreamed it was a bird's nest. I have always been grateful, though this is the next-to-smallest P.O. in the state of Mississippi, and I do not enjoy being referred to as a hussy by my own grandfather."

But Stella-Rondo says, "Yes, you did say it, too. Anybody in the world could of heard you that had ears."

"Stop right there," says Mama, looking at *me*.

So I drew my napkin straight back through the napkin ring and left the table.

As soon as I was out of the room, Stella-Rondo says, "She said it not once but repeatedly," and Papa-Daddy says, "Started growing it on the Coast when I was fifteen years old." He would of gone on till nightfall if Shirley-T. hadn't lost the Milky Way she ate in Cairo.

So Papa-Daddy says, "I am going out and lie in the hammock and you can all sit here and remember my words: I'll never cut off my beard as long as I live, even one inch, and I don't appreciate it in you at all."

Passed right by me in the hall and went straight out and got in the hammock.

II

It *would* be a holiday. It wasn't five minutes before Uncle Rondo suddenly appeared in the hall in one of Stella-Rondo's flesh-colored kimonos all cut on the bias like something Mr. Whitaker probably thought was gorgeous.

"Uncle Rondo!" I says. "I didn't know who that was! Where are you going?"

"Sister," he says, "get out of the way. I'm poisoned."

"Then stay away from Papa-Daddy," I says. "Keep out of the hammock. Papa-Daddy will certainly beat you on the head if you come within forty miles of him: he thinks I deliberately said he ought to cut off his beard after he got me the P.O., and I've told him and told him and told him, and he acts like he just don't hear me. Papa-Daddy must of gone stone-deaf."

"Well, he picked a fine day to do it then," says Uncle Rondo, and before you could say Jack Robinson he flew out in the yard.

What he'd really done, he'd drunk another bottle of that prescription; he does it every single Fourth of July as sure as shooting, and it's horribly expensive. Then he falls over in the hammock and snores. So he insisted on zigzagging right on out to the hammock, looking like a half-wit.

Papa-Daddy woke up with this horrible yell, and right there in the hammock he tried to turn Uncle Rondo against me. I heard every word he said. Oh, he told Uncle Rondo I didn't learn to read till I was eight years old and he didn't see how in the world I ever got the mail put up at the P.O., much less read it all, and he said if Uncle Rondo could only fathom the length he had gone to to get me that job! And he said on the other hand he thought Stella-Rondo had a brilliant mind and deserved credit for getting out of town. All the time he was just lying there swinging as pretty as you please and looping out his beard, and poor Uncle Rondo was *pleading* with him to stop the hammock, it was making him so dizzy. He was too dizzy to get turned against me as yet. He's Mama's only brother, never married, and is a good case of a one-track mind. Ask anybody. A certified pharmacist.

Just then I heard Stella-Rondo raising the upstairs window. While she was married she got this peculiar idea that it's cooler with the windows shut and locked. So she has to raise the window before she can make a soul hear her outdoors.

So she raises the window and says, "Oh!" You would have thought she was mortally wounded.

Uncle Rondo and Papa-Daddy didn't even look up. I had to laugh.

I flew upstairs and threw the door open. I says, "What in the wide world's the matter, Stella-Rondo? You mortally wounded?"

"No," she says, "I am not mortally wounded, but I wish you would do me the favor of looking out that window there and telling me what you see."

So I shade my eyes and look out the window.

"I see the front yard," I says.

"Don't you see any human beings?" she says.

"I see Uncle Rondo trying to run Papa-Daddy out of the hammock," I says. "Nothing more. Naturally, it's so suffocating-hot in the house, with all the windows shut and locked, everybody who stays in their right mind will have to go out and get in the hammock before the Fourth of July is over."

"Don't you notice anything different about Uncle Rondo?" asks Stella-Rondo.

"Why, no, except he's got on some terrible-looking flesh-colored contraption I wouldn't be found dead in, is all I can see," I says.

"Never mind, you won't be found dead in it, because it happens to be part of my trousseau, and Mr. Whitaker took several dozen photographs of me in it," says Stella-Rondo. "What on earth could Uncle Rondo *mean* by wearing part of my trousseau out in the broad open daylight without saying so much as kiss-my-foot,

knowing I only got home this morning after my separation and hung my negligee up on the bathroom door, just as nervous as I could be?"

"Well, what do you expect me to do about it?" I says. "Jump out the window?"

"No, I expect nothing of the kind. I simply say that Uncle Rondo looks like a fool in it, that's all," she says.

"Well, he looks as good as he can," I says, "As good as anybody in reason could." I stood up for Uncle Rondo, please remember. And I said to Stella-Rondo, "I think I would do well not to criticize so freely if I were you, and came home with a two-year-old child I had never said a word about and no explanation whatever about my separation."

"I asked you the instant I entered this house not to refer one more time to my adopted child and you gave me your word of honor you would not," was all Stella-Rondo would say, and started pulling out every one of her eyebrows with some cheap tweezers.

So I merely slammed the door behind me and went down and made some green-tomato pickle. Somebody had to do it. Of course Mama had turned both the Negroes loose; she always said no earthly power could hold one anyway on the Fourth of July, so she wouldn't even try. It turned out that Jaypan fell in Eagle Lake and came within a very narrow limit of drowning.

So Mama trots in. Lifts up the lid and says, "H'm! Not very good for your Uncle Rondo in his precarious condition, I must say. Or poor little adopted Shirley-T. Shame on you!"

That made me tired. I says, "Well, Stella-Rondo had better thank her lucky stars it was her instead of me come trotting in with that very peculiar-looking child. Now if it had been me that trotted in from Illinois and brought a peculiar-looking child of two, I shudder to think of the reception I'd of got, much less controlled the diet of an entire family."

"But you must remember, Sister, that you were never married to Mr. Whitaker in the first place and didn't go up to Illinois to live," says Mama, shaking a spoon in my face. "If you had, I would of been just as overjoyed to see you and your little adopted girl as I was to see Stella-Rondo, when you wound up with your separation and came on back home."

"You would not," I says.

"Don't contradict me! I would," says Mama.

But I said she couldn't convince me though she talked till she was blue in the face. Then I said, "Besides, you know as well as I do that that child is not adopted."

"She most certainly is adopted," says Mama, stiff as a poker.

I says, "Why, Mama, Stella-Rondo had her just as sure as anything in this world, and just too stuck-up to admit it."

"Why, Sister!" says Mama. "Here I thought we were going to have a pleasant Fourth of July and you start right out not believing a word your own baby sister tells you!"

"Just like Cousin Annie Flo. Went to her grave denying the facts of life," I remind Mama.

"I told you if you ever mentioned Annie Flo's name I'd slap your face," says Mama, and slaps my face.

"All right, you wait and see," I says.

"I," says Mama, "*I* prefer to take my children's word for anything when it's humanly possible." You ought to see Mama —she weighs two hundred and two pounds and has real tiny feet.

Just then something perfectly horrible occurred to me.

"Mama!" I says. "Can that child talk?" I simply had to whisper! "Mama, I wonder if that child can be—you know—in any way? Do you realize," I says, "that she hasn't spoken one single solitary word to a human being up to this minute? This is the way she looks," I says, and I looked like this.

Well, Mama and I just stood there and stared at each other. It was horrible!

"I remember well that Joe Whitaker frequently drank like a fish," says Mama.

"I believed to my soul he drank *chemicals*." And without another word she marches to the foot of the stairs and calls Stella-Rondo.

"Stella-Rondo? O-o-o-o-o-oh, Stella-Rondo!"

"What!" says Stella-Rondo from upstairs. Not even the grace to get up off the bed.

"Can that child of yours talk?" asks Mama.

Stella-Rondo says, "Can she what?"

"Talk! Talk!" says Mama. "Burdy-burdy-burdy-burdy!"

So Stella-Rondo yells back, "Who says she can't talk?"

"Sister says so," says Mama.

"You didn't have to tell me—I know whose word of honor don't mean a thing in this house," says Stella-Rondo.

And in a minute the loudest Yankee voice I ever heard in my life yells out, "Oi'm Pop-oi the Sailor-r-r-r Ma-a-an!" and then somebody jumps up and down in the upstairs hall. In another second the house would of fallen down.

"Not only talks, she can tap-dance!" calls Stella-Rondo. "Which is more than some people I won't name can do."

"Why, the little precious darling thing!" Mama says, so surprised. "Just as smart as she can be!" Starts talking baby talk right there. Then she turns on me. "Sister, you ought to be thoroughly ashamed! Run upstairs this instant and apologize to Stella-Rondo and Shirley-T."

"Apologize for what?" I says. "I merely wondered if the child was normal, that's all. Now that she's proved she is, why, I have nothing further to say."

But Mama just turned on her heel and flew out, furious. She ran right upstairs and hugged the baby. She believed it was adopted. Stella-Rondo had turned her against me from upstairs while I stood there helpless over the hot stove. So that made Mama, Papa-Daddy, and the baby all on Stella-Rondo's side.

Next, Uncle Rondo.

I must say that Uncle Rondo has been wonderful to me at various times in the past, and I was completely unprepared to be made to jump out of my skin, the way it turned out. Once Stella-Rondo did something perfectly horrible to him—broke a chain letter from Flanders Field—and he took the radio back he had given her and gave it to me. Stella-Rondo was furious! For six months we all had to call her Stella instead of Stella-Rondo, or she wouldn't answer. I always thought Uncle Rondo had all the brains of the entire family—a brilliant mind. Another time he sent me to Mammoth Cave, with all expenses paid.

But this would be the day he was drinking that prescription, the Fourth of July.

So at supper Stella-Rondo speaks up and says she thinks Uncle Rondo ought to try to eat a little something. So finally Uncle Rondo said he would try a little cold biscuits and ketchup, but that was all. So *she* brought it to him.

"Do you think it wise to disport with ketchup in Stella-Rondo's flesh-colored kimono?" I says. Trying to be considerate! If Stella-Rondo couldn't watch out for her underwear, somebody had to.

"Any objections?" says Uncle Rondo, just about to pour out the ketchup.

"Don't mind what she says, Uncle Rondo," says Stella-Rondo. "Sister has been devoting this solid afternoon to sneering out my bedroom window at the way you look."

"What's that?" says Uncle Rondo. Uncle Rondo has got the most terrible temper in the world. Anything is liable to make him tear the house down if it comes at the wrong time.

So Stella-Rondo says, "Sister says, 'Uncle Rondo certainly does look like a fool in that pink kimono!' "

Do you remember who it was really said that?

Uncle Rondo spills all the ketchup out and jumps up and tears off the kimono and throws it down on the dirty floor and puts his foot on it. It had to be sent all the way to Jackson to the cleaners and repleated.

"So that's your opinion of your Uncle Rondo, is it?" he says. "I look like a fool, do I? Well, that's the last straw. A whole day in this house with nothing to do, and then to hear you come out with a remark like that behind my back!"

"I didn't say any such of a thing, Uncle Rondo," I says, "and I'm not saying who did, either. Why, I think you look all right. Just try to take care of yourself and not talk and eat at the same time," I says. "I think you better go lie down."

"Lie down my foot!" says Uncle Rondo. I ought to of known by that he was fixing to do something perfectly horrible.

III

So he didn't do anything that night in the precarious state he was in—just played casino with Mama and Stella-Rondo and Shirley-T., and gave Shirley-T. a nickel with a head on both sides and tickled her nearly to death, and she called him "Papa" and he believed she was adopted. Men believe anything. But at 6.30 A.M. the next morning he threw a whole five-cent package of some unsold one-inch firecrackers from the store as hard as he could into my bedroom and they every one went off. Not one bad one in the string. Anybody else, there'd be one that wouldn't go off.

Well, I'm just terribly susceptible to noise of any kind; the doctor has always told me I was the most sensitive person he had ever seen in his whole life; and I was simply prostrated. I couldn't eat! People tell me they heard it as far as the cemetery, and old Aunt Jep Patterson, that had been holding her own so good, thought it was Judgment Day and she was going to meet her whole family. It's usually so quiet here.

And I'll tell you it didn't take me long to make up my mind what to do. There I was with the whole entire house on Stella-Rondo's side and turned against me. If I have anything, I have pride.

So I just decided I'd go straight down to the P.O. There's plenty of room there in the back, I says to myself.

Well, I made no bones about letting

the family catch on to what I was up to. I didn't try to conceal it.

The first thing they knew, I marched in where they were all playing Old Maid and pulled the electric oscillating fan out by the plug, and everything got real hot. Next I snatched the pillow I'd done the needlepoint on right off the davenport from behind Papa-Daddy. He went "Ugh!" I beat Stella-Rondo upstairs and finally found my slave bracelet in her bureau drawer under a picture of Nelson Eddy.

"So that's the way the land lies," says Uncle Rondo. There he was, piecing on the ham. "Well, Sister, I'll be glad to donate my army cot if you got any place you can set it up, providing you'll leave right this minute and let me get some peace." Uncle Rondo was in France.

"Thank you kindly for the cot, and peace is hardly the word I would select if I had to resort to firecrackers at 6.30 A.M. in a young girl's bedroom," I says back to him. "And as to where I intend to go, you seem to forget my position as postmistress of China Grove, Mississippi," I says. "I've always got the P.O."

Well, that made them all sit up and take notice.

I went out front and started digging up some four-o'clocks to plant around the P.O.

"Ah-ah-ah!" says Mama, raising the window. "Those happen to be my four-o'clocks. Everything planted in that star is mine. I've never known you to make anything grow in your life."

"Very well," I says. "But I take the fern. Even you, Mama, can't stand there and deny that I'm the one watered that fern. And I happen to know where I can send in a box top and get a packet of one thousand mixed seeds, no two the same kind, free."

"Oh, where?" Mama wants to know.

But I says, "Too late. You tend to your house and I'll tend to mine. You hear things like that all the time if you know how to listen to the radio. Perfectly marvelous offers. Get anything you want free."

So I hope to tell you I marched in and got that radio and they could of all bit a nail in two, especially Stella-Rondo, that it used to belong to, and she well knew she couldn't get it back—I'd sue for it like a shot. And I very politely took the sewing-machine motor I helped pay the most on to give Mama for Christmas back in 1929, and a good big calendar, with the first-aid remedies on it. The thermometer and the Hawaiian ukulele certainly were rightfully mine, and I stood on the stepladder and got all my watermelon-rind preserves and every fruit and vegetable I'd put up, every jar. Then I began to pull the tacks out of the bluebird wall vases on the archway to the dining room.

"Who told you you could have those, Miss Priss?" says Mama, fanning as hard as she could.

"I bought 'em and I'll keep track of 'em," I says. "I'll tack 'em up one on each side the post-office window and you can see 'em when you come to ask me for your mail, if you're so dead to see 'em."

"Not I! I'll never darken the door to that post office again if I live to be a hundred," Mama says. "Ungrateful child! After all the money we spent on you at the Normal."

"Me either," says Stella-Rondo. "You can just let my mail lie there and *rot* for all I care. I'll never come and relieve you of a single solitary piece."

"I should worry," I says. "And who you think's going to sit down and write you all those big fat letters and postcards, by the way? Mr. Whitaker? Just because he was the only man ever dropped down in China Grove and you got him—unfairly—is he going to sit down and write you a lengthy correspondence after you come home giving no rhyme nor reason whatsoever for your separation and no explanation for the presence of that child? I may not have your brilliant mind, but I fail to see it."

So Mama says, "Sister, I've told you a thousand times that Stella-Rondo simply got homesick and this child is far too big to be hers"; and she says, "Now why don't you all just sit down and play casino?"

Then Shirley-T. sticks out her tongue at me in this perfectly horrible way. She has no more manners than the man in the moon. I told her she was going to cross her eyes like that some day and they'd stick.

"It's too late to stop me now," I says. "You should have tried that yesterday. I'm going to the P.O., and the only way you can possibly see me is to visit me there."

So Papa-Daddy says, "You'll never catch me settin' foot in that post office, even if I should take a notion into my head to write a letter some place." He says, "I won't have you reachin' out of that little old window with a pair of shears and cuttin' off any beard of mine. I'm too smart for you!"

"We all are," says Stella-Rondo.

But I said, "If you're so smart, where's Mr. Whitaker?"

So then Uncle Rondo says, "I'll thank you from now on to stop reading the orders I get on postcards and telling everybody in China Grove what you think is the matter with them," but I says, "I draw my own conclusions and will continue in the future to draw them." I says, "If people write their inmost secrets on penny postcards, there's nothing in the wide world you can do about it, Uncle Rondo."

"And if you think we'll ever *write* another postcard, you're sadly mistaken," says Mama.

"Cutting off your nose to spite your face, then," I says. "But if you're all determined to have no more to do with the U.S. Mail, think of this: what will Stella-Rondo do now if she wants to tell Mr. Whitaker to come after her?"

"Wah!" says Stella-Rondo. I knew she'd cry. She had a conniption fit right there in the living room.

"It will be interesting to see how long she holds out," I says. "And now—I am leaving."

"Good-bye," says Uncle Rondo.

"Oh, I declare!" says Mama. "To think that a family of mine should quarrel on the Fourth of July, over Stella-Rondo leaving old Mr. Whitaker and having the sweetest

little adopted child! It looks like we'd all be glad!"

"Wah!" says Stella-Rondo, and has a fresh conniption fit.

"*He* left *her*—you mark my words," I says. "*That's* Mr. Whitaker. I know Mr. Whitaker. After all, I knew him first. I said from the beginning he'd up and leave her. I foretold it all."

"Where did he go?" asks Mama.

"Probably to the North Pole, if he knows what's good for him," I says.

But Stella-Rondo just bawled and wouldn't say another word. She flew to her room and slammed the door.

"Now look what you've done, Sister," says Mama. "You go apologize."

"No, I am leaving," I says.

"Well, what are you waiting around for?" asks Uncle Rondo.

So I just marched off without saying kiss-my-foot or anything, and never did tell Stella-Rondo good-bye.

There was a Negro girl going along on a little wagon right in front.

"Girl," I says, "come help me haul these things down the hill. I'm going to live in the post office."

Took her nine trips in her express wagon. Uncle Rondo came out on the porch and threw her a nickel.

IV

And that's the last I've laid eyes on any of my family or my family laid eyes on me for five solid days and nights. Stella-Rondo may be telling the most horrible tales in the world about Mr. Whitaker, but I haven't heard them. As I tell everybody, I draw my own conclusions.

But oh, I like it here. It's ideal, as I've been saying. You see, I've got everything cater-cornered, the way I like it. Hear the radio? All the war news. Radio, sewing machine, book ends, ironing board, and that great big piano lamp—peace, that's what I like. Butter-bean vines planted all along the front where the strings are.

Of course, there's not much mail. My family are naturally the main people in China Grove, and if they prefer to vanish from the face of the earth, for all the mail they get or the mail they write, why, I'm not going to open my mouth. Some of the folks here in town are taking up for me and some turned against me. I know which is which. There are always people who will quit buying stamps just to get on the good side of Papa-Daddy.

But here I am, and here I'll stay. I want the world to know I'm happy.

And if Stella-Rondo should come to me this minute, on bended knees, and *attempt* to explain the incidents of her life with Mr. Whitaker, I'd simply put my fingers in both my ears and refuse to listen.

DIAGNOSIS: *Paranoid psychopathic state.*

Here is condensed into one person—the heroine who tells the story—the sickness of her entire family. Her projection of blame onto the world; her sense of physical inferiority; her hostility and concealed longing, changed to hate and rejection; her distortions, which make her life more hateful and lonely—all are typical symptoms of paranoia.

You have seen early signs of this disease in the classroom—though possibly not so distorted as to indicate psychosis—in the boy (or girl) who is always right, never at fault, always put upon, and who retreats within a wall of resentment. These are hard children to reach. They need firm limits to take away their frightened sense of power on the one hand, and abject helplessness on the other. Their parents frequently are demanding, rigid, blaming, and rejecting—attitudes that must be avoided in the classroom. Also, the teacher must not get caught up in the infinite blaming, self-exonerating episodes. He should handle the situation with a quiet, firm "Let's forget who is to blame and get on with the job, OK?"

Mr. Dick

Charles Dickens

[*David Copperfield's aunt describes Mr. Dick and explains why he happens to be living with her under her protection.*]

. . . "Because his brother was a little eccentric—though he is not half so eccentric as a good many people—he didn't like to have him visible about his house, and sent him away to some private asylum-place: though he had been left to his particular care by their deceased father, who thought him almost a natural. And a wise man *he* must have been to think so! Mad himself, no doubt."

Again, as my aunt looked quite convinced, I endeavoured to look quite convinced also.

From *David Copperfield* by Charles Dickens, 1850.

"So I stepped in," said my aunt, "and made him an offer. I said, 'Your brother's sane—a great deal more sane than you are, or ever will be, it is to be hoped. Let him have his little income, and come and live with me. *I* am not afraid of him, *I* am not proud, *I* am ready to take care of him, and shall not ill-treat him as some people (besides the asylum-folks) have done.' After a good deal of squabbling," said my aunt, "I got him; and he has been here ever since. He is the most friendly and amenable creature in existence; and as for advice!—But nobody knows what that man's mind is, except myself."

My aunt smoothed her dress and shook her head, as if she smoothed defiance of the whole world out of the one, and shook it out of the other.

"He had a favourite sister," said my aunt, "a good creature, and very kind to him. But she did what they all do—took a husband. And *he* did what they all do—made her wretched. It had such an effect upon the mind of Mr. Dick (*that's* not madness, I hope!) that, combined with his fear of his brother, and his sense of his unkindness, it threw him into a fever. That was before he came to me, but the recollection of it is oppressive to him even now. Did he say anything to you about King Charles the First, child?"

"Yes, aunt."

"Ah!" said my aunt, rubbing her nose as if she were a little vexed. "That's his allegorical way of expressing it. He connects his illness with great disturbance and agitation, naturally, and that's the figure, or the simile, or whatever it's called, which he chooses to use. And why shouldn't he, if he thinks proper?"

I said: "Certainly, aunt."

"It's not a business-like way of speaking," said my aunt, "nor a worldly way. I am aware of that; and that's the reason why I insist upon it, that there shan't be a word about it in his Memorial."

"Is it a Memorial about his own history that he is writing, aunt?"

"Yes, child," said my aunt, rubbing her nose again. "He is memorialising the Lord Chancellor, or the Lord Somebody or other—one of those people, at all events, who are paid to *be* memorialised—about his affairs. I suppose it will go in, one of these days. He hasn't been able to draw it up yet, without introducing that mode of expressing himself; but it don't signify; it keeps him employed."

In fact, I found out afterwards that Mr. Dick had been for upwards of ten years endeavouring to keep King Charles the First out of the Memorial; but he had been constantly getting into it, and was there now.

"I say again," said my aunt, "nobody knows what that man's mind is except myself; and he's the most amenable and friendly creature in existence. If he likes to fly a kite sometimes, what of that! Franklin used to fly a kite. He was a Quaker, or something of that sort, if I am not mistaken. And a Quaker flying a kite is a much more ridiculous object than anybody else." . . .

Mr. Dick and I soon became the best of friends, and very often, when his day's work was done, went out together to fly the great kite. Every day of his life he had a long sitting at the Memorial, which never made the least progress, however hard he laboured, for King Charles the First always strayed into it, sooner or later, and then it was thrown aside, and another one begun. The patience and hope with which he bore these perpetual disappointments, the mild perception he had that there was something wrong about King Charles the First, the feeble efforts he made to keep him out, and the certainty with which he came in, and tumbled the Memorial out of all shape, made a deep impression on me. What Mr. Dick supposed would come of the Memorial, if it were completed; where he thought it was to go, or what he thought it was to do; he knew no more than anybody else, I believe. Nor was it at all necessary that he should trouble himself with such questions, for if anything were certain under the sun, it was certain that the Memorial never would be finished.

It was quite an affecting sight, I used to think, to see him with the kite when it was up a great height in the air. What he had told me, in his room, about his belief in its disseminating the statements pasted on it, which were nothing but old leaves of abortive Memorials, might have been a fancy with him sometimes; but not when he was out, looking up at the kite in the sky, and feeling it pull and tug at his hand. He never looked so serene as he did then. I used to fancy, as I sat by him of an evening, on a green slope, and saw him watch the kite high in the quiet air, that it lifted his mind out of its confusion, and bore it (such was my boyish thought) into the skies. As he wound the string in, and it came lower and lower down out of the beautiful light, until it fluttered to the ground, and lay there like a dead thing, he seemed to wake gradually out of a dream; and I remember to have seen him take it up, and look about him in a lost way, as if they had both come down together, so that I pitied him with all my heart. . . .

DIAGNOSIS: *Eccentric—schizophrenic thought processes of an obsessional and delusionary nature—nonviolent.*

Our society seems to have even less room for the extreme eccentric, the queer one, the wacky but kindly, possessd but harmless fellow, than in David Copperfield's time. However, even today, England has greater tolerance for eccentricity than we do. Like Mr. Dick's brother, we are more afraid, more ashamed, and more uncomfortable in the presence of deviations from our standard of well-adjusted, "normal behavior." David's aunt is not bothered by Mr. Dick's obsession with King Charles I or his delusion about the Memorial. Nor does she patronize him, or get caught up in his psychotic fantasies. She lets him be and appeals to the healthy side of him. She respects his kindness and his sagacity when—like many psychotics—he is sagacious or insightful. By contrast, our society harbors the fear that because someone is psychotic, he is psychotic all the time and needs to be put out of sight. Most psychotics have many lucid periods oriented to reality. In such periods their judgments are as worthy as those of the rest of us.

A teacher handling a junior Mr. Dick in the class would do well to seek professional help. Like David's aunt, the teacher should appeal to the healthy parts of him; be uninvolved in the unhealthy parts; and, like David, enjoy him despite his distorted thought processes. The teacher also would make sure that his peculiarities do not affect the rest of the class. Our society, with its insistence on uniform adjustment for happiness, is hardest of all on Mr. Dick types. We worry more, fuss more, accept less.

Silent Snow, Secret Snow
Conrad Aiken

Just why it should have happened, or why it should have happened just when it did, he could not, of course, possibly have said; nor perhaps could it even have occurred to him to ask. The thing was above all a secret, something to be preciously concealed from Mother and Father; and to that very fact it owed an enormous part of its deliciousness. It was like a peculiarly beautiful trinket to be carried unmentioned in one's trouser-pocket—a rare stamp, an old coin, a few tiny gold links found trodden out of shape on the path in the park, a pebble of carnelian, a sea shell distinguishable from all others by an unusual spot or stripe—and, as if it were anyone of these, he carried around with him everywhere a warm and persistent and increasingly beautiful sense of possession. Nor was it only a sense of possession—it was also a sense of protection. It was as if, in some delightful way, his secret gave him a fortress, a wall behind which he could retreat into heavenly seclusion. This was almost the first thing he had noticed about it—apart from the oddness of the thing itself—and it was this that now again, for the fiftieth time, occurred to him, as he sat in the little schoolroom. It was the half hour for geography. Miss Buell was revolving with one finger, slowly, a huge terrestrial globe which had been placed on her desk. The green and yellow continents passed and repassed, questions were asked and answered, and now the little girl in front of him, Deirdre, who had a funny little constellation of freckles on the back of her neck, exactly like the Big Dipper, was standing up and telling Miss Buell that the equator was the line that ran round the middle.

Miss Buell's face, which was old and grayish and kindly, with gray stiff curls beside the cheeks, and eyes that swam very brightly, like little minnows, behind thick glasses, wrinkled itself into a complication of amusements.

"Ah! I see. The earth is wearing a belt, or a sash. Or someone drew a line round it!"

"Oh, no—not that—I mean—"

In the general laughter, he did not share, or only a very little. He was thinking about the Arctic and Antarctic regions, which of course, on the globe, were white. Miss Buell was now telling them about the tropics, the jungles, the steamy heat of equatorial swamps, where the birds and butterflies, and even the snakes, were like living jewels. As he listened to these things, he was already, with a pleasant sense of half-effort, putting his secret between himself and the words. Was it really an effort at all? For effort implied something voluntary, and perhaps even something one did not especially want; whereas this was distinctly pleasant, and came almost of its own accord. All he needed to do was to think of that morning, the first one, and then of all the others—

But it was all so absurdly simple! It had amounted to so little. It was nothing, just an idea—and just why it should have become so wonderful, so permanent, was a

mystery—a very pleasant one, to be sure, but also, in an amusing way, foolish. However, without ceasing to listen to Miss Buell, who had now moved up to the north temperate zones, he deliberately invited his memory of the first morning. It was only a moment or two after he had waked up—or perhaps the moment itself. But was there, to be exact, an exact moment? Was one awake all at once? or was it gradual? Anyway, it was after he had stretched a lazy hand up towards the headrail, and yawned, and then relaxed again among his warm covers, all the more grateful on a December morning, that the thing had happened. Suddenly, for no reason, he had thought of the postman, he remembered the postman. Perhaps there was nothing so odd in that. After all, he heard the postman almost every morning in his life—his heavy boots could be heard clumping round the corner at the top of the little cobbled hill-street, and then, progressively nearer, progressively louder, the double knock at each door, the crossings and re-crossings of the street, till finally the clumsy steps came stumbling across to the very door, and the tremendous knock came which shook the house itself.

(Miss Buell was saying "Vast wheat-growing areas in North America and Siberia."

Dierdre had for the moment placed her left hand across the back of her neck.)

But on this particular morning, the first morning, as he lay there with his eyes closed, he had for some reason *waited* for the postman. He wanted to hear him come round the corner. And that was precisely the joke—he never did. He never came. He never had come—*round the corner*—again. For when at last the steps *were* heard, they had already, he was quite sure, come a little down the hill, to the first house; and even so, the steps were curiously different —they were softer, they had a new secrecy about them, they were muffled and indistinct; and while the rhythm of them was the same, it now said a new thing—it said peace, it said remoteness, it said cold, it said sleep. And he had understood the situation at once—nothing could have seemed simpler—there had been snow in the night, such as all winter he had been longing for; and it was this which had rendered the postman's first footsteps inaudible, and the later ones faint. Of course! How lovely! And even now it must be snowing—it was going to be a snowy day— the long white ragged lines were drifting and sifting across the street, across the faces of the old houses, whispering and hushing, making little triangles of white in the corners between cobblestones, seething a little when the wind blew them over the ground to a drifted corner; and so it would be all day, getting deeper and deeper and silenter and silenter.

(Miss Buell was saying "Land of perpetual snow.")

All this time, of course (while he lay in bed), he had kept his eyes closed, listening to the nearer progress of the postman, the muffled footsteps thumping and slipping on the snow-sheathed cobbles; and all the other sounds—the double knocks, a frosty far-off voice or two, a bell ringing thinly and softly as if under a sheet of ice —had the same slightly abstracted quality, as if removed by one degree from actuality —as if everything in the world had been insulated by snow. But when at last, pleased, he opened his eyes, and turned them towards the window, to see for himself this long-desired and now so clearly imagined miracle—what he saw instead was brilliant sunlight on a roof; and when, astonished, he jumped out of bed and stared down into the street, expecting to see the cobbles obliterated by the snow, he saw nothing but the bare bright cobbles themselves.

Queer, the effect this extraordinary surprise had had upon him—all the following morning he had kept with him a sense as of snow falling about him, a secret screen of new snow between himself and the world. If he had not dreamed such a thing—and how could he have dreamed it while awake?—how else could one explain

it? In any case, the delusion had been so vivid as to affect his entire behavior. He could not now remember whether it was on the first or the second morning—or was it even the third?—that his mother had drawn attention to some oddness in his manner.

"But my darling—" she had said at the breakfast table—"what has come over you? You don't seem to be listening. . . ."

And how often that very thing had happened since!

(Miss Buell was now asking if anyone knew the difference between the North Pole and the Magnetic Pole. Deirdre was holding up her flickering brown hand, and he could see the four white dimples that marked the knuckles.)

• • •

"Now Paul—I would like very much to ask you a question or two. You will answer them, won't you—you know I'm an old, old friend of yours, eh? That's right! . . ."

His back was thumped twice by the doctor's fat fist,—then the doctor was grinning at him with false amiability, while with one finger-nail he was scratching the top button of his waistcoat. Beyond the doctor's shoulder was the fire, the fingers of flame making light prestidigitation against the sooty fireback, the soft sound of their random flutter the only sound.

"I would like to know—is there anything that worries you?"

The doctor was again smiling, his eyelids low against the little black pupils, in each of which was a tiny white bead of light. Why answer him? why answer him at all? "At whatever pain to others"—but it was all a nuisance, this necessity for resistance, this necessity for attention: it was as if one had been stood up on a brilliantly lighted stage, under a great round blaze of spotlight; as if one were merely a trained seal, or a performing dog, or a fish, dipped out of an aquarium and held up by the tail. It would serve them right if he were merely to bark or growl. And meanwhile, to miss these last few precious hours, these hours of which every minute was more beautiful than the last, more menacing—? He still looked, as if from a great distance, at the beads of light in the doctor's eyes, at the fixed false smile, and then, beyond, once more at his mother's slippers, his father's slippers, the soft flutter of the fire. Even here, even amongst these hostile presences, and in this arranged light, he could see the snow, he could hear it—it was in the corners of the room, where the shadow was deepest, under the sofa, behind the half-opened door which led to the dining room. It was gentler here, softer, its seethe the quietest of whispers, as if, in deference to a drawing room, it had quite deliberately put on its "manners"; it kept itself out of sight, obliterated itself, but distinctly with an air of saying, "Ah, but just wait! Wait till we are alone together! Then I will begin to tell you something new! Something white! something cold! something sleepy! something of cease, and peace, and the long bright curve of space! Tell them to go away. Banish them. Refuse to speak. Leave them, go upstairs to your room, turn out the light and get into bed—I will go with you, I will be waiting for you, I will tell you a better story than Little Kay of the Skates, or The Snow Ghost—I will surround your bed, I will close the windows, pile a deep drift against the door, so that none will ever again be able to enter. Speak to them! . . ." It seemed as if the little hissing voice came from a slow white spiral of falling flakes in the corner by the front window—but he could not be sure. He felt himself smiling, then, and said to the doctor, but without looking at him, looking beyond him still—

"Oh, no, I think not—"

"But are you sure, my boy?"

His father's voice came softly and coldly then—the familiar voice of silken warning. . . .

"You needn't answer at once, Paul—remember we're trying to help you—think it over and be quite sure, won't you?"

He felt himself smiling again, at the notion of being quite sure. What a joke!

As if he weren't so sure that reassurance was no longer necessary, and all this cross-examination a ridiculous farce, a grotesque parody! What could they know about it? These gross intelligences, these humdrum minds so bound to the usual, the ordinary? Impossible to tell them about it! Why, even now, even now, with the proof so abundant, so formidable, so imminent, so appallingly present here in this very room, could they believe it?—could even his mother believe it? No—it was only too plain that if anything were said about it, the merest hint given, they would be incredulous—they would laugh—they would say "Absurd!"—think things about him which weren't true. . . .

"Why no, I'm not worried—why should I be?"

He looked then straight at the doctor's low-lidded eyes, looked from one of them to the other, from one bead of light to the other, and gave a little laugh.

The doctor seemed to be disconcerted by this. He drew back in his chair, resting a fat white hand on either knee. The smile faded slowly from his face.

"Well, Paul!" he said, and paused gravely, "I'm afraid you don't take this quite seriously enough. I think you perhaps don't quite realize—don't quite realize—" He took a deep quick breath, and turned, as if helplessly, at a loss for words, to the others. But Mother and Father were both silent—no help was forthcoming.

"You must surely know, be aware, that you have not been quite yourself, of late? don't you know that? . . ."

It was amusing to watch the doctor's renewed attempt at a smile, a queer disorganized look, as of confidential embarrassment.

"I feel all right, sir," he said, and again gave the little laugh.

"And we're trying to help you." The doctor's tone sharpened.

"Yes sir, I know. But why? I'm all right. I'm just *thinking*, that's all."

His mother made a quick movement

forward, resting a hand on the back of the doctor's chair.

"Thinking?" she said. "But my dear, about what?"

This was a direct challenge—and would have to be directly met. But before he met it, he looked again into the corner by the door, as if for reassurance. He smiled again at what he saw, at what he heard. The little spiral was still there, still softly whirling, like the ghost of a white kitten chasing the ghost of a white tail, and making as it did so the faintest of whispers. It was all right! If only he could remain firm, everything was going to be all right.

"Oh, about anything, about nothing,—*you* know the way you do!"

"You mean—day-dreaming?"

"Oh, no—thinking!"

"But thinking about *what?*"

"Anything."

He laughed a third time—but this time, happening to glance upward towards his mother's face, he was appalled at the effect his laughter seemed to have upon her. Her mouth had opened in an expression of horror. . . . This was too bad! Unfortunate! He had known it would cause pain, of course—but he hadn't expected it to be quite so bad as this. Perhaps—perhaps if he just gave them a tiny gleaming hint—?

"About the snow," he said.

"What on earth!" This was his father's voice. The brown slippers came a step nearer on the hearth-rug.

"But my dear, what do you mean!" This was his mother's voice.

The doctor merely stared.

"Just *snow*, that's all. I like to think about it."

"Tell us about it, my boy."

"But that's all it is. There's nothing to tell. *You* know what snow is?"

This he said almost angrily, for he felt that they were trying to corner him. He turned sideways so as no longer to face the doctor, and the better to see the inch of blackness between the window-sill and the lowered curtain,—the cold inch of beckon-

ing and delicious night. At once he felt better, more assured.

"Mother—can I go to bed, now, please? I've got a headache."

"But I thought you said—"

"It's just come. It's all these questions—! Can I, mother?"

"You can go as soon as the doctor has finished."

"Don't you think this thing ought to be gone into thoroughly, and *now?*" This was Father's voice. The brown slippers again came a step nearer, the voice was the well-known "punishment" voice, resonant and cruel.

"Oh, what's the use, Norman—"

Quite suddenly, everyone was silent. And without precisely facing them, nevertheless he was aware that all three of them were watching him with an extraordinary intensity—staring hard at him—as if he had done something monstrous, or was himself some kind of monster. He could hear the soft irregular flutter of the flames; the cluck-click-cluck-click of the clock; far and faint, two sudden spurts of laughter from the kitchen, as quickly cut off as begun; a murmur of water in the pipes; and then, the silence seemed to deepen, to spread out, to become world-long and worldwide, to become timeless and shapeless, and to center inevitably and rightly, with a slow and sleepy but enormous concentration of all power, on the beginning of a new sound. What this new sound was going to be, he knew perfectly well. It might begin with a hiss, but it would end with a roar—there was no time to lose—he must escape. It mustn't happen here—

Without another word, he turned and ran up the stairs.

Not a moment too soon. The darkness was coming in long white waves. A prolonged sibilance filled the night—a great seamless seethe of wild influence went abruptly across it—a cold low humming shook the windows. He shut the door and flung off his clothes in the dark. The bare black floor was like a little raft tossed in waves of snow, almost overwhelmed, washed under whitely, up again, smothered in curled billows of feather. The snow was laughing: it spoke from all sides at once: it pressed closer to him as he ran and jumped exulting into his bed.

"Listen to us!" it said. "Listen! We have come to tell you the story we told you about. You remember? Lie down. Shut your eyes, now—you will no longer see much—in this white darkness who could see, or want to see? We will take the place of everything. . . . Listen—"

A beautiful varying dance of snow began at the front of the room, came forward and then retreated, flattened out toward the floor, then rose fountain-like to the ceiling, swayed, recruited itself from a new stream of flakes which poured laughing in through the humming window, advanced again, lifted long white arms. It said peace, it said remoteness, it said cold—it said—

But then a gash of horrible light fell brutally across the room from the opening door—the snow drew back hissing—something alien had come into the room—something hostile. This thing rushed at him, clutched at him, shook him—and he was not merely horrified, he was filled with such a loathing as he had never known. What

was this? this cruel disturbance? this act of anger and hate? It was as if he had to reach up a hand toward another world for any understanding of it,—an effort of which he was only barely capable. But of that other world he still remembered just enough to know the exorcising words. They tore themselves from his other life suddenly—

"Mother! Mother! Go away! I hate you!"

And with that effort, everything was solved, everything became all right: the seamless hiss advanced once more, the long white wavering lines rose and fell like enormous whispering sea-waves, the whisper becoming louder, the laughter more numerous.

"Listen!" it said. "We'll tell you the last, the most beautiful and secret story—shut your eyes—it is a very small story—a story that gets smaller and smaller—it comes inward instead of opening like a flower—it is a flower becoming a seed—a little cold seed—do you hear? we are leaning closer to you—"

The hiss was now becoming a roar—the whole world was a vast moving screen of snow—but even now it said peace, it said remoteness, it said cold, it said sleep.

DIAGNOSIS: *Schizophrenic breakdown—delusions and hallucinations, both visual and auditory; gradual withdrawal from world of reality into autistic one, or world of his own.*

This secret world of snow is unbearably tempting or beckoning, like a siren to Ulysses, until the boy, age 12, is magnetized away from the world of home and school. Exactly what, in his middle-class home and daily life, was so painful for him that he needed to retreat? It could have been the clinging to mother or over-identification and unconscious hostility of one of the parents, so frequently found in schizophrenic breakdowns. We are told only how his delusionary cocoon spread from home to school. Mother, father, and teacher become aware of the increasing withdrawal of this boy, of his "not-thereness." The ways the doctor mishandled the child, the father showed understandable irritation under the strain of anxiety, are typical reactions to the frightening phenomenon of watching a child disappear into another world before one's eyes, unable to stop it.

The story indicates well the kind of child this is. In a classroom, he is shy, quiet, withdrawn—no behavior problem other than that more and more often he is miles away when a question is asked. Sometimes his answers are puzzlingly inappropriate, rooted in the question but winding off into outer space. He is the kind of child Miss Buell would describe in a conference as being very adequate sometimes, but just not there most of the time. The seemingly sudden onset of the illness is misleading. A keen and sensitive teacher could have recognized signs of increasing withdrawal if attuned to see them. A psychologically aware teacher would consult the psychological department of the school before actual break-down occurred.

Jordi

Theodore Isaac Rubin

. . . He woke up suddenly, looked around the room, and jumped out of bed. People were talking in the kitchen. The woman's voice was high-pitched, tremulous, and sounded very angry. The man's voice said, "Yes—OK, already, OK," and then the door slammed and it was quiet again. He felt like eating but was afraid to go into the kitchen. The garbage pail under the sink, with its greasy, gaping, smelly hole frightened him awfully.

Shaking miserably, he finally opened the door and walked into the room backward. The woman shook her head and said, "Why can't you walk like all of us, Jordi?" He couldn't answer—the pail might hear him. The big hole was like an ear, and it could hear everything—sometimes even his thoughts. If he kept quiet and thought nothing, maybe he could shut it out and make himself safe.

He gulped down his orange juice and ran out of the house. He made it—he was safe again—but he had to be careful of the garbage pails on the street.

And then he remembered that he forgot his jiggler. He had to have his jiggler if he wanted to get by the garbage cans safely. He knew that he had to face the woman again. She just couldn't understand why he wouldn't talk. Sometimes she hugged and kissed him. Sometimes she gave up and shook him.

He marveled at her fearlessness. She talked in front of the can, even picked it

up and shook it. But her voice—when that voice got loud and angry, the whole room shook. It felt like he would be crushed by it. It went through him and made him shake and scream inside—stop, stop, stop, stop, stop, but her voice would go on. Sometimes, though, the man's voice, which was kind and deep and smooth, would say, "Stop," and her voice stopped.

He tiptoed into the house, but she saw him and said, "God, Jordi, walk like the rest of us." He took the doorknob attached to a long string and ran past her out of the house. He had his jiggler and was now truly safe.

He let the jiggler hang down in front of him and waited. Soon it would tell his feet where to go. Funny, how his feet followed the jiggler without his even thinking about them. He walked and walked and felt that he was all alone even though there were people here and there.

•   •   •

He went to school each morning and returned in the late afternoon. This went on week after week, month after month. He was not aware of the passage of time. Nor was he aware of the change taking place in him. It wasn't a big change, and yet in a way it was. Because he was becoming more comfortable. There were fewer terrors, fewer voices, less hiding in himself. There was so much going on outside of him —so much going on between him and the world, the world and its objects—the world that used to be an emptiness, a nothingness, a hole full of potential disaster. But only he knew of this new world-relating, and

even he didn't "know" it. But he felt it—
yes, he felt it. And yet it hardly showed.
For, after all, as the months went by,
there they were, as before—Sally and Jordi,
Jordi and Sally—with only a few words
between them now and then. But the words
were increasing, and they were becoming
more and more important as steppingstones
between two people.

He called the week end the "different
days." One Sunday when the streets, lacking their normal week day hustle and bustle,
seemed empty, he had a thought, desert,
desert—the big Sahara desert he had seen
in the book. Then he thought, desert days,
desert days.

But then Monday would roll around,
and "Sally days" would be there again—
and he would feel full and be somebody.

And so the time passed.

"Yi, yi! Yi, yi! I'll break them all, all,
all. I'll break them all."

He put his heavy mittened fist through
one after another of the windows.

"Jordi," she yelled. "Jordi! Stop, stop!"
She caught him and pinned his arms
tightly against his body.

"What happened? Why did you break
them? Don't you know, Jordi? Why?"

"I'm not Jordi. Leave me alone—I'm
not Jordi. I'm me, but me isn't Jordi—not,
not today, not today."

"I'm Sally today."

"Yes, you're still Sally—but me, I'm
not Jordi, not today, not now."

"What's making you so angry?"

"This place is like an ice house, like an
ice house today. I'm keeping my coat on. I
won't take it off."

"Keep it on if you like, but that coat
is Jordi's coat, and you said you're not
Jordi, so why wear his coat?"

He ran over to the rack, tore his coat
off, and jumped up and down on it.

"This is my coat, this one," he said,
snatching the blue tweed overcoat off the
hook.

"That isn't your coat. That belongs to
Robert."

"It is Robert's coat and today it is
mine."

"How come it's yours today, Jordi?"
He didn't answer.

"Will it be yours tomorrow?"

"I don't know, I don't know. If I'm
Jordi tomorrow, then it won't, but I don't
know."

"Oh, I see. Then you must be Robert
today."

"Yes, I'm him—I mean I'm me—but
me is Robert."

"How come you are Robert?"

"I don't know. I just am Robert, that's
all."

"How did you become him?"
He didn't answer.

"All right, Robert," she said. "When
did you become him?"
He still ignored her.

"I thought you were Jordi when you
left here yesterday."

"I was," he said. "I was—but he took
Jordi away from me. He took him away."

"He?"

"Yes, he, Robert."

"Well, how did he, Robert, do that?"

"On my bus, on my school bus, that's
how."

"On the bus?"

"He took my seat, he took it from
me. He made me sit in his. I had to sit in
his. I said, 'Give me my seat, give me my
Jordi seat,' but they laughed."

"Who, Jordi?"
He ignored her.

"I mean who laughed?"
He still didn't answer.

"I mean who laughed, Robert?"

"Now I understand you, now I do.
It was the train man. The train man, he
laughed at me and said, 'Take Robert's
seat. All the seats are the same. We can't
waste time. Come on, kid, take Robert's
seat!' "

"Well, where is Jordi now?" she asked.

"Over there," he said, pointing to
Robert. "Over there, that's the Jordi boy,
the one that sat in the Jordi seat."

Sally walked over to the coat rack

and took down John's big brown coat. It was much too large for her. It came down to her ankles, and the sleeves flapped below her hands.

"I guess I've got the wrong coat on," she said, flapping the sleeves up and down.

"Yes, Sally, that coat isn't yours. That's John's coat—Lisa's teacher, John."

"Then who am I? If I'm wearing John's coat, who am I?"

"Oh, come on, you're silly."

"I'm silly. I guess I am silly with this great big coat on."

"I mean Sally—Sally silly, silly Sally."

"Yes, Jordi, I'm Sally. Maybe silly, but still Sally, and, no matter whose coat I put on, I am still Sally."

She went back to the rack and put one coat on after another. Each time she put another coat on, she asked, "Who am I?" And each time he repeated, "You're Sally, I know you're Sally."

Then she took his hand and said, "Let's go up to William's office." When she got to the director's office, she asked him if he could leave for a few minutes. He said, "Hi, Jordi," as he closed the door behind him. Then Sally sat down in William's chair.

"Whose chair is this?"

"William's chair."

"Where is William?"

"William just went out."

"So who am I?"

"You, you're Sally—silly Silly," he grinned.

She got up. "Sit here, in William's chair." He sat down.

"Where is William?" she asked.

"Oh, he's still outside, Sally. You know that."

"Well, where are you sitting?"

"I'm sitting in the big chair."

"Whose chair?"

"The William chair."

"And who are you?"

He looked into her eyes very solemnly. Then his face crinkled into a big grin, and he said, "I'm Jordi. Yes, Sally, I'm truly Jordi." . . .

Several months later he sat at his mother's sewing table.

He looked at the crayons and took out all the short pieces. That left him seven long ones. He couldn't make up his mind. First he started with orange, then red, then black. He finally started to fill the fish in with purple.

But the point was worn down. He tried awfully hard but couldn't stay within the lines. He held his hand stiff and tried not to bend his wrist, but this only made it worse. Tears streamed down his cheeks, and he could hardly see. He held his right hand with his left, but to no avail. Grief and hopelessness flooded him. He heard himself thinking, can't, can't, can't—Jordi can't. Jordi can't. No good, no good, no good.

There was little of the fish left now. The purple made wilder and wilder streaks all over the paper. This time there was no hesitancy in his choice. He took the red crayon. Holding it like a knife, he stabbed the paper again and again. Then he took the black and blotted out the remains of the fish altogether. He took the sharp pencil and stabbed and tore and stabbed and tore over and over again.

The paper was in shreds now. His sobbing tore out of him in spasms. It was interrupted only by short gasps of breath. His body twisted to and fro, and his shoulders heaved up and down. He felt himself drowning in anguish.

Through his tears he suddenly saw the tattered paper. It was monstrous. This torn-up red, purple, black, stabbed, blotted-out fish was horror itself. He screamed and ran. He could feel the thing chasing him. This bleeding, stumpy thing he had wounded. This monster he had manufactured.

The form and color of it kaleidoscoped. He pictured it short, round, fat, tall, black, purple, sharp, dull with jagged holes and hating him. He stopped. He hit his jaw with his closed fist. He hit himself again and again.

His face was very swollen, but the

monster had gone. Only a piece of colored paper remained. He crumpled it into a ball and dropped it into the basket.

He heard the key in the door, and then she came in. He heard her say, "Oh, God, oh God. My God. Why, why? Your face, your face, my baby, my baby. Why, why did you do it, why?"

He let himself be led into the bathroom, and the cold compress felt good. He heard her sobbing but couldn't understand why.

"But, Mama, I feel good. I do, I do feel good."

"Why did you beat yourself? Why, Jordi, why?"

"It was the fish monster. I had to get it away—I just had to. It was—oh, Mama, I don't want to hit myself. I don't want to. I don't know, I don't know—how—how. Oh, Mama, help me," he cried, and then she stopped crying.

He felt himself held by her and felt his bruised cheek being kissed. He snuggled into her arms. Then she led him into the living room and gave him the chocolate bar she had in her bag. He stopped crying, ate it, and felt better.

"I like you. Mom, I like you."

"I love you, Jordi. I love you very much."

"How much, Mom? How much?"

"A great big bunch and then some—more than anything, more than anything in this whole world."

"Gee, I feel nice, Mom. It feels good in here." He pointed to his chest. "It feels warm and good in here."

"I'm glad. I'm so glad, Jordi."

He went outside and walked to the water tower. He sat and stared at it for a while. Then he walked around it and looked at it some more. After a while he started to walk home. He made sure his jiggler was in his pocket but didn't take it out. Just knowing he had it with him made him feel safer.

On the way home he thought about Sally and wondered what words they would rhyme in school. Then he thought of the word "rhyme," and then "slime" and "climb." He pictured himself climbing the water tower. On top of it he would be away and higher than anyone else. But he would have to come down to see Sally and her and him too. Then he thought, her and him, Mama and Papa.

When they ate supper, his jaw ached, and he thought about it.

"Do you feel all right?" his father asked.

"Yes, yes."

"But your jaw, Jordi, does it hurt?"

"My jaw—yes, it hurts. It does hurt."

"I'm sorry it hurts, Jordi."

"Me, I'm sorry too. I'm sorry my jaw hurts."

He rubbed it a little too hard and winced.

After supper he was very tired. He lay on his bed thinking about things for a while. In a very short time he fell asleep.

He dreamed that he was walking on the kitchen floor. He walked up and back, swinging his jiggler to and fro. Suddenly he realized that the floor had a big fish outlined on it, and nearby lay a great big purple crayon. He took the crayon and started to color the fish. But then the crayon turned into a Pogo stick. Jordi rode the Pogo—jumping from spot to spot and depositing purple wherever he landed. Soon the whole fish was purple—and there wasn't a spot outside of the lines.

Then a funny thing happened. The fish rose up from the floor and became a real live purple fish. Then it said, "I like you Jordi. You made me a nice color, and I'll always be your friend."

Then he tied a long string all around the fish and led him through the deserted street like a dog on a leash. And people woke up and began to fill the streets. He wasn't afraid, though, because he had his fish friend with him, who was bigger even than a big dog.

He got up the next morning feeling that there was more to him. He felt as though there was more of him than his usual self—sort of like a piece had been added. He looked in the dresser mirror and felt disappointed that there was no addition to himself. His dimensions were all the same. He was no heavier and no taller.

But the feeling stuck with him. There was just more of him, even if he couldn't see it. Maybe there was more inside him—inside, where he couldn't see but sometimes felt different things.

The feeling made him walk differently. His feet moved more importantly; his steps were surer. Everything about himself felt more solid. When he got on the bus that morning, he almost felt it creak down in response to his added something. He remembered nothing of his dream. It was as if it never happened.

When he got to school, he and Sally rhymed words for a while and then sat down at the long low table.

"I feel funny, Sally."

"Oh?"

"Sort of like more."

"Like more, Jordi?"

"More—draw, draw. Let's draw, Sally."

She took down a big box of crayons and paper.

For a while he just drew lines—then broader lines, and then boxes and circles here and there. Then he drew a series of dots from one corner of the page to the other. Then he drew lines connecting the dots.

"Sally, could we fill in something?"

"Sure. What would you like to fill in, Jordi?"

He didn't answer.

"Here. Here is a triangle, Jordi."

"A triangle?" he asked.

"Yes." She explained how a triangle consisted of three sides and three angles—one between each pair of sides. Then she drew a circle and a rectangle and defined and explained each of them to him.

Jordi was intrigued with what he heard. Listening to her was great fun.

"Gee, I like this, Sally. I like to play this way."

"Me too," she said.

Then he took a purple crayon and started to fill in the large triangle—the one he now knew was an equilateral triangle. He was very careful, but, unwittingly, he moved just outside the lower left angle.

"Oh, oh," he moaned, "Sally, I feel funny. Oh."

"What's wrong, Jordi? What? Tell me."

He hit himself with his closed fist again and again.

"Hold my hand, Sally. Help me—hold me."

She held his hands between hers as he moaned, "Oh, oh." Then she managed to get him on her lap. She bent over him, held her arms around him, and hugged him tightly.

He felt warm and safe.

After a while he stopped moaning. But she continued to hold him. Soon she started to hum and sing to him—and after a few minutes he hummed along with her. They sat humming and singing for more than an hour. Then they walked around the room and looked at all the new pictures recently placed on the walls.

They had meat loaf, potatoes, and green peas for lunch. Jordi attacked it with relish and even ate some more potatoes before he gulped down his Jell-O.

When they were back upstairs—sitting at the table—Sally started to talk.

"Why were you angry at yourself, Jordi?"

"Angry?"

"Yes—before lunch when you hit yourself and asked me to hold your hands?"

"Oh—I was angry?" he asked with some wonderment. Then he answered himself. "Yes, I was. I went outside the line." Tears started to fill his eyes. "I went outside the line. I couldn't help it—I just couldn't."

"The line, Jordi?"

"Yes, when I filled in with the crayon."

"I see."

"Do you Sally?"

"Yes. I understand. But, Jordi, you don't have to draw perfectly. It's all right to go outside the line. I'll love you anyway.

"Jordi, you draw just for fun. If it has to be perfect, it's no fun."

"Perfect?" he questioned.

"Yes—you know—just so, all within the line—exactly so. Nothing—nothing is perfect."

"But, Sally, if it's outside the line the triangle won't be a triangle anymore. It will be all over. It will be like wild—like a panther."

"But, Jordi, even if it isn't a triangle anymore, it's OK. And a little bit won't matter anyway. It will still be a triangle. And anyway, Jordi, a drawing isn't a living thing. But, regardless of how you draw, Jordi, you will still be you, and I'll love you inside or outside the line."

"A drawing isn't a living thing," he repeated. "A drawing isn't a living thing."

"Draw an empty fish—draw a fish, Sally."

She outlined a big fish on a large white sheet of paper.

He filled it in with purple. Then he looked at her—and scribbled the crayon outside the outline. He looked at her again. And they both started to laugh together. And they laughed and laughed until their bellies hurt. Then she hugged him and hugged him and kissed his cheek. And it didn't feel bruised at all.

After several months Jordi had learned a considerable amount about addition, subtraction, and the multiplication tables and some facts about division.

One day he asked if they could talk more about the angles—triangles and rectangles. Sally told him all about degrees in angles. Then she went on and explained about circles and area and volume. Jordi was very attentive and absorbed it readily. But then Sally explained that this would be discussed later on in high school and college. She described high school and college and working. Jordi listened but wasn't too interested. Later on they resumed their reading work, and he liked the way she looked when he read a whole page from the reader without stopping.

Just before he went home that day he turned to her and said, "Sally, you really became a teacher in this room."

•   •   •

"Jordi, how do you feel about going to another school?"

"Another school?" he asked, obviously confused. "Will you be there? Will you be there with me, Sally?"

She went on. "Jordi, you don't understand. Do you remember we once talked about more grown-up schools, about high schools and colleges?"

"Yes, I remember, but will you be there, Sally?"

"No, Jordi, I won't be there—but you will learn a great deal more about angles, about history and many interesting things. And there will be other teachers there, and you will meet children your age there too."

"I don't want to go, Sally. I want to stay with you."

"You're not leaving yet, Jordi. It won't be for another six months."

"Do I have to go? Do I have to, Sally? Who will I talk to? Who will tell me I'm Jordi if I get lost—who, Sally?"

He began to cry, and she hugged him to her.

"You won't get lost, Jordi. You're lots better now. Your problem hardly shows anymore—that's why you don't have to stay. You can go to a regular school."

"You mean Lisa can't leave?" he said through his tears.

"No, she can't leave, Jordi. Besides, Jordi, you will have Dr. Mills to talk to. You will see him every day after school."

"Oh, Sally—oh, why did you tell me, why? Now my problems will show—now mine will show."

"Let them show, Jordi, and cry all you like. And, Jordi," she said, "you will visit me. You can come now and then, and I'll come and see you at home every few months. We can talk on the phone too."

"Everything hurts. Please, please, don't say any more, Sally."

But Sally said much more. They talked and talked about his departure from the school.

And then only two days remained before Jordi would leave. Four and a half years had passed since he entered the "ice house."

"Jordi, in two days you will go to your new school, but remember you can visit here."

He suddenly swirled about, faced her, and yelled, "You hate me, you hate me. You lied, you lied. You never liked me never. And I hate you, I hate you."

He picked up a blackboard eraser and threw it, shattering the nearest window.

Then he ran out of the room and out of the building. He just ran and ran, too dazed to think or watch where he was going. But he soon found himself on the subway and in the front car of the Lexington Avenue express.

He rode all over New York and cried most of the time. Then he thought about Sally and the times gone by. Then he thought about their talks of the last six months.

When he got back, it was six o'clock, but everybody was still there. Even his mother and father were there.

Then he saw her, and she said, "Jordi, I'm so glad to see you. I'm so glad to see you, Jordi."

He looked at her and said, "I came back, I came back. Sally, I came back to leave."

DIAGNOSIS: *Autistic child.*

This excerpt is taken from a subjectivized factual account of an autistic child who was rescued from his inner, noncommunicable world by the efforts of a group of devoted people, who work with autistic children and their parents. Not all such children are cured—not even a majority. Some can be helped. Some few can be reached and cured, Jordi for one. After grim setbacks and infinite pains, he gave up his own fantasy, his own distorted perception of objects and people to join the rest of the human race. The Jordis cannot stay in a regular school or maintain themselves in school. Their language, if any, is incomprehensible; their impulsive behavior, unpredictable; their gestures, bizarre and their look, wild and unrelated.

To teach them takes infinite capacity to mother and not smother; to charade, or act out, messages of reassurance through gesture, tone of voice, deed; to enter into the understanding of what a particular autistic child's world, his gestures, language, or silence means to him; to discover a link between our world and theirs.

The case history of Jordi is based on a child at the Brooklyn League School, run by Carl Fenichel. A few Jordis completely recover; a few improve enough to take an odd place in society; some become more useful and more satisfied patients at institutions.

Dr. Rubin worked at the Brooklyn League School. He portrays the horror, the nightmare-like days that schizophrenic and autistic children experience. One can sense the lostness of Jordi, his inability to conceive of himself as a person with boundaries. He becomes the objects and people in his environment, and they invade and become him.

Sometimes he helps himself find his boundaries by using a "jiggler," a typical device such children use to extend themselves to the outside world. It serves not only as a security blanket serves many children, but also as a moving force. When the jiggler moves, the child can move. It is as if the jiggler takes on the responsibility for what the child does; the jiggler does it and he must follow. The jiggler keeps him safe in an unsafe, unbounded world. Objects, machinery, toys are safer and more manipulable than people. However, since objects are given so much power, they can become threatening and dangerous monsters; a water tower, a street light, anything can take on life and hit back. The difference between live and unlive doesn't exist; even more remote is the difference between thee and me. This is seen in the excerpt about Robert and Jordi, so expertly handled by Jordi's therapist-teacher; the magic containment of self, demonstrated in the fish-coloring incident; the self-mutilation and destruction evolving from "going out of bounds."

Dr. Rubin outlines the cure, which is long in coming and often doesn't come. The last episode is the story of gain and loss, the necessity of leaving old things behind in order to grow. It also implies the toughness and faith necessary to help a child grow to the next step. Note that though a doctor and a school director are in the picture, it is the teacher—a specially trained teacher to be sure —who is the central figure in the child's daily school life. Teachers, like mothers, though to a less involved extent, respond with the same ambivalent feelings to these deeply puzzling, unhappy, anxiety-provoking children.

A Little Boy's Long Journey

Jules Romains

Clanricard had not seen Louis Bastide passing with his hoop. Louis Bastide had come up the rue Clignancourt from the corner of the rue Ordener, running all the way. The slope was very steep. Horses had to take it at a walk; and they pulled their loads up in jerks, straining for all they were worth and striking sparks out of the stones. One day little Louis had been there when a fire-engine with magnificent horses arrived at a gallop and attacked the slope. A few yards up the hill, they had to slow down like everybody else.

So it was obviously very difficult to roll a hoop up such a slope. It needed plenty of enthusiasm and stout-heartedness at the beginning; and then a determination not to weaken, not to give way to your tiredness—to say nothing of great skill in handling your stick.

When he got out of school, Louis Bastide had gone straight home to his parents, who lived in the rue Duhesme, on the third floor, quite near the boulevard Or-

Reprinted from *Men of Good Will*, Vol. I, by Jules Romains, translated by Warre B. Wells, by permission of Alfred A. Knopf, Inc. Copyright 1933, 1961 by Alfred Knopf, Inc.

nano. He kissed his mother and showed her his copy-books and the report on his work and conduct. He did not ask for anything, but his eyes shone. His mother looked at his pale little cheeks and at the fine sun outside; and she tried not to let him see how pleased she was that he wanted to go out and play.

"All right," she said, "take your hoop. Mind the traffic. Be home by five o'clock."

The hoop was big and substantial—too big for Louis's size. But he had chosen it himself after mature consideration. Long before buying it he had seen it in the window of a bazaar, and he had said to himself that nobody could want a finer hoop—perhaps because of the strong, healthy look of the wood, whose colour was clear and whose joints were well fitted. You had only to look at it to realize how it would run and jump.

Its dimensions had given him something to think about. But Louis expected to go on growing for some years yet; and he could not imagine that a hoop of which he got very fond might some day cease to be dear to him and simply strike him as a child's trivial toy. His only reason for ever discarding it would be its getting too small for him. In choosing a rather big one, Louis was taking thought for the future.

He went down the stairs, with the hoop hanging from his shoulder. Once he was out in the street, he stood it in the middle of the sidewalk, very straight up, holding it lightly with the fingers of his left hand. Then he gave it a smart tap. The hoop rolled away. The end of the stick caught up with it at once, keeping it in the right direction; and after that Bastide and his hoop had run one after the other; rather like a child running after a dog that he has on a leash; and also rather like a rider who lets himself be carried along by his horse, but at the same time keeps on spurring and guiding him.

When you have played for a long time with a hoop, as Louis Bastide had done, and you have had the luck to find one of which you are very fond, you come to realize that things are quite different from going out in the ordinary way. Try and run by yourself; you will be tired in a few minutes. With a hoop, you can keep tiredness at bay indefinitely. You feel as though you were holding on to something, almost as though you were being carried along. If you happen to feel tired for a moment, it seems as though the hoop imparted strength to you in a friendly kind of way.

Besides, you don't have to run fast all the time. If you know how to do it, you can go almost at a walking pace. The trouble is to keep the hoop from falling to the right or left; or clinging to the legs of a passer-by, who struggles like a rat in a trap; or lying down flat on the ground after going through extraordinary contortions. You must know how to use your stick, how to give the hoop very gentle taps, just as though you were stroking it and helping it on its way. Above all, in between your taps, you must keep control over any tendency of the hoop to waver, with the help of your stick, which must just graze the edge of it on one side or the other all the time, keeping it on the

move or changing its speed, with the end of the stick held ready to intervene quickly at any point where the hoop threatens to fall into a lurch.

Louis Bastide need not have kept all these details in his mind, for he had been playing with the hoop for a long time, and he had become skilled enough in handling it to trust to most of his actions being automatic. But there was a background of conscientiousness, of thoroughness in him which prevented him from doing anything in the least important without taking pains over it. Nor could he help taking pains even over his pleasures. Once he was interested in anything, he applied himself to it passionately, and the smallest details struck him with pulsating clearness, with a sharpness which made every one of them something unforgettable.

He was born to be a man with the utmost presence of mind. But his capacity for taking pains did not prevent him from taking fire. If his control of the hoop never ceased for a moment to be an operation of scientific exactitude, performed in a sphere of pitiless clarity, his running through the streets became an adventure luxuriant and mysterious, whose connecting thread resembled that of dreams, and whose inexplicable ups and downs led him little by little, and turn by turn, to moments of enthusiasm, or of intoxication, or of a melancholy in itself uplifting

Once he had crossed the boulevard, he followed the rue Championnet. It was, at that time, a rather out-of-the-way street, still full of whiteness and brightness. There were scarcely any tall houses. There were low, long buildings, opening on inside courtyards, with nothing but a window or a peep-hole in a door looking out on the street now and then. It was a street with gateways, with fences. A street whose habitual silence was broken only by the occasional rumbling passing of a three-horse truck.

The sidewalk was bright, and wide enough; and also it was empty. The long wall which ran on your right accompanied you like a comrade. There were only three or four lamp-posts between you and the next crossing. All this street was full of easiness, of security, of mute benevolence. The sky above it was spacious. The smoke of a factory, in the distance, emerged almost pure white and displayed itself to the right of the tall chimney like a banner floating in the breeze.

Happy the child of Paris who had the run of this quiet street. He could see the sky and the smoke. The sky, still blue and sunny, told you, all the same, that night was coming. It bent down over the roofs of the sheds, and so it came quite close to you. But away there where the smoke was, it was glorious, deep, distant.

That beloved sky, towards which your eyes kept straying, which you kept on finding from time to time—this evening it was like your idea of the future. It did not promise anything, but it contained, somehow or other, all kinds of promises which the heart of a child of Paris could divine. It reminded him of certain hazy but still remembered happinesses that he had known when he was still quite small, still more of a child than he was now, that were already a part of his memory, even while he was running behind his hoop, that were already his own personal, incomparable, secret past.

How lovely that smoke was! A quite regular series of puffs that rolled up and then spread out. Something like those magnificent clouds of summer, but with a will of their own, an aim of their own, an aspiration of their own. They conveyed to you the idea of a spring; and then that chimney, which you could see sticking out of the city—it was as though the source of the clouds, coming to birth in the depths of Paris, had been borne up there into the sky.

Sometimes the hoop took it into its head to run away. The end of the stick pursued it without succeeding in catching up with it; and the hoop leant over a little, it veered about. It behaved just like an animal which loses its head as it runs. You must know how to catch up with it not too

impatiently. Otherwise you ran the risk of running it up against a wall or of knocking it over.

When the time came to leave the sidewalk and cross the street, it was a delight to wait for the hoop's little leap and watch over it. It was exactly as though you were dealing with a sensitive, nervous beast. And afterwards, until it reached the opposite sidewalk, it never stopped leaping on the stones, in their cracks, with all kinds of capricious irregularities and changes of direction.

Louis Bastide pretended that he had a mission to accomplish. Somebody had commissioned him to follow a certain course, to carry something, or perhaps to herald something. But the itinerary was not easy. He had to keep to it, respecting all its unexpectedness, all its oddness, both because this was a law and also because there were dangers and enemies to be avoided.

Here was the immense wall of the freight station, and the rue des Poissonniers, whose gas-lamps were so strange. They had a crown, like kings; a halo, like martyrs. Louis's mission demanded that he should turn to the left, across the street, and go towards the fortifications, following the long wall and passing underneath those strange gas-lamps.

The day was declining a little. The street was beginning to be filled with bluish shadows and with an almost cold air. The sky remained luminous, but it was farther away. There was no further question of the promises that it might hold for a boy who raised his eyes. Louis slowed down to a little running step, very regular, scarcely faster than the walk of a grown-up. The hoop visibly helped him. That kind of slender wheel, which could run so fast, slackened its pace so as not to tire Bastide. At this rate he could keep on going to the other end of Paris.

The bridge over the Ceinture railway, encircling the city. What had his mission to say? That he should not cross it, but turn to the left along the rue Béliard.

The rue Béliard reminded you of a road running out into the country. Far away, in the provinces, there must be many a road like this, where travellers and coaches passed along at the fall of day. Louis remembered an engraving in a school-book; and also a picture in a postal almanac; and, most of all, a drawing in an old catalogue of the Magasins du Bon Marché.

It was fine to have got as far away as this. The houses at the side of the road looked at you with astonishment. They all looked at your face and said to themselves: "How tired he must be!" But they were wrong if they imagined that Louis had come there for their benefit. His goal was far beyond, and he must get there before night, "before night overtook him," as the books said.

The most that Louis would do was to call a brief halt here. The courier would not even dismount from his horse. He would let his beast go slowly, quite slowly; and as he passed the trough, he would let him drink a little. If anybody questioned him, he would make no reply; or he would content himself with "evasive words."

Thus his gallant little horse, so faithful to its master, recovered its breath. It was better not to pay any attention to the cutting of the Ceinture railway, which lay to the right. Otherwise, the spell would be broken. Unless, indeed, you thought of mountains. In mountain country the railway, penetrating any number of tunnels, made its way to a village. Once a day at the most, the mountaineers watched for the arrival of the train.

In the inn, which was that shed surrounded by a bank, opposite the cut, people were drinking and playing cards as they waited. They might be hunters who had come down from the mountain. They had not come down to take the train; for nothing in the world would they leave their own country-side; but, still, they were waiting.

Louis imagined himself going into the inn for a moment. He left his hoop outside, leaning against the wall; but he kept his stick in his hand, just as you keep your whip. "A glass of wine, sir?" "Yes, but I won't sit down, because I haven't time. . . . Good health! . . . Is it freezing in the mountains?" "Yes, they say that right at the top the pass is covered with snow. But you'll get through, if you don't let the night overtake you."

The courier set out on his way again. Here began the road that ran up into the mountains, that led to the pass blocked by snow.

How fine it was, a street that went up straight in front of you and ended far away in the sky! This one was particularly fine, because it was never-ending and made you think of a great precipice beyond it. Louis's father called it "chaussée" Clignancourt, not just "street" like the others. Louis did not know why, but he was not surprised that this marvellous street should have a name all to itself.

His mission now was to get to the top of it before he was "overtaken by the night"; higher even than he could see; right up to the top of the hill of Montmartre. Then it would be his mission to make a kind of reconnaissance by following the end of the rue Lamarck, like a road cut in a rock, from which you could see the whole of Paris across the new gardens.

Long before he reached the slope, there was still a fair distance on level ground, and, since the hoop was bowling along without his touching it, as though the wind were pushing it, Louis imposed a quite moderate pace upon himself. On the other hand, he made a vow not to slacken up the slope until he reached the pass "blocked by snow." After that he would be free to proceed as he chose. He would have left the road. He would be on paths where it was permissible and even prudent to dismount.

But that was still a very long way off! Bastide needed all his courage, and also all his skill. He resisted the temptation to go fast. He approached the dangerous street-crossings carefully. His mother had warned him to mind the traffic. Louis had no desire to be killed; but his mother's despair if he were killed frightened him even more than the idea of death. The stretcher being carried upstairs; "My little Louis! My poor little boy!" The wreck of the hoop, which they might put with his body; the stick, which he might still clasp in his hand.

Still, it is difficult to evade a law which you have laid down for yourself. Cross the boulevard Ornano with his hoop hanging from his shoulder—that was something which Louis could not bring himself to do. He even had a feeling that he would be punished in some way or other if he did. The laws which you lay down for yourself, or, rather, the orders which come to you from some mysterious depths in yourself, will not suffer you to infringe them or play tricks with them. You risk much less in disobeying a visible master.

Louis had the right to stop, he and his hoop, the one supporting the other. But so long as the course was not finished, the hoop must not leave the ground, must not cease to be in contact with the ground; for if it did, he would cease to be "true" to himself.

The rue Marcadet in its turn was successfully negotiated. The long climb began. Louis, who knew very little about any other neighbourhood, thought that in the whole of Paris there could not be any slope which it was more honourable to conquer. He who was capable of scaling it, without the hoop that he guided falling down or running away, need not be dismayed anywhere.

But the passers-by lacked brains. If they understood the value of the test, they would not hesitate about getting out of the way, instead of making those annoyed faces, or looking at the boy with contemptuous pity.

So it was that Louis Bastide came to the half-way house of the rue Custine. He saw Clanricard and saluted him hastily, raising his hand to his béret. The master was looking the other way. Bastide, very

fond of him as he was, could not possibly stop. The private law which he had formulated for himself at the bottom of the slope required that he should reach the "pass blocked by snow" without a halt. He would have liked to be able to explain to his master that he was not imposing such an effort on himself just for fun.

So he kept his stride and did not allow himself to take breath until he was at the top of the street.

After that it was almost a rest. Louis had the right to go up the rue Muller at walking pace. To help his hoop to keep its balance, he could even support it gently with his left hand, with the tips of his fingers grazing the edge of the wood. On mountain paths the most skilful horseman dismounts and, taking his horse, however good he may be, by the bridle, guides him and helps him not to stumble. All this was inside the rules.

When he reached the bottom of the rue Sainte-Marie, he asked himself whether he should go up the street itself or up the steps. He chose the steps. The other way was much longer and offered no opportunity of picking up new threads of adventure. So far as going up a flight of steps like this with a hoop was concerned, the rule to be followed was self-evident. While Louis himself used the steps, keeping as far over to the left as possible, the hoop made use of the granite curb. He helped it with stick and hand. It was a delicate manœuvre, the more so in that the principal role devolved upon the left hand. The hoop might escape you and hop backwards; in a series of hops it might run away altogether and go and get smashed under a carriage. But, to avert such a misfortune, it sufficed to be very careful—in other words, to be very fond of your hoop.

As he climbed up the steps, Louis met a keener air, less tainted with darkness. The cliff of houses on his right rose in successive surges, following the rhythm of the steps, and at its peak still received a slanting but dazzling light. The windows of the upper floors were still burning with reflections. Without stirring from their rooms women could watch the sunset.

And the boy wanted to raise himself up faster, as though up there, on the cornice of the hill, were all the joy, all the games, all the adventures of the future. The very noise of Paris passed into his body, though he was not aware of listening to it. Up with you, nimble hoop! Trains whistled in the suburbs in the plain. The child of the low streets recognized their cries without noticing them, as though he had been born among sea-birds. Roofs innumerable creaked in the wind; their creakings and cracklings sounded above the rustle of the leaves in the precipitous gardens. Like all these noises, the hoop, too, bounded and mounted. The child of Paris, as he stopped to take breath, drank in a sound of destinies that came to him from everywhere.

DIAGNOSIS: *Normal child—sense of play, fantasy control, power, discovery, curiosity.*

No more need be said. May every teacher have many children like Louis in his classroom, and may all teachers cherish and nourish such a child's imagination and curiosity, the sense of play, and sense of adequacy.

SUMMARY

The transfer from fiction to reality occurs in the classroom every day. The following paper was written by an 11-year-old girl who was sent to the principal's office because of sullen behavior and passive refusal to complete assigned schoolwork. The principal, a warm, supportive woman, had been helpful to her on several occasions. After spending half an hour of encouraging her to talk, the principal suggested that the girl might find it easier to express her troubles in writing. She responded slowly and quietly wrote the following statements.

May 18/1964

1. I don't like to be around many people.
2. I dislike some of people in my class.
3. I don't like boy.
4. I don't dream about boy.
5. ~~————————————————~~
6. I'm always doing the wrong things.
7. I wish people didn't ask about my family.
8. I always have to tell where I'm going when I go out to play.

1 I don't like to talk about me.

~~2~~
~~14~~

8. People always calling me names.
10. I don't like the people on the ~~my~~ the street I live on.
11. I'm ~~a~~ always getting in fight.
12. And I would want any wishes.
13. People always comparing me with my sister.
14. I don't cry at night.
15. I ~~————~~ sometimes ~~to~~ have nightmare.
16.

Notice the crossed-out sentences and the feelings of personal worthlessness that are expressed. How does it feel to be emotionally disturbed? There is only one answer. It is painful!

The rest of the book is devoted to describing or explaining how constructive intervention—in the classroom or in the doctor's office—may help to prevent or to ameliorate some of this pain.

2

How Can Disturbed Children Be Identified?

Of all the uncertainties regarding the disturbed child, the matter of identification is one of the most vexing. It has been demonstrated that the problem pupil in one classroom may even be on the "good-citizen list" in another. Parents often shop around from clinic to clinic, anticipating different diagnostic decisions from experts—and, disconcertingly, they frequently find them. Situational factors may play a large part in producing symptomatic behavior. A pupil who is no problem in a tightly organized setting may be hard to manage in a free, self-choice situation. A child who is relatively withdrawn and mute among peers in the school may warm up with a benign adult in a one-to-one relationship. Attempts to find a basis for understanding the "generating condition" in maladjustment are not as yet systematically planned.

Some children have a total adjustment problem in school, at home, and wherever they may be. Others are in trouble at home, but not in school. And some fail as a result of frustration in the face of a task or social demands at school. In other words, the setting may induce the stress. Thus, evidence from the school world does not always coincide with evidence from the out-of-school world of the pupil, another confounding aspect in the educator's study of childhood disturbance.

In the face of this complexity, what can the teacher do? In this chapter, we have broken the problem into two broad areas. The first, "Screening and Diagnosis," should sharpen the comprehension of adjustment-versus-maladjustment, and thus lay the foundation for subsequent material. The second, "Overall incidence of Disturbance," gives an insight into how much and what kinds of maladjustment one is likely to find in the child population.

SCREENING AND DIAGNOSIS

Screening is the process of selecting certain pupils who appear to be disturbed and significantly deviant. In diagnosis, the pupils are studied to determine the nature of the deviancy that is present.

Screening can be done at many levels beyond the mere I've-got-some-problem-kids-in-my-room type of generalization. Teachers can use various devices to check out all the children, rather than relying on the obvious symptoms that are exposed. Whole school systems can be surveyed by the teachers and the validity of their nominations judged on the basis of their evaluations of cases that are already known to the special services. While teachers have been criticized for being biased in their selection of cases, studies show that modern teachers are effective, particularly in picking out children who externalize their difficulties. Sometimes teachers are given categories to which they fit pupils. At other times they rate all pupils at various points on a continuum.

It has also been found that parents, often ignored as a source of information because of their biases, can contribute important information, and may be a better source of information for mental-health screening than generally believed.[1]

Whole state populations have been screened through the nominations of the disturbed by professionals who are in contact with children. Thus, there are reasons for doing "ad hoc" screenings of various types for particular purposes. The types of disturbance and their percentages will vary with the directions given and the rater's competency.

There are check sheets, tests, and scales for teachers to use in identifying the disturbed child. As has been described, certain disciplines rely on specialized tools, such as projective tests, while others rely on extensive interviews. The first selection, by Bühler and co-authors from the book *Childhood Problems and the Teacher,* has become a minor classic to many, because it does not substitute a list of simple symptoms for real understanding of the whole personality. Their book contains extensive material on cases, as well as discussions of therapy and the teacher's role, the group process, and projectives. The whole work is notable for its logical progression and the deep understanding presented without obfuscation. We have come to expect technical words often as a substitute for understanding. The quiet, simple, and direct presentation should not lead one to underestimate the wisdom of Bühler's concepts.

The selection here approaches problem behavior with the slant of the clinician but focuses on the school and the teacher's viewpoint. It should help teachers recognize their own personal biases.

The selection by Hollister and Goldston is in stark contrast to Bühler's psychodynamic approach to behavior. As much as we need to develop a picture of the child's inner life as it relates to his disturbance, we also need to learn what specific information contributes the nuances of understanding. It helps to know what methods can be employed and how teacher data are combined with information from other sources. The article tells, in outline form, what a comprehensive, multidiscipline, case study might contain. It is a preliminary taxonomy of items to be considered in designing a working procedure for selecting pupils for emotionally handicapped classes. It illustrates how screening for a practical purpose can be broken down to specific details.

[1] See J. C. Glidewell, H. R. Domke, and M. B. Kantor, "Screening in Schools for Behavior Disorders: Use of Mothers' Report of Symptoms," *Journal of Educational Research,* LVI, No. 10 (July–August 1963), 508–515.

What Is a Problem?

Charlotte Bühler, Faith Smitter, and Sybil Richardson

In psychological terms, a problem is a hindrance that disrupts the continuity of processes within the individual or in a group. A problem in school disrupts the work, the desirable cooperation of the group, or the individual's ability to function adequately.

Specific methods are needed to overcome the hindrance, but before methods are applied, the nature of the problem must be established and understood. The teacher has to interpret in psychological terms the problem as it appears in the classroom.

There are trivial everyday disturbances which teachers cannot study in detail. One morning two little girls may giggle constantly, or a boy may not be able to concentrate on his work or another may give an impertinent answer. These events cannot be submitted to elaborate psychological scrutiny but must be quickly met by educational group techniques. This is problem solution on the *behavior level,* or *level one,* where action is met by counteraction and the disturbance is thus eliminated.

While the level-one solution is adequate for many school incidents, this solution is applied too often to problems that require deeper understanding. All *repetitious* disturbances should be given psychological study. Constant giggling, repeated distraction, or impertinence represent complex problems which cannot be dealt with on the behavior level. Repetitive behavior is not just release of acute tension but indication of deeper and chronic disturbances in the child. *Repetitious disturbances must be interpreted as signs or symptoms of deeper underlying tensions.*

These deeper tensions may exist in the child who exhibits repetitious disturbing behavior. They may be found in the class situation, or they may have their origin in the child's relationship to other children or even in the attitudes of the teacher who is a part of the situation.

In addition to repetitious behavior, other disturbances require further study. *A serious single disturbance* gives a glimpse of a severe maladjustment in a child or of a deeper disorder within the group. For instance, one severe tantrum or a serious lie or a complete breakdown in tears may be significant and call for study.

A third type of disturbance is equally indicative of deep-seated tensions. A child may produce a *succession of different disturbances* which, superficially, seem unrelated. A child may today wriggle restlessly, tomorrow poke his neighbors, the next day sit and stare into space, another day masturbate openly, and still another complain of headaches. Each of these behavior disturbances may be different expressions of the same deep conflict or frustration in the child.

This succession of disturbances is generally not accidental, but follows a pattern based upon dynamics that are deep and complex. Such disturbances cannot be handled on the behavior level. Depending on the underlying emotional conflicts and on the whole situation, these problems must be handled on *level two* or *level three.*

Level two is an approach within the reach of the teacher who has the preparation and opportunity to devote time and study to personality problems. Level three is an approach for which the training and techniques of a psychologist or a psychiatrist are required.

AWARENESS OF PROBLEMS

Teachers are faced with an overwhelming number of different problems.

They see *disturbing behavior, social-relationship problems, emotional outbreaks, learning and other work problems,* problems connected with *ethical conduct, sex maladjustment,* problems resulting from *physical handicaps,* from *environmental handicaps,* from *cultural predicaments,* or indications of *incipient psychoses.* It is natural that their attention is drawn primarily to disturbances that prevent the progress of work or interfere with group harmony. The teacher sometimes overlooks the more severe and damaging disturbance, harmful to the individual or to the group, because it is less obtrusive.

A child who is timid and withdrawn is less disrupting than a child who constantly brags or fights. Yet he may harbor feelings and ideas more detrimental to himself and to others. Quiet children often pass unnoticed, even when on the verge of a breakdown due to their shyness and fears. Grown-up patients in psychotherapy sometimes reveal for the first time the agonies of their school years, when, inwardly shrinking, they were forced to speak to the class.

Children must learn to overcome timidity and should experience success in tasks they thought they could not master. There is, however, a limit to the use of encouragement for a human being who is deeply afraid, and the teacher must learn to know the limitation of the methods available to her. Pushing a fearful child by insistent prodding into a situation he dreads may achieve the opposite of the desired result, if the child's fear develops into a panic.

The teacher must be alert to the whole gamut of difficulties that a child may experience. The teacher's approach must be flexible and adapted to personality structures, for a mechanically applied general technique can never solve problems in different personalities.

EVALUATION OF PROBLEMS

Problems that an individual presents to others are due to problems that he experiences within himself. To evaluate the nature and the gravity of these inner problems is the difficult task that becomes partly the teacher's responsibility.

To define the extent to which the teacher takes this responsibility, several general principles are useful. The first rule is: Never assume that a problem can be explained by one specified cause. It is common practice to do this. To give an example, a popular explanation nowadays is to relate a child's maladjustment to the arrival of a new baby and to consider this the cause of the trouble.

The arrival of a new child is disturbing to the security feeling of the older child, but this disturbance is often absorbed if other circumstances are favorable. In all likelihood the disturbed child was insecure for several reasons, and the newcomer's arrival was only the most apparent of a number of experiences undermining this child's confidence. No chronic maladjustment, no repetitious misbehavior, no complex pattern of difficulties can be explained in terms of one single cause.

A second rule is: Never believe that explanations can be given without study of the individual situation. This is one of the most frequent mistakes made and occurs often in conjunction with another tendency that should be avoided.

This leads to a third rule: Do not give explanations that are not explanations. To say that a bragging child wants attention is no explanation; it is merely a description of the child's behavior. The child wants attention, but the reasons or motives for his need for attention must be sought.

Elaborate theories are sometimes developed without any study of the individual, on the assumption that a generalization may apply. For example, a girl with an average IQ is worried about her poor schoolwork and about not being popular. The teacher's theory is that demands at home are too high, that the child lacks the feeling of success, that the parents show their disappointment.

This may or may not be true. The explanation might easily be quite different.

The mother may have rejected the child before she faced school demands, or the child may be competing with a brilliant sister, or she may be emotionally disturbed for other reasons.

A little boy of seven, *Micky* had difficulties in learning to read and was aggressive with other children. After talking with the mother, the teacher concluded that the boy was intimidated by the superiority of his parents and his older brothers and felt inadequate at home. When the boy came to psychotherapy, he took one of the dolls representing a mother, lifted her skirts, shouted in profane language at her and squirted her with a water pistol after taking off her panties.

Undoubtedly he had more serious problems than superior brothers, which neither the mother nor the teacher could have discovered. Children live through experiences that require a third interceptor. In the meantime, mother and teacher must be guarded against explanations and theories. Careful studies by a trained psychologist should be initiated, if their preliminary reasoning proves inadequate.

A fourth rule is: Learn to weigh symptoms and consider their proportion to the assumed or known causes. This is the greatest art in the evaluation of problem behavior, requiring long experience.

If a boy is extremely resentful and aggressive and steals from other children, it is no sufficient explanation to say that he is overdisciplined and does not have enough freedom. The problem must be more serious. For example, this child may have suffered an injustice and may want to take revenge on others by being unfair too.

If a little girl vomits in the morning when she starts to school and says she is too sick to go, it is probably no sufficient explanation to say that she is spoiled, immature, and wants to stay with her mother. She must have more specific reasons to be afraid of school or to rebel.

If another girl is overambitious in class, worries a great deal, bites her nails, pulls her socks and her hair, and is restless, this cannot be explained by perfectionistic ambitious parents; other and deeper problems must be involved.

It is not easy to weigh the pain, anxiety, or guilt that a person feels against the existing frustrations or demands to which he is exposed. The assumption of the "average condition" of stresses and demands which clinical thinking used in the past— that is, the assumption that most children live in average circumstances and should behave in an average way—cannot be accepted by the conscientious observer. There are many unfair conditions of life with which a child cannot be expected to cope, and there are other situations which are less hard than an individual appears to find them. Study is always necessary before the reality of frustrations or demands can be judged.

Comparison of two very shy and withdrawing children, such as *Priscilla* and *Ingrid* reveals extraordinary differences. Ingrid takes things painfully because of her own interpretation of life, while Priscilla has actually a very difficult situation to face. Both children have perfectionistic parents, but Ingrid is loved and pressure is not exerted on her, while Priscilla gets more discipline than affection.

Elmer and *Julia*, who suffer from inferiority feelings, are both handicapped by objective conditions, Elmer by illness, Julia by the fact that her parents were immigrants and the father had an odd personality. While Elmer's physical handicaps were so great that the boy could do nothing but resign and withdraw, Julia unduly blamed her background. It was not her looks or her father's disagreeable personality that kept other children away from her, but her own withdrawing attitude.

Knowledge of the relationship of symptoms or clusters of symptoms to certain underlying disturbances is still incomplete. Correlations regarding certain symptoms and certain clusters of symptoms have been partially established. . . .

Pupil Selection and Study
William G. Hollister and S. E. Goldston

THE SCREENING AND DIAGNOSTIC PROCESSES

The processes of screening and providing a comprehensive diagnosis of both the psychological and educational assets and deficiencies of emotionally handicapped children involves group and individual procedures for the early identification of such children and subsequent individual study. The communication that develops between the staffs involved in the screening, referral, diagnostic, placement and interpretation components of the program vitally affects their capacity to mobilize the right resources to meet the needs of the individual children.

GROUP TO BE SCREENED

1. Criteria employed, e.g., age, sex, socio-economic data, grade level, etc.
2. Aspects of psychopathology, i.e., diagnosis, severity, prognosis.

SCREENING METHODS

1. Teacher nomination.
2. Psychological test data.
3. Educational test data.
4. Peer data, e.g., sociograms, peer ratings.
5. Cumulative record data.
6. Parent interviewing.
7. Home visits.

REFERRAL SOURCES

1. Major sources of referral; role of family physician.

From William G. Hollister and S. E. Goldston, *Considerations for Planning Classes for the Emotionally Handicapped* (Washington, D.C.: The Council for Exceptional Children, NEA, 1962).

William Hollister is Professor of Community Psychiatry, Department of Psychiatry, University of North Carolina Medical School. S. E. Goldston is Training Specialist, National Institute of Mental Health, Bethesda, Maryland.

2. Community agency participation in referral.

REFERRAL CRITERIA

1. Criteria and procedures for accepting referrals.
2. Priorities.

EDUCATIONAL DIAGNOSIS

1. Instruments utilized.
2. Types of data collected.
3. Diagnostic categories employed.
4. Role of classroom teacher.

SOCIO-PSYCHOLOGICAL, PSYCHIATRIC, AND MEDICAL DIAGNOSIS

1. Socio-psychological diagnosis to assess achievement, aptitude, attitude, social relationships, personality, and developmental factors.
   a. Instruments utilized, e.g.,
      Sociometrics
      Anecdotal records
      Diaries
      Case study
      Observations
      Interviews
      Parental reports
      Projectives
      Self-rating scales
      School history
      Personal history
      Family history
      Developmental progress charts
      Past teacher reports.
   b. Disciplines involved.
   c. Identification of ego strengths, talents, and social skills.
   d. Definition of conflict-free areas.
2. Psychiatric diagnosis.
   a. Descriptive psychiatric diagnosis according to APA Standard Diagnostic Nomenclature.

b. Inclusion of a dynamic formulation in the psychiatric report.
c. Inclusion of a prognostic statement in the psychiatric report.
3. Medical diagnosis.
   a. Physical examination by school or private physician.
   b. Use of other medical specialists.

THE PLANNING, PLACEMENT, AND CONTINUOUS ASSESSMENT PROCESSES

Following the initial screening and preliminary diagnosis, procedures must be employed to collate information on the educational, social, psychological, psychiatric, and medical status of the child. The determination of a recommended plan for care and suitable educational placement is contingent upon a detailed, multi-disciplinary analysis of the diagnostic data. Diagnostic emphasis needs not only to be on defining the child's problems but also to identify the strengths available for the psychological and educational rehabilitation of the child. After placement has been effected, it should be periodically evaluated.

ANALYSIS OF DIAGNOSTIC DATA AND PLANNING FOR CARE

1. Disciplines involved: use of case conferences to analyze data and plan for care—frequency, duration, staff involved.
2. Types of care recommended, outcomes projected, and goals set, e.g., special class; part-time classroom; resource room; home-bound teaching; counseling for parent, teacher, child; work-study assignment.

CRITERIA FOR PLACEMENT

1. Classification of pupil maladjustment used, e.g., habitually failing despite adequate intelligence; habitually unsatisfactory in attendance; acute disruptive behavior; seriously withdrawn and blocked in group setting; hallucinatory and delusionary and fugue episodes.
2. Premises for grouping.
3. Heterogeneities and homogeneities in grouping, e.g., age, sex, diagnosis, prognosis, grade level, IQ, reading ability, size of class, ratio of teacher to pupils, age range, degree and range of severity of disturbance, complexity of individual learning disabilities, possible inclusion of brain-damaged or mentally retarded children.

TRANSLATION OF RECOMMENDATIONS INTO ACTION PLAN

1. Procedure for implementing recommendations.
2. Written behavioral management plans.
3. Role of administrator, teacher, and parent.
4. Time lag between formulation of the recommendations and their translation into positive action.

INTERPRETATION OF FINDINGS TO SCHOOL STAFF AND PARENTS

1. Methods of communication, e.g., regular conferences.
2. Extent of sharing.
3. Opportunity for feedback.
4. Use of home visits.

MECHANISM FOR EVALUATING AND MODIFYING PLACEMENT

1. Procedures for evaluating and modifying placement.
2. Criteria for evaluating pupil's adjustment.
3. Stage at which evaluation is performed.
4. Parental involvement in evaluation.

CONTINUOUS ASSESSMENT PLANS

1. Procedures for periodic staffing of cases.
2. Participation of classroom teacher in case staffing.
3. Classroom observations by clinical personnel.

4. Schedules for retesting pupils.
5. Development of a record system.
    a. Progress notes.
    b. Inclusion in cumulative record files.
6. Feedback from parents.

1. Recording of final diagnosis.
2. Final outcomes in planning.
3. Providing data for future research.

Talking to a child is not equivalent to a psychiatric interview. Both plan and method are involved when the clinician interacts with a child.

To know how the psychiatrist goes about his work is not to know how to do it one's self. The intent here is not to make teachers into junior psychiatric interviewers. However, when a teacher reads a psychiatric report or has the opportunity for psychiatric consultation, the reaction is likely to be more productive if he understands the psychiatrist's approach. Of course, no two examiners would be identical in their procedure, but Dr. Shapiro covers the fundamental aspects in his article. We can see that the psychiatric examination is not rambling, random, or diffuse; unless the discourse, devious though it might seem to the outsider, covers a well-rounded series of items and leads to a substantial synthesis, it is not successful.

Psychiatric Examination of the Child

Marvin I. Shapiro

The psychiatric examination of a child may superficially bear very little resemblance to the psychiatric examination of an adult patient. Nonetheless, the interview with the child—although it may be conducted on the floor during a game of jacks or with the patient sitting on the examiner's lap sobbing over a broken toy—remains essentially a reapplication of basic principles of interviewing techniques in a different setting.

In developing an understanding of the emotional aspects of a child's difficulties, the pediatrician, general practitioner, psychiatrist or other worker may at first feel uncertain in his approach to the child. Many unexpected, disconcerting situations develop, and it is often not clear what to

look for during the contact with the child. Frequently all that is obtained from the examination is an impressionistic recollection of some outstanding trait or performance rather than a well-considered appraisal of the child and the problem. The mental status examination is useful in evaluating the personality of the adult patient. There has been no comparable standardized guide, however, for the psychiatric examination of the child.

The purpose of this communication is to present a form for the diagnostic evaluation of a child which organizes the many inferences that may be drawn from interaction with the child. . . .

BACKGROUND

Before taking up the examination itself, it will be useful to review some general concepts that help put the diagnostic activ-

Reprinted with permission from *Mental Hygiene*, 43 (January 1959), 32–39. Dr. Shapiro is assistant professor of child psychiatry at the Pittsburgh Child Guidance Center.

ity into proper perspective in the process of helping a child by means of psychiatric intervention.

The study of a child's difficulties must include an evaluation of the familial and environmental factors. In this paper, however, the focus is upon the child himself. It is helpful to keep in mind that while the doctor is going about his work the child is also busily appraising the doctor, and that the conclusions formed by the child will enter into the clinical behavior the doctor is observing.

The psychiatric examination differs from the medical or laboratory examination in that psychiatric examination, diagnosis and treatment go on simultaneously and cannot be separated from one another. Like a juggler, the examiner needs to coordinate the many aspects of his relation to the child. The emphasis in this outline will be upon organizing the information originating from the interview in such a way as to enable the doctor to act most effectively in behalf of the child and his problem. It is planned to consider what takes place during the psychiatric examination of a child, what is to be observed and tested. The problem of *how* to conduct the examination is outside the scope of this paper, as such skills are best gained under supervision and no fixed procedure for this can be easily described.

Prior to the examination, the doctor should have some general plans to help him organize the raw data of the child's behavior. He should have some ideas, obtained from a previous contact with the parents, as to what to expect. The purpose of the examination is to determine the nature of the problem, whether or not treatment is indicated and if so, who is to receive it—the child, the parents or both. An effort is made to categorize the problem in the classification system used in general psychiatry, and the doctor accumulates the evidence that permits him to diagnose the presence of organic brain damage, a psychotic disorder, a psychoneurosis, etc. When psychopathology is found, the doctor evaluates its severity, seeking to clarify whether the disturbance is a situational response and transitory or whether it has become part of the child's personality. The examiner's estimate of the treatability of the disturbance or of the child's capacity to change is just as important as the recognition of psychopathology.

With this as our orientation, we can turn to a consideration of the psychiatric examination. It is to be anticipated that the items suggested in this study are not to be used during the interview in the same order in which they appear in the outline. Rather, the form may be useful as a mental check list of the various elements which enter into the examination.

IDENTIFICATION

This is an orienting statement which forms the background and reason for the clinical evaluation of the child. The subsequent interview will attempt to answer the question implied here. Where the parent has a host of complaints regarding the child, it is important to identify the primary difficulty which is the most disturbing to the parent.

THE OUTLINE OF THE PSYCHIATRIC EXAMINATION OF THE CHILD

IDENTIFICATION
Name, age, sex, religion, color, ordinal position, reason for referral, who referred, first or second examination, etc.

APPEARANCE
Build, facial expression, clothing, health, defects in hearing, vision, etc., personality traits, mannerisms.

INTERPERSONAL RELATIONS

Interaction with parent—waiting room, degree and type of anxiety upon separation, response to reassurance, reaction upon rejoining parent.

Interaction with examiner—attitude: arrogant, suspicious, cooperative, etc.; capacity to relate; type of relation: trusting, controlling, erotic, etc.; role taken and role assigned to doctor; feeling aroused in reaction to patient; beginning compared to end of hour; first interview as compared to last.

CAPACITIES

Intelligence—estimated level: knowledge, imagination, grasp of situation; potential capacity.

Affects—mobility, appropriateness, predominant moods, shame, anger, depression, anxiety, etc., shifts in tension, somatic expressions as sweating, blushing.

Motor—coordination, gait, muscularity, use of hands, body, activity pattern, inhibited, immature, hyperactive, etc.

Speech—clarity of diction, of ideas, defects, vocabulary, pressure, spontaneity, voice quality, etc.

CONTENT (Attitudes, feelings, ideas, etc.)

Towards clinic visit—reaction to visit, grasp of purpose, awareness of difficulties, reaction to symptoms, feelings about return visits, participating in planning.

Towards self—Behavior, appearance, body, sex, intellect, worries, fears, preoccupations, etc.

Towards others—parents, siblings, relatives, peers, teachers.

Towards things—pets, hobbies, possessions, money, food, school.

PLAY AND FANTASY

Play—approach to and interest in toys, toys used, mode of play: incorporative, extrusive, intrusive, etc.; manner of play: constructive, disorganized, nurtural, etc., distractibility, play disruptions, etc.

Fantasy—wishes, dreams, daydreams, fantasies, ambitions.

CLINICAL IMPRESSION

Descriptive—summarize personality structure.
Dynamic—major areas of conflicts, mechanisms of adaptation.
Statistical—use standard nomenclature and code number.

PROGNOSIS

Benign, malignant, acute, chronic, with treatment, without treatment.

DISPOSITION

Further diagnostic studies, need for treatment, treatability, psychiatric therapy, environmental control.

TREATMENT

Individual, group, collaborative, consultative; frequency and estimated duration of therapy, goals, family management, countertransference impressions, general approach.

APPEARANCE

A vivid description of the impression that the child creates helps to establish a mental picture of the kind of child being examined. The items listed make no attempt to exhaust the descriptive possibilities. Some further items could include family resemblances in the facial expression, whether the child appears older or younger than his stated age, details of body care such as bitten nails or unkempt hair. Gross neurological signs such as facial asymmetry, disturbances of gait or nystagmus will suggest further medical investigation. The first few minutes of the interview may be regarded as having a far greater degree of intensity and therefore more significant influence upon the remainder of the interview than any other similar few minutes during the examination. Aichorn has emphasized the importance of the quick impression in the beginning moments of the interview when recognition of the dominant attitude and feelings of the child enable the doctor to respond most appropriately to the child.

INTERPERSONAL RELATIONS

Observation of the child in the waiting room often furnishes valuable clues as to the nature of the parent-child relationship. The physical closeness or apartness of the child and the parent, the attitude of the parent as expressed in voice tone and manner of handling the child, the reaction of the child and the parent to the separation— all these are noted in the first few moments of the study.

As a general procedure, it is preferable to plan for at least two diagnostic interviews. While one may be sufficient (and at another time three or four sessions may be indicated), two interviews permit the examiner to observe the changes in the child's responses to his visits. A child who remains detached and stolidly defensive in successive interviews presents a different task in the planning of therapy from the one who shows a progressive ability to relax and to relate. The former indicates that the char-

acter formation has already become involved and the child will probably require individual therapy regardless of any subsequent alteration in parental attitudes and behavior. In the latter case, the changing nature of the relationship indicates a greater elasticity of the child's personality. This in turn suggests that the attempt to change the parents' attitudes and relationship to the child will be an important part of the treatment plan.

The feelings aroused in the examiner in reaction to the child are another valid source of data. At the descriptive level, a child may appear to be silent and inhibited. Yet one child may be frozen with fright, another rigid with anger, and still a third provocatively teasing. The most sensitive recorder of these different moods remains the emotional response of the examiner.

CAPACITIES

Here is described both the endowment that the child possesses and his ability to use it freely. This includes the enduring assets as well as the outstanding liabilities which are observed in the child. The level of functioning and the degree of stability in maintaining this level form a base line against which future progress or regression can be measured. The manner of functioning that the child demonstrates may suggest the therapeutic approach to be used. One child may be over-intellectualized and need help in relation to isolation of emotional feelings. Another may act impulsively, indicating difficulty in controlling motor activities. Still another may be unusually sensitive and shrink from close contacts with people.

The examiner is alert for fluctuations in the level of performance—such as flashes of intelligence, which help in the differential diagnosis of a brain-injured child or a mentally retarded one.

CONTENT

It is helpful to gain some understanding of the child's ideas and feelings about coming to see the doctor. The preparation of the child for the examination should be reviewed beforehand with the parents. It is usually quite revealing to observe the results of preparation, not only in terms of the child's personality but also in terms of the parent-child relationship. There are many possibilities to explore: The child may not have heard what was said to him, or he may have distorted the information, or the parent may have been unable to be direct with the child in this matter.

During the examination the child should be prepared by the examiner for other procedures such as psychological tests, and for future visits. The child's ability or inability to express his feelings about such important figures as his parents helps the examiner to map out the sensitive areas in the child's living experiences. The overall total response of the child to the new situation throws light upon the character formation and the defenses that the child characteristically uses in meeting life's stresses. The child's appropriate or inappropriate response to the clinic setting furnishes an opportunity for estimating the capacity to adapt.

The doctor needs to be familiar with the series of problems that each child meets in growing up and to evaluate the current difficulties in terms of the successful or unsuccessful integration of these successive stages of psychosexual development. The individual problem may appear in the form of a currently unrealistic belief about the world or about himself. It may show up as an exaggerated feeling or absence of feeling, or an inability to act, or a preoccupation with one particular activity, or indeed any combination of any or all of these. Once identified, the tendencies should be cautiously tested to see whether it is flexible and reversible or whether it has become isolated from the influences of daily living and part of the character of the child.

Throughout all of his efforts to understand the child, the examiner does not simply probe for factual material but creates the atmosphere which is most favorable for

a spontaneous interchange of matters of interest to the child.

PLAY AND FANTASY

The child's fantasy life and play activity offer significant indicators of the unconscious determinants which enter into his behavior. Through these media, as through dreams, the needs and wishes that are too anxiety-provoking to be directly expressed find discharge. A child can be encouraged to share his fantasies by such questions as "If you could make three magic wishes, what would you wish for?" or "What do you want to be when you grow up?" or "What is your favorite program on television?" The doctor can express his interest in hearing about dreams which the child enjoyed and dreams which were frightening to him. This tension-releasing function of fantasy and play is not only of service to our diagnostic purpose, but also indicates the therapeutic openings which can be used in helping the child gradually express his desires and fears more freely.

While the emphasis in this paper has been upon a verbal interchange, at times it may be desirable to use play materials such as dolls, clay or pencil and paper to help the child express himself. The experience and personal preference of the examiner will help decide the choice of such aids. A few dolls in a family scene may help the child relate how he feels about an emotionally-charged aspect of his home life. If he shows an interest in drawing pictures he may be asked to tell a story about them. As the child talks, the examiner listens for the particular affect, such as shame or anxiety or anger, which appears as a persistent thread woven into the fabric of the stories and dreams. It is this thread that is so important in understanding the painful feelings against which the child needs to defend himself.

The mode of play item has been adapted from Erikson and refers to the principal way that the child functions or, to put it differently, to his main style of life.

For example, the hyperactive child who is unusually curious and prematurely pugnacious, who literally gets into everything, may be using this intrusive form of behavior to express unresolved phallic strivings. Sudden alteration or disintegration of a play activity is carefully noted as a sign of increasing tension, and the examiner relates the disruption in play to what has just preceded it.

CLINICAL IMPRESSION

These separate diagnostic impressions summarize the significant findings which have emerged from the examination. The child is described as to what type of a person he is and how he tends to deal with his difficulties. From the review of his observation and participation, the doctor also infers what the sources of the difficulties are. The value of a statistical diagnosis lies more in the direction of recording information about similar clinical problems in order to gain a broader base for our understanding, rather than of being of immediate clinical use with the child.

The diagnosis of psychopathology in the child is less definitive than the diagnosis of psychopathology found in the adult. The immaturity of the child and the flexibility of his defenses allow for a shifting of patterns of response to stress. An understanding of this prepares the doctor for the discrepancies he will often meet where the child's reported problem is so different from what is actually observed clinically. The interview is part of a total dynamic interplay of forces, and the relatively isolated sample of behavior which is noted will limit the scope of conclusions to be made. Still, a working hypothesis that allows practical, realistic action to be taken can almost always be synthesized from the various data that have been accumulated up to this point.

PROGNOSIS

A projected course of events may be considered in terms of a historical review of the problem as it has developed up to the present time. While the doctor is unable to predict every adaptive stress that the child will face, he may be able to anticipate some. For instance, it may be expected that an 8-year-old patient who shows a potentially psychotic disorder will have considerable difficulty in handling the problems of adolescence, and perhaps may be unable to manage them with success. Social and economic realities, the stability of the family unit, the intelligence and concern of the parents are some of the significant factors to be weighed in the prognosis. To these the doctor adds his judgment of the malignant or benign quality of the child's difficulty as it appeared during the examination.

DISPOSITION

Here the doctor recommends the next step to be taken in the management of the child's problem. The primary decision to be made is in regard to the treatability within the setting where the child is examined. In a clinic where different workers may see the child and his parents, the assignment of the collaborating therapist is considered. Recommendations for further medical studies are also made when necessary.

TREATMENT

Once the need for and the feasibility of psychotherapy have been established, further details of treatment are to be considered. The decision of who is to receive treatment—the child, the parent or both—is important. The type and frequency of therapy—whether supportive or uncovering, individual or group—should be considered. The goal of therapy and the problems that might be anticipated should be recorded as well. These matters are not regarded as fixed and unalterable but are to be changed when indicated.

DISCUSSION

While the technical problems of interviewing do not lend themselves readily to didactic analysis, it may be fruitful to reflect upon some of the special situations which often arise in work with children.

Recognizing that the child often comes unwillingly, the doctor is prepared to meet and help his patient, who is frequently most uncooperative. If possible, the doctor sees the child alone in order to observe how he handles himself when he is on his own. With some children, however, the separation may stir up such an overwhelming amount of anxiety as to threaten to disrupt self-control. In these situations the parent is asked to accompany the child until a tolerance for the separation is developed. The principle here is the same as is found in all fields of medicine: The doctor himself should do no harm and must not introduce a new traumatic experience into the problem.

Should the child angrily refuse to accompany the doctor to his office, the doctor responds as appropriately as possible to each specific situation. He accepts the child's anger as an expression of anxiety over the examination. At the same time, he helps the child avoid feelings of shame which could arise afterwards if infantile, regressive behavior were allowed to control the situation. This is accomplished by the firm insistence that the examination be carried out. By his own direct participation the child has the opportunity to see that his fears about it were unrealistic. In the case of a pre-school child the examiner may simply pick up the child in the waiting room and carry him into the office. This, however, would be humiliating for a child of school age, who is no longer accustomed to such physical control by parent-figures; here the doctor would be acting more appropriately to take the child firmly by the arm and lead him into the office. This illustrates an important point, namely, that the doctor needs to adapt his own behavior and expectations concerning the child's performances to the age and personality of each patient he sees. The needs and problems of the pre-school toddler are different from those of the adolescent, and each requires a modification in the clinical approach used by the doctor.

The question of the use of physical force is often a source of personal difficulty in professional work with children. The doctor is ready to act whenever necessary to keep the situation within limits of comfort and safety. If verbal controls do not suffice, then physical control may be required. The confident readiness and unambivalence of the doctor is actually reassuring to the child, who may have anxiety over his own lack of self-control.

The real dependence of the child upon adults requires that the doctor be aware of his dual role. He is both a parent-surrogate as well as a physician and cannot remain completely impersonal in his relation to the child. In an interview with an adult patient who breaks down and starts to cry, the doctor waits until he has regained composure. In the case of a young child, however, the doctor does not remain so detached, but offers the child his own handkerchief or draws him close for physical comforting. In working with the pre-school child, the physical nearness of the examiner may be used to help establish the relationship. It is often of value for the examiner to pick up a child who is sitting alone and feeling very alone and hold him on his lap. If a child remains absolutely silent in the face of the examiner's attempts to relate to him, it may be helpful to gently take the child's pulse rate. A racing pulse suggests that the child is struggling to control inner tension, while a relatively normal pulse rate indicates a greater degree of ego participation in the resistance.

In this fashion the diagnostic process demands active participation by the doctor so that bits of behavior can be properly evaluated. A careful consideration of the physiological factors, psychosexual development and cultural background is necessary for the analysis of any one clinical problem.

Since the major portion of this paper has been centered around the facets of examination and diagnosis, a reconsideration of therapy during the interview should be added to restore balance in this matter of helping a child in difficulty. Since the child is most often brought to the clinic because of the parents' concern, his initial position is a passive one. The symptomatology for which the parents are seeking help may in no way correspond to the worries or concerns that the child has about himself. Part of the purpose of the visit, therefore, from a therapeutic point of view, is to interpret the interview in terms of what the child himself wants or is worried about or would like to be helped with. We seek, at all times, to engage the child's own participation in the therapeutic process. If this concern with the child's own preoccupation is lacking, the examination will tend to remain an objective description of the child and his functioning, and the child's own emotional investment will be minimal. Ideally, his contact with the doctor should be a constructive experience in living for the child. It should expand his trust of adults and begin to supply the help he needs.

References

Aichhorn, August. *Wayward Youth.* New York: Viking Press, 1935.

Erikson, Erik H. *Childhood and Society.* New York: W. W. Norton, 1950.

There are reasons for planning studies to meet particular needs, and there are advantages to using systematic, standardized procedures, especially when one wants to compare findings with those of others.

Eli Bower leads the list of the researchers doing school screening for adjustment vulnerability. He and Nadine Lambert have designed and marketed, through the Educational Testing Service, devices which work K-12 (from kindergarten through twelfth grade). Anyone interested in either the theory or practice of screening should study these publications and instruments in detail. They are ingenious and practical.

Perhaps the most significant factor in Bower and Lambert's approach is the threefold study. Rather than depending upon teachers alone, personality tests alone, or peer perceptions alone, they use a combination. The problem in screening is to get behind the denials and defenses of a pupil, the possible biases of a teacher, and to somehow take advantage of the knowledge found in the peer culture. These are all access points within the confines of the school milieu:

1. *Teachers rate pupil behavior:* Using a normal distribution grid, the teacher indicates the relative position of each student on eight scales.

2. *Peer perceptions:* Finding out how other pupils feel about a given pupil is an important screening procedure. Several devices appropriate to the age level cover this area.

3. *Self-perception:* With different devices, it is possible to get self-concept data on all levels.

It must be remembered that these three data sources are to be collated and weighted through specific procedures that finally result in one total evaluation.

In-School Screening of Children with Emotional Handicaps

Eli M. Bower and Nadine M. Lambert

WHAT IS MEANT BY "EMOTIONALLY HANDICAPPED"?

An understanding of what is meant by "emotionally handicapped" is a prerequisite for effective use of the screening process. Mental or emotional health is inferred from the degree of freedom an individual has in choosing from among alternative kinds of behavior. Conversely, mental or emotional disturbance can be inferred from individual behavior which is limited, inflexible, and restricted. Such limitations or restrictions serve to reduce the individual's relative freedom of choice in social and educational endeavors. The reduction of personal maneuverability and flexibility in a changing environment increases the individual's difficulties in adapting to the pressures and changes of life. As a result, the emotionally handicapped person shows increasing susceptibility to behavioral difficulties and interpersonal friction. . . .

Specifically, the emotionally handicapped child is defined as having moderate to marked reduction in behavioral freedom, which in turn reduces his ability to function effectively in learning or working with others. In the classroom, this loss of freedom affects the child's educative and social experiences and results in a noticeable susceptibility to one or more of these five patterns of behavior:

1. *An inability to learn which cannot be adequately explained by intellectual, sensory, neurophysiological, or general*

Eli Bower is Deputy Director, Liaison and Prevention Services, California State Department of Mental Hygiene, Sacramento, Calif. Nadine Lambert is Professor of Education, University of California, Berkeley, California.

health factors. An inability to learn is, perhaps, the single most significant characteristic of emotionally handicapped children in school. Non-learning of this kind may be manifested as an inability to profit from *any* school learning experiences as well as an inability to master skill subjects. The non-learner may fall behind almost imperceptibly in the first few grades but finds himself in deep water by the time he reaches 4th grade. There are some students, too, who seem to be keeping pace until they reach junior high school, when they begin to flounder badly.

By whatever symptoms the inability manifests itself, we will, as educators, seek the cause or causes. And once we have ruled out intellectual, sensory, neurophysiological, and general health factors, there remain emotional conflicts and resistances to be investigated as major causes of learning disabilities.

2. *An inability to build or maintain satisfactory interpersonal relationships with peers and teachers.* It is not just "getting along" with others that is significant here. The term "satisfactory interpersonal relations" refers to the ability to demonstrate sympathy and warmth toward others, the ability to stand alone when necessary, the ability to have close friends, the ability to be aggressively constructive, and the ability to enjoy working and playing with others as well as to enjoy working and playing by oneself. In most instances, children who are unable to build or maintain satisfactory interpersonal relationships are noticed by their peers, or are most clearly *visible* to their peers. Teachers, however, are also able to identify many such children after a period of observation.

3. *Inappropriate or immature types of behavior or feelings under normal conditions.* Inappropriateness of behavior or feeling can often be sensed by the teacher and

peer groups. "He acts like a baby almost all the time," or "He acts funny lots of times," are judgments often heard that describe such behavior. The teacher may find some children reacting to a simple command, like "Please take your seat," in wildly disparate or incongruous ways. What is appropriate or inappropriate, mature or immature, is best judged by the teacher using his professional training, his daily and long-term observation of the child, and his experience working and interacting with the behavior of large numbers of children.

4. *A general pervasive mood of unhappiness or depression.* Children who are unhappy most of the time may demonstrate such feelings in expressive play, art work, written composition, or in discussion periods. They seldom smile and usually lack a "joy of living" in their school work or social relationships. In the middle or upper grades a self-inventory is usually helpful in confirming suspicions about such feelings.

5. *A tendency to develop physical symptoms, such as speech problems, pains, or fears, associated with personal or school problems.* Often, this tendency is first noted by the child himself. Illness may be linked regularly to school pressures or develop when a child's confidence in himself is under stress. Speech difficulties resulting from emotional distress are usually painfully audible to the teacher and parent.

To sum up, then: the significant patterns of behavior in children indicating a need for closer scrutiny by a teacher are: inability to learn, unsatisfactory interpersonal relationships, inappropriate behavior, unhappiness, repetitive symptoms of illness after stress. . . .

WHAT IS MEANT BY "SCREENING"?

A major caution in the use of the instruments and process described in this *Technical Report* is to be aware of the fact that this is a *screening* process, and is *not* intended for diagnosis or classification.

A second caution: the screening proc-ess has little to say about the causes of emotional difficulties. It has been designed to answer the question: Which children are not functioning well in a particular behavioral dimension? It cannot answer these questions: What caused the difficulty? Is the difficulty serious or minor and transitory? What can be done about it?

The purpose of screening in the area of emotional handicaps is similar to the purposes of other screening activities carried on by the school: for example, the screening programs for vision and hearing problems. To illustrate: the vision screening program in California public schools has four objectives which would be equally applicable in screening for emotional handicaps:

1. To insure early in their school careers a more adequate identification of pupils with defects;

2. To help pupils with defects to receive more intensive individual study and, if necessary, remedial services;

3. To help teachers become aware of such disabilities and to help teachers to cope with disabilities educationally;

4. To provide necessary educational adjustments for groups of pupils in the school who can profit from such programs.

Effective screening for emotional handicaps is dependent on procedures or instruments which can be administered, scored, and interpreted with the same ease and effectiveness as those for screening visual handicaps. The efficacy and economy of screening for emotional handicaps are based on the assumption that some defects or handicaps can be detected early and remedied with greater ease and less effort than handicaps allowed to develop fully.

The same thoughtful professional care and discretion need to be exercised in this type of screening as in any other. Parents need to be informed about the objectives of the process and to be assured that the school will follow up the screening by advising and consulting with those parents whose children may need additional help. The administrator and the teaching staff need to understand the purposes of the program and to carry out the procedures of the process in an informed and motivated manner. The entire procedure, including the administration and scoring of each instrument, has been developed to ease the burden of work for the teacher. Effective screening, however, does not occur through effortless magic. Teachers and administrators will need to put the same effort and attention into the details of this screening process as they would into testing vision, hearing, or achievement. . . .

Certain broad criteria emerged as likely to be important in any process for the screening of children subject to or susceptible to emotional disturbance, especially in a process to be used on a large scale in many schools:

1. It should be possible to complete the screening procedure with only such information as the teacher could obtain without outside technical or professional assistance;

2. The procedure should be sufficiently simple and straightforward for the average teacher to undertake without long training or daily supervision;

3. The results of the procedure should be *tentative identification* of children with emotional problems—leading the teacher to *refer* to competent specialists those children who could benefit most from thorough diagnosis;

4. As a corollary to 3 above, the procedure should *not* encourage the teacher to diagnose emotional problems, nor to draw conclusions about their causes, nor to label or categorize children; in fact, the procedure should actively discourage the teacher from undertaking any of these highly technical interpretations;

5. The procedure should be one which neither invades the privacy of individuals nor violates good taste;

6. The procedure should be one which does not offer a threat to any child;

7. The procedure should be inexpensive to use.

With these criteria, and others that emerged as the work progressed, develop-

ment was begun of screening procedures for identification of emotionally disturbed children at several different levels of schooling.

BEHAVIOR RATING OF PUPILS (All Grades)

One of the most important and useful kinds of information obtained by the school is the teacher's professional judgment of children's behavior. Teachers see children over a period of time in a variety of circumstances: in stress situations, at work and at play. Their judgment and observation have been sharpened by professional training and by day-to-day experience with the normal behavior of children. Often the teacher's rating can be the single most effective index of a pupil's growth and development.

Few professional persons, no matter how well-trained, can make ratings of others with absolute certainty and complete comfort. Don't spend too much time worrying about whether your rating for a particular child is "right" or "wrong." Make your best judgment of each student, then go on to the next. Remember that it is not your judgment alone that will be used to determine whether or not a pupil is developing emotional difficulties. Your perception of a child's behavior will be combined with the perceptions of the child himself and those of his peers—to make the final judgment about screening a child.

THE CLASS PICTURES (Peer Rating—Kindergarten to Grade 3)

After you have completed the *Behavior Rating of Pupils*, your next step in screening is to plan for administration of the peer ratings. The peer rating instrument for kindergarten and primary grades, *The Class Pictures*, must be given to each child in your class individually. This may take fifteen to twenty minutes of time for each child. Administration of *The Class Pictures* to the entire class, however, may be spread over a period of time—up to, but not exceeding, one month.

Administer the instrument to children one at a time when the rest of the class is engaged in seat work of some kind or occupied in other activities which do not require constant supervision. Such a schedule will require a minimum of interruption in your regular teaching program.

The Class Pictures are composed of twelve picture cards with a total of twenty scoring items (one or two items on a card). Five of the items are pictures of boys in situations related to emotionally maladjusted behavior; five are pictures of girls in situations related to emotionally maladjusted behavior; five are pictures of boys in situations related to positive or neutral types of behavior; and five are pictures of girls in situations related to positive or neutral types of behavior.

The Class Pictures have been developed as a means of analyzing, in a systematic and measurable way, how children are perceived or "seen" by their peers. The responses of most pupils to the pictures will not surprise you. Some responses, however, may seem unrealistic and inappropriate. *Accept each child's responses without comment unless the child obviously misunderstands directions.* Your role during the administration of *The Class Pictures* is one of test proctor and recorder of responses.

The Class Pictures are used with children who have not yet learned to read or write well. Therefore, the responses of each child will need to be recorded individually by you. You will, of course, have to make special provision for the rest of the class while you are administering *Class Pictures* to individual children. If an additional school person is available, he may work with the class while you administer *Class Pictures*. The actual administration should always be done by you. If you are able to organize the class into working groups, *Class Pictures* may be administered to a few individuals daily during such work periods—but you will decide for yourself how best to accomplish this task.

On the test each child is asked to consider which of his classmates is most like the child in every one of the twenty situations. Some children will pick twenty different names. Others may name one or two peers for several or many different items. Still others may make no response for one or more items. *Do not expect any fixed pattern of responses.*

When the responses for every child in the class are collected, the teacher can tally the number of times a particular child is chosen for each of the twenty pictures. The total number of times a child is chosen for *all* of the pictures indicates how clearly or how vividly he is "seen," or perceived, by his peers.

The number of times a pupil is picked for the ten *negative* pictures indicates the degree to which he or she is *negatively* perceived by his peers. By dividing the number of times a child is picked for the ten negative pictures by the total number of times he is picked for all twenty of the pictures, a per cent, indicating the ratio of negative perception by peers, is obtained and used in screening.

The mean or average number of negative selections of emotionally handicapped boys and girls has been found to be significantly different from the mean number of negative selections in the general school population of that grade and sex. Consequently, the per cent of negative perception has been found to be a reliable indicator of those children whose behavior, as observed by peers, indicates some degree of emotional difficulty. The higher the per cent, the greater the possibility that the child has emotional problems. The per cent of negative selections on *The Class Pictures*, when combined with teacher ratings and self ratings, has been found effective in primary grades for screening children with emotional handicaps.

A CLASS PLAY (Peer Rating—Grades 3–7)

A Class Play is a peer rating instrument with greatest applicability in grades 4, 5, and 6, though it has been used with success in grades 3 and 7. It should be administered reasonably soon after you have completed the *Behavior Rating of Pupils.* It should take no more than 35 to 45 minutes.

Section I of the instrument contains descriptions of twenty hypothetical roles in a play, with instructions directing each pupil to choose a classmate who would be most suitable and natural in each of the roles. A second section of the *Play* (Section II) elicits from each pupil an indication of the roles he would prefer, or which he thinks other people would select for him. This section has thirty different quartets of the twenty roles, with a question aimed at finding out how the child sees himself in relation to each role.

The scoring of *A Class Play* is very much like the scoring of *The Class Pictures.* Each pupil names a classmate for each of the roles in the play. By counting the number of times a pupil is picked for each of the roles in the play, and then counting the number of times each pupil is picked for the *even numbered* (negative) roles, a percentage is obtained indicative of the positive or negative perception of each pupil by his classmates. This score is used in the screening. . . .

STUDENT SURVEY (Peer Rating —Grades 7–12)

The *Student Survey* is the peer rating instrument for use in the junior and senior high schools. In order for this test to have validity, it is necessary to administer it to a class in which the students have had an opportunity for some social and intellectual interaction, as well as for observation of one another in a variety of classroom situations. Previous work with this test has shown that social studies or English classes are usually best for this purpose.

Some students in the junior and senior high school may be sensitive to the kinds of questions asked on the *Student Survey.* It is important, therefore, that you anticipate the possibility of such sensitivity and take steps to allay any suspicion or resentment. For example, some teachers have found it

helpful to have ready an envelope into which all the tests can be placed when the students are finished. This helps to reassure the class that the test results are confidential and reinforces statements made in the instructions that the results will not be discussed with others.

Section I of the *Student Survey* consists of twenty items. Ten are illustrative of maladjusted or emotionally disturbed behavior and ten are illustrative of neutral or positive behavior. For each statement of behavior, the students are asked to list the name of a classmate who is most like the student described in the item.

Section II of the *Student Survey* contains the same twenty behavior statements randomly arranged in thirty groups of four statements each. The student is asked to select one of the four statements in each group as the one which he thinks others in the class might apply to him, or which he thinks would apply to himself. The responses to Section II can be used to compare the peer ratings of a student with his self rating. The value of providing two sections in the *Student Survey,* a peer rating and a self-rating on the same items, is, that after scoring both sections, the teacher is able to measure and analyze how a student sees himself in relation to how he is seen by others. . . .

A PICTURE GAME (Self Rating— Kindergarten to Grade 3)

A Picture Game is designed to give a measure of young children's perception of *self.* It is used along with the *Behavior Rating of Pupils* (teacher rating) and *The Class Pictures* (peer rating) to identify pupils who are vulnerable to, or handicapped by, emotional problems.

A Picture Game consists of 66 pictures, including two sample pictures. Each picture is illustrative of normal home and school relationships and events. With the exception of the two sample cards and the first ten pictures, each picture is emotionally neutral in the portrayal of the relationship or event. The child is asked to sort each picture into one of two categories: "This is a happy picture" or "This is a sad picture." The sorting is done by placing each picture in the "happy" or "sad" side of a two-compartment box which has a happy face shown on one compartment and a sad face on the other. The child categorizes each picture in accordance with his perception of it.

The first ten pictures the child sorts are stereotypes: obviously happy or obviously sad situations. The purpose of including them in the test items is to check on each pupil's understanding of the task. If a child sorts the first ten pictures correctly, you can be fairly sure that he has understood the process well enough for you to use his score in screening. If, on the other hand, he does not sort the first ten pictures correctly, you will need to meet with him individually and ask him to sort the pictures again for you, making certain that he understands the process. Some children *choose* to place pictures differently from others. If you find that such children understand the process but continue, on re-administration, to sort the pictures in an independent fashion, make a note of it on the "Class Record Sheet," and use the child's score in screening. . . .

THINKING ABOUT YOURSELF
(Self Rating—Grades 3–7)

The purpose of *Thinking About Yourself* is to elicit from the pupil himself an *intra-self* measure of the relationship between a pupil's perception of his environment and his conception of what it ought to be. What is looked for is the degree of discrepancy between a pupil's self perception and an ideal self, between his perception of himself as he *is* and as he would like to be.

Many pupils with serious emotional problems cannot bring themselves to disclose their difficulties in writing, or are uncomfortable about disclosing them. Their

responses will therefore very much resemble those of other children in the class. These youngsters are most likely to be screened by teachers and peers.

There are other pupils, however, who do not manifest their difficulties to teachers or peers, but who rise to the opportunity to express inner discomfort and *can* communicate their disturbance on a self rating instrument. Since the average discrepancy between self and *ideal* self has been found to discriminate between pupils with emotional problems and those with normal behavior adjustment, *Thinking About Yourself* provides a meaningful and useful screening dimension not available from teacher or peer ratings. . . .

A SELF TEST (Self Rating—Grades 7–12)

A Self Test is intended to obtain a measure of the difference between the way a pupil sees himself and the way he would like to be—in other words, a measure of the difference between self and ideal self. To the extent that a student is able to disclose the differences or similarities between these two aspects of self, the instrument is useful in screening. However, some pupils with moderate or serious emotional problems cannot bring themselves to disclose the discomfort or dissatisfaction which this instrument invites them to disclose. Their responses, therefore, will very much resemble those of other students in the class. These youngsters are more likely to be identified by teachers and peers in the screening process.

There are other pupils, however, who do not manifest their difficulties to teachers or peers, but who rise to the opportunity to express inner discomfort and *can* communicate their disturbance on a self rating. For these students, the *Self Test* provides the opportunity. Since the average discrepancy between self and *ideal* self has been found to discriminate between pupils with emotional problems and those with normal behavior adjustment, *A Self Test* provides a meaningful screening dimension not available from teacher or peer ratings.

A Self Test contains forty statements describing people behaving in a number of different ways. In Section I, the student is asked to indicate how strongly he *would like* to be or *would not like* to be the person described. In Section II, the items are re-peated and the student is asked to indicate how strongly he feels he *is* like or *is not* like the person described. The two responses by the student (i.e., whether or not he *wants* to be like and whether or not he *is* like) are then compared in the scoring process, after which the amount of discrepancy between the two "selves" is compared. . . .

Now we turn to a highly structured diagnostic approach. The educator needs a specific diagnosis which will lead to educational "treatment." He needs to determine the pupil's assets and handicaps for doing class work. Academic progress is one index of adjustment, but the reverse is also true; academic functioning can be a method of facilitating adjustment. What are the educational capacities of the disturbed child? Can emotional and organic components be analyzed? Kirk and Bateman see this type of study as developing into a total system of differential diagnosis, as they indicate in their conclusion.

Diagnosis and Remediation of Learning Disabilities

Samuel A. Kirk and Barbara Bateman

Disabilities and disturbances in learning processes have long been of interest to various professions. The medical professions, especially neurologists, have been concerned with finding physiological and structural correlates of specific learning disorders. Pathology in particular brain areas has been related to certain disabilities. . . .

For the past several years, interest at the Institute for Research on Exceptional Children has been concentrated on the development of a scientific pedagogy in the area of learning disabilities. Psychological factors in language (psycholinguistic) functions with young children has been the specific concern. A scientific pedagogy in this field requires (a) the development of behavioral diagnostic instruments of such a nature that the specific psycholinguistic disabilities can be differentiated and identified; (b) validation of these tests by research studies; and (c) determination of the educability of psycholinguistic disabilities through longitudinal training of a select group of children.

At the present time the experimental edition of the Illinois Test of Psycholinguistic Abilities is itself being extensively tested, and a few children are receiving tutoring.

The test, its theoretical background, rationale, and illustrations of its diagnostic uses are discussed by Kirk and McCarthy (1961). The present edition of the ITPA assesses six psycholinguistic abilities involving meaningful use of language (auditory decoding, vocal encoding, auditory-vocal association, visual decoding, motor encoding, and visual-motor association) and three abilities involving automatic usage (auditory-vocal automatic, auditory-vocal sequential, and visual-motor sequential).

Three recent studies using the ITPA have demonstrated its usefulness and validity as a differential diagnostic test, and have also pointed out its limitations. Olson (1960) found that the test differentiates children who are deaf, sensory aphasic, and expressive aphasic. Bateman's (1962) study estab-

From *Exceptional Children*, XXIX, No. 2 (October 1962), 73–78. Reprinted by permission of the authors and the Council for Exceptional Children.

lished the usefulness of this test with children who have severe visual defects, short of legal blindness, and thus suggested that the test primarily measures central psychological processes which appear to be relatively independent of sensory processes or acuity. A study by Kass (1962) found that children with normal intelligence, but with severe learning disabilities in the area of reading, show deficits in the automatic-sequential, or second-level abilities, while they perform normally on the tests at the representational or meaning level. That is, their comprehension and association abilities to deal meaningfully with language are not deficient, but their performance on the automatic aspects of language usage is inferior. In addition to providing new, useful knowledge about some psychological correlates of severe reading disabilities, Kass's study also pointed up the desirability of expanding the ITPA to include more tests at the automatic usage level.

The present problem is to determine whether children who show significant deficits in some areas of psycholinguistic functions can improve in these functions if special training on their deficits is offered. Currently a case study method is used to (a) make a study of the child, (b) determine whether the child has a specific learning disability in the psycholinguistic area, (c) organize a tutorial remedial program for the purpose of ameliorating his deficits, and (d) re-examine the child with psychometric tests and with the ITPA. Through a series of such case studies, in a sense using a child as his own contrast, the investigators hope to define more clearly the patterns of disabilities found in children and the correlation of these clinical disabilities to other characteristics, and to determine the extent and the rate at which one can help to ameliorate these deficits.

To illustrate the present stage of research and the methods currently employed in a field in which conventionally controlled research is not feasible, a case study is given.

WH was referred to the institute by his parents when he was four years of age. He had been excluded from a nursery school because of his inability to adjust, and because the authorities felt he was mentally defective. He was the only child of parents of professional status. Observations and test reports by other agencies suggested that he was quite severely retarded in social development, motor coordination, and speech. Both walking and talking had been developmentally delayed. No physical abnormalities were noted by the medical examiners.

When initially tested, WH was 4–7. His Binet IQ was 82 and his Minnesota Preschool verbal IQ was 83. However, he obtained scores in the average range on the non-verbal Minnesota Preschool (103) and the Peabody Picture Vocabulary Test (97). The solid line in Figure 1 shows these psychometric results, converted to age scores, and his ITPA profile.

It will be noted from Figure 1 that his primary psycholinguistic deficits appear in the visual-motor association, motor encoding, and visual-motor sequential abilities. All of these disabilities involve the visual-motor language channel. Because his visual decoding ability was average and other observations suggested that perhaps the motor encoding difficulty was primary, it was decided to plan tutorial remediation in the area of motor encoding.

Early tutoring activities were planned to elicit gross motor activities such as marching, running, jumping, and hopping in a manner suggested by Kephart (1960) for brain-damaged children. Stages in developing these activities included alternately moving arms and legs, imitating the tutor's movements in such games as "Follow the Leader," and moving by verbal command and in response to music.

Readiness for motor encoding itself (expressing ideas motorically) included drawing, finger painting, directional drawing, and building with and arranging blocks.

WH was retested after three and one-half months of remedial work, as shown by the dotted line in Figure 1. Figure 1 shows that the only area in which WH showed appreciable gain in the test after the brief

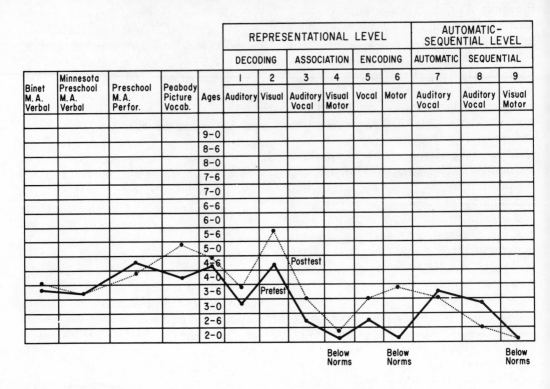

Figure 1. Comparison of Illinois Test of Psycholinguistic Abilities pretest and posttest profile for WH

three and one-half months of remediation was in motor encoding. (At this stage in research, we feel that a change of two years is the minimum that can be accepted as significant with children in WH's age range.) It is interesting to note that neither of the other abilities improved beyond the gain expected from maturation, in spite of the improvement shown in motor encoding. WH's tutoring will continue and perhaps, at a later date, it will be determined whether work on his motor encoding disability will irradiate to the presumably related disabilities, or whether it will be necessary to plan instruction for these areas directly. . . .

The case presented above is an illustration of a psychodiagnostic approach to some forms of learning disabilities in children, and the use of this diagnosis in deciding on the appropriate techniques of remediation for the child's major deficits.

There are two basic approaches to rehabilitation. One approach is to capitalize on the assets of an individual rather than to pay direct attention to his handicaps or deficits. For example, since mentally retarded children have difficulty in learning to read or to do arithmetic but presumably can accomplish handwork, the programs for the mentally retarded for years have emphasized handwork and minimized academic work. In the education of the deaf, teaching speech is a major area of difficulty. The tendency in some schools is to minimize speech and to emphasize manual forms of communication.

The philosophy of remediation which has been adopted here is to emphasize the development of the areas of major deficits found in the psycholinguistic profile. The hypothesis is that, although the child may have a biological or emotional factor which has inhibited the development of some functions, a part of the deficit in the child is the result of psychological withdrawal from activities requiring use of the deficient ability.

It is likely that during the growing stages the child exercises functions in which he can be successful, and avoids activities in which he faces failure. As a result he later shows marked deficits in some areas and normal performance in others. If a child has difficulty in speech and obtains his desired ends through motor encoding his profile may show low vocal encoding and high motor encoding. If he learns by and exercises his auditory decoding abilities, but does not succeed at an early age in understanding what is seen, or visual decoding, he will later have higher auditory than visual decoding ability.

The present problem is to determine whether the marked deficits found in some children can be developed, and to what extent these disabilities can be ameliorated. The remedial procedures that have been used are based upon two factors; (a) the major disability or disabilities that need amelioration, and (b) the level of functioning at which we have to initiate remedia-

tion. If the child shows, as did WH in Figure 1, a major deficit in motor encoding, that is one area that needs development. But the activities required to develop this ability had to start at the two year level where he was then functioning. . . .

References

Bateman, Barbara D. *Reading and Psycholinguistic Processes of Partially Seeing Children.* Monogr. Council Except. Child., 1, No. 5 (1962).

Kass, Corrine E. "Some Psychological Correlates of Severe Reading Disability." Unpublished doctoral dissertation. University of Illinois, 1962.

Kephart, N. *The slow learner in the classroom.* Columbus, Ohio: Charles E. Merrill Books, Inc., 1960.

Kirk, S. A., and J. J. McCarthy. "The Illinois Test of Psycholinguistic Abilities—an Approach to Differential Diagnosis." *Amer. J. ment. Defic.,* 1961, 66, 399–412.

Olson, J. L. "A Comparison of Sensory Aphasia, Expressive Aphasia and Deaf Children on the Illinois Test of Language Ability." Unpublished doctoral dissertation. University of Illinois, 1960.

OVERALL INCIDENCE OF DISTURBANCE

We do not know how many disturbed children there actually are. Criteria of disturbance and the personnel making the judgments differ from study to study. Furthermore, we do not agree on categorizations of the problem syndrome a pupil presents. There are almost as many schemes as there are researchers doing the studies. For these reasons, general incidence statistics are difficult to come by, and there have been many attempts to organize the welter of statistical data into some illuminating format.

One area to be examined in determining the overall incidence of emotional disturbance involves those who were excluded because they did not "fit" in the classroom situation. The fact that they *had* to be excluded, in essence, constitutes a definition of disturbance. The causes, of course, are many. However, those disturbed children who are not a problem to others, because they do not act out will not be numbered among those excluded, even though they may be very sick.

We seldom have an opportunity to study a large number of the "excluded" cases, and follow-up work with such a population is rare. Therefore, the survey done by Lyons and Powers is particularly valuable. They study pupils who are often candidates for special classes for the disturbed. The particular impact of the first grade is clear in their study, as is the fact that several early school months may pass by before teachers give up and exclude. Most of us consider exemption as a negative influence in a child's life. Unfortunately some educators think otherwise and even call it "suspension therapy." The importance of the particular teacher in the pupil's survival in school is all too clear.

Study of Children Exempted from Los Angeles Schools

Dorothy J. Lyons and Virginia Powers

Children who seem unable to profit from public school instruction because of behavioral or emotional problems are the focus of this report. Many of these children have problems that not only restrict their ability to learn but also interfere with the educational program for other children. During the 1960–1961 school year, 661 children were exempted from Los Angeles city schools for varying lengths of time because of extreme behavioral or emotional problems.[1]

In reviewing the recommendations for exemption of the 661 children, it seemed important to attempt to find answers to questions such as the following:

To what extent did the medical exemption reflect the problem of the emotionally handicapped child?

Was the exemption a necessary device to relieve the classroom of unbearable tensions? Was it a sign that the child was too disturbed to be contained in school? Was it an indication that he must have psychiatric help? Was it one of the necessary steps toward solving the problem?

Was the severity of the problem recognized?

From *Exceptional Children*, XXX, No. 4 (December 1963). Reprinted by permission. The authors wish to express appreciation to Dr. Louise W. Seyler and Dr. Donald J. Kincaid for their constructive suggestions.

Dorothy Lyons is Physician Supervisor for physically handicapped and emotionally disturbed children, Health Services Branch, Los Angeles City Schools; Virginia Powers is Guidance Specialist, Elementary Division, Los Angeles City Schools.

[1] The total of 661 pupils represented .2 percent of the Los Angeles elementary school population during 1960–1961.

Were necessary measures recommended? Were these recommendations implemented? Were community agencies utilized when indicated?

Did class size, teacher inexperience, work load, etc., preclude the use in the classroom of special techniques that might be helpful to these children? Did these children need special classes?

Did many of these children exhibit a brain-damage syndrome?

Certain of the children exempted by the school doctor because of emotional problems had been assigned to special training classes for educable mentally retarded children.

What are the implications for the school and special services personnel when these children continue to exhibit severe behavioral disturbances?

Are there implications for (a) educators regarding subject matter and techniques; (b) health personnel regarding the etiology of retardation (for example, brain-damage); (c) the school regarding the possible need for acceptance and recognition of these pupils; and (d) the counselor regarding conferencing of school personnel, parents, and pupils?

In an attempt to better understand the problems presented by these children and possibly to improve procedures whereby they might be helped, the Health Education and Health Services Branch and the Elementary Guidance and Counseling Section of the Los Angeles City Schools cooperated in reviewing exemptions for the school year 1960–1961 and in tabulating the recorded data. The tabulated data provided information in four areas: (a) types of diagnoses; (b) kinds of exemptions; (c) numbers of schools using exemption and frequency of exemption; and (d) characteristics of children exempted.

IDENTIFICATION AND DIAGNOSIS

The difficulty of identifying these disturbed children with a specific, unique diagnosis was reflected in the varied diagnoses used by both private and school physicians to describe the hyperactive, antisocial behavior which was the usual syndrome noted. This problem of classification is not a new one. The difficulty of differentiating between social and emotional maladjustment or emotional instability and a brain-damage syndrome has been discussed heretofore in other reports on this subject.

While cognizant of the pitfalls of such an endeavor, the medical diagnoses were examined carefully for possible classification for this study. The diagnoses seemed to fall into the following six categories:

Emotional instability. Physicians' diagnoses classified in this category included emotional disturbance, emotional disability, physical and emotional immaturity, social immaturity, nervous instability, severe psychological problem, erratic behavior, severe emotional disorder, extreme fatigability, wetting of pants, and temper tantrums or uncontrolled anger outbursts.

Hyperkinetic behavior syndrome. Physicians' diagnoses classified in this category included behavior difficulties, severe behavior problem, hyperkinetic behavior syndrome, organic brain syndrome, extreme hyperkinetic behavior, hyperactivity, psychomotor instability, brain-damage, cerebral palsy, postencephalitis, overactive, and neurologic disorder.

Antisocial behavior.

Aggressive abnormal behavior.

Psychosis and neurosis. Physicians' diagnoses classified in this category included schizophrenia, psychoneurosis, psychiatrically disturbed child, and anxiety neurosis.

Personality disorder.

With the completion of the study, four other categories seemed to emerge: immaturity, emotional disturbance, hyperactive-acting-out, and emotional disturbance associated with mental retardation.

The level of intellectual ability is always of interest when studying school presented problems. A comparison of the ability of the exempted pupils in relation to the diagnostic categories is shown in Table 1.

Pupils were most frequently exempted because of emotional instability and hyperkinetic behavior. Intelligence was not a discriminating factor in the diagnostic category. The greatest number of exemptions for any IQ range, however, was in the 70–79 group with 17 percent exempted. The next highest number was in the 80–89

TABLE 1. TOTAL NUMBER OF PUPILS EXEMPTED FROM SCHOOL BECAUSE OF EMOTIONAL PROBLEMS

DIAGNOSIS	IQ 79 AND BELOW	IQ 80 AND ABOVE	NO TEST DATA AVAILABLE*	TOTALS
Emotional Instability	159	138	133	430
Hyperkinetic Behavior	53	75	57	185
Antisocial Behavior	3	6	1	10
Aggressive Behavior	6	7	5	18
Psychosis and Neurosis	1	4	6	11
Personality Disorder	2	4	1	7
Totals in each IQ Category	224	234	203	661
Percent in each IQ Category	33.9	35.4	30.7	100.0

* Pupils not referred for individual psychological test prior to exemption.

group with 12 percent exempted. These are the borderline, slow learning children who generally have a higher potential than the average candidate for special training classes but have difficulty adjusting to the pace of the regular classroom. On the other hand, while emotional disturbance is not necessarily associated with a particular IQ level, only 13 pupils in the superior IQ range (120–149) required exemption because of emotional problems.

Kinds of exemptions recommended depended on the child's ability to tolerate school attendance and ranged from one or more hours attendance a day to total exemption. Of the 661 children exempted from school attendance, 405 or 61.3 percent attended on a part time basis, and 256 or 38.7 percent were out on a full time exemption. The duration of the exemption was adjusted as indicated by the child's ability to adapt to the classroom situation.

Of the 661 children exempted, 582 were boys and 79 were girls, emphasizing once again the difficulty many boys have in adjusting to the instructional program, a problem which research has repeatedly identified. More children were exempted at the lower than at the upper grade levels, and more were exempted from special training classes than from regular classes. It will be noted in Table 2 that 48.2 percent were exempted from kindergarten to grade three and 14.7 percent from special training classes. Immaturity and inadequate home training may be responsible to some extent for exemptions in the early grades. It was found that six year olds were exempted

TABLE 2. NUMBER OF CHILDREN EXEMPTED BECAUSE OF EMOTIONAL PROBLEMS BY GRADE LEVEL

GRADE	NUMBER OF CASES	PERCENT	CUMULATIVE PERCENT
Kindergarten	43	6.5	6.5
First	144	21.8	28.3
Second	78	11.8	40.1
Third	54	8.1	48.2
Fourth	49	7.4	55.6
Fifth	33	5.0	60.6
Sixth	23	3.5	64.1
Social Adjustment	4	.6	64.7
Special Classes for EMR	97	14.7	79.4
Grade not specified on form	136	20.6	100.0
Total	661		

most frequently, followed by the seven and eight year olds. The apparent increasing ability to adjust to a classroom situation may possibly be a reflection of maturation in some children.

The number of pupils exempted during each school month is shown in Table 3. The second school month of each semester shows the highest number of exemptions for that semester. The month of May is next highest in number of exemptions. Of the 421 elementary schools in the district, exemptions were used in 239. It was probable that certain schools had a greater number of children presenting severe problems because of transiency or socioeconomic conditions. . . .

TABLE 3. FREQUENCY OF PUPILS EXEMPTED BECAUSE OF EMOTIONAL PROBLEMS BY SCHOOL MONTH

	FIRST SEMESTER		SECOND SEMESTER			
	NUMBER	PERCENT	NUMBER	PERCENT	TOTAL	PERCENT
First Month	23	7.7	68	18.8	91	13.8
Second Month	110	36.7	98	27.2	208	31.5
Third Month	64	21.3	85	23.5	149	22.5
Fourth Month	43	14.3	97	26.9	140	21.2
Fifth Month	60	20.0	13	3.6	73	11.0
Totals	300		361		661	

QUESTIONNAIRE FOLLOW-UP OF PUPILS EXEMPTED

The statistical information obtained from the recommendation for exemption forms left unanswered questions regarding action taken during the interim of exemption and expected changes in behavior, if any. In an attempt to obtain these answers, a questionnaire was devised. The amount of information elicited by the questionnaire was limited by the necessity to simplify responses to the questions. The questionnaires were sent to the principals of the schools from which the children had been exempted, and responses on the 468 questionnaires (71 percent) returned were tabulated. The following discussion covers the topic areas in the questionnaire.

It appeared that in many cases full or part time exemption was recommended pending special placement, for upon return to school the child was placed in a social adjustment or educable mentally retarded special class or a child development center for severely mentally retarded. These assignments were frequently made on a trial or a limited day basis. It was found that children who did not return to school were in certain cases attending private schools, detained at juvenile hall, under psychiatric observation, or awaiting placement in a state hospital for the retarded. It was interesting to note that 28 children moved out of the district.

MEASURES TAKEN PRIOR TO AND DURING EXEMPTION

Measures taken prior to exemption included adjustment of the school program, parent conferences, referral to the school doctor and counselor, referral to community agencies, and part-day exemption. The part-day exemption which would permit the pupil to remain in school as long as he could tolerate attendance was not always feasible because of working parents or transportation problems.

Adjustment of the school program included placement in special classes such as social adjustment or special training, trial with different teachers, reading help, restriction from yard before school and during the lunch hour, grade or school change, and rest periods. In some cases the child was referred to the school guidance committee or to the welfare and attendance worker for help.

Schools reported many parent conferences with varying degrees of effectiveness. Lack of parental understanding and lack of cooperation were frequent complaints. It would appear that a great effort was made on the part of school personnel to help the child make an adequate adjustment to school and to assist the parents in understanding the child's problem prior to exemption from school attendance.

Measures taken during the interim of exemption included referral for physical evaluation or guidance to private or community physicians, hospitals, and/or clinics. Nineteen percent of the parents also received psychological help during the child's exemption. In some cases the only help received was from the elementary counselor. Seventeen percent of the children were placed on medication. Schools were not usually aware of the type of medication the child was receiving, nor were they able to evaluate its efficacy.

Here again there is an impression on the part of school personnel of lack of parental concern or understanding and refusal to accept responsibility. Comments include mothers' objection to special training for the educable mentally retarded (primary classes), parents' refusal of the psychiatric evaluation recommended by the physician, or parents' objection to the medication prescribed by their physician or clinic.

Where a low IQ was part of the child's history, both parents and school sometimes indicated that guidance was not needed. On the other hand, guidance clinics refused to accept special training youngsters because of mental retardation. It would seem that the mental handicap is aggravated by the refusal of needed guidance. Hence, where the presenting problem is mental retardation, the possibility that the etiology is centered in the emotional disturbance can rarely be explored.

It was apparent from the study that there were three problems related to community agency referrals: lack of parental cooperation, long waiting period for initial appointment, and limited services available in certain areas. An additional problem that became evident was perhaps a need to understand how community agencies operate. Bewilderment and frustration were expressed in comments such as "referred to three resources; all refused," "case dismissed after two interviews," "case refused; father did not participate," or "case refused because child not legally adopted."

PRESENT ADJUSTMENT IN SCHOOL

Factors listed in the questionnaire as possibly contributing to improved adjustment were maturation, understanding of the problem by teacher and parent, and appropriate school placement. However, comments indicated that possibly the reasons for improvement of school behavior were many and varied and could be classified as school, home, or health centered. For example, change of teachers, removal of older sibling to junior high school, parents' awareness and understanding of the problem, complete change of home environment such as foster home placement, or medication were some of the reasons stated as contributing to improved behavior. It appeared that most schools used every conceivable device to facilitate adjustment. Mentioned were "new grade, new teacher, new children," "same class placement; reading in another class," "goes home for lunch and rest as these were difficult periods for child in school," etc.

Further study of the comments regarding present adjustment at school revealed the emergence of a group of char-

acteristics which seemed to describe the exempted child. These comments, some of which follow, give a picture of an antisocial, compulsively acting-out individual with little self-control and poor academic skills in need of much individual help:

Appears to have no social conscience.
Antisocial, appears to prefer to play alone.
Has no respect for the rights of others.
Easily stimulated by others and has difficulty at recess and noon.
Willful but attempting to conform.
Moved too often to make any headway with a program.
Siblings now following pattern of conduct.
Needs individual supervision.
Must be kept busy.
Has more ability in oral type of work.
Argues, bullies, loses control of himself easily.
Wants to conform but can't.
May need to be exempted again.
Poor coordination.
Poor work habits.
Virtually a nonreader.
Has had three retentions but still academically and socially immature.
Needs to be isolated from others to be able to work.

Although 263 schools reported that the psychological study had been helpful at least to some degree to teachers and/or parents, 144 schools reported that it had not been helpful. Only one school gave a reason for this, stating that the psychological study was too limited. It would appear that more use of the counselor's time in counseling with parents and teachers of children with problems could be helpful in increasing understanding of these children—their ability in relation to school or home demands, realistic goals, and the strengths within the child that can be exploited for his benefit.

When the exemption could be used in a flexible manner, it appeared to be quite effective. This "conditional exemption" permitted the child to be excused when necessary, thus making him use his own resources for control. It may be of interest to note that a similar technique known as "suspension therapy" has been found successful in Modesto City Schools, California.

Here again, in discussing the adjustment of returned pupils, complaints were numerous regarding clinic referral. In addition to the unavailability of referral agencies, the travel problem presented by the long distances to available clinics was claimed to prevent follow-through on clinic referral. This was considered a serious problem when improvement possibly could be facilitated with guidance help.

SUGGESTIONS FROM SCHOOL PERSONNEL

Comments of school personnel encompassed not only suggestions but also observations on existing problems. These statements concerned use of the exemption, recommendations for special classes, and problems relating to community referrals and parent conferencing. Principals stated that frequently the exemption was effective because it (a) indicated to parents firmness in handling the situation; (b) involved the parents in the child's problem; and (c) emphasized the need for earlier guidance service for the child with the potentially handicapping emotional problem. Part time exemption was felt to be helpful in that it provided for flexibility in exemption and trial returns to school. It also involved the child in controlling the situation and made possible continuous follow-up and observation of his progress toward improved adjustment.

Principals stressed the strong, understanding, accepting teacher as the most effective factor in assisting the disturbed child in the classroom. The classroom atmosphere created by a calm, poised, relaxed teacher cannot be overestimated in the improvement of school adjustment.

Certain questions were raised regarding parent-school relationships. It was felt that the school's role should be clarified when home factors such as undesirable home situation and apparent lack of adult authority and supervision contributed to the child's atypical behavior. Ways were needed to help parents of young children gain understanding and acceptance of their child's limitations and of the need for special class placement. Insight as to the gravity of the child's emotional problem was needed. Especially was there a need to accept the child in spite of his behavior.

Principals stressed the need for special school facilities for long-term help. These included:

Additional social adjustment classes for younger and/or retarded children with specially trained teachers and specialist help.

More remedial reading classes.

Regular classroom environment with reduced enrollment permitting "one to one" relationship.

A diagnostic center and school with expert teachers.

Classes designed to meet the need of brain-damaged children.

Classes for children with emotional problems.

More classes for the educable mentally retarded with a shorter school day for the younger retarded child.

The need for more community agencies for referrals was emphasized. Suggested were more psychiatric facilities for average income families, less delay in obtaining appointments, guidance facilities conducted in Spanish, and up-to-date community agency directories. Needed also were additional PTA guidance resources such as increased diagnostic help, service for long term therapy cases, and guidance for mentally retarded pupils. Administrators stressed the fact that school personnel must be helped to accept inadequate and hostile parents. Parent conferences could be minimized when the parent appears ineffective or antagonistic to the child and help for the child sought through all available school resources.

The preceding observations, suggestions, and recommendations by administrators, counselors, and nurses completing the questionnaire indicated a keen awareness of the gravity of the problem which results in the removal of a child from school attendance and terminates participation in school activity and interaction with his peers. While included were many useful and valuable suggestions, many questionnaire comments implied on the other hand a lack of understanding of either certain aspects of the problem or means of solving it. For example, the suggestions regarding special classes for brain-damaged and emotionally disturbed children imply a specific diagnosis for each syndrome. However, the tabulation of diagnoses described earlier, it may be recalled, revealed the difficulties of the problem of creating a clear-cut dichotomy between a brain-damage syndrome and the hyperkinetic behavior of the emotionally disturbed or even the young unidentified mentally retarded child. Again, it must be remembered that in addition to the problem of accurate diagnosis, the grouping together of acting-out children without provision for their special educational needs, including instructional material geared to the level at which they can succeed as well as special teaching methods, can be both impractical and ineffective.

RECOMMENDATIONS

The following recommendations are based on the needs which appeared evident after evaluation of the statistical data and the questionnaire returns:

1. Step-by-step procedure should be planned prior to exemption. This should include the use of all school resources to attempt to identify the problem, to alleviate the problem, and to assure follow-up when exemption, a last resort measure, is used.

2. It should be recognized that some children are so seriously disturbed that continued attendance in school may jeopardize successful therapeutic results.

3. Teachers should be assisted to recognize the importance of their role in working with these children and every support possible be provided to them through consultant help, in-service training, etc.

4. The needs and special problems of the borderline (IQ 70–89) ability children who appear not to fit in the special training class or the regular class should be studied.

5. The feasibility of a lower class norm for this borderline ability group whose behavior problems seem secondary to their learning problems should be considered.

6. More special classes with limited enrollment and specially selected teachers should be provided for children with learning and behavior problems.

7. The possibilities and limitations of school-parent cooperation should be explored further. The school should realize that it must continue to help within its own framework when parents appear to be uncooperative or inadequate and that lack of parent acceptance of school problems and recommendations does not necessarily imply lack of concern.

8. School personnel should be helped to understand the uses and limitations of community resources, particularly the selection practices which are based on the agency's scope of service.

9. The child's return to school should be based on his improved behavior rather than the extent of the parents' cooperation.

10. Guidance services should be provided for the emotionally disturbed educable mentally retarded child and his parents.

11. Contact should be maintained between school and agency during the interim before intake appointment and/or during the treatment interval.

The following selection, by White and Harris, is especially pertinent for a general understanding of the overall problem of mental illness among school children. The authors have reviewed the research and interpreted the underlying difficulties before synthesizing the information. For example, age apparently makes a big difference in the amount of disturbance found. The authors' excellent critique of incidence studies will give the reader an insight for evaluating survey work done in local school programs.

In this discussion of types of mental illness, White and Harris present the frequency counts which provide an overall appreciation of what the school faces when we speak of emotional and social pathology. Their statistics help answer the questions: What are the major symptoms of disturbance? Is the significant problem child psychosis? How large a role is played by academic failure? What age variation might be expected in patterns? White and Harris have condensed the findings from many researches into a few pages.

Mental Illness in Relation to the Pupil Population
Mary Alice White and Myron W. Harris

In order to measure the emotional adjustment of any population, we need some reference points by which to judge. Psychologists are well acquainted with the difficulties in establishing such criteria. They are familiar with the problem that cultural values impose, knowing that what is adjusted behavior in one culture is considered abnormal in another. The same discrepancy in criteria may exist from one social class to another, from one geographic area to another, from one ethnic group to another. Despite these difficulties in defining what is good or bad adjustment, we also know that some people experience a failure in adaptation which leads to great distress, to treatment, to hospitalization, or to prison. Therefore the problem of inadequate emotional adjustment exists, even though we cannot measure it or define it accurately.

One way to gain perspective on this problem is to reacquaint ourselves with the incidence of known mental illness in the population, particularly of school age, before we take up the studies of maladjustment carried out within school systems.

INCIDENCE OF MENTAL ILLNESS

Figures of admission to mental hospitals are not a reliable indication of the prevalence of actual mental illness, because of the variation in criteria for admission and because admission rates depend upon the availability of other facilities. Admission figures, however, are about the only means we have for estimating the rate of known mental illness. Marzolf (1956) cites 1943 figures for New York State, based on first admissions to state hospitals, of 59 first admissions per 100,000 of persons between 15 and 19 years of age. Marzolf's figures reduce to a rate of .59 per 1000 for the 15–19 year range, roughly that of senior high school. Thus a school psychologist could expect less than 1 admission per year to a state hospital for each 1000 senior high school students, but this prediction is very crude indeed. Similar figures have been reduced to rates per 1000 in Table 1 in order to compare them to the school population.

Examining Table 1, we note that the estimated rates vary considerably by area, by type of admission, and by age range, and the utmost care must be taken in predicting from such rates. We could

TABLE 1. ESTIMATES OF INCIDENCE OF MENTAL ILLNESS
PER 1000 IN SCHOOL-AGE POPULATION

AREA	DATE	RATE	AGE RANGE	CRITERION
New York State[a]	1943	.59	15–19 yrs	First admission to *hospital*
England–Wales[b]	1956	2.98	0–20 yrs	First admission to *hospital*
United States[c]	1955	.70	0–24 yrs	First admission to public *prolonged-care hospital*
United States[d]	1955	3.35	0–18 yrs	Admission to *outpatient clinic*
United States[e]	1955	3.55	0–18 yrs	Under care in *outpatient clinic*

SOURCES: [a]Marzolf, 1956, p. 11; [b]adapted from Brooke, 1959, p. 897; [c]adapted from Kramer, Pollack, and Redick, 1959, Append. Table 1; [d]Eisenberg, 1960, p. 277; [e]adapted from Bahn and Norman, 1959, p. 945.

infer tentatively that less than 1 pupil per 1000 of our *total* pupil population might be expected to be admitted to a public mental hospital each year. Not included are admissions to private facilities, such as special schools for the emotionally disturbed, unless these facilities are required to report admissions to their state mental health departments. Further, between 3 and 4 pupils per 1000 of the total pupil population can be expected to be under care of an outpatient clinic each year. In addition there are private treatment resources, and agencies not required to be licensed as clinics. Rates, of course, will vary from one area to another. School psychologists tend to be hired by communities alert to psychological problems, and therefore these communities tend to have a greater number of facilities and more of their pupils seek and receive some type of mental health service. The rates we have just abstracted would probably be well below those in such communities. . . .

The rate of admission to these [outpatient] clinics for patients under 18 years was 335 per 100,000, whereas the rate for adults was only 171 per 100,000. Nearly twice as many children were treated as adults. This seems a curious fact when we have no reason to believe that mental illness is actually more frequent among children than adults. The high rate for children is possibly due to the attitudes of parents and schools in seeking treatment, or to the policies of the clinics in accepting a high

proportion of children as patients. The total rate of admission for children in such clinics is estimated by Eisenberg as 1 percent of the population, but admission does not necessarily mean treatment. Half of these children received psychiatric diag-

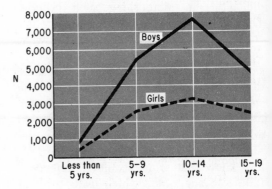

Figure 1. Terminations from Licensed Outpatient Clinics, New York State, 1959. (N.Y. State Dept. of Mental Hygiene, Robert E. Patton, Director, Statistical Services, personal communication, 1960)

nosis only, another quarter received services other than treatment, such as psychological testing or parent counseling, leaving one quarter who actually received direct treatment of some kind. . . .

MENTAL ILLNESS: TYPE OF DISORDER

Since there are differences in indices of mental disorder by age and sex in the school-age population, we might consider whether there is also a difference in the type of abnormal behavior which leads to admission. One of the most comprehensive studies of this problem was undertaken by Gilbert (1957), who surveyed 2500 consecutive cases in four metropolitan community and educational clinics in 1954. His data, which are shown in Table 2, repeat the high ratio of boys to girls as outpatients, but here we can see that this ratio is true for *every* type of referral problem. The ratio is particularly high for academic difficulties, where boys outnumber girls almost three to one, and for aggressive and antisocial behavioral problems, where boys outnumber girls almost four to one. What may surprise us is that boys outnumber girls even for passive and withdrawn behavioral symptoms by a ratio of over two to one. The age distribution indicates that problems appear most frequently in the 6- to 10-year-old group. This is not surprising since the most frequently reported symptoms are academic and aggressive ones, which are most likely to be recognized during the early grades. Of particular interest to school psychologists in Gilbert's data is the importance of academic difficulties as the basis for referral to child guidance clinics. Perhaps his data inflate the frequency of academic symptoms because two of the clinics surveyed were school clinics, which might be expected to emphasize academic adjustment. On the other hand, data from psychiatric outpatient clinics may underplay the role of academic symptoms because of diagnostic pathology. It is common for children who are admitted to psychiatric clinics to be diagnosed according to the pathology inferred, so that a low-achieving student may be reported diagnostically as a passive-aggressive personality with the presenting behavioral problem obscured by the diagnosis.

A distribution of psychiatric diagnoses for children terminated at 488 outpatient clinics in 1956 is shown in Table 3. The type of referring problem is almost impossible to ascertain from these diagnostic categories, even though we can estimate that a large percentage must include academic difficulties. If we restrict ourselves to this method of reporting maladjustment among treated children, we see that the pupil in the age range of the primary grades is again the most frequent patient in the psychiatric clinic, as he was in Gilbert's (1957) clinics. It seems unwise to make generalizations about the frequency of each psychiatric disorder for each age group, because the criteria for the diagnoses varies so widely. There is a tendency in most clinics, and this is suggested in Table 3 also, to refrain from the more serious diagnoses when a patient is young. They prefer to use less ominous labels than "psychotic disorders" or "personality disorders," the use of which rises with the age group.

SUMMARY

The difficulty in determining both the actual incidence of mental disorder and the precise nature of the abnormal behavior is almost insuperable when we attempt to establish base lines of abnormality in a school population. Diagnostic labels often fail to reveal the nature of the behavior for which a child is treated. On the other hand, referral problems are reported in multiple fashion for each patient. There is no adequate way to obtain a comprehensive view of how many school-age children are being treated for which mental disorders as identified by what behavioral pattern. Without accurate base lines we are in a poor position to evaluate studies which report maladjustment within a school setting, for in considering these latter studies we lack even the criteria of admission for treatment in clinics or in hospitals as proof of demonstrable mental disorder. We do not know whether aggressive behavior reported among classroom pupils is comparable to the aggressive behavior shown by treated outpatients. We do not know whether neurotic symptoms reported on a personality inventory bear any relationship to treated psychoneurotic disorders for the same age group.

TABLE 2. REFERRAL PROBLEMS OF OUTPATIENT CHILDREN

REFERRAL PROBLEMS	UNDER 6		6-10		10-14		14-18		ALL AGES			TOTAL AS % OF N	PERCENT OF ALL CASES IN 2 COMMUNITY CLINICS	IN 2 SCHOOL CLINICS
	M	F	M	F	M	F	M	F	M	F	TOTAL			
Academic difficulties	3	0	358	126	322	117	146	54	829	297	1126	45	27	56
Mental retardation	16	9	166	94	180	123	50	35	412	261	673	27	6	40
Aggressive, antisocial behavior	45	12	242	65	192	39	115	45	594	161	755	30	45	20
Passive, withdrawn, asocial behavior	38	15	174	74	110	50	60	25	382	164	546	22	32	14
Emotional irritability and anxiety symptoms	45	16	205	86	108	46	49	25	407	173	580	23	34	16
Hyperactivity and motor symptoms	24	12	139	59	69	24	20	5	252	100	352	14	22	8
Sexual behavior problems	6	1	12	10	13	6	6	6	37	23	60	2.5	4	1
Toilet training	27	7	50	25	36	14	0	2	113	48	161	6.5	12	1
Speech defects	25	9	62	19	26	9	10	1	123	38	161	6.5	6	7
Miscellaneous	14	17	90	38	71	51	34	29	209	135	344	14	20	9
Totals	243	98	1498	596	1127	479	490	227	3358	1400	4758	190.5	208	172

SOURCE: Gilbert (1957, p. 40). These data are based on 2500 children seen in 4 metropolitan child guidance centers, with an average of 1.9 complaints per child.

TABLE 3. PSYCHIATRIC DISORDER OF PATIENTS WITH A
DIAGNOSED DISORDER FOR WHOM SERVICES WERE
TERMINATED, BY AGE GROUP, 488 OUTPATIENT
PSYCHIATRIC CLINICS, 1956

PSYCHIATRIC DISORDER PATIENTS UNDER 18 YEARS OF AGE	TOTAL	AGE GROUP AT ADMISSION (YEARS)			
		UNDER 5	5–9	10–13	14–17
Number of patients	34,009	2,415	12,762	10,576	8,256
Percent with:					
Brain syndromes	7.4	16.6	9.6	5.4	4.0
Associated with convulsive disorder	1.7	2.3	1.9	1.5	1.5
All other	5.7	14.3	7.7	3.9	2.5
Mental deficiency	17.6	32.3	19.3	15.8	13.1
Psychotic disorders	3.5	2.7	2.4	3.0	6.1
Psychophysiologic autonomic and visceral disorders	1.3	1.3	1.1	1.4	1.3
Psychoneurotic disorders	12.6	4.8	12.4	14.3	13.2
Personality disorders	21.3	10.0	16.5	23.5	29.0
Transient situational personality disorders	36.3	32.3	38.8	36.7	33.2

SOURCE: Bahn and Norman, 1959, p. 948.

However, it is unquestionable that there is a high proportion of children being treated as outpatients, as compared to inpatients; that boys outnumber girl patients about two to one at every age level, and for almost every type of abnormal behavior; and that these ratios equalize as the children reach adulthood, when social class appears to emerge as a significant factor in the frequency and type of treated disorder. . . .

INCIDENCE OF EMOTIONAL MALADJUSTMENT IN THE SCHOOL POPULATION

We shall turn now to surveys of emotional maladjustment found in school settings. Let us make clear at the outset that these surveys do not bear any specific relationship to rates of treated mental disorder. However much we might believe that noted disturbances of behavior or of mood within a school population are the forerunners of later frank mental disorder, there is little evidence to prove that one population

necessarily produces the other. We must discriminate constantly between maladjustment as defined by rates for treated mental disorder, maladjustment as defined by judges within the school setting, and maladjustment as defined by tests or self-reports. Many school psychologists assume, and often without good grounds, that a maladjusted pupil is a potential mental patient. It is not yet known what proportion of maladjusted pupils—that is, maladjusted by the criteria of school culture—produce later frank mental disorder, later delinquency or crime, later maladjustment which goes both untreated and unlabeled, or whether school maladjustment merely represents either a phase of development or an inability to adapt to the peculiar requirements of the school setting. This is another area in which research by school psychologists is badly needed.

HOW TO ESTIMATE INCIDENCE IN SCHOOLS

First, a word about how maladjustment in a school setting is judged. Most of the better-known studies have used some form of rating by teachers or mental health experts. Maladjustment can also be estimated by rate of referrals to school psychologists or other specialists. Tests, inventories, questionnaires, academic marks, dropout rate, delinquency rate—all these can be used, singly or combined to produce some global score. These techniques have produced different results because of the technical problems involved. Who, after all, is to say whether a pupil is adjusted or maladjusted—his teacher, his peers, his parents, mental health specialists, or himself? If there is a difference of opinion, and in most studies there is, who is to say which judge is correct? If a pupil demonstrates behavior which is socially considered abnormal, such as a frank psychosis for which he has to enter a hospital, we would probably agree that maladjustment has been established, but this happens very rarely in a school population—at a rate of less than 1 per 1000 pupils. The area of maladjustment this side of frank mental disorder is an essential one to describe, count, and study, but it is, paradoxically, elusive. Adjustment by

school standards bears some positive relationship with later adult adjustment on a group basis, at least in terms of occupational success and the incidence of treated disorder, but the relationship is not 1:1, and many individuals disprove the group predictions. For the rest of this discussion, then, let us keep in mind that maladjustment is based upon opinion, opinion that is not yet established with adequate reliability or validity.

SURVEYS OF MALADJUSTMENT IN
SCHOOL POPULATIONS

The major surveys to date have been summarized in Table 4. They have employed teacher ratings, referral rates, specialists' judgments, and weighted indices which included testing instruments and school records. The first survey shown in Table 4 is that of Wickman's (1928) classic study. Later we will discuss in detail the series of studies which Wickman's work set off, evaluating the methodology. For our purposes here we need to know only that it was the first major attempt to survey pupil maladjustment in this country using

TABLE 4. ESTIMATES OF MALADJUSTMENTS IN SCHOOL POPULATIONS

SOURCE	DATE	CRITERIA	POPULATION RANGE	RATE IN PERCENT MILD	RATE IN PERCENT SERIOUS
Wickman	1928	Teachers' ratings	6–12 years	42.0	7
Hildreth	1928	Survey of school personnel	K–12th grade	— 7–8	
Rogers	1942	*Weighted index* based on teacher ratings, tests, marks, age, grade, attendance, etc.	Elementary	33	12
Mangus	1948	*Weighted index* based on teacher ratings, test, sociometry	3rd and 6th grades	— 19	—
Ullmann	1952	Teacher ratings	9th grade	—	8
Bower	1958	School specialists	4th–6th grades	—	4

a scale for teachers' judgments. Wickman found a rate of 7 percent of serious maladjustment, and of 42 percent of mild

maladjustment. We would probably question the latter figure automatically because, as statistically trained people, it is hard for us to conceive of abnormal behavior which is true of almost one-half of any population. Wickman's survey covered only the elementary population of 6 to 12 years.

Using Wickman's study as a first estimate, we can compare it to Hildreth's (1928) survey. Hildreth approached the problem differently by surveying an entire school population, the Lincoln School in New York City, in the period prior to 1928. In this school she reported 7–8 percent of the pupils listed as problem cases, not differentiated between mild and serious degrees. At the elementary level, boys were reported as problems three times as often as girls, which is fairly consistent with the figures reviewed above for outpatients. She also noted that there were three times as many children with IQ's under 105 reported as problems than existed proportionate to the total school IQ distribution, and the most prominent referral problem was an educational one. So, as early as 1928, we find the suggestion that emotional maladjustment is somehow related to educational maladjustment, that perhaps these are two different ways of describing the same population. Hildreth's rate of 7 to 8 percent, which is close to Wickman's (1928) figure, was obtained in a school that was probably more psychologically oriented than most in that period.

The next major study did not appear until 1942. It was by an investigator well known to psychologists, Carl Rogers. Rogers (1942a) surveyed 1500 children in Columbus elementary schools, of an age range similar to that covered by Wickman. He employed a weighted index composed of academic standing, CA, grade placement, a revised Wickman scale for teachers' judgments, truancy, and several personality tests. The results of this survey (Rogers, 1942b) showed that 12 percent of the pupils had serious maladjustment problems, and 33 percent had mild problems. He also found that 1 in 4 children had serious reading difficulties, 1 in 4 was an intellectual misfit in his grade placement, and 1 out of 20 was repeating his grade. His data on grade placement were, if anything, conservative. A more recent survey by Ypsilantis (1957) of all United States pupils revealed that 75 percent in 1950 were in their expected grade placement, 5 percent were in grades higher than expected, but 20 percent were a grade or more retarded. Ypsilantis' figures are for the nation as a whole, not one school system, and he reports more boys than girls, more rural than urban, more southern than nonsouthern, more nonwhite than white are retarded in grade. The sociological implications seem fairly clear. Rogers' (1942b) data probably represent a better than national average school population. It is all the more interesting to read the variation in rates which Rogers (1942b) found from one school to another, due possibly to differences in criteria, possibly to differences in educational policies, possibly to the characteristics of the local school population. Rogers (1942b) himself remarked that the more favored the neighborhood, the fewer the serious mental health problems. But his data also showed that the fifth grade, in all schools, was the most maladjusted by his criteria. This finding may bear some relationship to developmental factors, which we shall consider in the studies of normal children.

Mangus (1948, 1949) investigated a more rural population, that of 1500 children in the third and sixth grades in one Ohio county. He too used a teachers' rating scale, a forced choice using deciles, to which he added the California Test of Personality and a sociometric "guess who" technique. This was the first major study to employ pupils' per judgments. It lacked, however, the objective measures of school success employed by Rogers (1942a, 1942b), and as a study its methodology is difficult to follow. Mangus used a weighted index which showed some 19 percent of the pupils were poorly adjusted, but he did not differentiate between serious and mild cases. His data and Rogers' data do not seem at all comparable, so that we cannot generalize. But again we find in Mangus' report that boys showed two to three times as much maladjustment as girls and ". . . a close relationship between personality adjustment of children and their success or failure in school" (Mangus, 1948, p. 13). A corollary study which Mangus and Woodward (1949) carried out, apparently in 1948, and which does not appear in Table 10, was of 805 tenth-graders in one Ohio county. Here he used only the Mental Health Analysis, an adjustment inventory. But it is of interest that he found *high* adjustment scores in those pupils who were not retarded, who were more popular, and who had a high IQ, compared to those with low adjustment scores. The possibility is beginning to emerge that adjustment indices may actually measure educational adjustment itself, rather than emotional adjustment, unless we assume that both educational and emotional adjustment are dependent variables upon another unknown variable.

In 1952 Ullmann (1952a) undertook a survey of 801 white boys and girls who were in the ninth grade in a section of Maryland. Employing a forced-choice scale of adjustment with the teachers, and the SRA Youth Inventory, plus some interesting sociometric techniques with the pupils, he decided that ". . . the picture of maladjustment is a function of the type of instrument used to measure it" (Ullmann, 1952a, p. 40), which is a point that needed to be made. The teachers rated 8 percent of the pupils severely maladjusted, and again boys outnumber girls, this time four to one. The teachers' ratings, however, were closer to the pupils' sociometric ratings than to the inventory. Ullmann felt that the ratings were more accurate for the boys, the inventories for the girls. This is an interesting point, in line with our earlier question about possible sex differences in maladjusted symptomatology. There is some reason to think that boys display maladjustment in overt acting-out fashion, whereas girls tend to internalize their distresses, and such differences might be revealed better on inventories than on

behavioral scales. Ullmann (1952a, 1952b) recommends using both rating and self-descriptive data largely for this reason. In evaluating his study, we must remember that he was dealing with ninth-grade pupils, who are usually 13–15 years of age. Normal developmental patterns at this age may produce different results on behavioral rating scales—different from studies of younger children—and also marked differences between sexes. Sociometric techniques at adolescence may also have another meaning than they do for younger children, and inventories may be taken in a somewhat more sophisticated vein.

The most recent effort to evaluate maladjustment among school children was carried out by Bower (1958), who attempted primarily to test the ability of teachers to identify maladjusted children. We will discuss teacher ratings later, in reviewing the studies of the Wickman type, because this is an important but separate methodological issue. As a by-product of Bower's study, he identified 4 percent of the 5500 pupils in selected fourth through sixth grades in California as seriously emotionally disturbed. However, these children apparently had been previously identified by referral for diagnostic study, and identification was by clinicians rather than teachers. Bower's figure then represents the diagnosed rate, based on referrals, and may be useful for comparison with other referral studies, such as Hildreth's (1928).

After reviewing these six major studies, we may well ask ourselves: What is the incidence of maladjustment in schools? We might better ask: How can we define this type of maladjustment so we can measure it? If we restrict ourselves to the seriously maladjusted pupils, the rate is apparently somewhere between 2 and 12 percent. Recognizing the variation in criteria and in instruments, we would tend to accept, *as a working estimate only,* a range near the lower end of the scale, such as 4 to 7 percent. The degree of mild maladjustment is too difficult to define for us to accept any overall estimate. We could use the rates of grade retardation, of truancy, or of dropouts, which are more available as definitive statistics, but they do not necessarily describe "emotional maladjustment in schools" unless we so define it, and we are unwilling to make that assumption. . . .

In summary: The picture is a disorganized one. Ways of obtaining rates of emotional maladjustment among pupils vary so much that few inferences can be made. The rates appear to depend upon the instruments used and the population studied. There is no adequate way to compare these maladjustment rates with those for treated mental disorder. We do not know what relationship exists between school maladjustment rates and later mental illness, delinquency, or crime. Most lamentable of all, we do not know what these maladjustment rates mean in terms of normal development. Several attempts have been made to describe the nature or source of such maladjustment, a point we take up next. . . .

References

Bahn, Anita K., and Vivian B. Norman. "First National Report on Patients of Mental Health Clinics." *Publ. Hlth Rep.*, 1959, **74** (11), 943–956.

Bower, E. M. "A Process for Early Identification of Emotionally Disturbed Children." *Bull. Calif. State Dept. Educ.* (Sacramento), 1958, **27** (6).

Eisenberg, L. "Emotionally Disturbed Children and Youth." *Children and Youth in the 1960's.* Survey of papers prepared for 1960 White House Golden Anniversary Conf. on Children and Youth. Washington: 1960.

Gilbert, G. M. "A Survey of 'Referral Problems' in Metropolitan Child Guidance Centers." *J. clin. Psychol.*, 1957, **13**, 37–42.

Hildreth, G. "A Survey of Problem Pupils." *J. educ. Res.* 1928, **18**, 1–14.

Mangus, A. R. "Personality Adjustment of School Children." Ohio State Dept. Publ. Welf. Ohio State Univer., and Ohio Agricult. Exp. Sta., July 1948.

Mangus, A. R. "Mental Health of Rural Children in Ohio." *Res. Bull.*, No. 682. Wooster: Ohio Agricult. Exp. Sta., March 1949.

Mangus, A. R., and R. H. Woodward. "An Analysis of the Mental Health of High School Students." Hamilton: Div. Ment. Hlth, Ohio State Dept. Publ. Welf., July 1949. (Monograph)

Marzolf, S. S. *Psychological Diagnosis and Counseling in the schools.* New York: Holt, 1956.

Rogers, C. R. "The Criteria Used in a Study of Mental Health Problems." *Educ. Res. Bull.* (Ohio State Univer. Educ. Res. Bur.), 1942, **21** (2), 29–40. (a)

—————. "Mental Health Findings in Three Elementary Schools." *Educ. Res. Bull.* (Ohio State Univer. Educ. Res. Bur.), 1942, **21** (3), 69–79. (b)

Ullmann, C. A. "Identification of Maladjusted School Children." *Publ. Hlth Monogr.*, No. 7. Washington: Fed. Security Agency, Publ. Hlth Service, 1952.

Wickman E. K. *Children's Behavior and Teachers' Attitudes.* New York: Commonwealth Fund, 1928.

Ypsilantis, J. N. "Variations in Age-Grade School Performance." *Teach. Coll. Rec.*, 1957, **58**, 268–277.

SUMMARY

In this chapter, we have touched on very extensive territory. Teachers are key persons in the nomination of children for further study; they contribute part of the information used to judge the degree and nature of disturbance. Since special teachers play a more significant role in screening and diagnosis, they need to know, in addition, how other disciplines make their contributions.

The incidence studies offer the educator a general basis for examining the adjustment of pupil populations. Under "Screening and Diagnosis" we have illustrated ways in which teachers can systematize their judgments and sharpen their evaluative skills. Also, we introduced a new field which holds much promise for the future: "educational diagnosis," designed particularly to aid the teacher. We look forward to the time when there will be a total diagnostic scheme for teachers to parallel the present one for clinicians.

3

What Kinds of Help
Are Appropriate?

The children described in the last chapter—that is, children who have troubles or are troublesome, whether at home or in the classroom—can be helped. If circumstances go well, they may be helped by life or by growing up. However, if relationships or the children's understanding of them don't change, their troubles will probably remain or even increase, to cripple their own lives and possibly the lives of people with whom they come in contact.

Clearly, the most direct way, although often the most difficult, to alter a child's perception is to work with his parents. Help also can be obtained through friends, through the church, or through a teacher or principal. Often the parents cannot change their own perceptions or attitudes without specialized help. Then a child-guidance clinic, mental-health center, social case worker, psychologist, psychiatrist, or psychoanalyst may be called on to help the parents individually, together, or in a group of other parents with similar difficulties. The various forms of therapy illustrated in this chapter have usually been tried first with adults. The principles of therapy for both children and adults are, for the most part, the same; techniques differ in that interview through conversation is ordinarily used for adults, while for children, play, art, and acting techniques are more frequently used.

It is valuable for educators to understand in a general way what occurs when a child is referred for therapy; because the mental health disciplines and schools need to work together. The educators' awareness of the child usually precedes that of the clinic or the doctor. Therefore, the teacher's observations can be of great help to the clinic or doctor in selecting the proper treatment for the individual child. Also, the teacher can help dispel the mysteriousness that has clothed treatment in the past and led to the feeling that a child in treatment is "crazy." Teachers should understand that to get help for themselves or for a child implies only that a better solution to life is being sought. Also, an awareness of the therapist's goal can help the teacher handle the child.

At one time or another, nearly every teacher refers some child to a psychologist for testing. This is frequently the first step in an attempt to find out whether a child's difficulties are severe or temporary; whether they are caused by physical disabilities, mental handicaps, or emotional disorders; or whether they stem from a bad situation in the classroom or home. After a full diagnosis is made, a course of action is recommended that might include tutoring or having the child in a one-to-one relationship with a teacher a few times a week; changing his schedule, his teacher, or his school; or placing him in a residential or day-care treatment center. The decision may be to give the child psychotherapy from one to five times a week, or speech therapy. Glasses or a hearing aid may be recommended.

Perhaps the child's school program should be changed, or perhaps he should be placed in a foster home or merely have a separate room from his baby brother. His parents may need financial aid, marital counseling, or job placement.

Too frequently, the testing of a child is not reported back to the teacher in understandable language. This is partly because of language blocks between the professions and a mutually suspicious attitude of one profession toward another. It is the increasing responsibility of both psychologists, who test, and educators, who ask for information, to learn to speak each other's language, so that the information from a diagnosis can be put to valuable use.

It is suggested that educators become familiar with the instructions and interpretation of the tests used. A group intelligence test is the lowest possible denominator indicating a child's basic intelligence. In other words, if a group intelligence test states that a child has an IQ of 80, it may be because he comes from a nonarticulate background; or because emotional problems or physical handicaps make writing, being in groups, and testing itself a problem. Terman's book[1] about the history of his test, the Stanford-Binet, and what it means is a well-written document, of the essence for any educator who has ever dealt with a "slow learner." Wechsler's book[2] describing the Wechsler Intelligence Scale will acquaint a teacher with the principles behind measuring intelligence and explain why an individual test is often more accurate than a group test. Various personality tests, such as the Minnesota Multiphasic,[3] have preambles that may well be of interest. There is a wealth of literature on the projective tests, probably the most fascinating of all. The most familiar are Hermann Rorschach's inkblot test,[4] the Thematic Apperception Test,[5] and The Children's Apperception Test.[6] Other tests worth reading include the Goodenough "Draw a Man Test;"[7] the Blacky Cartoon Test;[8] the Jung "Free Word-Association Test;"[9] the Kuder Preference Test;[10] the Strong Vocational Inventory;[11] the Gates, or Monroe, Reading Diagnostic Tests;[12] Bender's Gestalt Test.[13]

Let us assume then that a diagnostic work-up and a case conference have been held on a child showing emotional disturbances. What might be done for him by the psychiatrist, the psychologist, the social worker, and/or the teacher? This chapter gives a picture of how this child might be helped, both outside of school and in school.

[1] L. M. Terman, *The Measurement of Intelligence,* the Stanford revision of the Binet-Simon Intelligence Scale (Boston: Houghton Mifflin Co., 1916).

[2] David Wechsler, *Measurement and Appraisal of Adult Intelligence* (New York: Williams & Wilkins, 1958).

[3] Starke R. Hathaway and J. Charnley McKinley, *Minnesota Multiphasic Personality Inventory* (University of Minnesota).

[4] Hermann Rorschach, *Psychodiagnostics* (New York: Grune & Stratton, 1942).

[5] H. A. Murray, *Thematic Apperception Test Manual* (Cambridge: Harvard University Press, 1943).

[6] L. B. Bellak and S. S. Bellak, *Manual of Instruction for the Children's Apperception Test* (New York: C. P. S. Co., 1949).

[7] F. L. Goodenough, "Children's Drawings" in *Handbook of Child Psychology,* 1st ed. (Worcester, Mass.: Clark University Press, 1931).

[8] G. S. Blum, *The Blacky Pictures: Manual of Instructions* (New York: Psychological Corp., 1950).

[9] C. G. Jung, *Studies in Word-Association,* trans. M. D. Eder (London: Heinemann, 1918); also, "The Association Method," *Am. J. Psychol.* XXI, 1910, 219–269.

[10] *Kuder Preference Record* (Chicago; Science Research Associates, 1946).

[11] *Strong Vocational Interest Blank* (Stanford, Calif.: Stanford University Press, 1938).

[12] *Monroe's Diagnostic Reading Examination* (Chicago: C. H. Stoelting Co., 1930).

[13] Lauretta Bender, *A Visual Motor Gestalt Test and Its Clinical Use,* Research Monograph No. 3, American Orthopsychiatric Association, 1938.

The reader who wants a variety of points of view (e.g., from individual therapists, case workers, and clinicians) is referred to a collection of child-treatment interviews: *Psychiatric Interviews with Children*, edited by Helen Leland Witmer (Harvard University Press, 1946).

For the views of the noted psychologist, Erik Erikson, the reader is referred to his *Childhood and Society* (W. W. Norton, 1950) and *Martin Luther, a Study in Identity* (W. W. Norton, 1961). Erikson helped create the school of thought that felt it necessary to work with the child's ego as well as the "id" (instinctual drives). Erikson placed great emphasis in treatment on a child's educational or intellectual processes, his defenses, and his strengths. According to Erikson's "theory of identity," a child's growth is seen as a search for himself in which the child learns to incorporate his heredity, his parental and peer relationships, and his cultural milieu into his own unique self. The concept of identity is particularly important in the study and treatment of adolescents.

Regardless of a particular therapist's point of view, an intimate relationship is formed between him and the child, by means of regular sessions at regular times, unshared with anyone else. The child, according to his age, his mode of action, and his needs, may communicate with the therapist by means of games, paint, clay, puppets, dramatization, writing, or direct speech. The therapist tries to choose a medium that will support the child's strength and health while also clarifying the child's problems and their causes. If the therapist is successful, the child's perception will become more healthful.

Therapists differ in how much or how little they want the parents in the picture and on how much they want to learn from the child's school, church, or camp. The trend now is for greater communication between therapist and school. Reasons for not contacting the school often stem from concern over social stigma to the child; making the child more "special"; fearing the child will feel betrayed or tattled on; ignorance of the school's contributions and the therapist's own fear of teacher or principal conferences.

Treatment is determined not only by the therapist's style, personality, and theory and also by the child's age. Treatment of a five-year-old, for instance, would probably be devoted to communication through games and painting activities. A fourteen-year-old would be expected (unless quite ill) to use speech far more. A full description of activity therapy can be found in Virginia Axline's *Play Therapy* (Houghton-Mifflin, 1947). Special forms of treatment for working with schizophrenic children can be found in Bruno Bettelheim's *Love Is Not Enough* (Free Press, 1950) and *Truants from Life* (Free Press, 1955). Special techniques applied in treatment with delinquent and acting-out children can be found in August Aichorn's *Wayward Youth* (Meridian, 1955) and Redl's *Children Who Hate* (Free Press, 1951) and *Controls from Within* (Free Press, 1952).

INDIVIDUAL PSYCHOTHERAPY

Freud predicted that he would be remembered for formulating a theory that really wasn't new—about the underlying forces behind human behavior. Particularly, he said, philosophers, writers, and artists knew and expressed a knowledge of the inner human drives. He felt his contribution was to take their observations and insights and systematize them into a way of thinking. His theory came from experience with hundreds of sick people who could not be helped by other medical disciplines. His prescription for treatment came from philosophy rather than pharmacology: "Know the truth and it shall set you free." The method rested on leading or helping the patient to become aware of the truths about himself.

Freud's theory might be called an education theory. The therapist is a teacher. His subject matter is the patient himself; his curriculum is the patient's past experience, present world, and unconscious feelings. The methods used to help the patient gain awareness, insight, and consequent change, while set down by Freud in specific terms for treating adult neurotics, have been modified or altered according to the empirical or convictional information gained by treating not only neurotic adults, but also psychotics and criminals, as well as children suffering from emotional illnesses.

Freud's basic premises resulted in an intense study of children and their development. His theory of the libido, which might be defined as affectional energy, starts at the breast. This energy can develop naturally in a child who is able to put up with the pressures of society; or it can be blocked, deterred, or turned in ill-fated directions. Freud's emphasis on early childhood experiences focuses psychoanalytic, psychiatric, and educational thought on parent-child and teacher-child relationships. His theory of the unconscious makes sense out of seemingly senseless behavior. Failure to achieve where potential exists, somatic complaints without perceptible causes, crime or misdeed without use or reason become understandable in the light of previously unsuspected human needs and conflicts.

Since in the psychoanalytic treatment of adults great focus was placed on childhood, it was natural that children themselves be scrutinized. If illness began in the early years, could it be prevented or caught before it developed further? Could society or education help from the outside? Could the therapist help from the inside? Could parents and teachers alter the course of a child's development to free his energy for constructive living in place of pathological living?

The first case of child therapy was undertaken by Freud himself. Little Hans was treated indirectly by Freud for a phobia of horses. That is to say, Freud supervised the treatment through Hans's father.

In the early years of psychoanalysis, Anna Freud, Sigmund's daughter, and Melanie Klein both worked with children. Although both based their work on Freud's formulations, they disagreed with each other on many basic questions of treatment, such as the relationship between therapist and child, the use of dreams and symbols, the length and conditions of treatment, and the handling of parents. Melanie Klein took the major part of Freud's adult theory and applied it to children. Anna Freud, however, modified her father's theory in a way which was consistent with the child's basic dependence on parents. She was more concerned with the child's total environment—his friends, his neighborhood, his teacher. The reader is referred to her *The Ego and Mechanisms of Defense* (Int. Univs., 1964). For Melanie Klein's type of interpretive therapy, refer to her book *Narrative of a Child Analysis* (Basic Books, 1960).

In the next excerpt Anna Freud discusses the three characteristic viewpoints of psychoanalysis with suggestions for pedagogy.

The Relation between Psychoanalysis and Pedagogy

Anna Freud

. . . Out of my summary, condensed from a great abundance of data and thereby probably often confusing, perhaps you will be able to retain for your guidance only three of the characteristic viewpoints of psychoanalysis.

The first of these ideas is concerned with the division of time. Psychoanalysis distinguishes, as you have already learned, three different periods in the life of the child: early childhood up to about the end of the fifth year; the latency period to the beginning of the prepuberty stage, about the eleventh, twelfth, or thirteenth year; and puberty, which leads into adult life. In each period there is a different emotional reaction of the child to those around him, and a different stage of instinctual development, each of which is normal and characteristic. A special attribute of the child, or his method of reaction, cannot therefore be judged without reference to the specific period of his life. An act of instinctive cruelty or shamelessness, for example, which belongs to the early period and to puberty, will cause anxiety to the observer if it occurs in the latency period, and if found in adult life will have, perhaps, to be judged as a perversity. The strong link with the parents, which is natural and desirable in the first period and in the latency period, is a sign of retarded development if it still exists at the end of puberty. The strong urge to rebel and to have inner freedom which in puberty facilitates the emergence into normal adult life may be regarded as an obstacle to the right development of the ego in earliest childhood or in the latency period.

The second aspect is connected with the inner growth of the childish personality. You have probably up till now

From *Psychoanalysis for Teachers and Parents* by Anna Freud, trans. Barbara Low (New York: Emerson Books, Inc., 1954). Reprinted by permission.

pictured to yourself the child with whom you have to deal as a homogeneous being, and consequently have not been able to explain the difference between what he wants to do and what he is able to do, the clash between his intentions and his actions. The psychoanalytic conception shows you the personality of the child as of a threefold nature, consisting of the instinctual life, the ego, and the superego, which is derived from the relationship with his parents. The contradictions in his behavior are to be explained, therefore, when you learn to recognize behind his different reactions that part of his being which at this particular moment predominates.

The third principle is concerned with the interaction between these divisions of the childish personality; we must not imagine this to be a peaceful process, but rather a conflict. The issue of such a duel, for example, between the ego of the child and an instinctive wish he knows to be undesirable, depends upon the relative strength of the libido at the disposal of the instinctive impulses compared with the energy of the repressing force derived from the superego.

But I fear, indeed, that these three principles for practical application which I have put briefly before you do not give you all that you hoped to get from psychoanalysis in the way of help for your work. Probably you see practical advice which will be a guidance to you rather than an extension of your theoretical knowledge. You want to know for certain which methods of education are the most to be recommended; which must be absolutely avoided if you do not want to imperil the child's whole development. Above all, you want to know whether we shall continue with more education, or give less than we have in the past.

In answer to the last question it should be said that psychoanalysis, whenever it has come into contact with pedagogy, has always expressed the wish to limit education. Psychoanalysis has brought before us the quite definite danger arising from education. You have learned how the child is forced to fulfill the demands of the adult world around him. You know that he conquers his first great emotional attachments by identification with the beloved and feared adults. He escapes from their external influence, but meanwhile establishes a court of judgment within, modeled on the authority of those beings, which continues to maintain this influence within him. This incorporation of the parent-figures is the dangerous step. When this takes place the prohibitions and demands become fixed and unchangeable. In place of living beings they become an historical background which is incapable of adapting itself to progressive external changes. In reality the parent-figures would be influenced by reason in their conduct and would be accessible to the claims of a new situation. Naturally they would be prepared to concede to the thirty-year-old man what was forbidden to the three-year-old child. But that part of the ego which has been formed from the demands and standards of the parents remains inexorable.

The following examples are given to elucidate these points. I know a boy who was extremely fond of dainties in his earliest years. As his passion for dainties was too great to be satisfied by legitimate means, he hit upon all kinds of unlawful expedients and dodges in order to procure sweets, spent all the money he possessed upon them and was not too particular as to how he procured more. Education was called upon to act; the boy was forbidden sweets, and his passionate devotion to his mother, who had interfered with his pleasure, gave special emphasis to the prohibition. His extreme fondness for dainties disappeared, to the great satisfaction of his elders. Yet today this lad, now an adolescent who has plenty of money at his disposal and the freedom to buy up all the sweetmeats of the Viennese confectionery shops, is not able to eat a piece of chocolate without

blushing furiously. Everybody who observes him is at once certain that he is doing something forbidden—that he is eating things bought with stolen money. You notice that the restrictions imposed upon him earlier have not automatically yielded to the changed situation. . . .

Or take another case. A tiny little girl develops an extreme pleasure in her naked body, shows herself naked to her brothers and sisters, and delights in running through the rooms stark naked before she goes to bed. Education steps in and again with success. The little girl now makes a very great effort to suppress this desire. The result is an intense feeling of modesty that continues in later life. When the question of choosing a career arises somebody suggests an occupation which would necessitate sharing a room with companions. She unhesitatingly states that this career is not for her. Behind the rational motive the fear is ultimately revealed that she will have to undress before the others. The question of qualification or preference for the career is of no consequence compared with the strength of the prohibition carried over from childhood.

The psychoanalyst who is engaged in his therapeutic work of "resolving" such inhibitions and disturbances in development certainly learns to know education from its worst side. Here, he feels, they have been shooting at sparrows with cannon balls! Would it not have been better perhaps to have given somewhat less value to decorum and convention in these various nurseries, and to have let the first child be greedy and the second imagine himself in the role of the father; to have permitted the third child to run about naked and a fourth to play with his genitals? Would these childish gratifications really have had any important adverse effect as compared with the damage wrought by a so-called "good education"? Compare them with the division which is thus introduced into the childish personality; the way in which one part of him is incited against another; see how the capacity to love is diminished and the child grows up incapable, perhaps, of enjoyment and of accomplishing his life-work. The analyst to whom all this is apparent resolves, so far as he is concerned, not to aid such an education, but to leave his own children free rather than to educate in this way. He would rather risk the chance of their being somewhat uncontrolled in the end instead of forcing on them from the outset such a crippling of their individuality.

But you are, I feel sure, shocked at the one-sidedness of my views. It is high time to change the standpoint. Education appears to us in another light when we have another aim in view—for example, when it is concerned with the neglected child, such as August Aichhorn deals with in his book *Neglected Youth.*

The neglected child, says Aichhorn, refuses to take his place in society. He cannot succeed in controlling his instinctive impulses; he cannot divert enough energy from his sexual instincts to employ them for purposes more highly esteemed by society. He refuses, therefore, to submit to the restrictions which are binding on the society in which he lives, and equally withdraws from any participation in its life and work. No one who has had to do with this type of child in an educational or psychoanalytical connection can fail to regret that in his childhood there had been no force from without which succeeded in restricting his instinctual life, so that these external checks would have been gradually transformed into inner restrictions.

Take as an example a child who for a little while occupied the attention of the Vienna Children's Court. This eight-year-old girl was equally impossible both at home and at school. From every educational institute or convalescent home she was unhesitatingly sent back to her parents, after three days at the most. She refused to learn anything or to share in the activities of the other children. She pretended to be stupid, and so cleverly that in several places she was diagnosed as mentally defective. During the lessons she lay down on a bench and played with her sexual parts. Any interruption of this occupation resulted in a wild howling horrifying to the grownups. At home she was ill-treated—this was the only idea the parents had of dealing with her. An analytic investigation showed two things. The external circumstances were peculiarly unfavorable to the development of any kind of emotional relations between the child and her environment. No one could offer a love that would have in any way compensated the child for giving up the gratification obtained from her own body. It also showed that the severe punishments from which the parents had obviously expected a restraining influence could not fulfill this purpose. Either owing to her own disposition or on account of significant early experience, the little girl had developed such strong masochistic tendencies that each beating could only become once more a stimulus to sex excitement and sex activity. Compare this case of neglect with the one of repression which I described to you earlier. You can see that a free and self-reliant human being does not evolve from this child either. She is nothing but a cowed little animal whose further moral development has stopped simultaneously with her mental growth.

Aichhorn mentions in his book *Neglected Youth* another severe case of maldevelopment—that of a boy who from about his sixth year onward had found every kind of sexual gratification in his mother, and finally, after reaching sexual maturity, lived with her in actual sexual intercourse. He had thus actually accomplished what the other children had enjoyed only in fantasy. Neither has this boy developed into a self-reliant, harmonious, vigorous human being, as we might have expected, considering the evil effects of education described above.

A kind of "short-circuiting" had occurred in his development. By the actual fulfillment of his childhood's wishes he had saved himself the necessity of traversing the whole circle of "becoming grown-up." The wish to become like his father in order to attain all the possibilities of the gratifications permitted to his father was now superfluous. He had indeed escaped the "splitting" of his personality, but in return for that he had given up any further development.

But you will find that the problem is not so difficult as I have represented it to you, and that disturbances in development and delinquency may be merely extreme results, showing, on the one hand, the injurious effect of too great repression, on the other the lack of all restraint. The task of a pedagogy based upon analytic data is to find a *via media* between these extremes—that is to say, to allow to each stage in the child's life the right proportion of instinct-gratification and instinct-restriction.

Possibly a detailed description of this new analytical pedagogy should have been the content of my lectures to you. But for the present no analytical pedagogy exists. We have only as yet individual educators who are interested in this work, and having been analyzed themselves they now seek to apply to the education of children the understanding that psychoanalysis has brought to them of their own instinctual life. It will be a long time before theory and practice are complete and can be recommended for general use.

But in spite of this you ought not to say that psychoanalysis has done nothing beyond giving indications as to the future; that it certainly does not profit teachers engaged in practical work to study psychoanalysis, and that probably it would be better to dissuade them from having anything to do with it. Nor should you say that they had better make enquiries in ten or twenty years' time as to what has been accomplished meanwhile in the application of psychoanalysis to pedagogics.

I maintain that even today psychoanalysis does three things for pedagogy. In the first place, it is well qualified to offer a criticism of existing educational methods. In the second place, the teacher's knowledge of human beings is extended, and his understanding of the complicated relations between the child and the educator is sharpened by psychoanalysis, which gives us a scientific theory of the instincts, of the unconscious and of the libido. Finally, as a method of practical treatment, in the analysis of children, it endeavors to repair the injuries which are inflicted upon the child during the processes of education.

The following example illustrates the second point, i.e. it explains the pedagogical situation by means of the unconscious background of the conscious behavior.

An excellent woman teacher began her career in her eighteenth year when, in consequence of unhappy family circumstances, she left home to take a post as governess to three boys. The second boy presented a serious educational problem. He was backward in his lessons and appeared very timid, reserved, and dull; he played a subordinate part in the family, and in contrast to his two gifted and attractive brothers was constantly pushed into the background. The teacher devoted all her efforts and interest to this boy, and in a comparatively short time had obtained a wonderful success.

The boy got very fond of her, was more devoted to her than he had ever been to anybody before, and became frank and friendly in his ways. His interest in lessons increased, and by her efforts she succeeded in teaching him in one year the subjects laid down for two years, so that he was no longer behind in his work. The parents were now proud of this child, whom until then they had treated with but slight affection; they took much more trouble about him, and his relations to them and also to his brothers improved, until the little boy was finally accepted as a most valued member of the family circle. Thereupon an unexpected difficulty arose. The teacher to whom the success was entirely due began now on her side to have trouble with the boy. She no longer gave him any love, and could not get on with him. Finally, she left the house, where she was greatly appreciated, on account of the very child who had been in the beginning the center of attraction to her.

The psychoanalytic treatment which she underwent nearly fifteen years later for pedagogic reasons revealed to her the true facts of the case. In her own home, as a child, she had, with more or less justification, imagined herself the unloved child—the same position in which she had actually found the second boy when she began her work with him. On the ground of similar slighting treatment she had seen herself in this boy, and had identified herself with him. All the love and care which she had lavished upon him meant that she was really saying to herself: "That is the way I ought to have been treated to make something out of me." Success, when it came, destroyed this identification. It made the pupil an independent being who could no longer be identified with her own life. The hostile feelings toward him arose from envy; she could not help grudging him the success which she herself had never attained.

You will say, perhaps, it was a good thing that this teacher, when she dealt with her pupil, had not yet been analyzed; otherwise we should have lost a fine educational success. But I feel that these educational successes are too dearly bought. They are paid for by the failures with those children who are not fortunate enough to reveal symptoms of suffering which remind the teacher of her own childhood and so make sympathy with them possible for her. I hold we are right in demanding that the teacher or educator should have learned to know and to control his own conflicts before he begins his educational work. If this is not so, the pupils merely serve as more or less suitable material on which to abreact his own unconscious and unsolved difficulties. . . .

Having a glimpse of the point of view of one of the founders of child psychoanalysis, we now sample an American child psychoanalyst, Dorothy Baruch. She works along the lines of Anna Freud's theory. The case excerpted here should be of particular interest to school people, since it is the story of a boy (Kenneth) who acted out his unconscious conflict by severe physical symptoms and by school failure. This child was operating on a 101 IQ at the beginning of treatment, at 140 at the close of treatment.

In this selection the parents' involvement in the child's pathology is emphasized. Dr. Baruch saw the mother (Cathy) individually on a regular basis, and the father (Vic) from time to time. Both parents also participated in group therapy for parents with children in treatment. Both of these techniques are used increasingly when treatment of children is undertaken. It is rare that children under the age of 15 are seen, save in hospital or residential treatment settings, without insistence that some form of regular therapy be administered to parents. Frequently, depending on the theory of the therapist, teachers are also interviewed by the therapist for the purpose of getting, and sometimes giving, information relevant to the child's growth. Sometimes parents are seen by the child's therapist, as in Dr. Baruch's case. Sometimes separate therapists are used. Sometimes multitherapeutic measures are used with parents as in the example given here.

The following selection was chosen for three major reasons. (1) It is the case of a child who got into treatment because of a learning problem—in reading and spelling. (2) It is an example of the most typical kind of therapy done in this country, work with a child and a parent in a child-guidance clinic. The child's therapist was a psychologist; the mother's therapist was a psychiatric social worker. (3) It is the record of one complete case.

One Little Boy

Dorothy Baruch

At home Kenneth wheezed steadily for the four days and nights between that session and the next. He was quiet. He was good. But he coughed and struggled for air during the night and breathed with painful tightness during the day. The doctor did what he could.

But Kenneth kept on wheezing.

The doctor questioned me: Were we moving too fast? I said I'd watch it; perhaps we were. Kenneth had been such a good boy for so long that it was frightening him to open up to his own view this other part of himself—a part that lies deep in every one of us—hidden but ready to splash out in the bitter word, in the twisted temper or in the flood-burst of mass riot, lynchings and war. In small or large measure we manage, each in our own way, to keep it underground, according to the smallness or largeness of the hurts we have suffered, according to the onus we have leveled at ourselves for unwelcome feelings and according to the quantity and depth of the bitter gall we have stored.

Kenneth had been hurt. I knew only part of it all at the moment. Anger had, as result, accumulated inside him, and had given rise to fantasies mixed with tremendous fear and guilt. He could not show this anger or he might do too much. He might lose the last remnants of his mother's love. Therefore, unconsciously he did let the anger turn back on its course till he himself was both donor and recipient in the pain of illness, in the tragedy of failure, and in the fantasied hurts more dreaded than that of the wounded soldier and more dreadful to bear.

He would have to bring anger to the surface where he could look at it and with my help gradually understand and inte-

grate it into the portrait that he painted of himself in his mind.

Release had to come as a primary step if he was to survive in wholeness. I knew this. But I knew also that if it came too fast, it would threaten to inundate him so that he might close up the floodgates anew with reinforced blockades.

In his next session, Kenneth again chose the soldiers. At the start, he dared not follow his impulse to strike down the enemy. Hesitance encased him like lead-gray fog. But at last his desire broke through—throwing a spotlight on terrain that had been veiled from view. And with it, his face was illuminated.

His bombs struck not only mountains but men. His bullets, born in swift flight by his hand from enemy to enemy, crackled mercilessly. Faster and faster. The open voice replaced the closed whisper. Free breath in and out of lungs replaced the stoppered sibilance of his wheeze.

"The bomb got em!" jubilantly. "One man. Two. Three . . ." He went down on one knee, crouching in triumph over the strewn men, his yellow head bent to inspect the havoc he had finally managed to deal after such struggle. His words spilled out. And with them, in the risen excitement, a small trickle of saliva dribbled from his mouth to the floor.

He looked at the dark spot of spittle on the linoleum in stunned silence.

"I—I'll clean it up," he whispered.

Stiffly he rose from his bombs and his soldiers. He walked to the closet hook where a cloth hung and to the sink where he wet it. He wrung out the cloth like a well-taught robot, and brought it back to the spot on the floor.

"I—I didn't mean to get the floor messy."

"I know it, Ken. But really, in here it

Reprinted from *One Little Boy* by Dorothy Baruch (New York: The Julian Press, 1952), by permission of the publisher.

doesn't matter. You can do lots of things in here that you think aren't proper outside."

But he could not hear me or dared not show that he'd heard.

Slowly and with painstaking thoroughness he mopped the wet space, went back to the sink, washed the cloth out, wrung it, mechanically hung it back on the hook. And without another word but with the rasp of his wheezes breaking the silence, he came straight into my lap.

I thought: To him messing means being bad. So also do injuring and killing, even in play, mean being bad. They're different sides of the same coin, different facets of resentment, or anger, or hostility—call it what one will. Inside of Ken, the reservoir was full to spilling over. In his play, when it was draining out through the drama of killing, it did not need for the moment to drain out in asthma. In such play, though, it showed more of its true form. Ken could not escape its meaning as completely as he could when it came out in sickness or failure. Sickness and failure were great camouflagers. With them he could say in the space beyond words where unrecognized thoughts exist more as feelings: I'm being good, not naughty. I can't help it, after all, if I fail or am sick.

Since messing was less bad than injuring or killing and since injury and killing had frightened him so much, it was obviously not the messy spittle in itself that had sent Ken back in fear to being a baby seeking arms' shelter. The spittle was merely the proverbial last straw.

I would try to help Kenneth get firmly acquainted with the milder forms in which his "badness" showed itself before tackling what to him seemed more dangerous. I would arrange materials and set up the playroom so that it would automatically limit what Kenneth brought out. Instead of waiting for him to get the soldiers from the cupboard, I would have clay or paints out on the floor in readiness, as an invitation to mess rather than injure or kill.

Then bit by bit as he tackled what was less frightening to him and saw that he could live through it without being overpowered by his feelings or deserted by me, he might perhaps gain courage to explore more deeply. I would try as we went along to help him feel less guilty and less afraid and to understand his feelings better, not through mere words of explanation but through the experiences which we would share. Perhaps then—very gradually—the more dreaded feelings might lessen until he could say, in effect, I can handle what's left of them. I'm not really so bad! I don't need to be afraid any longer that my feelings will push me into such terrible actions that I'll either be deserted or destroyed. I needn't turn them back on myself and punish myself with illness and failure. I needn't keep them walled off and hidden as if I were telling myself, "These feelings, they're *not* part of *me*." Instead, I'll be able to let them slip into place as part of what I am. If he could reach this point, he would no longer need to stand over himself, cruelly denying himself and trying to relish denial in place of pleasure. He would no longer have to drain energy from his school work, for instance, in order to keep reinforcing the walls. The energy that had been used for hiding would be freed for work and play, for enjoyment and laughter, for friendship and love.

All this I hoped might eventually happen. I would try to help Kenneth achieve it. But essentially it was Kenneth himself who had to do it. Would he be able to? Was there sufficient courage and vigorous urge left in him, not only for living but for aliveness? How far would Kenneth be able to go?

I had finger paints waiting ready for him next time, right in the middle of the floor.

"What are they? . . . Where are the brushes? . . . Where are pictures to color? . . . I don't do well in free art in school. I like paint-books better. I almost never go outside of the line."

Poor, tight little Kenneth, afraid of what his brush's unsteadiness might mean, feeling that he must not go beyond the line—seeking the shelter of its neat constraint.

I told him you did this kind of painting with your hands, that was why it was called "finger painting."

He wanted gray. And when we got a blob of it onto the paper, he touched it very gingerly with one finger. "Look how dirty my finger got."

He stared unhappily at it.

"Will my finger get clean again? Will the mess come off?"

"Let's try with the soap and water at the sink."

We did. And he saw.

He took a big breath. "It does come off."

He started afresh. With the tips of all the fingers on one hand. With whole fingers down. With palm in, slithering, until the sticky paint was covering the inside of his hand. "See how dirty?"

Again doubt. "Will *this much* come off?"

Back to the sink. "I'd better see."

He scrubbed until I wondered if he'd left any skin.

To the paints with both hands sliding in. Back to the sink. Again to the paints. Again to the sink. Paint and scrub. Prove that he wouldn't have to keep tell-tale signs of dirt on him, then he could get dirty. But the proof was hard to believe. And so it had to be sought again and again until he could finally say with more certainty, "I *can* get them clean."

Both hands went in, then, and the paint slid up past the wrists. "I'll make them real, real dirty." He was smearing the paint now, over the backs of his hands and between his fingers. "I'll get them all dirty. Ahrrr, ahhrrrr, I'm messy! Ahhrrrr!" He growled and stuck up his hands toward my face in a menacing gesture as if he were going to smear me. A pouncing gesture, his fingers spread like claws. His head was

back, his eyes guardedly on me, and a sound came from his lips. It was laughter but it was not the full-throated sound that rises from the gay heart. Rather the ghost-sound of an echoed, hollow denial of fear.

I wondered if he saw me swallow.

Even though it was thin and shallow, coming from no farther back it seemed than his palate, still this was the first time in the short long month he'd been with me that I'd heard Kenneth laugh. . . .

Blaine did not call Cathy. But he called Vic into his private office, and from behind Mr. Taylor's great mahogany desk, he told Vic that he was reorganizing the business and for the time being would not need Vic's services.

Vic said, "That's all right." Nothing more. Next day, however, he went back and doggedly questioned, "What's wrong, Blaine? Why are you letting me out? It's important for me to know."

Blaine had said there was nothing against Vic. Only right now he needed men of a different type, more aggressive. "You're the research type, Vic; the inventor, the investigator. Right now that's not what this place needs. We need people who can promote. Push. Why don't you open a consulting service? When we come up with a tough problem we'll use you. It's a deal. But at present we don't need your kind of a man here full time."

That night there was a group psychotherapy session. Cathy came in, the air of a crusader about her, her dark head high. Vic followed, dragging his feet.

Glancing around the already gathered circle, Cathy chose the straight-backed chair from the two that were still empty and Vic, looking helpless, sank into the low armchair and huddled over himself.

The hum of greetings between the group members stopped as the doctor glanced at his watch. "Well," he said, swiftly surveying each face in the circle, "it's time for us to get to work."

There was silence and a few moments of waiting for some group member to spontaneously start to talk about whatever lay on his mind. For into this warm, big room with the quiet of shadows on the wall and the circle of waiting faces, these people once a week brought their troubles and feelings and fantasies just as Kenneth brought his into the room where he played. Here, the doctor and I, as joint psychotherapists, had come to stand as a new father and mother. Under our guidance, these men and women with their diverse problems had grown to speak as freely as they would alone.

Tonight it was Cathy, not Vic, who began.

"It isn't fair," she protested. "It shouldn't have happened to Vic!"

She went on to recount what Vic had told her. She was angry, she said, at Mr. Taylor for not having protected Vic. "After all the years that Vic's been there. Why, he's been Mr. Taylor's right hand man. I think it's a darn rotten deal. Especially being told he's not the aggressive type!"

Cathy's voice was patiently sweet with martyred indignation. "That's like a slap in the face! What if Vic isn't the aggressive type? Vic's got a lot of other qualities . . ."

With quick perspicacity, several group members picked up Cathy's feelings. They now came out with thoughts that people ordinarily keep unsaid.

This is part of group psychotherapy. For when a person sees in the group how others react to him with the covers of pretense shorn off, he can at one and the same time see how he affects people outside the group. How he reacts in turn with hurt or anger, with impotence or with gestures of appeasement, stands out in clean silhouette. He can see more clearly what he is and how he is and what there is in him that upsets others and brings trouble onto himself. In the circle of the group he experiences safely and without harm in microcosm the undercover reactions which in the macrocosmic

circle of his life outside the group bring him trouble.

With perceptiveness reaching with honesty toward honesty, one group member now hit on the falseness in Cathy's exaggerated sympathy.

"Come on off your pedestal, Cathy."

And another, "You're damned mad at Vic for not being more aggressive and you know it."

"I'm not." Cathy sat straighter and stared around the circle of faces, her hands trembling. "I'm not mad at Vic. Why should I be? I feel sorry for him. I'm mad at that damned Taylor."

"How do you feel, Vic?" another group member asked.

"I *don't* feel, I guess. That's still the trouble. I don't think it matters too much, if you know what I mean. I think Blaine's suggestion about my opening a consulting office is a good one and that's what I'm planning to do, and some of the clients I've worked with will come to me, I'm sure, as soon as they know I'm on my own. I think Blaine himself will use me, and I'll do all right. I'm not really worried."

This time the group reacted to his feelings. Some were friendly, some were challenging, some were frankly angry at him for the absence of vigor in his response. He persisted passively, "It doesn't bother me!" He showed no anger at their anger. No backfiring to their challenges. No appreciation, either, for the friendly concern.

Finally the doctor pointed out, "You have the same problem here, don't you, Vic, that you had on the job? You take all the criticism here without protest. You don't work up any aggressiveness. Let's see, now, how does it really make you feel when the rest of the group jumps all over you?"

Vic looked at the floor and swallowed. He uncrossed his long legs and recrossed them. "It doesn't matter, if you know what I mean."

"What do you mean, Vic?"

He swallowed again and turned toward Cathy, his great hands hanging limply over the arms of his chair. "It doesn't matter," he said and added without change in pace or pitch, "It doesn't matter as long as Cathy thinks I'm all right."

The response rose quickly from various people.

"You sound like a little boy feeling fine as long as his mama says he's O.K. Just like me."

"As long as mother thinks you're wonderful, you don't have to struggle. The world can go by."

Vic's eyes were narrowed like blue slits of water almost lost in their hollows a great distance off. "My mother did think I was wonderful. My mother and Cathy."

His voice did not as usual plod on in monotone to indecisive end without ending. It paused in distinct waiting as if for something to rise from inside him rather than to come from the group.

"My father was away a lot, travelling for a firm he worked for. When he was at home, he was cold and aloof and disapproving of everything I did. I never felt close to him. I'd try to do things to please him when he was around, like getting his slippers for him or kissing him goodnight because he expected it of me, but I'd kiss him gingerly and notice how sharp his whiskers were, like barbed wires telling me to stay on my own side of the fence and not to get in his way or his territory or something, if you know what I mean. I tried to do things to please him, but it never did any good. He'd pack up and leave. I never really had a father. We never were close. I took Mr. Taylor as a father, I guess. I looked up to him and admired him and felt close to him and showed him I was there to do whatever he said. I guess that's got something to do with it, my always doing what he said. If I'd shown more initiative I might be managing the firm now. But I always looked to Mr. Taylor as the one who held the reins. He was so much older . . ."

"The man with the whiskers!"

"Well, I took him that way. As a father."

"And now the only father you ever had walks out and leaves you. But it doesn't really matter, you say, because you have Cathy. I used to say my father could walk out and go to hell and I wouldn't care. But I've seen recently that it mattered a hell of a lot. I was just covering up that I cared, so that the caring wouldn't hurt quite so much."

The doctor came in again. "You thought it didn't matter then, Vic, because you had Mother. You tell yourself it doesn't matter now because you have Cathy."

Vic nodded slowly. "Mother and I were close. But somehow I guess it did matter. I had to be man of the house, if you know what I mean . . ."

"What, Vic?" I asked.

"Well, I did things for Mother. Took care of the furnace and chopped wood and shovelled snow and other things, too, that were more just for her. Just between the two of us, if you know what I mean." He looked for all the world like a frightened overgrown boy who wanted to slink out and hide in some dark retreat with his guilty but cherished secret.

"What, Vic? What sort of things?" I hoped he could share with me now the secret things he'd shared with his mother earlier, only now show them openly in front of these other people, discovering as he did so that in reality he had nothing to fear.

"Well," he swallowed and cleared his throat, "things like brushing her hair. She had blond hair, long and like silk. When she had it unbraided it came to below her waist. She'd let me unbraid it. And I'd run my fingers through its length, straightening it all the way . . ." Vic's eyes were now very blue, focused as if off into distance. "She had a white ivory hair brush with a woman's figure carved on the back. Only a hole had been burned into the girl someway by a branding iron. That's silly, by a cigar or cigarette, I don't remember. And I forget where the hole was in her, what part of her was missing, just that there was a hole somewhere. I'd like to brush her hair; it felt soft and good and there were other things, too, like that, if you know what I mean."

"That felt good?"

He nodded.

"Well," he looked down at the floor. "Well, she'd like me to sleep in bed with her when *he* was away, and I'd wash her back for her when she bathed. She liked me to do it, take care of her, sort of . . ."

"She thought you were wonderful, Vic," the doctor said gently. "How did you feel, Vic? Protected and safe?"

Vic's eyes almost closed till the blue scarcely showed. He looked down at the floor away from everybody, as if he were afraid to meet anyone squarely. Then, in a voice that was duller and flatter and yet tighter and less flaccid, he answered, "No. Not safe really. No. I didn't really feel safe with my mother. I don't understand it. There was something about it. Well, it seems to me somehow . . . It came to me just at this moment . . . I never thought so before, but . . . Well, as if she had in some way expected too much."

"Like Cathy now?"

He scuffed his great feet on the floor in a helpless gesture, and very slowly shook his head. . . .

"I can't club her!" Kenneth had said. "But I can do other things."

"If I were Hamburger," he elaborated one day, "I'd show her I was angry. I'd jump on her bed and get paw marks all over it. I'd get real mad and growl and bark. I'd chew up her purse and get mud on it. I'd be a real mad and happy Hamburger. Real happy to be mad."

He looked at me soberly. "I'd like to be like that. I'd like to do things, too, to show her how I feel. I'd like to be a real-happy-to-be-mad-Kenneth. But if I got too outspoken it would just get me into a mess of trouble. I can't do it with her. I know that. But I can get the mad out in here with you."

He became freer and easier in report-ing what had gone on at home and in the neighborhood. "My boy friend Gene took me to a movie. He treated me. I feel more like a friend!" . . . "And me and a couple of other boys got some flower seeds and planted them in the empty lot." . . . "And we're working on a model airplane."

He was freer, too, in expressing his feelings. He was angry at his mother when she was late to meet him at the dentist's one afternoon. He was angry when she forgot to pick him up at school as she'd promised to do. He was angry at her and at his father when they proposed taking back his room for their study and moving him in again with Brad.

"It makes me furious," he announced, glowering. "It'll put me right down again at Brad's level, three years younger than I am. I'll have to turn the lights off earlier and turn the radio off earlier. Just the idea of the whole business makes me mad . . . They don't care how much Brad disturbs me. I don't know what I'll do if I have to move in with that brat . . ."

He stopped and a crafty look came into his face. "Oh, yes, I do know. I'll cough and I'll sneeze and I'll wheeze. I'll get the asthma again. I'll annoy them with it every night. Every night about every half-hour I'll call them in and I'll be such a nuisance keeping Brad awake that he'll be all peevish and shrieky and they won't be able to stand either of us together, and then they'll *have* to give me back my own room . . ."

Even though he thought he could not manage to talk about it to his parents, he had.

At dinner that evening when Brad was especially silly, Ken saw an opening. He threw a glance in Brad's direction, and then turning to his mother, he announced with utter disdain, "That there's my brother. I love him. I could murder him. And if you put me into that room with him, I will."

He reported to me a few days later, "I was surprised. She took it O.K."

He grew more expansive. "It's really remarkable. She really can take it from me better than she used to. I guess because she's learning to bring her own crossness out in little fire-cracker explosions. She doesn't hold it all in the way she did. You should see her at home sometimes. She looks like a witch.

"But it's still hard for me to say things to her. It's still easier to say them to you."

He looked pensive. And then very slowly, as if he were pushing to see his direction through fog, he struggled to bring into words what had long been one of his greatest fears. "Sometimes I want to let go. Over some little nothing, almost. Some little thing happens; only it isn't little when it gets to me. It seems big. I guess because it sets off something *big* inside me. The biggest wish to SOCK that you ever knew. It's so big that if I socked anybody with that much steam I—I—think I'd explode."

In great simplicity, Kenneth had elucidated what many people never come to understand. He had been so afraid that he might act on his inner anger and carry out to the full what it dictated that he had kept himself tightly in check. Immobilized almost. So afraid had he been of the push and the force of hostility in him that he had closed up and denied that any was there. In his unconscious mind, however, it had continued to propel him until again and again he had turned it back onto himself, punishing himself for the bad wishes and thoughts, getting sick, feeling guilty, cringing and failing.

If a child's emotional hungers are satisfied by his mother in the helpless beginnings of life when he cannot fend for himself, then he can take in better stride the necessary denials which must be imposed on him as he grows. If he were to put the matter into words, he might say, "I get angry, yes, at big people for their forbidding me things I want. But still I know they are fundamentally with me and for me. They care about me. They proved that to me when I was small."

On the other hand, when forbiddings follow early deprivations and a child has not come to the place where he feels he can trust his parents to love and understand him, he is apt to feel they deny him because they don't care about him. Then hurt and anger and rage and fury mount far more stormily. They must be barricaded all the more tightly. It's as if he said to himself, "I must not even look to see that these feelings exist. If I acknowledge them, they may burst and destroy me and my world."

Kenneth, however, had looked. With me to support him, he had come through pain and fear to a place of seeing. The pain and fear had grown small enough to endure, and Kenneth had built inner courage enough to tolerate the remnants that still were there and always would be. The trust in me that he had come to feel so profoundly had helped him to make up for his earlier lack of trust in his mother and father. It had helped him move forward toward trust in himself.

Now, since he trusted himself more securely, he could trust himself to manage feelings that he had not felt capable of managing earlier.

Before coming into therapy, he had built up a way of managing himself that was in truth self-demolishment. His way of checking himself had not lain in control but in paralysis. He had virtually immobilized effective functioning in his fear lest unwanted feelings come through. As a result he had not been able to bring out normal aggressiveness. The drive and the push had been so checked that he could not even tackle school subjects with the verve that comes when feelings flow freely into any act. It was as if he had posted a demon of punishment at the streets' intersection, always keeping the "Go" sign off and the "Stop" sign on.

But now he felt it less necessary to call on the demon. Kenneth felt himself more able to judge and choose and guide what he should do. He could use his eyes and look over the terrain and take into account what the traffic could bear. He could say to himself, "I'll not go up that street; it's better not to. I'll move along this other street instead. The first street's not safe; the second one is." He could say to himself, "It's not possible to let my feelings run along this action pathway. But along this other one, it's all right.

"I can't let my feelings run out in the act of clubbing my mother. That way is no good.

"But I can talk to my mother sometimes about my feelings. Though only very occasionally.

"I can talk my feelings out to you and to myself . . .

"I've been mad at my mother lots. I was mad at her the other day because she promised me I could go to the store with her and then she went off and completely forgot that I was waiting. I'd like to have called her an idiot. But I knew if I did, she'd get too sore. So I drew little idiot pictures and knew in my mind who they were."

Or again, "I'd like to sock her really. But she's a woman and so I can't. I went and socked my ball, though, all around the block."

He could manage these feelings now more consciously without shoving them all into his unconscious mind. He had acquired the basis for true *self-control*—for managing the outflow of feelings, neither denying nor letting them run wild. He saw what he could do and what he could not do in more realistic terms.

Kenneth had seen too that he could not gain good, warm sensations in his body through possessing his mother. But the deep and human universal wish to experience body-feelings of pleasure was in him. He needed to know, just as all of us need to know, that these can exist without a person's having to feel dirty and bad. He needed to know, just as all of us need to know, that he would have to steer and control the outlets in accordance with our culture's demands, again not by blocking or denying or paralyzing them, but by finding legitimate action-pathways for them to travel along.

We talked about this just as we talked about finding outlets for his feelings of anger. I reiterated what he already knew: that he wouldn't be able to make love to a woman until he was big. But that of course he would think of it and wish that he were already big all the time of his growing.

He made a finger painting in gorgeous colors, warm and glowing magenta-red against a background of aquamarine. A great shaft ran up the center with hands curved around it.

He stood off and surveyed it, and nodded in quiet satisfaction. "A penis with hands touching it. It feels good."

Then, dreaming forward into the future and back into the past, he bridged the time span between with the first marriage dream of every small boy. He worded it now without confusion, knowing it could not be. "Sometimes it wants to go into the mother's baby hole. But naturally it can't."

And then, musingly, he recalled other ways toward solution that he had essayed. "Remember, when I used to poke into the big job hole? I would pretend then that I was poking in the mother's baby hole, exploring, sort of. Trying to find out what was in there.

"And then when I thought how bad it was to want to go into the baby hole the hands would grab and hurt the penis to hold it back and punish it. That's the red . . ."

I wondered if I saw him flinch, ever so slightly? Were there still in the red of blood's tinge, some things that frightened?

He could see now, however, that hurting himself was not the answer. "That's no use!" he declared. "It's better to make it feel good with the touching. In bed at night. Instead of counting sheep!"

Here again was a legitimate action-pathway, owning up to the feelings and controlling their outflow; not needing to let sex any more than aggression remain a dark demon, unmanageable and bad.

"I can't poke her. But I can do other things."

He had brought out the wish and we'd

worked together. The baby wish of dependency on one hand, to push all of himself into his mother, to crawl back into her sheltering body. The man-dream of aggressive independence on the other hand. The wish to conquer and possess. He had faced his fear of letting either side of the impulse flow out into action. The fear of being engulfed and eaten as the baby guppies had been eaten by their mother. The fear of injury to a part of his body, his leg being amputated, hurt by an enemy whose identity even now he had not grasped.

He had explored his feelings and the fantasies enough to glimpse the comforting fact that he could keep them imagined. He had met the stirring in him enough to know that *he could impose restrictions on himself without imposing punishment.*

Kenneth had seen that he could not bring out his wish to "poke" into his mother. Not directly. But there were some more "reasonable" ways of solving the wish, some action-pathways along which it might legitimately go.

"Noises are more reasonable than noses going into ears," he announced one day.

"How do you mean, Ken?"

"Well, when Hamburger barks, his noises go into your ears. That's more reasonable than his little wet nose poking in."

I nodded and waited.

"My noises go into my mother's ears," he elaborated, "just like Hamburger's bark. I used to poke coughing and wheezing noises into her ears. Now I poke different kinds of noises in. The kind she likes better. Good noises, like when I told her yesterday that I'd gotten a spelling prize in school and good grades."

I commented that he was poking his nose into books apparently. He laughed and said he was getting quite nosy. At school, too, he'd wanted to find out what a couple of boys were whispering about and he'd gotten into a fist fight. "Not a bad one. Just enough to show them I could get

in on the show. Then, you know? The one I fought with deserted the other and whispered to *me!*"

I checked with the principal. "Yes. He actually did fight. I'd seen it coming; he's been ever so much more aggressive. Fortunately, I'd prompted his teacher that if he should fight, she should just stand by and not let it get too hot. But if possible not to stop him. He's needed so badly to get to where he *could* fight. He held his own, too, the other day when a boy tried to take his place in the line. He said 'No' and actually pushed the other youngster away. And he's getting along better now on the playground; takes more part in games and has made some good friends."

"How about taking a test?" I asked him one day.

"One of those I.Q. things?"

"Yes."

"To see how my mind works?"

"To see how well it's been poking its nose into all kinds of business, finding out about this and that."

He took it in stride as a challenge, eager to see what the test was about.

I was not surprised when the results came to me.

This boy, who two years earlier had been labeled too low to pass with the rest of the children, this boy who had been told to repeat his grade because his score was "only one hundred and eight"—*this boy's intelligence quotient now showed above one hundred and forty.*

I felt as if a gift had been laid in my lap.

Kenneth was now able to use the intelligence that had always been his. It was no longer blocked and tied down along with feelings that had to be held in. It wasn't the test result of itself that pleased me, but rather what it indicated of the general freeing in Kenneth. The test result was a sign that things were going well. So was the absence of asthma. Kenneth had

had no attack for over two months, ever since the session after he had painted the great elephant club that had killed his "bad" mother.

Kenneth put into his own words a few weeks later what was happening. "I think I'm getting healthy," he anounced. "If this keeps up, I'll soon be able to get a Life Insurance policy."

But Cathy and Vic were having a hard time and in my mind lay the question: was Kenneth healthy enough to take in his stride the things that might come? . . .

Three days later Vic called me again. His voice, half-raised, had stumbled back into the tense monotone. He had to see me today.

He came in.

Things were in a terrible mess, he said. He groaned and put his head down into his hands, burying the tears. He didn't know what to do. He hadn't phoned Loretta the next day but she had phoned him. The same urgency was in her as on the previous night. She had made up her mind to have him. She knew he loved her. This old-time business of honor was stupid. If he didn't do something decisive about it, she would. He had pleaded for her to wait in order for him to have time to work things out.

But she hadn't waited. She'd gone to see Cathy and she'd spilled things. And Cathy was furious. Cold and aloof in her now justifiable sense of having been offended.

He couldn't forgive Loretta for having done this. And Cathy wouldn't forgive him. She was keeping him out.

Cathy was bitter. "I can just see Vic giving Loretta what he never gives me. Spending time with her when he has no time for me. Talking to her when he won't talk to me. Loving her. Probably sleeping with her, though he says he hasn't . . ."

With me, Cathy was alternately cold and stormy. To Vic she was vindictively cold and hostile.

She became more depressed, feeling life had ended. "Except that I've got Ken. He's wonderful. He's been sweeter to me than he ever has been. As though he's sensed what's been going on."

And from Ken, who called and came in to see me: "I've been really afraid the last few days that Daddy might leave me with Mother. There's something all wrong.

"I keep wondering what it's all about. They still fight too much inside and not enough outwardly. Sometimes I think maybe they have financial worries and that's it. I know they have. But I think it's more the inside feelings that count.

"In the bedroom. That's where it's always the worst.

"They seem to be saying they wish it was all over with. They sit on the bed talking to each other. Maybe trying to love and having trouble. They've had too much trouble trying to love each other.

"I don't know what it is, but something happened. And I've been worried and scared that now they *will* break up the family and get a divorce. I'm mad at them for it. Why don't they grow up and get along? I'm mad at my father mostly for still not really trying to get at his feelings. He still pulls too much into himself, and that way he'll never get things straight.

"I don't like to think of their divorcing. It's frightening. Then I'd be my mother's only man."

For weeks Vic moved in a fog. And then something happened that, with its impact, brought long delayed decisiveness into his life.

It was a Saturday with the children home from school and Ken asked if he could go with his father to visit a job on which Vic was consulting.

Vic looked abstracted. "Why yes, Ken. Come on."

They went across the street together to where Vic had parked the car along the curb. Ken climbed in front in the seat next to Vic. Vic started the motor. And then it happened. With a racing engine Vic went crashing into the car parked ahead.

Ken was thrown forward against the windshield.

"I didn't know what had happened," Ken told me. "I only felt scared. I didn't know till afterward that I had a big lump on my forehead and cuts on my head and chin and fingers. I grabbed for the door and tried to open it. It was stuck someway, and that bothered me more than anything. I just had to get out and I finally did.

"I walked out and stood there and saw Mother coming across the street. And then I blacked out. When I came to, I was lying on the sidewalk. Daddy was walking away and Mother was still coming toward me. She came right to *me*. She didn't talk to Dad."

"I don't know how it happened," Vic said. "I don't see how it could have. The car parked in front of us was at least five feet away. Even a poor driver could have maneuvered out easily. But I crashed into it. As if it were a premeditated act."

But this was not all. A few weeks later it happened again.

Two accidents in such rapid succession!

"That coincidence," Ken muttered, "certainly had an awfully long arm."

He had stood the first accident with amazing fortitude, but this second one was too much for him. He came in wheezing. He felt that somehow the accidents had been his fault.

Why, I wondered, was he retreating to self-condemnation? For what was he punishing himself?

Soon I found out.

A few days before, Cathy had done an unusual thing. She had gone into the bathroom with Kenneth supposedly to help him into his pajamas. Quite incidentally, however, she had looked at his body in its eleven-year-old development.

"She looked at my hair there and told me I was growing big there. She told me I was growing into her man."

"So," I said, "you thought maybe that Daddy was trying to hurt you for that reason when he bumped the car. That he was jealous of your being Mother's man? And you're blaming yourself because in a way you'd like to be."

He assented and then retracted. "I did, I guess. But really it was all in *my* mind, not in Daddy's. I know my Daddy didn't mean to do it . . ."

For a moment I wondered whether to press truths that I knew he could grasp. But the horror and the terror of having to live with a father who wanted to harm him was too frightening as a certainty. Especially when he felt, as he'd said, that his father was not really working on his problems. Better to let it rest in the shadow of an imagined possibility from which Ken could choose to escape as he wished. Better to let him handle it by covering it over. For the present, at least. Of most importance for him now were his own feelings toward his father, rather than understanding his father's feelings toward him.

"How does the whole thing make you feel toward Daddy?" I asked.

He nodded knowingly and all at once the wheezing was cleared. "I guess that's one thing I've been hiding. I've been holding it in. He's so big. I've been kind of scared of saying it to myself. But I'm sore at him really. I'd like to do something violent to him. Maybe he didn't mean to do it. But I'm mad at him anyway. He should have been more careful. It *was* his fault. He had absolutely no excuse . . ."

As Ken went on angrily, he grew easier. He had not gotten at the ultimate reason for his anger. But he was at least placing his anger where he knew it belonged rather than turning it back onto himself.

To Vic, the impact of the whole episode kept growing. At first he tried to deny that unconscious motivations had played any role. Then something came out that helped him. One part of the first accident had bothered him more than any other. This stuck in his mind until one night, in the group therapy session, he confronted Cathy with it.

"*I* was in that accident, too, Cathy. I, too, was in the smash. It wasn't only Ken who was in the car. I was there when it hit. But you . . . how did you act? As if there were no one there but Kenneth. You came across the street, Cathy, and you didn't say one word to me. You passed me by and went straight to Ken . . ."

Cathy and Ken! Ken and Cathy! The combination made a pattern in his mind which met with another pattern. His own pattern long ago.

For days and nights the tremendous import of this filled him until from out of the crucible of the deep suffering in him there rose a conviction stronger than words.

At last Vic knew that he couldn't let this happen to his son, the thing that had happened to him. His father had left home. His father had left him with his mother. He himself had been leaving home virtually, seldom being there and when he was there not really being present. Being abstracted and away, his feelings apart. He was leaving Ken with Cathy as his father had left him with his mother.

He couldn't let this thing happen. He had to dig in and stop escaping.

Vic knew finally that he had to become a man.

Many months later Vic brought into another group therapy session something that had happened to him the previous night.

It seemed that the white moon had been shining in the window onto Cathy as she lay asleep beside him in bed. He had raised himself on his elbow and had looked down on her to see if she was all right, since she had just recovered from a rather heavy cold. A sense of eeriness crept into him as he watched the covers rise and fall with her breathing. Her face was relaxed, her lips slightly parted. From between them came the slightest of snores.

He caught his breath, his chest tightening, the dryness coming into his mouth.

Panic filled him. He wanted to run. To get up and get out.

This had happened before. With Loretta. But earlier also. With his mother when he was a boy. The rise and fall of her body as she breathed. Her closeness in bed. The small snore creeping out with its rhythmic hum.

How many had been the times when he had been filled with ineffable yearning to reach out and run his hand through her long, soft hair. Being with his mother was good and close and warm. Until his father came home.

Vic had told himself that his mother preferred him to his father. That when his father returned home and he, Vic, was shoved off into the small room across the hall, his mother's mood would slip from its ordinary unsmiling and serious quiet into sadness that held in it the quality of resignation.

And then Vic recalled an incident he'd lost long ago.

His father had come home on the previous night and Vic once more had been put to bed in his own room. The next day he got up before the pale morning moon was out of the sky. He'd dressed himself quietly, somehow vaguely planning to go outside in search of something. Something perhaps to fill the lonely void inside him.

He opened and closed his bedroom door and stood in the hall, the door to his mother's room darkly closed. And then it was that the sounds came to him which for all the years since he had been struggling to keep lost. Little chirruping unwonted sounds creeping out through his mother's closed door. And the sound of her laughter, secretively gay.

This quiet woman who, he'd always believed, was sexless. This serious woman who never laughed! His father was doing something to her to make her lips part in this gurgling enjoyment.

After his father had gone again and Vic was back once more in his mother's bed, night after night he would rise on his elbow and gaze at his mother sleeping.

Then the wish would creep into him along with the shadowed fear that made him slice off the wish before it pushed over the threshold into awareness—the wish to know what secret things he, too, might do to her to make her laugh.

Long after the episode lay buried, the wishes still prompted him to run away. He left home as soon as he was old enough to get a job. He travelled across many states to remove himself physically from that which he carried with him, ironically, in his innermost thoughts.

"I see it now," Vic said, a new composure showing in the increased easiness and strength in his voice. "Some of you people in this group take refuge in confusion. My way has been to take refuge in composure. My calm, cool quietness was a way of escaping the thoughts and feelings I felt I had to escape . . ."

He glanced at the doctor, smiling in sudden hesitance and letting his eyes drop, still somewhat fearful that this man whom he now took as a kind of father might punish him as his real father might have if he'd seen into his thoughts. The doctor might perhaps reach out and burn a hole into him with his cigarette, as his real father might have burned a far graver, deeper wound with a branding iron. Like the hole in the figurine on his mother's ivory brush. Like a hole his father might have slashed with his keen-edged razor.

"I can see now," Vic continued, "that any reaction I have had to any woman is essentially a reaction to my mother. I took refuge in the composed assurance that I'd solved my problem by leaving it when I left home. But I hadn't. I hadn't left my mother. She was still with me, inside me. I carried her across the country with me. And I carried along with her all my reactions of fear about getting close to a woman. Cathy! Loretta! It wouldn't have mattered who.

"But now that that's out in the open, I don't need to run after some Loretta-shaped promise to happiness. I can see that it's up to me to clear out the underbrush, and then the road to happiness with Cathy

won't be too hard. She's really the woman I want."

Gradually as the months passed Cathy, too, saw things. One night in the group something was said that made her slip back into what she had used as *her* refuge, the sweet, martyred, long-suffering air behind which she hid the feelings that made her afraid.

This touched off something in another group member, a man who was full of the fury he had carried from his past. He sprang up now and took it out on Cathy. "You're just like my mother," he shouted, "with your holier-than-thou attitude."

He rose and started across the room toward her, towering in his violence, his fists whitely clenched.

For a split second, Cathy's teeth flashed in white and gleaming exultation and the flush of excitement flooded into her cheeks. Then she flinched and paled and started trembling. She wanted to run, but she stayed.

She was frightened by violence and excited by violence, both. She veered from violence and steered toward violence, both. The happiest days of her life had been when her father had turned to her. And this he had done in violence more than in peace. Her only sure way of getting her father had been to provoke him to the point of violence. Then in the mad bursting of temper he became all hers.

"His spankings were the only way through which I could consistently get him."

His spankings actually had been his most dependable gift.

But violence could become too violent and hurt could become too grave. The fear had grown to overshadow the excitement, and Cathy had sought safety in marrying a man unlike her father, mild and retiring, with whom she could control her own feelings along with the control she exerted over him.

That she had needed also to control Blaine she came to see far more clearly, and why. She had wanted a man, yes. But only a man whom she could dominate. Otherwise, in her own excitement, she might provoke hurt beyond endurance, such as her father might have given her a long, long time since.

Gradually Cathy saw these things in their many-sided aspects with the shadows and the colors reaching from them. As she was able to show these to her doctor-father and her therapist-mother without being destroyed as she had feared in her childhood that her own father and mother might destroy her, she grew less fearful. She no longer needed to take refuge in tenseness and apologetic sweetness. Moreover, she could let her most impelling wish come to flower—her deep and basic wish to have a man.

Time moved on. Changes came into being slowly—almost imperceptibly. Like the shift of the seasons. Barely noticeable, the changing, till the change was there.

Vic was Cathy's man now. And she was his woman. There were fights between them as there always would be and always are in a marriage that has any vigor. But there were moments of ecstasy also, and moments of peace.

The following selection, from Beulah Ephron's *Emotional Difficulties in Reading*, represents a school-centered problem. In many cases this student would have been sent off for tutoring and nothing but tutoring. At times this answer succeeds, but in those cases where the emotional problems themselves make it impossible for a child to read, tutoring never gets off the ground. A long plateau of little progress sets in, and until the emotional problems are tackled, not much emerges other than defeat for tutor and child. Dr. Ephron handles her contacts with reading disabilities by therapeutic means. After the problem is discovered and the child becomes aware of the connection between his feelings and his poor school performance, she may then give actual tutoring during part or all of the sessions. Sometimes, this is not necessary. The non-reader begins to read after therapeutic intervention. More often, however, the child who has been a non-reader needs help in skills and confidence to catch up to his own potential reading level after his emotional blocks have been removed.

Emotional Difficulties in Reading

Beulah Kanter Ephron

. . . Mike was fifteen when he came to the Reading Center. He was failing four subjects, and one of his teachers, who had faith in the boy and great affection for him, sent him to us.

Mike was standing in a little hallway instead of sitting comfortably in the waiting-room when the counselor arrived. He

Reprinted from *Emotional Difficulties in Reading* by Beulah Kanter Ephron (New York: The Julian Press, Inc., 1953), by permission of the publisher.

smiled a shy, embarrassed, charming smile. He appeared much younger than his fifteen years. His small stature and peaked, almost elfin, face constituted a childlike rather than adolescent appearance. Walking down the hall to the interviewing room, Mike walked with a swagger, perhaps hoping to appear older, bigger, tougher, more athletic? He spoke with a swagger, too, pretending to take lightly matters which kept him close to tears. During the interview, the counselor occasionally caught on his face a strained look of pain and helplessness. He held his head at a jaunty angle and smiled almost continuously, trying to maintain composure. His eyes filled with tears from time to time.

The secretary had given Mike an application form to fill out while waiting for the counselor, since he had arrived almost an hour ahead of the scheduled appointment. He had written: "I want help with reading and spelling, and thinking before I do things. I do things and then think later. I want to find out how to study. I'd like to study." He also said that he had once had a year of tutoring in reading.

C-1: Have you any idea why you are here?

M-1: Yes.

C-2: Tell me about it. Let's hear it from you.

M-2: So I'll learn how to read better.

C-3: You feel that's your problem?

M-3: I guess so.

C-4: What's the problem as *you* see it? People come here with problems . . . what's yours?

M-4: I have a lot of problems.

C-5: Want to tell me?

M-5: Can't pass in school. (Silence.)

C-6: Tell me about it.

M-6: I failed.

C-7: When?

M-7: Last report card.

C-8: Is this the first time it ever happened to you?

M-8: Yeah. First time I ever failed *four*. I've failed English before. Never failed four.

C-9: Do you mind if this interview is recorded?

M-9: No.

C-10: Thank you. Now tell me, do you have any idea why it happened?

M-10: Well, I just didn't get the tests good. (Sounds extremely depressed and barely enunciates.) Didn't know the work.

C-11: Do you have trouble concen-

trating when you're reading? Can you remember what you read?

M-11: Well, I just read. I didn't remember everything word for word.

C-12: Nobody's expected to do that, are they? Everybody forgets a lot of what they learn. People learn to prepare for tests, and then they are expected to forget a lot afterward. That's how it is.

M-12: I don't know English . . . words. They put them on the board and they tell you to change them into adjectives and stuff like that. I know nouns, but I don't know the types of nouns.

C-13: Um-hum. You need grammar.

M-13: I don't speak clearly.

C-14: You don't speak clearly?

M-14: No. I get all mixed up when I talk. I don't know why. When I talk, words come out that I don't mean to say. It just comes out that way. I ought to think before I talk.

C-15: You mean you get nervous.

M-15: No, I don't get nervous. I get all mixed up. Talking sometimes about something that don't have to do with anything. Change and be on another subject. It just comes out when it comes in my mind.

C-16: Tell me more.

M-16: That's all. (Silence.)

C-17: What are you thinking?

M-17: Nothin'.

C-18: Is there anything new in your life that hasn't been there before, since this is the first time this has happened to you.

M-18: I don't know. (Thinks.) It might be moving to a new school.

C-19: You changed your school?

M-19: Moved into senior high school.

C-20: How do you feel about the change?

M-20: It's a lot freer than in the other school. There you had to be in the room when the bell rang and the doors closed.

C-21: Ummm. Is that right! (Sharing his tone.)

M-21: Yeah.
(Counselor offers Mike gum. He at first refuses, then accepts when Counselor says she is going to chew some, too.)

M-22: Thanks.

C-22: You're welcome. . . . Do you have the same friends in the new school as in the old one?

M-23: Well, the same, but they're just in some classes. Not home-room.

C-23: Well, tell me more. Tell me what things seem to be making a difference.

M-24: Actually, I was failing in English until I came to the story part, and I had a good imagination, so I wrote a good story. So I passed. That's the only way I got by. (Speaks with self-contempt.)

C-24: That's worth something, isn't it?

M-25: Well, the thing is, when it comes to spelling I don't get the spelling right. Red marks all over the paper.

C-25: We can help you with your spelling. But spelling isn't the most important thing. When you get to be a big successful man you can hire a secretary to correct your spelling.

M-26: I don't know whether I'll be a big successful man.

C-26: Sure you will. You're bright enough.

M-27: Everybody tells me I've got the brains. . . .

C-27: But you don't believe it?

M-28: No.
(Silence.)

C-28: What are you thinking?

M-29: My Dad wants me to get all 90's. I tell him it's impossible.

C-29: He's ambitious for you.

M-30: Oh, yeah. He can't figure out why he's so smart and I'm so dumb.

C-30: How do *you* figure it?

M-31: What?

C-31: I said, how do *you* figure it?

M-32: Why I'm dumb?

C-32: You just said your father can't figure it out. Wasn't that what you said?

M-33: I figure that he's so smart and I'm so dumb, and I can't figure out why.

C-33: Oh, I thought you said *he* can't figure it out. *You* can't figure it out. Does your father *call* you dumb?

M-34: Nah.

C-34: No. You call yourself dumb. When did you start doing that to yourself?

M-35: When? The first grade.

C-35: What happened in the first grade?

M-36: I was always in the third group in reading. I wasn't smart. I didn't know nothing. Knew 'rithmetic pretty good. English, nah.

C-36: You know, it's interesting how often that goes together. People who like arithmetic so often don't care much for spelling and English. . . . Please tell me more about you in the first grade.

M-37: They had one, two and three as far as our ability went. Like some could read fast, they would be in the first class. Every time the teacher gave a spelling test, I failed.

C-37: Umm. (Sympathetically.) Tell me more.

M-38: About what?

C-38: Oh, anything that comes into your mind. All about what's bothering you, so we can find out what's going on, what's cooking.

M-39: I don't know anything that's bothering me. I just don't want to disappoint my father.

C-39: That must be a worry to you.

M-40: He wants me to go to college. But I don't think I'm smart enough. . . . Really, I'm not too fond of school. I like to be outside. (Apologetically.)

C-40: Well, that's natural for a boy your age.

M-41: Some kids just keep their heads in a book.

C-41: That isn't so good either, is it. It is important for you to be outdoors at your age. You're growing. Studying isn't the most important thing at fifteen. To be healthy is the most important thing at fifteen, when your body is growing in all directions.

M-42: Yes. But I'm supposed to pass in school.

C-42: How much time do you put in on your school work?

M-43: An hour on each subject.

C-43: A day?

M-44: Yes.

C-44: That's quite a lot.

M-45: Oh, yes . . . ! About three hours a day. Last week one of the teachers was absent, so I only did two hours.

C-45: Do you have a gang you go with outdoors? Friends?

M-46: Yeah, a few. The gang hangs around with one guy. He has a car.

C-46: Big deal.

M-47: Yeah.
(Silence.)

C-47: What are you thinking?

M-48: Nuthin'. (Friendly but depressed in tone.)

C-48: You're under some pressure apparently, to please your Pop.

M-49: Oh, yeah. . . . And the kids tease me about my big brother. He teaches. He teaches in my school.

C-49: In your school?

M-50: Yeah. And my father teaches in a college.

C-50: Tell me more.

M-51: Well, nuthin'. . . . The kids just tease me about it.

C-51: Why do they do that?

M-52: I don't know why. Probably to suit themselves.

C-52: What do they say?

M-53: Oh . . . I say some funny things, and then they come back and keep on talkin' along. . . . I don't know how to explain. Just kiddin' around.

C-53: They like you.

M-54: I don't know. I don't know whether they like me or not.

M-55: The teachers bother me, too. Nag. They say, "You should be a smart, smart fellow, because your big brother is so smart."

C-55: It's not fair, to put that pressure on you.

M-56: I just tell them that as generations go down they get dumber and dumber. My brothers got ninety and eighty; my sisters were seventy and eighty; and I'm seventy and sixty. They don't really care much anyhow. Just give 'em reasons why I'm so dumb and don't pass.

C-56: You yourself feel that you are not smart.

M-57: Oh, I probably could be smart, but I don't want to spend time studying.

C-57: I don't think you should spend more than three hours a day studying. I think that's too much as it is. That gives you very little time to be outside, doesn't it?

M-58: Well, I work and then come

home. Maybe I play ball if I finish my work fast enough. Then I take care of my paper route and come home and listen to the radio a little bit. After I eat I go upstairs for the rest of the night. If I get done studying at nine or nine-thirty I'll listen again, maybe to a half-hour program.

C-58: Tell me some more.

M-59: I was thinkin' that I don't think I want to go to college anyhow. I don't even know what I want yet. I been tryin' to get some pointers on farming; I'd like maybe a dairy farm, or a chicken farm. I'd like to work on trees, too, maybe that tree surgery stuff. I *like* it—to be out in the air and not be cooped up in a little office!

C-59: Have you had any experience with farms?

M-60: (Brightening.) Oh, yeah! My uncle has a swell place. I go up summers and help around. Fill silo and do things around. Odds and ends. I haven't done anything big. Just helped around. I like it.

C-60: It sounds wonderful. Have you talked it over with your family?

M-61: They say if I want that, it's okay. They want to put me in something I want to be.

C-61: So you would not feel you would be disappointing your parents if you didn't go to college.

M-62: I don't know. I just hope my father don't expect nothin' from me. I don't want to be a teacher or anything like that. Or an office big-business man.

C-62: Yes.

M-63: I want a little house and farm.

C-63: I think that sounds lovely. Every person has to choose his own life, doesn't he?

M-64: (Thoughtfully.) Yeah. . . .

C-64: No matter what his parents want.

M-65: Oh, they don't interfere much.

C-65: But somehow you have the feeling you want to do what would please them.

M-66: Well . . . my big brother was so smart. They figure I should be smart like that brother. My other brother, he's an airplane mechanic.

C-66: What about your sisters?

M-67: They both work in offices. Type. Stuff like that.

C-67: So, with the exception of your big brother who teaches, the other children all work with their hands. So, you wouldn't be so different. I'm a little puzzled. Where do you get the feeling that more is expected of you?

M-68: I guess it's the teachers that nag—want me to be like the brother who teaches.

C-68: And I guess there's something inside yourself that's nagging you about it, too.

M-69: (Thoughtfully.) Yeah. . . .

C-69: Tell you what. We'll talk about it some more. Right now, let's hear you read something, so we'll get some idea of how you read. Okay?

M-70: Yeah.
(Counselor administers the Strang oral reading paragraphs. Mike reads the first one fluently and accurately.)

C-70: Good. Do you remember now what it was that you read? Can you tell me what it said?

M-71: (Mike shows good comprehension of the paragraph.)

C-71: Good. Let's try another.

M-72: All right.
(Mike reads both the second and third paragraphs with accurate pronunciation and good comprehension. Coun-

selor used the content of the third paragraph to stimulate further discussion. The paragraph dealt with the growing use of psychological and guidance clinics in meeting human problems.)

C-72: Very good reading, Mike. Now tell me what that was all about.

M-73: Well, it tells how a person like me can try to find out what's wrong. If they could find out what's wrong, they could make him ready for his future life.

C-73: Very good.
(Long pause.)
Would you like that kind of help? Are there problems in your life you'd like to have solved—that is, have help solving?

M-74: Oh, a few. But I like to solve them myself, but . . .
(Silence.)

C-74: What are you thinking?

M-75: Well, I oughta solve my own problems.

C-75: Everybody likes to . . . but sometimes it takes more courage to get help when you want it or need it. It doesn't hurt to talk things over with someone else . . . don't you think that's true?

M-76: Oh, I don't know. I mean, it's okay to talk to a friend. To have a buddy to talk to. But none of my friends listen when I talk. . . . I mean, I've fooled around so much, now you can't be serious. They say I'm stupid. (Tearful.)

C-76: That's a problem. Because you need to be taken seriously. Everyone needs to be taken seriously. And if you get into the habit of doing the joking business, so that nobody takes you seriously, it's hard to get out of it.

M-77: Yeah. But everything I say myself I almost laugh at. I can't blame anyone else for that.

C-77: In other words, you need to learn to take yourself seriously, don't you.

M-78: Yeah.

C-78: Don't you feel you're *worth* taking seriously? Perhaps you have some question about that?

M-79: I . . . well . . . I shouldn't judge myself. I should be taken seriously by someone else where it's up to them whether they take me seriously.

C-79: It's important that you take yourself seriously . . . that you have good respect for yourself as a young man. . . . Right?

M-80: Yeah. . . . (Thinking about it.)

C-80: You're a very *cute* boy, and I suppose you've gotten used to being treated as the cute little boy, haven't you?

M-81: I guess so. (Thoughtful agreement.)

C-81: The cute little kid.

M-82: (Smiles sheepishly.) It don't work no more.

C-82: You're lucky it doesn't. You wouldn't want to be a cute kid all your life, would you?

M-83: No . . . I used to be such a stupid kid when I was in the sixth grade, fifth grade. . . .

C-83: Who called you stupid?

M-84: Myself. I mean, I wasn't *stupid,* but I used to do funny things and people would laugh at me. I thought I was something big.

C-84: You mean you were the class clown.

M-85: Yeah! The teachers started calling me "show-off" and everything like that. I'd just get mad. But I don't fool around like I used to. I learned to be quiet.

C-85: And at home you're the youngest. . . . Did they treat you like a cute little kid at home?

M-86: I don't know.

C-86: It's hard to be the youngest in the family. I was the youngest in my family, and for years I was called "the baby."

M-87: Oh, they call me "baby."

C-87: Doesn't that make you angry?

M-88: Well, I just tell them to lay off. When we had our dog, I used to say, "The dog's the baby, I ain't no baby!"

C-88: (Laughs heartily.) I did the same thing exactly!

M-89: I mean, it doesn't bother me. (Shrugs.)

C-89: You feel you can shrug that one off.

M-90: Yeah. There has to be a baby in the family, no matter who it is.

C-90: Well, I guess we'll have to talk about it in our next meeting. Want to give me your address so I can write you a note about another appointment . . . ? Our time is not only up but well over.

M-91: (Mike gives address.)

C-91: Do your parents know you came here today?

M-92: My father brought me down.

C-92: Before you leave, I want you to know that anything you say to me is considered confidential. I will never tell your father or mother or teachers anything you tell me unless I get your permission first. It's between you and me, and therefore you can feel free to tell me anything you want. Okay?

M-93: Well, what I said today I'd probably not mind. . . . I mean, I could tell anybody. . . .

C-93: You haven't told me any secrets, you mean . . . but you might sometime want to, so I want you to know that you will

be treated as a young man whose confidence is to be respected. Understood?

M-94: (Smiles.) Yeah.

C-94: How would you feel about going to a school where your brother isn't teaching?

M-95: Oh, I don't know. It's just the same. When I was in school where he wasn't teaching, but they knew he was a teacher anyhow, they used to say, "I'm going to tell your brother about this." And if I did something wrong, "I'm going to bring this up to your brother." They used to say that down in the old school.

C-95: Goodness! What a thing to do . . . ! Oh, someone wants this room, so now we must stop. . . . Do you want to come back again and talk some more?

M-96: I don't care. (Voice is cheerful and louder than before.)

C-96: You don't have to unless you want to.

M-97: I *want* to get straightened out.

C-97: All right. Then you do want to come back. Instead of my writing you a note, let's go to my office now and look at my calendar and make an appointment.

M-98: Okay.

This is the kind of interview that student counselors find discouraging. They almost tearfully protest to their supervisors, "The boy wouldn't say anything. No matter what I did, he wouldn't open up." It is tempting, under such circumstances, to give up the aim of establishing a therapeutic relationship and flee to the certainty of exercises, tests and reading materials. To have done so with Mike would have been a mistake; he has had all the teaching and tutoring that one young lad can tolerate.

What are the criteria that immediately establish the fact that Mike needs psychotherapeutic help? His I.Q. is superior, yet he failed academically. This says at once that there is more to his failure than can be met with drill work. A boy with a much lower Intelligence Quotient might need assistance in picking up study techniques, or in learning vocabulary; but with his fine intelligence, Mike ought not to require tutoring for these simple procedures. Very early in his school record, he was in trouble with his teachers for what they called "laziness"—a word that, like a smoke-screen, hides whatever difficulties are causing inefficient living.

When so little is offered verbally, it becomes especially important to watch for clues—the spoken and the non-spoken. The tension in Mike's face, the tears springing to his eyes, the exaggerated swagger, the look of bewilderment that came and went like a cloud over his face . . . these tell a story. One wonders how he feels about his small stature, his childlike appearance. One wonders what started the "tough guy" facade, and what perpetuates it. His statement that he "gets all mixed up when he talks" calls for attention and clarification. Does he mean he has trouble with impulsiveness? Why does he feel he "ought to think before talking?" (M-14 and M-15)

It is an interesting commentary on the teaching of English, that Mike speaks of his "good imagination" with contempt. He says he can write a good story, but that he gets "red marks all over the paper" because of poor spelling. (M-24, M-25) How did it happen that the two were not kept separate? Why could he not feel proud of his story-writing ability, and keep this uncontaminated by his sense of failure in his spelling? Though spelling must be taught in a context, so that the purpose of communication is served by good spelling, thus giving purpose and meaning to the learning of words, still there ought to be some provision made for story-writing in which spelling is not corrected.

M-27, 29, 30, 36: These responses begin to reveal the perplexity and unhappiness of an adolescent boy who has superior intelligence but is unable to mobilize his energies to use his intelligence effectively for academic purposes. In M-39 he speaks key words, "I don't want to disappoint my father." He is in difficulty over wanting to be himself but also wanting to please his father in his father's terms. He is apologetic about expressing his own interests. (M-40, M-41)

He has a great deal to live up to. (M-49, M-50) Perhaps he feels, unconsciously, that he would rather not even try competing with these scholars in his family, that the competition is too great.

M-51 to M-54 gives some indication that he is not happy in his relationships with his friends, either. Later in the interview, from M-76 through M-85, there is further clarification of Mike's feeling that he is caught in a way of life which is not fulfilling to him; one gets the impression that he needs help to extricate himself from his old ways and to build new ones.

M-55 gives a clear picture of how innocently, yet devastatingly teachers may reinforce a student's fear of competition, believing they are stimulating him to greater effort, but in reality only heaping more burdens upon him.

M-59 through M-62 convey the story of the emotional trial Mike has been living through. He becomes quite animated when talking about his dream of doing outdoor work, but shortly afterwards he expresses the unhappy thought that perhaps following his dream will be a disappointment for his father. "I just hope my father don't expect nothin' from me." M-63 through M-69 air this problem further.

C-69 was a mistake. When the counselor read this interview, she was shocked to find that she had changed the subject at this point, when it would have been so much better to let the interview continue the way it was going. In an effort to reconstruct her reasons for introducing reading here, the only possible explanation the counselor can find is the following one:

When working with an adolescent, the counselor always makes it a practice to include at least ten minutes of reading work, for one reason: When the boy or girl goes home, he or she will be asked by the mother or father, "What did you do at the Reading Center?" He needs something specific to say, such as, "We practiced reading out loud," or "I read and she timed me," or "I worked on vocabulary." To say, "We talked," leads to the next question, "What did you talk about?" How can he remember what they talked about, when it was nothing very specific? Or, he may feel reluctant to repeat what he talked about, if he talked about embarrassing things like worrying about not disappointing his father.

One cannot help an adolescent unless he continues coming for help, and he will not be able to do so unless his parents send him. If parents send adolescent children for help with reading, they may become impatient with reports of "talk," not knowing that this talk paves the way for more efficient study. They know of reading help in terms of tutoring, and it is a good idea to satisfy the parent by including a little work with reading each time, until the adolescent has had a chance to know the counselor, to feel safe with her, to like working with her, and finally to approve of a visit with the parents, at which time the counselor's method of work can be clarified to the parents.

By this time, the adolescent will be so interested in his work with the counselor that he will want to continue it, counteracting any doubts the parents may have and reassuring the parents that something worthwhile is being achieved. This is important, since the mother or father sometimes has unconscious jealousy of the "intruder," which is consciously expressed as doubts in the efficacy of the treatment. It is the counselor's responsibility to make matters clear to them, to help them, and to win them over to a state of mind that will be helpful to the adolescent.

Everything the counselor does should have one guiding purpose: to help the adolescent boy or girl who is coming to her for help. Therefore, whether communicat-

ing with the school, or the teacher, or the parents, the manner in which it is done should be carefully worked into the treatment relationship in a way that makes it part of the treatment. For example, there is a world of difference between seeing a parent at the adolescent's request, and seeing a parent completely independently of the adolescent's knowledge or interest. If done in the latter way, the conference with the parent seems to the adolescent, when he finds out about it, to be just another version of the old, old story of parent-teacher get-together to talk him over, without their having any interest in his ideas. (The Case of Donald, presented later in this study, is a good illustration of how a conference with a parent can grow out of a boy's own wishes.)

Sometimes the adolescent would like the counselor to see the parents at once, without delay. This request in itself calls for its part in therapy. A young man of nineteen said, at his third visit to the Counselor, "*You* see my parents and tell them *it's not my fault* that things have gone wrong. Tell them they should leave me alone and let me make up my own mind about things." The Counselor encouraged him to make a list, which she wrote down, of things he wanted her to tell his parents. Then she raised the question of his inability and unwillingness to tell them these things himself. She suggested they wait a few weeks and work on the problem of his fears to speak up for himself. She promised to back him up and to support him in his efforts by seeing the parents directly after he had talked to them himself. She said to him, "*I* don't need the experience of talking to your parents in order to strengthen myself; therefore, I do not want to rob you of the opportunity to strengthen yourself by doing your own talking." This made sense to him, and he agreed to wait a while and try to discover why he felt so helpless in their presence. The complaint, so familiar in reading cases, sprang to his lips, "It's like talking to a stone wall."

Written reports back and forth, from

reading clinic to school, ought not to be documents hidden from the adolescents about whom they are written. The writer will never forget the look on the face of a fourteen-year-old boy when she said to him, "I have a report from your school about you. Want to pull your chair around and read it with me?" He looked stricken with surprise, then recovered and said eagerly, "Yeah!"

When a report is to be written to a parent or teacher, who is better equipped to help write it than the person about whom the letter is being written? He should have a part in thinking through what is important to communicate and what he would prefer not to have revealed. This activity becomes part of the therapy.

To return to Mike, from whom we digressed to explain why the counselor interrupted his valuable trend of thought: Mike suffered a great deal from lack of privacy throughout his school life. His teachers by-passed him to deal *about* him with his father and his brother, since both were in the academic world. The counselor felt it especially important in his case to keep his relationship with her completely his own, to do with as he pleased. She therefore gave him some reading work to provide him with something to talk about if questioned by his father, and thus make it easier for him to keep to himself, if he so wished, the more personal discussion that had taken place.

Returning to the interview: It is interesting to see the change in rhythm in Mike's speech as the interview progresses. His sentences become lengthier and clearer, less elliptic. M-95 is a long, complete expression spoken more soberly and more carefully than anything he has said thus far. Apparently he is beginning to take himself more seriously.

Finally, with M-97, he formulates his purpose in planning to return: "I want to get straightened out." He has come a long way from his initial request, that he wants to come, "So I'll learn how to read better."

GROUP PSYCHOTHERAPY

The history of ways to intervene in the lives of troubled children proceeded with greater flexibility than that for adults. It was clear from the start that the procedures, the geography, the physical positions used with adults were impossible to use with children. Children would not stay on a couch. Children like to see to whom they are talking.

Further, some children, who were impossible or difficult to reach in an individual relation, appeared to improve or overcome their problems when they were handled in groups. Some of them found help from their peers, others could work out angers and fears only with other children and not with adults. In addition, selected children profited (as do certain adults) in having both individual and group treatment, sometimes simultaneously, sometimes consecutively. Adolescent groups have been particularly successful. This age group, troubled with relationships with parents and difficulties in separating and growing up, often feel safer among their peers. Delinquents also frequently respond better when adult authority does not loom as the single relationship to be mastered.

In considering group therapy many factors are still being explored and studied. What kind of children work together best in a group? Should one mix boys and girls; should one mix ages? Should the withdrawn child mingle with the hyperaggressive? Does one kind of child increase another kind of child's anxiety to an intolerable extent? Are symptoms contagious? Do too many of the same kind of child tend to reinforce the illness or the symptoms? All these matters of grouping are of essential importance. Much has been learned. There is still much to be learned. Different group therapists succeed with different kinds of groups, some with activity groups for preadolescents, some with delinquent groups, and others with educationally focused groups.

This kind of information is of particular relevance to teachers, who have long been concerned with the groups they are handed each fall. Teachers talk of having a good group; of a group that never should have been put together; of the impossibility of holding a group with a certain Jane or a certain Johnny in the class. Teachers also have much information to contribute to the theory of groupings, although most are unaware of how much they know and how useful their knowledge could be to the psychologists and others studying optimal grouping.

Just as the teacher determines the atmosphere and progress of his class, the group therapist is essential to group work. He has the same basic goals as an individual therapist, but his skills and talents may differ greatly. His methods certainly differ. He must see that each member's dynamics be given a chance to show. The group can be compared with the human body, with legs, arms, eyes, and ears all functioning differently while the body acts as a unit. The total gestalt of the group is of great concern. Each group has a different "flavor" which changes in accordance with the philosophy, personality, and skill of the group therapist. His pace is of tremendous importance. How quickly can the whole group work? How can one protect Pete, who must move to awareness of painful feelings slowly, and at the same time push Carolyn, who is on the verge of insight but seems to be unhappily stuck in an old pattern.

Group therapy has, of course, not been confined to work with children. There is an increasing use of groups with adults. Alcoholics, marriage partners, divorced or widowed groups, parents, hospitalized psychotics, discharged mental patients—name the problem, there is now a group for it. Sometimes group therapy is the only therapy offered to a child. Sometimes children are seen individually and their parents in groups; sometimes the opposite occurs.

Because standard group-therapy techniques with young children are readily available in such books as Samuel Slavson's *Practice of Group Therapy* (International Universities, 1962), we present here an original article by Joan Colebrook on group work with a disadvantaged adolescent minority.

A Group Approach to Group Work

Joan Colebrook

During the last three winters I have led groups of teenagers and adults in Settlement House programs, and these notes are written to point up a method of working, which (for lack of a better name) I have called a "group approach to group work."

An original article used by permission of the author. Material may not be reprinted without permission of Joan Colebrook.

In general this method used (1) a concentration upon relationships rather than upon a leader-group relationship, (2) orientation of participants to bring about certain results and (3) in the case of the Inter-Cultural group, which I am using for illustration, a deliberate equalization of black and white members. For those who meet with group-work problems which are not mentioned in the "book," or for those who work in areas where there is considerable racial tension, this brief account may have some interest.

The Inter-cultural group was co-ed, and it met in Settlement House B in a neighborhood with a high percentage of crime, illness, alcoholism and pathology. It was formed of young Negroes from sixteen to twenty-two (indeed the greater percentage of the Settlement House members was Negro) and although this group first met to study dance and song, the interest in racial questions became so strong, that this became a catalyzing factor in group development.

We met at first upon an "open" basis (which meant that members could come to the meetings more or less as they pleased, and without pressure to be regular in attendance). The attitude in the house was very permissive and the members included some brought directly from street corner activities, so that an authoritarian approach was not at all feasible. Members wandered in and out of the office, congregated in the halls, did not check their coats, were late in coming and casual about keeping appointments, etc. I found that not much could be expected of members in a formalized way, and that by keeping the group upon an open basis, a larger attendance could be had, and more members reached. At the same time, a core group began to form, mostly males, all of them held together by the way they tried to solve their "Negroness" in a world hostile to their race.

My first experience with the group was not particularly happy. I found it hard to get and to keep their attention. They would wander in and out, drink Coca-Cola, turn their backs and talk during discussions. Many—particularly girls—would whisper their opinions to their neighbors. Some would enter the room singing loudly. Many would get up, bang the door as they went out, returning soon and opening the door just as loudly. This was quite in keeping with their behavior in other parts of the house, so that I did not feel it could be a special hostility. Testing-out was very no-

ticeable. During these days my problem was to involve the members, to keep them coming somehow or other to the meetings instead of to the pool room. It seems that the race discussions (which were an immediate success, in that the group grew from eight to about thirty on good nights) served the purpose of dissipating the free-floating hostility felt by members to life in a white world; they served also to put me and other white speakers or visitors through a testing period, necessary to the group's security. Discussions were generally—at first by my initiation, and later by the group's voting—about race problems; "integration," "lynching," "slavery and its history," "intermarriage," etc. These subjects brought out the submerged energy in the group and gave some illusion of participation. It was generally not possible to get onto other subjects because of the poor background of most of the members (many had not finished high school, and those who were at trade school or even at junior college, read very little). About race, however, these young people were somewhat informed, and even inaccurate information was buttressed by emotional knowledge.

At this point something should be said about the purpose of group work in Settlement Houses. Goals, of course, must vary from group to group, but it is necessary to face the fact that the social situation is changing and that the era which produced the Settlement House, long ago gave way to a different situation. The *kind* of disorganization which Jane Addams noted is not less evident but perhaps more so. Other social elements are operating in the slums, however; among them the activities of the welfare state, the disappearance of the old political machine, a constant shift of populations, and massive slum-clearance projects which are helping to break up the old fabric of human relationships.

According to statistics, the "disadvantaged" in urban areas are consolidating in special areas, but at the same time means of reaching the slum population are lessening—old patterns and ties are being disrupted, personal charity is giving place to impersonal state charity, and the individual needs the Settlement House less for entertainment. Isolation is growing. Morals are changing. Populations are more mobile. These factors make it harder for the Settlement House to operate. New methods of communication are needed, new kinds of programs, new and more effective ways of educating adults. At present private agencies operate in an unsurveyed confusion. While some needs go unfulfilled, others are served by three or four agencies which compete with each other.

In the group-work field as in other fields, overall studies are needed to estimate needs and to clarify goals. In many areas and in many agencies, group work is at once insufficient (that is, it does not reach enough people to be felt), is not regular enough (many teenagers and young adults in such areas only attend one or at most two groups per week), and is not of high enough quality (that is, the leader may not be a professional, nor have other necessary characteristics). Value judgments may vary from leader to leader and from supervisor to supervisor. This makes for an added confusion of goals, and although this may be fruitful if one takes a non-rigid attitude, it is at least necessary for all workers in one house to communicate well if a group member is present in two or three activities, each run by a different value-system. The general effect is not what it might be, considering the possibility of group work as a medium. And since the science of group work—if science it is—is still in its infancy, much research still needs to be done.

My problems in the house where I led the Inter-cultural group included the following factors. (1) There was a split between the concepts of recreation, education, and guidance. The group members felt that they were there for recreation, but were willing to accept a little education thrown in—and the House officers hoped for education, but there was little clarity as to how such goals would be reached under existing conditions. (2) The young people who joined my group were at first not ready to accept education, sometimes not even recreation, and they were often disturbed, hostile, maladjusted, and strikingly lacking in motivation. The group leader therefore had the task of "persuading" members to meet in an undetermined manner, as against the easy attractions of the pool room, card table and record-player. Lack of money and personnel made it hard for staff to separate activities so that the urge for recreation was duly met before the time allotted for group activities. This tended to add confusion and ambivalence to young people already ambivalent enough. (3) There was too much noise and confusion in the house itself and a difficulty in obtaining absolute privacy and a feeling of quiet and closeness. (4) There was always a time limit imposed upon the group, a feeling that the members could not really involve themselves in a discussion because it would be broken up at ten o'clock. My group tended to come late (being older and working they often had legitimate reason) but late or not, they had a great need to learn to involve themselves. (5) The atmosphere of the Settlement House was unsuitable for older teenagers and young adults in that it did not provide the feeling of freedom which was a psychological need for that age-group. (6) As a single worker I found it impossible, or at least difficult, to deal with so many individuals, especially because of a certain kind of lack of concentration which the atmosphere seemed to encourage. I found this a personal difficulty as well as noting it in the group. Because of this, though gains were made, these gains were extremely slow. Since I did not control the setup I could not try to obviate this difficulty.

These factors seemed to operate against a really dynamic program and I began to cast about for a means of alleviating them. It was relatively easy to hold large noisy discussions—in reality a kind of entertainment—in which much inaccurate information was produced, and hostility expressed along with laughter and good fellowship. However, this was nothing but a prelude to further development, and while it created a good impression in the house, individual growth was too slow, so that changes were indicated.

At this point there was a reorganization in the teen-age program, which meant that it was possible for me to concentrate upon a small nucleus of the core members of my original Inter-cultural group. There were six of these core members and two or three potential members. John and Sydney represented the middle-class-oriented, striving-for-education element. Robby and Todd were very aggressive color-conscious boys, one of whom, Todd, was a member of the Black Muslims (a pro-Negro, anti-white organization, with the specific title of Temples of Islam (T.O.I.). Jack and Dave, were, in their different ways, retreatists. Jack was simple and lacked self-confidence. Dave expressed cynicism and cloaked hostility, tending to remain always on the periphery, and studiously avoiding emotional contact. Ernie was a boy who had a difficult background, but who was slowly making intellectual gains. It is necessary to say more about Robby and Todd, who, with their adherence to the Black Muslim beliefs, had a sense of support lacking in the rest of the group. There is not space here to enlarge upon the philosophy of this organization, which has been much publicized, but it bases its concepts upon a mythology which pictures the white man as a mutant, weak and cruel, who through guilt alone, enslaved his stronger black brother. The Black Muslims believe in complete segregation, and Todd and his friend Robby never explained their presence in my group. Robby claimed that he was not a real member of the Black Muslims. He had an ebullient personality and was a leader in the hard core of the group. He had a certain charm and sought refuge from his doubts and frustrations in his racist beliefs, giving long dramatic speeches and trying to divert all attention in his direction. During the first winter it had appeared that the group was swayed by his dramatic harangues and his quick tongue—however at the same time

there was resentment at his platform-stealing techniques. The presence of these two members not only kept the other members guessing (they were not after all, sure that the solution offered by the Black Muslims might not be a suitable one for themselves) but it tended to keep the racial theme uppermost in the group mind.

It may well be that a superficial adjustment to society makes minority groups especially hard to influence. Several of these boys had attended the Settlement House since they were quite small (six years old) but they retained many immature and difficult characteristics. The great difficulty in bringing about changes in the forming personality—while at the same time unhealthy factors are operating at home or in society—is one of the problems facing a Settlement House staff.

I had noticed that when a young Negro dancer took part in a discussion with us, that he was very frank about the self-pity employed by Negroes to exonerate themselves for not progressing. This attitude caused a larger proportion of the group than I had expected, to agree with him, and to admire his objectivity, and I had wondered then how the group would be affected if transplanted into a whole new environment of such objectivity. The interplay suggested that if a new environment could be set up, the situation might act as group therapy, by automatically speeding-up the human dynamics. I argued that if a certain number of white participants could be added to the group, and if these participants could be oriented towards a healthy development for the group—towards interrelating, integration, new values, motivation etc.,—progress should be faster than when I, alone, tried to bring about slower changes. A continuous application of this interchange upon a large enough scale to suggest a *whole new world* should have a good result. I decided to experiment with a *group approach to the group* and to see what happened. Perhaps I felt most of all that the majority of my group members had grown up in a hostile and pathological world. They held the fighting stance in many of their human contacts. I felt that they had had no experience of a white world in which they could be warmly received. If a more sympathetic world, especially for them—for instance a white world without discrimination, a world where ideas operated and competed in a realistic fashion—could be built around them for a time, then the whole group would have an experience of knowing that *social worlds are not all the same*. This new world did not have to be perfect, but it would have to have some superior elements, and I needed for it participants who were warm, honest, unprejudiced and imaginative. These participants would have to provide for the group—at least once a week—a new family, a new society. They would have to commit themselves for some time to the group.

I should add here that I had noticed interesting results with one of the younger groups in Settlement House A when I had brought in a male volunteer. Several children began calling us Ma and Pa, and there seemed an effort to re-create a family atmosphere. It should be interesting to see whether in Social Agencies a more frank approach to family "caringness" would result in growth for group members.

To return to the Inter-cultural group, four Ivy League University students agreed on consultation to join us, as well as a girl from an excellent psychiatric clinic in the area, and these participants with the leader meant that the proportion of members to outsiders was roughly fifty fifty. I consider this an important fact. Also the meeting was moved from Settlement House B to my apartment in a suburb of the city, which, while it meant extra work to ferry members to and fro, meant also that we had a captive audience, a quiet atmosphere and an unrestricted time element. If we were to create a new environment I argued, we must create one where all who did so, came there purposefully, where no one could interrupt or present diversionist tactics, where one was not conscious of the clock, and where because the group itself was

inter-racial, racial matters were not necessary to hold the group together. These arrangements were of course artificial, but then so is the arrangement at Settlement House B. It seems actually less logical to gather together young people, hoping to guide them, than it is to put them into an environment which itself will tend to guide them.

Now in this new environment there was an immediate increase in involvement —a kind of total commitment which did not seem easy to achieve in the Settlement House. A discussion was generally managed with the intention of persuading, stimulating, or leading group members to express themselves freely. The members were given preference over the participants but the participants or the leader were, broadly speaking, guiding the discussion because of their broader interests. However the participants were so interested in the members that their attention was not forced. In other words, both members and participants were learning. While preference was given to the members in speaking, preference was also given to attitudes rather than facts in most discussions. As former leader, but now member of the group, I found that responsibility was taken upon many points which had been hard to manage alone. I was able to attend more easily to the dynamics of the group and to learn more about the personalities and lives of the group members.

The principles behind the dynamics of a group are similar, whatever the purpose of a group meeting. The presence of other group members provides support and enables the bringing forth of latent or suppressed feelings. The common elements of therapeutic action seem to be the same —(1) relation to others (2) catharsis (3) insight or ego-strengthening (4) reality testing (5) sublimation.[1] These elements seemed to be more operable now that the group was functioning in the new manner. The fact

[1] See S. Slavson, *Analytic Group Psychotherapy* (Columbia, 1950).

that we all sat in a small room, without glaring lights, some of us on the carpet, physically close and therefore emotionally accessible, was in itself an important point. Several psychiatrists have mentioned the importance of lights and furniture arrangement in group therapy. I had found this so with a girls' group when the members, coming from the Settlement House for an occasional meeting, liked to crowd around a small table by candlelight. Similarly the presence of other participants made value changes easier because the group from the Settlement House found themselves less supported than heretofore, yet not overpowered by these students who were less middle-class than most of the whites they had encountered before.

Technically we were not a therapeutic group—but now some therapeutic factors became more operative. It was easier to allow time for free association, to bring out doubts and hostility, to drop defenses, and to test reality. We were really using methods of informal education with a bias towards therapy.

No attempt will be made to describe the meetings in detail. The first three revolved more or less upon the race issue, though after this a more natural choice of subjects seemed to evolve. Joe L., a university student, had been to the Sit-ins in the South and talked of his time in prison along with Southern Negroes. Non-violence as opposed to violence was discussed and the members related back to a film shown about Gandhi. The film had made an impression, but here was the further impression of a white student who had used the method of non-violence. The Black Muslim members of the group engaged in dramatic argument—Robby asserting that no real friendship was possible with a white man; "Friendship is a leaky ship" was his constant statement. The conversation came around to the feelings of rejection which could cause such a philosophy and those members not of the Black Muslim group gained enough confidence to attack Robby and to make it clear that they did not

associate themselves with his fanaticism. This running argument was continued for some weeks—but even so the dynamics moved rather fast here and Robby was forced into a position from which he could not retreat. Robby had somewhat focused his attention upon Joe L. who seemed, with his activities in the Sit-ins and Southern picketings, to play the part of Robby's alter-ego (since Robby himself had activities of a segregationist nature). Very disturbed, partly by Joe, to whom he felt drawn even while he claimed that all friendships with whites was a weakness, and partly by the now clear desertion of his own black friends, Robby was unable to cope with the conflict. A further tension was created when a Negro from South Africa visited the group. And he, after his recital of experiences infinitely more horrible (at the hands of the white man) than those experienced in America by our group, yet firmly adhered to his belief in integration, brotherhood, intermarriage etc. This was too much for Robby. After an explosive scene, he and Todd left the group, their influence undermined. Robby told me later during a personal follow-up, that he rejected some of the Black Muslim ideas and was looking for new solutions. My impression was that he had been forced to see the conflict between his feeling of friendship for some white people and his political solutions, and that he was searching now for some fresh means of resisting this exposure.

The rejection of the Black Muslim ideas by the group took place quickly in comparison to the many meetings we had had in the first winter when two or three aggressive anti-whites dominated the group. Although now it meant the temporary loss of the two extremists, it was a healthy dynamic because the rest of the members could not develop when controlled by a philosophy of hate. After a period of catharsis, these remaining members settled down to relate more naturally.

Serious talks had shown up the limitations of the members, but the more striving boys, on the other hand, responded not only to the intellectual stimulus but also to the hopeful atmosphere. Sydney and Jack showed more interest in reading, made notes at meetings, took down the names of books and articles, and sometimes brought clippings to the group. I listened to both these members laboriously repeat what a former speaker had said in somewhat the same terms as the speaker, as if trying to conquer a new medium. Jack made and kept several appointments outside group meetings to attend political seminars, speeches, etc. One of the retreatist members, Dave, showed great uncertainty about coming to meetings, but was in his own way affected by the atmosphere of enquiry which prevailed. Although he read a good deal, he seldom committed himself to argument, but would say such things as "I know I could live under communism." However, when listening to a Polish visitor telling of her experiences in that country, his final comment was that he would "read some more." The extent to which emotions controlled his political beliefs was suggested by his breaking down after this argument and telling me that he didn't like to talk because his thoughts weren't clear. Indirectly he expressed gratitude for the group when he said that he liked it but "I hope you can all take my sarcasm."

One evening a particularly revealing discussion was held about "Crime and the Negro," headed by a research worker in delinquency. After a brief talk—skillfully given in hip language—we threw the conversation open and subjects such as drugs, the police, muggings, and so on were bandied about. This was "members evening." It was revealing to see them lapse into a language of their own, to recount an existence lived in a world they conceived of as threatening and disorganized, to grow lyrical about the dangers and "kicks," the flights from dance halls, the gangs lying in wait on various corners, the best methods of dividing up to meet later, the "tippin" across town, how they felt after drugs, how communication went between friends—a communication built upon an ironic and mocking recognition of their own ambivalent roles. Ernie gave an imitation of selecting a victim (an intruder on the "turf") of the preliminary greeting, the partitioning of his belongings ahead of time, of the wrong directions which led him into a trap, of the final robbing down to his pants and shoes. Such free discussion is not so easily found in a Settlement House environment unless it is in a set-up arranged to give an illusion of freedom—and this discussion gave real information necessary to understand the values members had absorbed. One boy, Vic, from a group in another house, who had often expressed to me anti-Negro feelings, came to the meeting at my suggestion to tell of the increase of tension in a nearby area because of the influx of Puerto Ricans. Vic expressed his resentment against these Puerto Ricans, complained about their knife-carrying and their language, and suggested that they were now getting too much attention from Settlement House B. ("They're going all out for the Puerto Ricans.") This gave an opportunity for an analysis of prejudice in general, and Vic left the group with two of the Negroes in his car. I reflected that the method I was using could also be used with groups of whites and Puerto Ricans.

The six-weeks-experiment of the "Group approach to group work" seems to have had a positive effect. The leader was able to get a much clearer picture of individual members and their cultural context, a primary necessity for further work. Involvement became automatic rather than only possible when the group was moved to a favorable physical environment where privacy, quiet, and a pliable time element were operating. The group approach made it possible for the members to experience a good inter-racial atmosphere and to test out in a controlled situation so that the unnatural concentration on race could lessen. The dynamic tended to be faster due to greater interaction. Personal relations became warmer. One member, expressing to me his love for one of the Ivy League

University men, then said "And I love you, too, just the way I love him." I think that he was trying to express his feeling of the general warmth of the group, where "love" could be something possible on a human level.

One of the negative aspects of removing the group from the Settlement House was that it was a fairly clumsy procedure, and tended to shut out floating members who might have eventually joined the group. However, the point which must be stressed is that the leader was, during this period, relatively satisfied with both individual and group development. She felt that in a controlled situation such as the above it was possible to demand enough from the group. Problems in structuring and programming are administrative ones; and it is not for the drifting or disturbed juvenile to dictate the structure, as so often happens in Settlement Houses. Rather, he must express his self-determination through the structure. It is only too possible in a busy, overburdened Settlement House to allow the member who comes in from the street to find not only shelter from the outdoors, but also a hangout where no real effort is required, no allegiance to person, duty, or idea. This may result in a deep inner conviction that nothing is hoped for him, that he is not (as he has already feared) worth anyone's belief.

In a brief evaluation, some of the members reactions were as follows.

Jack: "I enjoyed it a lot—it was educational—as I said I came eighty percent of the time—it was something you don't get out of books." Jack added that he had felt a "little tense at first—wondered what the university boys would think of us."

Sydney: "I enjoyed it very much—all the way through—enjoyed it like anything —it was sweet somehow—like a family."

Ernie: "It was boss—some nights were wonderful. I learnt things."

John: "Its been pretty alright. I've been enjoying it—I never felt left out. I felt I was welcome."

Robby: "I knowledged and I knowledged."

Dave: "I was grateful though I couldn't always talk—especially when you were all brainwashing me."

Todd was not there for the evaluating session.

It is possible that the group approach outlined here might be used in more than one way. This form of social education in a controlled setting has the advantage of being pliable in that it can educate through both interchange and identification. It sets up more possible roles than does group work with one leader. It might be very valuable in community work—for instance during urban renewal when it is necessary to rouse civic awareness. A teenage or young adult project would need the cooperation of several universities or schools, but if ten or more groups could meet in any problem neighborhood for a winter (each group made up of equal numbers of members and oriented participants) the effect might be of circles of democratic exchange, fertilizing a deprived and isolated neighborhood. Many different techniques have been used for adult education, but this particular technique has special emotional values for both members and participants. It is a *shared* experience. For the young adult or adult who has never related on an equal basis with contemporaries in more privileged areas, it provides a new world. Most adolescents who quit school do so not because they devalue education, but because of financial and psychological pressure. Such groups as ours described above offer a possible avenue of familiarizing them painlessly with areas beyond the cultural barriers, and this familiarity might make success avenues more available by breaking down prejudices and fears.

ADJUNCTIVE THERAPIES

Children are an active race. They communicate in a variety of ways, often less with words than in play, games, body movements, pictures, and all the things they make, from music to plane models. Adult psychotherapy is based on the ability of a person to communicate with others in words. However, sometimes a too great facility with words beclouds issues and conceals rather than reveals feelings. In such cases, it is the therapist's job to help the patient uncloud and reveal. Some analysts have used painting, body movements, and dramatizing as supplementary means of helping their patients communicate. Dr. H. G. Baines, a Scotch Jungian analyst, was particularly fertile in developing painting as a treatment tool. Moreno developed psychodrama in group therapy. Psychoanalysis was originally formulated to treat neurotics who were expected to be able to learn to verbalize feelings. When therapy expanded to the treatment of psychotics, with particular emphasis on schizophrenia, there were many patients who didn't speak for long periods and many who seemed to express their distress or conflicts by body movements. Dr. Frieda Fromm-Reichman developed particularly skillful methods with schizophrenic patients. Some of the tools developed with adults were borrowed from child therapy, while child therapists in turn borrowed the new techniques used with nonverbal adult patients.

We have talked about play therapy as the backbone of child treatment. Games, activities, toys, dolls are used along with speech of a supportive, probing, or interpretive nature. Also the art media, drawing, painting, finger painting, clay work, and mosaics will help a child willingly project his feelings, conflicts, fears, dreams, defeats, and aspirations. These can be used as communication by the therapist just as surely as any words. Sometimes the child's paintings are accompanied by words, sometimes not. Sometimes the therapist interprets the paintings to the child; sometimes he merely reflects back the child's feeling as shown in the painting. The way a therapist handles these questions depends partly on the kind of illness of the child and the stage of treatment and partly on the therapist's philosophy of treatment. Whether it is used as part of a child's therapy hours or as an isolated therapy in itself, art therapy has proved a fruitful means of communicating, of discharging feelings, of working out conflicts and resolving them. Clearly, the skill of the art therapist in relating to the child through understanding dynamics, translating psychodynamics into visual or plastic form, and handling the messages relayed is of prime importance.

Art therapy is perhaps the most commonly known adjunctive treatment, and there are a variety of schools of thought about it. It is done individually or in groups. It may be the only therapy used, but it is more likely to be used along with other forms of treatment. The principle underlying it holds true for all forms of adjunctive therapy—namely, that a patient (particularly a child) may be helped to express his problems, conflicts, and manner of operating by ways other than direct verbal communication and that through these means he may gain insight and be able to alter his perceptions and modes of behavior in ways that will be more satisfying to himself and others. Elinor Ulman defines the purposes and principles of art therapy in the following article.

Art Therapy
Elinor Ulman

It is always hard, sometimes impossible, to find the ideal name for any complex and subtle discipline. The title "art therapy" can easily be dismissed as inadequate or inaccurate, but I have not found a better one. Doubtful implications can only be resolved by careful, evolving definition. The purpose of this paper is an opening move in that direction.

"Art therapy" is currently used to designate widely varying practices in education, rehabilitation, and psychotherapy. Directors of special schools, psychiatrists, and even (in at least one case) the United States Civil Service Commission, refer to certain professional and volunteer workers as art therapists, even though no similar educational preparation, no set of qualifications, nor even any voluntary association binds these people together. Possibly the only thing common to *all* their activities is that the materials of the visual arts are used in some attempt to assist integration or reintegration of personality.

Yet competing and mutually exclusive definitions of art therapy have already been published by art therapists. At least one psychiatrist, objecting to the looseness with which the term is used, has attempted to tighten up its meaning. Psychiatrists also have suggested various combinations of new names to designate special uses of art materials in psychotherapy.

Art therapy is the only one of the many activity therapies to attract this kind of attention from psychiatrists. This, I believe, implies something important about the peculiar nature and potency of our medium. There is a considerable body of

From *Bulletin of Art Therapy*, I, No. 2. Copyright © 1961, Elinor Ulman. Reprinted by permission of the author.

A member of the faculty of the Washington School of Psychiatry, Miss Ulman was assigned by the Department of Physical Medicine and Rehabilitation to work in psychiatry at District of Columbia General Hospital.

literature describing the therapeutic use of patients' graphic and plastic projections in psychiatric practice. A number of these books and papers antedate the important publications of such art therapists as Naumburg and Kramer. Since art therapists have begun to publish, some psychiatrists imply that the term is being used to denote territory that belongs rather to themselves.

Direct attempts by art therapists to define art therapy demand first consideration. Whatever its deficiencies, our two-word title at least indicates the two main trends in existing practice and theory: some art therapists put the emphasis on art and some on therapy. The art people tend to exclude procedures where completion of the creative process is not a central goal; the therapy people often explain that preoccupation with artistic goals must be minimized in favor of a specialized form of psychotherapy. In the United States the second group—emphasis on therapy—found its spokesman earlier in the person of Margaret Naumburg. They are the ones who afford us the unique privilege of colliding squarely with psychiatrists who encourage their patients to communicate not only with words but with paint and clay. Among them also are the few who claim that art therapy can be an independent as well as an auxiliary technique in psychotherapy—a claim made, as far as I know, for no other activity therapy.

"SYMBOLIC SPEECH"

Naumburg's theory has undergone considerable evolution since the early 1940's; only a recent formulation will be quoted. Naumburg designates art therapy as analytically oriented, saying that it "bases its methods on releasing the unconscious by means of spontaneous art expression; it has its roots in the transference relation between patient and therapist, and on the encouragement of free association. It is closely allied to psychoanalytic therapy. . . . Treatment depends on the development of the transference relation and on a continuous effort to obtain the patient's own interpretation of his symbolic designs. . . . The images produced are a form of communication between patient and therapist; they constitute symbolic speech."

Naumburg cites the advantages of introducing painting and clay modeling into analytically oriented psychotherapy as follows: First, it permits direct expression of dreams, fantasies, and other inner experiences that occur as pictures rather than words. Second, pictured projections of unconscious material escape censorship more easily than do verbal expressions, so that the therapeutic process is speeded up. Third, the productions are durable and unchanging; their content cannot be erased by forgetting, and their authorship is hard to deny. Fourth, the resolution of transference is made easier. "The autonomy of the patient is encouraged by his growing ability to contribute to the interpretation of his own creations. He gradually substitutes a narcissistic cathexis to his own art for his previous dependence on the therapist."[1]

An informal inquiry made in 1960 revealed that of 30 art therapists working in the United States and Canada a substantial majority believed that a therapeutic endeavor where spontaneous graphic and plastic projections serve primarily as "symbolic speech" was an important goal of their own practice. About half of these, like Naumburg, minimized any other special contribution of art activity to the treatment of the mentally ill. Independent private practice appears to be rare;[2] most of these art therapists work as members of psychiatric teams. Conditions vary widely and

technique is modified in many ways. It is worth noting that Naumburg and others have applied similar methods both in individual treatment and in group therapy.

Naumburg's procedures overlap those described by psychiatrists who use painting and clay modeling in the course of psychoanalysis or analytically oriented therapy. These doctors share most of her convictions about the advantages gained by introducing these special materials and techniques, though in their reports I have found no mention of any change in the problem of handling transference. Max Stern and Ainslie Meares make it abundantly clear that they regard the interpretive use of patients' spontaneous productions in paint or clay as an integral part, but only a part, of their own basic therapeutic practice. W. L. Meijering assigns "expressive therapy," characterized as intensive and interpretive, exclusively to the "expert psychiatrist."

HEALING QUALITY OF THE CREATIVE PROCESS

The conflict here implied can be discussed better after considering another important theoretical formulation. Edith Kramer emphasizes art in defining the art therapist's special contribution to psychotherapy. In 1958 she became the second member of our nascent profession in the United States to publish at book length and to attempt rigorous definition.

The healing quality inherent in the creative process explains, in Kramer's view, the usefulness of art in therapy. "Art," she says, "is a means of widening the range of human experiences by creating equivalents for such experiences. It is an area wherein experiences can be chosen, varied, repeated at will. In the creative act, conflict is reexperienced, resolved and integrated. . . . The arts throughout history have helped man to reconcile the eternal conflict between the individual's instinctual urges and the demands of society. . . . The process of sublimation constitutes the best way to

---

[1] Margaret Naumburg, "Art Therapy: Its Scope and Function," in *The Clinical Application of Projective Drawings* by Emanuel F. Hammer et al., Springfield, Ill., Charles C. Thomas, 1958.

[2] See Margaret Naumburg, *Psychoneurotic Art: Its Function in Psychotherapy;* Grune & Stratton, 1953.

deal with a basic human dilemma, but the conflicting demands of superego and id cannot be permanently reconciled. . . . In the artistic product conflict is formed and contained but only partly neutralized. The artist's position epitomizes the precarious human situation: while his craft demands the greatest self-discipline and perseverance, he must maintain access to the primitive impulses and fantasies that constitute the raw material for his creative work.

"The art therapist makes creative experiences available to disturbed persons in the service of the total personality; he must use methods compatible with the inner laws of artistic creation. . . . His primary function is to assist the process of sublimation, an act of integration and synthesis which is performed by the ego, wherein the peculiar fusion between reality and fantasy, between the unconscious and the conscious, which we call art is reached."[3]

The complete artistic process thus exemplifies victory in the continuous struggle imposed on man by his basic nature. Therefore the arts have special value in the treatment of the mentally ill,

[3] Edith Kramer, *Art Therapy in a Children's Community;* Springfield, Ill., Charles C. Thomas, 1958, pp. 6–23.

but by themselves they cannot repair seriously damaged capacities for sublimation. No art therapist who places the emphasis on art considers art therapy a possible substitute for psychotherapy in the more conventional sense. Most agree with Kramer about a few salient qualities that distinguish the art therapist from the art teacher. In therapy the product is more clearly subordinated to the process than in teaching. Even more than the teacher must the therapist offer acceptance and respond to the special needs of every patient. His psychodynamic understanding shapes attitudes and actions in ways too subtle for brief recapitulation, enabling him to contribute both to the therapeutic program and to the understanding of each patient's total personality.

Of the 30 art therapists previously mentioned, a majority consider that providing adequate conditions for the creative process is an important part of their job, but only a small number appear to believe that it is their whole job. About twice as many aim only at the use of graphic and plastic productions as "symbolic speech." The largest single group—about half of those responding—believe in both these two main ways of using art. . . .

Music therapy is clearly related to all the above-mentioned therapies. If body movement and body rhythm are understood to be projections, as are painting, clay work, games, and use of toys, then clearly the making of music is also a projection. There are, however, some limiting factors. To be free to project what one wishes with music, one needs to know how to use an instrument or how to use his body as a singing instrument. However, the act of participant listening and responding projectively is often used therapeutically, both with individual patients and with groups. It is often used in mental hospitals and in treatment schools as part of the program.

Different types of troubled children respond differently. The schizophrenic child often relates through music. The neurotic or phobic child often finds release; the brain-damaged child appears particularly responsive to sound and rhythm. But the hyper-aggressive child and the hyper-active brain-damaged child often lose hard-fought-for controls on hearing some overstimulating instruments, such as the drum. Music, like body movement and art, has to be thought out carefully when used with different children. This fact is of particular importance to teachers who, after planning a program for a group, often find many of the group responding well while a few others fall apart, breaking up the whole activity. Study of the use of materials or modes in these areas when applied to a given kind of child should be useful to teachers on sub-grouping and lesson planning.

Dreikurs illustrates the use of music therapy in the following article with two case histories and an evaluation of the techniques used by therapists.

Music Therapy
Rudolph Dreikurs

Bobby, aged five, was aggressive—screaming, hitting, and kicking. In the first session, he ignored the instruments, screamed, kicked the doors and the walls. The therapist sat quietly, looking out the window. Bobby stole a glance at her, then intensified his volume. The therapist took a big bongo drum, played it softly at first, then overtook Bobby in volume and tempo. Bobby stopped, in a furious red-faced rage. The therapist said sweetly, "This time, louder and faster, Bobby." Bobby sat down on a chair, his head down, tense and depressed. After a silent pause, the therapist hummed a nursery rhyme. Its effect was quiet and calming. Bobby stood up, went to the farthest corner of the room, and, with his back to the therapist, swayed from leg to leg in perfect rhythm to her singing. She continued the same melody with the text, "Bobby is a fine big boy," over and over, with Bobby swaying in rhythm. Finally he turned around, smiled at the therapist and ran over to her. This had taken 50 minutes. They played another song on the phonograph, he jumping up and down with delight, and both singing the chorus together.

At the second session, Bobby again screamed at the sight of the therapist, this time in another room. He ran to the old room, screaming, and the therapist waited for 20 minutes before he came and joined her. He screamed and kicked, and tried to throw a record out of the window. The

Rulolph Dreikurs, M. D., and Dorothy Brin Crocker, "Music Therapy with Psychotic Children," in E. Thayer Gaston, ed., *Music Therapy 1955* (Fifth Book of Proceedings), (Lawrence, Kansas: The National Association for Music Therapy, 1956), pp. 62–73.

therapist used the same nursery song, *Mary Had a Little Lamb,* but this time playing it softly on a record-player. Bobby had to stop yelling in order to hear it, and then—spontaneously—sang the song with, "Bobby is a Fine Big Boy." Both continued singing and playing together, over and over again. The boy was delighted, and both added the line, "Bobby came down town," to the same tune. He looked happy, although from time to time he ran to the doors screaming and then hurried back.

During the following sessions, the therapist deliberately thwarted Bobby's compulsive expectations, by using the same room when he expected another and vice versa. She did the same with changing the music procedure. This upset his repetition compulsions. He shrieked each time in panic, "What's the matter?" and the therapist repeated his, "What's the matter?" as a recitative and then added, "Nothing," with her voice going up in a happy way. Then she chanted the old beloved chant, "Bobby is a fine big boy," and before long he joined in, "What's the matter—nothing—Bobby is a fine big boy," singing in a happy voice. Everything that Bobby accomplished was added to the chant, and he obviously looked happier and was more relaxed.

The first verbal communication occurred while beating the bongo drums. At first Bobby only repeated the therapist's last words, but gradually he started to express himself about food. They used new musical tunes to sing about foods, menu-planning, what he liked to eat and what went well together. At first, he was unable to make a choice. So they carried over to situations indicating possible choices. Since Bobby repeated the last words of the therapist, she frustrated him by making the undesirable things the last words. Then Bobby shifted to the next to the last word, and gradually made a choice.

The chants became more elaborate. Folk music songs were used with words about the things that "big boys can do," such as going down town, going out to lunch, and going to school, and all the things that babies do and cannot do. (Bobby had a brother, one year old.) He did not use pronouns, starting sentences only with his own name, so the therapist chanted the proper pronouns to him; and, without realizing it, Bobby began to use them. His musical taste alternated between the primitive chanting and rather sophisticated music. He learned folk songs and songs from musicals. The music and rhythm were used to accompany drawing, cutting out, tying knots, and playing with blocks and clay. Bobby is now beginning to participate in a group.

Stephan, a 14-year-old boy, was unwilling to speak with anyone except his family. His mother was completely defeated. He had stopped talking to outsiders and was considered feebleminded. At the age of seven, he had for a short time begun speaking and singing in school; but, as suddenly as he had begun, he withdrew again. He was stubborn, lost his temper, did not play, never worked at anything. He had been under psychiatric care for years without any results. Soon after coming to the child guidance centers for help, Stephan and his mother were referred to music therapy.

When he came for the first session, there was background music of folk songs. He appeared limp, droopy, slow-moving, except for the excitement shown in his eyes. He carefully examined all the instruments, went from one to the other, touching them, but was unable to choose one. He finally came to the therapist and acted out that she should pick one. His excitement increased. She put another record on, and he sat back in the chair and listened intently.

The therapist structured the music on the basis of his passivity. She started with passive listening, avoided doing things for him, but praised and encouraged him. In the second session, she asked him whether he would like to draw while listening. He made faint "two-year-old" scrawls on the paper. The music was changed from sedative to exciting—to calypso. The therapist picked up castanets and started dancing. He still sat, but imitated her movements. The therapist got behind him and propelled him by using rhythm instruments on his rear. At last he started moving. They began with an autoharp, Stephan accompanying the therapist's singing. Then she stopped singing, saying that she didn't know his favorite. "Isn't that a pity!"

This is the outline of two months' activities, after which the boy's speech returned. While encouraging him through praise, the therapist frustrated him constantly by ignoring his unwillingness to talk. She addressed questions to him as if she had forgotten that he didn't speak. After two months, he played the rhythm instruments with better rhythms and much more energy. He showed preference for certain pieces, and for the first time made a sound on a kazoo. He immediately dropped the instrument as if surprised at his own courage. Later he blew several times on a harmonica and then dropped it also. He made musical portraits on the bongo drums, describing moods, places, animals. In this way, he and the therapist began conversations between themselves on the bongo drums. Using musical background, they started acting out situations; going to the psychiatrist, preparing to come down town alone, meeting new people, the therapist changing the drum beats in accordance with the words, Stephan responding with his own rhythm. They played duets together on the recorder and listened to modern music, about which the boy drew pictures which suddenly became rather mature.

The therapist continued to frustrate Stephan by sometimes "not understanding" pantomimes or drawings. He tried to scrawl his communications; but the therapist accelerated her tempo of speaking, so that writing became impossible, and he threw his pencil and paper to the floor in frustration. Once, after two months, he was unable to plug in the phonograph because he needed to stand on the chair on which the therapist was sitting. She "did not understand" when he first tried to pantomime and then to push her gently off the chair. Then he bent to the therapist's ear and began to grunt, until after about 20 minutes of grunting he said, "Get up," in a whisper. After this experience, he always wanted to go back to the practice room where this had occurred. He began to talk in whispers. Once the therapist played on the piano, acting out a scene of being trapped in a burning building. He had to shout for help. Then he was to be furious because somebody had hit him, and he had to yell, "Scram." In the beginning he whispered both times, but finally he yelled. From that time on they played—with music—all kinds of experiences, taking a trip on the bus, buying tickets, buying various things. He began to sing louder and louder, and talked audibly, with his favorite music background, about his dreams, his daydreams, his loneliness and his fears. He felt that no one at school liked him because he was "dumb." He was ashamed of his puny, weak body.

Finally, Stephan was introduced into a group of younger psychotic children, where he began to direct them and to teach them in their music therapy activities. In school he began to function on a higher level.

EVALUATION OF THE THERAPEUTIC ACTIVITIES

It is impossible, because of limited space, to analyze and evaluate the various activities of the music therapist. Definite psychological principles underlie each step. Perhaps most important is the utilization of the pressure of the situation, a technique which the writer calls "natural consequences." Against the expectation of those who may consider any pressure on such children to be harmful, the children responded well to such situational pressures, probably because of the absence of verbal expressions. This distinction between verbal pressure and natural consequences is exceedingly important in the training of all children, but even more needed in dealing with psychotic children.

The corrective influence of reality comes almost automatically into play if the therapist resists passively the child's mistaken approaches. In order to do so, she must be able to recognize his goals and know how to cope with them. The four goals which the writer has described as underlying the disturbing actions of a child are: (1) the demand for undue attention and service; (2) the power struggle to defeat or overpower the adult; (3) the desire to hurt, as revenge for actual or imagined abuse; and (4) the flaunting of actual or assumed deficiencies to avoid another failure. These four goals are found in psychotic, as well as in other children. They can be recognized in the cases presented here.

The necessary passive resistance of the therapist naturally implies her ability to react to the child's suspicion, hostility or aggression, with interest, understanding, and lack of condemnation or censorship, but without yielding. In this way, the therapist exposes the child to new experiences in human relationships, conducive to better relationships with all.

Significant in some of the approaches described, was the technique of accepting the child's faulty behavior patterns as the basis for progress, entering into his private logic, swinging in tune with his actions, thoughts and feelings, and eventually redirecting them.

These cases are only samples of the work done by the music therapists working with the writer's patients. This work brought results where other approaches had failed. It seems that the pleasant experience with music, often merely in the background, stimulates participation, permits an increase in the child's attention span, and raises his frustration level. External and internal tensions disappear, as reality becomes more pleasant and less threatening. The demands for participation are so subtle that they are not resented or defied.

In this sense, music therapy may in many cases be the method of choice, the only method which has proved its efficacy in reaching certain children. Most important is the fact that this can be achieved with a few sessions a week, so that institutionalization no longer appears mandatory, unless the child is too destructive to remain

at home. But, even with such aggressive children, it is often possible, through firmness and stimulation by music therapy, to achieve sufficient improvement so that the child can continue in his natural setting.

Music therapy is still relatively young. Many new approaches and techniques will probably evolve in the process of exploration, experimentation and scientific evaluation of the results. The experiences gathered in working with the most difficult cases will undoubtedly provide new insight into the corrective potential of music in general.

One of the most interesting and most used adjunctive therapies is play acting. Actually, like art therapy and occupational therapy, it is used as frequently with very troubled adults as it is with children. It was discovered that many people are more able to express their honest feelings and conflicts when playing an imaginary role, or when in a situation among neutral people. They can project conflict-making or stress-making situations in a way that reveals their reactions to both themselves and the therapist. When children understand their own reactions they can learn to meet stress in more useful and satisfying ways. Psychodrama is often used with convalescing mental patients about to reenter society. Thus, the situations they may fear, or may be likely to meet are encountered first in play acting at the hospital.

Sometimes the more inhibited or concealed ones find the use of hand puppets, marionettes, or masks easier than direct play acting. One of the pitfalls that is particularly operative with children (where grasp on reality is less well formed) is the confusion between reality and fantasy; therefore, it becomes of prime importance for a therapist using this technique to define and redefine reality for the child. Many children benefit immensely from the skillful use of psychodrama—particularly neurotics, phobics, delinquents, acting-out children, and some schizophrenic children. Diagnosis and careful trial and error are needed to determine how much and when a child should have psychodrama, as Woltmann explains in our next article.

The Use of Puppetry in Therapy
Adolf G. Woltmann

"Hit him!" "Kill him!" "Watch out, he is still alive. He is going to kill you!" "Turn around quick. He is coming after you. He

Reprinted from Harold H. Anderson and Gladys L. Anderson, *An Introduction to Projective Techniques: And Other Devices for Understanding the Dynamics of Human Behavior,* © 1951, by permission of Prentice-Hall, Inc., Englewood Cliffs, New Jersey.

is going to bite you!" "Hit him again and kill him!" "You better run home to your mother. This place ain't safe!" "Kill him!"

Excited voices of children fill the room. Some children stand up with their fists in the air, ready to come to the rescue of the little character on the stage. Others sit quietly, but their flushed cheeks and heavy breathing betray their tense emotional state. A few hide their heads in their hands, as if afraid of watching the struggle between the little puppet and the crocodile. The fight on the puppet stage continues. With a stick twice his size, the little puppet boy subdues and apparently kills the fierce puppet crocodile. The animal sprawls lifelessly on the stage, but as soon as the puppet boy turns his back, it reopens its threatening mouth, lifts its head, and chases the little boy all over the stage. Another battle ensues. The crocodile is hit and killed again, only to come back to life and to harass the little boy until finally, the puppet boy is victorious over the fierce animal. This time the killing is final. The crocodile is pushed off the stage. The puppet boy bows and acknowledges the rousing applause from his responsive audience. The tense excitement is gone, the atmosphere relaxed. The children are happy that their beloved puppet actor has escaped unharmed from this life-and-death struggle.

An examination of scenes like the one just described raises a number of questions. Why do some children clamor wildly for killing, while others hide their heads? Why do some children move their hands as if they had to fight the animal aggressor on the stage, while others shrink away from such aggression and advise the puppet character to run away and to find safety and refuge in the sanctum of the home and the presence of the mother? Why do the children relax when their puppet hero is victorious? Why do some children urge the crocodile to eat up the puppet? Obviously, these puppets have specific meanings for each child. What determines these meanings, and what do they convey in terms of the child's thinking, reaction, and participation?

It is assumed that each child identifies himself, in a manner specific to him, with the puppet characters and with the actions portrayed by them. It is further assumed that this identification leads to projections in the sense that each child projects his own feelings, desires, wishes, and anticipations into the puppet show.

Before a fuller comprehension of these complicated processes is possible, the elements that go into a puppet show must be analysed. This calls for a discussion of puppets, the stage, the play, the psychological rationale of puppet types and of the puppet plays, the combination of acting and play content into a meaningful whole, the reactions of children to general and specific puppet play situations, and the possible therapeutic influence that puppet shows have on children.

PUPPETS

Puppets are divided into three large groups: shadow puppets, string puppets (marionettes), and hand puppets.

The *shadow puppet* is used predominantly in the Orient. It is made of translucent material such as parchment or thin leather, mounted on a stick. The shadow puppet is held close behind a translucent screen, and a light behind the puppet throws its shadow on the screen, so that the audience, facing the screen, does not see the real puppet but only its shadow. Most shadow puppets have arms joined to the body and moved by additional sticks. The puppeteer sits behind the screen and manipulates these puppets above his head. The shadow puppet is limited in its movements: it can only move from right to left or vice versa across the stage; it cannot turn around on the stage because it would lose its form and appear as a thin, black line on the screen; it cannot move into the background because a retreat from the screen toward the light would cause enlargement and distortion of the shadow. Its action radius is also limited. Shadow puppets cannot put on a good, convincing fight. Finally, the use of shadow puppets in this country labors under a cultural handicap. The oriental shadow puppet is endowed with color symbolism that is strange and alien to us. A shadow puppet in blue, say, might mean that the character is good and noble. The same puppet, appearing in red, perhaps, indicates that this good person has turned into a villain. Different facial features such as a pointed or a bulbous nose, a high forehead, a protruding chin, and so on, likewise have specific symbolic meanings commonly understood by oriental audiences and not requiring verbal explanations or specific deeds.

The *marionette,* or *string puppet,* is the best known member of the puppet family in this country. It is a jointed doll with movable head, arms, and legs. Elbow and knee joints allow for human-like movements and actions. The various parts of the marionette are fastened to strings gathered above the doll in a wooden control. The puppeteer stands behind and slightly above the marionette, his body hidden from view by the backwall of the stage. He holds the control in his hands, and by shortening or lengthening different strings, endows his puppet with lifelike motion. The feet of the marionette are heavily weighted down with lead. Quick and hasty string movements interfere with gravitational forces and result in a pendular swing. If the puppeteer does not possess skill and fine muscular control, the string may become entangled and seriously interfere with the planned action.

This brings to mind an anecdote related by Charles Dickens. During his travels in Italy, he saw a marionette show portraying the death of Napoleon. Dickens found this sad scene highly amusing because the physician who was attending the dying Napoleon suffered from entangled strings and hovered over Napoleon like a vulture. These remarks should not be interpreted as a slur on the artistic potentialities of the marionette, but should simply be regarded as a warning.

The marionette is the most artistic puppet type at our command. It appears in full view of the audience, in contrast to the shadow puppet and the hand puppet, which usually show only the head and the torso. It can run the whole gamut of human actions and emotions. Yet, the appearance of two or more marionettes on the stage calls for caution. Care must be taken that they do not touch each other too closely,

lest they become entangled in each others' strings. This potential danger, therefore, precludes close, lifelike, aggressive actions such as fighting, punching, or hitting. It also interferes with scenes in which puppets, through kissing, stroking the face, and dancing, demonstrate love and affection.

The third type of puppet is known as the *hand puppet* or the *glove puppet,* more commonly referred to as the Punch and Judy type of miniature actor. The anatomy of the hand puppet is very simple. It consists of a three-dimensional head with a costume or garb attached to it. The arms form part of the dress and are not joined to the puppet body as in the shadow puppet and the marionette. The hand puppet, as the name implies, is manipulated by the hand of the puppeteer, which is inserted into the puppet. The index finger moves the puppet head, the thumb and the middle finger manipulate the two puppet arms. This close connection between puppet and puppeteer allows for quick and direct action, because every move of the hand and the arm is immediately transmitted to the puppet. Neither the shadow puppet nor the marionette enjoys this intimate relationship with its master: movement transmitted through sticks or strings is indirect.

The hand puppet's simple anatomy, which makes possible easy manipulation, its immediate responses to the puppeteer's actions, and its lack of entangling strings and of sticks that inhibit free-swinging motility, makes this little actor an ideal medium for the portrayal of human problems, especially when the onlookers are children. Children do not need elaborateness and overdecoration. In order to drive home a point, a puppet show for children should consist of simple, obvious, direct, and forceful actions, so that, if necessary, a whole show can be acted out in pantomime and still be fully understood. A shadow puppet or a marionette is usually handled by one puppeteer. The hand puppet player can easily manipulate two puppets at the same time, one on each hand. This allows for closer coordination of action. In the above-mentioned scene, one puppeteer plays both the puppet boy and the crocodile. In this way, the crocodile is able to play possum when the boy looks at it, and move as soon as the puppet turns its head. This close coordination makes the actions look more convincing. The radius of puppet action is only determined by the reach of the puppeteer's arms. Movement can be as fast or as slow as desired without running into contrary gravitational forces.

The technical elements of building and constructing puppets are omitted. The reader is advised to consult *The Puppet Theatre Handbook*, by (Marjorie) Batchelder (Harper, 1947), for a comprehensive, detailed, and illustrated presentation of these technical aspects.

PSYCHOLOGICAL RATIONALE OF PUPPETRY

The following remarks are pertinent to a fuller understanding of the therapeutic application of puppetry. The three main puppet types were discussed at the beginning of this chapter. To that elaboration must now be added the fact that puppetry, regardless of geographical location and type, can be traced back to the cultural beginnings of mankind. Puppetry, like the folk song, the folk dance, the arts, and architecture, had its origin in religious rituals. It is not an artifact like the radio or the movies. Together with the other mentioned cultural manifestations, it has survived the rise and fall of nations and races. It has been modified by divergent cultural streams but has never been flooded out of existence; its survival to the present day testifies well for its inherent strength and general appeal.

Throughout its long existence, hand puppetry has retained a very important trait that has been lost by the marionette: hand puppetry still employs *types,* rather than *characters* created for a specific play. These types developed in various cultures and were modified by changes within those cultures, so that today the type remains al-though the original archetype may have disappeared.

It is impossible within the brief confines of this chapter to give a full historical survey of the development of puppet types, but as each important puppet type is discussed, short historical data will be included in the description.

The hero of all the puppet shows that were used in the therapeutic puppet shows at Bellevue Hospital is a boy by the name of Casper. His pointed cap and multicolored costume render him ageless, so that he can easily portray youngsters between the ages of six and 12. The origins of this type go back to about 5000 B.C., when it appeared on the East Indian shadow stage as a servant to a rich master. Basically, he is a comedian who causes his master to become involved in all sorts of compromising situations. The same type is also noted on the Greek and Roman stage, either as a living actor or as a puppet. He has become world-famous as the English Punch, having been introduced into Great Britain by Italian showmen during the time of Queen Elizabeth. In France, he has thrived under the name of "Guignol," in Russia, as "Petrushka," and he entertained German children first as "Hanswurst" and later on as "Kasper." The Turkish shadow puppet, "Karagöz," belongs to the same family. Basically, this type represents the man on the street with all his ambitions, strivings, and desires. He stresses primarily the earthy and material things in life. Like all of us, he oscillates between courage and cowardice. He seldom is at a loss for words, but more often than not, he uses physical force to defend himself and to settle an argument. He is both clever and naive, full of hope and in deep despair, trusting and rejecting. Since he is only a puppet, he can act out his audience's innermost wishes and desires.

This type was used in the Bellevue puppet shows as the main character. The nature of the therapeutic aims and the age distribution of the audiences made it necessary to change him from a man into a boy. Right from the start, we noted the great popularity that he enjoyed among the children of the ward. An investigation into the children's responses and reactions over a period of several years gave us pertinent clues to his popularity. We learned that most children identified themselves very closely with him. He seemed to express their wishes and desires, and his combination of words with actions was a real demonstration for them of how problems could be handled and settled.

Casper and his fellow puppets cannot simply be defined in psychoanalytical terms, but there is no question that the various sides of the total psychic structure are reflected differently in the various puppets. Casper is the expression of strong infantile desires which demand satisfaction. He knows that he must adapt his drives to the demands of reality. This satisfies the demands of the super-ego. We must therefore see in Casper something of the Freudian "idealized ego" which reaches for reality without being in conflict with the "id" or pleasure principle. The monkey, which plays an important part in some of the shows, gets his gratifications easily and corresponds in many ways to the "id" which has not been restricted. . . . Casper's parents take over the role of the super-ego. We believe that the child sees his parents as dual personalities. The Good father and the Good mother love and protect the child, feed him and show him affection. The Bad father and the Bad mother inhibit the pleasurable impulses of the child and train him in a manner not always agreeable to him.

In order to underline the superego function of the father, we made him appear as a plainclothes detective, connected with the police department. He thus not only represents authority in the family setting, but also personifies the controlling force through which law and order are maintained in the community. The Bad mother in the puppet shows is portrayed by the witch. She is the product of folklore and

fairy tales. As such, she does not need any specific introduction because the children immediately sense what Casper or any other puppet might expect from her. In one of our shows, she denies food and rest to Casper, makes him work hard, and belittles all of his attempts to please her by being orally aggressive to him. In another show, she helps Casper to get rid of his baby sister. "The part of the Bad father is portrayed by the giant, the magician, and also partly by the cannibals. The giant, through his enormous body, is a physical threat to Casper. The magician, through his magic and clever scheming, is intellectually superior to Casper." The cannibals show hostility to Casper and threaten him with oral aggression. They would like to cook and eat him. Cannibals appeared on the European puppet stage about 200 years ago, probably as a result of mercantilism and colonization, which brought Europe in contact with primitive cultures.

The crocodile or alligator plays a very important part in a good puppet show. This animal represents oral aggression in a twofold way. Those children who like the crocodile identify their own oral aggression with the big mouth and the sharp teeth. The child's oral aggression against the world is frequently met by counter-aggression, directed by the environment against the child. Therefore, those children who are greatly afraid of the crocodile usually express their own fears of counter-aggression. This probably appears to them as punishment and as fear of the harsh, forbidding forces in the world about them. Occasionally, children become overwhelmed by their own aggression. Fear of the crocodile might then be expressed in the words of an eight-year-old boy who said during a group discussion about a puppet show: "I am afraid of the crocodile. It might eat me up myself." The crocodile or alligator made its appearance on the European puppet stage with the cannibals.

The figure of the devil is another puppet character of long standing. Like the witch, he is a product of folklore and fairy tales, to which have been added theological identifications. He needs no special introduction, because every child immediately knows what he stands for. How intense the projection of youngsters into a puppet show can become is best illustrated by the example of a six-year-old boy. When the devil suddenly and without any prior warning popped up on the stage, this boy bolted from the room, shouting, "Casper, pray for Jesus Christ. The devil is here."

Added to these major actors are minor characters that serve to round out any specific plot. In one of our shows, Billy, the bad boy, and his mother appear. Billy is the negative Casper in the sense that he completely rejects authority, sasses and hates his mother, beats up Casper, and is very demanding and overbearing. The contrast between the good Casper and the bad Billy has served for many illuminating discussions about various family constellations, attitudes toward parents, and the consequences that might ensue if the balance of power were shifted toward the child. Another character type, General "Hitt-'em-and-kick-'em from bang-'em-and-slang-'em," serves as Casper's Prime Minister and Chief Executor when Casper tries to build up a government for children and finds it expedient to eliminate adult control and authority.

This enumeration of puppet types may suffice to stress that puppets are capable of representing specific personalities either directly or indirectly, or specific sides or aspects of personalities. With such an array of types, there is hardly any limit to the portrayal of problems.

Over and above the flexibility that is provided through the grouping of these various puppet types, there are other psychological factors that make hand puppetry an ideal medium for tackling and solving problems.

Puppetry is a make-believe affair. A puppet consists only of a head and a costume. The hand and the voice of the puppeteer give it a pseudo-life. A puppet might be beaten, but it does not feel real pain. It might be killed, but since it consists of in-animate material to begin with, killing is never real but only simulated. Situations may be very threatening, but puppetry carries with it the reassurance that everything on the stage is only a make-believe affair. This by no means detracts from the realness with which the children follow the actions, identify themselves with this or that character, and project their own wishes into the show. The make-believe nature of puppetry allows it to go beyond the limits of biological life. It is perfectly normal that a bad character like the crocodile is killed, comes back to life, is again killed, and so on. Children are not concerned about the killing, but clamor for the reassurance that takes place each time the bad and threatening character is killed. Solutions to problems have to be experienced again and again before complete mastery is achieved. However, should severely neurotic or psychotic children feel threatened by the show, one can easily reassure them by taking them backstage, where they can see for themselves that the puppets are not really alive, but are only doll-like characters guided by the puppeteer.

This make-believe nature of puppetry is further expressed by the combination of puppets used. A puppet show in which only realistic characters appear is too logical and does not allow for fantasy digressions. A puppet show in which only fantasy characters act is too unreal and fantastic and does not allow for identifications on a reality level. A good puppet show, like a good fairy tale, should therefore combine both realistic and fantasy factors. This mixture of reality and fantasy makes it easier for the child to enter into the spirit of the problem presented, and aids in the identification. Since parts of the show or some of the puppets (witch, devil, giant, and so on) are symbolic expressions of attitudes, the child himself feels free to project his own attitudes into the show.

Children, by and large, enter quickly into the make-believe nature of the puppet show. Yet it will happen that very disturbed and psychotic children object to a puppet

show because their own main problem consists of a severe struggle between maintaining a reality appreciation and giving in to
their own delusions. One psychotic youngster felt compelled to wash not only the
puppets, but also the stage. He claimed
that the puppets and everything connected
with them were dirty and had to be cleaned.
Dirt, to this child, represented the threat of
insanity, whereas clean and white stood for
reality. Another one of our young patients
objected to the puppet show as being too
mechanical, and called me the "mechanical
man." This little girl went through a rapid
phase of deterioration toward the end of her
stay in the ward and always went into hiding when a puppet show was given. These
and similar experiences taught us that severely psychotic children might conceive
the puppet show as a threat to their endeavor to hang on to reality. These children
were much more aware of the make-believe
nature of the puppet shows, and therefore
reacted in very marked fashion. They felt
threatened and had a strong desire of defending themselves against such make-
believe.

Another important prerequisite for a
good hand puppet show is the *close interaction between the audience and the puppets.* Several centuries ago, it was quite
common for the actors on the legitimate
stage to address some of their lines, and also
off-hand improvisations, directly to the audience, which, in turn, talked back. This
form of audience participation is no longer
practiced on the legitimate stage, but it

has been kept alive on the puppet stage. Before the show starts, the children are told
that they are expected to enter into the
show by telling the various puppets what
to do, suggesting modes of action, warning
of threatening dangers, and aiding the actors verbally in whatever way they can.
The puppets, in turn, speak directly to the
children. Casper, for instance, might ask
his audience whether or not he should play
hookey from school. He acts dumb, tells the
children that he never did such a thing, and
asks them to instruct him on how to go
about it. It is self-evident that the answers
Casper receives contain valuable clues to
the children's thinking and experiences. In
this way, material is produced that would
be extremely difficult to extract in an individual interview. The children are not
aware of the fact that they themselves give
away clues to their own behavior. On the
contrary, they feel highly flattered that Casper takes them into his confidence. They
really have the feeling that they themselves
are running the show. This makes it clearer
why it was said that a good hand puppet
show should consist of a skeleton-like, flexible script, because without this, such improvisations and audience interaction could
not take place. It is not uncommon for the
puppets to deviate temporarily from their
script to follow some suggestions from the
audience, and to return to the regular plot
at the proper time and continue with the
play until a new interruption causes another
deviation. . . .

Dance therapy has been used successfully particularly with schizophrenic
patients and inhibited neurotic patients. Since schizophrenia, especially in childhood, is frequently associated with a lack of, or a distortion of, verbal communication, body movement appears to be a very useful way of helping its victims to
communicate and to relate. Similarly, the inhibited neurotic whose verbal pathways are blocked to certain words or ideas may find himself liberated by body
movements. In the next article, Chace describes how dance therapy can be used
with children.

Dance in Growth or Treatment Settings

Marian Chace

While there are many similarities between the use of dance in the education of the child and its use with psychotic patients, there are also many dissimilarities. Children reach out for knowledge, and in teaching them one has a feeling that all of one's resources are called upon to feed this growth. Each dance session brings new awareness of body coordination, sensitivity to musical tones and rhythms, and alertness to new ways of using the body in dance patterns. All of this is on a conscious level. The world is a curious place to the child, and he wants to find out about it.

Children have always fascinated me in their ability to absorb and retain at a rapid pace. I do not know how many teachers feel as I do, but it always seemed essential to teach them with extreme accuracy and clarity because of their ability to quickly absorb and retain the learning material.

Children are in the period of transition from nonverbal communication to communication utilizing verbal symbols. They have not yet given up the use of their bodies in direct action in response to emotion. Consequently, when they dance they often are more spontaneous and more exciting to the observer than are older people, who can move with greater technical proficiency.

Most adults do not consciously employ body action as a means of communication. Consequently, they are far less alert to the meaning of movements of themselves and others. Because movement probably has less meaning to them, adults are slower in the learning process. One expects an adult group to retain no more than a third of the material given in a specific class. It is therefore possible for the teacher to make mistakes in instruction and correct the error

Reprinted by permission from *Music Therapy, 1958,* I (October 1959), 119–122. Marian Chace is Dance Therapist, Saint Elizabeths Hospital, Washington, D.C.

in the following class. If this happens in a children's class one hears from all sides, "but you said." I always felt that children's classes demanded the optimum in perfection to meet this quality of alertness in the absorption of knowledge.

The teaching process is one of reeducation in the clinical situation. While it is true that during a session one has the feeling of growth, that growth is measured in small degrees of progress. Contact is made through the nonverbal communication of body action, but the patients do little reaching to the world around them. They are similar to children in their use of movement to express immediate emotion, but their movements are an expression of their inner selves rather than a response to the world around them.

The body is involved in all emotional experiences, and psychomotor tensions reveal both feelings of security and insecurity. Naturally, if one is working with children who feel a lack of trust and security in their environment, one is dealing with a clinical situation just as one is with adult psychotic patients.

As the child attains better coordination, posture, and rhythm in his movements, he often develops a feeling of greater security and confidence in himself. Many children, who are lacking in the ability to function with other children without fear, are helped materially through participation in dance classes. Grace and poise are really other names for efficient, coordinated movement and awareness of self.

With both children and mental patients it is important to remember that the dance sessions which one is leading are for the purpose of building sufficient awareness of self through expressive movement. In sessions with either group one is working for creative expression and a feeling of well being, as well as improved coordinated body action. In neither group is one working to develop a professional performer. At intervals one will find, in either group, a "poet" who is able to express ideas for others in a way that demands a specific approach in order to develop his talent. In general, however, one is working for an experience in dance that will make members of the class more confident of functioning in the world of reality rather than in the world of imagination.

It is also disastrous to use authoritarian methods of teaching in both of these groups. In a class of children one would develop a group of robots, all of whom would be weak imitations of the rigid instructor. No matter how beautiful the movements of the individual child might be, they would be meaningless as an expression of his feelings. The child performers would be technically proficient dancers with the vitality of marionettes. No contribution toward their development as individuals would have been made. In conducting such a class with mental patients, one would have the patients going through movements in the characteristic dull manner of the schizophrenic. In neither instance would there be growth or regrowth.

Both groups, however, need structured classes. Each is composed of people who are dependent on authority figures and who are afraid of showing independence of action opposed to authority for fear the world will tumble in on top of them. Both groups need to be weaned from this dependency. However, both would be lost and bewildered without structure to the dance sessions. There is a world of space between rigid authoritarian domination and laissez-faire. Both groups need well defined limits of expected behavior and organized instruction in the use of the body. Horizons cannot be broadened nor can the ability to walk upright toward those far off hills be developed without both limits and structure.

I speak frequently of the development of the ability to express creative and spontaneous movement in the nonverbal medium of dance. I feel that I am frequently misinterpreted as recommending free move-

ment exclusively. Nothing could be less true. No one can speak and be understood unless he has a language which can be heard and interpreted by others.

The greatest difference in the structure of the classes for the growth of children in the educational process and the re-education of mental patients, lies in the leadership of the two groups.

The leader is first a teacher giving instruction to the best of her ability in the children's classes. Limits are very clearly defined no matter how much initiative and independence of action is encouraged. These limits vary greatly with the chronological age of the child. Great simplicity in the structure is needed with little variation from class to class for the young child. He feels secure with known factors. There is so little he has learned and there is so much that is bewildering. As he develops he can be encouraged to assume more responsibility for his actions as the limits established by the leader broaden and give him greater freedom. Even though these limits are nonverbalized and not at all times apparent, the child feels more secure in a situation where he knows they exist and where he must abide by them. The child will constantly test these limits, be rebellious at times, but will accept them and be lost without them. The child in seeking independence seems constantly to need to be sure that the leader is able to say "No" as well as "Yes."

While it is also important that the leader in a dance session with mental patients be able to set limits and, in so doing, occasionally say "No," it is far more important that he be able to set these limits so wide that they are visible only when a need arises. The person who has intense emotional problems is more frequently overdependent than overassertive. He will constantly ask that he be made to feel secure in a safe, restricted shelter. This may be done in many ways: sometimes with behavior that demands curtailment of his activity; sometimes with overpassivity that asks for constant attention from the leader; or sometimes by withdrawal from the group. The leader needs to try to help the patient to become aware of sufficient warmth and interest in order for him to dare to undertake his rightful independence and assume the responsibilities which he can fulfill.

Although the roads travel in almost opposite directions, in both education and reeducation the leader is attempting to use dance action as a means of building confidence. Both need support from the leader; both need encouragement and limits. In education the limits must be firm with a gradual widening as growth takes place, while in reeducation there must be constant alertness by the leader to attempts on the part of the patient to shrink these limits to the point where he can remain totally dependent and avoid any reaching out to the rest of the world. In other words, for the child the leader must hold firm limits which are slowly widened as the child develops naturally, whereas for the mental patient, the leader must both define limits and help the patient to push outward his own self-imposed narrow restrictions.

OCCUPATIONAL THERAPY

Occupational Therapy is one of the oldest forms of adjunctive treatment. Indeed, it precedes the organized discipline of psychotherapy in point of time. Patients in mental hospitals, in prisons, and in reform schools have always been given some kind of activity program. As the field of psychotherapy became more sophisticated, the kind of occupational work was observed and studied with greater care. Different types of patients at different times were given different activities. The symbolic meaning of the activities for each individual was investigated and there was an attempt made to intervene therapeutically in the choice or duration of activities.

A once helpful activity may no longer be beneficial for a patient and may even become a deteriorative agent. For example, the ripping of material is very useful for many patients working out the undoing of their own lives, or hostility towards others; however, it can (at a given point) come to be the only area of concentration and intensify perseveration or brooding. An aware occupational therapist will, even at the risk of resistance, try to change the activity to something more constructive as a means of conveying the message: "You are ready now to move on to a healthier phase." The significance, the timing, the value of using a variety of materials are of particular interest to occupational therapy. In this regard teachers might learn much from occupational therapists and vice versa.

Doyle's article presents a fascinating picture of how an O.T. works with an emotionally disturbed adolescent boy.

An Emotionally Disturbed Adolescent in Occupational Therapy

Phyllis Doyle

In this paper, psychiatric occupational therapy will be defined in terms of ego

Reprinted with permission from Phyllis Doyle, "A Commentary on the Behavior in Occupational Therapy of Two Emotionally Disturbed Early Adolescent Boys." Paper presented at the 1961 Annual Conference of the American Occupational Therapy Association.

Phyllis Doyle is Supervisor, occupational and recreative therapy, Children's Psychiatric Hospital, University of Michigan Medical Center, Ann Arbor, Mich.

psychology. The complementary roles of the psychotherapist and the occupational therapist in treating emotionally disturbed children will be touched upon. Finally, incidents from the records of two early adolescent boys will be presented to demonstrate the growth of ego skills and the shifting of the defensive structure which are observable in occupational therapy. These changes may be attributed, in part, to the intrapersonal and interpersonal transactions of the occupational therapy hours.

According to Erikson, when Freud was asked what a normal person should be able to do well, his succinct reply was, "To love and to work."

"To love and to play" could as well answer the question of what a normal child should be able to do well.

In the emotionally ill or maladjusted we look, then, to disturbances in the "feeling" and "doing" functions of the ego.

By definition Occupational Therapy is treatment through individual or group participation in creative and manual activities, or through training in activities of daily living. Through such of these activities as are appropriate to the emotional state of the patient, his age, his physical condition, his native aptitude and interests, the patient is helped to achieve greater mastery of his own body and a growing competence to cope with the social demands of the treatment situation.

The objectives of psychiatric occupational therapy may be stated as, "Helping the patient's ego to help itself"[1]—to achieve a more age-appropriate and more sex-appropriate mode of adjustment through:

1. "Doing" the *Activity*. One of the ways a person learns who he is is by learning what he can do. The patient is encouraged to improve existing skills and to acquire new ones. Such personality traits as desire for mastery, competitiveness, compulsivity, creativity, curiosity, pride may be exploited and channeled constructively. Specific activities may provide for basic

need satisfactions such as the obvious oral gratification inherent in the preparation and consumption of food.

2. "Feelings" toward the *Group*. Hopefully, the patient learns to modify his behavior and his demands in order to avoid negative group reactions. Ultimately, he may acquire the capacity to relate positively to his peers, thereby becoming not in, but part of a group.

3. "Feelings" toward an *Adult* who will make demands on him in terms of performance and behavior, who will recognize and reward real accomplishment, who will support him in his efforts toward a fuller realization of his potential as a creating and a relating being. Such a relationship can develop only in an atmosphere of mutual trust, understanding, and respect.

In the past five years the writer has worked with a number of preadolescent and early adolescent boys at the Children's Psychiatric Hospital, Ann Arbor, Michigan. We have speculated that the usually high degree of motivation in occupational therapy among this group of patients reflects their appreciation of the invitation to health which is implicit in the O.T. shop situation. In certain instances in which a patient has refused the invitation, directly or indirectly, it has been all too evident that he meant to remain sick (immature) at all cost.

Each child is seen regularly by his psychotherapist and we, in occupational therapy, have learned to recognize the heightened anxiety, the lability and intensification of mood, the state of flux, as signs of the child in psychiatric treatment. We are prepared to support him through the inevitable upheavals which mark progress in psychotherapy, but we are not permissive of acting-out or talking-out of those problems with which the child must come to grips in his psychotherapy hours. This does not mean that the child must leave his symptoms outside the shop. It does mean that realistic demands are made of him in terms of performance and behavior because he is a patient and not in spite of it.

It is not within the scope of this paper to deal with the role of the psychotherapist

[1] Paraphrasing Erikson, "to help a child's ego to help itself."

or of the other members of the treatment team at the Children's Psychiatric Hospital. The listener must bear in mind that the psychiatrist functions in the dual role of coordinator of the treatment team and psychotherapist to the patient. It is the psychotherapist who properly interprets, at a deep level, the child's behavior in the light of his past experiences and fantasies.

As occupational therapists, we may properly clarify for the child the facts of his behavior in the light of the immediate reality. We may, for example, point out apparent causal relationships; e.g., "Until a few moments ago you were working successfully with that saw but as soon as your attendant came to take you to your doctor's appointment you started banging it around and claiming that it was no good. It seems to me that you are angry with your doctor for taking you out of O.T. and not with the saw." We may point out inappropriate or missing affect; e.g., "Most kids would be mad if they dropped their pizza on the floor. You are smiling."

Since each child's use of the occupational therapy situation is uniquely his own we will, at this point, examine the O.T. records of two patients, each of whom was in treatment at the hospital for over a year. In each instance we will note the growth of ego skills and the building of more flexible defensive systems.[2]

The first patient, Melvin, was chosen because through him we can demonstrate his social isolation, his defensive use of fantasy, and his attempts early in treatment to solve his conflicts at a symbolic level. We will trace his movement from fantasy-orientation toward reality orientation. We will note his growing capacity to relate both to adults and to peers.

Melvin was a stocky, muscular lad of thirteen. He spoke in clipped phrases, laughed in an abrupt, harsh chortle. There was an air of tension and brooding about him.

From psychological tests and from the

psychiatric examination we learned that Melvin scored well above average in intelligence with indications of a superior potential. Projective tests indicated a diagnosis of schizoid personality pattern disturbance with passive-dependent features.

A summary of the problem on admission included: violent temper, poor school adjustment, stealing, jealousy of mother's attention to siblings, no friends. His major therapeutic tasks were, therefore, to gain control of his instinctual impulses and to learn to relate. His acting out was, in part, a denial of his passive-dependent needs.

Even before Melvin came to O.T. he had inquired about the possibility of making gun stocks and almost immediately on starting O.T. he began to construct a gadget which seemed already to exist in his fantasy—a cigarette lighter made in the shape of a gun. For five months, with two interruptions of several weeks' duration each, Melvin wrestled with the construction of this gadget. Melvin knew exactly how the gun-cigarette lighter was to work but was vague in his explanation of how he was going to make it. The occupational therapist's attitude toward the improbable task was that she did not see how it could be done but that she would help Melvin in every way she could. Her goal, at this point, was to establish a relationship at the only level which Melvin could tolerate, one of support and acceptance.

In the ensuing weeks he pursued his task with single-minded intensity. He referred to the gadget variously as his invention, his experiment, his dickie-gun. At times he cradled it tenderly and protectively in his hand. Later it was to be used as a prop for aggressive fantasy play as he stood holding the partially completed gun menacingly and swept it in an arc around the shop as if holding an enemy at bay. An admiring young peer told the O.T. that Melvin had featured the gadget in a fantasied escape from the hospital, imagining the police broadcasting this warning, "Watch out for Melvin Waters. He is armed with a cigarette lighter."

---

[2] Only one case is presented here.

Our young inventor was not to be permitted to work in peace, however. He was subjected to persistent, noisy, provocative intrusions into his obsessive task by one peer in particular. Irritated, hostile rebuffs only incited his tormentor to more, and more brazen affronts. Melvin's anxiety mounted to unbearable intensity. Since he was incapable of dealing with Conrad's aggressiveness directly, he was permitted to withdraw into an adjoining work area when possible, and the occupational therapist withdrew with him. He could not, at this time, ask for help nor could he formulate his wants, only indicate by frantic, futile activity that something needed doing. The O.T. had to sense what was needed and provide a ready-made solution. "Look, Melvin, will this metal strip hold the barrel upright?"

Eventually Conrad dared "accidentally" to knock Melvin's priceless "gun" out of a vise in which Melvin had clamped it. An outraged Melvin cursed Conrad roundly, turned on his heels and fled. Melvin was quite incapable of settling the score, and on the ward, immediately after the incident, he and Conrad were more friendly than ever. Because Melvin could not be safely and appropriately angry he had to defend himself by an excessive show of forbearance toward Conrad.

The gun-cigarette lighter which Melvin used initially to keep people away from him became, in time, an object through which he began to form relationships. Ward staff took Melvin on errands downtown to buy parts. The maintenance man's help was enlisted when some work involving a blow torch was required. Peers, instead of regarding the project and its perpetrator with awe, began to give Melvin advice and even began to predict that the lighter would never work.

On the day when all parts were in place, the culmination of five months of effort, Melvin had to concede with annoyance and irritation that the lighter indeed would not work. He was able to accept this bit of reality and to face in this instance his own limitations. He quickly undid weeks of work, commenting that he had wrecked Hell out of it. The O.T.'s role was simply to support him in this acceptance of reality. Even so, Melvin was reluctant to be done with it and for two weeks more he painted and embellished what was just a toy gun after all. Quite appropriately, in the light of Melvin's relationship with his mother, the gun was sent home with her for safekeeping.

This was not the last of Melvin's weapons, however. During periods of stress in his treatment he returned, again and again, to their production but never for long and never with the intensity of investment which marked this early phase in his treatment.

It was mentioned earlier that Melvin interrupted his work on the cigarette lighter only twice during five months. The second of these interludes coincided with a two-week absence of his doctor in the third month of treatment. Melvin did not mention that his doctor was away but came to shop in a quiet, dejected mood. He stood with his back to the group looking pensively out of the window, furtively wiping away his tears. He could not acknowledge that anything was wrong but got out his work, examined it briefly, then slipped it sadly into the O.T.'s smock pocket, murmuring that it was no use, he couldn't get the parts he needed to finish it. For the first time Melvin was accessible to the O.T. and seemed to be silently asking for suggestion and attention. A leather wallet was drawn out and Melvin compliantly cut and glued the parts as directed saying only that he didn't need a wallet. The next day on entering the shop Melvin greeted the O.T. brightly with, "I've been waiting for you to show me what to do next." Before his doctor's return Melvin had made two wallets and many, many trips to the O.T. office for additional instruction, extra materials, and more important, for much personal attention from the O.T. He had been able to accept, briefly, a warm, dependent relationship.

During the gun-cigarette lighter phase Melvin had accomplished several things. He had become more realistic, less withdrawn, and less absorbed in fantasy. He had begun to relate both to peers and to adults.

The next phase might properly be called "getting into treatment" with his doctor and was heralded by many and varied somatic complaints. Toward the O.T. he assumed a hypercritical, irritated bossiness and with peers Melvin needed to set the conditions on which he could relate to them, be it bully, buddy, or clown. There was a sense of unrest and the ever present depression.

Melvin indicated the content of his brooding when he asked about another of his doctor's patients who had improved markedly and had been discharged after a brief admission, "Does that mean he has a good doctor?"

He seemed to be asking if it was safe to form a transference relationship with this doctor. "Will he help me to get well, too?"

The O.T. responded to the question realistically by stating that some patients could be helped in a shorter period of time than others.

Two projects occupied Melvin during this time, each representing a distinct and characteristic mood. The first was a mosaic tile picture executed in black and white of an ambiguous, silhouetted male figure which appeared to be standing in a clump of trees. We speculated that this might have represented Melvin, himself, or his doctor. This was his thoughtful, pensive project which he ruminated over, put together bit by bit. Sometimes he praised it extravagantly, at other times threatened to smash it. "What damned good is it if I can't sell it," seemed to be his way of devaluing it. By noisily proclaiming his destructive intentions, Melvin seemed to be asking that the picture be spared and it was repeatedly put aside by the O.T. for another time. Eventually, he was finished with the mosaic, like the earlier gun-cigarette lighter project, though he never completed it. It seemed no longer to serve any useful purpose for Melvin. When he returned it to our office for the last time he remarked that he couldn't work on it, "I'm too sick . . . I mean I'm sick of this place." By this slip of the tongue Melvin acknowledged recognition of his need for help and a readiness to accept it.

Melvin's other project of this period was produced in a burst of hyperactivity and expansiveness in the midst of construction of the mosaic puzzle. It was a large wooden storage box, a "popular" project among the children. It seemed to indicate the strengthening of his identification with peers. It also indicated the surrender of some of his omnipotent and magic qualities. Melvin could maintain the fiction of superiority only so long as his projects were unique and mysterious. Melvin's pathology was, however, reflected in his various associations to the box project. It could be a retreat— "It would be nice to make a box big enough to put a chair, a lamp and books in and then I could read in peace." A "coffin" association was too threatening and Melvin quickly revised it to a "playpen." "The staff treats us like babies and now they have us making our own playpens." These comments were directed toward peers whom Melvin had enlisted in a patients *vs* staff campaign and required no response from the O.T.

Another and more trying phase of Melvin's therapy followed and involved an initial probing with his doctor of his feelings about significant people in his life and laying of the groundwork for eventual emotional autonomy. Now Melvin was talking, talking about his feelings and about people. He was no more the isolated genius. The bad people, he said, were in the hospital and the good people were at home. His true feelings were revealed when Melvin began a flurry of gift making for family members. His ambivalence was reflected in his inability to get these gifts completed in time for special occasions. If they were completed, the gifts could not be found until the occasion had passed. During this period Melvin began relating to the O.T. in a dependent, young boy fashion. He would appeal to her trustingly with, "You've just got to help me."

During the latter part of Melvin's hospitalization he was involved in establishing his identity, his independence, his maleness, his right and ability to be aggressive.

You will recall an incident some nine months before when Melvin, in the face of severe provocation from a peer, Conrad, could only run away when to lash out would have been more appropriate. He obsessively now licked old wounds by recalling humiliating defeats at the hands of skinnier but tougher adversaries both at home and in the early weeks of his hospitalization. He seemed, at this point, to be facing his own inadequacies and to be seeing himself more realistically. He constantly measured himself against peers, which one was taller, which one smarter, which one a better craftsman.

An incident occurred at this time which was indicative of the change in Melvin's mode of behavior. It serves, also, to illustrate how the roles of psychotherapist and of occupational therapist complemented each other in this case.

The O.T. had left the group, five patients and an occupational therapy student, to go into an adjoining room. On her return moments later she found a circle of patients, Melvin included, standing around the crumpled figure of one of the boys. When asked what had happened all eyes turned toward Melvin. He muttered that Ted must have had one of his seizures. Ted whispered that Melvin had hit him and the other boys concurred. Confronted with this evidence Melvin turned away abruptly and in a distraught tone said, "Damn it, I can't say anything. Can't you see I'm too scared?"

After making certain that Ted was not hurt, everyone was told to get back to work with a general reminder that this sort of behavior just didn't go in shop.

The occupational therapist, however, found occasion to leave the shop shortly

thereafter and took the still frightened Melvin with her. As they went on their errand Melvin was asked if he would like to talk about what had happened. Using the O.T. as his "victim" Melvin reenacted the incident. He showed how he had approached Ted, spanned his throat in a "playfully" menacing gesture with his hands. Ted had reacted by pushing Melvin's arms away sharply. Then it was that Melvin lashed out, landing a fist on Ted's jaw. The first time, Ted went crashing to the floor. In the reenactment, the O.T. was the recipient of a sharp but controlled blow on the jaw. It was indicative of the trusting nature of his relationship with the O.T. that he could repeat the act of aggression, confident that there would be no retaliation and that he could control his aggression.

The incident was recounted to Melvin's doctor and in the next psychotherapy hour Melvin reported this dream: The doctor was lying on the floor of the O.T. shop and Melvin was standing over him, hammer in hand. Melvin's explanation of the scene was that he was angry at his doctor because the doctor had been talking about sending him away to a boarding school.

When asked what connection there might be between the dream and the events of the previous day in the shop, Melvin became somewhat incoherent but in essence said he just couldn't apologize to Ted in front of the other boys or the O.T. because they would think he was a sissy. In fact, it was Melvin who might think himself a "sissy" if he apologized, thus undoing his aggressive act.

It is interesting to note Melvin's recognition of the difference in the roles of the O.T. and the doctor. With the O.T. he could review the events as they happened in reality and even use the O.T. to clarify for himself what had happened. With the doctor he recalled aggressive fantasies and related his anxieties about his masculine identification and about his future.

Melvin thus experimented with his new-found right to be aggressive. He had at the same time established a somewhat shaky leadership in the group. Much of his behavior could be classified as adolescence, acute. He could be high-handed and rejecting of the O.T. in the presence of the group, "*We* don't need *you*," but pleasant and respectful when alone.

He cultivated a "hoodish" look and in shop constructed masculine props—a cigarette holder, a pipe which was his masterpiece, a tobacco pouch, cigarette case. He remarked half-seriously to a peer, "I've got to get started on my career of smoking." He even asked if he couldn't make beer in the kitchen rather than his favorite pizza.

Many of Melvin's problems during this period were peer related. His own ego boundaries were not so firmly fixed nor was his own identity well established. He tended to become caught up in the pathology of peers and to act out their problems as his own. During this time he was frequently excluded from shop for part or all of an hour.

One of his last pseudo-scientific projects was a compressed air tank made from a large tin can, a project suggested to him by and lifted out of the fantasy life of his tormentor of nine months ago, Conrad. The two boys had, at this time, a close though scarcely healthy relationship. The compressed air tank was made as a conciliatory gesture to Conrad, who was at the moment excluded from O.T. Melvin thus attempted to relate to Conrad at a safer though sicker level of shared fantasy.

As time approached for him to leave the hospital Melvin directly indicated apprehension of the future and an honest recognition that he had still a long way to go to health. He returned briefly to the construction of a weapon but quickly rejected it.

Melvin, when he first came to the hospital, had lived essentially within himself. He could then in his omnipotent fantasy be scientist, inventor, genius. However, his magic worked only if he shared his secrets with no one. Immediately upon attempting to make his fantasy real, as when he constructed the gun, Melvin opened that inner door a crack and reality began to impinge upon him. Still far from well, Melvin had taken giant steps toward reality and relatedness and had established a tentative adolescent identity. . . .

MILIEU THERAPY

The concept of milieu treatment for children flows naturally from the theory of group work. The word milieu implies the total environment a child lives in, the whole culture that surrounds him, in other words everything that is done to, with, for, or by a child in the place where he finds himself. Quite simply, a public school in all its parts is a child's daily milieu from 9–3. A boarding school is a child's total milieu including his substitute home and substitute parent and siblings. The word is used in psychiatric terminology to describe the entire setting in which a child in residential treatment (or in all-day care treatment) lives. The therapeutic concept varies with the program of the setting. If it is a total therapeutic setting, then milieu treatment will consider: individual therapy; school, which is handled therapeutically as well as educationally; group-work and group-therapy activities; eating; bedtime and waking; incidental daily relationships with the staff. The premise behind milieu treatment is that a sick child needs more than just a few isolated hours of individual or group therapy. He needs to have every aspect of his life designed to build on his healthy parts and to transform his unhealthy parts. Insights can come at meal times as well as at play.

Clearly, a healthy, insightful milieu is a good thing for every child. It is what all schools strive for. When a child is troubled, however, it becomes vital that those dealing with him—parents, teachers, scout leaders—are sufficiently knowledgeable to handle him beneficially. The more ill the child, the more likely is it that essential parts of his milieu, such as his home, have been damaging.

When a child is very ill, or when his own environment increases or sustains ill health, he should be removed from it. To treat him optimally, his entire milieu must be designed therapeutically. Such a design requires a high degree of sophistication or clinical aptitude on the part of all members of a staff: the director must have knowledge, imagination and skill in dealing with adults as well as children; the therapists must be able to communicate with other members of the staff as well as their young patients; the teachers must be able to recognize the psychodynamic meanings of the child's intellectual development, blocks, assets, and failures. The social workers working with the parents need to understand the total treatment plan in order to make possible a healthier milieu for the child when he leaves the institution and returns home, or goes to a different environment. They must also interpret to the milieu staff the underlying emotional and cultural environment from which the child came.

Although this kind of total therapy is expensive, it is a faster method for those children who respond well to treatment than giving them custodial care with droplets of treatment scattered through the week. For those children who are the most difficult to reach, it appears to be one of the few methods that can work. The children most frequently receiving total milieu therapy are the schizophrenic and autistic; seriously hyper-active and delinquent; and some organic cases such as post-encephalitics, severe epileptics, and birth brain-damage cases. In cases where the physiological aspects of the children are severely disturbed, the children receive pharmacological or physiological treatment as part of their total milieu therapy along with psychological treatment.

Redl, who has been both provocative and creative in his many efforts to blend therapeutic knowledge and educational programs, details the many factors, both tangible and intangible, that must be considered in the therapeutic milieu.

The Concept of a Therapeutic Milieu
Fritz Redl

Speculations about the therapeutic value of the "milieu" in which our patients live are neither as new nor as revolutionary as the enthusiasts, as well as the detractors of "milieu therapy" occasionally want them to appear. If I may risk shocking you so early in the game, the most extreme degree of "holy respect" for the tremendous impact that even the "little things" in an environment can have is represented in the original

From Fritz Redl, Ph.D., "The Concept of a 'Therapeutic Milieu,' "*American Journal of Orthopsychiatry*, XXIX (1959), 721–734. Reprinted by permission.

description of the conditions for a Freudian psychoanalytic hour. The ritual of interaction between patient and therapist is certainly sharply circumscribed. Even items such as horizontality of body posture and geographical placement of the analyst's chair are considered important conditions. Of course, the "basic rule" must be strictly adhered to, there should be no noises from the analyst's children coming through from the next room; one would worry whether patients might meet each other on the way out or in. The idea that months of solid work even by the greatest genius of transference manipulation might be endangered if doctor and patient should happen to meet at the Austrian equivalent of a cocktail party, instead of in their usual office terrain, is certainly impressive evidence for the great impact classical psychoanalysis has ascribed to factors such as time, space, and other "external givens."

If you now want to argue with me by reminding me that all this is true only for the duration of the 50-minute hour, and that other "milieu" factors in the patient's wider circle of life have not been deemed as relevant, then I might concede that point. But even so, I would like to remind you that we have always had a holy respect for two sets of "milieu" factors, at least in child analysis: we have always lived under the terror that the parents or teachers of our child patients might do things to them which would be so traumatic that we could, of course, not analyze them while all this was going on; and we would insist we couldn't touch a case unless we could get the child out of the terrain of parental sex life and into a bed of his own, or unless the parents stopped some of the more extreme forms of punitive suppressiveness at once. These are only a few of the illustrations we could think of. You will find a much more impressive list of "milieu variables," which certainly need to be influenced by the therapist, in Anna Freud's classic, *Introduction to the Technique of Child Analysis*, though not under that heading, of course.

The other case in point of my argument that even classical psychoanalysis has not neglected concern with "milieu" influences as much as it is supposed to have, relates to our evaluation of failure and success. At least in our informal appraisals I have time and again observed how easily we ascribe the breakdown of a child analysis to the "negative factors in the youngster's environment," and I have found in myself an inclination to do the same with the other fellow's successes. If my colleague seems to have presented an unusual piece of therapeutic "breakthrough," I find the temptation strong to look for the good luck

he had with all the supportive factors that were present in his case and which, to my narcissism, seem to explain his success much better than the technical argument he put forth.

Now, seriously, if we secretly allow "milieu particles" to weigh so strongly that they can make and break even the most skillfully developed emotional therapy bridges between patient and doctor, hadn't we better look into this some more?

The fortunate fact that the answer to this question has, historically, been an enthusiastic "yes," however, has started us off in another problem-direction. Since more and more of us got impressed by more and more "factors" which in some way or other could be subsumed under the "milieu" term, the word has assumed such a variety of connotations that scientific communication has been overstimulated, but at the same time blocked in its development toward precision.

Since avoiding the traps of early concept confusion is an important prelude to a more rigid examination of meanings and their appropriate scope, we might allow ourselves the luxury of at least a short list of "dangers we ought to watch out for from now on," provided we keep it telegram-style, so as not to take too much attention from the major theme. Since time and space for argument is dear, I shall be presumptuous enough to confront you simply with my personal conclusions, and offer them as warning posts, without further apology.

TRAPS FOR THE MILIEU CONCEPT

1. The cry for *the* therapeutic milieu as a general slogan is futile and in this wide formulation the term doesn't mean a thing. No milieu is "good" or "bad" in itself—it all depends. And it depends on more factors than I want to list, though some of them will turn up as we go along.

2. It won't do to use our own philosophical, ethical, political convictions, or our taste buds, in order to find out what

really has or has not "therapeutic effect." Even the most respectable clinical discussions around this theme drift all too easily into A's trying to convince B that his setup is too "autocratic," or that what he called "democratic" group management isn't really good for those youngsters. Whether a ward should have rules, how many and which, must not lead to an argument between those who like rules and those who don't; I have seen many a scientific discussion end up in the same personal taste-bud battle that one otherwise finds acceptable only when people talk about religions or brands of cars.

3. Even a concept of "total milieu therapy" does not imply that all aspects of a given milieu are equally relevant in all moments in clinical life. All games, for instance, have some kind of "social structure" and as part of that, some kind of "pecking order" which determines the power position of the players for the duration of the game. Whether the specific pecking order of the game I let them play today had anything to do with the fact that it blew up in my face after five minutes is a question that can be answered only in empirical terms. I know of cases where the pecking order was clearly it; I have to look no further. I know of others where it was of no *clinical* relevance at the time. The boys blew up because they got too scared playing hide-and-seek with flashlights in the dark. In short, the scientific establishment of a given milieu aspect as a theoretically valid and important one does not substitute for the need for a diagnosis on the spot. It alone can differentiate between potential milieu impacts and actual ones in each case.

4. The idea of the "modern" and therefore social-science-conscious psychiatrist that he has to sell out to the sociologist if he wants to have his "ward milieu" studied properly is the bunk. Of course, any thoughtful appraisal of a hospital milieu will contain many variables which the mother discipline of a given psychiatrist may never have dreamed about. On the other hand, the thing that counts is not only the description of a variable, but the assessment of the potential impact on the treatment process of a given group of patients. That is basically a *clinical* matter, and it remains the clinician's task. The discipline that merges social science with clinical criteria in a balanced way still has to be invented. There is no short cut to it either by psychiatry's stealing particles of social science concepts or by selling out to the social scientist's domain.

5. The frequently voiced expectation that the discovery of what "milieu" one needs would automatically make it easy to produce that style of milieu in a given place is downright naïve. An instrumentology for the creation of "ward atmosphere," of "clinically correct policies of behavioral intervention," etc., has yet to be created, and it will cost blood and sweat to get it. The idea that all it takes to have a "good treatment milieu" is for a milieu-convinced ward boss to make his nurses feel comfortable with him, and to hold a few gripe sessions between patients and staff, is a daydream, the simplicity of which we can no longer afford. . . .

A "MILIEU"—WHAT'S IN IT?

Obviously I am not going to use the term in the nearly global meaning which its theft from the French language originally insinuated. For practical reasons, I am going to talk here only of one sort of milieu concept: of a "milieu" artificially created for the purpose of the treatment of a group of youngsters. Within this confine you can make it somewhat wider if you want, and think of the "Children's Psychiatric Unit" on the fourth, eighth, or ninth floor of a large hospital, or you may hold before your eyes, while I am speaking, a small residential treatment home for children that is not part of a large unit. Of course, I know that the similarity of what I am talking about to other types of setups may be quite great, but I can't cover them all.

Hence, anything else you hold before your eyes while I talk, you do strictly at your own risk.

So, here we are on the doorstep of that treatment home or at the keyhole of that hospital ward. And now you ask me: If you could plan things the way you wanted to, which are the most important "items" in your milieu that will sooner or later become terribly relevant for better or for worse? The choice is hard, and only such a tough proposition gets me over the guilt feeling for oversimplifying and listing items out of context.

1. *The social structure.* This is some term, and I have yet to see the psychiatrist that isn't stunned for a moment at its momentum—many would run and hire a sociologist on the spot. Being short on time, I have no choice, but let me hurry and add: this term in itself is as extendible and collapsible as a balloon. It doesn't mean much without specifications. So, let me just list a few of the things I have in mind:

a. A hospital ward is more like a *harem society than a family,* no matter how motherly or fatherly the particular nurses and doctors may feel toward their youngsters. The place I run at the moment is purposely shaped as much as possible after the model of an American camp, which is the only pattern I could find which children would be familiar with, where a lot of adults walk through children's lives in older brother and parentlike roles without pretending it to be an equivalent to family life.

b. The *role distribution* of the adult figures can be of terrific importance for the amount of clarity with which children perceive what it is all about. Outspokenly or not, sooner or later they must become clear about just who can or cannot be expected to decide what; otherwise, how would one know when one is getting the run-around?

c. The *pecking order* of any outfit does not long remain a secret to an open door neighborhood-wise toughie, no matter how dumb he may be otherwise. He also smells the outspoken "pecking order" among the adults who take care of him,

no matter how carefully disguised it may be under professional role titles or Civil Service Classification codes.

d. The *communication network* of any given institution is an integral part of its "social structure." Just who can be approached about listening to what, is quite a task to learn; and to figure out the real communication lines that are open and those which are secretly clogged in the adult communication network is usually an insoluble task except for the suspicious outside researcher. . . .

2. *The value system that oozes out of our pores.* Some people subsume that under social structure. I think I have reasons to want a separate place for it here, but let's not waste time on the question why. The fact is, the youngsters not only respond to what we say or put in mimeographed writing; they smell our value-feelings even when we don't notice our own body odor any more. I am not sure how, and I can't wait until I find out. But I do need to find out which value items are there to smell. Does the arrangement of my furniture call me a liar while I make a speech about how much at home I want them to feel, or does that gleam in a counselor's eye tell the child: "You are still wanted," even though he means it if he says he won't let you cut up the tablecloth? By the way, in some value studies I have missed one angle many times: the *clinical convictions* of what is professionally correct handling, which sometimes even questionnaire-clumsy workers on a low salary level may develop, and which become a motivating source for their behavior in its own right, besides their own personal moral convictions or their power drives.

3. *Routines, rituals, and behavioral regulations.* The sequence of events and the conditions under which people undergo certain repetitive maneuvers in their life space can have a strong impact on whether they can keep themselves under control, or whether their impulse-control balance breaks down. Since Bruno Bettelheim's classic description of the events inside a

child while he seems engaged in the process of getting up or getting himself to sleep, no more words should have to be said about this. And yet, many "therapeutic milieu" discussions still waste their time on arguments between those who like regularity and those who think the existence of a rule makes life an unimaginative drudge. All groups also have a certain "ritual" by which a member gets back into the graces of the group if he has sinned, and others which the group has to go through when an individual has deviated. Which of those ceremonial rites are going on among my boys, thinly disguised behind squabbles and fights, and which of them do adult staff people indulge in under the even thinner disguise of a discussion on punishment and on the setting of limits? Again—the mere discovery of phenomena fitting into this category is not what I am after. We are still far from having good research data on the *clinical relevance* of whatever specific practice may be in vogue in a specific place.

4. *The impact of the group process.* We had better pause after pronouncing this weighty phrase—it is about as heavy and full of dodges as the phrase "social structure," as previously pointed out. And since this one milieu aspect might well keep us here for a week, let me sink as low as simple word-listing at this point. Items that I think should go somewhere under this name: over-all group atmosphere, processes like scapegoating, mascot-cultivation, subclique formation, group psychological role suction, experiences of exposure to group psychological intoxication, dependency on contagion clusters, leadership tensions, etc. Whatever you have learned from social psychology, group psychology and group dynamics had better be written in right here. The point of all this: These phenomena are *not* just interesting things that happen among patients or staff, to be viewed with a clinical grin, a sociological hurrah, or with the curiosity stare of an anthropological slumming party. These processes are forces to which my child patient is exposed, as real as the oedipus complex of his therapist, the food he eats

and the toys he plays with. The forces producing such impacts may be hard to see, or even to make visible through x-ray tricks. They are there and as much of his "surroundings" as the unbreakable room in which he screams off his tantrum.

5. *The trait clusters that other people whirl around within a five-yard stretch.* I first wanted to call this item "the other people as persons," but I know this would only call forth a long harangue about feelings, attitudes—Isn't it people anyway, who make up a group?—etc. From bitter discussion experience, I am trying to duck these questions by this somewhat off-the-beat phrase. What I have in mind is this: My youngsters live as part of a group, true enough. But they are also individuals. And Bobby who shares a room with John is within striking distance of whatever personal peculiarities John may happen to throw at others. In short, we expect some children to show "shock" at certain colors on a Rorschach card. We expect children to be lured into excited creativity at the mere vision of some fascinating project outline or plane model seductively placed before their eyes. Well, the boy with whom Bobby shares his room is worse than a Rorschach or a plane model. Not only does his presence and the visualization of his personality do something to Bobby, for John not only *has* character traits and neurotic syndromes; he swings them around his body like a wet bathing towel, and it is going to hit whoever gets in its path, innocent or not. In short, personality traits remain psychological entities for the psychologist who watches them in the youngsters. They are *real things that hit and scratch* if you get in their way, for the roommate and all the other people on the ward.

We have learned to respect the impact of certain extremes in pathologies upon each other, but we are still far from inspecting our milieus carefully enough for what they contain in "trait clusters" that children swing around their heads within a five-yard range. Let me add: not all traits and syndromes are "swung"; some stay put and can only be seen or smelled, so they become visible or a nuisance only to the one who shares the same room. Also: we are far from knowing what this all amounts to clinically. For the question of just what "milieu ingredients" my ward contains, in terms of existent trait clusters of the people who live in it, is still far removed from the question of just which *should* coexist with each other, and which others should be carefully kept asunder.

6. *The staff, their attitudes and feelings—but please let's not call it all "transference."* This one I can be short about, for clinicians all know about it; sociologists will grant it to you, though they may question how heavily it counts. In fact, the attitudes and feelings of staff have been drummed up for so long now as "the" most important aspect of a milieu, often even as the only important one, that I am not afraid this item will be forgotten. No argument needed, it is self-evident. Only two issues I would like to battle around: One, while attitudes and feelings are very important indeed, they are not always all that counts, and sometimes other milieu items may gang up on them so much they may obliterate their impact. My other battle cry: Attitudes and feelings of staff are manifold, and spring from many different sources. Let's limit the term "transference" to those for which it was originally invented. If Nurse's Aide A gets too hostile to Bob because he bit him too hard, let's not throw all of that into the same terminological pot. By the way, if I grant "attitudes and feelings of staff" a place on my list of "powerful milieu ingredients," I mean the attitudes and feelings that really fill the place, that are lived —not those that are only mentioned in research interviews and on questionnaires.

7. *Behavior received.* I tried many other terms, but it won't work. There just isn't one that fits. In a sentence I would say: what people really *do* to each other counts as much as how they feel. This forces me into a two-hour argument in which I have to justify why it isn't unpsychiatric to say such a thing. For, isn't it the underlying feelings that "really" count? That depends on which side of the fence

your "really" is. The very fact that you use such a term already means you know there is another side to it, only you don't want to take it as seriously as yours. In short, there are situations where the "underlying feeling" with which the adult punishes a child counts so much that the rather silly form of punishment that was chosen is negligible. But I could quote you hundreds of other examples where this is not the case. No matter what wonderful motive—if you expose child A to an isolation with more panic in it than he can stand, the effect will be obvious. Your excuse that you "meant well and love the boy" may be as futile as that of the mother who would give the child an overdose of arsenic, not knowing its effect.

This item of *behaviors received in a day's time* by each child should make a really interesting line to assess. We would have to look about at "behaviors received" from other boys as well as from staff, and see what the implications of those behaviors received are, even after deducting from them the mitigating influences of "attitudes that really were aiming at the opposite." The same, by the way, should also be taken into consideration for staff to be hired. I have run into people who really love "crazy youngsters" and are quite willing to sacrifice a lot. Only they simply cannot stand more than half a pound of spittle in their face a day, professional attitude or no.

In order to make such an assessment, the clinician would of course be interested especially in the *forms* that are being used by staff for intervention—limit-setting—expression of acceptance and love, etc. The totality of prevalence of certain forms of "behavior received" is not a negligible characteristic of the milieu in which a child patient has to live.

8. *Activity structure and nature of constituent performances.* Part of the impact a hospital or treatment home has on a child lies in the things he is allowed or requested *to do.* Any given activity that is halfway shapeful enough to be described has a certain amount of structure to it—

some games, for instance, have a body of rules; demand the splitting up into two opposing sides or staying in a circle; and have certain assessments of roles for the players, at least for the duration. At the same time, they make youngsters "do certain things" while the game lasts. Paul Gump introduced the term "constituent performances" into our Detroit Game Study, and referred by this term to the performances required within the course of a game as basic. Thus, running and tagging are constituent performances of a tag game, guessing word meanings is a constituent performance in many a charade, etc. We have plenty of evidence by now that—other things being equal—the very exposure of children to a given game, with its structure and demand for certain constituent performances, may have terrific clinical impact on the events at least of that day. Wherever we miscalculate the overwhelming effect which the seductive aspect of certain games may have (flashlight hide-and-seek in the dark just before bedtime) we may ask for trouble, while many a seemingly risky game can safely be played if enough ego-supportive controls are built right into it (the safety zone to which you can withdraw without having to admit you get tired or scared, etc.). In short, while I would hardly relegate the total treatment job of severely disturbed children in a mental hospital ward to that factor alone, I certainly would want to figure on it as seriously as I would calculate the mental hygiene aspects of other factors more traditionally envisioned as being of clinical concern. What I say here about games goes for many other activities patients engage in—arts and crafts, woodwork, outings, overnight trips, cookouts, discussion groups, musical evenings, etc. Which of these things takes place, where, with which feeling tone, and with what structural and activity ingredients is as characteristic of a given "milieu" as the staff that is hired.

9. *Space, equipment, time and props.* What an assortment of names, but I know as yet of no collective noun that would cover them all equally well. Since I have

made such a fuss about this for years, I may try to be shorter about it than seems reasonable. Remember what a bunch of boys do when running through a viaduct with an echo effect? Remember what may happen to a small group who are supposed to discuss plans for their next Scout meeting, who have to hold this discussion unexpectedly, in a huge gym with lots of stuff around, instead of in their usual clubroom? Remember what will happen to a baseball that is put on the table prematurely while they are still supposed to sit quietly and listen, and remember what happens to many a well-intended moral lecture to a group of sloppy campers, if you timed it so badly that the swimming bell started ringing before you had finished? Do I still have to prove why I think that what an outfit does with arrangements of time expectations and time distribution, what prop-exposure the youngsters are expected to stand or avoid, what space arrangements are like, and what equipment does to the goals you have set for yourself, should be listed along with the important "properties" of a place where clinical work with children takes place? So far I have found that in hospitals this item tends to be left out of milieu discussions by psychiatrists and sociologists alike; only the nurses and attendants have learned by bitter experience that it may pay to lend an ear to it.

10. *The seepage from the world outside.* One of the hardest "milieu aspects" to assess in a short visit to any institution is the amount of "impact from the larger universe and the surrounding world" that actually seeps through its walls and finds its way into the lives of the patients. No outfit is airtight, no matter how many keys and taboos are in use. In our own little children's ward-world, for instance, there are the following "seepage ingredients from the world outside" that are as much a part of our "milieu," as it hits the boys, as anything else: Adult visitors and the "past case history" flavor they leave behind. Child visitors and the "sociological body odor" of the old neighborhood, or the new one which they exude. Excursions which we arrange,

old haunts from prehospital days, which we happen to drive through unintentionally on our way to our destination. Plenty of purposely pulled-in outside world through movies, television, pictures, and stories we may tell them. And, of course, school is a full-view window hopefully opened wide for many vistas to be seen through it—if we only could get our children to look.

There is the "hospital impact" of the large building that hits them whenever they leave the ward floor in transit, the physically sick patients they meet on the elevator who stir the question up again in their own mind: "Why am I here?" There are the stories other boys tell, the staff tells, the imputed secrets we may be hiding from them whenever we seem eager to divert attention to something else. As soon as the children move into the open cottage, the word "seepage" isn't quite as correct any more. Suffice it to say: the type and amount of "outside world" particles that are allowed in or even eagerly pulled in constitute a most important part of the lives of the captive population of an institutional setting, and want to be given attention to in an appraisal of just what a given "milieu" holds.

11. *The system of umpiring services and traffic regulations between environment and child.* Those among you who have a sharp nose for methodological speculations may want to object and insist that I am jumping category dimensions in tagging on this item and the next one on my list. I don't want to quarrel about this now. For even though you may be right, it is too late today to start a new chapter, so please let me get away with tagging these two items on here. In some ways they still belong, for whether there are any umpiring services built into an institution, and what they are like, is certainly an important "milieu property" in my estimation. . . .

In short, it runs somewhat like this: Some "milieu impacts" hit the children directly; nobody needs to interpret or translate. Others hit the child all right, but to have their proper impact someone has to

do some explaining. It makes a great difference whether a child who is running away unhappy, after a cruel razzing received from a thoughtless group, is left to deal with this all by himself; or whether the institution provides interpretational or first-aid services for the muddled feelings at the time. Some of our children, for instance, might translate such an experience, which was not intended by the institution, into additional resentment against the world. With sympathy in the predicament offered by a friendly adult who tags along and comforts, this same experience may well be decontaminated or even turned into the opposite.

A similar item is the one I had in mind in using the phrase "traffic regulations." Much give-and-take can follow naturally among the inhabitants of a given place. Depending on the amount of their disturbance, though, some social interactions which normal life leaves to the children's own resources require traffic supervision by an adult. I would like to know whether a given milieu has foreseen this and can guarantee the provision of some help in the bartering custom among the youngsters, or whether that new youngster will be mercilessly exposed to the wildest blackmail with no help from anyone, the moment he enters the doors to my ward. In short, it is like asking what medical first-aid facilities are in a town before one moves into it. Whether this belongs to the concept of what makes up a "town," or whether it should be listed under a separate heading I leave for a later chance to thrash out. All I want to point at now is that the nature of and existence or nonexistence of umpiring services and social traffic regulations is as "real" a property of a setup as its walls, kitchen equipment and clinical beliefs.

12. *The thermostat for the regulation of clinical resilience.* If it is cold in an old cabin somewhere in the midst of "primitive nature," the trouble is obvious: either there isn't any fire going, or something is wrong with the stove and the whole heating system, so it doesn't give off enough heat. If I

freeze in a building artificially equipped with all the modern conveniences, such a conclusion might be off the beam. The trouble may simply be that the thermostat isn't working right. This, like the previous item, is a property of a given milieu rather than a "milieu ingredient" in the stricter sense of the word. However, it is of such utmost clinical relevance that it has to go in here somewhere. In fact, I have hardly ever participated in a discussion on the milieu concept without having this item come up somehow or other.

The term under which it is more often referred to is actually that of "flexibility," which most milieu therapy enthusiasts praise as "good" while the bad men in the picture are the ones that think "rigidity" is a virtue. I have more reasons to be tired of this either/or issue than I can list in the remaining time. It seems to me that the "resilience" concept fits better what most of us have so long tried to shoot at with the flexibility label. A milieu certainly needs to be sensitive to the changing needs of the patients during different phases of the treatment process. It needs to "tighten up" —lower the behavioral ceiling when impulse-panic looms on the horizon; and it may have to lift it when self-imposed internal pressures mount. Also, it needs to limit spontaneity and autonomy of the individual patient in early phases of intensive

disorder and rampant pathology; it needs to throw in a challenge toward autonomy and even the risking of mistakes, when the patient goes through the later phases of recovery. Especially when severely disturbed children are in the process of going through an intensive phase of "improvement," the resilience of a milieu to make way for its implications is as important as its ability to "shrink back" during a regressive phase.

JUST HOW DOES THE MILIEU DO IT?

Listing these 12 variables of important milieu aspects which can be differentiated as explorable issues in their own right is only part of the story. I hold no brief for this list, and I am well aware of its methodological complications and deficiencies. The major value of listing them at all lies in the insistence that *there are so many of them* and that they *can be separately studied and explored.* This should at least help us to secure ourselves against falling in love with any one of them to the exclusion of the others, and of forcing any discipline that wants to tackle the job, whether it be psychiatry, sociology or what not, to look beyond its traditional scope and directly into the face of uncompromisingly multifaceted facts. . . .

SUMMARY

In this chapter on how disturbed children can be helped, we have shown the ways children may undergo specific treatment in clinics, or private offices for their emotional discomforts and illnesses. We did not include medical or drug treatment, because we are not equipped to convey detailed information on medication. Furthermore, most educators are content to know from a parent or physician when a child is taking a specific drug, why he is taking it, and in what ways the drug may affect his school behavior. The adjunctive therapies explained in this chapter—art, dance, music, puppetry, and occupational therapy—are winning clinical respect and undoubtedly will attract increasing interest from the educational and research fields as more school programs are developed. Milieu therapy, the most complex, offers a total therapeutic environment for children who cannot respond to outpatient intervention.

4

What Kinds of Schools and Programs Are Provided?

Once a child is identified as emotionally disturbed or socially handicapped, the educational recommendation usually includes both professional treatment and a modification of his educational program. The biggest problem confronting the schools is not in formulating the recommendation, but in carrying it out. Eli Bower, a consultant to the National Institute of Mental Health, recently reported on a national survey that of the half-million seriously disturbed children in our country only ten thousand were receiving treatment. The next logical question is: What is happening to the other ninety-eight percent? The vast majority of these children are fidgeting, fighting, itching, instigating, crying, and, incidentally, failing in the regular classes of our public schools. Treatment facilities are scarce and often limit their admissions to children who are "good cases." Even when a child is acceptable to a child guidance clinic, it is not unusual for him to wait more than a year for treatment to begin. By that time his teacher's hope for help has dwindled to despair; he has given up working with the child and is willing to accept a nonverbal exchange of no-work for no-noise. Thus a schoolroom, once the center of active learning, is forced to assume the role of an impersonal and passive babysitter.

To depend solely on clinics and professionals outside the school to solve the problems of the ever rising number of disturbed children, has become unrealistic. The school needs to develop its own re-educational facility and to admit that there are children whose behavior is so deviant that even special classes and programs will be ineffective. It needs to shout, without embarrassment, that the school is not omnipotent and cannot keep these children only because there is no other place in the community for them to go. The school needs to be relieved of the *major responsibility* for the deviant ones. The care of emotionally disturbed children is a community-centered problem, not just a school problem. The school, in close cooperation with other civic agencies, should campaign actively for additional facilities such as foster homes, detention homes, day-care programs, and residential facilities.

This chapter gives examples of the various types of psychoeducational settings for emotionally disturbed children. Included are methods of adapting the regular class, the use of special classes and special schools, and finally, the residential school or hospital.

Since ninety-eight percent of the emotionally disturbed children in the public schools remain in a regular class, the primary source of support should be for the classroom teacher. Historically, the first attempt was to provide the teacher with specialists who were not a part of the school staff (psychologists, psychiatrists, and social workers). As these consultants worked with the classroom teacher, the teachers began to feel that they were becoming an extension of a child-guidance clinic, rather than being helped by the specialists to understand and better teach groups of children. In short, the child-guidance approach created as many problems as it solved. For example, when a child was taken out of a classroom for individual therapy, the child's problem was placed outside the teacher's jurisdiction. The teacher's role was devaluated when the therapist, under severe time-limitation or because of a lack of interest, was unable to maintain a cooperative and continuous flow of information. Under these conditions, the teacher was relegated to a passive role where his insights and concerns were not considered. Also, the therapy given the child many times was fragmented and ineffective. As dissatisfaction set in, the school slowly shed its child-guidance approach.

The present trend is to re-design the specialists to function within the overall educational milieu of the school. During the last ten years, many experimental projects designed to bridge the gap between educational practices and mental-hygiene principles for the classroom teacher have been carried out. The emphasis has changed from treating individual children to helping teachers help themselves.

The following article describes a technique and a method of consultation designed to help a teacher (and other school staff) understand and deal with a. variety of professional problems in a hygienic way. This method was developed during a three-year research program involving many school settings, special and regular, from nursery school through senior high school.

Technical Assistance

*Ruth G. Newman, Claire Bloomberg, Ruth Emerson, Marjorie Keith,
Howard Kitchner, and Fritz Redl*

THE TERM EDUCATIONAL TECHNICAL ASSISTANCE CONSULTATION

First of all, the term "Educational Technical Assistance Consultation" has been criticized by some of our readers. We, ourselves, are not overjoyed with it. Our critics have claimed that it is too easily confused with other uses of the word, yet this is precisely the kind of thing we wished to avoid. We tried to find a descriptive phrase which would be a portmanteau term including a variety of roles and functions,

From *Technical Assistance,* a report by the authors to the Washington School of Psychiatry, Washington, D.C., 1964. Reprinted by permission.

while, at the same time, differentiating what we did from what other consultative services offered to schools. It would seem that the term cannot be made into the kind of Rube Goldberg invention which could do everything we wanted it to do. The following are the concepts we wished to cover.

THE MEDICAL MODEL

We wanted to distinguish what we were doing from the kind of consultation which takes place at intervals, may or may not go on for more than one session, but is strictly limited to a service done on call, on demand. The medical model of a doctor being called in to consult with another doctor on diagnosis or treatment of a patient is the most familiar example. In such a case the consulting physician and the patient may benefit from the specific interaction between consultant and consultee. The consultee may, through this interaction, learn how to look at a similar patient in a different manner. Thus learning, training and change may take place, but the session has not been called for that purpose and the consultant physician removes himself from the relationship as soon as the particular situation is ended. Many parallels can be drawn between this kind of consultation and mental hygiene or educational consultation, i.e., a consultant is asked to talk with the principal and teacher in order to help diagnose and appraise a case of a deeply withdrawn child in a classroom; or to examine the disability in reading of a whole group of seventh graders which has brought about a consultation between the English teacher, and the specialist remedial advisor, opthamologist and curriculum expert. The consultation ends when a specific course of action is determined.

We may do and have done this kind of consultation within the framework of Technical Assistance consultation, but we go beyond this function. We, as part of our major hypotheses, come weekly, meet with a variety of people on a variety of issues. We may continue our consultant relationship with the consultee(s) over a period of an entire year, or we may see a given teacher or school nurse at different times throughout the year, depending on his or her expressed needs or desire to see us. Training is not the focus of our interviews but is implied and is part of our purpose in being on hand regularly. In any event our continuous and reliable availability for consultation each and every week at the school itself is a distinguishing characteristic we wished to make clear.

CRISIS CONSULTATION

We felt that "Technical Assistance" differentiated us not only from the medical model, but the more intensive crisis con-

sultation developed by Caplan for mental health purposes. In Crisis Consultation a complete interaction is handled through consultation with all people concerned for a brief period. When the problem has been handled, the contact ends, save for followup interviews. With our method, the contact does not end but we are on hand to pick up other areas of concern to the same people or others within the school at other times. Thus, the goal of training is more central to our method or at least, the possibilities for training over a longer period and with more than one kind of incident are more readily open to us.

TRAINING CONSULTATION

The matter of training was basic to our entire design. We were in business to help train those school staff members who wished help, in small doses or large, to deal with problems of the emotionally disturbed or disturbing student in the school room. What is more, our aim was to do this in such a way that staff would be able not only to handle the specific problems more usefully, but so that they might, in time, be able to handle similar problems with other children, and/or to distinguish between what is a similar problem and what just looks like one. By continuous contact, we hoped to help differentiate to some extent how much the disturbance arose from the child, how much from the group, how much from the curriculum, the use of materials, the methods, the teacher-child relationship, the teacher personality, and the system at large.

Although our work was inextricably bound up with training, we were not and never wished to be in the role of the school supervisor, who, though he may also be a training agent, is used by the school systems to evaluate, rate, and by definition, sit in judgment on a teacher's performance according to certain school standards and in comparison with other teachers. Therefore, we very much wanted to differentiate our work from that of the school supervisor who often determines a staff member's tenure, salary, placement and rating. Though we were specifically and emphatically not doing this kind of job, there is no question that what we did in our consultation is closely related to what a good case-work supervisor does with his or her case workers; and what many training analysts do with their psychiatrists or psychologist trainees. Yet, we wished to avoid the term supervisor, and we felt the term consultant-trainer did not include all that we had in mind to do, nor all that we actually did.

DEMONSTRATION AND INTERVENTION CONSULTATION

We were prepared to take on other tasks related less directly to training and more directly with life on the job and inter-relationships determined by the job. Although our approach was non-judgmental in that we neither sat in judgment nor gave comparative ratings, we of course had and gave value judgments. We were often aware that a teacher or counselor had handled a child either ineffectively or even damagingly. When the time was appropriate, we said so, not in terms of a scolding but in terms of inquiring into what had gone wrong, what was misunderstood or not known, how the thing might have been seen from a different perspective—perhaps more fruitfully. When asked, or when given an opportunity, together with the teacher, we tried to help find alternate ways of looking at the teacher or student behavior. One manner of doing this was by simply talking things over, which is usual procedure for consultant relations. Another way was by demonstration and implication. In other words, the very form of the interaction between consultee and consultant could be such that the consultee could use it as an illustration of what might be done, or perhaps of what shouldn't be done, with the student. This method is often used in skillful case work supervision and is not new.

In addition, there were times when quite purposely, and for thought-out reasons, our consultants entered into the classroom, the parent-teacher conference, the management of a number of children in order to demonstrate various techniques, to explore what might be going on with the child or children that had temporarily stymied the teacher. Following such a demonstration, an interview between consultant and consultee was held so that the demonstration could be a joint endeavor and not simply a consultant taking over. Occasionally, because of time or pressure, this went by the board, but we made an honest effort to see that it was done whenever possible. This kind of interaction was handled as carefully as possible to guard against a halo effect in which the consultant was held as expert and the staff member as admiring on-looker. Mutual difficulties were gone into, different ways of seeing what took place were gone over. The relationship was directed into a two-way relationship between two specialists, each of whom had something to offer the other in order to attack the task at hand most effectively. Thus, although we tried to avoid advice-giving as wisdom from above, we did not hesitate, once a mutual view of roles was established, to give advice or make recommendations or referrals when we felt that the staff member could use them to help free him from additional frustration and to allow for his own sense of development, growth and independence. This kind of maneuver in consultation is ticklish. Because it is difficult, and can so easily slip over into unuseful attitudes, it is often avoided. We include it in our term and simply maintain that we try to use it carefully and with as much awareness of the possible dangers as we can.

POINT IV PROGRAM

Taking all our roles into consideration, we therefore developed the term Technical Assistance Consultation both to differentiate our roles from those of other people who functioned similarly in a different context, and to include, as proper under our roles, aspects of consultation which are not part of either the function or the purpose of other types of consultation. We chose the term Technical Assistance because we thought it was sufficiently elastic and descriptive to include all these functions. We borrowed it from the United States State Department Point IV Program because like the delegates sent out from the State Department, we came from outside a school system, having been invited to do so, and entered into a different environment, not only to advise but to lend technical knowledge and active participation. Like the Point IV Program, our assignment was continuous within a limited period of time. Like the Point IV Program we hoped that what we were able to communicate which was of use to our consultees would be carried over into their own system of operation, individually and over-all. In most settings, to a larger or a smaller extent, we arranged some way wherein either the school itself could carry on with the kind of work we inaugurated within their own ability to do so, or we found ways to follow up, or make check visits when we were invited to do so. We wished to imply the concept of the linkage of systems defined by Gilmore in her article on consultation where people (the consultants) come from one speciality, one environment, into another, wherein awareness of both cultures is essential. This was our purpose but some of our critics understood the idea as meaning that we were going as experts to an under-developed environment *and this we most emphatically did not want to convey.* If we have contributed to obfuscation by adding to already confusing terminology, we are most penitent. In our defense we can only say our intentions were the opposite and that it is difficult these days to find a term which satisfactorily describes a complicated process. For instance, no sooner has one accustomed oneself to thinking of a child who does not function educationally, partly because of his cultural and economic opportunities, as an "educationally deprived child," than a group of people is horrified and feels it is a belittling term so one proceeds to alter the phrase to "educa-

tionally disadvantaged" or "educationally inefficient"—all of which implies something similar but something different. If we have done the same thing with our term Educational Technical Assistance Consultation, we can only say that having committed this sin, we hope that what we have in mind is understood by the reader. To recapitulate, it is an interpersonal process involving consultation of a largely voluntary nature. It is regular, continuous within a limited space of time, the weekly or bi-weekly visits lasting throughout at least one school year. It offers a variety of consultative services and functions: active intervention, listening, observing, supportive, inquiring, directive and indirective methods, demonstration, individual and group sessions. It is based on an interpersonal interaction between consultant and consultee, directly related to the consultee's professional performance. In our case, the focus was on preventative, managerial, sometimes curative mental health measures to aid school staff in dealing with the disturbed and/or disturbing behavior of students within the school. . . .

TECHNICAL ASSISTANCE WITHIN A SYSTEM OR WITHOUT

Properly speaking, from the definition given above, when Technical Assistance comes from within a system it is not strictly Technical Assistance. However, for purposes of description here, since many people wondered whether it was better to have the Technical Assistance consultants come from within a school system or without, we will keep to the term. It is basic to the total concept that, whether from within or without, these services were not planned to supplant other existing functions. If such methods come from within the system, there might be a trained core of guidance people with social case work or psychological backgrounds, trained in the variety of skills needed for doing our kind of consultation. The Albuquerque System of New Mexico was attempting to do just such a job. Their difficulty was that it became mandatory for all schools to accept their services and this nullified the voluntary concept. This too is a problem which can be worked on, and they worked on it; but this is a possible disadvantage of having Technical Assistance consultation come from within a system. It is more threatening to the over-all process than is the other obvious objection which arises in considering school originated Technical Assistance consultation; namely, that school staff will view the Technical Assistants suspiciously as potential spyers and raters. Of course this can be a problem, but it can be ameliorated by skillful consultants who carefully and patiently iterate and reiterate their role and function. The consultants must be willing to live out the natural and expected testing period where the truth of this statement about their real roles and functions can be tested out and established. There are advantages to Technical Assistance consultants coming from within a system. There is familiarity with its rules and attitudes. There is also a possibility of easy rapport between consultant and consultee since they share many of the same problems. Furthermore, many principals originally feel uncomfortable about what seems to be washing dirty linen before strangers. It is less threatening to do so within the family, so to speak.

There are distinct advantages in coming from without a school system as we did. It is easier to deal with the bugaboo of power and status lines, to convince the school staff that hirings, firings, ratings, raises and placements do not in any way depend on the consultant's knowledge or judgment. It is easier to work for change with the staff itself instead of being caught up in the policy fights and financial difficulties coming from above. Since some battles are momentarily, if not permanently, unfightable, it is better to focus on those things a given staff member, or a group of staff members *can* do about their dissatisfactions with their professional work. It is

much like working with a wife who is married to a badly crippled man. If she wants to stay married to him, there is no use, other than catharsis and recognition of the feelings that go into such a condition of life, to get stuck within the unchangeable. The problem becomes how to better conditions within the person and within the relationship so that life can be fuller and give more satisfaction all around. Similarly, there is so much to be done by the staff members themselves that it becomes unnecessary to dwell forever on those aspects that can't be changed or those that can only be changed slowly or by group action and community help. Moreover, there is a push towards independence and growth in the consultee(s) since they are aware that they will be on their own within a given period. They are likely to take more responsibility and search out ways to maintain those aspects of the consultation work which appear valuable and use them after the departure of this particular Technical Assistant.

To work outside requires a trained nucleus of people. Where can these people come from? They can be a specialized and trained group as we were or they can come from mental hygiene clinics, thus uniting community and school, clinical facilities and educational facilities more closely. This is an area where trained personnel, if trained in school environment, if familiarized with school problems, school atmosphere, school language, could be strikingly useful in doing preventative and curative mental health work without needing to increase their bulging case loads and getting farther behind in their waiting lists. Of course this implies either additional staff or staff who would be allotted time for such services. It most certainly implies time for training a core of Educational Technical Assistance consultants. It would seem to us a most useful field of inquiry for mental hygiene clinics. Often, in order to please school or community, these clinics use trained staff to make detailed studies of problems such as school phobia or anxiety among kindergarteners rather than a more total mental health approach, which could be instituted at the cost of a little more clinic and staff time.

WHO CAN DO THIS KIND OF JOB?

Whether Technical Assistance consultation comes from within or without a school or a school system; whether the task is to work on communication, management, curriculum modification, in-service training, we have found certain basic qualifications to be essential for the consultants to be effective. This is most especially true if consultation is to deal with mental health problems (which in fact are a part of all the services mentioned above). Before going into these qualifications, it would seem only fair to the reader to mention our own theoretical bias (if it has not already been gathered through reading the text) since the qualifications we find primary are contingent upon our way of looking at the whole problem.

Our theoretical bias derives from the psychodynamic point of view. We, therefore, wished to include in our consultative attitudes and services a message to our consultees, whether they be teachers, principals, counselors, psychologists or social workers. The message states that a certain amount of self-knowledge and self-acceptance is essential for professional effectiveness. Therefore, throughout our work, we tried to create an atmosphere where increasing self-knowledge and self-acceptance could take place. Since, though we came from a different specialty, we engaged in an interpersonal process ourselves it became partly a matter of relaying attitudes and ways of observing, perceiving and consulting. Our bias includes a conviction about motivation which contains conscious, pre-conscious and unconscious forces. In actuality we rarely dealt with under-the-surface material and only attempted to do so when it directly affected the staff member's own professional, on-the-job behavior. Nonetheless, we came with the belief that these factors influence behavior. Some re-

action sheets claimed that it is equally impossible to do this kind of a job without considering unconscious forces: this is indeed possible. It is simply that this is not what we did and therefore our conclusions are colored by the manner in which we approached our job. These conclusions will be found in the discussion that follows about defenses, awareness level, interviewing techniques, the quality of observations, the quality of relationships, role definition, the boundary line that divides therapy from professional consultation, the phenomena of transference and counter-transference, of overdependence and overinvolvement, of resistance and withdrawal. An example of one of our concerns and conclusions should suffice to make the point.

HUMAN ERROR

Much consultation, especially mental health consultation, has to do with the process of listening, of being a wailing wall, of lending support or acceptance, or at least toleration of what is being said. Our particular emphasis with school staff, as stated above, was to give an awareness of what is going on, to develop a certain amount of self-acceptance of what one did at a given moment in time, even though we may have wished he had done differently. We felt this self-acceptance to be especially necessary in schools, since above and beyond other institutions, schools are most susceptible to the disease of outlawing human error. A mistake is wrong and must be concealed, an error must be rationalized, denied, projected or handled by an overload of mea culpa moanings. The all-too-rare statement that "everyone makes a mistake sometimes" is usually only mouthed. This attitude is conveyed in no uncertain terms to the children being taught, so that errors are feared and are not thought of as tools for learning. Among the teachers themselves, their concealment of lesson plans under their desks when supervisors come to call and the hurried bringing out of what is considered "right" is a case in point. "Don't tell on me" is as much or more a staff disease as it is a disease of the students. We feel this is most crippling and destructive to mental health, and in fact to honest intellectual attitudes for both staff members and growing children. It paralyzes learning and makes for pathology or dishonesty (the two are not too dissimilar).

In consultative work with social workers, psychologists, psychiatrists, it is part of the process to open up mistakes and to use them, not to sit in judgment, but in order to help the person find out why the mistake was made, what was good behind the mistake, what was not useful, what needed to be altered, and how one might proceed next time.

EXAMPLE OF ERROR

How is this applied to a teacher? Let us say a teacher has lost her temper at Billy when for the fourth time Billy has interrupted her lesson by bursting out in class with loud cat-calls. Her loss of control was unbecoming and she feels she alienated others in the class. She is filled with chagrin and self-loathing. A Technical Assistance consultant, after breaking through this defensiveness, tries to communicate the fact (a) that losing one's temper might have been a mistake in that instance but a very human mistake, (b) that nothing was gained for Billy or herself in doing so and that something might have been temporarily lost in her relationship with the class, (c) that Billy needs limits, (d) that the time to tackle Billy was the second cat-call not the fourth, before Billy got out of bounds completely and before the teacher had reached her level of frustration, (e) that records and reports of Billy's behavior with other teachers point to the possibility that Billy did this because he wanted attention and because he was conveying a message that the work was too hard for him at that given moment and that rather than be called on and appear dumb to his classmates, he was breaking up the class. The teacher has given the consultant knowledge of Billy; the consultant can support her observation powers and her ability to see, and can also relay the lesson the mistake itself teaches about motivations, timing and perhaps seating arrangements, sub-grouping in the classroom, materials more befitting Billy's level, etc. The mistake can be seen not only as not fatal, but helpful, and from its perusal can come suggestions from teacher and consultant concerning how to treat Billy and how rapport with the class might be reestablished.

This kind of interaction is basic in case work and psychological supervision, it is most lacking in most school milieus, regardless of statements to the contrary which may be said but not felt, experienced or acted out. Our bias towards self-awareness and acceptance made us particularly sensitive to this kind of problem. Other biases might be equally so. In our minds the need for such awareness is an essential finding about schools and school staff with vital implication for consultative procedures. One way in which we approached this problem, made possible because of our continuous, regular contact with the schools, was by using ourselves as demonstration models. That is to say we tried very hard to be aware ourselves of our own errors, to point them out where it was appropriate to do so, without dragging them in falsely, to indicate our acceptance of gaffes, mistakes, poor handling; to show where they had helped us to see more clearly if they had indeed done so, and what we were going to do about them. This was not only appreciated by consultees but, we hope, was a helpful learning tool. This concept returns us to the problem of who can do Technical Assistance consultation, for indeed, one necessary trait that needs to be trained into anyone doing this kind of work with schools is the ability to be aware of mistakes, not to conceal them but to use them.

INTERPERSONAL RELATIONS

The underlying kernel out of which all Technical Assistance consultative work flows or fails to flow is the quality of the interpersonal relation. It goes without saying that since, like teachers, Technical Assistance consultants will not be saints, they will relate differently with different school staff and not equally well with all. Yet, they must have the basic ability to relate well to most of the staff with whom they deal. Relating well implies an ability to form a warm, friendly, not overly but sufficiently, involved relationship which must be convincing—ring true, eliminate phoniness. A Technical Assistance consultant must be a good or participating listener. He must have developed skills, whether intuitively or by training, which will help him know when to listen and when to talk, when to sympathize and when to keep silent, when to intervene directly with a suggestion and when to gently push the consultee to find his own suggestions. He must know when to direct the consultee back to the point under discussion and when to allow rambling. He must know when to stop a conference and when to give extra time, at that moment or later in the day. He must know how to listen in either a formal or informal setting; and when to choose one and when the other. He must have the ability to wait and be sufficiently able to tolerate anxiety himself so that he does not get impatient with lacks of signs of change or with slip-backs on the part of consultees. Basically, he must have a fundamental belief that something can come out of interpersonal interactions, despite the sometimes discouraging look of things, the long delay in seeing results, the lack of pats on the back for himself. Not everyone, not even those who are usually good with interpersonal relations, has this quality. In order to build it in, a good bit of supervision or colleague shop-talk for the Technical Assistance consultant himself is necessary.

Clearly, if one is after self-awareness in others, the Technical Assistance consultant himself must have some ability to introspect and be able to recognize his own anxiety signals, his own defensive structure, his own needs and the ways in which his own counter-transference is apt to show up. For example, one of our consultants was

aware of her need to help and was frequently made anxious by her urge towards overinvolvement. The awareness helped up to a point. An overawareness can be unuseful too, so that at times she bent over backward so that there was too much caution in her moves. Her ability to spot this made it possible for her not only to overcome it, but to express her attitudes to the principal so that both could be on guard for what was a real threat to the effectiveness of the consultative process and what was imagined or feared.

One aspect of interpersonal relationships in which it is necessary to train Technical Assistance consultants is an awareness of boundaries. By constant reappraisal, he must know what the consultee is able to grasp at that time, what the organization—the school—can take, what the consultant himself can and cannot do. He must know how to keep the relationship focused on the professional task and to indicate the limits of what is appropriate in this relationship and what might be more appropriate in other nonschool-centered relationships. He must be able to convey the boundaries in time, in place and in role definition to his consultee(s).

It is obvious that any one in this position must be able, by training or talent or both to recognize and to tolerate hostility, direct or indirect resentment towards himself as well as counter-hostility or resentment in himself. He must be able to handle rejection, be it temporary or complete, to face failure or low levels of satisfaction. Peculiarly enough we have found this concept so drummed into consultants, especially by the psychological, psychiatric and social work disciplines, that the converse needs to be said. A Technical Assistance consultant needs to be able to accept improvement and even success without over-suspicion or self-belittling.

Other aspects of the interpersonal relationship which seem particularly pertinent to the job of a Technical Assistance consultant at schools, are the ability to recognize non-verbal cues and to sense the particular unique impact of one personality on another. By such skill the consultant may take informed guesses about how the personality of his consultee would affect a shy student, an aggressive student, an obsessive-compulsive student, an anxious student, a person in authority, a competing colleague or an underling colleague. Particularly important in working with schools, especially schools from cultures, background and economic levels different from the consultant's own, is some knowledge and awareness of cultural differences and what this means to the students and to the teachers who, like the consultant, may come from different backgrounds than the students. The particular conflicts, misunderstandings, mismanagements, prejudices, stereotypes which occur under these conditions are of the essence in a Technical Assistance consultant's job.

As soon as one begins discussions such as this, the qualities that evolve as necessary for Technical Assistance consultants sound like a girl scout honor oath. This is not what is meant at all. People with foibles and failings, disturbances of their own, and lacks in training can be good Technical Assistance consultants. Indeed, as has been mentioned before, there is much to be said for foibles, lacks and faults. The qualities mentioned may be latent and may be trained-in where a person has a basic talent for interpersonal relations or a sensitivity to them. There are many people from many backgrounds who relate naturally and easily, especially within a professionally-bounded context. There are others who may have many assets and virtues but cannot do this kind of job. This is to say that in selecting people to do Technical Assistance consultation, it is unwise not to be aware of these basic qualities which may exist because of training or simply *because*. Many schools, for instance, choose for their guidance and counseling personnel, people who were excellent gym teachers or social science teachers, because they had an ability to be friendly with kids in a given context. The result is too often that a good teacher is lost and a poor counselor gained. This too can operate in training for Technical Assistance consultant work unless careful thought is given to the particular personality traits, attitudes, backgrounds, and predilections of the persons selected. There are, for instance, many psychiatrists and psychologists, excellent within the rules of their own disciplines, who can not do this kind of off-their-own-territory-on-someone-else's-territory kind of eclectic interpersonal task. Sometimes, this is because they are, for the most part, unaware of the total school ecology (this could be trained-in presumably). But they are also often uneasy with other disciplines, uneasy with the wide open spaces of multiple demands from a number of people in a busy school atmosphere.

What we are saying then, is that we have found that it is not the specific disciplinary background that determines whether the Technical Assistance consultant will be good in the job. We ourselves had one consultant whose background included psychology, education, specializing in learning problems; a social worker interested in school social work; one teacher with a special education interest who had originally been a lawyer; one ex-nursery school teacher who had supervising experience and interview techniques for research purposes. Each had his assets and shortcomings. The common quality, despite special interest and training, was the kind of ability to relate flexibly, to be interested, to be aware of oneself as part of the relationship and an ability to throw oneself into the setting in which consultation was to take place. . . .

INTERVIEW TECHNIQUES

The basic tool needed for this job is the interview technique. Therefore, the greater the knowledge and experience with various forms and types of interviewing, the more likely the success. Interview techniques appropriate to this particular job are something that can be learned. Even though there is no specific body of knowledge built up for educational consultation of our kind, much can be found in the literature of social case work and clinical psychology, and in psychiatric source books, journals and articles. There are even low and high level courses in psychotherapy and case work connected with professional training schools, as well as some at a few universities, especially in certain graduate departments. They are not all of the same quality or depth but they can give a learner some foundation on which to build. If one has come to the Technical Assistance consultant job from any clinical background, it can be assumed that field work as well as course work in interviewing has been a basic part of training. The longer one has been in the actual business of interviewing, the more comfortable and flexible will be the ability to do this job. It goes without saying that once in the act, the Technical Assistance consultant himself will need supervision and consultation with colleagues at the same level of experience, or at a level of greater experience. The same conditions operate for the Technical Assistance consultant as for the consultee. There will be the same anxieties, defenses, hurdles. There are bound to be problems concerning when to intervene and when not to; how much to be involved; how deeply to go into something; how to define or redefine one's role; how to extricate oneself from school politics and interpersonal line-ups within the staff; how to break a deadlock; how, or if, one should see someone who pretends, or even feels he wants to see you but keeps breaking appointments; when to call limits and when to push on, etc. All these problems need to be looked at, talked over and dealt with just as much as the school staff needs to talk over professional problems if the job is to be effective. Moreover, shop talk or supervision either by colleagues or outside consultants, keeps one alert, through one's own experience, to defensive reactions and blind spots of one's own. Any training group, whether it be conducted by outside facilities or as part of a university, a clinic or a school system, would need to offer information and field work to familiarize Technical Assistance consultants with a variety of schools and school settings. If the field of consultation is mental health

needs or communication, the observed settings should range from residential treatment centers through private schools to public schools at all levels. How intensive such training could be would depend on the background of the particular Technical Assistance candidate. No matter how experienced, the person about to launch into such a job needs to spend a good bit of time at the particular school where the consultation is being undertaken. One's role while wandering in the halls, lunch room, lounges, parking lots and offices needs to be defined for the staff so that one doesn't look like a spy from administration or local newspapers. Here the principal's cooperation, statements and attitudes are of utmost importance.

Interview techniques for this job, in addition to the basic one-to-one relationship within a set structure (formal and informal) must include group consultation. One needs awareness of non-verbal clues and cues and training in the ability to take up asides or casual comments or jokes that will give the consultant some notion of the feelings of the place—the particular concerns and needs, the perception of staff members by other staff members, the point of view in relation to the principal, to special psychological or remedial services, to facilities in the community, and so forth. In this way the consultant may avoid leaping into pitfalls with perfectly good intentions. Without knowing the system he might barge into making sensible-sounding suggestions which happen to be utterly ridiculous in this set-up and simply underline his ignorance of what goes on. At the same time he needs to be able to be ignorant and ask questions, but to ask them in such a way that they can be answered as honestly as possible without embarrassing anyone too much.

GROUPS AND ROLES

We have found that in this kind of work, it is helpful to have special knowledge in group techniques, not only because as a consultant one will use them, but because teachers, who work with groups all day long and who may have absorbed some knowledge of groups and what one does with them, frequently have not examined their practices and are therefore unaware of the varieties of grouping, of the reason why certain groups work and certain groups fail. They are often unacquainted with translations of sociogrammatic techniques into the classroom, and are sometimes fearful of using the group either to manage ticklish situations or as a teaching device.

Another requirement for this kind of consultation is the ability to clarify or bring about awareness of teachers' self-expectations and what they perceive as being expected of them. What roles are they to play? What role has the principal in their eyes? What is the status hierarchy in their system of looking at things? What role has the consultant? What does the teacher feel the consultant should be doing, and how divergent is this from what the consultant feels he should be doing? . . .

BOUNDARIES OF CONSULTATION AND THERAPY

One of the questions which inevitably arises in our kind of consultation process is whether consultation of this kind does not slip over into therapy. If so, is this not a smuggling in of the kind of treatment which necessitates a course of action in which both parties have voluntarily decided to participate in a fully conscious manner? How can one protect oneself, either as consultee or as consultant from transforming some consultation sessions into therapy? There is also the corollary suspicion on the part of some of our readers that if we slip into therapy, since this is not what we have said we are doing, there is a factor of a hidden agenda, a manipulative marionette string pulling.

Of course, if therapy is defined as any interaction between people in which it is hoped that change in attitudes and behavior will take place to the satisfaction of the person receiving therapy, then Techni-

cal Assistance consultation can be thought of as therapy. But then, so can aspects of nearly any good relationship. But that is too broad a definition of therapy to concern ourselves with here. In this consultative relation do we try to reorganize the consultee's point of view, and personality structure? Do we tap his unconscious for clues, attack his defenses and try to substitute more satisfactory patterns? No, we do not. The question is one of role delineation. In therapy the relationship is based on the exploration of the patient in all his modes of behavior, thinking and feeling. In Technical Assistance consultations, where the personal relationship between people, or attitudes towards people, directly affect the specific job at hand (say a teacher-parent conference or the interplay between a teacher with segregationist attitudes and her Negro pupils) then we try to explore this interaction if the consultee wants to do so. If, as sometimes has happened, having explored such an interaction, the staff member wishes to pursue the subject and go on to further explore his motivations, or feelings, we call a halt. We define where our role begins and where it ends. Should he wish, for his own purposes, to go further, we make, *upon his request,* suggestions of facilities for doing so. The subject matter for our consultation is the job, the workday. The goal is to help a staff member perform his job in such a way as to be able to function more successfully with individuals or groups in his class. It is often both relevant and important to help him with his relation with other staff (those in authority over him, those with less seniority and those with equal status) in order that he may serve his students more adequately. It is sometimes imperative and relevant to relieve him of extra loads of tensions and strain which are affecting his performance as a teacher; these tensions may derive from particular crises in his own personal, nonprofessional life but neither the underlying subject matter nor the goal of the conference is his own personality reorganization. This needs to be very clear in the eyes of both consultant and consultee to avoid getting into too deep waters; to avoid misunderstandings and resentments and indeed, the unethical practice of using one kind of interaction to conceal another. Even if a teacher were to ask for what is essentially a psychotherapeutic relation, it would be improper and out of place to give this to her and slip it in as appropriate to Technical Assistance consultation. One certainly might, however, as part of the proper function, explore with her how she feels her present difficulties interfere with her job, and one might legitimately suggest sources for treatment or support her own desires to get help, and help her make the necessary arrangements. Unless the boundaries are defined and re-defined during the process there may be confusion and the basic Technical Assistance relationship will suffer.

It is true that many of the techniques used in psychotherapy are those that are used in the Technical Assistance relationship: listening, supporting, questioning, waiting, summarizing, and even—though with quite a difference—interpreting. The difference is that this entire procedure is focused on the job, students and other staff, not on the personal problems themselves. For example, a piece of behavior on the part of a teacher might be interpreted by a therapist as arising out of unconscious competition with a younger sibling. The same piece of behavior might be interpreted in a conference by a Technical Assistance consultant in terms of how the student experiences the teacher's constant nagging, or tearing down or belittling. The aspect of competition might or might not come to light: it would not be dealt with on the basis of overall attitudes. It would be dealt with as a question of continuing to teach this student without being destructive. Techniques which might alleviate this negative relation might be proposed. The therapist would be concerned with the woman's feelings about competition. The Technical Assistance consultant would only be interested in trying to decontaminate this relation and purify it of the teacher's personal

pathology. To suggest a comparable situation: a sanitation specialist might be able to purify the water feeding into one apartment house so that the water becomes drinkable, but not be concerned with the depollution of the water in the general system—this being a job for other sanitation specialists.

We would not deny that from our bias, we would subscribe to the hypothesis that unconscious factors, defenses against anxiety or break-through of unconscious material often directly affect a teacher's management of a child or a group of children or her own performance of her job. In our own work we devoted a great deal of time, thought and attention to how we approached such interactions—where our job began and where it ended; how to convey our boundaries and our role to the consultee. We found that when we had appraised the situation fully, we could usually set the limits without cutting the teacher off, still keeping the avenues of communication open to the factors which actually interfered with her doing her job.

Let us give two more examples from our files to make the point clear. Miss Gray teaches the second grade. She has tremendous difficulty accepting dirt. It actually repels her—it always has since childhood. Robert, her pupil, is a troublesome child whose emotional stability is shaky but who can, with support and good teaching, quite easily be maintained in class and be able to learn. He is doing badly and so is Miss Gray who is fully aware of Robert's potential for learning and potential for distress. Robert is repulsive to Miss Gray. He cannot get from her the kind of attention he needs, only the kind he cannot use. To make things worse, Miss Gray is looking at Robert as the pioneer of a long train of such children, for the neighborhood in which she has taught many years has changed, and more and more the poverty-stricken children, often dirty and unkempt will be filling her classroom and she can not abide the very smell of them. So Robert is getting a double dose of Miss Gray's own personal idiosyncrasy and anxiety. Now, in talking over the problem with the Technical Assistance consultant Miss Gray may be very well aware of the fact that she has always had a hyper-reaction to dirt and the smell of poverty. She may or may not know the background reasons for her dismay. She may be well aware, or not at all aware, that her attitude is at the crux of her difficulty with Robert. She may have thought of changing schools at the end of the term to avoid "Roberts." She may even have thought of stopping teaching entirely although she has been a good, bright and conscientious teacher. The Technical Assistance consultant need not dig out every facet of her childhood experience. It may not even be necessary to dig out very many. It is essential that she take a look at her attitudes, and that she be helped to overcome her repugnance *in the classroom with Robert or his counterparts.* She is quite free, as far as the consultant is concerned, to keep her repugnance in her home, with neighborhood children and with her nieces and nephews. But here, at school, with Robert she needs help. She may, with exploration, decide that this feeling of hers is unconquerable and then the consultant needs to help her face the fact that a change in neighborhoods might be a good thing. She may be sufficiently hampered by this phobia of hers so that she herself asks for a referral for further treatment. She may be able, with the help of Technical Assistance alone, to keep her phobia in bounds —that is to say, to disentangle Robert from his dirt or his odor sufficiently to be able to give him what he needs. In doing this she may be able to loosen some of her attitudes and she may find relief in this. But this is not the purpose of Technical Assistance consultations. It would be an indirect gain. Her ability to teach Robert in the way he needs is the goal, and if she has learned to keep her school behavior uncontaminated by the rest of her behavior so that she can handle future "Roberts" without dread, then the goal of Technical Assistance has been thoroughly met. If this be therapy make the most of it. To us it is not therapy,

but facing job-related problems which need to be dealt with. . . .

The job of the Technical Assistance consultant, therefore, is to be quite clear in his own mind whether a discussion is centered on a professional goal, even though it may seem to wander through the meadows and woods of family background, relationships and personal school experiences for a while, or whether it has jumped the path and is out of bounds. If a Technical Assistance consultant is comfortable and skillful enough in interview techniques and interpersonal relations, he will be able to encourage or to call a halt without too much risk of serious error. If he bends over in either direction it is best to choose the direction of less rather than more personal communication until he is quite sure of where the talk will lead. He will also be careful, in what we call a Beethoven's Fifth Symphony technique, to repeat and repeat themes, to iterate and reiterate what Technical Assistance is doing, how we see ourselves and our task, the proper limits of our role and the specific goals we have in mind at that particular moment so that each consultee becomes aware of what can and what can't be undertaken.[1]

PERSONALITY OR SKILLS

An equally interesting question leads out of the discussion above. It becomes important to distinguish when a professional problem arises out of a staff member's personality difficulties or personality traits and attitudes, and when it arises out of lacks in his teaching armamentarium which limit him in dealing with a particular kind of problem in the classroom. It is frequently true that the attack on one aspect of the problem affects the staff member's ability

[1] Our concept of talking with a consultee about his problems in the carefully and mutually defined limits of the appropriate role differs from the Caplan Crisis Consultation method of dealing with this problem only by using the consultee's object of concern (the child or parent) as a way of smuggling in the teacher's own problems. This method seems to us often artificial and evasive.

to deal with the other aspect. For example: a teacher appears disorganized and careless. Her room and her dress, her bulletin board and her manner of approach are all coming apart at the seams. This is communicated to a bunch of kids who cannot tolerate such disorganization without falling apart themselves. Is this because the teacher herself is a disorganized person and needs help in a personal way to deal with her disorganization? Or is it because she is dealing with a group of children who present her with problems with which she has never before had to deal and therefore, her defensive reaction is to become as disorganized as they are? Could she, by being given techniques and understandings of structure, or timing, of grouping and sub-grouping, pull herself together in such a fashion that her class would respond?

Those of us who come from a clinical background may be inclined to think of the difficulties observed as caused by personality dynamics, while those who come from a more educationally-centered background may be more likely to take the opposite view. In other words, a school-minded person might approach the problem by seeing that a staff member may need more help in lesson planning or in management techniques and that if given these, she may be able to organize her personality so that it will not interfere with her ability to function. The particular approach taken is less important than the ability to see that the problem might be approached either one way or another, and that if one way does not work the opposite approach might. If for instance, even with an intensive training in techniques which a teacher lacks, she cannot get the children to respond to her, and if her disorganization, rigidity, quick temper or whatever, remain, then her personality problems, as they relate to the job, need to be looked into in the Technical Assistance conference. Perhaps they can be solved by outside manipulation, i.e., by giving her a different grade level to work with or a different school placement; by changing her from business techniques to art

teaching or individual tutoring, if she has the skills to teach these other subjects. However, we have found far too often that consultants assume that it is the personality that must be fixed up for adequate jobs to be done. Sometimes consultants are unaware of the disorganizing effect on the personality when one has a task one feels inadequate to, because one doesn't have adequate materials, know-how, or time in which to do it. In such cases all one's defenses come into play, and what could be handled well and without overdefensiveness, given the proper techniques and tools, may, without such help, appear in the form of an amazingly destructive personality or an amazingly ineffective one. Take rigidity as an example. Many teachers or principals appear tremendously rigid. They cannot seem to put up with any change in schedule. Things have to go by the clock or in the way prescribed by the syllabus. Margins have to be kept exactly and headings on papers have to have just the correct centering or else the children get marked D. This rigidity often looks as if it were impossible to break through. Sometimes it is. Often it is a matter of panic on the part of the staff member. He often feels that since he does not have the ability to deal with groups, or to set limits, or to discipline, he must make barriers for himself from arbitrary outside sources which will give him props to deal with what he cannot handle. When he is helped with grouping, with seating arrangements, with his own ability to time, to set limits, to be effective with a troublemaker, it is amazing how rigidity can diminish and how much more effective and comfortable his teaching can be, especially with that kind of disturbed child who needs flexibility as a method or as a precept. A teacher needs tools to deal with mayhem in the classroom or he is bound to respond in ways that may be destructive to himself or his students. Therefore, frequently the personality disability may be contingent on the lack of tools or the lack of skill in dealing with a given kind of problem. Again the personality disability may exist, but it may be kept within bounds if the teacher has sufficient tools. Sometimes, of course, it just plain is the personality disability—in which case that must be dealt with. But that is frequently not the first thing to approach. The Technical Assistance consultant must be aware of what needs to come first; this takes time, continuing relationships and skill in observation. . . .

OVERALL ISSUES

We have been discussing issues that arose during our three-year experience which bear on the Technical Assistance consultant-consultee relationship and the process of consultation. We have tried to discuss these issues in terms of anyone doing, or planning to do, this kind of consultation with school staff, especially in relation to mental health problems. There are many other issues which have been referred to directly or implied in all the other chapters which could be discussed at length here. For instance there are the issues of transference and counter-transference, dependency, resistance, hostility, suspicion, over-expectations, interdisciplinary jealousies and frictions, stereotypy. There is the danger of being caught up in staff politics and staff wrangles, or running afoul of other "authorities" such as the diagnoses of school psychologists which run counter to one's own findings or the teachers' observations. We experienced all of these and have indicated all of them and more within the text. We feel that at this point, the picture has been sufficiently filled out and the factors sufficiently outlined for others within and without the schools to proceed to investigate in a more detailed fashion.

In the light of our experience, however, a bit more needs to be said about what school staffs need in order to deal with disturbed and disturbing children. In large part this has been dealt with in our section on teacher training needs, including the teacher diaries and our chapter on consultation, as well as the separate sections which give a description of the year's

consultation in each setting. A few more issues need to be pointed out or underlined.

In all cases, whether a teacher is new or old, *on-the-spot, in-service training of a continuous kind* needs to be included if teachers, or other school staff, are to be expected to deal with the kind of and number of disturbed children with whom they are increasingly confronted. We do not mean to discuss here whether the problems of disturbance are on the increase. We mean only that the teacher is burdened with more of these cases, that classes are bigger, although all known facts indicate that they ought to be smaller especially when they include the ill child. We know that expectations and demands concerning the handling of disturbed children are greater, that expectations for prevention, diagnosis, recommendations, parent contacts, community contacts, relationship with curative agencies are all part of the demands made by the community on the teacher. These further demands make it next to impossible for a teacher or other staff to cope adequately, unless on-the-spot training is given wherever and whenever problems arise. These problems cannot be dealt with in the abstract. Moreover, no teacher-training course, no matter how thorough nor how skilled, can cover all the kinds of problems which arise daily and increasingly within the schools. Obviously, in thinking about training, university courses need to be re-evaluated and new types of courses, to catch up with our state of present knowledge and our needs, instituted. Courses with a great deal of practicum and supervision are essential; but over and beyond all this course work, theoretic and practical, once a teacher is teaching, he or she needs continual on-the-spot help in order not to get bogged down by overload, by anxiety, by despair. *This is the only way to insure that teaching can be more effective both for the ordinary child with ordinary problems and for those having more than an average share of problems.* Since mental health and learning needs are closely allied, emphasis in on-the-spot training must be placed on both. What form this on-the-spot, in-service training is to take is a question which needs further exploration and further modification according to the needs of the particular school or school system which is considering inaugurating it. Our own form, described in detail in this report, was on a regular weekly basis, largely focused on individual consultations although sometimes dealing with groups both small and large. One of the reactions to our manual suggested that it could be done by training supervisors in the use of Technical Assistance. Perhaps it could be done by a lengthened form of Crisis Consultation. From our own experience we are convinced it could be done through our methods. There is an experiment, centered on other forms of school interaction, which is focusing on on-the-spot, in-service training of a selected group of young teachers (trainees coming home from Peace Corps overseas work). These people are given supervision, instruction in subject-matter teaching by master teachers, classes to teach and seminars in personal dynamics, in sociology, in curriculum and psychology for which they are given graduate credit. This may be a useful way to go about training new people and might be adopted in universities and college teacher-training programs. How much can be carried over to train older staff is a subject for further investigations. Our bias for Technical Assistance methods includes the absolute conviction, borne out by all our experience, that good, thoughtful, on-the-spot, in-service training for new and old teachers, for other staff besides teachers, for purposes of communication, for purposes of interdisciplinary understanding, for remedial teachers, for specialists, for school nurses, for teachers of the disturbed, along

with guidance people and regular teachers, and especially for administrators is an absolute essential if the mental health problems of school and child are to be met with more frequency. Usually one case in ten referred is seen (no one knows how many should have been referred). When referred, the minimal three months waiting period for each child further slows procedure.

From our experience, we are equally convinced that the more complicated the organization, the greater the need for the kind of on-the-spot training potentially afforded by Technical Assistance consultation. The junior high school and the senior high school are more needy than elementary schools and pre-schools. This is not to say that these lower-level schools do not need regular Technical Assistance. They not only do need it, but they use it extraordinarily well; because of their relative sophistication in human development they are able to use the help more intensively. However, *more* frequent visits or *more* use of group methods are needed in the high schools and in residential or day care treatment centers. In fact, since the treatment centers are more inclined to be aware of their need for this kind of work, it is more likely to be built into the original design of the center, or if not built in originally, to be inaugurated out of desperate needs. It is in the junior and senior high schools that the idea needs careful elaboration and demonstration and indeed requires further investigation to see how it can best be employed. If this can be done, it will alleviate the serious problems of fragmentation and lack of communication which affect the total organization and seriously affect the students who, at best, suffer from fragmentation and lack of communication in their lives. . . .

In the next article, Stark and Bentzen describe a project in which emotionally disturbed children were maintained in the normal school setting with the assistance of a psychiatric team and a project teacher. The project teacher was not to function as a specialist, but to help selected children upon teacher request. It is interesting to note that on the first day the project teacher was sent twenty wild children whom she could not control. The paper provides an excellent illustration of the conditions to avoid in beginning a modified classroom program and the need to clarify the project teacher's role.

Integrating the Emotionally Disturbed Child in the School

William Stark and Frances Bentzen

There has been increasing awareness of the significance of psychological factors in the satisfactory and healthy adjustment of children, and the incidence of "problems" and "problem behavior" has pyramided sharply in recent years. The need and the demand for professional help have outstripped the availability of appropriately trained and qualified professional personnel. From a community and public health standpoint, such disproportion between recognized needs and resources presents serious problems. The present study is an attempt to meet certain aspects of this problem and to determine to what extent the ordinary school and its staff, supplemented by a team of professional workers, a project teacher, a clinical psychologist and a psychiatrist, are able to learn how to deal with problems of the emotionally disturbed child in the normal school setting.

The immediate goal of this paper is twofold: (1) to define and to delineate a point of view concerning specific policies, methods and techniques utilized in a program of work with emotionally disturbed children and considered appropriate to the educational framework and teaching goals of the normal school environment; (2) to present for exploratory evaluation certain therapeutically designed group controls and limits found useful in establishing and maintaining the teaching role of a consultant psychiatrist in joint professional relations with a teaching staff.

A long-range goal (hardly confined to

Abridged from William Stark and Frances Bentzen, "The Integration of the Emotionally Disturbed Child in the Normal School Setting," in Morris Krugman, ed., *Orthopsychiatry and the School,* American Orthopsychiatric Association, Inc., New York, 1958, pp. 82–95. Reprinted by permission.

this particular presentation), shared by educators and psychiatrists alike, results from increasing awareness of the unremitting need for better communication and greater understanding of the meaningful *content* of psychiatric concepts and terminology and their specific applicability to general problems of growth and maturation among children.

The methodology of presentation selected by the authors for this communication may be described as documentary and developmental. The presentation will cover the following general areas of data and experience: (1) the general descriptive material necessary to identify and explain the stated nature and goals of the research project and the basic data involved; (2) a developmental report of the shared experiences of the combined clinical and teaching staff, documented from the recorded observations of the project teacher and the seminars led by the consultant psychiatrist.

THE RESEARCH PROJECT

The project was a 2½-year study of the integration of children with emotional difficulties functioning within classroom groups of "normally" adjusted children.

LOCALE AND SUBJECTS

The setting was a private school with an average enrolment of approximately 150 students ranging from kindergarten age and placement through junior high. During the first half year of the project the top group junior high members were excluded as participants inasmuch as it was agreed that contact with them was to be of such short duration it would prove of little value to the research goals.

The nursery or kindergarten age children were excluded from the project although their group teachers made frequent use of the research staff for consultation and guidance, and frequently requested the clinical psychologist's help for testing and evaluating behavior problems and the help of the consultant psychiatrist for handling the acting-out aspects of children's problems.

Out of the total school enrolment and over the 2½-year period, 75 children shared in the assistance provided by the research staff. Of this group two thirds were male and one third female. This sex ratio represents the enrolment pattern of the school. The ages of the children ranged from 6 through 12, and, since the school was interracial, race was not a factor considered by the staff as relevant to the research. The pathologies dealt with included hyperactive, aggressive, acting-out, explosive types of behavior, psychosomatic symptoms, schizoid adjustment patterns, panic episodes, behavior problems, problem behavior, learning difficulty, etc.; in other words, a wide variety of child behavior and symptomatology.

PERSONNEL

The teaching staff consisted of 12 teachers, the school director (also the initiating director of the research project) and an administrative assistant. The research staff consisted of the consultant psychiatrist, psychologist, and project teacher. The psychiatrist gave two hours a week to the combined staff needs, acting in the capacity of consultant, teacher and guide to the teaching staff and the project teacher in her work with the children. He provided assistance to the director of the project on problems of planning and integration of the research program into the school framework. The psychiatrist collaborated with the clinical psychologist in evaluating and interpreting the specific nature of the emotional problems of the children to the teaching staff.

The project teacher, although not clinically trained, had considerable professional experience and background in interviewing, counseling and remedial work with children. It was important that the project teacher's previous experience include training in observing and reporting accurately, as the need to select and record pertinent data became increasingly apparent as the research progressed. The project teacher was the only full-time member of the research team.

The clinical psychologist, in addition to the assigned duty of giving and interpreting the psychological test data, also worked in an individual tutoring capacity with a number of the project children and shared with the project teacher many of the parent interviews. . . .

DEVELOPMENTAL REPORT

Prior to the actual initiation of the project in the school setting a preliminary meeting was arranged by the school director for the purposes of planning and organizing the program with the combined staff. It was agreed by all members that any structuring of the children into a "special" class was to be avoided at all costs; and, further, that to be scheduled for time with the project teacher should mean no more to the children than to be scheduled for music, art or sports. It was hoped that with regularly scheduled programs of arts and crafts, as well as taking over such total school duties as recess supervisor, the project teacher would not be identified as a "specialist" nor the children assigned to her designated as "problems."

The need for predictable scheduling and for discussion of individual children in terms of planning for careful grouping, and the therapeutic value and function of established limits in the life of a child, particularly a disturbed child, were accepted eagerly by the staff as helpful concepts and "good ideas."

When the project teacher reported for her first day's work, however, she found herself the "teacher" of approximately twenty wildly excited and combative children who appeared to be certain of only one thing—that they were supposed to be there and nowhere else. There was no equipment, and no space other than the auditorium bare of all furniture except a piano. At the first formal staff meeting, the project teacher reported on her experience and the resultant feelings of anxiety, helplessness and confusion; and on the chaotic, destructive, hysterical acting-out behavior of the children assigned to her by the teaching staff because of their "problems."

It was apparent that the verbal agreement and seeming understanding and acceptance by the teaching staff of the therapeutic value and importance of "limits" in the work with disturbed children were superficial, because the *meaningful content* of the terms used by the consultant was not part of their experience. Without the content experience there was no implementation of the original plans for scheduling and planned grouping, and hence, the "dumping" of children whose behavior created classroom "problems" regardless of whether the problems were the child's, the teacher's, or simply an expedient use of a new resource.

It was also apparent that there was a need to establish an avenue by which the teaching and research staff could, through consensually validated data, acquire meaningful understanding of psychiatric concepts and insights. This step, retrospectively, represented the most valuable in accomplishment of project goals.

It became clear that there was a need to disband the present grouping of children and eliminate project teacher contact with *any* child until specific methods and practical plans had been established for implementing the previously planned program of work in terms of the research goals, rather than of the immediate needs for teacher relief.

During the months following, as the staff worked through these problems, a few of the principles of operation and planning for working with the children reflected a point of view that can now be formulated into standardized policies and procedures felt to be compatible with the teaching-

classroom situation, and at the same time contributing to the health and comfort of the children *without exclusion* from peer groups and at times without individual psychotherapy. (The following remarks and observations are not relevant to special classes for physically handicapped, retarded or brain-damaged children.)

It seems pertinent to consider some of the implications and practical problems created by a "class" for emotionally disturbed children—so far as our experience is concerned—for the child, the therapist, the teacher, the school and the two disciplines of psychiatry and education. The kinds of questions posed here are concerned with the results of what may be descriptively referred to as the "acting out" aspects of the psychiatric profession in the field of education, and the confusion resulting for both the psychiatrist in the field of education and the educator in the field of child health when treatment goals are substituted for the more appropriate goals of teaching, and when the classroom becomes primarily another therapeutic medium rather than a primary educational device.

For example, a "class" of emotionally disturbed children has the single factor of pathological behavior as its *raison d'être*, which is justified in terms of "clinically orientated" treatment goals. This type of grouping—or group—is appropriate and "normal" to the goals, needs, and personnel of treatment centers, hospitals, clinics and group therapy centers; and within this type of framework, the members of the group, the personnel and the sponsoring organization are integrated and motivated toward health and stability.

Aside from the conflicts resulting from the inappropriateness of treatment goals in an academic framework, children assigned to special classes for the emotionally disturbed are excluded from their classroom groups and the healthy support of their better-adjusted peers. Furthermore, it is the shared opinion of the authors that the "normal" classroom grouping, scheduling, and program of learning activities under the direction of a "good" group teacher constitute a powerful therapeutic device in themselves.

It is unfortunate but wholly understandable that children given to the type of behavior response where hyperactivity and aggression are prime characteristics constitute a high percentage of the referrals to "classes" for the emotionally disturbed. Their expulsion from the classroom provides relief for the teaching staff and removes from the group a type of behavior inimical to learning—on anyone's part. Their behavior, in interaction with other children with like difficulties in a numerically much smaller group, frequently takes on an aggressively hysterical pattern of explosive violence totally at variance with any of the respected and accepted standards of conduct of a "class" in any school.

The justification for continuance of this type of "special class" is curiously enough frequently assigned to the therapeutic benefits derived from a "permissive" atmosphere in which disturbed children are permitted to work out their "sibling rivalries" or "parental hostilities," or "feelings of rejection," with the goal ostensibly to "cure" emotionally sick children.

In presenting the point of view subscribed to by the authors, which emphasizes a method of teacher education and a supervised program of work with individual or small groups of children as contrasted with "special classes for emotionally disturbed children," one of the main points of difference becomes immediately apparent. The child remains *in the classroom situation* except for regularly scheduled periods when he receives individual attention geared to his particular needs and obtains relief from academic and group standards. This type of program allows the *child* to indicate when his comfort with his peer group and himself has reached a point where he no longer needs or wants "to leave my group."

Within such a framework of operation it is possible for the consulting psychiatrist and other clinically trained personnel,

through the use of teaching seminars, to coordinate supervision of the work with the children with a program of teacher training in the meaningful content of psychiatric insights and terminology. As the understanding develops, the seminars assist the teaching staff in implementing the practical aspects of handling the behavior of the disturbed child in the *classroom* in line with these same insights and concepts of behavior.

This is no short-term affair; but one of the more important aspects of this type of technique and approach to working with disturbed children is the use, in the seminar situation, of data derived from the teachers' own observations, the project teacher's recordings and reports, the psychological testing data, family and school contacts and the early developmental history. The use of these data implements the meaningful interpretation of behavior, not only of the disturbed child, but of children in general. Only through such sharing of data and interpretation by the consulting psychiatrist does the teacher come to understand that the emotionally ill child is not "abnormal" but rather a "normal" child with a sickness, and to understand the symptom in relation to the total personality.

One of the major temptations for the psychiatrist conducting a project such as this is to become involved in the direct evaluation and diagnostic study of individual children. It is our impression that the best use of professional time is made when the psychiatrist's role as "teacher" and as consultant to the school is maintained rather than clouded by the additional role of therapist and diagnostician. The individual evaluation is best carried on outside the school setting.

To remain the consultant to the staff and school alone precludes the psychiatrist from being endlessly entangled in diagnostic evaluations and places the emphasis of service where we feel it is of greatest help and use, particularly with limited professional facilities, namely, the teacher and thence to her pupils rather than specifically to a given child. Thus one avoids the pitfall of serving a few to the exclusion of many.

One of the major problems the consulting psychiatrist will find himself aware of, and occasionally involved in, regardless of his initial awareness, is the temptation to use the teaching seminar as a vehicle for group therapy. This may happen either through pressure from the members of the teaching staff, his own needs, or a combination of the two. The therapeutic soundness, validity and importance of maintaining and supporting at all times an individual teacher's feelings of adequacy and competency in her professional role—regardless of her personal problems—cannot be overemphasized. However, where indicated, psychotherapy is a self-appointed task best carried on *outside* the framework of education and in a setting unrelated to the academic setting.

This point is made because of the growing interest on the part of psychiatrically trained and oriented individuals in identifying with and working in school systems. Too often, as a result of occupational naïveté or unawareness, or even personal bigotry, the clinically trained individual assumes that *his* job and role is to "bring the light" of his professional insights to bear on the personal problems of the members of the teaching profession instead of adding his contributions and "light" to the profession itself.

The job of the teacher is to educate the young. To question the validity and importance of this goal either directly or indirectly is to attempt to change the goals of the profession rather than to clarify roles and *teach* the teachers who work with the child what the psychiatric profession knows concerning mental illness. There are, then, two jobs to be done for the emotionally disturbed child in the school system. One is to teach him. This is the province of the school staff. The other is to provide to the best of our ability therapeutically sound measures to increase his health and productivity. The combined goal of the consult-

ing psychiatrist and teaching staff is to work and learn together, not to proselytize.

The use of organized written data about a child for the beginning of each seminar seems to act as a control and limit against the release of excessive and disorganizing teacher-anxiety, a frequent phenomenon in the absence of such data.

The most frequent temptation is to deal at the outset with the teacher's role in relation to a specific child and his need. This we find to be most threatening to the teacher, and in a program devoted to teacher training this aspect of learning could well be the last, rather than the first. For just as in individual psychotherapy, where insight is gradual and integrated only with appropriately timed interpretation, so is the teacher's insight acquired only through techniques of teaching which involve use of this principle with respect to the group's learning. Ill-timed educational interpretation is as disorganizing to the teacher as it is to the patient.

The introduction of concepts related to the child configuration could occur effectively only when group cohesiveness, rapport, and lack of defensiveness with one another, and with the psychiatrist, occurred. This was the least threatening climate and therefore the best for such discussion. When such concepts were discussed, the need to keep them within the framework of the teacher role was most important.

The temptation at this time to make the teacher or to invite the teacher to become an adjunct therapist needs to be assiduously avoided. It should not be the intent of the psychiatrist to use the schoolteacher as an adjunct "therapist" any more than it should be the intent of the teacher to ask that the psychiatrist become an adjunct "educator," a trap most inviting with the special class framework. Each of these professions has an important function in the life of the child and need not usurp or transgress upon the role of the other. The effective fulfillment of each role to the benefit of the child, however, is dependent upon mutual interest in the child, concurring about child development and behavior, and respect for each other's roles and responsibilities.

In order for communication to be meaningful concerning aberrations of behavior, there must be some reasonable understanding of behavior dynamics. Just as it is unrealistic for parents to ask the psychiatrist for specific techniques in dealing with a part of a child's behavior as a panacea for the child's total difficulty without self-understanding of the contributing factors, so it is unrealistic for the school to make similar requests without similar self-understanding, in the hope that the psychiatrist's response will constitute the ultimate answer to the child's difficulty.

In the final analysis the selection of a technique for dealing with a piece of behavior is based upon some diagnosis of that behavior. The usefulness and success of any technique are dependent upon accuracy of diagnosis, and accuracy of diagnosis is dependent upon a relatively carefully developed picture of the child's personality, including an evaluation of the nature and intensity of his conflicts and his own capacity and technique for handling his conflicts.

To understand this picture also necessitates some understanding of the role of the unconscious in human behavior. Comparing the diagnoses of school and psychiatrist, we are not at all sure but that they disagree more often than not; and, what is worse, there is little mutual communication, and consequently no consistently directed effort in behalf of the child, but rather confusion or disappointment on the part of the school and the psychiatrist.

The kind of data which describes the child's behavior in school without describing the teacher's behavior and feeling is describing but half of a process that is two-sided. However, for a teacher to be able to communicate freely her own anxiety, her own real feelings about her pupils, and her own inadequacies in a teacher-child rela-

tionship, necessitates, first, that the teacher be comfortable in her own right with children; second, comfortable in her relationship with superiors and colleagues; and, finally, that she certainly be comfortable with the consulting psychiatrists.

The recommendations of the psychiatrist frequently are felt to be unreasonable, because the psychiatrist and the school do not talk the same language. At the Georgetown Day School, where we dealt directly with communication problems between education and psychiatry, we were able to establish an increasing understanding and consensus about the dynamics of a child's behavior, and the dynamics of a child's conflict. The teachers in their own role were increasingly able to avoid behavior which intensified conflict, and also devised processes which alleviated sources of conflict for the child in school.

From our experience with a school staff these types of communication occur not during a telephone conversation, nor through intermittent conferences, but through regular and continuous communication, and therefore something needs to be stated about frequency of contact between consultant and staff. A minimum of once a week is essential. A greater interval, at least in the beginning, permits a mobilization of resistance difficult to overcome. As in psychotherapy, where frequency of contact is an important element determining the efficacy of therapy, so in teacher education, the frequency of contact is a factor in the efficiency of learning. Only through such continuous contact does the language of the psychiatrist become meaningful to the teacher, and the language of the teacher become meaningful to the psychiatrist.

The process of establishing such meaningful communication is dependent upon: (1) A mutually genuine desire to meet the child's need. (2) Mutual sensitivity to the child, his conflicts, and his need. (3) Mutual respect for one another where neither feels threatened by the other. (4) Finally, teacher and psychiatrist must feel free to express their anxiety and frustration without feeling on trial or needing to defend their positions.

The work with the child must be directed where one discipline does not sit in judgment on the other, but where both are in a position to contribute their mutual skills to the benefit of the child. Communication such as this is the result of time and effort, but is essential for constructive work with and for the child.

This kind of communication has the following results: (1) The preparation of a family by a school for psychiatric help becomes more meaningful and less threatening. (2) A school comes to appreciate the fact that symptoms do not disappear after the first consultation with the psychiatrist. (3) The teacher can become aware of numerous resources within her own capacities to deal with children's behavior. (4) Psychiatry and education can contribute toward the development of consistent and meaningful attitudes and environment for the child. (5) Finally, psychiatry and education can increasingly integrate their respective skills to the ultimate benefit of the child, his family, and the community.

Thus the seminars, as a basic structure in this program, became a meaningful forum of interchange between the project staff and the school staff. Children selected for seminar study served as a focal point to demonstrate the significant aspects of childhood development. They served to demonstrate the characteristic conflicts of the growing child and the significance of fantasy in the child's life, the significance of adult attitudes, the significance of unconscious motivation in behavior, the significance of teacher attitude and of the teacher's unconscious as a determinant in the child's behavior. Through the seminars, teachers were able to discover for themselves meaningful "answers" to some of their "problems." What was most encouraging and helpful was that through the process of *seminar education* and through the *individual* and *small group work with children,* the children discussed showed significant improvement in their social adjustment and accompanying academic progress. The children who showed outstanding problem behavior accompanied by inadequate academic performance made such improvement that the project staff and the school staff were most satisfied. They were aware that this improvement may have been a peak in what might be a long adjustment, but they were tremendously encouraged and reassured that the methods employed could bring about significant results.

It may be of some significance to quote one child's experience in the trailer (the project's locale) during his last session as he voluntarily gave up the trailer to return to his class:

This is a pretty crazy letter to a person who is right here. I think the trailer was a very big success and I believe that all of the children who took part in it enjoyed it very much.

Personally, to me, I took it as something like a little piece of home here at school. I enjoyed it very much because of the fact, well—there were facilities for doing everything that the children liked and also it was a relief from the classroom. Even now, this very minute, it is a relief to get away from the classroom. You may wonder why I say this, but in the classroom you are sort of confined. But here in the trailer you are free to move and no one is going to yell at you if you get up to stretch or yawn. I also believe that children in other schools need this. Even at recess you have to do the same thing, but in the trailer you are the person who decides the choice of what you do. . . . *At this point Arnold indicated that there was something to be added here but he wished to write it at the bottom of the letter. He then wrote:* . . . She is somebody you can talk to and you say things that you can't even say to your teacher—or to your parents sometimes.

At the end of this portion and before the signature Arnold whispered the following: This is a secret! I believe you love me. That's the really special thing about the trailer but don't put that in the letter if it's for anyone I know. Well, that is it, isn't it? The end of my periods in the trailer.

It was nearly the end of the research project when one of the teaching staff remarked to the assembled group, "Why don't we staff one of the youngsters *not* on the project just to see if there's any difference in what we can learn from *them?*" thus reflecting their own relative comfort with symptomatic behavior and awareness of pathology as being a quantitative difference rather than a qualitative difference from the normal.

It was through weekly seminars and conferences that a teacher who had referred to the seminar discussion the problem of a "lazy" child who needed to have additional tutoring was able, a year later, to "remove academic pressure" and demands from a "withdrawn" child and to discuss with the parents the possible helpfulness of psychotherapy to them and the child and the school.

And finally, it was as a result of the seminar learning experience in methods for working with emotionally disturbed children that the project teacher, upon conclusion of the research grant, moved into the public school system and has been able effectively to implement a program of work with disturbed children.

The project teacher in the last article is prototypic of the crisis teacher advocated by Morse in the next article. Well-trained psychologically and educationally, the crisis teacher functions as the school's resource person who is responsible for handling on-the-spot conflicts.

It is predicted that many children who are referred to a special class could be taught and managed in a regular class if a crisis teacher were available to provide these children with temporary support and controls during their disorganized periods of fight or flight.

The Crisis Teacher

William C. Morse

One of the most encouraging aspects of recent Michigan public school planning for emotionally disturbed pupils is the flexibility which is anticipated. Suggestions include special classes, consultant teachers, and individually designed experimental programs. It is recognized that these new programs are supplemental to efforts for overall school mental health and the services of visiting teachers, psychologists, school nurses, and guidance workers.

A few school districts have already been operating small classes for the emotionally disturbed: in several instances evaluative efforts have been incorporated. The

From William Morse, " 'The Crisis Teacher,' Public School Provision for the Disturbed Pupil," *The University of Michigan School of Education Bulletin* XXXVII (April 1962), 101–104.

whole role of therapeutic education is being explored. An outpatient school program has been in operation at Hawthorn Center for several years and the Children's Psychiatric Hospital is ready to start an outpatient school as soon as finances are available. In addition to this interest on the part of the inpatient psychiatric institutions, the child guidance clinics are studying the feasibility of school-oriented day care programs as a part of their effort. In short, Michigan is in the vanguard of a growing national interest in school programs for children too disturbed to be helped in the regular classroom.

The plan presented in this new report is not a substitute for any of the present services or their anticipated legitimate expansion. Nor is it proposed that the school become a psychiatric institution. Rather, the plan is an immediate school rescue operation designed for the point of problem origin through the use of a new educational device, the crisis teacher. If the regular school is to function, it is mandatory that we keep the classrooms as free from teacher-exhausting, group-disrupting pupils as is possible. Conversely, the school has recognized the responsibility to offer additional assistance to these pupils when they cannot benefit from a well-modulated classroom learning situation. The small but appreciable educational "fall out" presents a difficult situation: authoritative handling seldom resolves the problem, and many cases go year after year until a negative school adjustment becomes fixed.

What are some of the school conditions which are necessary to keep a reasonably constant learning flow in classroom? First, there must be an immediate resource for the teacher when there is significant deterioration in the classroom group learning process. Help must be available without stigma or recrimination or even the implication of overburdening the administrator. The truth is, so many duties now devolve on the principal that his availability is limited. A new hand is required, but of a special type. Not only must the new person help the school at large, but he must provide immediate succor to the pupil as well. It is easy to forget that the pupil is in real need at his time of stress. And he needs help with two things—his school work and the feelings which distort his efforts at the moment. Of course, this is true for the acting out child who disrupts the class. But it is also true for the withdrawn, unhappy, quiet underachiever.

The "crisis teacher" is the school resource designed to meet this situation. This teacher must really know curriculum at the school level served, must be steeped in remedial teaching techniques and must be skilled in life-space interviewing, a style of interviewing essential for the teacher who must handle diverse types of behavior problems. The space provided may include a small classroom with a pleasant anteroom. Books and materials of all sorts are at hand.

Since each school is unique, modus operandi are derived from the specific needs of a given school. There are several observations, however, which may serve as guides.

1. The crisis teacher can be effective only to the degree that the whole staff is concerned about understanding and helping the deviant child. Case conference and strategy planning meetings involve all the teachers. Some planning for particular children can be done on a sub-group basis. The general principle is, that all the adults who deal with the pupil take part in devising the plan and evolving the strategy. Many failures in school relations are due to faulty communication among teachers who do not work together on their common problems. Merely providing another specialist will not make the necessary impact on the school environment. Also, regardless of what is accomplished in the special work, its real purpose is to help the child to get along properly in the regular classroom. The classroom teacher continues to spend more time with the pupil than any specialist does, and plans for assistance will have to consider her work as well as the time the child spends with the crisis teacher. Since many pupils are skillful manipulators, little will be gained unless all adults are aware of the case dynamics and have thought through the most appropriate management procedures. Frequently, after an encouraging start, an improvement plateau is reached and new plans must be evolved on the basis of a more complete understanding of the pupil and how he reacts.

2. Referral procedures are the responsibility of the total staff. When a teacher feels that a pupil cannot be helped in the classroom alone, this pupil becomes a potential candidate for the crisis teacher. It is important to note that this does not await a complicated diagnosis or parental permission, because the pupil is not in the usual sense a special case. His behavior "in situ" makes the referral. If possible, plans for

assistance are worked out in advance; but the regular teacher may take the pupil directly to the crisis teacher and present the situation in a nonrejecting nonmoralistic but frank manner. This special service is not a dumping ground or a discard heap. Rather, the two teachers discuss sympathetically the educational complexity at hand. Cues relative to the pupil's attitude about the referral are faced directly and the crisis teacher goes over possible goals. Afterward the pupil returns to the classroom only when he is considered ready to resume his progress in that setting.

Thus, the crisis teacher does not have a regular class or group. Pupils may come and go, sometimes on a more or less regular basis as seems advisable, but often on an episodic basis when specific pressure accumulates. Of course, at particular times, the special teacher may be working with more than one pupil. As crisis demands decrease or vacillate there are always underachieving children to be given individual help.

3. The work which goes on in the special setting is determined by the pupil's problem. Children seldom compartmentalize their relationships or their quandaries. Home, school, and play are all intermixed. General attitudes and schoolwork motivation are a confused combination. Consequently, the teacher has to take a broad humanistic approach in crisis teaching. The interaction may take on characteristics of a "man to man" talk, a parental surrogate, or a counselor, besides involving the general teacher role. Free of large group responsibilities, immediate achievement goals and time restrictions, the able teacher can operate with a new flexibility. Perhaps it will be individualized tutoring, an informal talk, a diversionary activity, or an intensive life space interview session around the feelings and tension evinced in the pupil. In short, what is done is what any teacher would want to do were it possible to determine action by the needs of the child rather than the large group learning process in a classroom. At times several children may be involved, and

group work is called into play. The difficulty may turn out to be a learning frustration, an interpersonal conflict, or an internal feeling. As the crisis teacher sizes up the situation, plans are made for immediate and long term steps. This teacher may get the outpouring of the child's inner conflict and must be prepared to handle whatever the child brings, as well as to refer special problems to other services. It is particularly important for the child to learn that he will be listened to and that his problem will be considered, even to the point of initiating joint sessions with his regular teacher to discuss conditions as he sees them. There are few of the secrets and confidences which some professional school workers make much of at the expense of exchanging information needed to solve the pupil's school problem. While it is obvious that this work takes utmost skill and sensitivity, it should also be clear that co-equal members of a staff can be open with the child, and no professional worker is "handling" another. All too soon we are faced with the fact that the total staff, with all the insight we can muster, will still not be able to influence the lives of some of these children at any better than a surface level. On the other hand, if we can help a pupil meet what are for him reasonable social and academic school expectations, this is itself a worthwhile goal, though other problems remain.

4. While a child does not have to be certified as any type of a special pupil for this service, some of the clientele will already have been studied intensively in the normal course of events. Other pupils will present baffling difficulties to the crisis teacher and staff. Here psychological study, visiting teacher investigation, or material from a psychiatric examination may be in order. Perhaps it becomes evident that the pupil's needs are for individual case work or family contact which can best be done by the visiting teacher or counselor. Since these specialists participate in the planning meetings, trial decisions are the product of mutual discussion. The sharing of cases

becomes the sharing of a problem-solving venture. In this way, the school principal, specialists, crisis teacher, and classroom teacher work as a team: possessiveness and contention are a luxury schools cannot afford.

With adequate research it may eventually be possible to predict which pupils will respond to such a program. At present the value is in the improved learning climate provided for the whole school, as well as helping the particular child.

The next selection, by Rosner, describes a different way of using the school milieu to handle difficult children. Once again we see the need for more intensive on-the-spot clinical service in volatile school situations. The concept of the all-day neighborhood school explained in this article offers an excellent example of how the community and school can cooperate with each other. These deprived Puerto Rican children in New York City, who have been termed unreachable, demand a very different kind of program than do the children found in the traditional clinics. The overwhelming number of reality problems at home and in the community make it extremely difficult for the teacher to establish and maintain rapport with these children.

Therapy with "Latchkey" Children
Joseph Rosner

"Latchkey" children are those who come from homes where parents work all day. After school the boys and girls let themselves into empty homes with keys provided them by parents who will not see them until the day's labor is done. From the end of the school day at three o'clock until the parents return home, these children are on their own. The adults are generally employed in a factory in unskilled or semi-skilled work. Homes are usually overcrowded and small; economic want exists in a tangible fashion. The emotional deprivation is just as obvious to the interested observer. This paper is an attempt to describe a program available in the community for treating some of these children

Reprinted with permission from Joseph Rosner, "Therapy with 'Latchkey Children,'" *American Journal of Orthopsychiatry*, XXVII (April 1957), 411–419. Copyright the American Orthopsychiatric Association, Inc.

Joseph Rosner, formerly school social worker with the Bureau of Child Guidance of the New York City Board of Education, is now Director of the Department of Psychology of the Sherwood-Trimble Medical Group and an Instructor of Education for the UCLA Extension School.

who present rather severe behavior disorders without recourse to institutionalization. Specific interview techniques will also be described as part of the total treatment plan. The problems to be discussed are not limited to "latchkey" children, however. Hence the material in this paper may find wider applicability in a field where children of similar background are known to need help.

In recent years the problem of "reaching the unreached" has been discussed in the literature. The New York City Youth Board has described the problems that the usual child guidance clinic faces with resistive children and parents. This agency has devised new casework and group work techniques to meet the challenge.

It is thus recognized by those close to these situations which present severe social pathology that traditional child guidance clinic treatment methods, with the emphasis on psychotherapy with child and parent, need to be studied and probably revised. It has been suggested that more intensive work by school social workers and school psychologists right in the schools, using psychiatrists as consultants, may offer more help to these children, who are the victims of very disturbed social conditions. In the areas where these conditions exist, schools tend to refer those children who constitute a source of disturbance to the teacher, in other words, children who have failed to respond to remedial efforts made by the school. This does not always mean that the parent is also distressed. She may not even care. In cases in which the mother is disturbed by the child's behavior, she often desires placement.

To treat such children in the community presents formidable problems. In view of the severe pathology present in the total environment, the question arises as to the effectiveness of weekly or even semi-weekly interviews in child guidance agencies. Yet these children may present serious problems to their families and communities alike. Placement in institutions is one solution. However, in New York City at any rate, the resources do not nearly meet the need for such facilities. If treatment is to be undertaken in the city, something more than the isolated contact of a child guidance agency, located away from the central area of infection, is needed. A place where children can be reached in the midst of their hostile aggressions is essential. Such a place does exist. While the setting described in the following paragraphs concerns itself with Puerto Rican children, it should be noted that the symptoms presented are prevalent among many other groups of disturbed children.

The treatment of these children took place in an elementary school setting. In this environment neither the children nor their parents came for help with their problems. The school authority referred the child to the school social worker, who had the facilities to carry on treatment directly in the school setting. A private room with a telephone was available in which to see children and parents. The population of the school referred to in this paper is approximately 98 per cent Puerto Rican. Since chil-

dren can be seen in the school, they are available for treatment during periods of resistance, when they might otherwise avoid agency contact. School hours from 7:45 A.M. to 5:00 P.M. make it possible to see children as needed rather than on a rigid weekly schedule, as must be done in the usual child guidance clinic. Because of the great deprivations present in this area, it has been designated by the New York City Board of Education as one of the six All Day Neighborhood Schools in the city. In addition to the 45 regular teachers for 1500 children, there are 6 ADNS teachers and a coordinator. The latter arrive at the school at 10:45 A.M. and leave at 5:00 P.M. During the regular school day, their duties include special programming with the various classroom teachers. They take an active part in helping to blend the Puerto Rican culture of the children with the American culture that the school represents. At 3 o'clock these 6 specially trained teachers take charge of 6 afternoon clubs, each of which is limited to 25 children. The children are involved in a diversified program of sports, arts, crafts, and music. Food is an integral part of the program, and the children in each club have a supervised daily snack, consisting of a sandwich, milk and fruit. The club leaders become acquainted with each child's behavior in the classrooms as well as the club rooms. The child's adjustment at home and in the community is also often known by the teachers in the ADNS program. Approximately 10 per cent of the total school population is thus served. The ADNS program represents an effective and critically important attempt to meet the group needs of these children.

The children in individual treatment, referred by teachers from regular classes, are often members of the afore-mentioned clubs. They are referred to the social worker, who is placed in the school on practically a full-time basis by the Bureau of Child Guidance of the New York City Board of Education. Psychological services and psychiatric consultation are available one day each week. In addition, certain mandatory services are carried out by the social worker, psychologist and psychiatrist working as a team. In this setting, beset by numerous social problems, the social worker acts as the coordinator for the other members of the team, who are not at the school full time. The psychologist tests children in the school one day each week, and the psychiatrist is available in the Bureau's unit office located in the area. The psychiatrist in this setting is the person responsible for any treatment carried out in the school, and is kept informed of the treatment process through regular weekly treatment conferences.

In order to treat the children referred to in the above setting, it would be of importance to involve parents in the treatment process. However, here one of the realities of working in such a setting becomes obvious. In this area few parents are available during the day for treatment. Almost every parent who is not receiving aid from the Department of Welfare works. The difficulties of living under severe economic hardships often make any psychological relationship insufficient for these people and ineffective in meeting their total life needs. This is especially true when parents and relatives do not see the needs as their own, but rather as related to a child who is a problem to them. While the maximum constructive objective might be reached in working with adults associated with children referred, this is not often possible. Since this is a demonstrable fact, it has been necessary to evolve substitute plans that will be effective in helping a child adjust realistically and in a personally satisfying manner.

There are some children who have such violent outbursts in the classroom or playground that they sometimes seriously injure other children. Cases of skull lacerations are by no means rare; fist fights are common. These are the children who need help for themselves, but from whom others need immediate protection. It should be stressed that while many children with diverse problems are referred for treatment, the type of child of greatest concern to the teachers of this socially and economically deprived area is the one displaying overt physical aggression as one of his symptoms.

Children emerging from such total deprivation react quite differently from children who come from less disturbed and deprived backgrounds. The severe physical aggression to be noted in such children is not wholly determined by "unconscious chaos." It is not just symptom behavior, but is a way of life. The aggressive behavior of these children is not always the result of repressed hostility; they suffer instead from imperfections of ego development. The more primitive types of experiences available to them have not afforded these children an opportunity to integrate more socially acceptable forms of behavior. Their entire social cultural milieu has thwarted their efforts at psychological growth.

The setting, in which the children are in school from eight to nine hours a day, sets the tone for the general framework of treatment. All services offered by the school are considered from the guidance point of view for each child. Cooperation exists with the Spanish Auxiliary Teacher, who is in the school three days a week. His firsthand knowledge of the language and culture of Puerto Rico is a valuable contribution to the school's efforts to understand and integrate Puerto Rican children and their parents. The classroom teacher and the ADNS leader, as well as the principal, custodian (a crucial person), lunchroom attendants, nurse, speech teacher and teachers of special classes, such as health improvement, all work cooperatively with individual children. Planned conferences are held with the afore-mentioned personnel as necessary. The social worker is available for this purpose three work hours a week. This is in addition to regular lunch hours used by the social worker to see the classroom teachers. Community resources (i.e., clubs, camps) are utilized in the attempt to help each child.

The careful thought given to the use

of every resource available is important in the treatment plan of each child. It is necessary to help the child obtain basic satisfactions from as many areas as possible. The case records adequately point out the glaring inconsistencies and unmet needs in the lives of these children.

The program as thus far outlined is predicated on the basis that with full use of agency, school and other community resources, severely disturbed children can be kept at home without recourse to institutionalization. This means, however, that the children need to obtain further support through community-sponsored opportunities, in order to obtain personally satisfying experiences. When this is a planned and constructive action, it results in solidifying home relationships, insofar as possible. Such a program eases strains and tensions when the child is in the home, and shows community planning at its best.

The question of the age at which it is best to begin this type of intensive treatment with children in the community deserves full study. It appears that very young children (five through eight), who are still physically dependent on their parents, benefit less from such a total program than children above this age group. Young children can often be kept in the school as long as the older children, but cannot go to clubs in the evening. They are less able to mobilize (or may not have) ego strengths against the destructive onslaughts of hostile, emotionally destructive parents or parental substitutes, who are themselves deprived. This appears to be a direct result of the fact that parents are not available for individual or group treatment.

Children of nine or ten usually appear able to accept the rather long period away from the home which is necessitated by home conditions, and seem to benefit from the facilities made available to them. Even without discussion on the part of the caseworker, they appear to understand the need for outside programming and cooperate in this action. They often express positive feelings about staying in school all day and

express satisfaction with the school lunch program.

In individual therapy another time factor becomes obvious. These children relate slowly in treatment. It takes from 6 to 9 months and sometimes much longer for a child to accept and trust the caseworker. This is very similar to establishing a relationship in an institutional setting. Unlike the institution that cares for the child on a 24-hour-a-day basis, this is not possible in our setting, since children still live in the larger community. The lack of trust sometimes prevents children from benefiting from positive experiences, as the following example will make clear.

D was referred for aggressively attacking a number of girls. He had blackened the eyes and lacerated the skulls of at least three girls. His suspicion of the worker was obvious. He feared being sent away by the worker and was unable to accept an opportunity to go to camp when it was first offered to him. This offer was made after D had been in treatment approximately two months. He gave no explanation for his refusal although the worker attempted to explore his fears in this area. Six weeks later, D spontaneously requested that the worker arrange for a camp vacation for him. The worker pointed out the delay and questioned whether camp was available at this late date. D explained that he had previously refused camp out of fear of being sent away from home. He had changed his mind when some of his friends had told him that camp was "on the level."

The problem with such children is further complicated because of their anti-social behavior and the need for the application of limits long before a relationship is established. Here the caseworker's role as a permissive person is jeopardized. It conflicts with the realistic need to impose limits on destructive and aggressive children. Yet the children so limited are not lost to treatment. They continue to return and are usually relieved that the caseworker exists as a limiting person who will restrain their antisocial impulses. They have failed, and are comforted that someone else is available to help them control themselves. The ego support given by the worker makes him an ally of the positive and healthy aspects of the child's personality. The necessity of discussing the negative aspects of the child's behavior, long before a relationship has been established, is a reality that cannot be ignored in treatment. Further it is important, it seems to me, that the worker state his position clearly to the child. This places the worker in an authoritative role, but nevertheless must be risked in order to clarify where the worker stands. It is not done punitively, but rather as a matter of fact. No threat is involved, nor is guilt emphasized, but the realistic attitude of the worker is made known to the child. This is quite different from the punishment of a hostile adult who basically rejects the child. It should be emphasized that the worker's opinion should be made known to the child only where a definite need exists. Actually the child is also being helped to see the consequences of his action. The two examples cited below will perhaps help clarify where the worker must make his opinions known to the child, and where the realistic consequences of a child's actions will lead him within the larger framework of the school's authority.

D, referred to above, displayed such severe outbursts of aggression toward other children that the worker had to discuss them with him quite early, and could not wait until D brought the episodes to his attention. Instead the worker had to use the teacher as source material. When D became hostile and wanted to know why the teacher was "squealing" on him, the worker pointed out that what D did was common knowledge and not a private matter. The worker insisted that this was unacceptable behavior and would have to be modified.

W was referred by the attendance officer for truancy. His truancy had lasted almost his entire school career. He was referred because it was felt that he came from a stable family unit and would respond to therapy. Careful exploration of this boy's activities by the caseworker disclosed that his family relationships were tenuous and that he was not a "lone wolf" in his truanting from school. He was a member of a club that was open during school hours. It was not possible to see this boy in the school setting. When the principal was informed that it might take six months to bring this boy back into school, he decided to transfer him to one of the special schools for maladjusted children in the area. This matter was discussed with the boy as a reality facing him. It was not done in a punitive fashion, but the caseworker pointed out the realistic limits of his own ability to continue seeing this boy in his present school setting.

The above examples not only show the need to set limits early, but also that there is a limitation of activity on a worker's part in every existing setting. Helping the child see the realities facing the worker also helps him accept limitations applied to him.

It is also necessary to identify for these children common meeting grounds with the worker treating them. While consistency between word and action is the principle involved here, it is not the specific. The child has to understand the worker's consistency in terms of his own experience. A promise must be kept, but this is not enough. In order for the child to identify himself with the worker on a fundamental level, the worker must understand the child and meet him on that level. In this instance the fact that there are subcultural values and value identifications is important. The worker must be alert to cultural similarities and differences in the total treatment process. The example below is an illustration of the above principle. It helped accelerate rapport between caseworker and child, and recognized the child's reality on a level understandable to him.

M was referred because of a wide range of symptoms. He was extremely suspicious of adults and aggressive toward other children. He displayed sexual preoccupation in the classroom. Later, severe sibling rivalry toward his younger brother came to the fore. While playing catch with the worker in the room one day, he asked why the worker did not remove his jacket. Before an answer could be given he answered his own question, saying that the worker did not really like playing with him. The worker said that he couldn't afford a fresh shirt every day, and was trying to keep his shirt clean for the next day. The boy laughed and said that was what his mother made him do.

In the treatment of children in a school setting, the changing of symptomological patterns may be a preliminary step in helping a child. Adjustment to the school setting is one of the purposes for which a child is usually referred to the school social worker. This factor must be given consideration in accepting a child for treatment. This is true of the aggressive child who is not manageable in the classroom, and of the truant who does not attend school. In both cases a change of symptom is necessary if the child is to remain in a school setting.

C was referred by his aunt and his grandmother for truancy. The social worker's contact with him was made when the boy was brought to school forcibly after a three-week period of truancy. When left alone with the worker, C gave him what the boy later described as "the silent treatment." It was finally agreed, after a great deal of effort on the part of the worker to reach this boy, that C would come in for his first real interview that afternoon after school. He left and truanted for the rest of the school day, but returned for the interview. He stopped his truancy that day.

For the past year and a half he has not truanted. A number of other symptoms of an aggressive and sexualized nature have come to the fore and are being handled. To emphasize the need of stopping the truancy, this boy recently told the worker that during school hours he had gone to a club. He was on his way to becoming an habitual truant.

It is necessary to emphasize again and again the role played by aggressive behavior in the lives of these children. Quite often the child referred for help with aggressive behavior has no knowledge of other social defenses. He simply does not know how to handle legitimate aggressions that more mature children take in their stride. Without attempting to give a detailed history concerning the need for aggressive or assertive actions, it should still be emphasized that some aggression in and of itself is necessary. As new satisfactions replace old frustrations, however, the need arises to help children handle legitimate aggressions in everyday life. This is especially true of children between nine and twelve years of age, who are dealt with in this paper. With the increase in relationship strength, there is increased ability to verbalize about the sensitive areas of life, as they concern the individual child. At this point the ego is open to new realities and new defenses. Verbal communication is the channel of expression for these children. They begin to differentiate between an authoritarian personality and inherent authority. They can then use this ability constructively whereas before they saw only direct aggression as the way of meeting life situations.

For the most part, the children referred for treatment come from rejecting families of low economic level; hence it is important to consider the approach in treatment that will lead to desired results. Not only are the children rejected and not trusting of adults, in the beginning, but the rejection is often overt, without the niceties usually associated with the rejection of middle-class children. A word is quickly followed by a blow in many cases, and there is not the suspense of trapping the adult into displaying the rejection, which is so often found in the case histories of middle-class children. This has implications for the worker involved in establishing a relationship with these children in treatment. Most adults are openly authoritarian figures to these children. The risk is therefore not too great if the worker does not try to disturb this conception at the beginning. In fact since it is usually the only type of relationship known to these children, it is the only one they will form. The reality and limits faced in treatment are support for a weakened ego. It appears to be a comfort to the children to know that the caseworker is not too different from the other adults they meet in everyday life. This extends to the language used by the caseworker. The change occurs slowly as the child recognizes the accepting nature of the caseworker and forms an attachment to him. The worker is not the authoritarian person the child expected to find in the beginning. By this time it is almost too late for him to withdraw from treatment. The child has become trusting and dependent on the worker. It is at this point that the caseworker can afford to become very permissive and emphasize the type of relationship that he might have wished to express earlier. To have done so when treatment was beginning, however, would probably have lost the child for therapy. He would not have trusted the worker's professions of interest, and any emphasis on the voluntary nature of the relationship would have given him permission to break off the contact.

The following two examples illustrate the relationship between worker and child during the early phases of treatment.

F was referred for constant fighting in the classroom and refusal to do work. While quite ready to discuss his fighting, he was quick to point out that it was the "other kid's fault." Questioning was not always successful in bringing out his provocative behavior. At times the worker repeated his story exactly as he told it, and F was quite content with the repeated version until the worker would ask if F thought the worker was a "sucker." F would ask what the worker meant and would invariably fill in

slight details that clarified his role in the many fights in which he became involved. Eventually the fighting stopped and he was able to gain some insight into his own behavior and establish some control over his own aggressive impulses.

A was referred for truancy and inability to adjust to the school routine. During the interviews, he delighted in telling the worker stories about the gangs that roamed the area. When the worker was able to identify some of the gangs, and expressed a thorough knowledge of the neighborhood, A was visibly impressed. The worker's knowledge of the slang used and of the very houses used in the exploits helped A express himself more easily, and eventually brought about his acceptance of the worker in the role of a giving, understanding person.

Whatever the example, the important point with the children described is to foster a dependency relationship in the early phase of treatment so that growth, integration and independence can occur in the end. This paper has been an attempt to present the problems and show possible designs for action that will be oriented to meet the specific problems presented by the children described. Much more work has to be done with these children before new treatment techniques can clearly be established. All too often it is contended that the usual mental hygiene clinic was not established to cope with such aggressive children. It is nevertheless these severely aggressive children who fill our institutions, and who must be treated in the community wherever possible, if institutions for disturbed children are not to be extremely overburdened.

Since 1950, special classes for emotionally disturbed children throughout the nation have grown and expanded like glamour stocks in electronics. During the next decade, we predict even greater growth. National training and research grants, state aid, and changing attitudes about mental illness all are helping. It is now possible for many school districts to set up special classes without serious community resistance and without having to assume the entire expense of the program.

What concerns many of us the most now is not the quantity of special classes, but the quality of these classes. If the community feels they can be used to "get rid of" all the "rotten, dirty, foul-mouthed children" who are "contaminating" their youngsters, "degrading" the building, "destroying" teacher morale, the chances are that these classes will not be therapeutically organized. We have observed some special classes so ill-conceived that they were offensive. We have seen special classes taught by teachers who were personally so disturbed that they were not allowed to teach in a regular class. We have observed special classes held in basement rooms so poorly equipped, so barren, and so depressing that the entire school staff as well as the children referred to the room as "the dungeon." We also have observed classes where the grouping of children was so inappropriate that explosive conflicts were the logical result. We have talked to well-trained, healthy, dedicated teachers who were made to feel guilty by the administration if they had any difficulty in their class. Some of these special teachers have been told never to send one of their children to the principal's office, and not to expect any professional consultation.

If the community cares about its emotionally disturbed children, if the community feels that these children have suffered enough and deserve a chance to learn to live more comfortably with others and themselves, then poor programs are inexcusable. We firmly believe that a poorly designed special class is worse than no special class at all. To prevent these conditions from developing, William Hollister and S. E. Goldston have written a pamphlet entitled, *Considerations for Planning Classes for the Emotionally Handicapped* (see Chapter 2). In this brief pamphlet the authors attempt to describe the essential components of a special class.

In the following article, Louis Hay describes the Junior Guidance Class Program in New York City, an excellent example of how special classes can be designed to re-educate children rather than serve as a dumping ground for the "misfits." Since its conception in 1950, the Junior Guidance Program has expanded to include 62 schools, 149 classes, 217 teachers and approximately 1,850 pupils. Three teachers are assigned to each unit of two classes. Thus children in conflict are provided with essential on-the-spot support, clarification, and controls. A closed-register class, consisting of 12 to 15 pupils, doesn't admit additional pupils after the class begins. An open-register class, consisting of 7 to 10 pupils who need emergency placement, admits pupils during the year. Group work with the parents, consultative help, curriculum specialists and complementary recreational program give the teacher support in depth. They also illustrate the conviction of the administration that these children need something more than a small class with a benign teacher.

A New School Channel for the Troubled Child

Louis Hay

The prospects of referral of most troubled children for therapy are slight. There is little reason to believe that in the foreseeable future the gap between need and help will be bridged adequately. The

Abridged from Louis Hay, "A New School Channel for Helping the Troubled Child," *American Journal of Orthopsychiatry*, XXIII (October 1953), 676–683. Copyright, the American Ortho-psychiatric Association, Inc. Reprinted by permission.

Louis Hay is psychologist for the Bureau of Child Guidance of the New York City Board of Education.

question, therefore, might well be raised, whether closer cooperation between clinicians and better trained school personnel might not tap new resources for helping these children.

The community must recognize that teachers are the only trained social representatives who are in a position to contribute toward the better adjustment of the greater number of disturbed children. The school is the child's first and most sustained contact with a social institution, other than the family. Can early detection and more appropriate management, within the school setting, aid in the reduction of the number of troubled children? Clinical knowledge has a contribution to make in determining the answer.

Despite the multiplicity of the symptoms of maladjustment, troubled children might be nurtured to more adequate functioning in guidance classes designed to meet their needs. This is the underlying thesis of the present proposal. . . .

What is proposed here is not offered as a substitute for individual therapy, when available and acceptable. Most educationally oriented mental health projects are conceived for normal populations. Their program is usually limited to special periods of verbal content. On the other hand, the stress in the guidance classes is on all of the content and all of the relationships, of the entire day, within the school, for a select population. There are, of course, extremely well considered plans and efforts to help certain types of troubled children. Several of the best known are well represented by members of this panel. These are usually on a custodial basis or in institutions divorced from public school systems. They are concerned with the delinquent or with those of more profound psychopathology. Agencies that work with children similar to those in the guidance classes have long waiting lists and their cooperation with the schools is peripheral. We are also concerned with adjustment problems not as yet necessarily personality-rooted nor thought worthy of intensive consideration; if these are detected and worked through during the early grades the establishment of patterns of maladjustment may frequently be prevented.

The New York City school system has been experimenting with several projects in a school setting. In one such program, poorly adjusted children are selected by the teachers of the kindergarten, first and second grades. Each child is studied by a clinic team. The parent is interviewed by the social worker. In groups of four or five the children spend two hours a week in a playroom with the group teacher. The planning for the child then becomes a group responsibility that involves a group teacher, the class teacher, the principal and the clinic team. The results have been most fruitful in pointing up new ways of helping school personnel to help children in need.

In September 1950, we initiated a guidance class program in a Brooklyn school (kindergarten–sixth grade) of approximately 1600 children. The school's socioeconomic composition, although widely diversified, is largely lower middle class. We started with a third-grade group and added two classes a year later. Today the three original groups are in the third, fourth and fifth grades with a total of 60 children.

The early plans envisaged one class for each of the six grades. Thus about one hundred of the most poorly adjusted children would make up the population of the guidance channel. By following the regular grade sequence they would be kept with their age mates and there would be minimal interference with the attitudes of the community, the parents and the school. The withdrawal of these children from the regular grades should be recognized as a major contribution to all the children because disturbed youngsters frequently control a disproportionate focus of class and teacher.

The children selected included those who were withdrawn, submissive, of low vitality, hyperactive, or aggressive; those with school phobias or with marked speech defects; those with notable physical disabilities such as asthma and epilepsy; and the academically retarded. The candidates often revealed clusters of symptoms. All of the original third-grade group manifested a reading disability as well as marked personality difficulties. The reading disability prerequisite was modified for the later groups.

Teacher referrals, record cards, health histories, standardized tests and conferences with teachers, past and present, as well as with some of the parents, and in some cases the psychologist's classroom observations were the primary sources of selection. The problem of grouping was recognized from the outset as most crucial. An attempt was made to avoid overweighting these classes with the overtly aggressive and the hyperactive children. All of the children were of average or better intelligence.

There has been an annual re-evaluation to determine whether the child shall continue in the guidance channel or return to the regular grades. Gains for some children have been sufficiently marked to permit their return to the regular grade after one year. Many need a longer stay. There are others who will need a supportive environment beyond the sixth grade. We feel, however, that when they leave the guidance channel they will be stronger in many respects.

The involvement of the teachers is both selective and voluntary. They serve by invitation, with the understanding that they may leave the project at the close of the school year. Teachers are considered in the light of the following criteria: an ability to relate well to children; a maturity evidenced by a capacity to work as a constructive team member; professional interest and flexibility that evince a respect for learning; and skills in the arts and crafts.

We have been fortunate in finding teachers within the school who enjoy experimenting and learning. Their association with the project has fostered a greater interest in the dynamics of child development. They have read more, have attended conferences, and have taken related

courses. The teachers, the assistant principal, who is expert in educational techniques, and the Bureau of Child Guidance workers (social worker and the psychologist, who also acts as coordinator) are the basic members of the team. For specific purposes we are joined by other specialists. Channels of communication are kept readily available through weekly meetings of the team and individual teacher conferences. All of us know only too well that these children generate emergencies routinely, and additional meetings to cope with such emergencies are not infrequent. The teachers have retrospectively evaluated their initial contacts with these children as among their most harrowing experiences. As one who has spent many years in the classroom, it is especially pleasant to report that they have survived—scarred but unbent. To date, no teacher has asked to leave the channel.

The curriculum for the child guidance classes is determined by the needs of the children and the special abilities of the teacher. The teachers have shown a keen consciousness of emotional readiness in approaching all activities. They try to avoid pressing an individual child in any area before there is acceptance on his part.

Nonacademic units are stressed to help the child who is not succeeding in formal schoolwork to develop self-confidence. With each new group much of the school day is devoted to music, painting, ceramics, carpentry, block-building, housekeeping, playing store and similar activities.

Academic work is not overlooked. The reading program is an outgrowth of experiential and language arts activities. These include well-motivated projects as well as other selected social experiences that are particularly meaningful in nurturing reading readiness. The experience chart is the basic tool. Into this the teacher tries to weave the vocabulary of the reading text. The reader itself is not used until the vocabulary has been mastered and successful reading is assured. The new developmental mathematics program is most helpful in these classes. Again the work is adapted to the individual students. There are as many as three or four groups in each class arranged according to current levels of academic achievement.

Small registers are considered essential. There is now a maximum of 20 to a class. Next year we hope to set the limit at 18, with 15 as the eventual goal. In order not to disturb established relationships there are very few pupil changes during the year. We believe that the children are building significant bonds that are worthy of more intensive study. For related reasons the teacher has remained with the same class for more than one year.

The largest classrooms in the building are assigned to these classes. They are about as large as a good modern kindergarten room. There are sizable corners for housekeeping and carpentry, space for rhythms and dancing, and room to move about and engage in varied activities. Art materials, lumber, tools, and other daily educational needs are abundantly supplied. There is a piano in each room, one of them a contribution from the parents' association. The cooperation of this organization has been sought from the beginning. As a consequence their support, financial as well as sympathetic, gives the channel substantial backing in the community.

The role of the school administration has been very important. The principal has participated in the over-all planning and in all crucial matters of policy. The assistant principal has been involved in the day-by-day planning and application, and has been available for conference to any member of the team. Unless the administration shows a real understanding of mental hygiene goals and practices such a project must founder.

Because of its interest in exploring new ways of extending mental health knowledge to the schools, the Bureau of Child Guidance has assigned a social worker and a psychologist to the project on a part-time basis, in spite of serious personnel shortages.

The New York City school system has curriculum specialists in art, music, reading, mathematics, etc. These specialists were invited to help us. Time spent with the guidance classes varied from a day to a week, and in one case an educational counselor came once a week for a term. Frequent consultations with the school nurse are an integral aspect of the project.

We know that parents of troubled children are by and large seriously troubled, often defensive, and with little insight into their children's problems. In this area of parent-school relationship we encountered the most difficulty. The parents resisted a special school grouping which they felt to be a reflection upon them as parents, and a threat to their child's and their own status. As the gains of the children became more apparent, the parents began to feel less threatened. We discovered, pleasantly enough, that the early resistance, almost violent at times, receded gradually and the parents became increasingly cooperative.

We all know that disturbed parents, who can afford private therapy or who have access to agencies, may resist therapy for their children. I feel, however, that through their contacts with a setup like the guidance channel they may be helped to accept referrals to agencies and psychiatrists and working with school clinicians. The social worker of the staff has also helped to reduce parental pressure. The principal in a recent report stated: "Many parents of these children have become more active in the parents' association. They spark many stimulating questions at parent meetings. It has been interesting to see the shift in the direction of their questions from those dealing previously with school situations to those involving the home. This change indicates a degree of confidence in the school which was just a faint hope when the Child Guidance Project was launched."

Among the gaps we regret most is the lack of a control group. What follows in the way of an over-all summary is in some respects more "impressionistic" than we would have liked. In January of this year, we made a study of teacher personality ratings of our 60 youngsters throughout their school career. The New York City rating cards list 15 personality areas. Improvement is noted here only when the child had a consistently unsatisfactory record in the particular trait prior to his entering the guidance classes, and when the progress was subsequently maintained.

The greatest improvement was listed under the heading "Self-Confidence." Of the 60 children studied, 24 changed from "Lack of Confidence" or "Needs Frequent Encouragement" to "Usually Works with Confidence." The second greatest improvement was in "Aggressiveness." Here 21 children changed from either "Does Not Assert Himself" or "Overaggressive, Fights Frequently" to "Moderately Aggressive." There were many who shifted from "Shy" to "Overaggressive." In the next position we find "Responsibility" with 18 cases of improvement noted; "Leadership" with 17; and "Social Adjustment" and "Work Habits" with 16 each.

Academic progress was evaluated by means of standardized tests and teacher judgments based on the reading texts used by each youngster. Reading was not given any special emphasis. Current techniques familiar to all alert teachers were used. These children, although of at least average intelligence, were, with a few exceptions, retarded one or more years when they entered the guidance classes. Most of the youngsters were below the reading readiness level at the end of the first grade. By the middle of the third grade, almost all achieved reading readiness. By the middle of the fourth grade there is a wide range of achievement: 5 are doing third-grade work; 5, second-grade work; 6, first-grade work; and 3 are at a reading readiness level. In the fifth grade the wide range continues but there is steady and appreciable progress, with one exception in whom we suspect some organic involvement. In the fifth grade, 3 are reading at fifth-grade level; 4 at fourth; 10 at third; and 2 at first-grade

level. Academic progress can be considered another indicator of better adjustment.

The following are brief excerpts on several children chosen at random:

David, nine, is now in the fourth grade. When he entered the third-grade guidance class in September 1951, he manifested real panic with spells of weeping and the clutching of his mother's arm. Now, his independence and vitality are quickly apparent. He comes to school alone, makes friends readily, and appears happy most of the time.

Roberta was so withdrawn and fearful that she had to be escorted into the classroom. She would sit isolated in a corner. When she walked, she hugged the walls. She is still shy but mixes with groups and will approach adults in whom she has confidence.

Ellen is Roberta's classmate and equally frightened. Recently she remarked to the psychologist, "Roberta told me not to be afraid of the dentist. Before, I was. My mother told me to stay with Roberta. She teaches me stuff and I'm not afraid so much. She always keeps telling me, 'Don't be afraid.'"

Joseph, eight, was withdrawn, did not participate in class activities and did not speak. He became involved in fights but could not hold his own. Now, he talks, but in a functional way, to meet specific purposes. He is more relaxed and is getting along better. At home, he runs errands without a written note.

Donald has a long history of asthma. His work is poor and he, too, is withdrawn. The family background is seriously disturbed. Asthmatic attacks are rarer and he has begun to fight back and hold his own with other boys.

Martha has a history of shyness and poor academic work. One day, she surprised her mother and the Sunday School teacher by volunteering to sing "Onward Christian Soldiers" as a solo in the church auditorium. At the end of the school year, Martha returned to the regular classes.

Henry was unusually aggressive and destructive from the beginning of his school career. After a year and a half in the guidance classes he has become more socialized and able to participate in group activities. There is less evidence of chronic hyperactivity. He is particularly proud of his ability to handle a primer.

What the warmth and security of the guidance classes mean to these children is best demonstrated by the words of one of the youngsters. In an interview with the psychologist Thomas said, "First I'm scared of school and then I got used to it. When I was in the second grade I was scared of reading. Then in the third grade with Miss O, I wasn't scared. I didn't feel like reading when I was scared. When I got used to reading, I said, 'Why can't I have more reading?' and she said, 'No, it would be too much.' So, I went to the desk and read by myself. I used to be scared to read to children. I'm still bashful to get up and tell the children what I did yesterday and other days [show and tell period]. I'm not scared to play now. I talk to other kids. I read out loud. Many times I know the right answer, but sometimes I'm scared to say it. It's true I'm scared I'm wrong and I don't want to say the answer and get into trouble. I'm not so sure I'm right. I am scared again and then I get happy again. When I was in the third grade I became happy all the time. I had another book and I felt scared. Then I got happy and I wasn't scared of the book. Then I went to Mrs. K's class and I'm still happy."

Every child in this group offers a dramatic story of unique combinations of inadequate homes, physical disabilities, arrested ego development, destructive compensatory mechanisms, and varying degrees of resilience and promise of more desirable adjustment.

Two questions that have been raised repeatedly deserve consideration. There is some fear that such a channel has segregative features. Segregation is usually viewed as a coerced deprivation of valuable opportunities in contrast to those of a more favored group. Deprivation is intensified when there is little or no mobility in the relationships. As this project has been en-

visaged from its inception there has been a keen awareness of this aspect. We feel, however, that since none of the elements usually associated with segregation is intrinsic here, the term does not apply. There is no coercion; neither child nor parent who is resistive need be included. Periodic reassessment allows for optional continuation. We have discovered that the reservoir of such children is so large as to allow for the inclusion of only those who are accepting. Furthermore the opportunities for these children are richer than usual. Hence there is neither coercion nor deprivation.

There is, however, a type of segregation that is extensively current and is seriously traumatic, namely, the functional segregation that is the lot of many of these unhappy children. The child who is not functioning well, academically or socially, stands out frequently as the proverbial sore thumb. Such an arrangement is much more segregative than the one in which an attempt is made by specialists to assess the child's needs and provide a healthful climate. At present the guidance classes are integrated into the school in such manner as to preclude stigmatization. In practice this has not been a serious problem.

The question is also asked whether the proposed plan is not simply good education. "Should not all children have the benefit of moderately sized classes, teachers who are aware of their emotional needs and a program that provides for activity, crafts, arts, etc., in addition to the three R's? In short what is the difference between this and a good private school?" We must remember that even the best of schools have disturbed children whose needs cannot be met by educators alone. The salient difference then is the intimate identification of clinicians with the educative process. This means close teamwork with the school and the teacher and supplemental clinical help for children and parents when necessary. Clinical case histories for each child are developed, the dynamic movement of the classroom is studied, conferences with teachers analyze the daily impact upon the child and the group, and various types of treatment are planned both individually and for groups of children and parents. The programs and pace that have a therapeutic rationale in a guidance class cannot be permitted in a regular class. The tolerance and limits of the one are not to be expected in the other. Since this is essentially a clinically oriented project the over-all direction and the individual patterns are invested with perspectives derived from psychiatrists, social workers and psychologists.

We hope that this report will be seen as that of an exploratory project that is working with limited resources. We are keenly aware of the limitations but we feel that what we are doing opens the door for more careful research into new ways of helping the troubled child. We believe that what is learned from these children can be of help to all children.

When a child's behavior is so deviant that he is excluded from public school, there are, unfortunately, very few resources available. However, if you happen to live in Brooklyn and your child is schizophrenic, he may be considered as a day student in the League School. The director and founder of this extraordinary school, Carl Fenichel, believes that a therapeutic day-care program can find new ways of working with seriously disturbed youngsters without placing them in a residential center. This school has successfully maintained fifty children who were so seriously disturbed that no private school would admit or retain them. Here is another example of the value of personal conviction and community support in creating new facilities for seriously disturbed children.

A Day School for Schizophrenic Children

Carl Fenichel, Alfred M. Freedman, and Zelda Klapper

The role of a day school must be considered within the framework of other services available to children who are diagnosed as schizophrenic. Considering the wide variety and range of intensity of clinical syndromes, it is obvious that no single facility or program can meet the needs of all such children.

On the one hand, there is the less seriously disturbed child who lives at home and manages to function in a public or private school; on the other, the severely disturbed child who is confined within an institution. Until recently there has been no facility for the child who does not belong to one of these two groups.

Carl Fenichel, Alfred Freedman, and Zelda Klapper, "A Day School for Schizophrenic Children," *American Journal of Orthopsychiatry*, XXX, No. 1 (1960), 130–143. Copyright, the American Orthopsychiatric Association, Inc. Reprinted by permission.

While a residential center is a necessity for certain children, it has many disadvantages: (1) Separation from the home is often traumatizing for some children and parents. (2) The child removed from his home loses the positive aspects of family life. (3) The child becomes accustomed to institutional life and this may create difficulties when he is ready to return to community living. (4) While the child is away, the family may become so reorganized that it can no longer accept the schizophrenic child back in the household. (5) Residential centers are often some distance from the home, thus making it difficult to work closely with the parents.

In an effort to overcome these objections and to explore new ways of working with seriously disturbed children within a community setting, the League School was founded in 1953. We are presenting our experiences at the School to demonstrate that the needs of many seriously disturbed children and their families can be met by a day school within the community.

The League School grew out of the desperate need of schizophrenic children and their parents. Psychiatrists who had seen these children had stressed that it was desirable for most of them to remain at home while in treatment.

Although most parents wanted to keep their mentally ill child within the family, the many overwhelming and exhausting problems they had to face each day, with little or no relief, made this almost impossible. Public and private schools had excluded these children as "uneducable." Nor was there any available day care program to relieve parents even for a few hours so that they could regain their energy and handle their child more positively.

Few of these children were getting any kind of professional help or therapy. Clinics rejected them as untreatable. Private psychiatric treatment was too expensive for most families. Even when parents could afford such treatment, it was the opinion of many psychiatrists that treatment without the support of a planned day care and school program failed to get results.

The League School started with the working hypothesis that many children diagnosed as schizophrenic can live at home and be helped in an adequate day care or day hospital setting. Such a setting required a school program in a therapeutic environment which could treat and educate these children under psychiatric and educational guidance.

The School opened in February 1953 with 2 children, a director, a teacher, a psychiatric consultant and a part-time social worker. Additional children were screened and admitted one at a time. An additional teacher was appointed for every two children. Within a year the capacity enrollment of 12 children was reached.

The purchase of a larger building in 1955 made possible much needed expansion of treatment and research facilities, includ-

ing the organization in 1956 of a nursery group. The League School, with 38 children and a professional, administrative and house staff of 28, now occupies a three-story building which formerly housed a private elementary school. The professional staff includes a director, a psychiatric director, 2 clinical and research psychologists, a psychiatric social worker, a dance therapist, a music therapist and 14 teachers.

SCHOOL POPULATION

Only children who have been diagnosed "childhood schizophrenia" by an outside psychiatrist or agency are considered for admission to the School. Children who have been diagnosed as primarily organic or retarded are not accepted. However, among the children with the label "childhood schizophrenia" numerous clinical pictures are seen. We therefore look for certain general features that we feel are essential in the diagnosis of all schizophrenic children, whatever their manifest behavior.

First we look to their history for evidence of disorders of development—that is, regression, or precocity and retardation existing simultaneously. Then we look for the presence of the three fundamental psychological problems in the schizophrenic child: (1) anxiety and the variety of defenses for handling the anxiety; (2) problems in relationships and identification, including impaired communication with others; (3) the presence of body-image problems, including confusion of body boundaries and uncertainty of orientation in time and space.

On the basis of manifest behavior or secondary symptoms, we can describe several categories of children at the School.

1. *The autistic child.* A large group of our children are autistic, with their primary source of stimulation derived from their own body. They have little or no speech, rarely display any affective awareness of people, and maintain a level of activity which has the barest relation to objects or events in the real world. We distinguish two subgroups:

a. Those who have been retarded in

maturation from birth. The differential diagnosis of "childhood schizophrenia" from mental deficiency is often a difficult one. The differential is based upon the presence of the primary symptoms.

George is an attractive, bright-eyed eight-year-old with no speech, little toilet training, and few interests. His developmental history contains no evidence of normal development at any period. He is always in motion, displaying extraordinary physical agility and coordination with exquisite judgment of his own body position in space. If he is not interfered with, he comfortably occupies himself with the sensations derived from his own motility. His interest in the outside world is more likely to take the form of a pursuit of small glittering objects, such as beads, than involvement with a child or adult. He makes no apparent distinction among people and relates to no one. He asks for little from the outside world and gives little.

b. The child who has a history of regression. These may be children with allegedly normal early development who began regressing seriously at some time. A few of the children in this group remind one of the "symbiotic" child described by Mahler. According to Mahler, early maturation in such children can be considered normal up to the point of preliminary ego differentiation, at which point the threatening effects of such growth or the actual experience of separation from the mother panics the child and precipitates regression.

Bruce is an extremely thin, frail nine-year-old boy with a normal speech pattern, enormous charm and pitiful vulnerability. In his developmental history there are two periods of regression noted before the age of five. Each of these periods of regression followed enforced separation from the mother.

Bruce walks on his toes as if chronically on the brink of disaster. He is usually observed moving around slowly in a detached preoccupied manner, rolling a rubber band or a bit of clay in his hand, and droning a song to himself. His separation from the outside world is quite definite,

even to the point of his refusing to eat. He eats almost nothing. All he asks of the outside world is the impossible: that it never change, and that it make no demands upon him. His reactions to change and to pressure are devastatingly extreme. He maintains a peripheral awareness of people, objects and events, and with gentle stimulation from very familiar and trusted sources, can occasionally enter into a give-and-take relationship with the outside world. During these brief interludes, he displays warmth, intelligence and even humor, and appears to be accumulating pleasant experiences from these skirmishes with the real world, meager as they may be.

2. *The organic type of schizophrenic child.* While these children present no clear-cut history of cerebral damage or dysfunction, they manifest certain of the symptoms associated with organic children, for example, distractibility, short attention span and motor drivenness.

Grace, a pretty, well-built, five-year-old girl, is in perpetual motion. She speaks well and constantly. Her contact with the outside world is an intense and overreactive one. She cannot shut out or screen impulses from the environment. As she frantically washes her dolly in the tub, her head is turned to the right to watch the little boy hammering there, and at the same time she is announcing to the little boy on her left that the teacher is calling him from the back of the room. An atmosphere of bustle and excitement is created in any room in which Grace is present. Not only is there a drivenness to respond to all stimulating aspects of the external environment, but there is also the continual impact of internal pressures on this small child. Her confusion about herself, her vagueness about the order of her universe, and her chronic anxiety affect her total person, casting her relationships with people into an impersonal mold, and constantly interfering with the development of her capabilities.

3. *A neurotic variety of schizophrenia.* This category is similar to the pseudoneurotic schizophrenic described by Lauretta Bender. Some of these children have

at one time been autistic. However, the clinical picture is marked by anxieties and anxiety defenses such as phobias, obsessive compulsive symptoms and bodily preoccupations.

Shelly is a methodical 11-year-old boy who has successfully developed structured anxiety defenses and thereby achieved a measure of self-sufficiency and independence. Every movement and every word is measured and deliberate for Shelly. When he walks down the stairs, his slow-footed, cautious gait gives him steady assurance that each step is where it is supposed to be and he will not fall. Before he puts on his jacket he wards off danger by placing the jacket on the table in a certain position, raising it, and then lowering it again four times before putting it on. In place of the wildly assaultive, disorganized, autistic child he was in earlier years at the School, he is beginning to present the picture of a well-groomed, pedantic, ritualized young man who is able to participate in academic work.

4. *An asocial aggressive type.* These are generally somewhat older children who are poorly related, aggressive, difficult to manage, often somewhat paranoiac. This group corresponds to those described by Lauretta Bender as pseudopsychopathic.

Sandy is a very bright, tall, owlish-looking 12-year-old. As he strides through the School with an air of enormous self-assurance, eager to describe his most recent Superman achievements, he never once loses hold of the small straw horse he carries in his hand. Although he can find his way through closets up to the school roof, can easily climb the highest tree, and complete a complex scientific experiment, he sleeps in a bed filled with the tiny stuffed animals he places in it before retiring. He lies and steals on a petty level, and leads some of the older boys in planned escapades which invariably include the basis for detection. His relationships with people are superficial and he never asks anything of them except that they give him ample

opportunity to exhibit his physical and mental omnipotence.

5. *The schizophrenic child in transition.* These are children who have a meager relatedness but are distinguished from the remaining children by their maintenance of continual contact with their environment, however meager this contact may be. Although anxiety-ridden, they have not yet developed any structured defenses. It is likely that these children will move in the direction of the neurotic variety of schizophrenia.

William is a small, slim, bright five-year-old with a freckled, elfish face and no conversational speech. Although he has some language, he depends upon pantomime and squeals to get what he wants. William appears to be aware of everything that is going on and seems to manipulate people and objects in a goal-directed way. He seems more in contact with the outside world than most of the other children in the School. Although constricted, anxious, and hostile, he is cooperative to an extent which makes it possible for him to work in an organized manner for short periods of time. Thwarting or failure has a disorganizing effect upon him, however. He tries to maintain his distance from people and does not permit more than a limited intrusion on his own privacy. He has still to develop safety mechanisms for some form of protection against the overwhelming effect of anxiety.

Thus, despite a common diagnosis, the children reveal great diversity and marked contrast in their levels and patterns of functioning. For those who function on a very primitive and infantile level, the School is more of a day hospital. On the other hand, there are two classrooms in each of which one teacher and three children work in a structured academic program. Many of the children show normal or superior intelligence but this is usually scattered and fragmented. There may be precocity in mathematics, science, art or music, and retardation in other areas.

Fourteen of our children do not talk at all. Some talk only to themselves, or just repeat unrelated phrases. Others talk incessantly but what they say is often inappropriate or confused.

A few of the children are completely withdrawn. Some just stare into space; others cover their eyes or ears with their hands to shut out the world. Many whirl around or rock back and forth in perpetual motion. Some laugh for no appropriate reason or make crying noises that seem to result from inner tension rather than from outside cause.

Many are not toilet trained; others are completely self-managing. Some show extremely tight and awkward motility; others have amazing dexterity in the use of big and small muscles. Some are hypersensitive to sound; others seem to ignore it.

Many ignore toys; others pervert their use by incorporating them into their mouths or limit their interest to minute parts of the toy. Play is usually isolated or parallel. For most of the children social play is meager or nonexistent.

PROGRAM

A tentative plan for the study and treatment of each child is established at the time of his admission to the School. Continual revisions of the plan evolve from the joint thinking of the clinical and teaching staff at weekly staff conferences and teacher-director conferences. The assignment of the child to a specific group is based on the child's needs, levels of functioning, the potential impact of the group on him, and his impact on the group. In the assignment of a child to a teacher, consideration is given to the teacher's skills, abilities, interest and suitability in working with this particular child and group.

The daily six-hour program is one of living-playing-learning experiences and activities that offer continuity, stability and security. It is a program of remedial or therapeutic education utilizing as many of the activities and techniques of preschool and elementary school as possible. Some techniques of play therapy, relationship therapy, group therapy, and music and dance therapy are applied.

The program is divided into two phases: a preliminary or preparatory phase, to make the child as comfortable as possible by removing stress situations and relieving anxiety; and a re-educational or rehabilitation phase, to stimulate maturation by helping the child to cope with inner needs and tensions, and with the outside world.

In such a program, the teacher-child relationship is basic. To be effective, such a relationship demands one teacher for every two or three children. Often a child needs the exclusive attention of one teacher for many weeks or even months. Therapy at the School is, to a great degree, the cumulative impact of the feelings, attitudes and behavior of the teacher with whom the child has contact six hours a day, five days a week, in the significant functions and activities of eating, playing, dressing, toileting, washing, resting, dancing, singing, painting, and, wherever possible, the more traditional academic activities.

Teacher-child relationships are initiated on whatever level the child is functioning. Often this is on a most primitive, nonverbal level with the teacher acting as an accepting, comforting, mother figure who holds, fondles, cuddles, rocks and feeds her child. Teachers have to be alert to any signs of response from a child. Contact with the outside world is often begun by body contact with the teacher.

A teacher may have to use her body as part of the child's to produce different types of motility until the child can do it on his own. Teachers need to know when to encourage a child to approach, explore, and try a new experience or activity. Care must be taken to avoid pressing a child beyond his fragile hold on reality. A new stimulus or experience may be too threatening and be met by withdrawal or increased resistance to outside contact.

New play experiences and academic activities provide a basis for reality testing. Every satisfying experience or mastery of a new routine or activity makes for decreased anxiety and increased self-awareness and confidence.

A disturbed child needs help, too, in experiencing and coping with the give-and-take of human feelings. A teacher must be able to recognize and identify with a child's feelings of anger, fear, confusion, frustration and aggression. Freedom to express and work through these feelings has often led to a lessening of anxiety and greater relatedness and response to the environment.

Teachers must know when to stimulate and permit such expression and how to deflect, dilute or control it before it becomes too overwhelming. The gradual imposition of limits upon a child's impulsive outbursts can be reassuring if applied in a nonpunitive manner. Limits and controls can also help in ego development and in differentiating the self and the outside world.

It is difficult to separate the teacher-child relationship at the School from the specific program and activities prescribed for the child. The conscious and unconscious influences and impact of the teacher and child upon each other are much too difficult to measure. Efforts are being made to develop sufficiently sensitive and accurate tools of observation to determine the relative contributions of specific play, educational and treatment techniques in a child's improvement and growth.

Much of the work of the League School centers around efforts at play activities. To the seriously disturbed child whose verbal communication is limited or distorted, and whose world is most confusing and threatening, play is vitally important for growth. By manipulating, organizing and reorganizing the small world of blocks, water, clay, dolls and puppets, the disturbed child may learn more effective ways to handle his inner needs and impulses and the complex world around him.

As we observe the play of these children we are struck by its impoverished quality, in marked contrast to the richness, spontaneity and creativity that characterize normal play. The very term "play" has to be used cautiously with our children, since a given activity which suggests play may, in reality, be obsessional in character. The play of these children is usually stereotyped in selection of activities and in patterning. There is a tendency to respond to the same few objects in the same way, day in and day out. For example, one child who is accustomed to arrange his blocks daily in a linear pattern reacted with anxiety when the teacher added a curved block to the building, and he compulsively returned the block to the shelf every time it was introduced.

In evaluating play interests in our nursery, we find that the children tend to favor material like water, balloons, balls, rocking boats, and musical instruments. The majority of the materials favored fall loosely into three categories: those with mobility, those having a granulated texture like sand, and those connected with sound. Of these, mobile toys are especially popular. Even the most autistic child is likely to show some response to a spinning top, a rolling tire or a bubble floating in air. As a matter of fact, the nursery children often convert almost any object in the classroom into a mobile one by throwing it.

By applying limits and pressing a child at the opportune moment, we can often help the child to change a particular play pattern. Slowly, cautiously, with proper dosage and timing, new materials and routines become part of the familiar, lose their threat and are accepted.

Because of their withdrawal from or limited response to the world, their desperate need for sameness, and their inadequate relationships with people, most of the children at the School lack the background and experiences that are essential for reading readiness and other academic work. As a child begins to feel comfortable with his teacher and his surroundings, he is encouraged to approach, meet and explore more of the world. A rich variety of experiences is presented: trips to neighborhood stores, playgrounds, parks, the firehouse, museums, and subway and ferry rides to other places of interest. These experiences help to enrich, enliven and expand the interests and background of a child preparatory to any academic work.

All academic work must be highly individualized and timed to fit the personal interests and needs, special preoccupations and the life experiences of each child.

Leonard is compulsively preoccupied with lights, switches, strings and fans. When these stimuli are near he manifests intense hyperactivity and disorganized behavior patterns. For several months he refused to participate in any activity for more than a few minutes at a time. Whole days were punctuated with uncontrollable outbursts of aggression and subsequent anxiety.

When he was not disabled by his obsessions, Leonard revealed a highly intelligent personality and good learning potential. Since he was quite verbal and keenly aware of his environment, it was felt that he was ready to learn to read. Like most of our children, he was tremendously threatened by any new learning situation.

Instead of waiting for his conflict to be worked through, it was decided to utilize Leonard's pathology in the learning situation. Leonard started learning words through picture associations—but only words that had special meaning for him: light, string, fan, parachute, etc. After these words became part of his working vocabulary, he accepted the idea of learning enough to be able to make a sentence. Slowly, neutral words like "cup," "ball," "house," "street," etc., were introduced. Former anxiety was mobilized for a short time every morning into excitement over mastering a new skill. Compulsivity was directed into printing a list of words every day. Leonard now has a definite reading period every morning which gives new structure to his day and to which he reacts with great enthusiasm and interest.

Karen for a long time resisted all efforts at academic work. She wanted to be a baby, she said, and preferred to spend much of her day with the very young children. She loved to eat and went down to the kitchen every morning to ask: 'What's for lunch?" This interest in food was exploited and Karen was soon eager to help make and print the day's menu. Playing around with the words in menus and recipes was the beginning of reading readiness. Within a year she was reading at the fourth grade level.

Karen's interest in scissors, paste and crayons and her love of color were used to get her interested in arithmetic. One day while her teacher and another pupil were making multiplication flash cards, Karen asked if she could make some with her scissors, crayons and colored paper. Interest in multiplication began. Flash cards in addition, subtraction and multiplication followed. Arithmetic is now part of Karen's program, and each day she brings in homework done artistically in a variety of colors.

Shelly clings to his teacher for protection and support whenever he is faced with an unfamiliar or threatening situation. He is extremely fearful of any new academic experience, convinced that it will be too difficult for him. Trial-and-error learning is rejected by Shelly because he cannot accept the frightening possibility of failure.

Shelly's daily ritual of academic work and homework must have sufficient sameness in it to make him comfortable. He must always sit in the same chair, to the left of his teacher, and with his ever-present shoelace that he jiggles in his hand. His previous day's homework must always be checked before his lessons can start. "I don't enjoy this," "I'm bothered," and other distress signals and reactions follow the introduction of anything new. Slowly, cautiously, gradually, with proper dosage and timing, new materials and routines become part of the familiar, lose their threat and are accepted.

OTHER THERAPIES

While every aspect of the School's environment and program has a therapeutic potential, there are some children at the School who are ready for and could benefit from more intensive individual psychotherapy. Since the School does not at present have the personnel or facilities to provide this service, six of our children are receiving individual psychotherapy, either privately or at outside agencies. Efforts are being made to obtain psychotherapy for four more children who are now ready for it. Unfortunately, child guidance facilities have long waiting lists, and the fact that there is a diagnosis of "schizophrenia" is apparently an additional deterrent to accepting referrals from the School.

The administration of drugs to some of our children is considered an integral part of the therapeutic program at the School. Ten of our children are receiving tranquilizers so that they can profit better from the total school program. Stimulant drugs are administered to six children who are severely withdrawn and regressed.

TEACHER SELECTION

Since there is as yet no well-defined or organized teacher-training program in our colleges to help teachers acquire skills, techniques and competencies for work with seriously disturbed children, it is no surprise that our teachers have a varied professional background. Some of our staff have been trained as nursery school teachers. We have found that nursery school training, with its emphasis on early childhood development, is ideal for working with most of our children, no matter what their age. Seriously disturbed children are children who have failed to grow up. To help a child move and grow, a teacher must have a clear idea of the level on which a child is currently functioning and what her specific developmental goals for that child should be. Others on our teaching staff have had elementary school training and experience, supplemented by courses in special education, remedial techniques and play therapy. A few have been trained in psychology rather than in education.

Far more difficult than evaluating the academic training and background needed for our teaching staff is the still unanswered question of personality criteria for selection of our teachers. We know that working with our children demands a combination of skill and art, and much of it is still an art rather than a science. Such essential qualities as imagination, intuition, spontaneity and sensitivity are not easy to detect or measure at the time a teacher is interviewed or selected for the job.

While we have had a few teachers who were equally at home with normal or disturbed children, we do not believe that a teacher who is effective with normal children can necessarily work well with seriously disturbed children. Conversely, not every teacher at the League School is suited for work with normal children.

Our teachers must feel at home with dirt, destruction, hostility, and all kinds of deviant and bizarre behavior. A child at the School may eat his mucous, smear food all over himself, or play with his urine. If a teacher reacts with disgust to such behavior, it can damage any relationship which she may have established with a child. In panic, a child may smash windows or throw things. Such behavior can be quite threatening to a teacher who interprets it as defiance or rejection of herself personally.

A teacher may understand intellectually that for a child's emotional growth he should be permitted to play with dirt, and yet the teacher's real feelings about cleanliness may get in the way. The child will sense that while he is being permitted to play with dirt, there is something in the teacher's own feelings that doesn't quite accept the activity. Often a teacher's unconscious needs and standards are imposed on a child. This may make the teacher more comfortable, but it isn't necessarily helping the child.

Our teachers need sufficient ego strength to absorb large quantities of provocation, hostility, aggression and negativism without feeling threatened or rejected. They must have adequate personal and professional maturity and insight to examine and constantly reappraise their own feelings and reactions to the children with whom they are working. While they must have genuine feelings of warmth, acceptance and kindness, teachers must not become overprotective, oversolicitous or "smothering" as a reaction to the strong dependency needs of the children.

Teachers at the School do not have the support of syllabuses, courses of study or lesson plans with clearly defined academic objectives. Blueprints and answers are not readily accessible in our work. We have had a number of highly skilled and experienced teachers who have found this lack of sufficient structure most threatening. There is compensation for our teachers, however, in the feelings of creative spontaneity, autonomy and self-direction which such an uncharted situation encourages and demands.

Our teachers must believe deeply and sincerely in the possibility for growth and improvement in the children they work with. A hopeless or negative attitude toward a child's growth potential would make the teacher's role ineffectual and untenable. However, because of their strong belief that they can help a schizophrenic child, our teachers must be on constant guard against seeing improvement where none has taken place; they must have the capacity for objective observations. These children change slowly. Satisfaction for the teacher comes in tiny doses, and when it comes there is always the possibility that regression may follow. The teacher's investment in time, skill, physical and emotional energy makes lack of progress or regression hard to accept. The frustration that may follow must not be allowed to be turned into feelings of failure or inadequacy toward oneself, or hostility and blame toward parents or supervisors.

PARENTS

Space does not permit a presentation of the School's work with parents, i.e., the counseling and guidance services of our psychiatric social worker, the referral of some parents to community agencies or to psychiatrists for individual therapy. Mention must be made of the initiation at the School of weekly group therapy sessions for parents which have proven helpful to the parents and the children. At first, par-

ents come to these sessions to find out more about their child's illness and to get blueprints for managing the child.

An intellectual probing of the origin of the illness, the prognosis, and methods of treatment dominate the early sessions. Information and discussion on mental illness provide an intellectual basis for relieving some of the parents' feelings of personal responsibility for their child's illness. Later, various expressions of shame, anxiety, inadequacy, isolation and resentment are aired, explored and often worked through, with group interaction becoming more prominent.

Direct guidance in the daily management of the child emerges from the interchange among parents. Some insight into the parents' feelings about themselves and their own conflicts contributes to increased personal comfort.

PSYCHOLOGICAL EVALUATION OF PROGRESS

The specific features of the School's program can only be evaluated in terms of their effect upon the individual child. It has been possible to maintain a record containing psychiatric, educational and psychological data for each of the children in the School. Of the 38 children, 16 can be tested by the use of standard tests of intelligence and of personality, applied in the prescribed manner. With flexible handling of instructions and test material, it is possible to use some parts of these standard test materials with 7 additional children. The remaining children cannot be tested by using any standardized test material. Instead, "controlled observations" have been used. These children are observed in the classroom, playground, and dining room for the purpose of recording the child's state-of-being in these various situations. His relations to objects, children, adults; his patterns of behavior during music therapy, or in transitions from inside to outside the School, are examples of the types of notations made periodically. Ten-minute periods of exposure to a standard playroom structure provide additional sources of observational data.

The psychological observations are integrated with data from other staff members for final analysis. Other sources include the teacher's daily observations, reports and anecdotal records, the staff conferences on the individual child, the psychiatrist's observations, and the parents' accounts of the child's pattern of functioning at home as outlined in a "Parent's Journal" submitted by each mother and father at the beginning and end of the school year. This journal records the child's behavior from the beginning to the end of a typical day at home.

FOLLOW-UP STUDY

Since its opening five years ago, the League School has admitted 50 children. Thirty-eight are presently enrolled; 10 have been discharged; 2 were withdrawn because of transportation difficulties.

Four children were discharged after they had passed the 12-year age limit at the School. The parents of these four children would have preferred to keep them at home and have them attend a day school for adolescents. However, no such day school existed. One of these children had to be placed directly in a state institution since no other facility would accept him. The other three were accepted at a residential center where two of these boys are doing very well in their relationships with children and adults, and are progressing in academic work and in other areas. The third boy could not adjust to the residential center and was subsequently placed in a state institution.

Three other children at the School were so disrupting to their families, particularly to their siblings, that the School recommended institutionalization. Another child was institutionalized because improper care and lack of cooperation by the parents negated all that the School was trying to do for the child.

Two other boys had made sufficient progress so that they no longer needed such a special environment; they are living at home and attending regular private

schools. Both have made excellent social and academic adjustment; one of them has just received an award for achievement from his school.

CONCLUSION

In reviewing the first five years of the League School, one is struck by the unusually rapid growth of the institution. The pressure for further expansion, as evidenced by the ever-increasing number of applications, is an indication of the need for such a service within the community mental health program.

The School has been able to maintain 50 children within the community for varying periods of time. These children were so seriously disturbed that no private or public school would admit or retain them. A great many of these children would have had to be institutionalized had it not been for the existence of the School. The establishment of the League School made it possible for such children to remain at home, participating in family life, and attending a therapeutically oriented school.

The children's experiences in the School have been varied. For a few, the School has been essentially custodial; for most, it has been therapeutic.

Many of our children have achieved self-management for the first time in their lives. Children with poor motor coordination have learned to play ball, swim, roller-skate, ice-skate, ride a bicycle and manipulate woodworking tools. Children with overwhelming fears and aggressions have learned to control impulses and tolerate change and frustration. Children who were afraid to cross streets, go into stores or playgrounds, ride a subway, and meet people, have overcome these specific fears and taken first steps toward socialization. Children who were considered "uneducable" have learned to read, write, do arithmetic and other academic work.

References

Bender, Lauretta. "Treatment of Juvenile Schizophrenia." *Proc. Ass. Res. Nervous and Mental Dis.*, 34 (1934), 462–465.

Mahler, Margaret S. "On Child Psychosis and Schizophrenia: Autistic and Symbiotic Infantile Psychoses," *The Psychoanalytic* *Study of the Child,* VII (New York: International Universities Press, 1952), 286–305.

Residential treatment in the United States began in 1920, when the Child Guidance Home in Cincinnati was founded. The tremendous growth of residential care for emotionally disturbed children has created a romantic and unrealistic idea that any such care can treat successfully any kind of child irrespective of the problem. While this illusion spreads, the fact remains that residential centers differ widely regarding the type of child they accept, the philosophy of operation, the size of the physical plant, the standards for the staff, the type of educational program, and the standard fee. Among private centers, the cost for residential care ranges from $6,244 to $19,055 per year. Since there is no universally accepted criteria for residential care, we could define it in financial terms and say that residential treatment is a setting where "wealthy and welfare children" are placed when they cannot be helped by the local community services.

A residential school program for emotionally disturbed children has opportunities and problems quite different from a special class within a school system or an independent therapeutic day school. The first assumption is that a residential school should have the total spectrum of activities and resources that exists in a regular school, plus a lot more. The second assumption is that the child in a residential center is exposed continuously to a variety of therapy—individual psychotherapy, group psychotherapy, activity therapy, and school therapy. It should be made clear that what the school offers a child is different from other forms of treatment, but there must be a basic unity of approach to the child, derived from a common understanding of his life history, dynamics, defenses, and assets. This unity is extremely important, because the emotionally disturbed child is by definition fragmented, disassociated, and confused. To give him a program which is also fragmented, disassociated, and confused is to feed his pathology and fortify his defenses. Although a unified-milieu program for the child is harder to achieve than a departmentalized program and demands much more from all the staff members in all the disciplines, the united effort pays off with greater inner-disciplinary respect and understanding.

The third assumption is that the teachers use all their skills to develop a child's ego, to clarify his identity, and to increase his ability to cope with the world by giving him skills, a broader horizon, means of staying intact, and interests of his own. Most important, the teacher works on the child's current level of need which may have a great deal, or nothing at all to do with his I.Q., potential, or present skills. Basic educational decisions are the responsibility of the treatment team and must not be forced or appropriated by teacher or therapist. For example, if a child prefers to read all day long, following a suitable educational curriculum, the decision to continue or interfere with this desire should be made within the unified appraisal of the child's treatment program. Perhaps the child needs to develop some distance between the continuous relationship that exists in a residential center, or perhaps the reading preoccupation is the solution to avoid listening to his fantasies or feeling his unacceptable impulses.

In any case, it is a serious error for school people to say to a group of therapists, "You fix them, and I'll teach them." Total treatment implies simultaneous treatments directed towards the various levels of the child's personality.

Various parts of treatment may often overlap, but there are distinct differences in approaches and roles.

In the next article, members of the Hawthorne Cedar Knolls School describe the difficult task of re-educating the hard-to-reach delinquent boy, even in a controlled environment.

Changing the Delinquent's Concept of School

Jerome M. Goldsmith, Harry Krohn, Ruth Ochroch, and Norman Kagan

The interrelatedness of the school to every other aspect of the treatment team must be borne in mind. Some of the teaching approaches would not begin to "jell" if the child did not have the opportunity to convert some of his modes of delinquent behavior into verbal activity with his therapist. The school-day experiences provide constant grist for the treatment mill.

Individualization within the structure has the same validity and application for the school program as with all other aspects of the environment. The interplay of both processes, individualization and group planning, as they are developed clinically, has an impact upon the methodology and content of the school's effort. The attitude of the children toward their setting is an additional factor that feeds from the cottage, play, and individual therapy situations to the school, and from the school back to these other areas. As we have been able to achieve an atmosphere of treatment and self-help, as opposed to one of antagonism and a conspiracy against the adults, we have been able to have a more positive attitude about school which in turn has contributed toward the shifting cultural attitudes of the children. The acceptance of the smooth successful delinquent into our environment is not easily absorbed by the children, nor does the tough newcomer with his talk of great exploits become a hero to the others. This matrix or existing environment has much to do with the school's initial ability to cope with the delinquent. But it should also be borne in mind that the school itself, because of its personnel, attitudes and structure, has contributed to the formation of this environment in which the new tough delinquent child finds himself somewhat of a stranger among his peers rather than an enviable hero.

The healing process in our environment, which embraces the concept of hour-by-hour management of the child in all phases of his living, forces the school to think in terms of healing, understanding, reorientation of values of the child, acquisition of skills and, above all, stimulating him toward higher aspirations and achievements.

Our clinical understanding and processes have finally been assimilated and sorted out sufficiently so that they assist the teacher with an understanding of the child, of his defenses and his way of affecting adults negatively. This knowledge has strengthened the teacher's ability, not only to tolerate, but to demand, to be optimistic, and to teach delinquent children effectively. What remains ahead of us is the continued need for study and review of these insights so that we can wittingly design more purposeful programs in classrooms for the different kinds of children whom we attempt to treat.

From Jerome Goldsmith, Harry Krohn, Ruth Ochroch, Norman Kagan, "Changing the Delinquent's Concept of School," *American Journal of Orthopsychiatry*, XXIX (1959), 249–265. Copyright, the American Orthopsychiatric Association, Inc. Reprinted by permission.

DEVELOPING A CLASS FOR AGGRESSIVE DELINQUENTS

Mr. Krohn: With the expansion of clinical services at Hawthorne in the late

1930's, it became apparent that not only could the treatment interview be a therapeutic tool, but so could the entire environment. The school, where most of the children spent a major portion of the day, was part of the New York City school system, and as such, operated as a completely independent unit. The school program was structured in much the same way as in the school from which our children had come as hopeless failures. There was virtually no integration of functions of the two professional disciplines, casework and education, and as a result the educational life of the child continued to be a destructive experience. As a matter of fact, since the school operated as if it were in New York City, the punitive device of dismissal from school for serious problems was constantly used. Many children who, in addition to their emotional problems, had been truants, and in some cases had been brought to court for truancy, now found themselves in an institution where they were excluded from school. They had had difficulty in accepting not going to school as an antisocial act in the city, while at Hawthorne removal from school seemed to be acceptable if the community wished it.

In 1939, at the request of the Hawthorne Cedar Knolls Board, the state incorporated the area covered by the institution as The Union Free School District #3. A Board of Education was elected from the larger board, and the school opened in September 1939, with a completely new teaching and administrative staff. The first years were difficult. Limited funds kept the teaching staff to a minimum and classes of 30 and 35 were not unusual. Teachers were expected to be expert in many areas since such luxuries as music, art and dramatics departments were beyond the financial scope of the district. During this early period, there were many doubts as to how wise the move to an independent school district had been since the quality of education had not improved, and the scope of the program had actually decreased. The one big gain, however, was the close cooperation that was possible between the clinicians and the educators, and this outweighed all other considerations.

I remember the first year and the years that followed; what was encouraging to all of us was the ability of the staff to examine its school and make the necessary changes to fit the needs of the population. Every September saw changes in program and organizational structure which had resulted from the previous year's experience. The staff experimented constantly with new educational methods and techniques; many were discarded but over the years we have learned how to organize and implement educational programs. That is an integral part of the treatment approach.

The breakdown of our population educationally is as follows:

1. Boys aged 8½ to 13. This group has an IQ distribution skewed slightly below the normal but not significantly so.

2. Boys and girls aged 13 to 18. A normal distribution of IQ's exists, with the girls skewed somewhat below normal and the boys slightly above normal, but in both instances, not significantly so.

3. The degree of retardation is severe in all groups. Ninety per cent are retarded from one to six years in their basic skills in reading and mathematics. This is based on chronological expectations.

4. Ninety per cent had been serious school problems, and had developed learning problems years before they came to Hawthorne.

5. Most of the older boys and girls had become serious management problems in school. Our intake summaries included incidents of hitting school personnel, running the gamut from teacher to principal; vandalism; serious incidents with other children—in many instances acts of violence or sadism—stealing, etc.

6. School records indicate that our children had been failing year after year. The extreme case was that of a boy with an IQ of 90 who hadn't passed a subject since the second grade. He came to us from the eighth grade and he was illiterate.

Many of our older children begin failing in the seventh, eighth or ninth grade. Those that reach high school have difficulty in meeting the rigid standards of the school.

The present school population totals 200 children: 45 Junior boys, 50 girls, 105 Intermediate and Senior boys. Planning a program for the Junior boys presents little difficulty. Most of the children came from chaotic homes and were, therefore, unable to mobilize themselves for school when they were in the city. At Hawthorne, the security of cottage life plus the consistent behavior by the adult helps the child to live a more ordered life almost from the very first day. This is reflected in the attitude of the children toward school. They are placed in groups where the emphasis is on improving oneself and the element of competition is removed. The focus is upon the child and he competes against himself. All children in the Junior School remain with the same teacher throughout the morning and afternoon.

The older boys and girls present a much more serious program problem. A small group are motivated toward continuing a formal academic program for one reason or another, and for them a modified core program has been developed on the ninth and tenth grade levels. The core subjects are English and social studies. The children assigned to these classes are of at least average intelligence, and their level of achievement is eighth grade or above in language skills. The children in this group are not delinquents and are more fragile than the rest of the population.

At the other extreme, a class has been designed for the older, aggressive, extremely delinquent boys. The achievement level in this group ranges from the third to the eleventh grade. Their attitude toward school is hostile and they have all given up any idea of continuing with their high school education. Most of the boys in this group are severe management problems, both in and out of school. This group usually works on large projects, and the boys acquire various skills and knowledge in relation to the specific project on which they are engaged.

Classes for boys and girls that belong somewhere between these two extremes are called activity classes and are in a sense like one-room schoolhouses. The groups are made up on the basis of age, social functioning, degree of aggressivity, etc. Their achievement levels range from the second through the eighth grade. Children in these classes are ambivalent about school, and have experienced so many failures that they will only try to involve themselves at their own pace. There is a definite class organization, but within this organization exists a great degree of flexibility as to curricular materials, length of time spent on particular activities, demands made by the teacher for production, etc. One of the primary goals of this class is to provide a successful learning experience and by so doing to encourage the boys to expand their educational field of endeavor.

A review of the program over the past few years revealed that we were providing a good school program for most of our population. The intelligent, aggressive delinquent was the one for whom we still had to design a more adequate program. At the time, if he expressed a desire to continue high school training, he was assigned to the tenth grade group. Here he rebelled against the formalized atmosphere that was necessary for the more fragile, disorganized members of the class, and in most cases his very presence terrorized the others in class. The other class available was the one mentioned above, in which control and physical work were the keynotes, with little if any stress on academic material. After a review of the program on all levels, administrative and staff, involving both clinicians and teachers, it became apparent that some of the techniques and educational principles in the other classes had to be combined to develop a new philosophy and methodology. Our thinking was as follows:

1. They needed status as a socially acceptable group since they had always been labeled by the community as delinquent, aggressive, hostile, etc. They were told from the beginning that they had the highest intellectual potential of the school and that we were going to help them make use of it. Knowledge, they were told, was society's most powerful tool. It was not the brawny bulldozer operator who was responsible for changing the face of the earth, but the scientists and engineers who designed the bulldozer. These specialists could actually dispense with the man by designing automatic equipment to replace him. Time and again, knowledge was equated with power.

2. The curriculum used in the academic class had to be modified; a greater number of subjects should be made available and the courses should not be formal in presentation. Since the delinquent is always trying to outmaneuver the adult, we decided that the boys, in order to prove to themselves that they actually had learned the course material, would have arrangements made for them to take the Regents' examinations at the local high schools.

3. As in the class of the older aggressive boys who were not academically oriented, and who worked on many community service projects, we felt that this new group should undertake community projects. When this was discussed with them, they immediately anticipated that we meant heavy muscular activity. When they found out that what we had in mind for them was organizing and working on committees for a school dance, they accepted the full responsibility—arrangements, publicity, preparation of food, including blue, green and red hors d'oeuvres, and entertainment. They also produced a class newspaper and wrote and produced an Election Day assembly.

4. From our experience in the activity classes, we learned how to set varied goals and then to make demands that would keep the boys producing. The only difference in

the new class was that, instead of a flexible curriculum in basic skills taught in the activity class, we were now applying the principle to intermediate algebra, advanced biology, senior English, trigonometry, etc.

5. One of our junior classes has an enrollment of six autistic schizophrenics. We had difficulty at first keeping them apart when we wanted them to work. We learned after a while to place the furniture, materials, etc., in such a way as to keep them away from each other. In laying out this classroom, we gave a great deal of thought to placing certain activities in specific areas so as to keep plenty of space between the boys when necessary.

The next area of importance was supervision of the teacher and the role of the supervisor with the class. The role assigned to the supervisor, myself in this case (in the future it could be the school counselor), was that of a benevolent authoritarian. The boys in the class, and all of them wanted to remain in class, were aware that the teacher consulted with me from week to week and that I reviewed the progress of each boy and of the class as a whole. In order to make sure that the boys did not lose sight of their objectives, three-way conferences were held to review the goals of the boys and what they were responsible for. The emphasis was on what the boy had to do to meet goals he had set. The possibility of removal from class was ever present, but it was always handled by turning the question of removal back to the boy. On one occasion a boy said, "You can take me out of class; you have always wanted to anyway." I countered with: "If I had wanted to take you out of class, I could do so by virtue of my position, without looking for an excuse. You were aware of what was required. If you can't meet the demands, you are removing yourself."

An important aspect of supervision is the weekly supervisory conference. At this conference I review with the teachers the weekly progress in the class, both from the standpoint of the individual children and of the class as a whole. This conference is important because the impact of the delinquent culture of the class upon the teacher is so great that it is necessary periodically to review what is going on, and thereby help the teacher to see the direction in which the class is moving. For instance, at one such meeting it became apparent that each boy was putting pressure on the teacher to reduce the required academic work. When viewed individually it did not seem significant. However, the total effect, if it had continued, would have been to destroy the minimum limits of academic achievement that had been agreed upon. The process was reversed by reviewing the request of each individual child. Except in those cases where we felt that the impact of disturbance in a child was so great that it was absolutely necessary to reduce the requirements, we decided to hold the line. In the following weeks it was apparent that what we had done was to raise the level of academic expectations, and that the class was able to meet this expectation.

Another important area in supervision is for the supervisor to be an enabler in the sense of providing certain skills that the teacher does not have. For instance, I frequently gave demonstrations and lessons in auto mechanics, practical electricity, etc. Providing materials and equipment when needed is frequently crucial in implementing both individual and class projects. The delinquent usually looks for an out, and will make demands that he hopes will not be fulfilled so that he can rationalize that his failure was due to someone else's inadequacy. In one instance, a boy felt that in order for him to continue a certain course, a specific textbook was necessary, and since the textbook was not available, he would have to give up the course. While the boy was in my office, I placed a call to the publisher and asked him to send the text by special delivery. The following morning it arrived, the teacher was able to

assign material for the day, and the boy actually completed the necessary assignment that day. . . .

CASE HISTORY OF A CLASS

Mr. Kagan: Establishing a classroom for the emotionally disturbed and delinquent boys whose behavior at rare times betrayed some vague academic interest was difficult. My goal as teacher of these 16 adolescents was not different from the goal of any other teacher in any other school: to transmit knowledge and facilitate the socialization of children. My role, however, differed somewhat from that of teachers in more typical classroom settings.

This paper is based on an analysis of a teacher's daily anecdotal records and represents an attempt to describe briefly as much of the methodology employed as could be inferred from these records. The classroom behavior of the boys, my role and use of curriculum are the general areas discussed.

These boys were not amenable to ordinary classroom procedures. Their attitudes, values, beliefs and myriad personality disorders made life in any classroom a difficult situation for a teacher and an almost impossible chore for the boys.

They perceived of schoolwork as something sissyish, in line with adult values and unreconcilable with their role as "tough guys." Almost every rule of the class and institution was denounced and tested.

The boys seemed to believe that all adults were negative, mean and selfish. They hated and defied adults and adult values. Members of the staff were referred to in the most profane, hostile terms. At least one third of the vocabulary of the boys was supplied by the slang form of a single noun, modified when necessary to serve as adjective, verb, adverb and conjunction.

They were apathetic, moody, and occasionally dropped their delinquent bravado to express feelings of complete worthlessness. They seemed to feel that they couldn't possibly produce anything worth while; that any productive efforts would be in vain.

They seemed to live from day to day without serious plans or goals for their future. Inquiries about occupational choices were responded to with the almost universal Hawthorne reply, "Man, I want to become a pimp." A few of the boys responded more seriously but not more realistically. Gerry and Sonny wanted to become atomic physicists despite their inability to function in an ordinary classroom. The prospect of putting out any real effort to achieve these goals was improbable as long as they remained on the fantasy level.

Another problem presented by the boys was their wide range of achievement levels and vastly different modes of functioning. . . .

Some of the boys were well attuned to therapeutic phraseology and could reason and argue their way out of nearly anything; for example, "I'm real upset today," or "I'm under a great deal of pressure in therapy right now, so please don't make me do anything."

Another area of difficulty for the accomplishment of educational goals was the lack of any real group cohesiveness. Each boy seemed too encysted in himself to care about such things as group enterprises or group prestige. The boys were even unwilling to share the teacher; frequently several vehemently demanded attention at the same time.

Finally, there was the pecking order. The strong ruled the less strong by virtue of physical prowess.

Each youngster needed to learn that which was in line with his level of functioning, was of interest to him and which he needed in order to stimulate some realistic aspiration. Each needed to learn from the classroom as well as from therapy that

adults and adult values were not all bad. Most important, each needed to accomplish positive, tangible or measurable productivity to belie his belief in his worthlessness. The physical classroom, the teacher-student relationship and the teaching techniques were organized around these presumed needs.

Obviously, typical classroom procedures would be as unsuccessful with these boys now as they had been in the past.

Initially, the room contained two potential working areas. A general craft area was located near the entrance to the room. It contained a large workbench and some basic woodworking tools. The academic area was at the end of the room and consisted of four tables and chairs closely lining the walls, in recognition of the preference of many of the boys to sit with their backs to the wall or off in a corner. I tried to develop a physical plant which took the factors of comfort and control into account.

The activities and equipment of the room were introduced as the boys manifested interests which could be translated into productive classroom activities. Before the end of the semester, an automotive section, complete with tools, books and two automobile engines, was evolved within the craft area. Model airplanes were suspended from the ceiling. Bookcases, made by the boys, lined the walls. A tropical fish unit was set up and carefully maintained. The academic area, too, became meaningful. Texts and workbooks on remedial English and math, algebra, geometry, biology, high school English and social studies filled the bookcases.

A teacher's use of his personality with a group of students is, at least partially, an "intuitive" process. The analysis of class anecdotal records helped me to better understand my attitudes toward the boys and how I transmitted them.

I had seen enough of these types of youngsters improve markedly, in the past, to be optimistic about their abilities and future. I placed as little emphasis as possible on the negative aspects of their behavior and as much as possible on whatever positive areas or achievements existed. With each boy, constant appraisal was made of his academic and social progress. When a youngster did well, I took pains to let the director, the principal, the cottage parents and the youngster's therapist know about it. This was a novel experience for these boys since, in general, attention for misdemeanors was the story of their lives.

I respected the boys and addressed them in terms of normal social amenities —please, thank you, would you mind, etc. Many of my personal likes and dislikes would be freely discussed with any boy curious enough to ask about them. I made many mistakes in working with the boys but was willing to discuss my actions with them, accept criticisms and apologize when I felt I was wrong. My respect for the boys was also transmitted through my expectations of them. I empathized with them but did not exonerate nor accept their asocial behavior. True, they were allowed to operate within a broad framework of activities based on individual interests but the class contained very definite limits. They could move quietly around the classroom, go from project to project, but they could not become so noisy as to disturb others, smoke, leave the class nor enact any aspect of the "pecking order" without serious reprimand or punishment. The boys seemed to know that, if need be, I could control them physically and that my respect for them was not based on fear.

Despite their bravado, the boys frequently asked for T.L.C. (tender, loving care). For example, one day Winny plaintively explained that he had been unable to sleep the night before. I suggested he put his head down on the table and try to rest. I tried to deal with each boy individually, but it was not always possible to spend a lot of time with each; however, a brief nod, smile, or slap on the back as I moved about the room let each know that I was there and concerned.

Although most of the boys in the class were openly aggressive, two were extremely withdrawn. For them, a different atmosphere was created than for the others. I approached them only when they asked me to. When, on occasion, they were irritable, I did not try to squelch their outbursts. I wanted them to discover that nothing terrible happened when a person became somewhat aggressive. I often involved these boys with the others by asking them to help another boy with a subject in which they excelled.

Slowly, the boys came to like me and the classroom. In this atmosphere, certain techniques seemed effective. The boys were encouraged and helped to explore their interests and occupational goals even when these goals were rather fantastic. I slowly helped them modify these goals to make them more realistically attainable. Pertinent information and materials were provided, and a *modus operandi* for goal achievement through activity in the classroom was established.

Although each boy was a unique individual in many ways, there seemed to be only two types of boys academically: those who could handle the work easily (unimpaired learners) but who didn't want to, and those who couldn't handle the work and didn't want to (impaired learners). Sonny had little difficulty in passing four one-year subjects in six months after his attitude toward school changed. Ed, who seemed equally motivated and intelligent, took three months of continuous effort to master fractions.

With those boys who were unimpaired and seemed to be made of "sterner stuff" than the impaired group, a deliberate process of confrontation was instituted. When they used the "I'm disturbed today" routine, I usually asked them if they hoped to solve their emotional problems within the next few years. Invariably, the answer was "Yes." "Fine," I would retort, "then you'll be a healthy person but an unemployed one. How happy do you think you'll be?" The impaired youngsters seemed more convinced of their own worthlessness and this technique was not used with them; rather, they were reminded of whatever progress they had made and were encouraged ad infinitum.

Subject matter, of necessity, was taught individually. There were as many courses as students. For the unimpaired boys I had to relearn geometry, algebra, social studies, English and biology. For the impaired boys, ungraded worksheets in basic skills had to be found or created so that a boy of 16 would not be ridiculed by his peers for using a book labeled "Grade Four."

Attempts to have the boys determine and execute group projects failed; however, the boys were able to sponsor a very successful school dance when I determined the goal and constantly focused each boy's attention and efforts on his specific job. For instance, Capp had to be reminded frequently not to eat all of the chartreuse hors d'oeuvres he had created. A class newspaper which resulted from my "tying together" varied individual interests, as well as the dance, became a source of pride for the boys.

The results of the various examinations at the end of the year seemed to indicate that knowledge had been transmitted to the boys. Eight of them took a total of twelve New York State Regents' examinations. Eleven of these were passed. The rest of the boys had been given achievement tests at the beginning and end of the school year. One boy showed no change. Four showed gains of from one to three years.

In assessing the effect of the classroom and its procedures on the socialization of the boys, it is impossible to divorce the school's influence from the influence of Hawthorne's total milieu. I feel certain, however, that the classroom activities played an important part in changing "Hey, teach!"—the defiant call of the delinquent —to "Hi, Norm!"

Another type of residential program is the therapeutic camp. The Salesmenship Club Boy's Camp at Hawkins, Texas, is an interesting example of therapeutic camping. The club admits delinquent boys between the ages of eight and sixteen, for an average period of eighteen months. These boys live in tents in pioneer fashion and are responsible for much of their own personal comfort and satisfaction. Each group consists of six to ten boys under the supervision of two counselors. In the evening the groups hold a "pow-wow session" around the campfire, when the boys express their feelings and discuss their reality problems. This form of group therapy certainly deviates from the orthodox approach, but has obtained rather startling results.

At the opposite end of the continuum, we would place the University of Michigan Fresh Air Camp, which functions as a training center for graduate students in all disciplines, offering the counselor-student individual supervision and didactic seminars. The campers are referred by social agencies because of problems they have had at school, home, or in the community.

A third approach, which combines both a residential school and a camp program under the title Project Re-ED, is the subject of our next article. This is a demonstration project sponsored by an eight-year National Institute of Mental Health grant, through the cooperative efforts of George Peabody College for Teachers, the State of Tennessee and the State of North Carolina. One of its purposes is to train teachers to staff a residential school with the support of mental health consultants. Although the goals of Re-Ed are limited, the project is stimulating and merits careful study.

How the Re-ED Plan Developed

Nicholas Hobbs

A study of resources for mental health training and research in the South, conducted in 1954 by the Southern Regional Education Board, revealed an acute shortage of facilities for emotionally disturbed children in the region. At that time facilities for residential services for children in all sixteen southern states combined were not sufficient to meet the needs of the least populous state. The situation has improved since the 1954 study, but the problem remains a serious one. In general, emotionally disturbed children are cared for by various inadequate emergency arrangements in the community, or are kept in detention homes, on wards with psychotic adults, or in institutions for the delinquent and the mentally deficient. Where specialized facilities have been built, they are costly and difficult to staff. The problem is nationwide. . . .

In 1956 the principal investigator for Project Re-ED studied programs for disturbed children in Europe. The object of the inquiry was to get ideas that might be useful in the United States. In Glasgow, Scotland, and in a number of communities in France were found patterns that might be adopted to help solve the mental health manpower problem in this country.

For more than twenty-five years Glasgow has had a school psychology service that has grown to impressive dimensions because of distinguished achievement. It is staffed by carefully selected teachers who have been given about two years of on-the-job training and then put to work in one of their eleven guidance clinics, or in their residential treatment center at Nerston, on the outskirts of the city. Nerston was established during World War II to care for children who could not adjust to evacuation and placement in foster homes. After the

war it was continued as a residential treatment center for children who were too disturbed to be cared for by the guidance clinics. Nerston is staffed entirely by teachers called educational psychologists, who teach regular classes as well as care for the children after school and at night in an around-the-clock therapeutic endeavor. There is one psychiatric consultant for the service. The program appears to be effective and has been a stable one for twenty-five years.

In France a much more elaborate program for all kinds of exceptional children, including the emotionally disturbed and delinquent, has been developed. Under the aegis of the *Union Nationale des Associations Régionales pour la Sauvegarde de L'Enfance et de L'Adolescence*—a quasi-public body that coordinates much of the French effort for the welfare of children—new patterns have emerged that are not yet widely known in America. The *Sauvegarde* administers funds, publishes a journal, and sponsors regional and national conferences and congresses. Because of its influence, one finds well conceived facilities for children throughout France. In the absence of an effective program for foster home placement, numerous residential centers are serving various functions. The centers, each with 40 to 60 children, are housed in old chateaux and are staffed largely by *educateurs*, a professional group having no counterpart in the United States. The *educateurs*, of whom there are some 3,000 in France, are carefully selected and trained workers with children. Having some of the skills of the teacher, the social worker, the psychologist, and the recreation worker, the *educateurs* take heavy responsibilities for the operation of observation and treatment centers. They suggest a pattern for a new professional group for mental health and educational programs in the United

Nicholas Hobbs, professor of psychology, Peabody College, is director of Project Re-ED.

States, called, in Project Re-ED, the Teacher-Counselor.

Re-ED had its origins in these early studies. Since then many organizations and individuals have contributed to its development. The first discussions of the possibility of developing residential schools for disturbed children, following roughly these European patterns, took place in the Commission on Mental Health of the Southern Regional Education Board. Several meetings were devoted to the topic, thus initiating the process of shaping the idea for later adoption by two states in the region. The SREB staff has continued to give the project strong support and to assist materially in planning for its realization. After the plan had been debated and found promising in these early discussions, it was presented to the officers of the National Institute of Mental Health, who expressed interest and encouraged the development of a proposal for possible grant support. Drafting a proposal took many months and involved the faculty at Peabody College, the Commissioners of Mental Health of the states of Tennessee and Kentucky (which was an original participant replaced later by North Carolina) and their staffs, and the mental health staff of the Southern Regional Education Board.

Invaluable consultant help was provided continuously by the National Institute of Mental Health. After the proposal was submitted a review committee not only evaluated it but made many useful suggestions for improvement of the plan. In the meantime the Joint Commission on Mental Illness and Health had endorsed the idea as representing a type of experimentation with new patterns of care that should be undertaken in a nation-wide effort to improve mental health services. A grant was approved by the National Mental Health Council in March of 1961. As the plan has moved from the proposal stage to the stage of actual operation it has of course undergone many modifications. The Commissioners of Mental Health of Tennessee and of North Carolina, the Advisory Commis-

sion for the project, the consultants in psychiatry, education, social work, and psychology, and especially the staffs of the two schools, have refined, elaborated, and in some instances creatively altered the initial plan. Re-ED is the product of many people who believed in an idea, and who have worked indefatigably first to discover the possible and then to make the possible an operating reality.

Despite some changes in external form, the following assumptions that guided early planning remain the foundation for the present program:

The problem of providing for emotionally disturbed children is a critical one requiring bold measures. Society will not continue to tolerate the assignment of disturbed children to detention homes, to hospitals for adults, or to institutions for the mentally deficient. The social need for imaginative planning is acute.

The United States does not have and will not be able to train a sufficient number of social workers, psychiatrists, psychologists, and nurses to staff residential psychiatric facilities for children along traditional lines. It will not be possible in the foreseeable future, with the manpower shortage becoming increasingly more acute, to solve the problem of the emotionally disturbed child by adhering to limited patterns. The problem must be redefined if it is to be solved.

For effective work with children the worker's personal attributes weigh more heavily than his professional knowledge and technical skills. Fully adequate programs for the reeducation of emotionally disturbed children can be developed by (1) emphasizing selection of workers, (2) providing condensed, highly specific, functional training, and (3) backstopping the workers' day-by-day activities with a dependable system of consultation by top-level professional personnel.

The model provided by education with its emphasis on health rather than on illness, on teaching rather than on treatment, on learning rather than on fundamental personality reorganization, on the present and the future rather than on the past, on the operation of the total social system of which the child is a part rather than on intrapsychic processes exclusively, may provide an effective as well as feasible approach to the problems of a substantial number of emotionally disturbed children.

ORGANIZATION OF THE PROJECT

Project Re-ED is organized around four semi-autonomous units: the Office of the Principal Investigator, the Training Program in the Department of Special Education of Peabody College, Cumberland House Elementary School in Tennessee, and Wright School in North Carolina. Peabody is the coordinating and fiscal agent for the project, as well as a participating member. The basic grant from the National Institute of Mental Health was made to the College.

THE SCHOOLS

The two schools in Project Re-ED have many characteristics in common, reflecting their commitment to a central idea. Each school also has a number of unique features, reflecting a commitment to planned diversity that capitalizes on local resources and refreshes the project with new ideas.

The two schools are an integral part of the mental health programs of their respective states, being in each instance the responsibility of the Commissioner of Mental Health. Grant funds are paid by Peabody College to the two states, which augment the funds and expend them in accordance with an established budget. The issue of state autonomy, within the general framework of organization and purpose of the project, is underscored here because a main goal of the demonstration is to show that the basic Re-ED plan for residential schools for disturbed children is realistic and practicable, that it can be adjusted to the political and administrative realities and requirements of different state or local governments. The North Carolina

school is 600 miles from the project headquarters, indicating that the ideas of Re-ED are exportable, that they can be put into effect without the daily supervision of the central staff. The goal of the project is not simply to get two schools into operation. The central purposes are to demonstrate that carefully selected teachers backed by consultants can do effective work with disturbed children and that the schools developed in accordance with the plan are viable social institutions, capable of being financed, staffed, and operated independently by any state or community.

The schools are designed to serve forty children of elementary school age, 6 to 12, organized into five groups of eight children each, with a rough division according to age, and with an expectation of about four times as many boys as girls. The children are in residence from Sunday afternoon until Friday afternoon, most of them returning home to their families for the weekend. This arrangement is regarded as exceedingly important since it keeps the family owning the child and the child his family, preventing the alienation that so often occurs with institutionalization of a child. It also provides a needed period of rest and refreshment for the staff. Of course not all children can go home every weekend, and provisions are made for them to continue at school with a modified program.

Two teacher-counselors are responsible for each group of eight children. They are assisted by teacher-counselor trainees, aides, student volunteers, or resource people in art, music, crafts, and physical education. The team of two teacher-counselors, with assistants, is the basic functioning unit for the schools; the team is responsible for the program around-the-clock. One teacher-counselor is responsible for the school day; the other is responsible for the child after school, through the afternoon and night until school time the next day. In the Re-ED plan, heavy emphasis is placed on formal school work, modulated to the needs of each child, on the conviction that school represents one of the two most important concerns of the child, the other being his family.

Schools such as proposed in Project Re-ED should not be thought of as replacements for psychiatric services for children. Indeed, the operation of the school should increase public awareness of the need for other specialized services. It has a clearly complementary function to the residential treatment center which requires the services of the traditional psychiatric team. It should serve as a buffer against hospitalization and as a means of speeding the return to school and community of the child who has been hospitalized for psychiatric reasons.

Project Re-ED is not a sufficient service for all disturbed children. It is seen as one unit in a complex of services that is needed for an optimum community program for disturbed children. Such a complex would include special consulting services for the regular classroom teacher, special classes in the public schools, day-care centers, child guidance clinics, residential schools for disturbed children (like Project Re-ED), acute and intensive treatment centers for disturbed children, and long-term care for severely disturbed children who do not respond to other forms of treatment.

THE CAMPING PROGRAM

Camping in Re-ED started out as a way to introduce variety into the year's activities but it has developed at Cumberland House into a major new dimension of the total program and may be continued the year around.

An opportunity to experiment with camping was provided by the availability of the H. G. Hill Camp, owned by Peabody College. The camp is located about fifteen miles from the school on a wooded bluff on the Harpeth River. Four cabins, a dining hall, and several smaller buildings constitute a base for operation, but the activities are centered primarily in the woods

and on the river. The College has renovated the camp and has leased it to the State of Tennessee for use in Project Re-ED.

The entire program at the camp is built around purposeful activities worked out by groups of children and their teacher-counselors. All groups build for themselves comfortable and attractive campsites in the woods, carry out nature study projects, plan and go on trips, and do some school related work. There is a minimum of formal scheduling at the camp. The children rise with the sun, work on meaningful tasks the day through, and get to bed early without need of persuasion.

In the summer of 1963, a group of older boys (who called themselves the Confederate Aviators) lived all summer in the woods in a primitive camp that grew quite comfortable with handmade furniture, ovens, etc., scorning the comforts of a cabin. Another group (the Bobcats) started in a cabin and gradually moved to their campsite in the woods. They built a rope bridge, over a sink-hole, of which they were immensely proud. A mixed group of girls and younger boys (the Whippoorwills) built one of their tents, appropriately, on a high platform in the trees, and won the admiration of all. One group started a fossil collection, another studied mushrooms, a third used river clay to mold and carve figures.

The activities of the camp have great appeal so that motivation for most children stays high. The tasks tend to have intrinsic rewards and punishments; if all members of a group do their assigned tasks well, the group has a good meal, if not, the meal may not be so good. There are no scheduled games, tournaments, awards, or elections. What the children do grows naturally out of the setting in which they are living. Teaching and learning are a continuous process. There is some formal instruction in reading and arithmetic but this too is tied to camping problems. Since the campsites are widely scattered, the groups are more cohesive than in the regular school year. The entire operation has a purpose-fulness and serenity that captures both children and staff.

Camping is a less central part of the program in the North Carolina school at the present time. Because of its unusual setting with an expanse of pine woods on its property, Wright School can combine its regular program with camping activities. The woods are used for cookouts, camp-craft instruction, nature study, and over-night camping. Again, the diversity of program within an overall pattern is seen as a realistic and desirable development, providing other states and communities with an invitation to adapt the plan to local circumstances and to invent new ways of realizing the basic objective.

THE TEACHER-COUNSELOR

The teacher-counselor is the central person in Project Re-ED. It is he who works with the children, at school, at play, at night, in camp, on trips to a museum, to a swimming pool, to a state park, to a concert. He is teacher and counselor and friend. He needs many skills: how to teach fourth grade arithmetic, how to help a child with a reading problem, how to manage a group of eight children in the evening after dinner, how to pitch a tent, pack a canoe, make a monkey-bridge, how to calm a child who has lost control of himself and comfort a child who is afraid or despairing, how to lead group singing, how to throw clay on a potter's wheel, how to operate a teaching-machine, how to understand a psychiatrist, psychologist, or social worker, how to help a teacher plan for the return of a child, how to talk constructively with a distraught or distrustful or overdependent parent, how to do all this and many other things as well. It is a demanding and truly professional role. There is no greater responsibility than for the welfare of a child. The working day is often long, with no counting of hours; weekend work is frequent; it is a year-round job; concern is ever-present.

To be successful a teacher-counselor must have a deep commitment to children. He must value service to others above gain for himself. He gets his main satisfactions from seeing a child open himself up to experience, gain some control, grow in competence and trust, and find some measure of joy in the world. He must reckon constructively with the fact that he will work each day where stress is high, where a child or a colleague or perhaps he himself will not be able to live up always to the demands of the situation. He will be paid reasonably well, about 15% more than he would make on a twelve-month job as a public school teacher, but anyone who would take the job primarily for financial gain would be foolish, perhaps irresponsible. In the face of a demanding, draining life, he must be a person of inner richness, who is able to re-create himself from sources external to the job. Integrity in human relationships, equanimity of spirit, an abundance of sheer physical stamina, considerable trust in self, an ability to give and receive affection yet stand being hated day after day, a well of good humor, an affinity for joyousness—these are some of the requirements for being a teacher-counselor.

Of the requirements listed above a few can be taught but most cannot. A person can be taught how to teach reading, tie a clove-hitch, and talk with a psychiatrist, but that's about all; the important things in the role of the teacher-counselor are the things that he has learned in the living of all of his life. Thus selection is most important in the making of a teacher-counselor.

Selection of the first teacher-counselors for training at Peabody was done on the basis of the applicant's record and in some instances on interviews and visits to his school. Now that the two Re-ED schools are in operation it will be possible to put into effect a selection procedure envisioned in the initial planning of the project. Applicants who have passed a preliminary screening will be invited to live and work in one of the schools for a two-week period.

This will give them an opportunity to see if the work feels right and the staff an opportunity to judge their suitability for the task. Heavy emphasis will be placed on self-selection in this new plan.

The training program at Peabody leads to a Master of Arts degree in special education. It requires three quarters of graduate work. In the past, trainees have spent six months in course work at the College and three months on internships in residential treatment centers in the United States, Scotland, England, and Denmark. The internships in varied settings have been an important source of ideas for the programs of the schools. Starting with the academic year 1963–64, the training program will be changed to take advantage of the ongoing Re-ED program at Cumberland House in Nashville. The internship will be spread over the three-quarter period. The trainee will combine didactic instruction at Peabody with supervised work as an assistant teacher-counselor at Cumberland House. The program will be enriched by seminars, visits from local and national consultants, attendance at professional meetings, and visits to outstanding institutions serving disturbed children.

Trainees receive a fellowship in the amount of $3600 plus $400 for each dependent up to a $4400. They must pay their own tuition. The Re-ED schools in Tennessee and North Carolina are now substantially staffed. Thus graduates of the training program, as well as experienced teacher-counselors from the staffs of the two schools, will be available for positions in other programs similar to Re-ED, to initiate Re-ED-type programs, or to serve in public schools, day-care centers, and hospitals.

Re-ED represents an explicit break with the predominant philosophy of developing professional people in our society, a philosophy that minimizes individual differences and relies most heavily on extended and expensive periods of training to assure competence. The Re-ED position represents an effort to test the hypothesis that, in providing professional services to children, a substantial measure of competence can be achieved by maximizing the contribution of individual differences while limiting professional training to a calculated minimum. It is a tactical stance that can clearly be justified in the light of the acute and widespread shortages of personnel in the service professions in the United States today. It is also an hypothesis that can and should be tested not only in programs for disturbed children but also in other areas (in mental retardation, in care of the aged, in treatment of chronic psychoses) where the manpower shortage is such that neglect of people is a consequence.

THE PROCESS OF REEDUCATION

The best way to describe what is meant by reeducation is to be explicit about the goals of the program and the means by which the goals are expected to be achieved.

The goals of Re-ED schools are purposely limited. There is no expectation of a radical reorganization of the child, such as might be achieved by intensive and prolonged psychotherapy. The objective is to help the child, the family, the school, and the community to achieve just sufficient reorganization with respect to the requirements of each from the other to make the whole system work in a reasonably satisfactory fashion and without undue stress. These limited goals are sought by the following means:

1. Restoring to the child some trust in adults, some competences to meet demands of family, school, and friends, some confidence in self, and some joy in the morrow.

2. Helping a child maintain normal progress in school when possible and providing him with remedial work in reading, arithmetic, and other subjects as needed to arrest the downward trend in school achievement so often observed in disturbed children.

3. Mobilizing resources in the child's home community in the interest of the

child, especially by giving assistance to his family.

4. Assisting the staff of the child's regular school to understand his problem and to make such reasonable adjustments in the school program as may be required to make possible an early and successful return of the child to his own school.

5. Helping the child to unlearn some specific habits that cause rejection by family, school, and friends, and to acquire some specific habits that make him more acceptable to the people who are important in his life.

6. Helping the child gain some cognitive control over his behavior by helping him identify specific goals and reviewing each day as it is lived to identify sources of satisfaction and dissatisfaction and ways of behaving likely to bring more success to the next day.

7. Helping a child to achieve a sense of belonging in his home community, to perceive favorably and respond to the institutions provided by society to assist him in growing up: the schools, churches, libraries, health services, parks, museums, recreational areas, theaters, youth programs, and other similar agencies.

WORK WITH THE CHILD'S FAMILY

Work starts with a child's family at the time a child is being considered for admission and continues throughout his stay and for a followup period after discharge. Placement in a Re-ED school can be most useful at a time of crisis in the life of a child, to help the child get himself functioning more adequately and to help the family, the school, and the community mobilize their resources for his earliest possible return to a reasonably normal living situation. The family is pivotal in the matrix of forces that sustains a child and makes it possible for him to develop. Thus a major emphasis in Re-ED is placed on work with the family. On the faculty of each school there is a full-time, fully qualified psychiatric social worker. Her major responsibility is to help

mobilize the resources of the child's home community to provide such help to the family as may be needed to get it operating above threshold with respect to the needs of the child, in order that he may return home as soon as possible. Ordinarily the social worker tries to find an agency or a qualified person in the child's community who will take responsibility for helping the family. In some instances, as when a family is too demoralized to be able to care for the child, the agency is requested to help find an alternate solution, such as placement in a foster home. The social worker also plays a central role in the selection of children for admission to the school, in interpreting the school program to parents, in helping teacher-counselors locate community resources needed in the child's program, and in planning for a child's return to his home.

WORK WITH THE CHILD'S SCHOOL

The child has two major concerns in our society. The first and most important is his family. The second is his school. In many mental health programs for children there is a large gap between the program of the specialized agency helping the child and the program of the child's regular school. In Re-ED an effort is being made to bridge this gap by the development of what is believed to be a new professional role and position, the liaison teacher. The liaison teacher is a fully trained teacher-counselor with several years of experience in public school work. His full-time responsibility is to articulate the efforts of the Re-ED school and the child's regular school in order to ease transitions and to make the Re-ED program of maximum help to the child in furthering his personal adjustment and his educational development. The liaison teacher visits the child's school prior to his admission and finds what kinds of behaviors were hindering the child's normal development in school, what remedial instruction he may need, and what he must achieve while at Re-ED to keep up or catch up with his class. The liaison teacher arranges for visits by the child to his regular school after enrollment in Re-ED to keep him in touch with people there and to keep alive the expectation of an early return. Finally, he visits the school to help make arrangements for the child's return, the objective being to encourage the school to make an extra effort at a time when the child is on the up-grade rather than to spend extra effort only when a child is getting into trouble. Re-ED schools operate in an area midway between the educational and the mental health services of a state; education is the central mechanism for achieving both mental health and educational ends. This position is most clearly exemplified in the work of the liaison teacher. . . .

LENGTH OF STAY

The Re-ED schools are designed to provide a short-term, intensive reeducational experience for a child in a period of crisis. It is expected that children will be in residence from four to six months. Some children may stay for two months, some may stay for two years, but the average stay should be relatively brief. A four-month's experience in a residential school makes sense only if one appreciates objectives of the Re-ED program. The purpose is not to effect a "cure" or a profound reorganization of the child's character and personality, but rather to give the child a special 24-hour-a-day environment in which he can grow in trust, competence, confidence, and joy, and to give the child's family, school, and community an opportunity to regroup their forces in the interest of the child's development in a relatively normal setting. Re-ED assumes that normal life circumstances are more conducive to healthy growth than is an institutional placement; it further assumes that there are occasions when a period of partial disengagement may be good for a child and for his family, school, and community as well. Children normally go home on weekends, a procedure adopted to prevent the alienation that sometimes occurs with removal

from the home. The schools often set four months as an expected period of stay to provide child and staff alike with a clear goal for work; but this is a tactical arrangement made to ensure full use of time and can be modified in either direction as may be indicated by progress of the child or by improved conditions in his home and school. . . .

COSTS AND FINANCING

The project is made possible by a grant of approximately two million dollars for an eight-year period by the National Institute of Mental Health. The grant provides funds for the operating costs of the two schools, for the training program at Peabody including fellowships for approximately 60 teacher-counselors, and for research and evaluation. Each state is responsible for providing, furnishing, and maintaining the physical plant for its school. It is difficult to estimate the cost of land and buildings for a Re-ED school since the circumstances in the two states in the program are quite different. However, the value of the investments made would be between $300,000 and $500,000. Each state will contribute to the annual operating costs of its school the approximate amount it would pay to maintain a child in an established facility, such as an institution for the mentally retarded. This amount has been set by the two states at $50,000 a year to care for an average population of forty children. In the last three terminating years of the project, each state will assume additional responsibility for operating costs at the rate of 25% for the first year, 50% for the second year, and 75% for the final year. If the project is judged to be successful each state at that time would assume full responsibility for operating costs.

The situation in the two schools has not yet stabilized to the point where it is possible to get a firm figure for the cost of maintaining a child in the program. The staffs of the two schools are approaching full strength but the population of children is currently (September 1963) about half the planned capacity of the schools. This means of course that the per diem costs are higher than they will be when the schools are operating to capacity. Experience thus far suggests that it will be possible to realize the initial estimate of a cost per day per child of from $12 and $15. . . .

SUMMARY

In order for a community to develop an adequate treatment program for emotionally disturbed children, it will need an array of coordinated services that include the school, but also extend well beyond the responsibility of the school. A model program should include a diagnostic and treatment center; assistance to the regular classroom teacher through consultation and program modification; special classes staffed by special educators; psychiatric day-care facilities for children who have intact homes but are too disturbed for the school programs; therapeutically oriented detention homes for children who are in a crisis; residential schools, hospitals, and camps for children who need intensive treatment in a milieu setting; and finally, a custodial institution for children who are unable to respond to intensive treatment. Such coordinated services would make it possible to give the child the type of treatment he needs, rather than forcing the child to adjust to the type of service that is available. It is encouraging to know that a few communities are planning for these varied and necessary services.

5

How Do You Manage
These Children?

The teachers a child has can make the difference in how he sees himself and how he grows. Of all the people aside from parents, it is the school people, especially teachers and classmates, who help or hinder his mental health.

The school is more than a community. It is a child's image of society. It has people and places that represent safety or danger, growth or regression, excitement or boredom. The child has contemporaries whose opinions and regard usually mean more to him than those of other people. There are his underlings, the younger or the weaker members of his class. And, as in any political or social structure, towering above him in layer upon layer of increasing power and decreasing personal acquaintance are "the authorities"—pedagogues and principals. They are the law, the judgers, the evaluators who largely determine one's view of oneself, as well as the way one is seen by others.

To fail in this first society is to start with a mind set toward failure. Whether one is destined to become president or pauper, the first total experience of society determines the child's perception and is his springboard to life in the community.

The children we are concerned with may enter school already unable in one or more ways to cope with society. Perhaps they are not ready yet for the complexity of living outside the small community of home; perhaps they are ready intellectually but not socially; perhaps their patterns of fulfilling their needs, of handling frustration, or of postponing present satisfactions for future goals (which very probably are not their own personal goals) are such that they are not acceptable to school authorities and/or peers. Some children come to school functioning adequately; but either school itself or home life, or both in combination, induce such distress that the process of social growth is arrested. Indeed, if the impact be too threatening, a child may revert to infantile behavior.

If his difficulties show up in behavior, the school will know them soon. The encompassing phrase "character disorder of childhood" indicates a multitude of behaviors from stealing, breaking, fighting, and spitting to lying and rudeness—behaviors that might be appropriate for a baby but are not acceptable to school society. If the child's conflict is held inside, his distress may be more difficult to determine, emerging perhaps in physical symptoms, speech or learning disorders, withdrawal, excessive shyness, absenteeism, and tardiness, or excessive strain at tests and grading periods.

However the disturbance appears, whether it be deep or temporary, it is the school's responsibility to note it and try to understand it and deal with it, for the sake of the individual child as well as the society which the school community represents.

We expect the majority of students who review this book to turn to this chapter eagerly, because most of them wonder about their ability to control their feelings when confronted by irritating, explosive behavior over a period of time. There is a hidden hope that these articles will reveal inner secrets of discipline and management, which can be digested like a vitamin pill, to provide protection against the dangers of teaching.

Unfortunately, magic works only for children, not adults. To make matters more complex, the intellectual absorption of psychological knowledge is rarely useful in an emotionally charged situation. The human animal is designed to react first and think later. This is true for adults, as well as for emotionally disturbed children who live in a fiery world of conflict and possess a short fuse of control. Where does this leave the students who are looking for specific techniques and solutions? The very best we can offer is exposure to new dimensions of behavioral conflict and its management, which previously have been out of their awareness. Thus, with intensive experience and excellent supervision, the student will find that his focus on specific techniques and pet solutions gives way to a broad analysis of the dynamic interactions of individual and group forces acting on a particular child (schizophrenic, neurotic) with a particular history, in a particular setting (schoolroom, playground, psychiatric ward) during a particular period of a day. This implies that the management of behavior is an individual matter determined by understanding the multiple forces operating within and on the child rather than by implementing a list of rules and regulations.

The first article, "Psychoanalytic Aspects of Discipline," by Sperling, clarifies the abundant confusion about the Freudian view of discipline and explains why many uninformed people feel that psychoanalysis is designed to free the impulses and to soften self-controls to the point that an uninhibited child flaunts discipline and conformity. Perhaps this grossly distorted view of psychoanalytic theory is fostered by adults who refute the Freudian interpretation of human behavior because it seems too threatening to them. If they can succeed in relegating this theory to the ranks of the foolish, they feel protected against looking beyond their own moral interpretations, which label all behavior as either right or wrong, acceptable or unacceptable.

For teachers of emotionally disturbed children, the understanding of behavior must reach into an awareness of the unconscious motives and the deep emotional patterns which develop over the years between parents and child. Sperling illustrates the parent-child interaction by showing how acting-out behavior of children is unconsciously stimulated and encouraged by parents. For example, if parents have much difficulty controlling their own impulses, they will find it equally as difficult to help their child control his impulses. Unless parents can tolerate tensions without repression or acting out, they are unable to offer the child an example which should lead to self-control. A variation of this problem occurs when one parent who is unable to express a forbidden impulse unconsciously sanctions this behavior in his child. Unless this parent participates in treatment, any attempt to work with the child usually brings only marginal improvement.

Psychoanalytic Aspects of Discipline

Melitta Sperling

Not only to the general public, but also to psychiatrists and even psychoanalysts, is the concept of discipline enmeshed in considerable confusion. Lay critics of psychoanalysis have based their opposition among other things, on the assumption that psychoanalysis aims at the elimination of disciplinary controls, with a consequent deterioration of the moral fibre of the individual. To "lose one's inhibitions" is considered by dilettantes to be the frivolous aim of psychoanalytic therapy and psychoanalysis is in this vein made the butt of numerous jokes.

The need for clarification of the dynamics of discipline as viewed from the standpoint of psychoanalytic theory and practice is of utmost importance in the present phase of child analysis, when therapeutic techniques have to be used in the handling not only of the classically inhibited patient, but also with the patient whose behavior disturbance is characterized by a *lack of inhibition*. Historically, psychoanalytic techniques were applied to the neurotic for whom the cathartic method was employed as a means of eliciting the repressed material. In the handling of disorders involving uninhibited (undisciplined) behavior of children, we have learned to use modified psychoanalytic techniques based on the understanding of the therapeutic role of the analyst who functions as a support to the child's ego and where the treatment method is not the acting out and release of repressed impulses but rather the integration of conflicting impulses into the ego, and a strengthening of its synthetic function.

Discipline has been equated with a repression of instinctual demands and has

From Melitta Sperling, "Psychoanalytic Aspects of Discipline," *The Nervous Child,* IX, No. 2 (1951), 174–185. Reprinted by permission.

implicitly been repudiated as a component of sterile educational methods. Liberation of instincts is equated with lack of discipline and is erroneously regarded as the aim of psychoanalytic therapy. True discipline requires that the instinctual energy be at the service of the individual so that he is not afraid to use his impulses, and is independent of the pressure of the environment (parents, teachers) in the control of his impulses. When this is achieved, we have an internalization of superego commands, resulting in real discipline and personality growth. Psychoanalysis does not regard the release of impulses as a way of life, rather it aims at a liberation of impulses bound in repression so that they are made available to the individual for use in his life's pursuits.

It seems to me that the core of confusion regarding discipline lies in the fact that the defenses against repressed impulses (aggressive and sexual) and particularly reaction formation are looked upon as representing discipline. In reaction formation there is a transformation of the repressed impulses, usually into the opposite of the original instinctual drive, as for instance, over-concern for cleanliness as a compensation for the wish to be dirty, extreme kindness as the disguised wish to be sadistic. The person is constantly on guard against the return of the repressed temptation and uses up his energy in order to maintain the repression. In lifting the inhibitions through analysis, the repressed energy is made available to the individual who in the course of treatment has developed sufficient confidence in his ability to maintain control, so that he can either suppress these impulses consciously or use them on a sublimated level.

Some of the modern trends in education and pediatrics reflect the misleading application of the concept of freedom, namely, release from discipline, e.g., in the exaggerated permissiveness of the progressive schools, nurseries and in the self-demand system for infants. In abandoning rigidity and authoritarianism, the tendency has been to abandon all restraint and, consequently, unduly severe responsibilities have been imposed, particularly on the younger child who needs to feel that there is a stronger person to support him in his struggle with his own impulses. The child feels safer when there is a ceiling to his impulses and becomes anxious when his forbidden impulses seek release. To give in to the child's demand is easier and pleasanter for the parent who unconsciously feels that the child could not possibly tolerate the tensions which he has himself not mastered. The parents through identification with the child subtly transmit their fear or unwillingness to tolerate the force of their own impulses. Such parents may encourage in their child, the lawlessness which is forbidden to them as adults and which they act out unconsciously in the child. Case histories provide ample material to illustrate the provocation of the child by the parent to engage in destructive acts. The parent in such a case usually does not mete out punishment appropriate to the offense, but punishes the child for something inconsequential.

Where the mother has no faith in her ability to control her own (objectionable) impulses, she can have little expectation that the child can achieve control. Only absence of fear from one's own impulses and ability for self-control make it possible for parents and educators to give leadership to the child. The ability to tolerate the frustrating tensions in the early training periods may be viewed from the standpoint of the normal expectation set up by a mother who feels confident that even the young child can tolerate some measure of instinctual discomfort. She will then not fall back into over-protective pampering. The personality of parents and educators who themselves are afraid of their impulses is recognized in the undue harshness with which they ruthlessly suppress manifestations of impulses in children because they represent a threat to themselves; there is a fear in the adult that the act of the child may provoke a break-through of their own repressed impulses. The strict parents and judges are those who fear themselves and mete out punishment in accordance with the degree of panic elicited by the original feeling as reflected in the offender. To punish severely is to keep the impulse adequately repressed.

The inconsistency of undue severity and undue permissiveness reflects the weakness of the ego of the parents. Undue permissiveness and leniency of many parents is not interpreted by the child as a sign of love or respect for its democratic rights. On the contrary, the child rightly perceives this attitude as an indication of weakness in the parent and a certain lack of concern for the child. In the struggle to achieve true discipline, namely control from within not from the outside forces, there has to be a positive identification with the restraining or prohibiting personality. In order to help the child to achieve this, it is necessary, as a first step in transmitting standards of discipline, to strengthen and support his immature ego in its efforts to tolerate the tensions of the instinct without immediate release. It is in this area that so many parents fail.

It is also in this area of the early training of the child that the insight gained from psychoanalysis is of the utmost importance. While it is not possible to give parents a blueprint which would tell them how to handle each specific problem in a specific way, we can give to the parents and educators a basic understanding of the child's emotional struggles and a dynamic orientation toward the problem of discipline.

It was left to the genius of Freud to discover and to formulate for us, first in reconstruction from the analysis of adults and later from direct observations on children, the basic dynamic concepts of child development. This has effected a complete reorientation in child psychology with regard to the role of the instinctive urges in the development of the child. Psychoanalysis has shown that these innate drives are of the utmost importance in shaping the child's personality and character. Psychoanalysis has further taught us that the personality development of the child depends largely upon the interplay of these internal forces with the forces coming from the environment, particularly those coming from the most important people of the child's environment, namely his parents; in short, the significance of the parent-child relationship for the personality structure of the child. This is not to be understood however, in the sense that the child merely mirrors the parental attitudes like a neutral agent but rather that each child reacts to his environment in a specific way, dependent upon a complexity of factors, internal and external ones, of which the child's emotional relationship with the parents reflected in the degree of his security is a most important one.

It is not possible within the framework of this paper to give a complete psychoanalytic exposé of child development, but it will be necessary to mention at least some important facts. From a dynamic point of view, the fusion of the two fundamental instincts—sex and aggression—is most important. These two instincts combine forces, thereby producing the characteristic manifestations of each of the child's developmental phases, eventually leading him into maturity. Any disturbance of the proper fusion of these instincts create severe disturbances in the development of the child. From this it becomes clear that the proper handling of the aggressive and sexual impulses in children are of paramount importance. The fusion of sexual impulses with aggression makes it possible for the child to assert his rights to the possession of his love-objects and for the mastery of reality in general. Without the admixture of aggression, sexuality would be ineffective; passivity and weak object relationships with impotence of the individual would be

the result. On the other hand an insufficient admixture of sexual (libidinal) impulses to aggression would manifest itself in destructive and uncontrollable tendencies, making the child anti-social and criminal. It is precisely in the areas of sexuality and aggression where parents and educators make the most harmful blunders.

How much expression of such impulses to allow and how much to deny and when to allow and when to curb is one of the most difficult tasks for parents and one in which even the most well-meaning parents will err unless they have a dynamic understanding and are not too much disturbed by their own emotional conflicts. There is this Scylla and Charybdis in the training of the child where indulging the child without restraining his instinctual demands, will make him unfit for living in a social group and a parasite and menace to society. Or, too early and too severe restrictions by setting up massive repressions, will deprive the child of the energy which he needs for adequate functioning.

Yet the task of the parents in the education of the child in our society is to enable the child to tolerate a certain amount of frustration and also a necessary degree of control of impulses so that the child can live in a group and in conformity with required standards. Failure to achieve this essential adjustment of the child, is a phenomenon so very frequent now that many child analysts have stated that child neuroses are disappearing in favor of severe behavior disorders and child delinquency. Parents who themselves do not accept and are unwilling to conform with the standards of our society are unable to achieve this in their children. Particularly difficult for the child is a situation where each parent takes a different attitude. In such a case the child behaves as if pulled all the time into opposite directions.

Tolerance for the expression of hostility and manifestations of infantile sexuality in children is very limited in parents who have difficulty in conceiving that their own offspring should at times hate them and should want to be destructive and dirty. This is even so with many of the so-called progressive parents who have an intellectual acceptance of these expressions but reject them emotionally because they experience them as a danger and threat to their own repressed, objectionable impulses. This rejection may be masked by a liberal use of terminology and lengthy technical explanations given to the children and by what would appear to be free and uninhibited behavior. Yet the child is not deceived by the pseudo-freedom but very keenly senses the parental anxieties which are a result of incomplete repressions. Children often feel seduced by their parents' behavior, for instance, the indiscriminate bodily display in which many parents indulge for "the sake of the child," "so that he will not be bashful" or the close physical contact which many parents maintain even with older children under the slogan "love your child." Such practices only over-stimulate and increase the child's own anxiety and certainly do not support him in the struggle with his own impulses.

One mother, who had difficulty in disciplining her 12-year-old son, was amazed to find that her son experienced taking showers together as a seduction. Even then she could not get herself to frankly tell him that this was not proper, but would try to avoid it by excusing herself with a headache. She had found nothing wrong with his affectionate kissing her on the mouth and in this situation also resorted to excuses, such as he shouldn't do it because of lipstick. Another mother, who complained that her 3½-year-old son would not allow her any privacy, was astounded to find that it was really she herself who did not allow him to have any privacy. She was a woman with very strong anal impulses, and would not allow her son to use the bathroom alone. She was startled to find how well he understood and respected her privacy when she allowed him to have his. . . .

For a real understanding and acceptance of the child's instinctual nature, not only an intellectual, but an emotional acceptance of psychoanalytic concepts, is necessary. Without this, much of the behavior of the child, especially when it is motivated by unconscious drives, remains unintelligible and inaccessible to change. It is obvious that child training and education and pedagogy in general, have gained and have still much more to gain from psychoanalysis. This does not mean that psychoanalysis is to take the place of ordinary child rearing. Psychoanalysis cannot substitute for this, not only for practical but also for theoretical reasons. Psychoanalysis is a method of investigation and treatment of the mentally sick. Training and discipline however, are methods for the healthy child who is still in the process of growth. Through correct application of psychoanalytical thinking, training and discipline should be practiced so that the child can remain healthy during these formative processes and yet with the understanding help of his parents and educators, acquire the internal controls and the inner freedom, which are necessary to make him a happy child and later a mature adult. . . .

Eight-year-old Martin was a severe behavior problem, a terror in school and in the neighborhood. His mother suffered from a functional heart condition which she attributed to the excitement which Martin caused her. At home he was rather well-behaved and affectionate with his mother and his three-year-younger brother. Psychoanalytic investigation revealed that Martin was acting out his unconscious, very intense resentment of his mother with his teachers. In this way, he managed (similar to the way a phobic would) to live comparatively free from anxiety with the real objects of his hostility. In this case, guidance of the mother alone, who was willing and cooperative, would have been insufficient, without the child's understanding of the unconscious motive for his behavior. It was possible to interpret comparatively easily to the child, why he was acting in this way, and with the changed attitude of the mother, who allowed Martin to verbalize some of his feelings regarding the brother, the vicious cycle could be reversed.

In another, on the surface, very similar situation, the dynamics were somewhat different and required more intensive work, especially with the mother. Eight-year-old Robert was constantly in trouble with the neighbors and in school, but he was also disobedient and difficult at home. The mother claimed that she could get him to do things only with corporal punishment. Robert, who to some degree was openly expressing his hostility towards his younger brother and his resentment of his mother, was also a nail-biter and although of superior intelligence, not able to apply himself in school. He was a very insecure child who felt rejected by his mother. It was brought out that his mother had identified Robert with her husband in the traits which she resented very much in him and punished in her child, using Robert as a substitute for her husband. The marriage was unsatisfactory. The mother was unconsciously castrating both her husband and Robert, while the younger boy was spared because he submitted passively to her. Robert tried to resolve his difficulties in a masochistic fashion. Some very insecure children develop such an attitude as a reaction to the unpredictable and explosive behavior of the mother, who in excitement threatens to leave the child, give him away, kill herself, etc. Through their provocative or negativistic behavior they try to bring on the very reaction in the parents that they fear most. They have an unconscious need to "make" them lose control and the parents usually comply very promptly. The parents as a result of their own helplessness, now try to assert their control over the child at all costs. When this happens the parents have lost the battle because the child now unconsciously operates by the masochistic formula, "I must be in control of the situation. So they can't do anything to me unless I want them to." This control over the parents is then proven by "I can get them angry when I want to and even though they

punish me, it is because I want them to." There is no way out of this vicious cycle for either child or parent unless they are helped to recognize why and how they got into it and unless the parents are willing to make the first step to stop it. It is a difficult situation for the parents who expect the child to change instantly while the child from his previous experience has learned to mistrust the stability of the parents and will try through provocation to test them again and again until he is convinced. Psychoanalytic insight made it possible to recognize the different underlying dynamics and mechanisms used by these two children and to resolve them, although on surface observation the two cases appeared to be very similar.

Another typical difficult situation for parents and therapists, yet inevitable in the course of therapeutic re-education of a child, is the transitory phase of the freeing of repressed, destructive energy in the treatment of the neurotically inhibited child. In such a case the analyst sometimes has to take over the role of the parents in order to achieve at a belated date with the child what his real parents failed to achieve. Anna Freud, in discussing the technique of child analysis states that the child analyst in some cases also has educational functions which should be carried out, preferably in conjunction with the parents. In order to get the child ready for this, a part of the neurosis or character deformation first has to be removed. This implies work with and transformation of the unconscious of the child for which neither parents nor educators are equipped and for which the therapist himself requires special training. This makes it obvious that our ordinary means of education are not sufficient in such cases.

The analyst has to be able to establish a relationship with the child which enables the child to make a positive identification with his analyst in the important therapeutic aspects and to be willing to accept discipline from him. Only then, will the analyst be able to convey the feeling to the child that the child can tolerate his destructive impulses in consciousness without having to act them out instantly. There seems to be a naive belief that psychoanalytic therapy with a child is permission given by the analyst to the child to act out all of his impulses. If this were so, such a therapy would certainly not only not help the child, but would increase his internal and external difficulties. Being at the mercy of his impulses, he would only get into more serious conflicts with his environment in his attempts to act them out. The child must feel that the analyst, while understanding his urges and his need to release them, will stand by and not let him be overwhelmed by them. If the child does not feel safeguarded in this way by his analyst, he will be anxious and distrustful, looking upon the analyst as a person who seduces him into being "bad" and thus getting him into conflict with himself and his environment. Also the child always, and rightly so, interprets complete permissiveness of the adult, as weakness, and as a result may become increasingly destructive in order to test how far he can go without being stopped. Every analyst has had the experience in the treatment of children that the analyst's permissiveness is felt as a threat by the child. The child, like the adult patient, wants the analyst to be as afraid as the child himself is, of his impulses, so that the analyst will not insist upon bringing these dangerous impulses to the fore. The analyst must not fail in this test because it is this specific experience which so many children have never had in actual life with their parents who are afraid of their child's impulses.

Misinterpretation of psychoanalytic principles and mistaking an intermediary phase of treatment for the goal of analysis, led to such attitudes in education as held for instance by Neill, who advocates complete abandoning of inhibitions and unrestrained behavior for children. There are cases in which for purposes of therapy it may be necessary for the therapist to withstand the incessant provocations of the child, which are aimed to break down the

therapist so that he finally will become angry and retaliate, and thus confirm the child's belief that all adults are the same, unreliable, sadistic and punitive and that therefore the child's anti-social behavior is justified and need not be changed. . . .

What seems to me the basic therapeutic principle here as well as in any psychoanalytically oriented psychotherapy, is the fact that the therapist has to prove himself to the child as a person different from anyone else the child has known before. He must be not afraid to allow nor to restrict if necessary, but at any rate one who understands the child and the unconscious motivation for this behavior and who can be patient enough to tolerate the child's behavior, so that through him the child eventually can be helped to understand his own behavior and to change it actively. Parents of course often have a valid cause when they complain, "You only treat the child, but I have to live with him," but while the parents' plight is a difficult one, we must remind them that what the child is today is in most cases the result of years of faulty upbringing and that the parents themselves have a very hard time changing even their most obvious attitudes towards the child.

In fact, I have often marvelled at how many children change through treatment, in spite of their parents. I think that this is probably due to the fact that the identifications in children are not too rigidly established and that the child therefore can still modify these, or establish new ones if a suitable object is presented. With younger children it is desirable to provide these suitable objects for identification in the child's parents and therefore, work with the parents, especially in behavior and disciplinary problems of the young child, is the treatment of choice. But even with older children and adolescents, it is sometimes necessary and possible through psychoanalytic treatment of the parent, to modify the child's identification with this parent by turning him into a more suitable love-object for the child. . . .

The following excerpt describes the teacher: the teacher with some types of emotionally disturbed children, the teacher's own problems and image of his or her job. The selection does not attempt to define the teacher's job; nor the teacher's role in all its complexity; nor the teaching process per se. It attempts to give a set of pictures of the teacher who confronts a class, especially when that class contains disturbed children. Long and Newman look at the demands made upon a teacher, his reactions to these demands and the consequent effect on the children being taught.

The Teacher and His Mental Health
Nicholas J. Long and Ruth G. Newman

Considering the contradictory concepts included under the image of a good teacher, it is little wonder that a teacher is confused about his role. Confusion is often a step on the road to mental health, but it never is, in itself, mentally healthy. At this moment, many teachers seem to be caught in a trap of confusion, not knowing which way is out. It would help them on their journey to define mental health in a most specific sense. For there is no question that a teacher's mental health is of primary importance. His influence over the developing personalities of the children in his charge is a basic determinant of the future he creates, and there are subtle as well as obvious reasons for his influence—more of that later. But let it be emphasized that it is a bad mistake to define mental health as the same for all people. Mental health is a statistical average to which everyone ought to try to conform, not as a norm; it is the quality of mind, body, and attitude that, on the whole, usually leads a person to feel reasonably comfortable—that quality which frees him to use whatever capabilities he has much of the time and which leaves him open and sensitive to what is going on around him instead of needing to defend his own structure.

Mental health does *not* mean, as so many of the statements in education textbooks and lectures imply, that every teacher must mold himself into a pattern of smiling, calm, responsive patience, and have no quirks and no off-beat notions. As a matter of fact, some of the best teachers in the past, as in the present, are, in other realms of life, considered eccentric or painfully shy (see *Goodbye, Mr. Chips*). But in the classroom, "odd ball" or not, many of these people seem to be able to marshal all their resources. Their pupils often love them and/or learn from them. It is not necessary to come off a mental health assembly line to be a good teacher. It is no more necessary (or possible) for teachers to be alike than for individual children to be alike. Uniformity is not the goal for which to strive. It is, rather, to see that teachers like teaching (most of the time), because when one likes doing something one is apt to be fairly good at it; to see that they get pleasure from the children they teach—not all of them, but most of them; that they feel satisfied enough with their work and their lives so that they can view their own successes and failures with some objectivity; and that they feel hopeful enough to keep the capacity to learn and grow, and are comfortable enough to ask for help and to use it.

HUMAN BEINGS AND TEACHERS

Focusing then on this specific definition, one may agree with that theme mentioned more than any other in all the literature concerned with the mental health

From Nicholas J. Long and Ruth G. Newman, "The Teacher and His Mental Health," *The Teacher's Handling of Children in Conflict*, Bulletin of School of Education, Indiana University (July 1961), pp. 5–26.

needs of teachers, namely, that teachers are human beings. This would seem a self-evident statement, yet the very fact that it is stated so often implies that in practice it is not so accepted or acceptable a tenet after all. Unquestionably, the insistence of the culture that its teachers, like its ministers and its psychiatrists, be better than everyone else contributes to the contradictory notions concerning a teacher's right to be human.

Common sense, intuitive understanding, and artist's insight, along with present-day contributions from psychology, sociology, anthropology, and psychiatry, have informed us that human beings have a good many feelings they are not proud of and that our culture frowns upon. People feel anger. They feel fear. They feel hate. They feel these things when they are threatened (and indeed they would not have survived as a species had they not experienced these feelings). Being a somewhat more complicated species than other animals, and being more adept at manipulating their environment to fit their needs, they are not so frequently threatened by the enmity of nature as they are by forces inherent in the culture: by approval and disapproval, by need for love and ego enhancement, by need for control, adequacy, and self-regard, for belonging, and for nourishment and warmth of a psychological as well as physiological kind.

This being true of human beings in general, how does the teacher's humanness especially affect his job, and what particular threats does the teacher experience more than, or different from, those of people in other occupations? How can these threats which determine his behavior affect the children he teaches?

Well, take the simple fact that teachers deal with children of all ages and that children, having not been around the earth as long as the teachers, are more primitively organized. They have not yet learned to hide, to control, and to repress their feelings (and considerable mental health time is spent worrying about ways to help them

use their feelings and not repress them in unhealthy fashions). Children, directly or indirectly, cry out their needs; perhaps they cannot define them, or place them correctly, or even do anything useful about them, but they make demands one way or another. The teacher must meet those demands, not only of one child, not only of many children, but of groups of children. He must meet these demands or divert them and at the same time teach subject matter. He must do this every day—even when he and his spouse have had a devastating fight the night before; even when he is worried sick about the fact that his own child has been moping about the house and has developed a stutter; even when his mother has become ill and has moved in on him. Even when he has not slept all night worrying over the unpaid bills and comes to school only corporeally, Mary will still need the extra attention she does not get at home before she can start in to work; Bill will still need to be set straight and quieted down before he can launch on algebra problems; Warren will need a hand on the shoulder to bring him back from outer space into earthly contact; and that group of devils in the back row will have to be brought into line.

If these management tasks are not done with some humor, warmth, firm quietness, or cheer, they will not work; and if they do not work, the class will collapse, and it will be one of those days in which everyone would better have stayed home in the first place. To be sure, this is not too different from any business man in any office, except that children are more obviously demanding and they react more readily to the first signs of irritation, disquiet, or panic. Their reactions are less clothed behind social masks, so that their fear, disturbance, or counter-anger is more immediately transferred back to the teacher, who in turn reacts as threatened organisms usually do, with fear or with flight, or, in the exceptional case of someone aware of his feelings, with an ability to see what is occurring and to put a behavioral thumb in the already leaky dike and start afresh.

A TEACHER'S SELF-AWARENESS

The ability to perceive what is going on outside oneself is no small matter and does not fall naturally like the gentle rain from heaven. It is precisely that ability which is built in by successful psychotherapy and allied techniques. It is what psycho-therapy and mental health is about.

This psychological premise is based on the well-documented assumption that the human being is influenced by a multitude of forces from within and from without. A person can afford to be aware of some of these forces, but, because of his culture, his upbringing, his individual personal experiences, and his picture of himself, he cannot afford to be aware of other forces. These latter forces are at least as powerful as those of which he *is* aware, and they may lead him to do all sorts of things which he himself may well not approve of. Moreover, since he cannot accept these things as part of himself, he can have no notion whatsoever of the effect of these actions on people around him, for good or for evil. For example, he probably does not realize that something about Joe in his class reminds him of his brother, Phil, whose very existence made his life utterly miserable all the years of his childhood, and that, without knowing it, he is quite unable to speak to Joe without irritation or to be aware of what *this* boy really is asking for. He may be equally unaware of the fact that the kids in the class are right when they accuse him of playing favorites. He may not know all the times he quite unconsciously smiles benignly at Margaret, how extra patient he is with all her questions and her need for special help. If someone should comment on his treatment of Margaret, he would ask, "Is this not good teaching?" Without special insight, he will never relate the fact that dependent Margaret is most appealing to him because he himself had always longed for someone to answer his dependent needs. He cannot afford to be aware that Margaret has become unpopular with her class because of the favoritism he has shown.

In a different context, Jules Henry[1] has reported a study in which teachers of middle-class children have been observed over long periods of time, their techniques of management noted, and their own self-report of their styles of operation recorded. Two cases out of many were specifically cited in which both teachers thought of themselves as strict disciplinarians. One teacher was quite unaware of the reassuring physical touches she continually gave to a child the minute he began to get out of bounds or the second he needed some extra push, and thus she controlled her class in a manner quite unknown to her. The other teacher was equally unaware of the number of times she pleaded with the children to do what they were asked, because she so needed their assistance. These two teachers would have been just as unaware that they used these techniques out of school with their sweethearts, their mates, their own children, or the clerks at stores with whom they dealt. They had no notion of how they actually went about the business of relating to people. Each had created a picture of himself, as all people do, having little to do with observable reality.

Actually, many of the things that teachers, along with other human beings, do unconsciously are helpful and useful things. Simply because they are done unconsciously does not mean they are bad. It is curious the amount of distrust people have of their unconscious. It is as if they began, as early as possible, to bury there all the things they did not like—their hate, their fear, their anger—and in so doing, they managed to forget that not only these qualities but other feelings have been buried there as well. All those feelings are closeted in their unconscious which, from infancy on up, have made them uncomfortable, have hurt them, or have left them open to attack or criticism. Often these feelings are affection, warmth, tenderness, humor, sym-

[1] Jules Henry, "The Problem of Spontaneity, Initiative and Creativity in Suburban Classrooms," *American Journal of Orthopsychiatry,* XXIX (April 1963), 266–279.

pathy, non-conformity, creativity. Frequently, when they have succeeded in locking the skeleton in the closet, they forget that in that very same closet lie their jewels and warmest or loveliest clothes. Teachers who receive more than the usual share of criticism from so many sources tend to be more vulnerable and therefore more fearful of letting their unconscious feelings come to the surface.

THE TEACHER'S PERSONALITY STRUCTURE

Although there are many teachers who have a natural self-awareness and an inborn talent enabling them to see what really is occurring, there is no one who cannot use additional tools to be able to better see and to better evaluate his own actions. There is no one who does not have shutters in his mind that go down when a particularly threatening experience occurs. What is threatening for one person may be entirely different for another. The way the shutters go down may also be quite different. This is what is meant by the patterns of defense talked of in psychiatry: repression, denial, projection, rationalization, displacement, identification, and the rest. What a person does when his defenses are set into motion may be quite different too. He may greet the threat with flight, with withdrawal, with despair, with increased energy, with extra control, with rigidity, with hostility, with tears, with illness, with laughter, or with sarcasm. These methods of behavior are not lost on the children he teaches, regardless of what the teacher *thinks* he is teaching. Johnny *may* learn arithmetic, but he *surely* learns that Miss J. quickly changes the subject when he says something in a loud voice. In other words, the child learns patterns of behavior more surely than he learns academic subject matter. The younger the child, the deeper the learning.

Of course the child learns his patterns of behavior from home first and foremost. But the school is the child's first venture into a foreign society. It generates in him some new pressures, sets alien standards, and arouses strain in him. Moreover, he spends a large part of his waking life with the teacher—in most cases a larger part than he spends with his parents.

So, if it is an accepted premise that children identify with meaningful adults and that their growth is determined by those people with whom they identify, it is clear that the teacher's ways of reacting are of utmost importance. Furthermore, although it would be nice to think that the child only identifies with the best part of adults, this is not necessarily the case. Since the teacher is in authority and appears to have power, and a child invariably seeks strength or support for his own helplessness, he will identify with, or try to be on the side of, strength; therefore, he may well identify with the more unpleasant parts of a teacher, the very parts, as a matter of fact, that the teacher may have kept out of his own awareness. Or the child, finding a teacher displeasing or too weak to help, may negatively identify. That is to say, if the emotional tone of the teacher has been, in a direct or an indirect way, threatening or non-need-fulfilling, the child may adopt a reverse image and try to become just those things the teacher is not. Thus, what a teacher is, who he is, and how he reacts to the hundred million situations, crises, and interactions that occur in class everyday is the child's armory of knowledge of the outside world. From this he learns how the whole world works and how one copes with anxieties and drives.

Fundamentally, it is not that a teacher is or is not a human being that is at question; it is what kind of humanness he exhibits and how his breed of humanness can be most effectively used in the classroom. The very humanity of teachers makes saintly behavior impossible. No human is always cheerful, patient, and carefree. Moreover, it is not such a good thing to be constantly euphoric. Indeed, if the teacher consistently represses his anger, the children may become increasingly convinced that their own angry and hostile feelings are unique and singularly evil.

Repressed, unaware, unusefully-directed rage and hostility, whether experienced by teacher or child, cannot forever be denied. It comes popping out, at most inappropriate moments, much too much, much too distorted, much too ineffective, much too overwhelming. Or else it appears in physical symptoms such as stomachaches, asthma, headaches, or dizziness. It may appear in nonlearning, in tics, in pretense and indirection, in lying, stealing, or truancy. The more we know about emotional health, the clearer it is that a teacher who gets angry appropriately is apt to be far less harmful to his class than a teacher who is generally irritable. A teacher who can face his own hostility toward a school task, or even toward the behavior of an annoying child, is likely to be one who can warmly take a child's sorrow or dilemma to heart. A teacher who is aware of his own vanity can laugh at himself and is likely to be able to keep the facts of school life in proportion. A teacher who knows he has acted crabby all the morning, because of a squabble at home, can pull himself together and keep the squabble where it belongs. He can proceed to make something more pleasant for the rest of the day. The teacher with awareness knows that, when too many people have been sent to detention hall that week, something may well be wrong not with the class but with himself.

FIRST AID FOR TEACHERS'
MENTAL HEALTH

It is the need for precisely this kind of awareness that a new kind of in-service program for teachers tries to meet. The open demand for a more personally and professionally meaningful type of help began, as it so often does, with the teachers who teach special classes—the physically and mentally handicapped, the braindamaged, the diagnosed emotionally and socially maladjusted. In these classes the extra burden on the teacher and the consequent risk to the pupils is more readily recognized. It has become clear, especially in teaching the emotionally disturbed, that a teacher can not function adequately for long without an informed shoulder to lean on, without an on-the-spot human wailing wall at which to gripe, to rage, to express fears and confess mistakes, to ask questions and wonder aloud. Where such a service is not provided, teacher drop-outs increase; where the human wailing wall is carefully conceived and consistently offered, where the people who are provided are educationally and psychologically informed, sensitive, sympathetic, and understanding, the turnover among teachers, even under the most incredibly difficult conditions, is remarkably lowered. The teachers themselves become aware not only of their own assets and shortcomings but of the exciting possibility of enlarged horizons, personal growth, and professional maturation.

A good thing does not remain quiet for long. So teachers in general, and even principals, have begun to seek some such help for themselves. Some enlightened school administrations have begun to take seriously the question of the loss of trained and often skilled teachers in their systems. There is evidence that salaries and other stated reasons for departure are not always the reasons for a quit job and certainly are not the only reasons. More and more schools have begun to recognize that not all the changes that need to be made can be effected soon enough, and that both staff and children are suffering because of this. There are long waiting lists for psychological services to diagnose and re-place disturbed children, there are over-crowded schools and classrooms, too heavy teacher loads, unhygienic class conditions, poor communications between principals and teachers or between teachers and parents, and untenable stress conditions of many kinds. All of these things need changing, but all take time. An enlightened in-service program, it has been discovered, not only expedites a more intelligent program of change but makes it possible for the changes to be significantly shared by the teachers. The long wait between what needs to be done and what can be done can thus be made bearable, and even useful, where the school staff is given an informed personal service. More and more schools use a new kind of consultation and supervision which properly leans on not one but all areas of the arts that underlie the science of human behavior.

THE STRAWS THAT BREAK
THE TEACHER'S BACK

What first appears in applying informed personal services is the variety of things teachers find particularly frustrating in their classrooms. Ask a teacher to report honestly what most drives him to distraction: sometimes it is the big things like overcrowdedness, or having no time to do a job; sometimes it is the personal idiosyncrasies that make life unbearable. There is no use in placing a heirarchy of importance on the gripes. As anyone knows, a spilled glass of orange juice at breakfast can, at a given moment, be just as upsetting as not receiving a pay raise. It is possible for both kinds of events to be devastating for the time being, or to be met and handled in proportion when awareness and support are available.

Below are some examples of teachers' frustrations as they expressed them. They represent the kinds of frustrations which carefully planned in-service or consultative programs try to meet, in an Androcles and the Lion kind of way, by seeing them as thorns which can, temporarily or permanently, cripple the teacher and keep him from performing, and can consequently hold back the child. A truly good consultative service to teachers could be of help, regardless of which of the following complaints one chooses:

Overcrowding is experienced with a sense of helplessness by some teachers:

In our school district during the past school term there was an overflow of children in our school causing most of the classes to have from 39 to 45 children. There was a constant assignment of new children from other schools in the city as well as from surrounding areas. This impact was felt tremendously in the school program and its operation to accomplish certain goals. As for me, this kind of "bargin'-in" (that was my inner feeling) of from one to two children each week was quite frustrating, as my concern in meeting individual differences was thwarted and my anticipated goals seemed out of reach. I found myself unconsciously resenting the fact that the child was sent to my room, and I became quite peeved if he did not have command of the skills expected of a second grader, for this meant that my job was to take time to help him if I could or at least to provide opportunities to expose him to the skills. I was not even willing to take him where he was and to work from that point, as that would take time, and time was what I didn't have, especially since time had already been sacrificed to register, enroll, and welcome him to the class.

I dread going to school these days—210 children a day, about 40 kids in a class. They tell me a new school is being planned to take up all the kids from the new housing settlement, but until then just try to teach English to 180 kids: the slow ones, the fast ones, the noisy ones. I thought you were supposed to know the kids you teach. I hardly know most of their names, let alone what they need from me. I love English. I have theories about teaching it. All that's been scrapped. Now I'm lucky to simply follow the prescribed dull study plan. I feel I'm not doing a thing for these kids. I'd give my soul for five classes of 20 children each!

I teach kindergarten. Once was, when I had a nice small 16 in a class group. Now I have two sessions: 50 in the morning, 42 in the afternoon, a volunteer parent helper for each class—when they show up. By the end of the day I feel as if I have the D.T.'s, with hundreds of moppets instead of pink elephants passing by. They call this teaching? Not in any child development course I ever had.

Special rules of personal and social behavior, as well as extra and menial chores and low salaries imposed on teachers, are often bitterly resented:

Then there is the "universal" frustration, not so much of salary (although everyone agrees that we are grossly under-paid) as of the benevolences I must cater to. I honestly hold in high esteem the virtues of the YMCA, YWCA, Boy Scouts, Girl Scouts, Red Cross, United Fund, and professional organizations, but somehow they seem to lose their flavor when I am aware that I *must* join in order to be considered a "good, cooperative" teacher. How nice it would be to join these wonderful organizations simply because I want to join them by choice only!

In the community in which I reside, teachers are somewhat expected to be "saints." This notion, to me, is ridiculous, for teachers, like everyone else, are human. It struck me as funny when I was interviewed for this particular position that the principal mentioned rather pointedly that this area had many people who drank in it, but that pressure was put on to get rid of any teacher who did so. He suggested that if I drank, not to drink in this area.

It would be nice to go into school in the morning and just teach and not have to be collecting money, taking attendance, playing nurse, and trying to discipline those who do not respond to the classroom role. It is difficult to be satisfied with doing just half a job all the time. It is difficult to realize that we cannot be 100 per cent effective but have to settle for much less. It is difficult for me to adjust to this situation as I am more of a perfectionist and like to get the best results all the time.

I hate to quit because I like to teach, but like it or not, I have to resign. My wife is expecting our second child and can no longer work. Since our first child is ill the doctor's bills and living expenses are just too much. I am overtired, tired trying to meet expenses by working at the post office in the Christmas rush and in a factory during summer times. I've been offered a job in an insurance company and, like it or not, I've got to take it. You've got to be rich to afford to teach if you've got a family.

The policy of administration is sometimes felt by teachers to be so outrageous (whether right or wrong) that their total teaching attitudes are affected:

To teach under an administration which focuses its attention upon creating benevolent public relations, even at the expense of school standards, seems to be my outstanding frustration. How is it possible for a high school principal to condone a student's laziness, slowness, and apparent lack of interest in subject matter, in a conference among the child's parents, the child, the teacher involved, and himself, and to state explicitly that possibly the reason for the child's failure was due to the lack of motivation and severity of grading done by the teacher. Mary, the student concerned, was a high school senior. She had failed sophomore and junior English and she was retaking both of these courses during her senior year as she needed both to graduate. Miss T. had Mary for sophomore English. She passed Mary because, as Miss T. said to me, "You can't fight city hall." I did not pass Mary, but when she graduated, she had no record on her permanent record of a failure in junior English. She had instead a "C."

The procedure of giving a contract for eight or nine months seems to have a decidedly negative effect upon the teacher. The implication read into the action is that the employer doesn't trust his judgment and has little faith in the training and prior experience of the applicant—that there is so much possibility that the teacher will be unsatisfactory that he cannot afford to hire her for a longer period than a year at a time. The result is an undermining of the teacher's performance, self-confidence, and feeling of security.

Most permanently established teachers would not have been asked to take such a teaching load, but many principals feel that they can ask a beginning teacher to accept almost any situation. This is a particularly hard thing to do, because a beginning teacher needs all of the help and encouragement that she can get, and even in the most pleasant situation will have many problems to cope with anyway. I feel that for a teacher, especially a teacher in her first year of teaching, to be so totally out of her teaching field is an injustice not only to the teacher but to the students.

The emotionally disturbed child in the classroom often generates despair and helplessness in the teacher:

There is a child in the classroom who suffers from an emotional problem. He is withdrawn, sensitive, and nervous—a condition which I know results from his home environment—a broken home, rejection, poverty, etc. I try to work with this child, give him projects that will display his self-worth, encourage him to join in the play activities of other children, give him extra "slaps on the back" for work well done, etc. All of this I do in the limited time the child is in school and under my jurisdiction. After school he goes home, back into the same surroundings that have caused him to be emotionally disturbed in the first place. My work, seemingly, becomes undone; the child enters the classroom the next day in the same condition as he entered the day before. I know the mind, soul, or body cannot be cured in one day, but as this chain of events goes on and on each day, I cannot help but sense a feeling of failure and helplessness.

Suzy was sent to me as an incorrigible seven-year-old who followed no rules, fought with all children, and caused constant room disturbance. She had an I.Q. of 78 on the Kuhlmann-Anderson and 79 on the Stanford-Binet. She was hostile, and yet on the first day of school she threw herself on me, nearly suffocating me with an embrace. Inquiring into her background, I found she lived in a house with seven or eight adults and as many children, seemingly all related, yet no definite relationship could be determined. I could not find out where the father was or even if he were living. Three women claimed to be her mother, but none would talk to me about her. Each said that her grandmother was responsible for her and she went to work at three in the afternoon and worked all night. I was never able to contact the grand-

mother. The frustration came about because I could find no one who seemed to care enough about Suzy to talk about her or try to help her. During the year I worked on the theory that if I loved her enough, she in turn would feel more secure and want to conform. I felt both I.Q. scores were invalid, because Suzy could think and reason. She was quite capable of finding information and presenting it when she desired.

I can't stop worrying about one little girl in my first grade. She behaves so peculiarly. She doesn't talk most of the time, though she can talk. She answers the other children and me with animal sounds. She hides under chairs like a dog and barks at people. She even bit one little boy. She draws pictures of dogs and insists on eating her lunch on all fours. I've talked to her mother who is frantic about her behavior, but they have no money to see a psychiatrist. She's been on a clinic waiting list for six months, and I've had the child up for Special Service to test her for three months. In the meantime, the class all laugh at her, and she just gets worse, and I don't know what to do.

Parents are often experienced by teachers as an impossible cross to bear, whether this is because of the teacher's own unresolved feelings about his parents or whether the parents actually are obstructionists:

As a teacher, I try to give all the love, energy, consideration, and understanding to each pupil that I possibly can. To have a parent question my attention to another child over his makes me quite frustrated, baffled, and thwarted. If only parents would understand that some pupils require more attention than others and that it is not that the teacher is partial in any respect.

The most frustrating thing I've encountered has been parental attitude. Some, and I must say generally speaking it's the mothers, feel as though their children are bordering on genius. When the mothers classify their dear offsprings as such, the teacher shouldn't expect them to do such trivial things as study a lesson or do a class assignment, but should give the child superior grades in subject matters and satisfactory for attitude.

I have a parent who calls me every night to complain about her child's behavior. At first I tried to be nice and tell her what to do, but nothing is enough. Can't she see I have a right to my evenings, and can't she handle her own child? But I can't seem to cut her off, and I feel helpless to do anything. I've told the principal, and he doesn't seem interested in helping me. "Oh, she'll stop," says he. But when?

Interpersonal relations with staff, where there are differences of opinion or approach or personality conflicts, can be of determining importance to a teacher:

Although students may have difficulty in other subjects, social studies presents quite a problem to several of my students. I believe it is because it involves a great deal of reading and comprehension. Extra time is needed to give those students help who are having difficulty mastering social studies. But what is most frustrating to me is the fact that many of our teachers frown on me for giving special help to the students because the teachers feel that the administration will require them to help with special problems also. Then too, some teachers have accused me of trying to impress the administrators because I give some special help.

The school was more of the traditional type, and, although I did try many new ideas and techniques, I found that I began following a somewhat "middle-of-the-road" position. Rather than actually teaching according to the way I had planned, I began to lean more and more to the type of teaching which was customary in the school system. There was not any real pressure from my critic teacher or from the superintendent, who was a personal friend, but I somehow felt that my efforts pleased them more when I followed the line of "traditional" teaching. At the same time, I felt that I was not doing a good job when

I did not follow the practices which I had studied in my methods classes. Discipline seemed to be the main objection to the newer methods. Whenever the boys and girls were working on their committees and the room was "noisy," I noticed that I worried about distracting the other rooms nearby. I even began to question the worth of my opinion. I sometimes felt that the older teachers humored me in conversations when I voiced my approval of modern methods and theory. This was not always the case, but I occasionally detected an attitude of "You'll learn. You may think this way now, but wait until you've taught several years." Perhaps this is why I began my graduate work right away rather than beginning teaching as I had previously planned.

I could do my job all right if that sixth-grade teacher would stay out of my way. We have a school where the principal is with us two days a week and with another school three days. When she's not here, that bossy, nosey Mrs. D. just takes over, calls down my kids in the hall when they're not doing anything, criticizes my bulletin board, disciplines my children in front of me, and undermines my authority. The principal is so dependent on Mrs. D. that there's no use talking to her. Anything Mrs. D. does is fine!

Sometimes deeply experienced personal conflicts can overwhelm a teacher:

I do not like having things on my desk looked at or handled. My desk is verboten. There are always children who want to rifle the papers or just look. They do not want anything, it just seems to be something they do. It doesn't matter to me that I never have anything on my desk that I do not want anyone to see or handle, I just don't want anyone to bother anything that is there. Inside, I have the feeling of "It's mine—hands off!" I know that this is silly, but I feel it strongly. The same feeling carries over to my personal things at home. I want them left alone.

When I may be about to come to a climax in a science experiment, or in the explanation of a transitive passive verb, or have all the attention of every eye and am about to express the punch line, there comes a knock at the door. I may as well answer it, because all hope of competing with that unknown factor of "Who's at the door?" is to no avail. Upon answering, I am handed a clarinet by a mother who says, "Would you please give this to Jeanne? She forgot she had band today." About that time I feel like a plugged-up volcano unable to blow the proverbial top.

If I were to name frustrations, they would come not from teaching but from the fact that I feel my family is shorted. I find myself, at the end of the day, weary physically and mentally, often unable to cope with home demands. I will give a short answer to those at home, whereas at school I would weigh my words and answer with a smile. Meeting the needs of two sons, ages 15 and 6, and a husband who is far from well could be a full-time job in itself. I feel frustrated in that I have little enthusiasm and patience to give at home after a full day of being enthusiastic and patient with a room full of children.

The other area of frustration is a difficult one to explain and also to admit. When I entered teaching, I had no intention of making it a career. I had hoped eventually to marry and raise my own family. After four years of teaching, I realized I would not meet many eligible men in the classroom. I realized I had to make a choice as to the type of career I wanted for myself. I knew that teaching was the one in which I would feel the happiest and gain the most satisfaction. I am going into guidance and counseling. I like working with people and think I have a reasonable amount of understanding of them. However, at times I feel very unloved and unwanted. I know this is going to hinder my working relationship in some cases. I can remember during my first few years of teaching that I threw myself wholeheartedly into helping students with extracurricular activities. I know I was looking for their appreciation and affection

as an outcome of my work. But in most cases the students forgot about my help and enjoyed the activities themselves, letting me sit on the side and watch. How does a single person manage to fill this need for love and affection without becoming the embittered old maid that is often used as a stereotype for teachers? I feel this is an important problem with me. I know the solution cannot come in a short time, nor can anyone else solve it but myself. I would like some suggestions as to possible solutions.

I know one should not dislike a child, but there is one in my class who so offends me that it spoils my whole day. She is sloppy and fat. Her hair is stringy and unkempt. She sits sulky and slumped in her chair, never shows any pleasure in anything, answers in a fresh way, if at all. I know she must have a hard time at home, and I bend over backward trying to be nice. But at the end of the day, I am exhausted from the effort. I even dream about her nights.

As different as these personally recounted examples of frustrations are, there is not one of them that could not be to some degree alleviated by on-the-spot, psychologically sophisticated supervision, consultation, or whatever is called the process of airing one's difficulties, looking at them honestly with an informed and sympathetic person, and being helped not to deny them or let them grow to giant size but to perceive them in a fresh context. Whether by new pathways of communication, or by a reshuffling of the way one sees things, or by simply getting the jumble of enraging feelings into a framework of words, or by a sense of human support, *something* can grow out of this process for the teacher and the pupils. But this can only be effected when the school and the teachers are openly hospitable to this kind of help, and when the help itself becomes, with increased experience, the kind a teacher asks for. To be of use, it cannot be poured down the throat like medicine; to be nourishing, it must be sipped slowly like the good wine that it can be. . . .

THE DISTURBED AND DISTURBING CHILD IN THE CLASSROOM

Another of the classroom teacher's common frustrations is the disturbed and disturbing child. Any teacher with the slightest grasp on reality knows full well he will have some difficult children in his class. The course of education, like that of true love, does not run smooth.

But it is true that even *difficulty* is a term that should have *normal* in front of it. There are some children far too sick to be in a regular class. They may be without impulse-control, or their behavior may be bizarre, or they may be withdrawn to the extent of being unreachable. Increasingly, special attention is being given and special provision being made for such children. But where is the severity of their disability first discovered? Rarely in the home. Rarely in the doctor's office. Mostly, severe emotional disturbance is first diagnosed in the classroom.

This means that a teacher—certainly a teacher of the early grades—has to live with, and try to teach, the child who is too ill to be lived with or too ill to be taught. Such a child disrupts the class, demands constant attention, and fills the teacher with a sense of failure and confusion, to say nothing of rage and sometimes of terror or revulsion. All of this causes him to feel guilty as well as inadequate. With the waiting lists of children on special services as long as they are, it is the rule, not the exception, that sees this child in the classroom for months before diagnosis, and longer before replacement. In the meantime, child, class, and teacher are often badly harmed. A growing awareness of this condition indicates the possibility, through teacher training, of earlier diagnosis, a better use of consultation, and increased skills for the

teacher to help him recognize and deal with these disturbances on an emergency basis. (The emergency often lasts the whole school year!)

Merely relaying to the teacher the fact that he cannot hope to teach this child and that it is not his fault that the child behaves or feels as he does or learns poorly, is sometimes enough to improve matters. Just knowing this often relieves the teacher, and the child's behavior relaxes in direct proportion to the lessened tension of the teacher. But teaching such children is no easy matter.

Ask any psychiatrist how anxiety-provoking it is to be around very ill people. The teacher is in this spot daily; his anxiety rises sky-high just at a time when he is also forced to deal with his usual load of problems and tasks, and his anxiety makes him less able to do so. Again, to play variations on our theme, the teacher's self-awareness may make all the difference between his survival in school and his collapse, just as it may determine the way a class will survive or the amount of damage the sick child experiences.

Some teachers—often the best motivated—court trouble by becoming overinvolved in the child and then feeling rejected and angry when their efforts fail. For some, particular symptoms are too evocative of repressed impulses or hidden childhood experiences of their own. Often, a child placed with a different (not necessarily a better) teacher fares better. Each teacher can take certain kinds of abnormalities and has his own personal aversions, the causes of which may be hidden from his awareness.

To make matters for contemporary teachers even more threatening, the notion of disturbance is even more complex than it used to be. There are, of course, the usual (though difficult on sight to distinguish) characters who are basically healthy but temporarily disturbed over a situation arising at home or at school with which they cannot cope, one which sets them into behavior very like the most disturbed child. The Johnny who throws a book at Peter may be a disturbed child or he may be suffering from an overload of criticism from Papa at the breakfast table. The act is a disturbed and disturbing one, but it can mean anything on the continuum from health to illness.

There are those with disturbances which are indeed very serious and severe but which are not too disturbing to the teacher in the classroom unless he is more than averagely conscientious: these are the too quiet, book-buried, non-social, shy and fearful children, whom teachers are learning increasingly to note, but who do not disrupt class activities as a rule, do not set an entire group into panic or mayhem, and therefore are not so quickly noticed by the teacher.

But in addition, a new phenomenon of disturbance has come to school and makes for a serious fraction of irritation for the class and the teacher. These are children who may not be intrinsically as emotionally flooded as some of the others mentioned, but they are disturbed and most surely are disturbing. They make up the increasing group of lower-class and upper middle-class children who, in a world much more mobile and less rooted than heretofore, have parents who move from place to place on jobs or who are looking for jobs. These children sometimes come from immigrant families (such as constitute a severe educational challenge in large cities like New York), or sometimes from indigent farm or unskilled labor families whose work is seasonal, or from military service people who move from post to post, or from the families of highly skilled young engineers or businessmen whose companies move them back and forth to branch offices in many states. These children have lacked the security of a place and a constant in their lives; they tend to make thin and superficial relationships, to be either desperate followers in order to belong, or desperate leaders in order to shine and to

make a mark while the brief candle of their stay burns brightly. Often they make up the gangs and the cliques and the socially worrisome element. Teachers have not yet found ways, other than by trial and error, of dealing with this phenomenon. They have not learned how to relate to these children, how to motivate them for long-term goals or long-term relationships. The very task of doing so, when one thinks about it psychodynamically, borders on the impossible. For these children have learned the hard way not to invest too much in relationships that are bound to change, not to count too much on any way of life when next month or next year the way of life will have to be quite different. Being basically healthy animals, they have learned to adapt superficially to everything in some way or other, and they convey an impenetrable wall when a teacher tries to help them invest themselves emotionally in work, in projects, or in relationships. This problem has just begun to be recognized as a severely frustrating aspect of teaching today.

REASONS BEHIND CHOOSING TEACHING AS A PROFESSION

From all that has been said so far, the reader must be beginning to feel as swamped with helplessness as the teachers themselves feel with some of their classes. Why, one begins to ask, would anyone choose teaching for a profession? It is a good question and has been the subject of some study. A teacher's reasons for choosing his profession often underlie the last frustration to be discussed here. What does a teacher hope to derive from teaching? What conscious and unconscious forces may lead to his decision to become a teacher?

There was a time when most teachers were women—when the only respectable job a woman could have was teaching. (This is still in large part true through the elementary grades.) In taking the orders, so to speak, she knew that she virtually sounded a death knell on her hopes for marriage, but she did retain respectability and a sense of usefulness. Unconsciously, a woman might go into teaching to avoid marriage. This may be the case today, as well as in times past, but it is not so easy an escape as it once was, since many teachers are married and the social restrictions on teachers have been modified. However, married or single, respectability is still achieved by the woman teacher. Years ago the rarer man teacher often took to teaching when he found himself to be bookish and unaggressive. This situation still exists, though it is less prevalent than it used to be. Some teachers took to teaching out of a sense of mission or dedication: it was a way to make the world, which did not look so good, better for the future. This is still true, fortunately, and is often found coexisting with many other reasons.

Some teachers fall into teaching. They begin with other fields, find other experiences unsavory, or feel they cannot succeed in them. A job of teaching is open and they attempt it.

Despite the pitiful salaries teachers have always been paid, there are people who feel more secure working on state, county, or city salaries than in business—a teacher's salary, though low, seems reasonably certain. But since low salaries are the rule, the teaching field has become increasingly attractive to many married women. These people often can supplement a limited income by teaching. They can buy the extras at home, or they can contribute to the necessities without the full burden of having to support a family on a teacher's salary. Education schools these days have more and more students who are middle-aged and have children past the toddler stage themselves. For these people, the economic strain tends to be less, but the strain of filling two full-time jobs, teaching and family life, often brings with it its own frustration.

A man or woman may take up teaching because a teacher has been so important in his own development. When he was in school, a particular teacher may have made a great difference in his life, may indeed have become someone to pattern himself on. Some people, contrariwise, take up teaching because of their own school sufferings and because they remember with chagrin and bitterness the poor teaching to which they were exposed, and they resolve to live life over for themselves through others, and this time to do it right. Some people seem to get along beautifully and comfortably with young people of different ages, but they may do very poorly, feel awkward, out of place, and inadequate in adult groups. Such people often make excellent teachers, especially of the very young (though they are frequently the ones who have the most trouble with the parents of the children they teach). These people may be reliving what was a real or a fantasied happier time of their lives. They may be educational Peter Pans and find it necessary to ally themselves with the young folks against the adults. Many of these people, though by no means all, often find it difficult to deal with the authorities in school. They are still carrying on childhood or adolescent rebellions.

Some people are much happier without people. They fall in love with subject matter, with mathematics, or physics, or ancient history. They may have discovered that real, present-day life is simply too much, that relationships demand a closeness that is too frightening; high school or college teaching allows them to legitimately drown themselves in their subject. They are often very skilled in their subject matter, and show a passion and love, when involved in content, that may well be inspiring to some of their like-minded students. These teachers are practically never the ones who find satisfaction in relating to the children in their classes, either as a group or as individuals, unless they find someone who is the budding image of themselves or who seems to be as interested in falling in love with that particular subject matter as they themselves are. These teachers (and some of them are very gifted, if one accepts their limitations) are virtually never interested in the psychology of children or interpersonal relations.

The fact that a teacher may have all sorts of reasons he does not recognize for choosing his profession does not differentiate him from anyone else. It is, again, part of his humanness. The same kinds of reasons, or equally unconscious ones, may impel a person to become a nurse, a doctor, an engineer, a bus driver, an executive, a secretary, a salesman, a plumber, a cattle raiser, a lawyer, or a fireman. The crucial difference for the teacher is that, because he must constantly deal with children and cannot avoid having an important effect on them, he, more than most of his fellow human beings, must be *aware* of the possible reasons for his choice of profession.

Redl and Wattenberg[2] have made a list of 15 of the more commonly stated reasons people tend to go into teaching.

1. Status
2. Family pressure
3. Love for subject field
4. Identification with a former teacher
5. Love of children
6. Fun in teaching
7. Helping to build a better world
8. Self-sacrifice for an ideal
9. Correcting the shortcomings of one's own past
10. Reliving childhood patterns
11. Desire for affection
12. Need for security
13. Halfway house to other ambition
14. Need for power and group leadership
15. Guaranteed superiority

[2] Fritz Redl, and William W. Wattenberg, *Mental Hygiene in Teaching* (Harcourt, Brace and Co., New York, 1959), pp. 479–482.

In the discussion above, merely some of these factors have been mentioned. One might not only discuss the rest but add many more. The fact is that people's motives are rarely, if ever, single-purposed, and most people make these decisions on many counts, on a series of personal, rational, irrational, and coincidental factors. Moreover, the reasons a person gives himself for doing something are nearly always the reasons his own self-image can tolerate. People have a great stake in hiding from themselves other reasons, perhaps just as strong or even stronger, which they do not want to face. A teacher afraid of his own aggression may be quite unable to see that he went into teaching not only for love of subject matter but just as much because he had a need for power unfulfilled in other areas. A teacher who takes great pride in his independent, controlled handling of life may not be able to recognize his loneliness and his need for affection as a driving motive. To restate the theme as a coda, the awareness mentioned earlier comes back into the picture again; for the more aware a teacher is of the hidden, as well as the obvious, reasons for teaching, the more fully will he be able to do his job and face its frustrations; for he will be more aware of the areas of satisfaction from which he derives pleasure and will not need to feel so resentful that he is not getting what he intended to get when he took his teaching certificate. Through awareness, he will have either given up impossible goals and substituted more realistic ones, or he will have found ways to reach the goals unanswered by his job in other areas of his life. . . .

Now that teachers are being exposed to the principles of psychodynamics, they are becoming aware of the important concepts of transference and counter-transference that develop as the child forms a meaningful relationship with his teacher. Too often teachers are surprised when a child, who has been showing significant change and has given evidence of liking them, suddenly becomes aggressive and even degrading. During these stressful times, important aggressive and counter-aggressive interactions inevitably take place between teacher and child. When a teacher is asked to explain the incident, a natural reaction is to protect his sense of adequacy rather than to admit that he lost control, or that the child manipulated him into an impossible situation. While these self-protective techniques are understandable, they also are destructive to the re-education of the child and must be discussed openly.

No teacher can handle all conflict situations successfully. In our supervisory work with well-trained, experienced teachers, a good share of the time is spent discussing how a teacher can be trapped in the child's web of secondary defenses of aggression, sexuality, and guilt. In teaching emotionally disturbed children it is not essential to strive for control in all situations, but rather to feel comfortable with one's psychoeducational interpretation of the child's behavior and to admit feelings of confusion, anger, panic, and helplessness when they occur. This honest attitude is one of the major attributes of the teacher who is emotionally, as well as intellectually, prepared to work with these children.

In the next article, Solomon discusses how teachers meet their own personal needs in the way they react to children's behavior and how with supervision these interactions can be used in a positive way in a school situation.

Neuroses of School Teachers

Joseph C. Solomon

I shall draw on experience I have had with teachers over the last quarter of a century both in teacher-training and in group and individual psychotherapy. I shall quote mainly from tape-recorded sessions of a teachers' workshop that has been in process since March 1954, in which teachers from kindergarten through high school have dealt particularly with children's feelings and their own.

The most frequently disturbing pattern of transference-countertransference interaction . . . accrues when children act out hostility—indirectly and unavowed— through disobedience, inattentiveness, not turning in assignments or turning them in "messed up" or late, through whispering, quarreling, "goofing off" and "horsing around."

In some instances the situation gets out of hand because in the attempts to maintain an ego-ideal of the "giving" parent the teacher unconsciously wishes to overthrow the introjected, authoritarian, demanding parent. And so, he or she [the

teacher] fails to provide the firm leadership that children need. Says a first-grade teacher, "I feel like a witch when I'm strict. I keep backing down then and the children invariably take advantage." Says a sixth-grade teacher with greater insight, "I had a big struggle with myself in working out where strength was good and where strength was bad, and where I was being like a bad mother and where I needed to be strong. And I came to see that what I had thought was punitive really wasn't. It was actually sticking to needed rules. Since I worked it out for myself, my children work much better."

Sometimes too great permissiveness appears to be a defense against a teacher's revealing hostilities toward actually demanding objects in his past. To quote one teacher, "The children loom up like 37 monsters, each yakking as loud as my mother did." "Demands, demands," says another. "I feel as if they're beating me with their demands and that I have to keep on sweetly saying 'Yes.'"

On the opposite side, some teachers carry out in the classroom the same sort of thing that we have seen youngsters depict in paintings where they draw themselves

From Joseph C. Solomon, "Neuroses of School Teachers," *Mental Hygiene,* published by the National Association for Mental Health, XLIV (January 1960), 87–90. Reprinted by permission.

as gigantic figures beating or smearing their parents, whom they draw very small. Such teachers make the children into parent figures shrunken into nonthreatening dimensions. They carp and criticize and use the children in one way or another as objects of their own ancient hostilities.

As a flagrant example of a teacher's taking hostility out on children, a fifth-grade male teacher read a story to his classroom in which a Corsican boy accepted bribes from a thief, which so offended his father's pride that the father shot the son. Totally unconscious of the sadism involved in the story, this teacher avowed that he read it "just to have a little fun. I like to see their reactions." My workshop members questioned his motives, and during the discussion that ensued he came out with "My own frustrations have always overwhelmed me." Meanwhile, his rigid classroom discipline and sadism had led his pupils to displace their aggression onto each other. "Someone is always beating someone else up as they come in the door." Concomitantly the achievement level in this teacher's classes was consistently low.

A man teaching the fourth grade has all his life "been in revolt." He permits pandemonium in his classroom. He says, "I think a certain amount of naughtiness in children is desirable." But he lets it get too extreme and then has to "use the paddle, which," he says, "relieves us all." Thus in the countertransference he acts out; he lets the children be naughty and then he gains restitution by punishing them as representatives of his guilty self.

Occasionally a teacher appears to take children as siblings. A high school teacher, for instance, finds herself "picking on" a particular popular girl. "My sister was glamorous; I wasn't" shed light on the matter when it slipped out one day. Another teacher, who had had numerous younger siblings to care for, continuously complained that "the children weigh me down."

In contrast, we have worked intensively on how the transference-counter-transference interactions can be used as assets in the school situation. We include such qualities as understanding and acceptance—of feeling "with" a child because within oneself one knows how he feels. It enables the teacher to react in positive fashion to transferences from the child.

We have found that it helps to make the countertransference positive when the teacher can see that often children want from him what they have emotionally wanted at home. It helps the teacher to see that often transference behavior attempts to elicit attitudes that the individual has not had at home. What we have found helps most, however, is for the teacher to recognize that children transfer onto him their negative and hostile feelings towards their parents. This often relieves the teacher of unrealistic guilt, self-condemnation and a needless sense of failure.

In short, meaningful awareness of the psychodynamics of childhood and how children bring a multitude of feelings from home into school often enables the teacher to give to the children, in ways appropriate to the school setting, adaptations of what Franz Alexander has called the "corrective emotional experience."

Teachers are helped, too, to make such adaptations when the difference between indiscriminate acting out and "channeling" of feelings is clarified.

In a B-11 United States history class —that is, with 15 and 16-year-olders—the subject of freedom was being discussed. There were muttered swear words, throwing of erasers, sly passing of notes, general disorder. These the teacher recognized, to quote his own words, "not as an affront to me, as I might have formerly. But I knew they were mad. And I thought: Better get it out legitimately. So I said, 'You seem bothered and mad at me or at somebody in connection with this business of freedom. Suppose you write out how you really do feel. Anything goes in the writing. But no more swearing, etc. Here is a way to get out your anger.'" To give just a simple single sample of the transference evident, I quote in part one boy's paper: "There is supposed to be freedom in the U.S. But the teachers tell me what to do. The principal tells me what to do. We can't talk. We can't be late. We can't chew gum. We can't do anything but our own school work which is terrible. It's the same at home. The old lady tells me mow the lawn, sweep the patio, do this, do that. The old man comes home. 'You forgot to do this. You forgot to do that. Leave your car in the garage and walk to school.' And there it starts all over."

To skip down to lower levels, a number of teachers have given children chances to bring out how they feel about their polio shots. In one kindergarten several children made clay mothers and clay teachers and "mashed them up because they hadn't ought to let the doctor do it," showing mother and teacher taken as one. (Incidentally, at all elementary levels teachers report that children inadvertently address them as "Mother" or "Father," "Mommy" or "Dad.")

In another kindergarten a little boy persistently buried a ball in the sandbox, kicked it and hit it. "I'm spanking you, Mrs. Hall," he announced. The teacher said, "You'd like to do that sometimes." He hit some more, "I'm hitting your husband. I'm angry at your husband." The teacher nodded. "I think maybe you're angrier at somebody else's husband." And he said, "Yes." He was "angry at Mrs. Webster's husband"—his father—and he added, "Angry at Mrs. Webster too. Just like at you." "I know" said the teacher, "All little boys get angry at their mothers and fathers sometimes and want to hit them or hit their teachers instead. They can't really. But they can hit the ball . . . or?" she turned and questioned the cluster of children who had gathered around. "They can paint hitting pictures," one child volunteered. "Or throw bean-bags," said another. "Like we'd like to do at you sometimes. But can't."

In handling stress situations between children, it helps also for teachers to realize that derivatives of the sibling relationship are often involved.

Another question current in psycho-

therapy is also important in the school situation: Shall the therapist—or in this instance the teacher—share countertransference reactions? In the classroom we have come to see that the teacher's verbalization of feelings makes for more positive interactions. We have found that the atmosphere remains more wholesome and the children's work progresses better when teachers are able to share their feelings, not to absolve the venting of anger but as one means of offsetting the necessity to do so.

Children in the classroom acutely perceive how the teacher feels.

In a first grade, for instance, a teacher slammed a book down on her desk, feeling she'd like to slam one of the noisy little children. The children caught it. One said primly, "It's no good for us, Mrs. Allen, when you slam books." Another said more resolutely, "I feel like you're slamming me."

In a mixed grade of elementary school children with hearing disabilities, a teacher found herself feeling very annoyed and abused because the children were not jumping in to help her clean up the paints they had used in a harbor unit. To give her own account: "They sat like little mummies, all staring. No one did anything. Finally I caught myself and I said, 'I'm mad at you.' And Nina said, 'Boy, you *are* mad. I guess you feel like when your mother used to make you do all the work!' She knew! . . . I said, 'Yes.' Then they all started grinning. And boy, they buzzed into it! And we all felt very solid and good."

As a fourth-grade teacher summarized it: "If I say how I feel, the children seem to feel safer. Even though I don't know what it goes back to or why, it's there."

Obviously what we have been talking about here are the conscious derivatives of the countertransference. In some teachers the unconscious parts may call for far deeper psychiatric help.

Not all teachers, however, can have the benefit of psychotherapy. But all teachers could benefit by having the psychiatrist become one of the important teachers in the education of every teacher today. . . .

No one can argue effectively against the view that teachers want to develop additional skills in managing individuals and groups in a classroom. The day of moralizing and physical punishment is passing and needs to be replaced by more useful diagnostic techniques backed up by administrative support. Otherwise, many intelligent, zestful young teachers who could make a significant contribution to the welfare of children will become overwhelmed by the inappropriate behavior of disturbed children in the regular class and end up discouraged and bitter. A young graduate student gave us a perfect example of this point. She writes in a way that can only come from a true sense of frustration.

My first year of teaching was a crushing and enlightening experience. I entered that spanking new first-grade classroom with all the enthusiasm, drive, confidence, and background that derive from a very happy student-teaching experience, cum-laude record and Master-teacher parentage. My goals high, filled with graduate idealism, I was sure that I would be an excellent teacher. By November, my idealism and confidence were shattered and I was verbally wishing that my husband would receive a job-transfer thus escaping one of the most difficult contracts of my life. Though many factors entered into my disenchantment with teaching (such as inadequate materials, absence of help and supervision) by far the greatest discouragements were concerned with establishing rapport, understanding, and discipline with six disturbed little boys whose problems ranged from extreme immaturity to parental desertion. The various ways in which they chose to disturb the class made group work (that oft' repeated phrase of the college professional year) unsuccessful, and I discovered that most of my energies were being spent smoothing out conflicts which they initiated or keeping a running pace ahead of them to avoid unpleasant situations. I might have won the race against two or three aggressors, but the room was square not hexagonal, and it was impossible to keep the sextette separated, busy, and happy for long periods of time. Naturally I sought help. The principal, a former junior high school teacher, and scared for her own job, tried to assist. She recognized my difficult situation since it was apparent the year before, and we studied the background on each child, interviewed parents, and became acquainted and sympathetic to the causes for the behavior patterns of the boys. But the big mystery remained (*How do you work with disturbed problem children to help them adjust to society, accept themselves, and establish self-discipline for the total group?*) The principal kept on saying, "Jody, you must just keep trying different techniques. If one doesn't work, try another. There are no pat answers." She did not believe in touching a child but she did believe in giving them cookies when sent to the office for disciplinary measures, as a way of softening them up. I tried firmness, kindness, separation, interesting personal projects (Oh, for more books on prehistoric animals!), giving responsibilities, personal talks, plus mouthwashing when Gary started calling the children "damn bastards."
Help in the nature of a reading consultant was never provided. Help in the way of a psychological consultant was promised and finally arrived in April. Dr. F was a slim, elegant, cashmered woman, with coffee cup in one hand and cigarette in the other. She tested and interviewed my boys and returned in May with her expert diagnosis. Pencil poised and eyes interestingly intent, I waited for her words of counsel on Gary. Finally she spoke slowly and earnestly, "You have a very disturbed little boy here." Rather a profound grasp of the obvious, I thought, since anyone could have deduced that upon passing him in the hall. I waited for concrete aids in approaching the problem but none came. We just went over his background again. It was obvious that the psychologist did not have the answer either, and if she did, she had little or no time to work with the teacher and/or child privately and give them the help which they so desperately needed.

The plight that this teacher faced is not unusual, and reflects a growing need to define the school's responsibility for discipline, the subject of the next article, by Morse.

The School's Responsibility for Discipline
William C. Morse

For a beginning teacher, the control and management of pupils is often the foremost problem. Most seasoned teachers have found one way or another to achieve adequate discipline, but still they are frequently faced with a particularly recalcitrant student or class. Field contacts with teachers serve to impress the educational psychologist with the fact that, in recent years, ever increasing effort is being put into the discipline aspect of the educational task. This phenomenon is general, refusing to be confined to one or another locale or age group. It used to be that there were "rough" schools and "normal" schools; now there are difficult children in all schools, whether the setting be the slum or the suburb, and whether the class be kindergarten or high-school senior.

Increasing cultural disorganization has come to be so commonly accepted as a normal condition of the American scene that we are inured to its consequences, one of which is this growing problem of disciplining each new group of youngsters. The state of acquiescence is about over, for certain immediate conditions are forcing educators to give renewed attention to discipline. First, there is the frightening specter of delinquency, so well advertised in the congested cities but evident in the hinterland as well. The school is seen as a major agency in any all-out effort to stem this tide. At the same time, the school itself is making a direct contribution to the problem. The clamor for a return to "basic" or "hard" education is provoking current school discipline problems too. When homework is piled up, demands raised, and

From William C. Morse, "The School's Responsibility for Discipline," *Phi Delta Kappan* (December 1959), pp. 109–113.

rates of failure increased, certain students are stimulated to a frenzy of work, as the proponents hoped. But for many other students with attitudinal and ability handicaps, the school, where they spend much of their waking day, has become less hospitable. Reactions have already been noted in increased school referrals to guidance clinics and pediatricians. Direct rebellion in schools is also more commonplace. There are signs that the post-Sputnik panic is abating, so that this self-imposed school discipline burden may take care of itself.

However, no one supposes that the overall problem of delinquency will take care of itself. There will be demands that schools take action, and simple panaceas will be offered. Already there are signs of anxiety attacks, and in some localities even parents are enjoining the school to resort to more corporal punishment. School boards are being admonished to "crack down." In the last analysis, the burden for such action will rest largely upon the classroom teacher, for it is in the classroom that school behavior is first condoned or criticized. It must be somewhat perplexing to classroom teachers, after attending many mental hygiene revivals where they hear the gospel of love, acceptance, permissiveness, and self-expression, to now be told to restrict, restrain, forbid, and punish. Of course the proponents of soft pedagogy and hard pedagogy both declare that what they advocate is all for the child's own good.

Faced with this dilemma, the vast majority of teachers are eager to find helpful guidelines for their work with resistant pupils. These teachers need the leadership of responsible and well-trained professionals in their analysis. They also need training in new skills so that they can do something in keeping with new understanding. This brief paper presents certain observations which have come from direct in-service work with teachers in the area of control and hygienic management of children.

There are many teachers who possess the level of psychological sophistication needed to make a creative approach to the discipline crisis. They have taken courses, read books, and listened to lectures on group dynamics. Teachers now know that if one wants only surface conformity in school, the answer is simple: establish an educational Gestapo. At this level, as long as a pupil behaves, no concern is wasted on the conscious or unconscious feelings which may be generated. Discipline becomes simply the application of control measures to insure behavior that appears to be acceptable. Threats, monitoring, and punishment play leading roles. One can find that minority of teachers who actually operate on this primitive level, to be sure, but even those who do are frequently unsatisfied and would change. Like the vast majority of teachers, they aspire to do work with the student on a deeper level, recognizing the presence of attitudes, feelings, and unconscious motivations which may underlie certain behavior. But they do not know how to do other than what they now do. By and large, teachers hope that their management of problems will result in students who will be able to control their behavior in subsequent similar situations. In short, and to use old-fashioned terms, teachers would like to effect some degree of character change. In psychological terms, they would foster the development of an adequate superego or conscience. They hope that students will identify with and incorporate values held by the adult, in this case the teacher. And, as the wise teacher well knows, this means bringing into play psychological processes still little understood. Small wonder that the master teacher becomes uneasy at the thought of the responsibility inherent in the process of discipline as we understand it today. For the truth is, the issues are very com-

plex and without easy solution. No single pattern will meet the requirements of all classrooms or every school. Each practitioner and each staff will have to work through to a program which will meet the local demand.

UNDERSTANDING THE CHANGES

How did schools come to be in such a difficult position? The plain fact is that school discipline has become much more complex over the years. The reasons why this is so take us back to certain basic changes which have taken place in education. Only by understanding these changes are we in a position to break the present stalemate of stereotyped attempts parading under the guise of a "new look" in discipline.

One basic change has been an increase in total concern for child behavior now delegated to the school: Parenthetically, it should be noted that educators did not request this increased assignment. Outside conditions and pressures dictated it. Since American education is characterized by loose boundaries of responsibility, the accretion was in the natural order of things. A change in the school clientele coincided with this change in the school's responsibility for the child's life. Schools expanded to include all children. Over a few decades we moved from a select school to a school encompassing education for every child. From stimulating the intellect, we moved toward nourishing the whole child, his feelings as well as his intellect. We became concerned about out-of-school behavior as well as in-school life. With this depth of involvement, discipline requires attention to all phases of the pupil's life, including the fundamental values which underlie behavior. It is no longer possible for the school to depend merely upon utilizing social sanctions initiated by the home and other cultural institutions. It is only too obvious that many pupils come to school without a set of values sufficiently molded to govern their actions properly. For example, appropriate relationships to authority, reasonable motivations for school tasks, or acceptable ways of treating peers can no longer be universally assumed. Consequently, the school has been put in the position of *creating* the actual standard, sometimes in cooperation with the home, but many times operating *in loco parentis*. This indeed represents an educational revolution the implications of which we have largely failed to face.

While responsibility changed, new methodologies lagged behind. We have kept the same basic assembly line and have tried to perform the expanded task by altering a few of the feeder sub-assemblies, such as special service departments. There are many statements of intent, but we have not tooled up to the new tasks. For character is not to be taught like spelling. If we are serious about this responsibility, we must be ready for vast changes in curriculum, methods, teacher-pupil contacts, and time distribution arrangements—to mention a few areas.

Such pronounced changes are vitally needed but they are not likely to come. A more realistic and sober position is to examine what part of the total discipline of the child the school can actually assume as its task, and what processes can be employed to this end. Specific issues must be identified and the relevant psychological knowledge brought in focus. Discipline becomes the keystone, but there are such related elements as motivation, the effect of class differences on behavior, and the impact of cultural agents such as magazines and television. What, in the total matrix, is the school's charge, and how can the responsibility be met?

It becomes obvious that the new classroom teaching role implied here is complex and demanding. For example, teachers need help in determining how much "acceptance" the school can supply a child when the home gives none. How far can teachers go in setting standards for adolescents? Most of all, *how* can we do these things? After a meeting at which some of these issues were discussed, a social worker in the audience stood up and declared, "We are asking too much. Were I teaching, I would have to go home and resign tonight. I could never meet the expectations for a teacher today." It is the classroom teacher who must make a reality of the philosophy blithely mouthed in fall pre-school conferences. Yet the demands on the teacher far outstrip the training we provide.

COURSES IN CONDUCT ARE NO ANSWER

In a recent provocative work, Erikson states, "An expert, it is said, can separate fact from theory, and knowledge from opinion. It is his job to know the available techniques by which statements in his field can be verified. If, in this paper, I were to restrict myself to what is, in this sense, *known* about the 'healthy personality,' I would lead the reader and myself into a very honorable but very uninspiring austerity."[1] Later, speaking of why we do not tell parents in detail how to foster certain developments in the personality, Erikson says, "The answer is because when it comes to human values, nobody knows how to fabricate or manage the fabrication of the genuine article."[2] No wonder the teacher treads softly. Attempts to help children by offering courses in conduct or social relationships are no answer.[3]

In summary, education faces a crisis in discipline because the type of effort needed to build character is more profound than the effort needed merely to control surface behavior. Also, the school can expect less in the way of already made character; it must create as well as sustain and utilize.

Without our realizing it, some of the steps already taken to meet this revolutionary expectation of education have netted as

[1] E. H. Erikson, "Identity and the Life Cycle," *Psychological Issues*, I, No. 1 (1959), p. 50.
[2] *Ibid.*, p. 71.
[3] *Promotion of Mental Health in Primary and Secondary Schools: An Evaluation of Four Projects.* Group for the Advancement of Psychiatry, Topeka, Kansas.

much confusion as solution. Schools tried to meet the situation by hiring experts who were specialists in psychology, social work, and guidance. In order to make them part of the school, social workers became visiting teachers. Psychometrists and clinical psychologists were re-christened school psychologists. A profusion of guidance workers augmented special services. Emphasizing as they do one-to-one contacts, these services soon became saturated and one has yet to hear of a school with enough personnel to relieve the classroom teacher of the responsibility of handling problem situations. Much could be said about the impact of these specialists on the total problem of school discipline. True, they "take care of" many difficult children. In certain schools, the services assume aspects of the child guidance center, offering counseling and sometimes therapy. The number of children given special services varies from school to school, from zero to several per cent. But the culture has succeeded in producing more and more of the serious maladjustment which is reflected in discipline problems. There are increasing numbers of pupils with partially formed characters where considerable additive or corrective effort is required. The school needs the specialists, for they have training and time which few classroom teachers have. But the school needs to put these experts at the service of the classroom teachers far more than has been the case thus far. The day of the independent special department, operating in its own isolated way, will perforce need to end. The first step in meeting the discipline crisis is to examine very carefully the use of our school specialists. This will have to be more than a counting of how many children are "seen" or how many hours of contact can be tabulated. Fortunately, some of these professionals are already re-orienting the view of their role.[4] But a good many are still intrenched behind barriers of spe-

[4] Jeannette Vosk, "The Clinical Psychologist in a Difficult School," American Journal of Orthopsychiatry, XXIX, No. 1 (January 1959), 157–165.

cial technique and jargon. Some will be threatened when they are asked to consider the rightful perimeters of school responsibility and what services the school should supply or the role the specialist should play in helping the classroom teacher. In some states, even the law protects them from meeting the actual problems which the school faces. The parent disciplines from which the specialties are derived will put up smoke screens and cry contamination. This promises to be a real struggle, but there are signs that some specialists have already realized that one-to-one relationships are too costly, that cooperative work and consultation with the teacher will serve more pupils.

As we cast about, are there other inklings of constructive effort? An obvious need is to rebuild the prestige of the classroom teacher in matters of discipline. We already have some cues. This will not be done by more lectures, or more verbalistic courses. It will mean improving support to the teacher from the administrator. By successfully exploiting the distance between these two authorities many pupils evade corrective effort. But more than this, teachers will need new training. Direct work by the specialized experts is needed to help teachers develop a clinical approach to specific problems. This can be done by in-service seminars and supervisory sessions, starting always with the teachers' own perceptions of their difficulties in classroom management. Teachers must learn clinical skills, beginning with a working knowledge of unconscious phenomena and progressing to analysis of their own classroom conditions.

LEARNING NEW DISCIPLINARY SKILLS

But diagnoses by the teacher, or the study of their own situations by various devices, important as this is, is only half the job. At the present time, unfortunately, most of the work stops with diagnosis. The other and more important half is the learning of new skills in actually managing individual students and handling groups. For a long time we have been stymied because we have lacked a conceptual framework for the teacher as a representative of the on-the-line worker in contrast to the specialist. The specialist has his tests and therapeutic techniques. The teacher has been left with unproductive old-style moralizing. Teachers need unique diagnostic and interview techniques by way of methodology. Many writers, Jersild[5] being one of the foremost, have illustrated diagnostic procedure for the use of the classroom teacher. Teachers have also needed a method to work with what they discover if they are to discipline pupils. Redl has supplied this much-needed technique framework under the rubric of "life space interviewing."[6] Essentially, this is the process by which the person who lives hour by hour with children and youth can get at the difficult behavior and handle it in a hygienic manner. Teachers can talk effectively with children without resorting to ineffectual moralizing or punitiveness, the usual stock in trade. We knew that these methods were not effective, but we needed a conceptual framework for something new. Attempts on the part of teachers to apply analytic or Rogerian methods in the action setting of the classroom have at times been unfortunate even to the point of disaster.

There is nothing simple or easy about this essential technique of life space interviewing. It is as sophisticated as the sister technique used in individual therapeutic interviews. But it is a skill teachers can learn to practice effectively. Properly trained in

[5] A. T. Jersild and K. Helfant, *Education for Self-Understanding.* Teachers College, Columbia University, 1953.

[6] F. Redl, "Strategy and Techniques of the Life Space Interview," *American Journal of Orthopsychiatry,* XXIX, No. 1 (January 1959), 1–19.

its use, teachers will have the basic instrument for hygienic management. Once they begin to know not only what is the matter (diagnosis) but what to do (remedial methodology), a certain percentage of the current disciplinary problems will come under control. Of course many other changes will be needed too, for time must be made available, and the number of individual student contacts a teacher has every day must be brought in line. The teacher must have the right to exclude and readmit to his classroom, for there is no control possible these days in a power vacuum. If the principal does not support the teacher, the child learns circumvention and will practice it assiduously. But the teacher will have to do a great deal of the work himself, which is why this new interviewing skill is so vital. Yet well-trained teachers and effective specialists will not meet all the school's discipline problems. . . .

We have been told that it is not democratic to separate. What is democratic about keeping deviate children in the normal classroom? Perhaps the single most needed step in education today is to restore the classroom as a place where normal, relatively normal, and manageable disturbed children and youth can learn together. It can only be done by providing special classes for seriously disturbed youngsters. Of course, those who cannot be helped in the regular classroom will not all fit into any one group, for they include emotionally disturbed, acting out, delinquent, and non-learning children. Schools will have to reassert the right of the professional educators to consult with parents about behavior which requires removal from the regular classroom. The special teacher and ancillary services may then be able to help these children. . . .

As Morse indicated, the most needed educational step for school communities is to re-define their limits on deviant behavior. They must decide what behavior can be tolerated and accepted in their particular psycho-educational setting. For example, an eight-week record of disciplinary cases that were seen by an elementary school principal showed the following range of eighty-two school offenses. This school is located in a transitional neighborhood, in a large urban setting.

OFFENSES	FREQUENCY
Fighting	22
Hitting a child while others held him	5
Biting other children	3
General disorder (pushing, pulling out a chair, screaming in the lunchroom and halls)	30
Rudeness to teachers	6
Obscene notes	3
Obscene language	5
Carrying a knife	1
Urinating in a waste basket	1
Preventing the class from working because of erratic behavior	6
TOTAL	82

In this school, the majority of offenses can be classified as aggressive acts which fall within the range of manageable, deviant behavior. The twenty-two incidences of fighting are not too disturbing to these children, nor to the teachers who are aware that the children are taught to strike back if they are hit and to defend their mother's name when threatened. In other schools, the same amount of aggression and sexuality would be intolerable and would be dealt with in a very different way.

In training teachers to work with emotionally disturbed children, considerable emphasis should be placed on the dynamics of aggression and sexuality. Most teachers, as middle-class children, were taught to deny these impulses. As a result, most teachers are unprepared emotionally to understand and accept the skillful, aggressive tactics of a child who has learned to live with hate and like it. In Redl and Wineman's *The Aggressive Child,* the authors provide many excellent examples of this defense.

McNeil's article describes various aggressive devices and techniques that antisocial, anti-adult boys use as an effective way of communicating and responding to threat. The latter part of the article suggests how adults can intervene to deter aggression and to restore interpersonal peace.

Personal Hostility and International Aggression
Elton B. McNeil

. . . Living with a group of 70 aggressive, antisocial, anti-adult boys provides, in miniature, an unparalleled opportunity to

From Elton B. McNeil, "Personal Hostility and International Aggression," *Journal of Conflict Resolution,* V (September 1961), 279–289. Reprinted by permission.

Elton McNeil is graduate chairman of the University of Michigan Department of Psychology.

experiment with the natural history of aggression and its deterrence. The setting for these observations was The University of Michigan Fresh Air Camp. The camp is a clinical training center for graduate students drawn from the fields of clinical psychology, psychiatric nursing, psychiatric social work, and special education; the campers are boys recruited from detention homes, training schools, mental hospitals, and clinics throughout the State of Michigan. The camp specializes in children who hate. Since it is a diagnostic and therapeutic training center there is an "unnatural" element to the interaction of these aggressive children; their most violent and gross expressions of hostility are obstructed by the adults for reasons of common humanity. In almost all other respects (except for physical punishment) the camp duplicates the normal life-setting of the child who is in violent protest against the form society has taken, the demands it makes on him, and the forces who represent the present world order. The camp, then, is an arena in which each child acts out his destructive pathology in relating to himself, his peers, and the rules of peaceful living.

THE COMMUNICATION OF THREAT

At the beginning of the camp season, our angry young men are usually strangers to one another. While each has a long record of war-like proclivities, he has only a dim awareness of the details of the hostile encounters of the other boys. Each boy has organized his perception of the world and his position in it along the dimension of toughness, fierceness, fearlessness, and resistance to the influence of others. It is these ingredients that come to flavor the social mixture which shortly emerges. At once, the boys begin a pattern of militant probing of one another in their individual and group relations seeking to establish a basis for dominance and submission.

The camp aggressive pecking order is established by the boys through a number of interpersonal devices which resemble those used by nations to establish their position in the world. A description of some of the most prominent devices and brief case illustrations of their use will be presented here but no reliable objective data are available. . . .

SABER-RATTLING

Most often, sabers are rattled on a to-whom-it-may-concern basis. Tall tales of aggressive prowess, violation of the law, defiance of adults, and resistance to requests all communicate threat to the eager listeners. They constitute a declaration of readiness to act violently as well as a demonstration of fearlessness. As soon as some recognizable order begins to emerge in the group, the saber-rattling becomes increasingly target-oriented and these subtle communications of threat focus on that person perceived as most powerful. The art of saber-rattling is practiced with great finesse by these boys, and they are careful to make their threats ambiguous and not easily challenged. At this stage in their relations with others they cannot afford, nor do they intend, to have a showdown. They rather are seeking to detect saber-rattling-induced fear in others. This device is the least expensive and least dangerous form of establishing dominance over others. It is also, by its very ambiguity, the least effective. Its most usual consequence is heightened saber-rattling by the intended victims. If at this point the threat is reinforced by sudden, violent action, the dominance pattern quickly crystallizes with the advantage going to the aggressor. The cost of an ill-timed or poorly prepared assault is immense. The aggressor who fails is pounced upon by the others and forced to suffer further humiliation and loss in status. Being aware that this fate awaits the loser, saber-rattling is intense and prolonged but the point of no return is carefully avoided.

The most usual form of saber-rattling is the threat of massive retaliation if any other boy tampers with one's personal possessions. This is done before any tampering occurs. Tommy, for example, walked into his cabin the first day, distributed his possessions on his bed, coolly surveyed his new cabin mates, turned to the counselor and announced, "If anyone touches this stuff he's going to be minus some teeth." The

fact that these were the first words he uttered made his aggressiveness have greater
impact and the generalized nature of the
threat was such that no other boy felt personally challenged. In this instance the
counselor was taken aback and erred by
stating that he didn't think anyone would
touch his property. When the counselor
failed to deal with the fact that threatening
others was improper behavior and responded, rather, by assuring the threatener
he would not have to carry out the threat,
the other boys could only conclude that the
threatener was indeed powerful. In the
first few moments of his diplomatic contact
with the other boys, the threatener had
gained an enormous advantage; an advantage that could have been limited by a
proper and well-timed response.

RECOUNTING PAST GLORIES

A refined version of the communication of threat is to be found in the recital of
glory attained in great historical conflicts.
This device has a quality of the "Terrible
Turk" about it and is not subject to critical
or objective appraisal by the listeners. To be
sure, the audience regularly discounts these
tales of heroism and power, but a lingering
doubt is planted in the mind of the consumer and this doubt can grow vigorously
when nurtured by the intended victim's
fears. The potential combatants match
story-for-story while they eye one another
warily to judge the degree of current prowess that remains from this colorful history.
I have seen boys literally come to believe
their own propaganda and act hastily and
ill-advisedly while swept up in their delusion of capability. As their fictions wax more
incredible, the level of threat perceived by
others increases apace and the probability
of open conflict becomes assured. Once
these tribal tales have become excessive
and when the dominance-seeker is confident
of his ground, he can force the issue simply
by announcing publicly that the other is a
liar. This grievous insult can only be re-
venged by battle or backing down. Either
alternative fixes another portion of the rank-
ing of dominance and submission. Again,

the challenger has the advantage and usually eliminates the other as a competitive
threat. A bold course of action, particularly
when it is excessively violent, acts to inhibit
similar behavior among the observers and
to force them to soft pedal their accounts of
ancient heroism.

Harold had been sent to the detention
home (for two days) when he was caught
extorting money from younger school children. One evening he was regaling his cabin
mates with stories of a series of fierce fights
he had with bigger boys at the detention
home and of how he had used judo to best
them. As the other boys listened with fascination and asked detailed questions, he began to elaborate in an unbelievable fashion.
One other boy vied for attention by telling
similarly exaggerated tales, each one top-
ping the other. As the audience became split
between the two, the boys began to accuse
one another of lying and fell to fighting in
an attempt publicly to demonstrate their
prowess. They remained enemies for the
duration of camp since each had unfor-
givably wounded the other psychologically.

THE ROLL CALL OF ALLIES

Early in the process of social maneuver the child can increase his potential
threat by making unsparing reference to
his "gang" at home or other allies who
would join him in an aggressive adventure.
This roll call of allies tends to be highly unrealistic since their capacity to deliver military support and their willingness to become embroiled in a purely local contest
are highly speculative. In itself, the reference to allies is an admission of weakness
that does not go unnoticed by those exposed
to such claims. Unless some convincing
demonstration of allied solidarity is forthcoming, our aggressive children demote the
users of such a threat to a submissive status.
The usual response of the threatener is then
to redouble his effort to frighten others with
the strength of his allies and this action
serves only to confirm the group's original
low estimate of his capacity.

Allies prove to communicate the greatest threat when they are obviously present, certain to act immediately in retaliation, capable of inflicting substantial damage, and are not paraded out of fear. To accomplish these ends, groups of boys consolidate their relations with others into a gang structure and a group code which binds them together. By institutionalizing their aggressive behavior and becoming interdependent on one another, they increase the risk of becoming involved in a personally meaningless conflict but the price is always judged well worth the benefit they receive through the strength of unity. The formation of gangs in the camp makes the roll call of allies a more meaningful threat and one that serves as a focus for the endless tug-of-war of dominance-submission relationships. As the gangs come to resemble nation-states, the quality of aggressive interplay shifts to a different dimension with altered characteristics. To judge the individual's readiness to respond with hostility you must now account for his relationship to his social group and the complexity of the prediction increases immeasurably.

Few leaders are lone wolves. There is a reassurance in the existence of a gang and we never encountered a child for whom the notion of submerging individual desires to the group good was not already a familiar idea. Tony (one of our most accomplished delinquent leaders) began, with the aid of a single lieutenant, to form a loyal group by what now seem to us to be a classic series of steps. Once the broad outline of dominance and submission had been established he forced the weakest boys to join him or suffer punishment. At the same time, he bribed those of middle power by sharing stolen candy and cigarettes with them. Having assembled a hard core of five boys, he consolidated them into a loyal group by leading forays (night raids, attacking lone younger children, forcing adult decisions in their favor, etc.) which made the group both disciplined and visible to others. The remaining three boys, who had been strong enough to resist Tony's leadership, soon joined the ranks with the others since they found the array of Tony's allies too powerful to withstand. Tony's visible display of allies forced the cabin holdouts to line up with him but it also acted to threaten neighboring cabins whose borders he regularly trespassed. Other gangs formed (using the argument of mutual defense against Tony) and open warfare soon resulted. As an interesting sidelight, those groups formed only with the common motive of defense suffered more internal bickering and never developed a coherent policy of meeting Tony's threats and invasions.

OUR GROWING MIGHT

For both groups and individuals, threat is apparent in communication to others about growing prowess and might. In camp this most frequently takes the form of description of exotic weaponry secretly available. Thus, a real or imagined switchblade knife that a boy implies he has available to him is a source of considerable anxiety to others. If he is known to be weaponless, he can resort to claiming that, out of common cause, others are planning to supply him with the means of destruction. The core of this threat is mystery and the wise propagandist lets the threat spawn its twisted offspring in the fantasy of his victim. A knife or other weapon is a meaningful threat since it tends to equalize the more obvious and observable dimensions of size, age, and strength. In much the same fashion, psychological warfare about strength is conducted via the enhancement of observable properties. The boys spend hours practicing boxing or muscle-building in highly public places and they work to achieve and accomplish feats of ability in fields related to aggressive capacity (i.e., athletics). The threat of growing might usually spurs the intended victims to engage in an armaments race with the threatener. If this course is taken and not restrained by some outside force, the inevitable consequence is open warfare. As each hostile child successively increases his threat to the other, the process reaches a point where it is intolerable to both and the tension becomes mutually unbearable. At this juncture, the need for relief from the tension of threat is greater than the deterrence provided by fear of the consequences of warfare and combat soon is joined.

A favorite (and regular) method of accruing additional might for a gang is to steal table knives from the dining room. These are sharpened, surreptitiously, for a later "rumble" of unspecified dimensions. In one such incident, a single table knife was stolen at lunch and the word spread so rapidly through the grapevine that forty knives were missing after supper. We forced a general disarmament by offering amnesty to all who would surrender their weapons and we recovered all but a few. The most determined of our aggressive leaders insisted they were "clean" and kept their knives hidden. Throughout that particular summer we were plagued by the continual theft of knives and as each culprit was apprehended he would insist that he needed it for self-defense since the staff had been unable to disarm the others. While the weapons were *never* used in combat, the threat posed by their possession caused a succession of fights and provoked extreme distrust among individuals and gangs.

DETERRENCE BY ATTACK

The single most effective device for spreading threat throughout the group is to be found in deterrence by attack or what might be described as the vicious example. The usual sequence of events involves the conscious selection, by a determinedly aggressive boy, of an innocent victim who possesses exactly the proper characteristics and potentialities. Once selected, the victim is provoked into a hostile act (usually over possessions) and then is soundly beaten by the attacker. The original hostility on the part of the victim is used by the attacker as a guarantee of immunity from authority and the victim's savage defeat spreads like wild fire through the community and acts at once as a threat to everyone. The aggressor need not repeat this demonstration again since he has dramatically and violently established his dominance and conveyed a widespread threat. He then proceeds to prey on any and all unprotected boys using

saber-rattling as his chief and highly effective weapon. The only limit on his capacity to aggrandize against others is the aggressive strength he had to begin with. If he is not very powerful he will be deterred by bigger and more powerful boys unless he converts his victims into satellites who will fight as he commands them. It is interesting that satellites achieved by conquest become, before long, willing allies who share a common sense of purpose with the aggressor. They soon "forget" the basis of their association with the aggressor and as they share the benefits of association with him, become convinced they are partners rather than prisoners. Attempts to explain the true nature of their relationship to the aggressor fail to dissuade unless the benefits of dissociation are made as attractive as those available as a satellite. The satellizing person, whatever his original motivation, tends to be actively well informed about the advantages of his status and only vaguely able to comprehend the abstract possibilities of other arrangements. This is no accident; it is a routine aspect of dominance-submission relationships.

Aggressively delinquent boys rarely attack their victims without first provoking them to some hostile act. Deterrence by attack is judged in terms of the transparency of the rationalization that is used to justify the assault. Among boys who hunger for power, the flimsiest of excuses is deemed sufficient and they are constantly on the alert for the proper opportunity. The most vicious illustration was the case of a boy who hit a "friend" in the mouth while the "friend" was taking a mid-afternoon nap. The inhumanity of this act was so threatening to the other boys that the aggressor became the undisputed leader of the group. It became a major task to demonstrate to the boys that they followed out of fear rather than respect.

THE RESPONSE TO THREAT

The most usual response to threat is the experience of fear. Fear in turn stimulates counter measures designed to remove the threat and it is these counter measures that produce warfare between boys or gangs. The classic obverse case is that of the small boy who rattles his saber, recounts his past glories, calls the roll of his allies, and defines his growing might only to be greeted by raucous laughter and amusement on the part of the "victim" who is twice his size. The hollow threat provokes no fear and no retaliation. When faced squarely with a meaningful threat the victim usually responds in kind. He threatens through a series of "if" propositions. He threatens to deprive (if you attack, I will withhold things you want). He threatens to retaliate in kind or he threatens a horrible but unspecified fate for the attacker. This exchange of ultimatums is always halted by combat if one of the two boys is certain of his capacity to win. It is halted short of combat if the ultimatums are face-saving and clearly recognized as such by both the stronger and the weaker parties. In any event, the weaker party must be the first to cease issuing ultimatums (thus tacitly admitting defeat) if he wishes to avoid open hostility of a physical sort.

Given the perception of threat by others, aggressive boys indulge in all the familiar national patterns of response. They threaten massive retaliation, they engage in brinkmanship, they openly discuss first and second strike capabilities, they engage in armament races, they recruit allies, and they assume a succession of defensive postures in their search for security and freedom from fear. They tend regularly to underestimate the capacity of the enemy as they concentrate on what *they* will do in retaliation for attack. They tend to stereotype the enemy and simplify his thought processes in order to be able to plan easily for defense. When the threat is directed toward a group or gang, there are long arguments about policy and defense with the actual behavior at the time of open conflict being quite spontaneous, unthinking, and not according to plan.

The most common first reaction to threat is an unfortunate one—communication with the enemy ceases. The immediate effect of this withdrawal from direct contact with the opponent is to render the determinants of action as much a consequence of fantasy and fear as of an appraisal of reality. Corrective information about motives, tools, or plans are left to speculation and the machinations of fear and anxiety. Preparations for defense are always misinterpreted by the antagonist as preparation for attack and a vicious circle is closed. The catalogue of reactions to threat is a familiar one and need not be detailed. It is at this point in the interpersonal relations of children who hate that mechanisms for the deterrence of aggression become mandatory.

THE DETERRENCE OF AGGRESSION

The attempt to head off disorder or to restore peace is an unending process with these children. Ideally, all our efforts should be directed toward prevention and the construction of a world in which there would be no need for assault as a part of interpersonal diplomacy. This, unfortunately, is not possible in a situation in which individuals have been allowed to develop an aggressive style of life and have had experiences which assure the development of hatred toward the world as it is. We must start, then, with the fact of aggression as a way of life; aggression that has proved a profitable device in the past or aggression that has been the single alternative offered to the child in his early life. A power-hungry potential leader finds in aggression the path to his aims.

The devices we use to control aggression are mostly stop-gap in nature. They are attempts to limit the expression of hostility so that the long process of reorganizing the individual and of providing him with alternatives for achievement other than war can be begun. The catalogue of deterrents to be described is not rank-ordered in terms of effectiveness since the usefulness of each technique varies immensely with the specifics of each situation.

DISENGAGEMENT

This deterrent to aggression has the advantage of controlling the intensity of hostile interchange and the flaw of severing communication between the warring parties. We make an attempt to prevent complete communication loss by restricting contact only when it is absolutely necessary. In many instances we can find neutral zones of activity in which the activity itself acts as a cushion to the mutual aggression. Group activities that do not require one-to-one contact can, if properly supervised, absorb much mutual antagonism. The purpose of disengagement is to eliminate the possibility of head-on encounter while encouraging interaction that can have a positive outcome. Transient aggressive outbursts that are a consequence of passing frustrations frequently dissolve in the midst of the substitute activity and then need no further attention. If no better than neutrality is achieved, each of the boys tends to store up hostility for a later encounter. Disengagement without constructive re-establishment of communication between the warring parties becomes nothing more than a temporary stand-off and increases the tension and perceived threat between them.

In order to disengage two combatants and yet maintain communication between them, we appoint a neutral third party (a counselor) to act as intermediary between them. In this fashion, each boy is prevented from directly provoking the other or responding directly to provocation since direct contact of any sort is a violation of the rules to which we have agreed. In order to break the hostile deadlock, the counselor arranges a series of highly gratifying situations in which they both can participate (ice-cream making, special trips, etc.) without competing for the gratification. Activities that work best are those in which their independent contributions produce an otherwise unobtainable end product which

they can then mutually enjoy. Preparing and cooking food for a cook-out is effective if their individual hungers are not allowed to become too intense.

a. *Demilitarized Zones.* When the level of mutual hostility is extremely high, disengagement must take a more drastic form than the simple and general admonition to stay away from one another. The stated specification of situations and areas to be avoided becomes necessary. The purpose of the demilitarized zones goes beyond reducing the possibility of open conflict. It serves as an indication to the fighters of the seriousness with which an aggressive solution to their problems is viewed. Frequently, the complexity of the arrangements for disengagement and demilitarization of certain zones impresses each child with his own power (why else all the adult attention?) and, in a sense, both get carried away with admiration for their own "wanted" posters. It is an excellent face-saving device for all concerned and it is greeted with a sigh of relief by the combatants.

b. *Secession.* Failing all else, we sometimes allow small groups to secede from the larger society for brief periods of time. This is an extreme form of disengagement which permits a gross reorganization of the individual or group relationships free of the stimulation to aggress provided by others. Such a move must be a voluntary one and communication about the meaning of the secession and plans for eventual unity with the larger society must be continuous. The most usual outcome of such secession is that of a growing awareness on the part of those involved of their own contribution to their difficulties. Secession is most effective when blame for interpersonal difficulties is being attributed solely to the actions of others. Secession amounts to a process of eliminating the supposed causes of the difficulty in order to examine the individual's behavior free of stimulation and provocation. The effectiveness of this device depends in great part on the willingness of adults to allow aggressive children to prey on one another rather than the larger society. Humanity dictates that such experiments be done with caution since they regularly prove to be painful to all concerned.

TREATIES AND TRUCES

Cease fire arrangements can be made with some success either on an implicit or explicit basis. As with most instances of aggressive conflict, we can depend on the existence of considerable fear in both boys. The explosive and uncontrolled character of open hostility is such that no one can really be comfortable with it and it is this fear-inspiring quality which brings our antagonists to the diplomatic table. The willingness to negotiate is stimulated further by the awareness of disapproval for aggressive behavior by the outside world. In any event, the meanest and toughest of our clients has always welcomed the opportunity to protest his innocence and to accuse his opposite number. We have discovered that any form of treaty or truce has a limited future. They tend to last only as long as it is to the mutual interest of the parties to maintain them. The moment of rupture is never fully predictable since it is a function of any of a number of situations which can act to light the fuse. Continued communication, positive experiences, and therapy focused on the reasons for the mutual hostility are needed. Without these reasoned attempts at a solution of the relationship, treaties and truces do no more than provide time for the emotions to fester and for both sides to prepare anew.

OCCUPATION TROOPS

In the most severe instances, disengagement, demilitarization, or truce and treaty are not sufficient deterrents. A stronger third party is required to police the terms of the agreement. These watch dogs need to be vigilant in the early stages of their task and be sensitive to the developing situation in order to pass control on to those being policed. If vigilance continues beyond the demands of the situation, the watch dogs become the recipients of hostility issuing from both sides. Efforts to anticipate difficulties and to head off trouble are resented since they take place at a point in time where the consequences of a failure to interfere are far from apparent. Such peace-making is trying to the most expert of men.

Our use of occupation troops is usually on a territorial basis; members of warring gangs are not allowed to be in the cabin area without adult supervision. This third party is always resented as an inhibitor of the right to self-determination and receives not only aggression displaced from the true target but is hated for what it represents as a symbol of parent-like interference. In part, the resentment arises because the occupation troops are a constant reminder that the child is not considered capable of managing his own affairs. This visible insult to one's maturity is a frustration that evokes aggression which gets heightened every time a dispute is settled in favor of the enemy.

INSPECTION

Occupation troops also act as inspectors to assure that the terms of agreement are being kept. Inspection is resented in the extreme by innocent and guilty alike. In instances when contraband is being sought (cigarettes, knives, stolen property, etc.) the victims of the act of inspection use the act in an attempt to establish a basis for emotional blackmail against the inspectors. Cooperation tends to be sullen or coupled with resentment and inspectors soon are torn between their need to enforce the law and an equally compelling need to establish friendly and unsuspicious relations with those being inspected. We have discovered no way to make threat of inspection appear to be other than what it is—an expression of distrust of others. The more thorough the inspector, the more hostility his acts engender. In an effort to circumvent this situation, we do not ask those who have a good relationship with the child or who must deal with him in other circumstances to act as inspectors. We try to leave negotiation and diplomacy for those who are neutral or whose relationship is uncontaminated.

In addition to the psychological damage which inspection seems to do, it happens also to be fairly ineffective as a means of controlling behavior or discovering contraband. Among boys with records of delinquency, the normal channels of intelligence are as effective as, and if done properly, free of the stigma and indignity of, inspection. If the participants agree to the inspection and cooperate with it, we can deduce either that the inspected have decided to match wits with us or that inspection is unnecessary. The hostility generated by inspection hardly makes it worth the effort.

SOCIAL ISOLATION

In the tradition of all blockades, social isolation acts to deprive the aggressive child of his victim. This is a last resort used only for totally unmanageable children since it is essentially a punitive act. Being deprived of the society of his peers is an especially painful event since the average child is without the requisite skills for tolerating aloneness. Isolation is usually entered into with bravado by the child but this soon passes into intense longing for companions. We isolate the child from those with whom he cannot relate peacefully but we do not remove him completely from human contact. There are advantages to positive contact with other non-combatants and all the child's contacts are supervised by an understanding adult. The role of adult supervision is not that of police and prisoner, it is rather that of a friend to a child in trouble. All of the adult's efforts are directed to understanding the source of the child's conflict and to providing insight about it to the child. In this manner, we again pursue our policy of expanded rather than restricted communication about the problem to be solved. In our search for the sources of irritation we need always to probe beneath the surface of the distasteful behavior. To the degree that we stereotype

and over-simplify, we fail at our task and hostility breaks out anew.

Social isolation is used only for violent and dangerous children. When a child is isolated socially, he is removed from his cabin and while he has access to all of the facilities of camp he is never allowed to contact (or be in the vicinity of) those toward whom he has hostile feelings. Two conditions are imposed: (1) he must work actively to solve his problem of relating to the group, (2) he must make enough progress to be able to return to his group within a three-day period. If we fail to succeed in this effort we send the boy back to the detention home. In essence, sending him home is the equivalent of establishing a complete blockade so that we no longer render him any service. With all the resources at our command we find we are forced, at times, to take such extreme steps.

AN APPRAISAL OF THE DETERRENCE OF AGGRESSION

With all the skill and experience we have accumulated in the management and deterrence of aggression, we must still report cases that resist the best of our efforts. Aggression with an admixture of psychosis or aggression with deep roots may require lengthy treatment without much hope for success. When such children reach the age when they are more able to instrument the hostility they feel or when they rise to positions of power in a society, the problem of curbing them is intensified incredibly. Their hostility evokes an echo in the unexpressed anger of those who follow them and the cloak of rationality and righteousness soon descends over their behavior.

The behavior of an aggressive individual can be controlled, as we have demonstrated, but only under special circumstances. In our case, the aggressive child is relatively powerless against adults experienced with hostility in all of its forms and almost all of our control issues from this relationship. The older and more experienced the child, the less effective are our controls and the more we must rely on repressive measures.

Our observations of this microcosm of aggression have taught us several things. We have come to know of the intimate connection between fear and aggression and have learned never to deal with one without the other. We have discovered that the most usual error is that of underestimating the fear component in aggressive acts. It is most often for this reason that solutions to aggression tend to fail. We have been forced to face squarely the powder-keg-and-lighted-match character of hostile persons. Their emotions and their capacity to aggress are ever-present dangers to peaceful existence and form the basis for seemingly trivial incidents that trigger great explosions.

The role of fear has its greatest impact when communications are severed between the hostile units. A rise in tension regularly accompanies the failure to communicate since the anchoring points in reality are eliminated. Ignorance gives fear free reign and elevates tension and the perception of threat to the point that the reality of capacity to attack becomes less vital than the promise of freedom from tension.

Deterrence of aggression we have found always to be a part solution and an unstable one at best. Unless the basic causes of aggression are remedied, deterrence can bring only a false sense of security. Positive deterrence in the form of need satisfaction and acceptable alternative forms of behavior must be a necessary second step.

While it is apparent that man is unlikely to discover a cure-all for his aggressive nature, it is also true that the world is populated by persons for whom aggression is not a problem. For nations of men this enviable state of affairs is achieved when the standards of behavior they value are such as to exclude aggression as a proper means of solving problems. While we are able to accomplish this in individuals more often than we fail at it, the process by which it is achieved is not so clear that we can draw up a set of fool-proof specifications for the mass production of such persons. This is an instance in which we cannot afford to fail in the process of socialization as often as we do. The nature of societies is such that the exceptions often prove to be our undoing. The task of socialization is an unending one since each generation grows to confront us with exactly the same dilemma we have faced since the beginning of time.

While the management of aggressive behavior is difficult in its own rights, the fusion of aggression and sexuality in overt behavior has an effect on most teachers that is equal only to the blast of the dirty bomb.

When a child shouts at a teacher to perform certain physical tricks with his body that are anatomically impossible, the child not only gives way to his impulse. He also enjoys the underlying motivation of this verbal aggressive sexual obscenity—to shock the teacher by striking him in a forbidden area. Unfortunately for the untrained teacher, the sudden exposure to primitive sexuality does hurt and the teacher is shocked. Temporarily his feelings are frozen, but they quickly become thawed by a heatwave of anger. If the teacher acts on his feelings and becomes counter-aggressive, the child's offensive move has been successful. Since adult retribution in the last analysis is more powerful, the child may lose the war, but he will always remember the victory of this battle. Once again, we see the necessity for understanding the dynamic interpretation of behavior. Perhaps in no other area do teachers receive less help than in understanding the dynamics of sexual behavior.

Another facet of this problem occurs in permissive treatment settings where children are allowed to verbalize obscenities and profanities under the naive guise that this is therapeutic. The only justification for such permissiveness may occur during an individual or group therapy session. Rarely, should it be tolerated in a group design like a classroom. *If the limits are not set on this behavior, the adults are failing to protect the children from subsequent feelings of guilt and to protect the group from becoming intoxicated by sexual and aggressive excitement.* In both cases, the lack of protection against a flood of excitement can only lead to program deterioration and destructive acting out.

In the next article, McNeil and Morse describe their clinical experience at the University of Michigan Fresh Air Camp. They discuss the various forms of sexual expression and describe ten typical adult reactions to sexuality. This article should be followed by an active class discussion, which should include the specific methods that special classes, special schools, detention homes, psychiatric hospitals, and state hospitals use in managing sexuality in children.

The Management of Sex in Emotionally Disturbed Children
Elton B. McNeil and William C. Morse

Surprisingly, the many volumes written about the institutional care of emotionally disturbed children rarely make systematic reference to the problems of dealing with sex. An examination of the indexes of such books would give little clue to the seriousness of the problem of behavior among institutionalized children. While sex is discussed and commented on, it is not delineated as systematically as are other impulse systems such as aggression. Most descriptions of sexual attitudes, feelings or behavior are limited to the confines of a case history format and suggest that problems, when they occur, are individual rather than group issues. The paradox presented by this relative lack of attention arises from the fact that professionals experienced in caring for emotionally disturbed children regularly report that sexual behavior is a delicate and difficult psychological problem requiring sensitive management by responsible adults. In theory, sex is accorded the role of prime mover; in the literature

From Elton B. McNeil and William C. Morse, "The Institutional Management of Sex in Emotionally Disturbed Children," *American Journal of Orthopsychiatry*, XXXIV (January 1964), 115–124. Copyright, the American Orthopsychiatric Association, Inc. Reprinted by permission.

of practice it does not seem to be accorded this status.

In rare instances, clear and detailed accounts are given both of the nature of sexual behavior among institutionalized children and of the techniques and principles of adult response to it. There is substantial question whether these reports reflect practices typical of most institutions but the norms for comparison are not readily available. Probably the most extreme statement of practice and belief is to be found in A. S. Neill's description of Summerhill. He maintains, for example, that "sex is the basis of all negative attitudes toward life" "that heterosexual play in childhood is the royal road . . . to a healthy, balanced adult sex life," and that "at Summerhill, nothing is unmentionable and no one is shockable." The discrepancy between his theory and practice is made clear when he notes, "If in Summerhill I approved of my adolescent pupils sleeping together, my school would be suppressed by the authorities." It is difficult to find a modern, systematic and detailed representation of the more conservative point of view, which probably characterizes the average institution.

The scarcity of careful delineation of

the principles of institutional management of sex in emotionally disturbed children exists with good reason. In part, it occurs because professional views of the sexual attitudes and behavior of children are probably more "radical" and "permissive" than those held by the average member of society. Then too, institutional life is a highly artificial sub-society that has unique needs and demands that must be met if it is to maintain an operational stability. A vital additional force promoting the avoidance of this aspect of clinical management can be traced to the fact that, even among professionally "liberated" child-care workers, sexual behavior in children is not responded to with as much psychological comfort as are other forms of behavior. Finally, there is an illusion that extensive agreement exists regarding a psychologically healthy approach to sex education for children—an illusion that retains its apparent substance by avoiding close scrutiny.

THE VARIETIES OF SEXUAL EXPRESSION

As an example of the problems of institutional management of sex, we will refer to some aspects of the behavior of the population of emotionally disturbed boys who attend the University of Michigan Fresh Air Camp. The camp is a clinical training center for graduate students drawn from the fields of clinical psychology, psychiatric nursing, psychiatric social work and special education; the campers are boys recruited from detention homes, training schools, mental hospitals and clinics throughout the State of Michigan. As a short-term diagnostic and therapeutic training center, we deal with a broad spectrum of symptoms and degrees of emotional disturbance.

The range of sexual behavior that may eventually emerge among some campers in this setting includes sexual language and gestures, "playing the dozens," group and individual masturbation, homosexuality, exhibitionism, attempts to promote hetero-

sexual experience and some standard and not-so-standard perversions. Lest the wrong interpretation be made, it should be noted that this kaleidoscope of sexuality is a range of behaviors and not the mode.

Unlike a "closed" institution, the camp is an "open" setting, which tends to exaggerate or highlight the range, frequency and intensity of sexual expression. The camp community is effectively isolated from the traffic of persons who usually enter and exit from the typical hospital ward while performing their specialized duties. The pattern of shift working is less pronounced and 24-hour-a-day contact through the sharing of meals and recreation areas breeds a quick familiarity among all community members. Thus, while a clinical camp for disturbed children is not representative of other institutions, the uniqueness of its social and psychological structure is particularly advantageous for the study of sexual behavior in its full-blown form.

At camp, the first few days constitute a nonsexual "honeymoon." During this time of ferreting out the social and sexual mores of the institution, a polite facade masks the underlying motives of some campers. Before long, there is an outburst of rage on the part of one of the children and this rage is accompanied, naturally, by profanity or sexual reference directed at a fellow camper or restraining counselor. The ripple of shock that accompanies this action is apparent in the other campers even when it is treated casually by the counselors. The ability to shock or to take others aback carries with it a substantial prestige value and what was done in rage soon becomes the product of cold calculation. Rapidly, sexual reference is employed in behalf of aggression, resistance and defiance of adult authority and the degree of contagion is substantial. While many of the younger children know the words but not the music of sexual swearing, its spread and elevation to the commonplace is rapid.

Sexual language, when repeated with sufficient frequency, tends to bleach out the affect associated with it. It soon suffers the impotence of the commonplace and thus the originator is forced to a new level of innovation. This often takes the form of sexual gestures. The advantage accruing to these manifestations of sex lies in the space-conquering capacity. An emotionally disturbed child can signal some insult across the length of a dining hall and accomplish his nefarious ends at long distance. Any form of sexual expression at these lower levels must be promoted constantly to a new, more complex and more dazzling achievement if it is to maintain the interest of the peer audience. Sexual language may evolve into "playing the dozens" as an exercise in verbal sexual proficiency, it may take the form of peer sexual invitation, or it may find its outlet in an exhibitionistic display of sexuality on the part of the child. Sexual conversations often focus on fantasies about adult sexual behavior and it is apparent that these contain thinly veiled anxiety and curiosity about parents, rather than adults in general. For the child, aggression has become a paramount issue and sex is pressed into its service. Physiological events such as enuresis and encopresis become suspect as subtle sexual expressions (or at least complications in the direct expression of sexuality) and, because of the varying levels of psychological and psychosexual maturity among the witnessing children, confusion reigns.

What was an individual sexual enterprise often becomes a group phenomenon within small subgroups. The level of dynamic group excitement that can be provoked by sexual overtures is unparalleled. The final phase of this burgeoning sexuality for the minority of the children expresses itself in two fashions: (1) an intense concern with the personal life (translated "sexual life") of the counselors and (2) an attempt to promote sexual experience with the female counselors. This latter has a quality reminiscent of the early 1900s about it. The male children view the female sex impulse as something akin to a raging beast that needs only to have the bars of its cage

rattled. Sex talk and exhibitionism (pulling down one another's trousers, provocative dances, and the like) are viewed as potent stimuli that will somehow sexually excite the female of the species. The fact that the reality never matches the fantasy does not deter a child who may be acting out a seduction fantasy.

It must be emphasized that sex constitutes only one of the huge variety of problems we deal with among our disturbed boys. There are many of our 70 clients who *never* get involved sexually at any level and while a steady undercurrent of sexuality may exist for some cabin groups it may remain fairly quiescent in its expression, flaring up only occasionally. Our clinical efforts are directed, primarily, toward the management of aggression and in dealing with a number of kinds of neurotic conflict.

The management problems posed by these sexual expressions can be arranged under three broad headings: (1) the management of sexuality, (2) the fusion of sex and aggression and (3) the adult response to various sexual actions.

THE MANAGEMENT OF SEXUALITY

Perhaps the single greatest error made by adults dealing with disturbed children is in underestimating the amount of guilt and anxiety that is generated by sexual activities and thoughts. These emotions complicate the process of management, since they serve to produce an emotional hangover which, in turn, becomes motivation in other situations. It is difficult to deal with sexual events and achieve closure for specific incidents in the short run. In most institutions the child comes into continuous contact with a variety of persons, and a sexual situation mishandled by one adult can trigger a chain of emotional outbursts the source of which is almost undetectable. The subsequent mishandling compounds and complicates the original event.

The attempt to short-cut the intensification of psychological distress follows a general set of principles at the Fresh Air Camp. We start with an assumption of the naturalness of the urge to sexual expression, an awareness of the extensive social prohibitions that apply to it and a wariness about the overdetermination of sexual behavior. Sexual language, for example, is not reacted to with shock or surprise but it is *not* encouraged by any staff member. Since such behavior is socially unacceptable, attempts are made to analyze its source, to help the child understand the motivation behind it, to substitute some more acceptable form of expression and to restrict its appearance to private situations if it does not abate. The logic of this modified form of social control is that public sexual language, or behavior for that matter, infringes on the freedom of others, is socially disapproved and produces emotional difficulties for other disturbed children. Thus, although the fact of sexuality is not disapproved, it is classified as a private activity and the source and nature of public views of sex are explained. Children—even most emotionally disturbed ones —seem to be able to comprehend the logic of firm but understanding social control of sex. This is not to say, of course, that this necessarily results in adequate control.

Sexual information is supplied to the children whenever it is requested and the request is deemed legitimate. More than once our graduate student counselors have been duped by the children in this respect. The counselors' emotional investment in education, learning and the "facts" of life makes them leap to the unwarranted conclusion that childish ignorance is the prime offender and prime source of sexual activity. Disturbed children as well as normal ones can use a sex education lecture as a sniggering, leering, vicarious source of sexual excitement. While there is a vast amount of misinformation mixed with patches of sophistication, even the child who needs information needs more than that. He needs a thorough exploration of his attitudes, beliefs and feelings, since it is in that area that he suffers most.

A usual device for the management

of sexuality is to reduce the level of temptation to which the child is exposed. This need not be perceived as "spying" or "patrolling" by the children although, in fact, it achieves this end. The presence of adults during most of the waking hours of the child, if it is not restrictive, helps him past times he could not otherwise manage comfortably. These adults ought to be able to deal with sex in a calm, unemotional and intelligent way.

FUSION OF SEX AND AGGRESSION

The problems of controlling sexual behavior and its attendant anxiety and guilt come primarily as a consequence of the fusion of sex and aggression. Among disturbed boys, both the sexual behavior and its concomitants soon are tinged with aggressive overtones. The camp specializes in "children who hate" and most of their psychological problems sooner or later become focused on aggression, yet any disturbed child is an easy prey for this admixture of motives. The male sexual role is normally one of enterprise and domination and its regulation and balance require a high degree of sensitivity to the more passive female partner. The blunted sensibility of damaged children blurs the distinction between self-assertion and hostility; in this way, sex and aggression become almost indistinguishable. Whether his excursions are homosexual, heterosexual or exhibitionistic, they have an assaultive quality about them. Sex language and gesture become almost desexualized in these children as they use them to offend adults and peers alike. The child who hates adults, who have always been viewed as punishing, finds sexual acting out a natural weapon.

The sorting out of sex and aggression is difficult for both the therapist and the child since sex has a physically pleasurable side to it. The child maintains that the excitement and gratification is a sufficient end in itself and the attempt to outline its aggressive components meets a wall of resistance. Adults suffer the same confusion of interpretation of motives and this complicates the task of therapy of sex problems. It is necessary to distinguish clearly between these motives since control is otherwise impossible. Even anger uses sex as a weapon. Since the most potent taboo is that referring to incest, it comes as no surprise that in almost every culture—as well as a delinquent one—the accusation about the sexual relations between mother and son are the most provocative. We have never seen a delinquent subculture whose members were not immediately ready for combat at the imputation that one of them had intercourse with his mother. The taboo adds vitality to the level of offense and this pattern is repeated over and over. In much the same way, homosexuality via intercourse or fellatio usually requires substantial aggression to accomplish its aim. Acts of this sort are dealt with as one part of the total manifestation of the sexual impulse but their socially disapproved nature is made quite clear. An attempt is made to teach the child—without criticism—the reality of social life, and it is usually a tempered version of middle-class reality.

ADULT RESPONSE TO SEXUAL BEHAVIOR

Some of the general principles involved in adult reactions to sexuality can be described even though an exhaustive list is beyond the scope of this paper.

The dangers of suppression. The most common method used by child-care workers in institutions as a whole takes the form of a generalized suppression of sexual behavior in the child. While motives for this action may be credible, its effect is seldom therapeutic. It acts first to ignore the meaning of the sexual act. Any such single remedy must necessarily omit consideration of the causes and be ill-adapted to the individual case. There is much too thin a line between "you shouldn't" and "it is wrong" for the child to discern, and the ease with which such adult actions can be misinterpreted by the disturbed child is too great a risk to take. Suppression, too, is self-defeating, since it attempts to cover up symptoms rather than to deal with causes and sets the stage for a much greater outburst at some later time.

Protection of the innocent. This becomes the basic reason for dealing in detail with disapproved forms of sexual expression and there are many "innocents" to be protected. Innocence in this respect can refer to the kind, quality and timing of the child's previous experience. The unsophisticated child who is introduced to advanced levels of sexuality without comprehending what it is all about cannot put the experience into a meaningful or reasonable perspective. In such circumstances the emotions he will experience will not match the behavior he displays or to which he is exposed.

Among the innocents are the adults whose own adjustment may be perilous in the sexual area and for whom such events are a threat to their personal defenses. The child can provoke highly negative counterbehavior in the adult and then use this as a source for subtle and unspecified psychological blackmail in future interpersonal transactions. Parents of institutionalized children who witness or hear reports of overt sexual expression in the institution can use this as the basis for countermeasures directed against the institution and its staff, and this continuing threat undermines the child-care worker's resolve to deal dispassionately with youthful sexual expression. Objections to the sexual acting out of institutionalized children may even come from professionals unacquainted with the facts of life of living with disturbed children and not just from disturbed parents. All sexual incidents are potentially explosive since they may produce so much injury to "innocent bystanders."

Criterion for intercession in sexual behavior. It is apparent that all the usual concerns about understanding the individual child should be invoked here, but the question of determining the exact moment of interference has ramifications that go beyond the individual case. If the effect on the group is the determining factor rather than the act itself, then we must consider dimensions such as the cohesion of the group, its leadership structure, the role of the child in the group, the social class of the group's members and the sociometric character of the interaction of the individuals. The style of life of the group and the group mechanisms for meeting threatening situations must all be considered. It is apparent that an act that would be dangerous if viewed solely from the vantage point of the individual case history may be rendered innocuous by group support. The decision to intercede and the timing and technique for doing so are, of course, functions of the clinical experience and philosophy of the worker. No rule of thumb is applicable but a general tendency to ignore the structure of the peer group in such decisions is too widespread for comfort.

The role of neutrality. It is axiomatic that there is no neutral zone for adults dealing with the sexual expressions of children. Adults who lean too heavily on a device such as ignoring low-level expressions of sex will soon find the child taking advantage of this tacit permission to promote a more advanced form of behavior. Too, adults react to sex as though legal rules of evidence were necessary for it to be discussed. Where a child will be queried about the possibility that he stole or aggressed against another child, adults may require incontrovertible evidence before initiating an inquiry about sexual misbehavior; the children capitalize on the adult's reluctance to probe the area of sexual behavior and use this lack of adult attention as a lever against the adult. Exploration of possible sexual incidents is, of course, an extremely tortuous task. Children obfuscate, lie, cover up and deny with an unspoken agreement to maintain a wall of silence toward the controlling adults. The tentativeness of the adult's approach to the task often is a sufficient cue for the child and he reacts accordingly, that is, he launches his most powerful weapons at what he detects to be a flaw in the adult psychological structure. Adult neutrality most often is a defensive avoidance of sex; true neutrality is an infinitely complex therapeutic maneuver.

Combined individual and group management. Sooner or later in every institution, pairs of children or small groups of children will present the staff with a problem of management of sexuality. The jumble of accusation and counter-accusation that usually emerges from the attempt to "get the facts" requires a substantial amount of time to straighten out and the group structure must be put back together after its chaotic falling apart over such incidents. The children must continue to live with one another, and a shared, public, group understanding must be reached. Each member of the group must be aware of what every other member of the group has agreed to and now understands about the situation, if further group decay is to be warded off.

Achieving a group understanding is only the first step in the process. The individual reaction of each child must be dealt with, since he views his relationship with the group in a highly personalized way. His emotions must be "mopped up" and the impact of the group incident must be interpreted in terms of the details of his individual case history. There are always a host of personal reactions that cannot comfortably be exposed before the other members of the group without jeopardizing his standing in it and his relationship to its power structure. This is a step that may be neglected only at considerable cost to the future of adult-child therapeutic transactions, yet it may easily be omitted under the press of time that combined group and individual working-through requires. It is our impression that, on the average, less than the necessary time is devoted to exploring all the ramifications of sexual incidents and that they are inadequately handled as a consequence.

Adult denial of reality. There remains the estimation of relative risk in having the adult over-react to sexuality or having him deny its existence. Denial differs from being neutral in that its appearance is seemingly unconscious. Evidences of sexual activity that would set off an alarm bell in the consciousness of an experienced worker, most often are overlooked by novices. It often seems that those closest to (that is, have a relationship with) the child are unaware of sexual material that seems blatant to an outside observer. Most often, erotic arousal in the child is "therapeutically" permitted with an unclear view of what is therapeutic about the passive acceptance of overt sexual expression. The distinction between acceptance and permission is an indistinct one and, when an adult is willing to sanction moderate sexual expression, he may not always be willing to sanction the excess to which it may shortly lead. The subtle encouragement provided by remaining passive at the first stages of such expression always exists as a high contrast to the later restrictiveness that appears when the bounds of "propriety" have been trespassed.

Sex education. We have followed a frequent institutional practice of calling on the pediatrician or medical representative for educational efforts around the topic of sex. While it would seem that the weight of medical authority would ease the tensions in such a situation, we have met with variable success with such an approach. It is lamentable that sex should be classified as a physiological problem in such a cavalier fashion. It may be that if we are to be completely honest with children we ought to teach them sex at the level the average child-care worker understands it rather than at the sometimes awkward, esoteric and somewhat clinical and anatomical level of the medical specialist. The continuing efforts to substitute obscure, Latin-derived terminology for sexual parts and functions is again some measure of our own inability to face the reality of sex as adults know it. It seems more rational, psychologically, to rely less on clinical terminology than to use commonplace terms while focusing on the

emotional and attitudinal components of sex. This seems logically to involve a frank discussion of the children's own personal sex habits and practices when called for and suggests that the average child-care worker needs more than casual instruction about the means and methods of sex education. The most usual assumption is that every "normal" adult comes fully equipped with the capacity to educate the young in our society about such matters—an assumption that hardly seems warranted by the facts. The discomfort of adults (as well as the lack of essential vocabulary) should not be underestimated but it regularly is, because of the discomfort most professionals feel about breeching this taboo topic. If we are truly interested in convincing disturbed children that sex is not an area of extensive taboos, then we must look to an extensive reorganization of our current methods of sex education; the reality we all know must be inserted in the sex-educational process.

The need for supervision. This category refers to the supervision of adult workers rather than of the children. In any institutional setting a certain amount of sexual by-play will exist between the adults and these events are highly subject to misinterpretation by the children. Not only must the usual level of social interplay be supervised and regulated, but continuous observations of the day-by-day interaction of adults and children ought to be subject to scrutiny. The stimulus value of an attractive female with an unconsciously provocative manner should not be overlooked. The contagion of sexual behavior is great and an originally innocent action can trigger a totally disproportionate reaction in a group of disturbed children. We have found again and again that female child-care workers make friendly overtures to male children in a manner that may be indistinguishable from the seductiveness that is more appropriately expended on male courting partners. In much the same fashion, male adult child-care workers can fall easily into a pattern of relationship that closely resembles that of a peer member of the "gang." Swapping tales of early sexual experiences and using a "one of the boys" approach has its dangers if it is not lodged in a properly mature adult worker. Consciously or unconsciously, the male and female child-care workers may slip into a form of relationship that is hardly calculated to contribute to the development and growth of the child. It is in this area that careful supervision is an absolute essential and, at the same time, it is an area that may be neglected. Adults need to distinguish between these personal and clinical sex attitudes and come to some understanding of the congruence between them.

The balance of freedom and restraint. A working institutional code always must walk the tight rope of freedom and restraint. In institutions dominated by the personality of a single outstanding theorist or director, for better or for worse, policy becomes clear if not always coherent. Most institutions are not organized in such an hierarchical fashion and practice becomes the fashioner of theory. For whichever side of the freedom-restraint continuum the policy leans, reasonable theoretical justification can be found, since the objective facts are so hard to ascertain.

The credible arguments for controlling and restraining the overt appearance of sexuality in children tend to focus on the acting-out quality of such expressions. The point is made that institutionalized children (particularly those in psychiatric institutions) usually suffer a substantial degree of regression to begin with and sexual acting out serves only to drive them deeper into their regressed state. These children need to be protected from the confusion, guilt and anxiety attendant on the deepening regression. The suggestion is made that children need and want to be controlled until they are capable of managing themselves and to deny this control is to abandon the child to his pathology and its destructive effects. While sexual acting out may be cathartic, such expressions may defeat the therapeutic goal of substituting thought processes for socially disapproved action. This line of reasoning suggests that the institution's responsibility for establishing a socially acceptable patterning of child behavior requires that from the beginning it make such behavior ego-alien, not ego-syntonic. An equally cogent set of theoretical principles can be used to defend just the opposite institutional policy; it is this adult theoretical uncertainty that encourages a vacillating policy that shifts with the fashions of the times.

The circle of guilt. It has been noted that sex can be pressed into the service of aggression and thus become a two-headed therapeutic issue. Perhaps a source of equal difficulty is to be found in the regularity with which sexual expression induces a guilt that can be assuaged only by some concrete punishment. Confession and discussion may not seem adequate atonement for what the child may see as the enormity of his transgression. In the magical thinking of the unconscious, the violation of a powerful taboo can be cleansed only by an antidote of equal power. In such instances the offending child may embark on a program of violence and provocation calculated to force the adult to punish and thus "even" his psychic score. The almost compulsive nature of the child's relentless search for freedom from guilt and anxiety can continue until his goal is reached and the adult finally disciplines the child (perhaps days later) for (in the child's mind) his sexual infraction. By this time in the child's sequence of behavior, he may have provoked so much anger and resentment among his peers or adults that the whole issue circles back on itself in a prolonged series of retaliations and counter-retaliations that can be traced to the original sexual transgression. In much the same fashion, children who commit sexual acts that produce substantial feelings of guilt may redouble sexual as well as aggressive activity in an attempt to relieve guilt by sharing it with many others. The psychic isolation of being the lone offender is intolerable to most children and they feel less guilt-ridden if others share their plight.

CONCLUSION

At the very least it must be concluded that the institutional management of sexual expression among institutionalized children has not received the theoretical attention so vital a topic warrants. It seems evident that the social taboos decried by professionals as prime sources of emotional disturbance have their counterpart among professionals in institutional life. The taboos appear in various guises ranging from the absence of professional concern in the literature through the lack of provision for training of child-care workers to the inadequate supervision of workers who make important daily decisions about managing sex in the institution. The illusion that there exists a high degree of agreement about the principles of hygienic management of sex would be dispelled quickly by any concerted attempt to discuss the issue.

Unless a teacher has thought through his concept of discipline and understands the theoretical basis for it, he is likely to become entangled in unnecessary verbal battles with parents who are quick to exclaim that the teacher has too little or too much discipline in his class. Often, the cause of this difficulty is the word "discipline" itself. It has different meanings to different people. From our framework, discipline means an extended process of incorporating adult standards within the child in a way that will leave him free to express his impulses independently but also in a socially acceptable way. Discipline is viewed as an internalized process that comes with maturity and not as an external phenomenon administered by adults.

When discipline is defined as the method of punishment a teacher uses when a child violates school rules, the teacher is provided with a label that can hide a host of adult outbursts, personal vengeances, and an aggressive power showdown. For example, in a study at Indiana University, 182 teachers were asked, Why do *other* teachers hit children? The majority of responses cited psychological defenses which protect teachers from facing their real motives for inflicting physical pain on children. Some of the more common rationalizations were: (1) It's the only way some teachers can get certain children to know that they (teachers) mean business. (2) Parents expect the teacher to paddle children. when they are bad. (3) The teacher has tried everything else and feels it is the only technique left. (4) The child's behavior is so repulsive that he deserves it. (5) Some children ask to be punished.

Studies on the effects of physical punishment have shown again and again that it brings no significant improvement in the child's behavior. Deeper analyses of some teachers' reasons for resorting to physical force indicated the following causes: (1) School policy, (2) Counter-aggression, (3) Teacher sadism, (4) Teacher displacement and projection, (5) Teacher unawareness of cause-and-effect relationships.

In the next article Redl presents an original paper describing the conditions necessary for punishment to contribute to the child's internal control system. He emphasizes that the significant variable in punishment is not what adults do to the child, but what the child does with the punishment. If punishment is to be effective, it must be unpleasant but the child must be free from perceptual distortions. Redl brings into focus the complexity of punishment.

The Concept of Punishment

Fritz Redl

PROFESSIONAL USE OF THE WORD PUNISHMENT

As Educators or Clinicians, our behavior toward children deserves the name "punishment" only if it is done with a *clearcut goal to help the child.* Thus, it is always a means to an end, and is always employed for the sake of the basic welfare and growth needs of the individuals involved. Whether the actual punishment administered under this policy was correct or helpful; or whether it was stupid, mistaken, wrongly handled; or whether it backfired in its intended effect, is not the point here, as we try to *define* our terms.

It is equally obvious that the use of punishment implies an attempt to produce an experience for the child which is *unpleasant.* It is based on the assumption that sometimes the affliction of an unpleasant experience may mobilize "something" in a child that gets him to think or change his behavior, a change which, without such a "boost" from without, would not have occurred. Tying those two aspects of punishment as viewed in the tool cabinet of the professional educator or clinician together, we might arrive at the following definition, which I think serves our purpose for the time being.

I refer by the term "punishment" to: *a planful attempt by the adult to influence either the behavior or the long-range development of a child or a group of children, for their own benefit, by exposing them to an unpleasant experience.*

The inclusion of the statement that it has to be a "planful attempt, guided by the benefit of the children as a goal," excludes all simple outcropping of adult sadism, bad temper, or personal vengefulness, as well

From Fritz Redl, an original article presented at the American Orthopsychiatric Association meeting, 1959, pp. 9–44.

as the use of the child as a prop to assuage one's own anxiety. The statement that all punishment aims at using the production of an "unpleasant" experience in the child marks this intervention technique as different from others. It also raises the crucial question which underlies all speculations about the wisdom of punishment as a tool in a given case: Just what is there to the underlying assumption that producing an unpleasant experience in a child is going to help him rally better to reason and control than he was able to before? For this is obviously the *only assumption* on the basis of which any educational or clinical use of punishment makes any sense at all.

ANALYSIS OF THE PUNISHMENT EXPERIENCE

"You can lead a horse to water, but you can't make him drink." This age-old saying is rather trite, but many a punishment discussion I have been in would have benefited if this had been written in bold script on the blackboard before it started. For what counts most in punishment is not what we do to *the child,* but *what the child does with the experience to which we have exposed him.* To make a long story short, *This is what must happen within the child if things go well:*

1. *The child experiences the displeasure* to which we expose him. This "displeasure" can be the loss of a privilege or pleasure he took for granted, or the exposure to something that is unpleasant or even "painful" in some way or other. Or both. For instance, I can take away his dessert, I can sock him one, or I can insist that he stay in his room while he hears the others playing outside.

2. Whether the displeasure be in the form of frustration or pain on some level, it is bound to produce an *upsurge of anger* in the child. This anger may not be con-

scious, nor does it have to be strong. But it is normal for the human to react to frustration or pain with an upsurge of fury.

3. The child clearly perceives—at least after the first few moments, the difference between the *source of his predicament* and *the real causes*. The source of his predicament is obviously the adult who inflicted the punishment, or the institution which made him do so. The cause for his predicament, however, is equally obviously *his own previous misbehavior*, for without it the adult would not have imposed the punishment to begin with.

4. The child now directs the anger produced in him by his predicament, not against the source of his trouble but at its cause: *he gets mad at himself* and realizes he would have avoided all this had he only shown more impulse control and wisdom in his actions to begin with.

5. He does however, not only get a little "mad at himself," but he *transforms* this self-directed aggression into *energy that can be used* for his own benefit. By "transforms" we refer to a process by which what was originally personalized fury or self-hatred can be changed into neutralized energy, now available for a multitude of more sublimated ends.

6. He uses this energy, drawn from his fury about his predicament for two purposes: (a) he forces himself to regret what he did; (b) he forces himself into a sort of "New Year's resolution": "I'll sure not be dumb enough to get myself into a situation like this next time."

7. In a future temptation of somewhat similar kind, he can make use of the image left from the previous incident, and can mobilize self-control power before the act. The previous punishment experience has helped him, not only toward better insight, but also left him with increased energies for temptation resistance.

These, basically, are the steps every child goes through each time a punishment experience to which he was exposed is "handled well" by him—even though these steps are, of course, not really experienced

clearly in the process. They are the *condition* for a constructive use of a punishment experience by a child.

How do we know if this can work? It would be easy, with above outline in hand like a "map," to predict exactly just what could go wrong with the way a child handles his punishment experience, and what conditions must be met within a given punishment plan to make a successful ending most likely. It would be easy—but it would take an estimated 80 pages to do it, so let's skip it for the time being. Let's select what seem to me the five most crucial items in this picture—leaving a dozen or so just about as crucial ones unmentioned for now:

1. From what we know about the child, is the specific *form of displeasure* which we selected for a given punishment situation likely to be used by him as an incentive for concern, or is it either going to roll off him without impact, or throw him into a tizzy of irrational response?

Examples: Some children prefer to sit in their room and masturbate anyway, rather than participate in a competitive game with dubious results for them. Sending such a child to his room won't even be experienced as punishment, no matter what *name* we may want to give the procedure. *Or:* A really good moral masochist *loves* to feel sorry for himself and nurse his grudge against the world, which has "done him wrong." Most punishments, for him, do not hold much displeasure, and what little they hold he turns around into self-pitying delight or juicy gratification of a perverted need. *Or:* Being sent back to stay in one's room as punishment for some misdeed or other, might, in itself, be a good "displeasure dose" to rattle a given child into more thoughtful self appraisal. Only— we sent him back while his neighborhood gang was just coming to pick him up for a ball game, and the things we said while we sent him back would be likely to make any self respecting and emancipation-hungry teenager cringe with unconquerable shame. *Or:* Some children are "allergic" to being alone in a small room. Being sent into one for punishment would produce unbearable panic in them. They are allergic to this type of experience, so you can't use it on them no matter how well they may have "deserved it."

2. From what we know about the child—is he going to be able to *differentiate between "source" and "cause" for his predicament* under the impact of the specific punishment experience which I have provided for him? If the answer to that is no, then you had better save yourself the trouble. Your punishment won't work, and whatever momentary benefit you draw from it will be badly outweighed by the negative side-effects.

Examples: Very little children do not have such discrimination well developed yet. A small child, bumping his head against the table, is likely to turn around and hit the table in revenge for "what it did to him." He is incapable of differentiating the source of his trouble (the contact with the table) from its cause (his own clumsy movement, and not looking where he was going). Some older children regress to that level under the *impact of displeasure or pain.* If that is so, punishment has no chance to help. *Or:* Some people are quite capable of making such distinctions, but they don't want to make them. It is much more gratifying to hate the cop who gave one the ticket than to admit one wasn't driving as one should have. Especially children who are still in the grip of a concerted effort to view the adult as hostile and to deny their own participation in the events of their lives, will construe any experience of displeasure as a "personalized wrong coming from a hateful opponent" rather than consider it a challenge to revise their own style of life. As long as they are in that stage, even the most clearcut form of punishment is going to backfire.

3. From what we know about the child—is he going to be able to *turn his aggression in the right direction,* under the impact of the punishment experience? By the "right direction" we mean, of course,

toward that part of himself that made him misbehave, instead of toward the punishing adult, the institution, the world at large, God, or the Universe—or the child in the upper bunk.

Example: Some children are quite capable of knowing and admitting that they were in the wrong and "deserved what they got." Yet, their ego is still totally incapable of coping with any amount of frustration or aggression in a constructive way. Thus, even when correctly mad at themselves, they will have to pour their fury at the people and things around them, or they simply explode into an orgy of diffuse and frantic aggression-discharge. This is especially true for our hyperaggressive child: even at the stage when they begin to feel guilty for what they did, as we hoped they eventually would, they still have not developed enough ego skills to cope with guilt feelings adequately. So, even though they know they are at fault themselves, their aggression still is poured toward the world outside them. As long as that is true, even otherwise well planned "punishments" are of no avail.

4. From what we know about the child—is he capable of sifting and transforming the anger we produced in him through our punishment, into the type of energy that can be used for increased insight and self control? Among all the puzzles, this is probably the most serious one. For, even if the child gets correctly mad at himself instead of at me the administrator of punishment, or at the institution and its laws, the crucial question still remains: what is he going to do with the fury he now directs against himself? For the fact that aggression is turned against ourselves alone is not enough. It depends very much on just what we do with the aggression we turn against ourselves. Unless the "sifting and transforming gland" for internalized aggression functions well, a child is not going to benefit from punishment received. By "sifting" and "transforming" I am referring to two separate tasks: by "sifting" I mean that the child's

ego must be able to decide just how much should be discharged as a waste product. Some children, for instance, discharge all of it as a waste product—none of it sticks and is internalized. Others can't allow themselves any "waste product discharge," so the full brunt of their anger is turned against themselves, which means they are *flooded with much too much repentance, discouragement and self accusation.* The normal child has glands which operate well that way: punished by an adult he can vent some of his anger by mumbling under his breath or slamming that door, some of it by a quickly produced "revenge fantasy against the punishing adult," some of it by diffuse discharge motions, such as, restless pacing of his room, rough manipulating of a ball, etc.—*and only the right amount is then sent to the transformer* to be turned into internalized energy for self-insight and self-control.

Examples: Some children *know* that they are to blame but if the punishment, pain, or frustration, or their already existing proclivity toward guilt feelings is too strong, they simply get *paralyzed* by their repentance and regret, drift into orgies of self-accusation, or they end up feeling no good, incapable of ever amounting to anything, or not worthy of the adult's love or their own self-confidence.

In that case, all the previous steps of punishment worked well, for they *should* have admitted they were wrong, as they did, they should have got "mad" at their own bad behavior, as they did. *Only,* they *did so too much,* and in a totally ineffective way. For simply being mad at oneself is no good, unless one has the energy for doing something about it. *Or:* Some children get angry at themselves, as they should, but they puff out this anger in waste motion rather than in an increase of energy available for self control. That means they punish themselves by slip actions and "accidents," by losing their favorite toy, breaking their prize possession, but they cannot use their self-anger for the purpose of more impulse control.

No matter how "repentant" they seemed to be in their immediate reaction to the punishment, they are as helpless as they were before at the next onslaught of temptation. Whenever things are wrong with the sifting and transforming machinery in the child's ego, a punishment experience cannot be benefited from.

5. From what we know about the child, is his ego in good enough shape to cope with the complications of the "time" element in punishment? In my estimate, the misfiring of punishments which were otherwise well designed because of this very factor of timing is the most serious trouble source in educational as well as clinical practice. I guess I had better lay this one out a little more in detail. By "time element" I refer, here, to three entirely different issues—all of them, however, equally crucial to the constructive use of punishment by a child.

a. The time relationship between punishment experience and offense. Public opinion is wildly confused on this issue. It either assumes that the two should be in high proximity—or else the child forgets what he is punished for—or that they should be far apart—so that the basic issue has time to sink in, and the adult has enough time to check on guilt, on issues of justice, and to get his machinery in motion. As is frequently the case, there is a kernel of truth in both extremes, but neither of them is *it.* The reality of the situation is more complex than either theory would like to have it.

In life with our hyperaggressive children we have learned that there is great importance to the issue of timing, but whether proximity or distance is of the essence depends on many items in each case. Talking about punishment: some children's awareness that they did something wrong—or even what they did—evaporates so fast that the act of punishment hits them after it is entirely evaporated. Then, the displeasure felt during the punishment experience makes little sense, it is likely to be perceived as rank meanness of an irritable adult rather than as punishment one has "deserved" for something one "did." On the other hand, some children's "offenses" were entangled in so many issues, soaked with so much affect, anger, confusion, delusion, etc., that no punishment experience can have much chance to do its trick, unless that confusion is disentangled first. Knowing this much about the ego of a child will make it clear that certain forms of punishment that create complications in the time relationship between punishment experience and offense, are by that very fact counter-indicated.

b. The timing of exposure to the punishment experience, is of crucial concern. Some of our children, for instance, might well "understand" that they deserved to be sent to their room, and might be able to "take" that part of it without distortion of the real facts, at least on occasion. The question to be asked next, however, is clearly: What will they do with themselves while exposed to the punishment condition, such as staying in their room, paying back for a damaged item out of their pocket money, or staying home while others go on a fishing trip, etc.

Many children's egos are not in shape enough to take the time exposure involved in a given punishment. In such cases, this specific form of punishment is counter-indicated, no matter how good it may look from all other angles.

Public opinion, unfortunately, is caught in a hopeless confusion on this item, too, which causes no end of trouble even in professional discussions on the issue. Namely, public opinion has assumed a fixed relationship between length of exposure and seriousness of offense. Thus, for a little offense in the swimming pool, one might assume that a child should be sent to his room maybe for just 5 minutes. For a bigger offense, maybe it would be "fair" if he were told to stay out of activities for 2 days. Well, it may be "fair" all right, but what effect will it actually produce? As long as Johnny sits there watching the other youngsters splash around happily while he is

sulking about his predicament, but still under the impression that he "had it coming" because of the freshness of the memory of what he did, all may be fine for a while. The moment the self-perception of what he did is evaporated, though, the experience assumes an entirely different shape. From then on it is not: "too bad I had to get myself into this trouble," but, "see, that bastard waterfront guy lets all these other kids have their fun, it's only me that doesn't get a break, hell with *him*."

In short, the psychological weight of a time issue has to be weighed with psychological scales, not with judiciary ones, and the psychology of timing belongs among the trickiest issues I can think of.

c. By "timing" we sometimes refer to the fact that the real test of the efficacy of a punishment lies in the question whether a child can make use of what he learned from it in the next temptation situation. Thus, its major effect is hoped for from its impact on the future event. This however, means no less than the question of whether a child can, at all, learn from experience, especially from an unpleasant one. And, beyond this, whether he can not only "learn" a lesson from the experience, but whether his ego can supply him with the necessary control energies to make use of what he learned when the next crucial moment comes around. It ought to be clear by now, that this is quite a lot to be expected, and I can't help being amazed time and again, that adults are so naively anticipating all the time that a few little punishment tricks do not show that long-range effect. The question whether a given child has it in him to "learn" from a given punishment experience is an important one to estimate correctly. For punishment, contrary to popular fantasies, does not teach a thing unless the recipient is in any shape to do the learning. In the case of children with severe ego disturbances, it is clear that this is one of the reasons why one would not expect much help from the punishment department. The ability to tie up a well interpreted experience from one's past, with an equally clearly perceived experience from the present, and on top of that mobilize just the right quantity of energy for self control and send it into just the right control-direction—this is obviously a task which a messy ego is likely to flunk. Yet—the use of punishment now makes little sense, unless we have some expectation that its impact can be utilized at some moment in the future tense.

In summary: About this issue of the "time element"—we want to assess just how well a child is likely to do in all three aspects of the time issues: Can he take the time relationship between a given offense and a given punishment without getting confused; can his ego sustain him for the *duration* of the punishment experience with all the specifics a given case involves; and is there a chance for some *future usability* of the experience to which we expose him now. If the answer to this is no, punishment isn't worth the effort you put into planning and suffering through it, to say nothing of the complications in the lives of children.

d. *Punishment and the problem of in-situational and post-situational support.* At this point, I hear you moaning: "Are you trying to tell us that punishment is as complicated as all that? What ever happened to the idea that it was a 'simple' technique, sort of clearcut and very concrete, and much more 'definite' than most of the other intervention techniques we talked so much about"? The answer to that is: Yes. That's exactly what I am trying to convey. The idea that punishment is a simple, clearcut technique belongs in the chapter of optical illusions. What the *adult* does in an act of punishment may be as simple and clearcut as a kick in the pants. What the kid does with this experience and how he reacts to it is anything but simple and clearcut. It involves the most sensitive and vital organs of his psychological organism, as I have just tried to show. In this respect, punishment is much more comparable to a case of surgical intervention than to what you see happen when the guy at the delicatessen

slices that salami for you with a sharp knife.

Unfortunately, I have to make it even more complicated, especially when we think of punishment in relation to a disturbed child. The prevalent thinking of the layman still puts most of his effort into finding the "best" form of punishment, having the educator impose it on the child —and from here on in he expects the effect to be sort of automatic.

Fortunately, we already know better than that. We know that even a well planned play experience for a child may need constant support during the time when the child is supposed to be exposed to it, or may need some post-situational followup. This principle again, is not new. Remember the time spent not only on figuring what game should be selected in the evening, but also on just how we give the children the support they need to live through the game successfully once it gets under way? Remember how important we felt it was not only to physically hold a child when that becomes necessary, but to help him get through this experience without misinterpreting it? Remember how important it was to stick around all through their tantrums, even after we didn't have to hold them anymore, just so we can catch that moment when the child needs or is ready for some activity he can hang onto and pull himself together again?

All this is as true of "punishments" as it is of other experiences in our children's lives. Thus, our responsibility is not ended with the decision to send that child to his room, or to tell him he has to pay part of the damage he has done to the other boy's toy for the next two paydays. The safeguarding of the right *effect* of a punishment experience is a job that continues as long as that experience lasts, and the real help to make sense out of it all often occurs much later in a post situational exploitation of the kid's reaction to it. Whenever we figure on any kind of punishment for our children, therefore, it is important to plan just as much for in-situational and post-situational support, as it is to decide what kind of punishment should be tried to begin with. Even a well designed punishment will backfire badly, if for some reason we are not able to give the child the support he needs going through it, without distortions, and "learn" from it what we wanted him to learn. With the act of punishment our work with the child on this issue does not end. It only begins. . . . If you ever thought of using punishment in some situations because it "saves trouble" or makes things work more simply, you'd better give that daydream up in a hurry.

LOOSE ENDS FOR SALE

The "analysis of the punishment experience" which I just presented was not meant to be a photograph; only a map. It makes no pretense of answering your question of just what to do. It only tries to point out a few salient points you will run into if you get into this terrain. . . .

Next, I would like to brush lightly past a few issues that I remember having come up in our staff discussions.

The usage of the term punishment being as loose as it is, we often discuss under the same label situations where we demand that a child "make up" for a hurt he has inflicted, or a damage he has caused. The form this takes may vary. We may insist that he at least "apologize" or show he is sorry; we may want him to clear up the mess he has caused and which inconveniences the other boy in his cabin or room; we may demand partial payment for damage done, etc. I personally do not like to see these arrangements thrown into the same pot as punishments, for they have only a small part of the process in common with them. But I won't quibble about words at the moment. Suffice it to remember that such procedures are actually much more rituals for the restitution of the individual into the grace of the group or of his victim, including an attempt to help him come to peace with himself. The following are the *three major goals* one has in mind when using this technique:

1. We may want to help the child get the taste of some *consequences* of his behavior, and at the same time offer him a way to *do something about it* that is more or less apt to re-instate the status quo.

2. By giving the child a chance to "make up for it," we also help him to reduce his guilt feelings and to restitute the previous relationship between him and the person or group against which he has offended.

3. We also make it easier for the victim of the kid's misbehavior—be it individual or group—to "forgive him," to terminate their own state of wrath against him, and to stop whatever revenge measure they in turn might have in mind. We sort of offer the victimized kid or group a pound of his psychological flesh as a premium for their "forgetting" what he had done to them.

It must be obvious by now, that this technique may have a number of great advantages and may well be used at times to restitute what had been disturbed, which may be a great relief for all concerned. It is also clear, of course, that this only would work where the child has some guilt about what he had done to begin with, where he is clearly aware and admitting that he was in the wrong, is basically ready to wish it hadn't happened, and is himself relieved at the idea of having it all "repaired." The major danger of the technique lies with the case of a child who not only has few guilt feelings, but defends himself against the development of such by a system of "pay as you go" arrangements. Offering this type of child too many opportunities to "pay off for what he did" is inviting his exploitation of this technique to feed his own resistance against real insight and awareness of right and wrong. Great care must be taken in those cases where such "restitutional arrangements" seem feasible, that the youngster gets all the help he needs to interpret his own "making up" correctly, and that we make no mistakes in the nature and duration of the restitutional rituals we may choose. . . .

When a child teases, threatens, pinches, pokes, hits, swears, runs away, or refuses to move, the teacher must be equally concerned with what to do about the *behavior* and the underlying *causes* of such behavior. Unfortunately, very little clinical attention is given to the former concern of teachers. Teacher intervention often is necessary in order to protect a child, a group, a program, or property from injury, contagion, disappointment, or destruction. The method of intervention and how it is perceived by both the child and the group raise many fundamental clinical questions that need to be examined with the same care as the theoretical discussions of the underlying dynamics of the child. In the next article Long and Newman have applied Redl's four-notched scale to the management of surface behavior in a school setting. The techniques presented are not new, but are particularly well organized to help professionals conceptualize within a given framework.

Managing Surface Behavior of Children in School

Nicholas J. Long and Ruth G. Newman

There are four major alternatives to handling behavior. They are: permitting, tolerating, interfering, and preventive planning. Redl emphasizes that no one of these alternatives is better than any of the others. The task is to find the right combination of techniques for each child.

Permitting behavior. Most rules in a school are made to inhibit and regulate the impulsive behavior of children. During the day, they are told in many ways to stop, slow down, and control their behavior. No one would argue against the importance of these rules in a group setting. If it is important for children to know what they cannot do, it is equally as important for children to know what they can do. For example, children should be told that it is permissible to run, shout, and scream on the playground, to be messy when they are fingerpainting, to have some degree of movement within the classroom, to go to

Abridged from Nicholas J. Long and Ruth G. Newman, "A Differential Approach to the Management of Surface Behavior of Children in School," *Teachers' Handling of Children in Conflict,* Bulletin of the School of Education, Indiana University, XXXVII (July 1961), 47–61.

The organization of this selection is taken from Fritz Redl's training notes at the Child Research Branch of the National Institute of Mental Health, Bethesda, Maryland, 1957.

the lavatory when necessary, to show some freedom of expression in their creative works, and to express an opposing view without being ridiculed or chastised. Children are reassured when they know in advance that their activities will not meet with adult frowns, shouts, or physical interference. More important, the sanctioning of behavior by adults eliminates much of the children's unnecessary testing of limits. A teacher who permits children to leave their desks and go to the book corner after they have finished the assignment should make this privilege clear. Then a child does not have to sneak a book and feel guilty about it or feel victorious about squeezing more freedom from the teacher than the child thinks he would expect.

Tolerating behavior. A lot of classroom behavior must be tolerated, but children should have no reason to believe that teachers approve or sanction it. The more common basic assumptions behind tolerating behavior are (1) learner's leeway, (2) behavior that reflects a developmental stage, and (3) behavior that is symptomatic of a disease.

1. Learner's leeway: Whenever a child is learning a new concept, experimenting with ideas, or trying to win status in the group, the teacher should expect that

the child will make mistakes. He should not expect that the child will do it perfectly. For example, many sensitive teachers tell their class that they are not going to be upset when children err in trying to master new academic and social skills. With some groups, the more mistakes they make, i.e., on an arithmetic assignment, the easier it is for the teacher to help them clarify their misunderstandings. This was found to be true in the following incident:

I have noticed that Carole (third grader) became very upset if she made a mistake on an assignment. The children were writing to a railroad company for some free material, but they did not know how to address an envelope. I went to the board and showed them the proper form and asked them to practice. In a little while I noticed that Carole had her head on her desk. When I asked her what was the matter, she said that she couldn't do it and that she already had made three mistakes. I asked her to show me her work. (She had misspelled one word, did not capitalize one of the words, and had the return address crowded up in the upper left-hand corner.) I told Carole that these are the kinds of mistakes that many boys and girls make and that I did not expect her or any of the other children to do it perfectly the first three or four times that they tried. With this encouragement, she started again.

Sometimes it is helpful to talk about "good mistakes" versus "poor mistakes." A good mistake is made when a wrong answer has come out of some sense, so that the logic shines through the error. A poor mistake is one which rests largely on effort or has not even the semblance of logic.

2. Behavior that reflects a developmental stage: Some behavior is age typical and will change as the child becomes more mature. Any attempt on the part of the teacher to alter or inhibit this behavior results in such negligible changes that it usually is not worth the inevitable fight. For example, children in the early grades are impulse-ridden and motor-oriented. Every kindergarten teacher knows this and has accepted the fact that very little can be done about it except tolerate it. This state of tolerance should not be confused with sanctioning it or permitting wild behavior. Another example is that children in the late third or early fourth grade, caught between group pressure and allegiance to the teacher, are notorious for tattling; i.e., "Miss Jones, Johnny hit Mary," or "Johnny pulled a leaf off your flower when you were in the hall." Other illustrations of age-typical behavior are the unscrubbed, unhygienic appearance of the pre-adolescent boy, the primping of sixth-grade girls, the secrets of pre-adolescent girls, and the sex language and behavior of adolescent boys. A classroom example of age-typical behavior is presented below:

At noon, several fifth grade girls came bursting into the room relating a story about the fifth grade boys. The boys had discovered several pictures of nude women which were hidden in a bush on the playground. In small groups, they were examining the pictures in detail when a few of the fifth grade girls "worked their way in" to see what was taking place. The girls screamed and found their way to my room. They related the story; then the bell rang.

The boys entered (without pictures), as though nothing had happened. Silence prevailed. They knew that I knew. Finally, I asked one of the boys where the pictures were. He explained that they had hidden them in the bushes and planned to secure them after school for more detailed study. I asked another of the boys to bring the pictures into the room. This he did and I, *without looking*, threw them in the wastebasket.

Then we discussed the situation, emphasizing the value of good literature. The children themselves brought out the idea that such material was available at all newsstands and that anyone could buy it; however, the individual who is attempting to be a good citizen will by-pass such trash. Even the curious boys agreed with the majority viewpoint.

The pictures remained in the wastebasket until after school. Several students sought me out at the teacher's desk, casting glances at the wastebasket all the while. Others, whom I had never seen before, entered the room and quickly left upon finding me there.

Next morning the wastebasket was empty; the pictures were gone. I didn't see them again until I entered the boiler room, where they were on the wall—property of the school janitor.

3. Behavior which is symptomatic of an illness: When a child has a respiratory infection, the chances are that he will cough in class and that the symptom (coughing) will continue until the child is well. This cause and effect relationship is accepted among teachers; however, when a child who is emotionally disturbed shows the symptoms of his illness, such as recurring temper tantrums, fights, and irrational fears, the child is likely to be unpopular with his classmates, his teacher, and even with himself. A psychologically oriented teacher realizes that, when a child suffers from emotional problems, the symptoms are rarely conscious forms of meanness but are simply an explainable outlet for his intra-psychic conflicts. For example:

Some of the things that Martha did were fighting, tearing up other children's property, walking the floor constantly, tearing pages out of her book, name calling, and spitting. Although Martha makes me angry and caused all of us many problems, I feel we have grown a little in understanding that we all have problems and that the class is simply not divided into good and bad, accepted and unaccepted. Martha's behavior has improved during the year and, if I did anything to help it, I was doing it with kindness, firmness, and accepting her as an individual, rather than judging her on the basis of her actions.

Interfering with behavior. While the psychologically trained teacher is aware of long-range goals and is sensitive to the child's core problems, the teacher still has to handle the spontaneous behavior that occurs in the classroom. Some behavior has to be stopped if the classroom learning is

to take place. A child cannot continue to act out all of his feelings. The task is to find ways of interfering with the behavior so that it does not disrupt the group greatly but still may be helpful to the particular child. Redl and Wineman in *The Aggressive Child* have listed 21 specific influence techniques that they have been able to identify in their work with aggressive boys. Twelve of these techniques will be developed as they apply to the positive management of children by the classroom teacher.

Before suggesting ways of intervening, the question of when a teacher should intervene needs to be considered. While this question cannot be settled without considering many variables, school psychologists have observed that too many teachers never set limits or intervene until they are choked with counter-aggressive feelings toward a child. When this happens, the teacher is likely to intervene in a way which is unhygienic and too severe. On the other hand, teachers have not been given any guide lines to help them with this difficult problem. They are not really sure whether they should interfere in a particular bit of behavior. Once again Redl gives us the direction and suggests the following criteria for intervention.

1. Reality dangers: Adults are usually more reality-oriented than children and have had more practice predicting the consequence of certain acts. If children are playing some crazy game, fighting, or playing with matches so that it looks as if they might injure themselves, then the teacher moves in and stops the behavior.

2. Psychological protection: Just as the adult protects the child from being physically hurt, he also should protect the child from psychological injury. If a group of boys is ganging up on a child, or scapegoating him, or using derogatory racial nicknames, then the teacher should intervene. The teacher does not support or condone this behavior and the values it reflects.

3. Protection against too much excite-

ment: Sometimes a teacher intervenes in order to avoid the development of too much excitement, anxiety, and guilt in children. For example, if a game is getting out of hand and continues another 10 minutes, the children may lose control, mess up, and feel very unhappy about their behavior later. Once again, the teacher should intervene to stop this cycle from developing.

4. Protection of property: This is almost too obvious to mention, but sometimes it is easy to overlook. Children are not allowed to destroy or damage the school property, equipment, or building. When the teacher sees this, he moves in quickly and stops it. But at no time does he give the impression so common in our society that property is more important than people. Protecting property protects people.

5. Protection of an on-going program: Once a class is motivated in a particular task and the children have an investment in its outcome, it is not fair to have it ruined by one child who is having some difficulty. In this case, the teacher intervenes and asks this child to leave or to move next to him in order to insure that the enjoyment, satisfaction, and learning of the group is unimpaired.

6. Protection against negative contagion: When a teacher is aware that tension is mounting in the classroom and a child with high social power begins tapping his desk with his pencil, the teacher might ask him to stop in order to prevent this behavior from spreading to the other students and disrupting the entire lesson.

7. Highlighting a value area or school policy: There are times when a teacher interferes in some behavior not because it is dangerous or disturbing but because he wishes to illustrate a school policy or rule which may lie slightly below the surface of the behavior. For example, he might want to illustrate why it is impossible for everyone to be first in line, or to point out how a misunderstanding develops when there is no intent to lie or to distort a situation. The focus is on poor communication.

8. Avoiding conflict with the outside world: The outside world in school can mean neighboring classrooms or the public. It is certainly justifiable to expect more

control on the part of your children when they are attending an assembly or are on a trip than when they are in their classroom.

9. Protecting a teacher's inner comfort: Inner comfort is not the first thing to be considered by a teacher. If it is, he is in the wrong profession. For example, if a certain type of behavior makes a teacher feel exceptionally uncomfortable, the behavior may not need to be totally inhibited, but the teacher may have to learn to be more comfortable with it, whether he likes it or not.

It would be foolish, however, for a teacher, given limits of human endurance, to put himself in a situation in which he is abused constantly or serves as a punching bag for the class. This would not be healthy for anyone. The problem is to distinguish between behavior which is developmental or momentarily cathartic from behavior that is pathological in origin. Once a teacher recognizes his personal idiosyncrasies and realizes that he is over-reacting to the behavior, in the long run, he might better stop the behavior than do nothing and inwardly reject the child.

It is obvious that a teacher does not consciously work through all these hygienic steps before deciding to stop a behavior. However, the nine points listed above can serve as a guide or reference point against which one can examine his actions. What makes this whole process challenging and complicated is that the child behaves in a way which, according to the proposed list, ought to be stopped but under certain psycho-physical conditions the teacher does not stop it. After all, life is flexible and usually cannot be condensed into an orderly list of psychological procedures.

What are some of the counter indications against interfering, assuming that the behavior is not dangerous? (1) The fuss that it would create at this time is not worth it! The group confusion that is certain to follow might disguise the real purpose of the interference. In such a case it might be better to wait for another time. There is a written guaranty that it will come. (2) The teacher decides to wait until the behavior deviates to the point where it is obvious not only to the child but also to the entire group. This way the child's typical defenses, such as projection, i.e., "You're always picking on me," or "I never get a fair deal," are clearly inappropriate. (3) The teacher is in too good a mood today. He cannot work up enough genuine concern to impress the child and/or the group with the seriousness of the child's behavior. While this feeling is a common one, it should not be the barometer for intervention.

Before returning to the discussion on how to stop inappropriate behavior, there is a need to impress upon the readers that the following techniques are designed to help a teacher maintain the surface behavior of children over some rough spots. They only are stop-gap methods and do not substitute for a well-designed program or replace the teacher's knowledge of individual and group psychology.

The 12 influence techniques to be discussed are planned ignoring, signal interference, proximity control, interest boosting, tension decontaminator through humor, hurdle help, restricting the classroom program, support from routine, direct appeal, removal of seductive objects, antiseptic bouncing, and physical restraint.

1. Planned ignoring: Much of children's behavior carries its own limited power and will soon exhaust itself if it is not replenished, especially if the behavior is designed to "get the teacher's goat." Assuming that the behavior will not spread to others, it might be wise for the teacher to ignore the behavior and not feed into the child's need for secondary gratification. In the following example, the teacher is aware of the underlying meaning of the boy's behavior.

One technique that I find successful is to ignore disruptive behavior. It works most successfully with Frank. When he starts dropping his pencils, or tapping his feet, I know that it is a signal that I had better get over there in a few minutes and help him. I have found, however, that if I confront him with this behavior, he usually argues with me and causes additional problems.

In this example, the teacher responds to the motivation of the behavior and not to the manifestations of the behavior.

2. Signal interference: Teachers have developed a variety of signals that communicate to the child a feeling of disapproval and control. These non-verbal techniques include such things as eye contact, hand gestures, tapping or snapping fingers, coughing or clearing one's throat, facial frowns, and body postures. Such non-verbal techniques seem to be most effective at the beginning stages of misbehavior.

When a student is acting up in a mild way, I have found that a glance in his direction will usually stop the behavior temporarily. Usually I do not have to look at a child for a long time before he is aware that I am looking at him. I have also found that this technique is most helpful with those students who like me. Another signal that I have used is to stand up from my desk when there is a lot of whispering. I hasten to add that there are some children who would have me stand and look at them all day without it helping them control their behavior one bit.

3. Proximity control: Every teacher knows how effective it is to stand near a child who is having some difficulty. Just as a crying infant will stop crying when he is picked up by his mother, although the actual source of discomfort still exists, the early elementary child usually can control his impulses if he is close to the teacher. The teacher operates as a source of protection, strength, and identification. As one of the teachers explains:

One technique I have found helpful is to walk among the children. As I walk down the rows, I help the children having trouble with their work, or I give the bored ones something else to do. My closeness and help show that I am interested and concerned. It creates a better atmosphere and rapport and diminishes problems. I have found it very helpful and more effective than just standing behind the desk and telling them what to do. When I have a child who needs more than the usual help, I usually put his desk close to mine so that we are both aware of each other.

There are some children who not only need to have an adult close by but who also need the adult to touch them before they are able to control their impulses. This is done by having the teacher put his hand gently on the child's shoulder. This action should not be confused with the teacher who leaves five red marks after he has made physical contact with the child.

The advantages of these three techniques, planned ignoring, signal interference, and proximity control, are that they do not embarrass or even identify the child in the group. The teacher may use all three of these techniques while maintaining his classroom program.

4. Interest boosting: If a child's interest is waning and he is showing signs of restlessness, it is sometimes helpful for the teacher to show some genuine interest in the child's classroom assignment, asking whether problem 10 was very hard for him or mentioning his personal interest in athletics, cars, etc. Tapping a child's area of interest may help him mobilize his forces and view the teacher as a person whom he wants to please. One teacher described an experience with a child with whom he used this technique as follows:

Craig was crazy about dinosaurs. He read about them; he drew pictures of them; and he even had a plastic collection of them. As you can guess, Craig was a problem. He did not bother the boys or girls or defy me, but he would spend his class time either daydreaming or else drawing pictures of dinosaurs. I talked to him many times about this and he promised to stop, but the following day he was back at his drawings. I decided that if I could not fight him, perhaps I could join him in his

interest. That night I spent the evening reading the *Encyclopaedia Britannica*. The next day I told Craig that I was very interested in dinosaurs, too, and even had a course in college that studied them. Craig was somewhat skeptical of my comment, but after I mentioned some vital statistics about dinosaurs he was impressed that I was an expert in the field. Together we studied dinosaurs but structured the work so that it would only take place after he had completed his regular assignments.

5. Tension decontamination through humor: There is nothing new about this technique. Everyone is aware of how a humorous comment is able to penetrate a tense and anxiety-producing situation. It clears the air and makes everyone feel more comfortable. The example below shows how one teacher used this technique to advantage.

I walked into my room after lunch period to find several pictures on the chalk board with "teacher" written under each one. I went to the board and picked up a piece of chalk, first looking at the pictures and then at the class. You could have heard a pin drop! Then I walked over to one of the pictures and said that this one looked the most like me but needed some more hair, which I added. Then I went to the next one and said that they had forgotten my glasses so I added them, on the next one I suggested adding a big nose, and on the last one a longer neck. By this time the class was almost in hysterics. Then, seeing that the children were having such a good time and that I could not get them settled easily, I passed out drawing paper and suggested that they draw a picture of the funniest person they could make. It is amazing how original these pictures were.

This example illustrates the phenomenon of group testing. The pictures were put on the board to test the vulnerability of the teacher. Some teachers would have reacted with sarcasm. They might have said that this was infantile behavior and not becoming a fifth-grade class. Other teachers might have given the class extra work or administered a group punishment, such as denial of recess or free time. However, this teacher demonstrated that she was secure, that a drawing could not cause her to regress or to become counter-aggressive, and that she could be counted on during stressful periods. Here is another excellent example of tension decontamination:

As soon as I entered the room two students who had remained in the room during the playground period informed me that Stella and Mary had a fight in the girls' restroom and were at present being seen by the principal. Since both of these girls are good pupils and are well liked by the class, I imagined that they and the class were wondering what I would do when the two girls returned to the room. Fifteen or 20 minutes elapsed before the girls returned. They entered and took their seats and the room became very quiet. I closed my book, looked at one of the girls and said in a rasping voice of a fight announcer, "And in this corner we have Stella, weighing 78 pounds." Everyone laughed. The tension vanished and we proceeded with our work.

Once again humor was used to communicate to the class that everything was all right, that there was no need to worry about it, and that the children could relax and return to their lessons.

6. Hurdle lessons: Disturbing behavior is not always the result of some inner problem. Sometimes the child is frustrated by the immediate classroom assignment. He does not understand the teacher's directions or is blocked by the second or third step in a complicated long-division problem. Instead of asking for help and exposing himself to the teacher's wrath for not paying attention or for exhibiting his educational inadequacies, the child is likely to establish contact with his neighbors, find some interesting trinket in his pocket, or draw on his desk. In other words, he is likely to translate his frustrations into motor behavior. The solution is to provide the child with the help he needs before the

situation gets to this stage, as was done in the following example.

Sonya was very stubborn and usually persisted in not doing her work. After making an assignment, I would give the students some time to work on it in class. I would walk around the room and casually stop at Sonya's desk. Noting that she had not started, I would ask her some of her ideas and would suggest that she write those thoughts on paper. She could do the work and would do it if I explained it to her and personally got her interested in it. If I let her alone, she would usually sit and begin filing her nails or looking at the boy next to her who would become quite flushed. While this technique meant more work for me, it finally paid off because, as soon as she began working, she worked without assistance and began making passing grades.

7. Restructuring the classroom program: How much can a teacher deviate from his scheduled program and still feel he is meeting his "teaching responsibilities"? Another way of asking this question is, "Does the teacher control the program, or does the program control the teacher?" For example, some teachers feel compelled to follow their class schedule with no "ifs," "ands," or "buts." Otherwise, they feel they cannot hope to complete the assigned course of study. Besides, they feel children must learn not to be affected by every passing emotion. They must learn how to concentrate even under undesirable circumstances. Other teachers voice a different position. They feel that the complexity of life and the many extenuating forces make it impossible to follow a standardized course. The task is not so much to teach children as to provide the conditions under which learning can take place. Perhaps these are straw arguments and the question that needs to be raised is, "Does restructuring a program ever facilitate learning?" "If so, under what conditions?" This takes the task out of the realm of "either-or" arguments and places it in the teacher's ability

to predict the tension level of the class in terms of feelings of irritability, boredom, or excitement. If the teacher feels that the class is tense but that the tension is decreasing, he may decide not to redesign his program. However, if he decides that the tension needs to be drained off, i.e., verbalized or channelized, before the class can involve itself in the next assignment, he may change his program immediately. Two interesting examples are presented below:

Shortly before a grade school basketball tournament I was forced to cancel basketball practice for the evening. This met with much disapproval from the team members. The lesson for civics that day concerned labor strikes. As I walked into the classroom, I detected the basketball boys were signaling for everyone to remain silent. It looked as though they were going to have fine cooperation from the rest of the class. Seeming to be completely unaware of their intentions, I cancelled our discussion period and proceeded to assign them the written work at the end of the chapter. This work, I explained, was necessary before we could discuss the chapter adequately. The period was spent in constructive work and avoided a head-on clash. Later I talked to the boys and explained why I had to cancel the practice.

The next example of restructuring illustrates how a teacher created an atmosphere of comfort and relaxation.

The children were just returning to the room after the recess period. Most of them were flushed and hot from exercise, and were a little irritable. They were complaining of the heat in the room, and many of them asked permission to get a drink of water as soon as the final recess bell rang. I felt it would be useless to begin our history study as scheduled. So I told all of the children to lay their heads upon their desks. I asked them to be very silent for one minute and to think of the coolest thing they could imagine during that time. Each child then told the class what he had been thinking. The whole procedure lasted roughly 10 minutes, and I felt that it was

time well spent. The history period afterward went smoothly, the atmosphere within the room relaxed, and the children were receptive.

8. Support from routine: We all need structure. Some children need much more than other children before they can feel comfortable and secure. Without these guideposts for behavior, some children become anxious and hyper-active. This is especially true during unstructured times, when children are moved by every wind and breeze of classroom behavior. Most beginning junior high school children find themselves in this state during the first few weeks. One boy summarized his feelings by saying, "It's like one great big surprise. Each hour you go to another teacher and you don't know what's going to happen until it's too late." To help these children, a daily schedule or program should be provided, as this may allay some of their feelings of anxiety. They can predict what is expected of them and prepare themselves for the next activity. As one teacher says:

Each morning I outline the activities for the day with one "leading question." I find that this is helpful to some of the children. When they come into class, they start thinking about the activities we have planned, instead of waiting for me to announce them. This saves time and eliminates the majority of random behavior.

9. Direct appeal to value areas: One of the most frequent mistakes of an untrained teacher is that he feels he must intervene severely and drastically in order to demonstrate that he has control of the situation. We know that this is not desirable. Another alternative is to appeal to certain values that the students have internalized. The conflict is that some children have not internalized the same values that the teacher has internalized. For example, a teacher cannot appeal to the child's sense of fairness, if the child feels he has been "gypped" out of something he has a

right to possess. A partial list of some of the values that most teachers can appeal to includes: (a) An appeal to the relationship of the teacher with the child, i.e., "You are treating me as if I did something bad to you! Do you think I have been unfair to you?" (b) An appeal to reality consequences, i.e., "If you continue to talk, we will not have time to plan our party," "If you continue with this behavior, these are the things that will probably happen." In other words, the teacher tries to underline cause and effect behavior. (c) An appeal to the child's group code and awareness of peer reaction, i.e., "What do you think the other boys and girls will think of that idea?" or "If you continue to spoil their fun, you can't expect the other boys and girls to like you." (d) An appeal to the teacher's power of authority. Tell the children that as a teacher you cannot allow this behavior to continue and still want to take care of them. The trick is to learn how to say "no" without becoming angry, or how to say "yes" without feeling guilty.

10. Removing seductive objects: Teachers have learned that they cannot compete against such seductive items as a baseball in a group of boys or a picture of the latest crooner in a group of pre-adolescent girls. Either the objects have to be removed or teachers have to accept the disorganized state of the group. It is not entirely the children's fault. Certain objects have a magnetic appeal and elicit a particular kind of behavior from children. For example, if a child has a flashlight, it says "Turn me on"; if he has a ball, it says "Throw me"; if he has a magnifying glass, it says "Reflect the sunlight"; if he has a whistle, it says "Toot me"; if he has a pea shooter, it says "Shoot me"; and so on. These objects feed into the child's impulse system, making it harder for children to control their behavior. One of the most exasperating experiences in a teacher's lifetime is to set up a science corner only to have it fingered to death in the first five minutes of bell time.

11. Antiseptic bouncing: When a child's behavior has reached a point where the teacher questions whether the child will respond to verbal controls, it is best to ask the child to leave the room for a few minutes—perhaps to get a drink, wash up, or deliver a message. This was done in the following situation.

I had only one occasion to use antiseptic bouncing. One morning during arithmetic study period I became aware of giggling in the back of the room. I looked up to see that Joyce had evidently thought of something hilariously funny. I tried signal interference, and, though she tried to stop, she succeeded only in choking and coughing. By now most of the children around her were aware of the circumstances and were smothering laughter, too. I hurriedly wrote a note to the secretary of the principal's office explaining that Joyce "had the giggles" and asked that she keep her waiting for a reply until she seemed settled down. I asked Joyce if she would mind delivering the message and waiting for an answer. I think she was grateful for the chance to leave the room. When she returned, she appeared to have everything controlled, as had the class, and things proceeded normally.

In antiseptic bouncing there is no intent of punishing the child but simply to protect and help him and/or the group to get over their feelings of anger, disappointment, uncontrollable laughter, hiccups, etc. Unfortunately, many schools do not have a place that would not connote punishment to which the classroom teacher can send a child. To send him to the principal where he sits on the mourner's bench is not very helpful and defeats the purpose of nonpunitive management. However, with staff planning, it is amazing what alternatives can be found.

12. Physical restraint: Once in a while a child will lose complete control and threaten to injure himself or others. In such emergencies, the child needs to be restrained physically. He should be held

firmly but not roughly. Once again there is no indication of punishment, but only a sincere concern to protect the child from hurting anyone. If a feeling of protection is to be communicated, such techniques as shaking, hitting, or spanking him only make it harder for him to believe that the teacher really wants to help him. Some teachers who are ignorant about psychodynamics feel that a child should be punished for such inappropriate and deviant behavior. However, if these same teachers ever had a chance to observe a child who has lost complete control over his impulses, they would soon realize how frightening and fearful this experience is for the child. These teachers would see the suffering and anguish these children go through. It is no game with them, but strikes at their basic feelings of survival.

The preferred physical hold is for the adult to cross the child's arms around his side while the adult stands behind him holding on to the child's wrists. Occasionally it is necessary to hold a child on the floor in this position. There is no danger that the child can injure himself in this position although he might scream that you are hurting him, or causing him considerable physical pain. Many of the children who need this type of control, go through four different phases. First, the child fights being held and controlled. He becomes enraged and says and does things that are fed by feelings of frustration, hate and desperation. He may swear, bite, and carry on in a primitive way. Most teachers who are not used to being treated this way, find it difficult to absorb this much aggression without becoming frightened and/or counter-aggressive. While we can be sympathetic towards this teacher he must provide the child with non-aggressive handling that he needs during this crisis situation. A professional nurse doesn't take away a patient's antibiotics because he happens to vomit on her. Likewise, a teacher does not reject a child when he needs adult controls the most. The teacher's control sys-

tem must take over for the child's until his controls are operating again.

During the first stage it is sometimes helpful for the teacher to tell the child softly that he is all right, that in a little while he is going to get over his angry feelings, and that he (the teacher) is going to take care of him and not let him hurt anyone or anything. Once the child realizes that he cannot break away and that he *is* being controlled, the rage usually turns to tears. This is phase two. At this point the child's defenses are down, his coat of toughness has vanished and his inadequacy and immaturity become evident. After this period the child usually becomes silent or asks to be let go, which is phase three. If the teacher thinks the child has control over his feelings and is not going to start the cycle all over again, the teacher should release his hold on the child. It must be emphasized that the teacher, not the child, makes the decision. One evidence that the child is gaining control over his impulses is that his language becomes more coherent and logical. If the child knows who he is, where he is, and what has happened, he is usually on his way up the ladder of integration. As he gains controls, the child usually has to save face, which is often accomplished by pulling away from the teacher or making a sly remark. This is phase four and usually a good sign that the child is ready to move on his own power. Next, the teacher may ask the child to go to the washroom and clean up.

Occasionally, a child may have to be held in the classroom, but this should be avoided whenever possible. If it cannot be avoided, one of the students should get the principal immediately so that the child can be removed from the class. Later, the teacher *needs* to explain to the class and to the child exactly what has happened in order to counter any delusional interpretations of the teacher's behavior.

An important point to remember is that whenever a teacher holds a child and is able to control his own personal feelings of anxiety and aggression, the chances are that his relationship with this child will improve significantly. The message the child receives is: "I care enough about you to protect you from your own frightening impulses. The fact you had to be held is no point against you. I'm not angry, but pleased that you are feeling more comfortable and are in control of your emotions." This kind of support can only foster the child's feeling that the teacher is a person whom he can trust.

Preventive planning. The fourth of Redl's four alternatives is preventive planning. Sometimes disruptive behavior can be avoided by developing a better school and classroom procedure. If a teacher always has difficulty during transitional periods, if there is undue conflict on the playground or in the corridors, the disturbing behavior cannot be attributed solely to "problem children"—perhaps the school program is inadequate. For example, if a teacher bores, fatigues, or regiments children into acting out, their behavior cannot be explained in terms of inner conflicts but simply in terms of a poor living design for healthy children. One teacher solved her problem as follows:

In a large elementary school in the heart of Detroit, the staff's major problem during the snowy months was snowballing. Although more teachers were scheduled for playground duty and the severity of the penalty was increased, the problem did not diminish. The children still threw snowballs, but they were much more clever about it. One teacher who was unhappy about additional playground duty suggested that they paint a huge circular target on the back brick wall of the two-story school and actually program more snowballing. After much discussion and apprehension, the idea was presented to the students. They thought it was a wonderful idea, so a student-faculty committee was appointed to draw up some rules and regulations. Once the target was drawn, the problem of snowballing was virtually eliminated. The children threw all their energy into hitting the bull's eye rather than one another. Some children would actually come to school early just so they could have the highest daily score. One teacher commented that many of the "problem children" were very active in this activity and threw themselves out by the time school began. He reported that they were even easier to teach. . . .

We have already indicated the major contribution Redl made in delineating the nature of the milieu. A second major contribution is his concept of LSI, or Life Space Interviewing. It is one thing to speak in theoretical terms of the proper function of a teacher who has to manage children; it is quite another to describe the basic skill needed to infuse the milieu with hygienic relationships. You will note the contrast with the traditional therapeutic interview but recognize that the author's concept of LSI does not involve an either-or choice, but supplements the total of what we know about managing and changing behavior. Teachers have found his description very useful in spelling out the general proposition as well as indicating particular functions to be performed.

Two words of caution are in order. First, to read about LSI does not provide the training necessary to develop skill in practice. Second, the lucid description may make it seem easy to practice. In actuality, since LSI requires recognition of action overtones as well as dynamics, it is at least as complicated as traditional therapy. However, LSI is in keeping with the role, responsibility, and understanding of teachers and it outlines concrete action beyond mere suggestions to teachers to "accept the child," "love the child," or some other simple generalization. LSI is a method of talking effectively with children, whether it be for control and disciplinary purposes or for understanding more completely how the child feels.

While Redl does not stress the point in this material, the adult must have an empathic potential—that subtle capacity to see and relate to the deeper feeling rather than the defensiveness of the child—to make the technique effective.

The Concept of the Life Space Interview

Fritz Redl

It is our contention that life space interviewing plays an important part in the lives of all children. All adults in an educational role in children's lives find themselves in many situations which could correctly be thus labeled.

It is our contention that the life space interview assumes a mediating role between the child and what life holds for him, which becomes just as important as the interviewing that goes on within the pressurized cabin.

It is our contention that in work with seriously disturbed children, even if they are not exposed to the special type of pressurized cabin therapy over and beyond their exposure to milieu therapy, the strategically wise use and the technically correct handling of the life space interviews held with the children are of foremost clinical importance.

It is our contention that even where children are exposed to clear-cut pressurized cabin therapy, for special therapy of one phase of their problem, the wisdom of strategy and technique used by their natural home or school life personnel in mediating life experiences for them is of major strategic relevance in its own right.

It is, before all, our contention that what goes on in a life space interview, even though held with the child by somebody not his therapist, in the stricter interpretation of the term, involves as subtle and important issues of strategy and technique as the decisions the psychoanalyst has to

make during the course of a therapeutic hour.

It is our contention, last and not least, that any application of total life milieu therapy as supportive to individual therapy, or undertaken in its own right, will stand or fall with the wisdom and skill with which the protectors, teachers, and interpreters in the children's lives carry out their life space interview tasks.

It is for this reason that we shall try to subject some of the occurrences during the process of a life space interview to the same type of scrutiny that psychiatric therapy techniques have for a long time been exposed to in our technical seminars. By the way, one more word about the *term:*

What we have in mind when we say "life space interview" is the same thing as what my staff, my friends, and my co-workers, while I still lived in Detroit, referred to under the name of *marginal interview*. The reasons for the change in terms are many, and seem to me so strong that they outweigh the equally obvious disadvantages of the switch in name. When I, and many of us in the same type of work, started talking about the marginal interview, it was pretty clear, out of our own context of operation and to us personally, what we felt it was "marginal" to. We meant, at first, the type of therapylike interview that a child may need around an incident of stealing from the "kitty" in his club group, but which would be held right around the event itself by the group worker in charge of that club, rather than by the child's therapist—even though the material around the incident would probably later be getting into therapy, too.

Abridged from Fritz Redl, "The Concept of the Life Space Interview," *American Journal of Orthopsychiatry,* XXIX (January 1959), 1–18. Reprinted by permission.

So—it was "marginal" in two ways: marginal in terms of the rest of the life events around which it was arranged; and marginal in terms of the overall job expectation of a group leader, who uses casework or therapy technique even while functioning in his group leader role.

Since I moved into the operation of our residential treatment design[1] within a huge hospital setting, the term "marginal" has lost the clarity of its meaning entirely, besides other disadvantages which the low-status sound of the word "marginal" seems to assume for many people.

In changing to the term "life space interview," we apologize for the possible confusion that might be created because we are using the term here with an entirely different meaning from the one Kurt Lewin had in mind. In spite of this disadvantage, we feel that the term is at least frank in its emphasis on the major characteristics of this type of interview we have in mind: In contrast to the interviewing done in considerable detachment from direct involvement in the here and now of Johnny's life, such as the psychoanalytic play therapy interview, the life space interview is closely built around the child's direct life experience in connection with the issues which become the interview focus. Most of the time, it is held by a person who is perceived by the child to be part of his "natural habitat or life space," with some pretty clear role and power-influence in his daily living, as contrasted to the therapist to whom one is sent for "long-range treatment." We are fully aware that none of the similarities or differences implied here are truly characteristic for the two operations; in fact, to find similarities and differences is the goal, not the starting point for our research. For the time being, and until someone with more imagination and linguistic know-how gives us a better clue, we think the term is as good, or bad, as any we could think of to connote what we have in mind. Frankly, we aren't quite used to it ourselves, and you may find us slipping back into calling the whole thing by its old Midwest-flavored name of the "marginal" more often than we may be willing to admit.

GOALS AND TASKS OF THE LIFE SPACE INTERVIEW

First, I want to select for discussion two major categories of goals and tasks for life space interviewing: (a) Clinical Exploitation of Life Events; and (b) Emotional First Aid on the Spot. The difference between these two categories does not lie in the nature of the event around which the need for the life space interview arose —we shall in the future refer to this event as the "issue"—but in our decision as to what we want to do with it; it is also defined, of course, by the question as to just what the situation itself allows.

Let's assume that a group of children are just about ready to go out on that excursion they have anticipated with eagerness for quite a while. Let's assume there is, due to our fault, somewhat more delay at the door because of a last-minute search for lost shoes, footballs, etc., so that irrita-

---

[1] Whenever in illustrations the "children on our ward" are mentioned, this refers to the following setting: Closed Ward within the premises of the National Institutes of Health, a large research hospital. The children referred to here: a carefully selected group of six boys ranging in age from eight to ten years at the time of intake, chosen as representative of "borderline" disturbances commonly referred to as "explosive acting-out type of child." They are children of normal IQ, however, and are expected to be free from traceable physical pathology, characterized in their behavior by a rather extreme volume of aggression, extreme forms of reckless destruction, and loaded with an amazing array of learning disturbances and character disorders to boot. The ward on which the children lived was staffed and operated more along the lines of a camping program, with the hospital as a base, but not ultimate limit for the activities. At the time of the presentation of this material, the movement of the children into a newly constructed open residence was imminent. The treatment and research goals of the operation included the study of the impact of intensive individual psychotherapy (four hours per child per week), of observations in our own school setting (individual tutoring as well as group school), and exposure to "milieu therapy" in their life on the ward.

bility mounts in the gang that is already assembled and raring to go. Let's further assume that in the ensuing melee of irritated bickering two of our youngsters get into a flare-up, which ends up with Johnny's getting socked more vehemently than he can take, furiously running back to his room, cursing his tormentor and the world at large, all educators in particular, swearing that he will "never go on no trip no more in his whole life." We find him just about to soak himself in a pleasurable bath of self-pity, nursing his grudge against people in general and adding up new evidence for his theory that life is no good, people are mean "so-and-so's" anyway, and that autistic daydreaming is the only safe way out.

Well, most of us would feel that somebody ought to move into this situation. The staff member who tries to involve the sulking child in a marginal interview at this time has a choice of doing either of two things:

He may want to be with John in his misery, and to assist the child in disentangling the complicated web of emotions in which he is so hopelessly caught, simply in order to "get him over it" right now and here, to get him back into his previous enjoyment-anticipating mood. This situation seems to be quite comparable to the concept of "first aid"; the organism is capable of taking care of a wound produced by a minor cut, but it might be wise to help it.

On the other hand, depending on how much time there is and how Johnny reacts to the adult's interview strategy, the adult may suddenly find that this opportunity gives him a long-hoped-for chance to help John to come to grips with an issue in his life which we so far have had little possibility to bring to his awareness. Thus, he may forget about his intention of getting John back to his original cheerful excursion-anticipating mood; he may even give in to his sulky insistence that he "wasn't going to go nohow," but he may decide to use this special opportunity to start on an interpretational job. He may begin to tie this event

up for John with many similar previous ones, and thus hope to help him see how John really "asks for it" many times, even though he has no idea that he does so, and how his irritably rude provocation or lashing out at other children often gets people infuriated, or whatever the special version of this perennial theme may be. In short, half an hour later our interviewer may be driving after the rest of the group with a somewhat sadder but wiser companion at his side, or he may at least have laid the groundwork for some such insight to sink in at a future opportunity, or to be picked up by his "therapist" at a later opportunity in case John happens also to be "in individual therapy" of the more classical style.

By the way, most of the time we can't be sure before an interview under which of the two goal categories it will eventually have to be listed, for we may in the middle of an interview find good enough reason for a switch from the original intent with which we entered the scene.

This differentiation between "Emotional First Aid on the Spot" on the one hand, and "Clinical Exploitation of Life Events" on the other, however, still leaves us with two rather comprehensive categories before us. I feel that the practitioners among you would like it better if we broke those wider concepts down into smaller units and thus brought them closer to the observational scene.

THE CLINICAL EXPLOITATION OF LIFE EVENTS

Our attempts at pulling out of a life experience, in which a given child is involved, whatever clinical gain might be drawn from it for our long-range treatment goal, may assume some of the following special forms:

Reality rub-in. The trouble with some of our youngsters, among other things, is that they are *socially nearsighted.* They can't read the meaning of an event in which they get involved, unless we use huge script for them and underline it all in glaring colors besides. Others are caught in such a well-woven *system of near to delusional misinterpretation of life* that even glaring contradictions in actual fact are glided over by their eyes unless their view is arrested and focused on them from time to time. More fascinating even, are the youngsters whose preconscious perception of the full reality is all right, but who have such well-oiled ego skills in alibi-ing to their own conscience, and rationalizing to any outside monitor's arguments, that the picture of a situation that can be discussed with them is already hopelessly repainted by the time we get there. It is perhaps not necessary to add how important it is, strategically speaking, that such children have some of this "reality rub-in" interviewing done right then and there, and preferably by persons who themselves were on the scene or are at least known to be thoroughly familiar with it.

Symptom estrangement. In contrast to their more clearly neurotic contemporaries, our children's egos have, in part at least, become subservient to the pathological mechanisms they have developed. They have learned well how to benefit from their symptoms through secondary gain, and are therefore in no way inclined to accept the idea that something is wrong with them or that they need help. A large part of the "preparatory" task at least, without successful completion of which the magics of the more classical forms of individual therapy are rather lost on these children, consists in alienating their ego from their symptoms. Hopeful that there must be somewhere a nonpathology-swallowed part of their ego functions waiting for a chance to speak up, we use many of their life situations to try to pile up evidence that their pathology really doesn't pay, or that they pay too heavily for what meager secondary gain they draw from it, or that the glee they are after can be much more regularly and reliably drawn from other forms of problem-solving or pursuit of life and happiness. By the way, the assumption in all this is

not that one can simply argue such children through well-placed life space strategy into letting go of their symptoms; part of the job needs to be tackled, in addition, by many other means. However, we can *enlist* part of their insight into helping their ego want to liberate itself from the load of their pathology. To make it possible for them, even after they want to, to shuffle off the unconscious coils of their neuroses, is an issue in its own right. We also ought to remember at this point how important it is that symptom estrangement be pursued consistently by all the staff all the way down the line. It would do little good to *talk* in interviews about the inappropriateness of their symptomatic actions, if the social reality in which they live made it too hard for them to let go of those very symptoms. Our action definitely has to be well attuned to our words in this task more than in any other.

Massaging numb value-areas. No matter how close to psychopathic our children may sometimes look, we haven't found one of them yet who didn't have lots of potential areas of value appeal lying within him. But while the arm is still there, circulation has stopped. Value sensitivity in a child for which his inner self has been liberated still needs to be *used*, and something has to be done to get circulation going again. Admitting value sensitivity, just like admitting hunger for love, is quite face-losing for our youngsters. There are, however, in most youngsters some value areas which are more tax-exempt from peer group shame than others. For instance, even at a time when our youngsters would rather be seen dead than overconforming and sweet, the appeal to certain codes of "fairness" within their fight-provocation ritual is quite acceptable to them. Thus, in order to ready the ground for "value arguments" altogether, the pulling out of issues of fairness or similar values from the debris of their daily life events may pay off handsomely in the end.

New-tool salesmanship. Even the most classicism-conscious therapists confess from time to time that they spend quite some effort helping a youngster see that there are other defenses than the ones he is using, and that doing this may at least partially widen the youngster's adaptational skills. The therapist, however, who operates in the "pressurized cabin" of a long-range classical style individual therapy design cannot afford to waste too much of his effort in this direction, or he would puncture the pressure-safe walls he has spent so much time building up to begin with. So, as soon as the potential to use such mechanisms has been liberated in individual therapy, the adults who "live" with those children can begin to use many of their life experiences to help them draw from them the vision of a much wider range of potential reaction to the same mess. Even the seemingly simple recognition that seeking out an adult to talk it over with is so much more reasonable than to lash out at nothing in wild fury may need to be worked at hard for a long stretch of time with some of the children I have in mind.

The life space interview offers a chance to leave the more general level of propaganda for better adjustment tools, and to become quite specific in the demonstration of the all too obvious inadequacy of the special tool previously chosen by the child. In this respect we feel the same advantage that the salesman may feel who, besides having leaflets to distribute, is given the opportunity to demonstrate.

Manipulation of the boundaries of the self. From time to time one invariably runs into a child who combines with the rest of his explosive acting-out type of borderline aggressive pathology, a peculiar helplessness toward a process we like to refer to as *group psychological suction*. Quite vulnerable to even mild contagion sparks, he is often discovered by an exceptionally brilliant manipulator of group psychological currents, and then easily drifts into the pathetic role of the perennial "sucker" of an exploitation-happy subclique.

The life space interview, of course, offers a strategic opportunity to begin to move in on this. To illustrate what we mean by this concept of "manipulation of the boundaries of the self"—and leaving out all the details as to life space strategy employed in the case—the following example may serve:

Several months ago, we felt that the time was ripe to "move in" on the problems of one of our youngsters around "group psychological suction" described above, so we decided to exploit incidents of this sort, wherever they might happen, through an increased use of "life space interviews." We felt good when eventually the following incident occurred one day in school: Two boys of the subclique that enjoyed exploiting this youngster were hard at work to get him to "act up" for them. This time their wiles didn't seem to get them anywhere; in fact, in the process of accomplishing their job they got out of hand themselves and got themselves "bounced." They were hardly out of the room when the youngster in question turned to the teacher, with a relieved look on his face, and declared, "Gee, am I glad I didn't get sucked into this one."

Many of our children are more ready than one would assume at first sight to expand their concept of the wider boundaries of their self into including other people, benign adults, their group, or the whole institution to which they feel a sense of belonging, and so on. In an entirely different direction, again, we may want to use life incidents to help youngsters with the problem of acceptance of their self, or of hitherto split-off parts of it. Anything that educators describe under terms such as "encouragement," "inculcating a feeling of worthfulness and pride," and anything that betrays confused attitudes of the children toward their "self" in the form of despondency coupled with megalomanic illusions, etc., might well be grouped under this heading.

In summary, we should underline the implication that these five goals for the use of the life space interview were meant to be illustrative rather than system binding. In all the instances we have raised so far, the real *goal* of what the life space interviewer did was the clinical exploitation of a given life event. It meant making use of a momentary life experience in order to draw out of it something that might be of use for our long-range therapeutic goals.

EMOTIONAL FIRST AID ON THE SPOT

While children are exposed to therapeutic long-range work on their basic pathology, it is important to remember that they are still forced to live with their symptoms until they finally can shed them, and that child development is also still going on. For, while it is true that our children are sick enough to deserve the term "patients," we must never forget that child patients are still *growing youngsters.* This means that the adult, who accompanies them during the various phases of their growth, is also needed as an *aid on the spot* in those adjustment demands of daily life that they cannot well manage on their own. It is our contention that this in itself is an important enough task to deserve special technical attention, and that the opportunity for such "aid in conflict" includes the situations which we term "life space interview." The emphasis here lies in the fact that emotional first aid in itself is a perfectly valid reason for a carefully planned life space interview, even if this special issue around which the interview is built promises no long-range gain in the same way in which we described it in the previous section. As illustration of the goal which a given life space interview may set itself, we should like to enumerate again five randomly assembled subcategories:

Drain-off of frustration acidity. Even normal children experience easily as something quite infuriating the interruption of the pleasurable exploit in which they happen to be engaged. This is especially unfortunate with our type of child who has such low frustration tolerance, for he is overaggressive and hostility-projective to begin with. It is here that the life space interview

has an opportunity to serve as an over-all hygienic device. In sympathetic communication with the child about his anger or justified disgust at the discomfort of having been interrupted, we can drain off the surplus of intervention-produced hostility, and thus avoid its being added to the original reservoir of hate. Such situations offer themselves especially when something has gone wrong with a planned enterprise, or if the mere need to maintain a schedule may force interruption.

Support for the management of panic, fury, and guilt. The trouble with many children is not only that they *have* more feelings of anxiety, panic, shame, guilt, fury than they should or than the normal child would experience, but also that they don't know what to do with such states of mind when they get into them. We have already complained, in *Children Who Hate,* about how difficult it is to help such children to react correctly even if they do feel guilty when they should. It is important, then, that the adult intervene and give first aid as well as therapeutic support whenever heavier quantities of such emotions hit the child or the group. In our own over-all strategy plan, for instance, we consider it important that an adult always stay with the child, no matter how severe his tantrum attack may become. The knowledge that we are just as interested in protecting him from his own exaggerated wishes, as from the bad intent of other people, has been found quite ego supportive in the long run. By being with the child right after the excitement of a blowup abates, the adult can often help the child "put things back into focus and proportion" again. He can also aid him in the return to the common course of activities or social life of the day without the sour aftertaste of unresolved hurt.

Communication maintenance in moments of relationship decay. There is one reaction of our children to experiences of emotional turmoil which we fear more than any other they may happen to produce—and that is, the total breakoff of all communication with us and full-fledged retreat into an autistic world of fantasy into which we are not allowed to penetrate. We get scared, because with children at the borderline of psychotic withdrawal from any and all reality this weapon of defense against help from us is the most efficient one.

It is used especially frequently when events force us to a clear-cut form of intervention in a youngster's behavior, the nature of which seems, at first sight, to offer an especially "clear-cut" point of argument or interpretation to the child. Yet, at this very moment he is liable to drop all relationships with us, and thereby makes us quite helpless in our attempt to offer sympathy, explanation or support. Often, for instance, after a particularly vicious attack upon another child, a youngster will misperceive the motives for the intervention of a protective and battle-interrupting adult to such a degree that he interprets even the most well handled interruption of the fight as rude and hostile "betrayal." To this he reacts with such resentment that the breakdown of all previously established relationships with that adult seems imminent. It is important that this process be stopped right then and there and that we prevent the *next step* in the youngster's defensive maneuver, namely, the withdrawal of all communication and the total flight into autistic daydreams. Often, in such a moment, it is obvious that nothing we could do would make any impact on the hopelessly misconceived image in the youngster's mind. However, our attempt to involve the youngster in some form of communication may prevent the next level of retreat from us right then and there. So we surrender any plan to "talk to the point," but simply try to keep communication flowing between child and adult, no matter on what theme and no matter how trivial or far removed it may be from the issue at hand.

Regulation of behavioral and social traffic. This specific task of the life space interview doesn't look like much, and we have become painfully aware that people have a tendency to consider it too "superficial" and undignified to be included in items as status-high as the discussion of

"interview techniques." Yet, our respect for the clinical importance of our service as *social and behavioral traffic cops* has gone up, if anything, over the last ten years. The issue itself is simple enough and doesn't need much explaining. The performance of the task, however, may get so difficult that it is easily comparable to the most delicate problems that might emerge in individual therapy of either children or adults.

The facts of the situation are these: The children know, of course, what over-all policies, routines, rules of the game of social interaction are in vogue in a given place. Only, no matter how well they "know," to *remember* the relevance of a given issue for a given life situation is a separate task, and to muster enough ego force at the moment to subject impulsivity to the dictates of an internalized concept of rules is still another. Thus, the service they need becomes very similar to the job the traffic cop, when functioning at his best, would perform for adults, and even the most law-abiding ones amongst us may need such help from time to time. He reminds us of the basic rules again or warns us of the special vicissitudes of the next stretch. He may point out to us where we deviate dangerously even though we happen to be lucky this time. Since people do not necessarily learn even from dramatic experience, unless they are aided by a benign and accepted guide, it may be important to go, in a subsequent session, through a stretch of behavioral confusion and to use it for reinforcement of our over-all awareness of the implications of life. Since our children are especially allergic to moralizing or preaching or lecturing of any kind, it would not do to offer them a condensed handbook of behavioral guidelines. It is important to subdivide that phase of their social learning into a number of aids *given on the spot* when needed most.

For example: we have a clear-cut policy on our ward about the child's going to our school sessions, and about the reasons for this, as well as the course of events which will take place if a child gets himself "bounced" for the time being. We have spent great effort to have everybody live this policy consistently so that the unanimous attitude of all adults involved could serve as an additional nonverbal reinforcer of the basic design. Yet, in order for all this to become meaningful and finally incorporated and perceived as part of the over-all structure of "life in this place" for our children, it took hundreds of situations of life space interviews surrounding school events.

Umpire services—in decision crises as well as in cases of loaded transactions. The children often need us for another function, which may sound simple though the need for it may be emphatic and desperate: to *umpire.* This umpiring role in which we see ourselves put may be a strictly internal one. It sort of assumes the flavor of our helping them decide between the dictates of their "worser or their better selves." For those instances, our role resembles that of a good friend whom we took along shopping—hoping he would help us maintain more vision and balance in the weighing of passionate desire versus economic reason than we ourselves might be capable of in the moment of decision-making. However, we wouldn't want to restrict this term to its more subtle, internal use. We envision it to go all the way from the actual umpiring of a fight or dispute, of a quarrel about the game rules in case of conflict or confusion, to the management of "loaded transactions" in their social life. Into the last category fall many complicated arrangements about swapping, borrowing, trading, etc., the secondary backwash from which may be too clinically serious to be left to chance at a particular phase. Many such situations, by the way, offer wonderful opportunities to do some "clinical exploitation of life events." But, even if nothing else is obtained in a given incident of this kind, the hygienic regulation and the emotionally clean umpiring of internal or external dispute is a perfectly legitimate and a most delicate clinical job in its own right.

Summarizing all this, we should like to emphasize what we tried to imply all along: All these "goals"—the strategic exploitation type, as well as the moment-geared emotional first-aid ones—may be combined sometimes in one and the same interview, and we shall often see ourselves switch goals in midstream. We probably need not even add that the type of goal we set ourselves at a given time in our project would also be strongly influenced by the phase the children find themselves in in their individual therapy, and of course, just where they are in their movement from sickness to mental health. In fact, the "stepping up" as well as the "laying off" in respect to selecting special issues for life space interview or for purposely leaving such materials untouched is in itself an important part of the over-all coordination of individual therapy and the other aspects of our therapeutic attack on the pathology of a given child.

SPECULATIONS ABOUT STRATEGY AND TECHNIQUE

The importance of a clinically highly sophisticated concept of *strategy and technique* in regard to the life space interview is taken for granted in this discussion by now. That this short symposium cannot hope to do more than open up the issues and point at the need for more organized research seems equally obvious. In view of this, it may seem most advisable to concentrate on one of the core problems of all discussions on strategy and technique, namely, the question of *indications and counterindications;* and to draw attention to some of the most urgent aspects that need further elaboration soon. If we say "indications and counterindications," by the way, we mean to refer to both: indications and counterindications for the *holding* of a life space interview to begin with, as well as indications and counterindications for a specific *technique* or for the establishing or abandoning of a specific strategic move. The question "Should I keep my mouth shut or should I interpret this dream right now?" which is an issue so familiar to us from discussions of individual therapy, has its full analogy in the orbit of life space interview work.

The following criteria seem to turn up most often in our own discussions of technique:

Central theme relevance. By this we mean the impact of over-all strategy in a given therapeutic phase on the question of just what situations I would move in on and what issues I would select for life space interview pick-up. It would not do to surround the children with such a barricade of attempts to exploit their life experiences for clinical gains that it would disturb the natural flavor of child life that needs to be maintained; and too much first aid would contain the danger of overdependency or adult intervention oppressedness that we certainly want to avoid. As an example for this: At certain stretches we would purposely keep away from "talking" too much about our previously quoted youngster's proneness to allow himself to be played for a sucker. It is only after certain over-all therapeutic lines have emerged that we decide in unison that such incidents should from now on be exploited more fully. It was felt, at that particular time, that the child's individual therapist would welcome such supportive rub-in from without.

Ego proximity and issue clarity. The first of these two is an old standby, well known from clinical discussions in classical psychoanalytic work. One simply does not sail interpretatively into material that is at the time so "deeply repressed" that bothering it would only unnecessarily increase resistance or lead to marginal problems in other areas. On the other hand, material of high ego-proximity had better be handled directly, else the child might think we are too dumb or too disinterested to notice what he himself has figured out long since on his own. The same issue remains, of course, an important criterion in life space interview work.

The item of *issue clarity* is a more intricate one and becomes especially complex because of the rapidity with which things move on the behavioral scene of children's lives and because of the many factors that may crowd themselves into the picture. Just one brief illustration of what we are trying to point out:

Johnny has just attacked another youngster viciously, really undeservedly. The other child's surprise and the whole situation are so crystal clear that this time we are sure that even our insight-defensive Johnny will have to let us show him how he really asked for it all—So, here we stand, our clinical appetite whetted while we watch the fight. But—wham—a third child interferes. He happened to run by, couldn't resist the temptation of getting into the brawl, and he is a youngster Johnny has a lot of hostile feeling about anyway. Before anybody quite knows what has happened, Johnny receives from that interfering youngster a blow much too heavy and unfair for anybody's fight ritual, and so, of course, Johnny leaves the scene howling with fury, pain, and shame about losing face. Obviously, we had better assist Johnny in his predicament, but the idea of using this life space interview for a push in the direction of Johnny's self-insight into the provocativeness of his behavior seems downright ridiculous at this point.

Role compatibility. Children who live in an institutional setting do not react to individual people as "persons" only. There is also a direct impact brought to bear on them from the very "role" they perceive a particular adult to be in. This issue has long been obscured by the all too generalized assumption that the personal relationship between child and adults is the only thing that counts. To illustrate this point:

When a camp counselor finds her whole cabin up on the roof where they know they shouldn't be, she may have trouble getting them down no matter how much the children may all love her. I, as the camp director walking in on that scene, may find it much easier to get them off the roof; in fact they may climb down as soon as they see me coming along. This does not mean that they have a less good relationship to their counselor or a better one to me. It simply means a difference in their role expectation. The counselor for them is seen in the role of the group leader, which heavily contains the flavor of the one who plans happy experiences with them. It is true that on the margin of this role they do know that the adult counselor also has certain "overgroup-demanded" regulations to identify herself with and to enforce. However, that part of her role—and for the sake of a happy camp experience we hope so—is less sharply in focus than the program-identified one. In fact, if that counselor got too fussy or too indignant about the youngsters' not responding immediately, or used the argument of the over-all camp regulations against her gang too fast, this would create resentment and a loss of subsequent relationship for a while. The role of the camp director, no matter how cordial individual feelings toward him may be, is much more clearly loaded with the expectation that it is his job to secure over-all coordination of many people's interests. The children would therefore expect the director to make a demand for them to get off that roof, and would not hold it as much against him that he does interfere with the pleasure of the moment or considers the whole camp more important than "Cabin 7" at this time.

The compatibility of the major role of a given adult with the role he is forced into by the life space interview is an important strategic consideration. In our present operation, for example, we felt, during the first year or so, that it was quite important that the role of the *counselor* be rather sharply set off from that of the *ward boss*, the *teacher, the therapist. . . .* During that phase it also seemed important for us to protect the counselor from too many unnecessary displaced hostilities, since she has enough to do to handle those that would naturally come her way. In short: During that period of time we felt it important that all requests for going home or for special prolonged week-end visits, etc., were steered to the psychiatrist, who was seen as the ward boss by the children. The transference character of many of these requests and the terrific ambivalence of the

children about them, thrown on top of all the aggression manipulation a counselor has to cope with anyway in her daily play life with the child, would have increased the ensuing confusion. The arrangement we created allowed the ward boss to absorb some of the extra frustration acidity unavoidably generated during such interviews, while the counselor was, so to say, "taken off that hook." At the same time, however, we did feel that the counselor is the most natural person to assist the child in *first aid* interviews around his concern about home, mother's not turning up for a visit, etc.

Mood manageability—the child's and our own. With due respect to all the clinical ambition any staff member can have about managing his own mood, there is a limit beyond which he cannot be forced any further. Such limits need to be recognized. Oversimplifying the issue for purposes of abbreviation:

If I work for an hour in order to get the children finally in shape to be quite reasonable and have a good stretch of quite happy and unusually well modulated play with me, I can't possibly act concerned enough if one of them does something that needs a more serious "reality rub-in" for good measure. This is especially the case where we allow a child to play his "cute antics" for the service of everybody's entertainment, and where he suddenly begins to go too far. Even a serious talk with someone who quite visibly found the same antics cute two minutes ago will not have the same strategic chance as a talk with one who *was not involved in the original scene.*

The item of mood manageability is, of course, an even more difficult one as far as the mood of the children is concerned. The issue may be clear enough, and the event beautifully designed to draw some learning out of it. If the youngster in the meantime gets overexcited, bored, tired, or grouchy, the best laid-out issue would be hopelessly lost and we had better look for another occasion for the same job.

Issues around timing. One of the great

strategic advantages of the life space interview is the very flexibility in timing that it offers us. We don't have to hope that the child will remember from Friday noon until his therapy hour next Wednesday what was happening just now. We can talk with him *right now*. Or, having watched the event itself that led to a messy incident, we can quite carefully calculate how long it will take the youngster to cool off enough in order to be accessible to some reasonable communication with him, and move in on him at that very calculated time. Or we may even see to it that he gets enough emotional first-aid from us or from our colleagues so that he can be brought into a state where some insight-focused discussion with him is possible at last. One of the most frequent dilemmas that aggressive and explosive children force us into is the fear of waiting too long to talk about something, because we know how fast they forget, as opposed to the need to let some cooling off take place, lest the interview itself get shot through with the aggression debris left over from the original scene. Sometimes external things happen and the "time" aspect may often work against us. I shall never forget the painful experience several years ago in which I finally had succeeded in working a bunch of quite recalcitrant delinquents into a mood conducive to my talking with them about an issue they didn't want to face. Just then the swimming bell put a rude end to my efforts. To keep them one minute longer while they heard and saw everybody else running down to their beloved free swim would have made shambles out of my carefully built up role as interpreter of the rules of life.

The impact of terrain and of props. Both the life space interview and the more classical styles of individual therapy believe in the importance of terrain and props. In the long-range therapy, after we have figured out the most goal-supportive arrangements, the problem of terrain and props loses its importance because it can easily be held constant or can at least be kept under predictable control. While the most favorable terrain is always the one in which both partners feel most comfortable, in life space interviewing the terrain may be terrifically varied, and neither it nor the selection of props is often within our power.

In fact, more often than not, terrain as well as props are on the side of the child's resistance, rather than on our side. This is, of course, especially true when we move in on a situation involving extreme behavioral conflict.

For the child, the most comfortable place may be the one behind his most belligerently cathected defenses. From bathtub to toy cabinet, from roof or treetop to "under the couch," his choice of terrain seems endless. In all cases the problem of what emotional charge the surrounding props may suddenly assume remains of high technical relevance. Besides what is going on between the two people, what is going on between *them and space and props* can become of great relevance.

In summary, the choice of a given technique must be (1) dependent on the specific goal we have in mind (2) within a given setting (3) with a specific type of child (4) in a given phase of his therapeutic movement.[2] There is no "odd" or "bad" technique in itself. The very procedure that "made" one situation all by itself may be the source of a mess-up in another, or may have remained irrelevant in a third. However, this reminder, while disappointing, would not be too hard to take, for we have learned that lesson from the development of concepts of strategy and techniques for the psychiatric interview long ago. Rather

[2] Many of the illustrations used in this paper need to be understood as limited by the specific conditions under which the observations were made. For their full evaluation, a detailed description of the over-all program and ward policies for the clinical management of the children and for the guidance of staff behavior would have to be added here. It is, therefore, expected that most of our illustrations will have to be read with this reservation in mind. While literal translation into practice with other children in different settings is not intended, we do imply emphatically that the basic principles we are trying to illustrate here should hold for a wide variety of designs.

than relearn it, we simply need to remember the difference between a pseudoscientific technical trick-bag, and a more complex, but infinitely more realistic concept of multiple-item conditioned choice of criteria for the selection of strategy as well as of techniques.

In teaching emotionally disturbed children there will be times when a crisis situation occurs that involves an entire group rather than a few individuals. In order to understand the dynamics of the situation, the teacher will need to hold a group interview. One technique that has been developed at the University of Michigan Fresh Air Camp clearly defines this type of group interview as a form of Life Space Interview. The specific goals of this technique include clarifying confused issues of social reality; breaking through individual and group alibi mechanisms which protect them from recognizing their impulsive behavior; ventilating group emotions; and freeing and strengthening the group's self-image which has been undermined by current conflicts. It is our belief that training institutions are aware teachers need to be provided with more useful knowledge of the group process, including group interview techniques. This area is no longer a luxury but a necessity for those who work with emotionally disturbed children.

Group Interviewing in a Camp for Disturbed Boys
William C. Morse and David Wineman

When a camp plays host for the summer to ninety disturbed boys the staff must be fully aware of the potential volatility of this group. Since the cabin group of seven boys and their three counselors forms the basic social unit of camp it is important that the individual characteristics of each be matched to produce maximum group harmony. The membership of each cabin is planned after a careful study of the records of the individual child, and particular attention is given to counselor assets and liabilities. Grouping is a task of major importance in therapeutic camping, and a number of criteria have been developed out of our year-to-year successes and failures. Since behavior in camp is predictable only to a limited extent from the agency data, even theoretical best-fits produce a group far from perfect. Even with as hygienic a

From William C. Morse and David Wineman, "Group Interviewing in a Camp for Disturbed Boys," *Journal of Social Issues*, XIII (No. 1, 1957), 23–31.

grouping as we can attain there is no way of avoiding the emergence of the basic behavioral disturbances for which the child is sent to camp. These disturbances, when they occur, are not viewed as interruptions in a smooth camp session. Instead they provide the raw material for helping the boys in their personal and social adjustment.

The problems that appear may range from periodic minor conflicts to sustained and painful disruptions which threaten to disintegrate the group. Since the staff aim is to maintain the group as an intact and relatively peaceful social unit, and since many of the individual personality difficulties appear most sharply when confronted with the challenges of group living, much time is spent in emergency interview sessions with the cabin groups. We have found that these interviews have been most effectively conducted by a staff member who embodies both administrative and therapeutic responsibility.

Naturally each group session runs its

own course over a period of forty-five minutes to two hours and great flexibility must be used in working each one through. Frequently such sessions open in a gentle fashion by some searching for "Why are we here?" This phase of the group interview is soon abandoned by the campers as it becomes clear that they must get at the basic difficulty before they return to other camp activities.[1] A second natural stage of the session is likely to run to ventilation and catharsis—sometimes germane to the problem, very often irrelevant escapism. As anxiety increases a varying administration of permissiveness and control is needed to prevent this phase of the session from becoming disorganized and hysterical. As in individual interviews, tempers vary, blocks are frequent, vital material may rush out or be repressed. The process may shuffle back and forth between group and individual case histories.

To usher in the third phase of the session it is necessary for the therapist to select out significant and usable material which will provide a focus for the group. It is possible to make something of a rough classification of the various foci which can emerge out of such interviews, comprising, in effect, a summary of the *functions* of the group interview. Thus, the interview may provide a setting for:

1. Clarifying confused issues of social reality.
2. Helping the group to develop skills for both admitting and coping with guilt.
3. Breaking through individual and group alibi mechanisms which protect them from recognition of their impulsivity and asocial behavior.
4. Interpreting mental content, either of a group or individual nature, with the goal of specific insight into psychic problems.

[1] Except for pressing emergencies we are careful to avoid substituting a group session for highly valued activity such as swimming, eating, or movies. In this way the group energy is not diverted against the staff and away from the central problem of their inability to live with one another.

5. Ventilation of individual and group emotion.
6. Recognition that problems are common to all, and mutual identification fostered by group discussion of these difficulties.
7. Freeing and strengthening of healthy group and self images which have been undermined by the current conflicts.

These descriptive categories tend to be separated less clearly in practice than on paper but they provide a convenient schematization for selecting the theme of the third phase of the group session. Thus, for example, when a group has been aggressively exploiting a counselor and taking refuge behind a welter of self-justification such as "this is a lousy dump anyway and she's an old bag who doesn't want us to have fun because she hates us," the group interview had better address itself to "breaking through the individual and group alibi mechanisms" from which such a distortion is fabricated. This means that priority must be given to the task of having them see that their argument about the camp and the attitude of the counselor is, in their own language, "strictly screw-ball" and only exists so that they can continue to "goof off."

In individual therapy certain processes within the client are crucial for the interview, e.g., his own value system, the degree to which he is reality oriented, his ability to form relationships, etc. In the same way the fate of the group interview is geared to certain vital group processes. Among these are the following:

1. The prevailing group code.
2. The degree of group cohesiveness.
3. The interaction patterns between subgroups, or cliques of individual members in the group.
4. The interaction patterns between the child leader and the group.
5. The power distributions in the group.
6. The degree to which individual case histories are compatible with each other.
7. The degree to which group roles (leader, scapegoat, clown, isolate, etc.) are established.

The group interview must show considerable selectivity regarding which of the group processes is to be manipulated. This list serves us primarily as a reminder of the complexity of the situation we face so we do not err in the direction of over-simplification.

As with any therapeutic tool, there are certain clinical cautions that should be followed in the application of the group interview. These can be divided roughly into two groups: (1) those contingent on the need for psychological protection for the individual, and (2) those governed by the need for group psychological hygiene. Maintaining an adequate balance between the two is the most difficult and perplexing aspect of group interviewing. Since group disintegration often comes into the open with a rush most interviews are emergency measures which have not had the benefit of careful, logical planning. Split-second diagnostic and therapeutic decisions must be made, and here there seems to be no substitute for lengthy clinical experience in interviewing groups of disturbed boys. For the interviewer the group interview offers a microcosm of the group's social organization, its healthy processes, and its pathology. These interviews, plus individual casework and various group management strategies, form a therapeutic design which can balance off the contesting forces at work within the children so that they may have a pleasurable summer camping experience which contributes to their psychological growth.

Let us turn to a sample of a group interview at the Fresh Air Camp. Although in dialogue form, this is not a transcript of an interview. It is a post-situational recall of the essential material. It is very much condensed, since the particular interview ran about one and one-half hours, but many of the expressions are verbatim and we feel the style itself contains few, if any, distortions. The group represented in this interview were senior boys between the ages of twelve and fourteen. The following member by member thumbnail sketch may serve to identify them sufficiently to clarify the dialogue.

Tony: leader of the group—a slick, manipulative delinquent—detention home background—has a well-oiled, pleasant manner with adults except in moments of sudden negative rapport—can exert positive effect on the group when motivated to do so.

Rusty: overtly aggressive—a bully—distrustful—Tony's lieutenant—highly dependent upon him—at rare times betrays an almost infantile need for adult attention and affection which is usually under very expert concealment.

Jim: sole Negro in the group—detention home background—dangerously violent during outburst of rage—sadistic—once, before camp, beat a younger boy so badly with a lead pipe that he had to be hospitalized. In the cabin he is teased and scapegoated by Tony and Rusty; he in turn vents his fury on weaker members of the group.

"Ears": so-called by the group because of the large size of the members referred to—ironically enough he has developed an ear infection, carrying around huge wads of cotton which he has stuffed in them—a compulsive stealer—dependent and insecure—he tries to avoid aggressive situations—scapegoated by Tony and Rusty when they are not attacking Jim.

Howie: a reserved, truculent boy—plays the role of an isolate in the group—jealous of Rusty's lieutenancy to, and intimacy with, Tony.

Chuck: an infantile, inept kid—the group stooge. Two other quiet boys who, together with Chuck and Ears, form a more subdued group in the cabin. As a group they are frequently scapegoated by Tony, Rusty, and Jim.

From these descriptions the reader can make an accurate guess about the nature of the problem facing this group. By the second week in camp the group is becoming progressively more disturbed because of Tony's corrupt leadership. Neighboring cabins are disturbed by the depredations of Tony and Rusty; these two, however, finagle events so that their innocent cabin-mates are the ones subjected to reprisal by the enraged victim. Due to progressive needling from Tony and Rusty, Jim has had severe blowups in which he recklessly tries to maim less powerful group members, such as Ears, with whatever weapon is at hand. As the group disturbance gains momentum the staff is alert for the appearance of a fresh incident which might serve as a basis for a group interview.

It should be emphasized that waiting for a typical episode which the group interview will seek to exploit is a deliberate strategy. It is not enough simply to know the general tenor and shape of group action in a cabin. The utmost concreteness and temporal immediacy is necessary or else the alibi experts in the group will quickly seize the opportunity to accuse you of being a fussy autocrat who wants only to bore them with discussion. If you say, "Yesterday there was some trouble," this is not enough. "Well what the hell are you talking about that for? Christ, that's over. Let's get outa this goddam joint," will inevitably greet you. And even the most miserably scapegoated and protection-hungry member of the group will be swayed by this lure and chime in, echoing, "Yeh, let's get out of here," turning his energies toward gaining acceptance from his tormentor by joining in the attack on the adult.

In this case an incident soon made its appearance. Before supper, between the time they come out of swimming and the actual serving of the meal (about 45 minutes), Jim has had one of his sadistic temper outbursts against Ears, cutting him by hurling a chunk of plaster at him. We learn from the counselor that during most of the day Tony and Rusty have been needling Jim. A contagious wave of unrest and impulsivity has spread even to the quiet youngsters in the group. Tony and Rusty are riding high on the crest of this choppy sea, finding it amenable to both their tastes and talents.

An interview is held in the evening after supper, the injury to Ears having been reported to the main lodge. The interview proceeds as follows:

Discussion Leader: I called you guys together so we could talk over some of the things that are happening in the cabin. Today, for instance, there has been a lot of wild stuff and Ears[2] got hurt.

Tony: (immediately assuming the role as group spokesman) Yeh, Ears here got hurt, didn't you, Ears?

Ears: (excitedly) I'm sitting on my bunk reading a comic book and this boy (pointing to Jim) starts foolin' around.

Tony: That's right.

Jim: (heatedly) Yeh, goddamit, them two bastards are always fussing around with me (indicating, of course, Tony and Rusty).

Discussion Leader: What do you mean, Jim, fooling around with you? What do they do?

Jim: Rusty started with me when we were in the boat—shoving me and grabbing my line and trying to throw my bait away. I ain't gonna take that, so I shoved back and then he beat the hell outa me. Boy, if they get my temper up I'll grind them so full of holes that they'll look like they was put through a sawmill.

Discussion Leader: How about it, Rusty?

Rusty: I don't have to say a goddam thing.

Discussion Leader: Look, you guys have got almost three more weeks out here at camp. The way things are going now, I don't think you can live with each other that long without working out some of the things that are bothering you.

Let us take our first brief recess from the interview at this point. The discussion leader is stressing as vividly as possible an elemental piece of social reality. In their present state of tension this has yet to penetrate the group's awareness. The keynote for the meeting is set: to survive to-

---

[2] The discussion leader never refers to the camper as "Ears" although it is printed here for purposes of easy identification.

gether for the next three weeks we have to get down to the business of working out our problems. Let's return to our meeting and observe the impact of this on Rusty's defiant, clam-up mechanism.

Rusty: Well, that S.O.B. (pointing to Jim) doesn't have to insult me.

Discussion Leader: How does he insult you?

Rusty: (smiling in embarrassment) He keeps calling me "stale crusty."

Jim: (in great indignation) Oh, you bastard, how 'bout when Tony calls you that? I don't see you smacking him around and he even tells other guys to do it.

Discussion Leader: How about that, Rusty?

Rusty: I can let whoever I want to call me that. I don't have to take it from Jim though.

Discussion Leader: I don't mean that part of it. I agree with that. But how about the other thing that Jim said, that about Tony egging on the other guys to call you stale-crusty and then you turning around and pounding them for it?

Tony: I suppose you're gonna tell us what we can say or not! Did you ever hear of freedom of speech?

Here we see Tony suddenly taking up the defense. For, trained as he is in the logic of group behavior, as befits a good delinquent leader, he sees the interviewer's last statement for what it is—a beginning attack on his manipulation of the group power structure.

Discussion Leader: I'm only asking Rusty how he squares it with himself to pound other guys for what *you* seem to put them up to.

This is a feint by the discussion leader which has a double strategic purpose. It alludes to Tony's petty Machiavellianism while it confronts Rusty with something of a value issue: is it right to vent on other guys a fury which is really inspired by Tony? But Tony, not Rusty, carries on the counter-attack with a swift change in tactics.

Tony: (with menacing facial leers and yet, with a hint of childlike indignation)

Listen—I have moods. When I was in the detention home I talked to the psychiatrist about them but I don't have to talk to you about them, see. And when I have moods I do what I want, see!

Here we are beginning to obtain a picture of Tony's rationale. He is a sick guy —certified as such by no less an authority than the psychiatrist at the detention home. And he maneuvers himself away from guilt about his acts as nimbly as he maneuvers the group into doing what he wishes. He fights fire with fire. In this case the admission of sickness is turned against the clinical invaders. When he has moods he can do what he wants. And now, let us watch Rusty, who having been cued in by Tony, springs alertly into the breech.

Rusty: Goddamit! He has moods and I have a brother who pounds hell outa me at home and I'm not gonna take anything from anybody out here. And I told it all to a visiting teacher at my school, whatever that bag's name is, and I don't have to talk about it out here and I'm not.

Jim: (with a fine sarcastic fury) Oh, sure. HE (pointing to Tony) has moods and HE (designating Rusty) has a brother who beats hell out of him so he turns around and beats hell outa me and around and around we go and where does that leave me?

Now we have one of the fascinating spectacles of the group interview. Here are these three tough, anti-verbal, casework-hardened youngsters one after another spitting out vital case history information. They don't want to talk, least of all about themselves, but even when they use their case histories to defeat our clinical effort, as Tony and Rusty are doing, they bring a valuable piece of grist to our clinical mill. They confront us with the spectacle of their case histories clashing with one another. The scene they draw for themselves (better than a trained therapist could) can now be turned into a tool for surgery on their group pathology. Let's return to Jim, who, having so acidly etched out for us his plight in the pincer of Tony's moods and Rusty's brother hatred, waits sardonically for the discussion leader to reply.

Discussion Leader: O.K. Jim, you're a good psychiatrist when it comes to Tony and Rusty, let's see what you can do about yourself. Whom do you turn around and pound?

Jim: (who knows his Fifth Amendment as well as the next one) I don't have to talk a damn word.

Discussion Leader: Yes, Jim, but how did the trouble start with Ears today?

Ears: Yeh, ask him, ask him. All I'm doing is reading my comic and this guy Jim starts climbing up on my bunk and yanking at my feet and yelling, "Hey Ears!" And when I say please get off and he don't, I push him and then he blows his top and starts heaving around and I get hit.

Discussion Leader: Isn't that part of the answer of where you're left, Jim? You turn around and pound Ears.

Jim: (angrily) Well, I'm not gonna take it from those bastards.

With this resistive remark Jim shows that he has understood our interpretive maneuver designed to clarify the chain of aggression between Tony, Rusty, himself, and Ears. What we will have to try to show him is that just as he shouldn't take it from them, he has a certain moral blindness in taking it out on Ears. This will be, perhaps, the topic of some of the post group-interview case work sessions we will have.

The interview continues:

Discussion Leader: How about the stale-crusty crack?

Howie: Aw, hell, Tony started that this morning.

Discussion Leader: How about it, Tony?

Tony: (refuses to comment). The other group members look at Tony and remain silent.

Discussion Leader: All the guys here seem to want to stay in good with you, Tony. They won't say anything.

Tony: (jeeringly) Because they're my friends, that's why.

Discussion Leader: Well, Tony, I think that's swell, but it also seems like it's part of the trouble too. Let me tell you how it looks to me from what you have been

saying. The guys like you; they want you to like them. O.K., then you have moods. Why you have them I don't know. But when you have them, for some reason you seem to get kind of mean. You have learned how to make guys fight with each other to stay in good with you. I guess when you have these mean moods you want them to do that.

Tony: Who do you think you are, a psychiatrist or something? Hey, let's call him psycho, guys.

The interpretation threatens Tony. No leader wants his own psychology to be clearly understood by his submissive following. So what he does is to try to defame the discussion leader. For who is more to be feared and despised by the acting-out delinquent than a psychiatrist? Tony's subtle yet clear challenge to the group is: "Going to believe what he says—this imitation psycho?" It is now clearly the time to anoint Tony's wound and to take the pressure off while we simultaneously summarize the group problem as this part of the group interview has highlighted it:

Discussion Leader: Look, Tony—this is not pleasant. I don't blame you for being a little sore. But let's be reasonable. It seems that you have a problem that we are going to have to work out if the guys in the cabin, including you, are going to have a decent time in camp. And you're not the only one with a problem either. Rusty here has a brother that pounds him so he is ramming around looking for a fight. Jim has a bad temper and he'd knock somebody silly if he wasn't stopped when he blows his top. Each guy is handing it out to another guy who either doesn't like to fight or who can't fight so well. Certainly you three guys— Tony, Rusty, and Jim—are going to have to work on that. Can anybody tell me why Ears has to take it from Jim, or Jim from Rusty, or Rusty be teased into fighting by Tony? (no group comment.)

Discussion Leader: My suggestion would be to talk it over with your counselor and also with some of the special people we have out here to help with your problems (here the casework staff, whom they all know, are specified). Anytime you want to get together again as a group I'll be glad to talk to you.

We have tried to illustrate, through a synopsis of one type of group session at the Fresh Air Camp, the role of the group interview in the clinical management of the kind of boys who comprise a significant percentage of our clientele. Children with different pathologies of course react much differently than this group did. Some are quiet, some anxious and guilty. Some of the older boys seem to develop a fascination for the "round table" and ask for sessions on their own. There are times too when skilled adult leadership is needed to manage the intensity of emotional outbursts during the sessions. Seen in terms of the total clinical design of the camp, the group interview emerges as a valuable tool in coping with the problems these youngsters bring with them to the camp setting. It is seen as serving a variety of functions and as utilizing various processes that are specific to the group psychological scene. These processes serve to concretize individual pathologies which may become sources of conflict for the group. While it is a valuable tool, the group interview is still only one of many strategies that must be woven closely together for the most efficient clinical action against the pathology in these children. The most important aids to group interviewing are the followup by individual casework

and the counselor handling of these issues when they arise again. The group interview seems to pave the way for an easy entré to these problems on future occasions, and the campers seem willing to use material from these meetings as a starting point for further discussion.

It should be recalled that each group session, and series of sessions with the same cabin, has its own characteristics. With the eight-year olds it is difficult to produce any problem-solving pattern while with the ten- and eleven-year olds there is discernible movement, during the session, from savage attack to workable solution. We are currently studying tape recordings of these group sessions to gain a fuller understanding of the shifting dynamics of the group in this situation. A particularly interesting phenomenon we have observed is the shift in content in the interviews following the discussion leader's understanding acceptance of guilt-producing behavior on the part of the boys. Hostility and tension seem to melt, and the campers reveal real empathy when, out of concern over the meaning of their own behavior, they discuss individual and group needs and problems. More needs to be known about how these defenses are penetrated and of the subsequent effect of such sessions on the group life.

SUMMARY

A major function of teaching emotionally disturbed children is to develop an effective hygienic management model for inappropriate classroom behavior. The teacher cannot rely on pseudo-psychological techniques, such as loving the children, or giving them special responsibilities in the classroom. The management of behavior must be based upon a psychoeducational interpretation of individual and group forces in order to provide the teacher with a differential approach that will consider both long-term goals and the immediate classroom conflicts. In this chapter, we have shown the psychoanalytic concepts of unconscious acting out by children and the roles of transference and countertransference in the classroom. The school's use of discipline was examined in the light of how children use aggression and sexuality as both defensive and offensive weapons, frequently causing teachers to react in a punitive way. Finally, specific psychological skills and techniques for translating theory into practice were explained.

6

How Do You Teach
These Children?

Once you understand the personal dynamics of these children and have their behavior under control, how do you teach them? Should the curriculum be redesigned, or only modified? How should the school day be divided between academic content and therapeutic play? How "structured" should the classroom activities be? Should the teacher let a child who is depressed or overtly angry regress academically? How does the physical design of the classroom facilitate or interfere with learning? How stimulating should the classroom be? Should individual study booths be constructed? How do you select educational material for a pre-adolescent who reads on a second-grade level? These are just a few of the many questions that educators, psychologists, and psychiatrists are beginning to answer.

The issues are sure to generate arguments, even among friends. Since the general field of education is far from precise about its goals, methods, and curriculums even for normal children, it is natural for the field of special education to have greater conflicts over theories and practices. For example, remedial procedures such as speech correction, art therapy, trampoline therapy, auditory drills, sand tracing, phonics, special diets, music therapy, coordinated crawling, field trips, machine learning, visual-motor drills, and psychotherapy are recommended by specialists who have found them successful. However, a closer look at the proposed theories and practices often shows that they are based either on a limited research project (usually with pre-adolescent boys of a selected pathology) or on the personal experience and wisdom of one "expert" in the field.

Three of the most accepted approaches to teaching emotionally disturbed children are presented in this chapter: the psychoeducational approach, the interference method, and the Rhodes approach. One way of comparing these three educational approaches is to examine their apparent answers to the following questions: (1) How authoritarian or permissive is the psychological atmosphere of the classroom? (2) How much flexibility and consistency does the program have from day to day? (3) What specific tactics does the teacher use to motivate the students educationally? (4) How much individualization is there in the curriculum? (5) How is a lesson presented to the pupils? (6) How is play used in the curriculum? (7) What happens when a pupil refuses to complete an assignment?

The last three articles of this chapter discuss teaching techniques that can be used with emotionally disturbed children regardless of the basic approach chosen.

In the first article, Morse presents the psychoeducational approach, which permits the educator to think within a theoretical model and teach by the problem-solving method. The teacher is an active member of a team that operates in a framework based upon understanding of the child. The teacher does not function either in isolation or on a trial-and-error basis, because he wants to know as much as he can about the child's developmental history, present conflicts, and strength, in order to formulate appropriate educational expectations and methods. For example, a highly verbal psychopathic child who is more interested in manipulating adults than in mastering educational problems needs a very different kind of educational program than either a schizophrenic child who is withdrawn and uncommunicative, or a neurotic child who has severe conflicts with his peer siblings and unattainable academic standards. How a teacher approaches each of these children depends upon his ability to translate clinical information into educational terms.

From psychological and psychiatric data, the teacher should be able to understand the operation of the child's impulses; the social values he has internalized and the extent to which they serve as brakes in situations that are tempting or frustrating; the characteristic ego defenses the child uses to avoid pain and maintain pleasure; and the complexities of the child's self-image. By combining this information with educational diagnostic tests, the teacher hypothesizes why the child is not learning and plans accordingly. He must decide what relationship is needed (close or distant), what kind of behavioral limits are necessary (firm or minimal), and what type of curriculum (active or structured) will attract the child's interests.

Education of Maladjusted and Disturbed Children
William C. Morse

Recently the teachers in a school for the emotionally disturbed were asked what it was they taught. After a pause they replied that they taught everything, and they added that they taught by just about every known method. The relaxed tone and the sometimes amorphous form of the work in a special school should not be misunderstood. Behind this lies teaching with thought-out goals and planned content. Relating the goals and content to the children's capacities is a most complex task.

In over-all perspective, the curriculum for the disturbed child follows a modern,

From William C. Morse, "The Education of Socially Maladjusted and Emotionally Disturbed Children," in *Education of Exceptional Children and Youth,* by William M. Cruikshank and G. Orville Johnson. © 1958. By permission of Prentice-Hall, Inc., Englewood Cliffs, N.J.

well-planned educational program. The skills of reading, language, numbers, and social relationships are always vitally important. The arts, social studies, and science studies are major concerns. More separation of content takes place throughout the junior high school level where material may be organized around the unified studies, English and social studies on the one hand, and science and mathematics on the other. Manual activities may be incorporated directly as a school experience or appear in related activities such as crafts or occupational therapy. Usually homemaking activities and practical arts are introduced here. With adolescents, some content dealing with social manners should be included. With older adolescents vocational preparation assumes major importance. Again, following the philosophy of modern education for normal children, a broad range of play activities, physical education, and extracurricular programs round out the picture.

In short, the educational birthright of the normal certainly belongs to the special pupil as well. The old idea that, since they were different, one must wait until they are in good mental health before they can be taught has been left behind. Some of the fear of their actions which used to make schoolrooms more like prisons has also been lost. If what is being done in modern education is useful, interesting, and supporting to normal children, it certainly has a place with the disturbed.

It is interesting how well most children grasp the significance of school as a reality factor. When they begin to improve, one of the first signs is often the request for a school like "school." They ask for homework and are eager for evaluation. This suggests that the school room is neither recreational therapy nor group therapy, although it contains traces of both. The therapeutic educator's implicit concern for the child and warm acceptance makes this reality palatable for these upset children.

THE EDUCATIONAL TONE OF THE SPECIAL CLASSROOM

The classroom is a social and learning milieu where tone and balance are crucial. Group interaction is utilized to encourage the child's socialization. Fortunately, educators have passed through the period when permissiveness was considered the *sine qua non* of hygienic atmosphere. It is now recognized that a pattern with implicit limits is necessary for the security of normal children, and even more so for disturbed children. With the disturbed child, pattern is not expected to mean the elimination of classroom problems. But the problems should be those which stem from the child's pathology rather than from equivocal conditions established by the teacher. It is equally important for the teacher not to resort to rigid form. The teacher establishes

and maintains the reality focus of school as a place for learning. At the same time the teacher's empathic recognition of pupils' feelings allows for flexibility within the broad pattern. Periods of regression, outbursts of frustrations, and short attention spans are all accepted as normal. The teacher is sensitive to over-all moods, such as those occurring at holidays when the school is enveloped in seasonal excitement. Daily routines, which were established to give security, go by the board to capture the emotion of the moment. Fun is as much a subject in the curriculum as is arithmetic. Nevertheless, the teacher remains the manager rather than the managed, fostering pupil initiative and resourcefulness, yet limiting energy here and channeling it there.

The teacher must have the permission and personal ability to enforce necessary limits even to the point of temporary exclusion of a pupil when he cannot make use of the classroom. The removal is talked through with the pupil without hostility in the hope that he will come to understand why.

Whether the teacher is more controlling or more permissive not only changes from time to time, but changes in relationship to the clientele. As has been seen, a group of asocial children require different handling than a class of anxious, withdrawn children. Usually they are both found in the same class, meaning differential treatment is required within the same group. If this sounds as if special schooling runs along like regular schooling, nothing could be further from actuality. The child who is immersed in his own preoccupation, or the child who is fighting society is unlikely to be ready to sit down at a desk and work gayly at his tasks. The necessary energy is at the service of other involvements. Such children are often far behind academically and frequently have blocks to learning. There are wide variations. Some never accomplish too much academically, while others concentrate on this avenue holding on tenaciously to this "normal" experience or even overcompensate through school-work.

Good teaching methodology which exerts a sustaining and directing force on normal children, may have no effect at all on these children. To plan the reading therapy for a 12-year-old who cannot recognize words or sounds, who never has gotten along with teachers or peers, while he is moving into a significant therapeutic relationship requires circumspection of the highest order. Perhaps one pupil can only fill out a work book exercise after first testing his answer through the teacher; another storms into a classroom announcing she and her friends have as of now seceded from school. A boy carries on his anti-authority tirade at the teacher arguing first that he was not told he had to do a given lesson, then that it is a crazy assignment anyway, and finally that he just won't do it. Yet these pupils can be taught and are being taught successfully. A few specific programs are described in the literature, and the reader will be referred to them in a later section. The material which follows immediately is organized around basic principles of this type of special education, regardless of the setting. They constitute the educational psychology in teaching the socially and emotionally disturbed. While this stratum is being examined separately, it should not be forgotten that it cannot be thought of apart from the role of the teacher or the grouping designs discussed elsewhere.

SPECIAL TEACHER'S CONCERN WITH PUPIL MOTIVATION

The teacher is far more consciously involved in motivational problems when working with disturbed children than would be necessary with normal children. Frequently, though by no means always, disturbed children have a history of poor school adjustment. Their attitudes toward teachers may be negative, and any sense of self-accomplishment through formal learning is lacking. Consequently a primary goal is to develop pupil-teacher rapport and to restore the sense of pleasure in learning. These attitudinal changes are also necessary preparation for return to regular schooling.

There is no methodological magic to motivate these pupils. Motivation is, in fact, a part of everything the teacher does. The teacher must recognize how much problems of motivation underlie all educational effort. To be effective school must come to be a place of pleasure and gratification. As this problem is examined, it will be shown how much the ordinary school implicitly utilizes an important but little recognized capacity of normal children. Stress on "democratic procedures," "pupil initiative," and "self-planning" sometimes obscures the fact that most of the teacher's purpose is really accomplished through a kind of motivational contagion. The expressed and tacit enthusiasms and purposes of the adult are responded to by the pupils. Sometimes the response may come through another pupil rather than through the teacher directly.

The child's dependent status predicates this contagion. While the normal child may object to being told directly, he does seek the comfort he gets by doing what pleases the adult. At adolescence, when the peer group has more power to induce goals than adults, the normal child is often caught between the two forces and school motivation becomes more complex. At times this wish to please the teacher is itself a problem, as in the case of the over-dependent child who is upset when he has to be on his own and is afraid to displease. In the normal process of maturing, pupils incorporate and reflect adult values until they end up feeling self-satisfaction when they do the task. This is the psychological substratum of school motivation, for it is known that many necessary school experiences do not have inherent appeal. In fact, it is a source of never ceasing wonderment how many educational tasks pupils assume which have little intrinsic satisfaction. Between the task and the child is the teacher and the group.

With emotionally and socially disturbed children the development of this capacity is aberrant. Often they are immune to catching work-minded attitudes from either teachers or peers. The psychopath cannot identify; the partially socialized sees the teacher's goals as alien; the neurotic is frequently in conflict with authority and his peer group siblings; the psychotic is not in communication. Since most of them are having a very difficult time handling their impulsivity, they are much more likely to be influenced by negative examples. For example, one child starts a diversion from the educational tasks, and the next thing the teacher knows, they are all getting wild. For these reasons the teacher must go far more than half way if the problems of motivation are to be solved. Somehow the pupil must become involved. Endless patience and careful use of situations over an extended period of time are required to create the proper pupil-teacher rapport. Meanwhile, the child always tests the relationship, sometimes with quiet persistence and sometimes with desperate frenzy. Newman suggests that the uneven course toward accepting school and the teacher is preceded by a period of regression. At any rate, the actions suggested under the role of the special teacher are intended to give substance to what the teacher does to establish a useful relationship with pupils. The point to be born in mind is that this relationship is valuable not only as an interpersonal feeling, but as a mode of helping the pupil with his motivational defects.

INDIVIDUALIZATION OF THE CURRICULUM

Each child is a school unto himself; the work of that school is dictated by the abilities and limitations of that pupil. It is known that the general diagnostic formulations require the skills of the psychiatrist and psychologist. But over and above these are particular things which the educational staff needs to know in planning the individual pupil's school experience.

To begin with, there is the over-all learning ability which the psychologist assesses by adding his insight to the results on his performance and verbal scales. When appropriate, achievement tests indicate the base line for skill and content lessons. Teachers are just beginning to recognize the importance of special psychological factors in individualizing school work. It is just as vital to select procedures fitting to the individual as it is to select material at his level. For example, he may think in concrete terms rather well but fail with abstract concepts. Perhaps he has idiosyncratic ways of problem solving or perception. These may condition his approach to arithmetic or reading. A good many of these specific factors can be worked out jointly by the teacher observing and the psychologist analyzing classroom work. This type of diagnostic teaching is especially needed in cases of stubborn failure to make progress under accepted teaching methods; it puts a new cast on the term individualization. As an illustration, some need not only visual cues but auditory cues and kinesthetic cues to learn to read. The special teacher cannot simply rely on general application of methods having proven worth. The application must be specific. Pupils often provide evidence for the teacher. When a child wants to go back to easy material, or lingers long at a particular level before being willing to move on, the special teacher sees this as the need for security, in the face of fears of failure. When gentle support and encouragement do not free the pupil, the teacher waits and lets the pupil know that he understands. Terms like laziness are not applicable. Allowing one child to regress would be in sharp contrast with the program for a child who needs pressure at the proper time—the psychopath or the child retreating from reality. Without such diagnostic data, teaching is blind.

There are other aspects of individualization. While there are many group projects for a whole class, subjects are frequently studied at the same time by several pupils; but each studies on his own level, like the parallel play of young children. Individualization may go much further with 10 discrete lessons going on simultaneously for 10 students. This resembles the one room school rather than the typical elementary or high school class where it is common for all pupils to be doing the same exercise in the same book and this at the same time.

Since most emotionally and socially disturbed pupils are academically retarded, the material must be more than just cut to the performance level. While the difficulty level is reduced, it still must be stimulating to the pupil, at his interest and level of sophistication. A 14-year-old nonreader may be destined for work at the pre-primer level, but not the pre-primer for 6-year-olds. Lists of material used in this regard are very valuable.

Many times the only answer lies in material designed for the particular pupil by his teacher. Time spent with children is effective only if there is time provided to prepare material for them.

There are other facets to individualizing the program. Attention spans differ. The periods of school may be short and interspersed with play, crafts, or free time for one child. Another has the sustained integration to keep at the task longer and can use more schooling. Many have times when they cannot stand the group situation in a classroom at all. Individualization may mean the exclusive one-to-one relationship with a teacher. Here school fears, fears of exposure to failure in a group situation, or need for psychological support can be provided for through a more intimate situation. Sometimes as with a psychotic child, it may take the complete energies of a teacher to bring about any of the communication which must precede teaching proper. Understandably, this one-to-one tutoring often takes on a more therapeutic coloring, although it still focuses on school learning difficulties rather than emotional problems *per se.*

At least in the initial stages, the frequent cases of reading failure need this individual therapeutic tutoring. Here, more than elsewhere, the stigmata of failure is apparent. It cannot be hidden and represents such a handicap that the child's defenses are most difficult to break through. Every educational program for the maladjusted must make special provision for reading therapy. More than a few disturbed children have reading failure as the core problem, and when this is true, reading offers the key to therapy. Other types of disturbed children may be approached through reading.

The history of the child's reading problem is most important. It may stem from a primary maturational lag or perceptual idiosyncrasies which make learning to read very difficult. Perhaps failure is due to secondary factors, such as poor teaching or emotional blocks. Both primary and secondary factors may be involved. Whatever the first cause, after years of failure there is bound to be an emotional component, hence the need for reading therapy. In most instances multi-sensory approaches are used so that visual associations may be combined with auditory and kinesthetic cues.

Claims for success in remedial reading are made for highly directive methods and for nondirective techniques as well. Close inspection would probably reveal that there are failures, too, when one uses only a given method. Some programs rely heavily on the reading games and special devices, while others think in terms of interrelationship. To overcome the defeatist attitudes of the child, a good deal of emphasis is placed on infusing the teaching situation with new hope. Once aroused, hope will die unless the child achieves, even though it be minor growth. Generic to success is a comfortable, nonthreatening atmosphere; without this the techniques and devices, whatever they are, will be rote mechanical exercises, forgotten even as they are done. After a time, new progress will show up in the regular school class, and there will be the courageous demonstration to his teacher of the breakthrough. Then the teacher can supplement the tutoring which may be needed for a long time before the child has anything like the level of confidence and achievement he needs to be on his own in reading. Even though reading failure may have been the starting point of emotional difficulty, one does not expect the improvement in reading to offset the inadequacy which has accumulated. New feelings about the self have to be learned too.

STRUCTURING THE CONTENT

One of the characteristics of special schooling is the unsystematic way content comes to be presented. The actual nature of the teaching units depend upon two factors: the general maturity of the pupils and the degree of integration which these pupils possess.

In the elementary work, considerable time is given over to units, frequently on a contemporary topic of some general concern, or a particular interest evidenced by one of the pupils. Since they tend to tire of a theme quickly, no long period is devoted to one unit. The work seldom goes smoothly. When projects are included, the operations are often wasteful and destructive. They may ruin their own product or someone else's. Tools and materials are dropped when they cease to be needed, but a blow-up is likely to ensue if they cannot locate what they want immediately. The teacher becomes a master at innovation and substitution, keeping a watchful eye to see that supplies are available for the more or less spontaneous ideas which develop. Within all of the confusion, the unit concept provides a start and a finish to an educational experience. From this the children get the much needed sense of accomplishment. It also provides a focus for the class group at the same time allowing for contributing subgroups and individual work. Since topics are broad and boundaries are flexible, the unit organization permits different members to work at different levels and emphasize different aspects and yet be a part of the group. Manual skills, dramatics,

visual aids, and excursions can be easily included. Reading and composition skills are practiced functionally.

But incidental learning alone is not enough to teach most of the basic skills. Brief but frequent sessions are needed on spelling, reading, arithmetic, and so on. For older children, who are integrated enough, the content may be divided into various subjects taught in separate periods. But too much shuffling from one teacher to another is contra-indicated for children who are very disturbed. A few teachers who have relationships with them can net more by handling various subjects than can several teachers, experts in their fields, only casually related to the pupils. Relating to one teacher may be all that a child is able to do at first. Consequently the design is adjusted to his needs.

The school program must be compatible for the levels of the pupils' integration rather than their age. For example, older children who are functioning at the nursery level of behavior, while they cannot be grouped with the preschoolers, may need a nursery school-like situation, where formal learning requirements are not imposed. On the other extreme, a child may have much disturbed behavior but still be able to follow a train of curiosity in science, or learn to type. Regardless of the organizational difficulties, these interests should be fostered. Significant gains are often made quite out of the context of the teacher's intended program. One boy, for example, who fell apart in the classroom during a crucial stage in his therapy, was most purposeful and controlled in a self-chosen art project of major proportions. Here he was no problem. He worked on his own and the recognition and satisfaction he obtained through this effort far outweighed the hours of class missed during this period. He was ready to return to the regular school program at the conclusion.

While the individual child may deviate, and plans are shelved time and again, the teacher must organize the accomplishment expected for the semester. Otherwise it becomes a chaotic hodge-podge. The plans may not be realized in the sequence or way intended, but the teacher has even more obligation to set goals than the regular teacher who can depend more on curriculum guides and books to provide much of the format. When time permits, the special teacher keeps an individual educational log on his pupils so that there are adequate guidelines. Periodic assessments of progress may be in order.

PLAY IN THE SPECIAL SCHOOL

There is a vast difference between "recess" and "play" as used in special education. Many of the children do not know how to enjoy play, and literally have to be taught wholesome play. The function of play is not intermittent freedom from the discipline of tasks, but a therapeutic and creative effort in itself.

Play has powerful potentials. In nurseries for schizophrenic children, for example, the play of a few normal "control" children may start the cycle of recovery. Through play the child experiments with self-control, with control of his environment, with fantasy, and with legitimate disregard of reality. Play therapy is based upon the reconstructive nature of play. The motor components are useful channels of tension release. Play and games, free and structured, offer many opportunities for self and social learning. Some children are particularly responsive to games with music.

Craft work is an extension of play. The special school makes much use of creative crafts with various media: paper, clay, wood, and metal. Exhibits enable the child to drain the last possible ounce of recogni-

tion from his work. Puppets and dramas offer expressive play opportunities. Like any child, these boys and girls enjoy dressing up and will work diligently on a paper bag costume. The meaning of expressive productions in painting, drawing, and clay work are not interpreted to the child in school. In the children's psychiatric hospital and other institutional settings it is common to separate occupational and recreational therapy from the school proper. The special teacher cannot help but use these at times anyway, even though there is ample opportunity for the child to experience them elsewhere. Aggression through hammering and sawing or athletics is far better than pounding a desk. Play activity blends into educational activity in another way. With girls, playing house and making candy moves into homemaking skills and eventually life experience preparation. With boys, the making of models may give way to shop activities which may in turn move into vocational preparation. It is not possible to divide play and school in the perception of the child or the mind of the modern teacher.

Because these children always strain the educational program, they are frequently cheated out of the extracurricular fun of a regular school. This is in reverse to the order of their need for such experiences. Clubs, special interest groups, and hobbies on a self-chosen basis are very useful to them. Sometimes the special teacher disregards the curricular-extracurricular difference: photography becomes the way to teach science and the school newspaper becomes the class in English. The program needs to include the elements which the regular schools find exciting to the pupils: organized sports, music, art, clubs, assemblies, and parties.

The "interference method" of educating emotionally disturbed children is proposed by Norris G. Haring and E. Lakin Phillips, who believe that a highly structured, well-organized classroom, which has proved effective in the education of brain-damaged children, can also be used successfully for hyperactive, emotionally disturbed children. In this structured-classroom program, the key techniques are the control of any extraneous stimulation, reduction of social activity, and the assignment of specific educational tasks with constant follow-ups until their completion.

The authors' research and related theoretical implications present a point of view that we believe all students should know about. Since Dr. Haring told us that subsequent clinical work somewhat altered his original views, we invited him to write comments to the original article. He did more than this. He and Richard Whelan reworked the material so that we now present what really constitutes an original article. Basically, the authors expanded the "interference method" to incorporate the "reinforcement" theory of education. They have defined four stages of behavior change: *orientation, shaping, cognition,* and *integration.*

On the surface, the interference approach appears to be very simple, economical, and logical; and it appeals to many teachers who find it consistent with their classical training. Also it offers a school community what appears to be a direct solution to the complex problem of educating emotionally disturbed children. In our experience, however, the actual design of a useful classroom has seldom been reducible to any single approach that can adequately accommodate the many variants found in disturbed children.

Experimental Methods in Education and Management
Norris G. Haring and Richard J. Whelan

This article is concerned essentially with the Arlington County Experiment conducted with emotionally disturbed children. We are re-affirming the position set forth in the Arlington study with particular attention to the classroom structure and the control of stimuli and the consequences of responses. These comments are based upon empirical data which have been accumulated over the past three years in classes for emotionally disturbed children at the Children's Rehabilitation Unit, located at the University of Kansas Medical Center. The experimental demonstration setting of the Children's Rehabilitation Unit has provided information about change in behavior that we feel will make a significant contribution when added to the previous ex-

An original article by Norris G. Haring and Richard J. Whelan, "Experimental Methods in Education and Management of Emotionally Disturbed Children," 1965.

Norris Haring is Educational Director of the Children's Rehabilitation Unit of the University of Kansas Medical Center.

perimentation. Specific consideration will be given to learning procedures, classroom methodology and the measurement of behavior.

We have become interested in the results obtained by researchers utilizing a modern learning theory paradigm in their efforts to ameliorate the debilitating effects of emotional disturbance in children. These behavioral scientists usually conduct experimental programs which involve exposure and programming for one individual at a time. Controlled, precise data from these experiments have many implications for educators who must apply specific remediation techniques in day-to-day classroom situations. However, translating results with individuals into group situations needs further analysis, clarification, and sophistication before effective use of such methods can be implemented. Birnbrauer, Bijou, Wolf, Kidder, and Tague (1963) have initiated group application of learning theory technology, and the reported results are quite encouraging. The commonalities, i.e. prosthetic environment and isolation, between Birnbrauer's design and the one used in the Arlington County experiment (Haring and Phillips, 1962) are readily apparent.

Examination of evidence from small group experiments, plus numerous studies involving individuals, leads us to believe that approaching the education of emotionally disturbed children from a learning theory behavioral model will produce positive and sustained results. The close, daily observations of children at the Children's Rehabilitation Unit, which provides a well regulated environment, have revealed information which indicates that there are several distinguishable developmental stages through which these children progress to more organized and productive behavior. These stages will be explained in detail subsequently.

Emotionally disturbed children are, for the most part, controlling, disorganized, unproductive, and unilateral in their approaches to daily expectations, relationships with peers, and authority figures. A systematic, organized, planned routine which replicates the program emphasized in the Arlington County experiment provides a pattern or model which enables disturbed youngsters to meet the responsibilities of daily living, as well as take their rightful position in the social community. The behavior model presented in the classroom provides techniques for the child to *acquire* and *maintain* appropriate productivity and relationships with others.

Learning theory applications (Eysenck, 1960; Ferster and DeMeyer, 1962; Levin and Simmons, 1962), social reinforcement (Lindsley, 1963), operant conditioning (Wolf, Mees, and Risley, 1963), and schedules of reinforcement (Ferster and Skinner, 1957), to problems of emotional disturbance, can only be mentioned; examination of these sources yields theoretical and practical techniques for classroom management of emotionally disturbed children. Objective data recorded at the Chil-

dren's Rehabilitation Unit have indicated the necessity of differentiating between two distinct processes in planning educational-therapeutic programs. These two processes are the *acquisition* and *maintenance* of behavior (Lindsley, 1964). "The conditions necessary for acquiring behavior are different from those necessary for maintaining the same behavior—there is a great tendency today to confuse the acquisition of behavior with its maintenance (Lindsley, 1964, p. 4). Shaping or generating a specific behavior response requires reinforcement of that response whenever it is emitted; behavior is acquired by utilizing this technique. After an individual has included the response in his behavioral repertoire, a one for one ratio of reinforcement to response is not necessary for maintaining the behavior. At this juncture, intermittent reinforcement can be utilized to sustain behavior at the desired level (Ferster and Skinner, 1957).

Classroom application of an operant-conditioning behavioral model has pertinent implications for special education. Lindsley (1964) has observed that special educators often reinforce behavior to superfluous degrees, i.e., they do not delineate between the number and timing of reinforcements necessary to acquire and maintain behavior. They provide continuous reinforcement even though intermittent application of reinforcement is the appropriate technique needed to sustain desirable behavior. A goal of special education is to enable an individual to approach and solve problems independently. An individual will need continuous reinforcement to acquire behavior which is applicable to solution of specific problems. However, intermittent reinforcement is all that is needed to maintain problem-solving behavior. In the classroom, the teacher could assume a peripheral role with a child whose behavior needs only to be maintained. The teacher's time and energy could then be devoted to children who need to acquire a particular behavioral pattern.

This rather cursory review is included

to provide a practical, philosophical rationale for the subsequent discussion of an educational program for emotionally disturbed children. The order of presentation has been so arranged as to present the Arlington County study (Phillips and Haring, 1959) first and then to follow by presenting some evidence which we hope will refine this position toward more effective and expedient procedures for the education and management of emotionally disturbed children.

THE ARLINGTON COUNTY EXPERIMENT[1]

Efforts to develop special classes in average school settings for emotionally disturbed children have been few. In a practical way, all schools have to cope somehow with emotionally disturbed children, whether they exclude them from school, demote them, promote them, or just permit them to flounder. In the past, the emotionally disturbed child has been considered almost completely outside the pale of the school's responsibility. This attitude is beginning to change, giving rise to experimental programs for dealing with emotionally disturbed children in the school setting. Since so few can afford expensive residential centers or prolonged psychological or psychiatric help, it appears necessary that schools move in the direction of providing practical services for this group. An experiment in Arlington, Virginia, was a step in this direction.

This project was initiated two years ago. The interim results, both qualitative and quantitative, are encouraging. Plans for expansion of the program are under consideration.

[1] This section of the Arlington County Experiment has been taken in toto from the article prepared by E. Lakin Phillips and Norris G. Haring, "Results from Special Techniques for Teaching Emotionally Disturbed Children," *Exceptional Children*, 26, Oct. 1959. A more detailed description of this experiment may be seen in Chapter 4 of the volume entitled *Educating Emotionally Disturbed Children* by the same authors.

PROCEDURE

Working within the confines of the average school, a proposal for classroom management and education of the school system's most severely emotionally disturbed children was activated. Referrals came from principals, classroom teachers, visiting teachers, school psychologists, and in a few cases, from parents. The school assumed the obligation of developing ways to cope with the behavior of the child as well as stimulating them educationally. Thus a two-fold purpose—improvement of the emotional and educational condition of the children—made up the objectives of the special classes.

The major hypothesis in handling the emotionally disturbed children was that such a child lacked *order* or *structure* in his environment and in his emotional-educational life. To remedy this condition, and to help promote growth, ways were sought to increase the definiteness, the structure of the daily classroom experiences. It was also necessary to involve the parents through parent-discussion group meetings approximately once a month to assist in the undertaking and to help with continuity in handling the children between home and school experiences.

CRITERIA FOR SELECTION

Criteria had first to be set up as to what types of children would be acceptable. Four criteria were arrived at after much preliminary discussion. They were:

1. Children showing hyperactive, distractible, attention-getting behavior; or withdrawn, uncooperative behavior; or those showing both tendencies.

2. Average or near-average intelligence (recognizing, however, that tested intelligence may be an underestimate owing to the emotional disturbance).

3. The child having been in the school making the referral at least one year (preferably two) and having been one year (preferably two) educationally retarded.

4. The likelihood that the parents

would and could cooperate and attend parent-group meetings and generally support the school's efforts.

Since the study was done with elementary age children, grade levels two to five, an implicit criterion was that the referred child not be too near the junior high level in order that follow-up time would be available before the child moved from the elementary school level.

ORIENTING THE TEACHERS

The procedure was to orient and carefully instruct the two teachers of the two special classes in methods of handling emotional and educational problems. Closely following the general aim . of increasing order or structure, many details were worked out pertaining to the daily routine. Preliminary conferences with the teachers were held by the authors, and weekly conferences and observations of the classroom climates were carried on for several months after the activation of the classes at the beginning of the fall term, 1957. As the teachers settled into the routine they posed increasingly specific and far-reaching questions of procedure, method, purpose. These questions forced us to come to terms in more specific ways as the general aim of the structured classroom environments got under way. Some specific problems were the following:

Assignments and skill limits of each child. This was determined initially on the basis of intellectual and achievement tests, and on the basis of the personal file. Modifications were necessary in case that a child would, for example, dislike arithmetic, or one was especially poor in spelling. The children often tried to postpone work on disliked subjects, or acted as if they did not understand direction sufficiently well to proceed on their own. To remedy these conditions assignments were made that were very brief and a close, consistent follow-through was maintained by the teacher. As the teacher got the "feel" of each child's attitudes, she could gradually give the child more independence in his

work. Piece by piece, day by day these tolerances and limits were extended until by the end of the first year nearly all of the group were able to work alone for long periods of time.

Seating and movement limits. In addition to regular seats in the classroom (for 8 boys), there were two small work tables, about 2½ x 5 feet, and five "offices" or booths. The booths were used to get the child to work under minimum distracting conditions, to increase the tolerance for independent work, and to handle restless, hyperactive and socially disturbed behavior. Sometimes, too, the children considered their "offices" as a haven when they felt poorly or were possibly the object of derision from others. The booths lined one wall of the classroom and were about 3½ x 3½ feet with a movable chair and a fixed table-level desk across the back of the booth. Sometimes children stored their supplies in the booths as well as in the assigned desk each had.

Play and recreational limits. Children were held to the completion of assigned work before play or recreational opportunities were available. Most of the academic work was done in the morning; physical education, art, music, free play periods, etc., came in the afternoon, *provided* the child's work was up to par. Brief periods allowing for free play with art materials, or clay were sometimes sandwiched in during the morning work periods if the child had completed work assigned him. Care was exercised not to allow the recreational pursuits to crowd out assigned work, and assigned work had a constant, first-order priority at the beginning of each school day.

Free-moving privileges. These privileges include access to the rest rooms, moving about in the classroom, moving from group to individual desk work, occasional errands to the school office, and getting in line for lunch. Children asked permission to leave the room. Tasks and errands were distributed weekly among the children so that all got a chance to carry on "official business" with the school office. The children were free to move from desk to "office" to workbench provided the move was closely related to the assigned work. Free roaming about or movement in lieu of doing work was kept to a minimum. To preclude the development of fatigue, the group would be taken at appointed times for a walk, for a "seventh inning stretch" during the morning work period. Water in the classroom sink was kept off; art materials were kept under cover so as to minimize distraction. The children knew these materials were available after they qualified to use them, and it did not take long to establish these elementary limits on the use of supplies.

Social-emotional conduct limits. Some of the children provoked others unrelentingly, especially at first. Others often came to school in a "bad mood" and hypersensitively interpreted classroom problems personally and might refuse to work, to communicate, to participate as a retaliative measure. These were difficult situations to control effectively and constructively. Several guidelines helped: Do early what you would normally be required to do later (in the way of setting behavior limits); do not participate with a child who is upset about his upset—let him calm down first; give one warning, then act; isolation was normally the preferred, and most effective, technique when a child's behavioral disturbance adversely affected others; and a specific emphasis on solution or resolution to a problem was always held by the teacher in contrast to queries of why the child did thus-and-so.

With the recurrent conferences each week or two, the teachers could accumulate instances of problems they had handled, in contrast to those they felt they had not coped with successfully. It was helpful to have contrasting success-failure instances for discussion; in time, this procedure cut down on the failure instances and increased the confidence of the teachers that they could deal with about any problem that might present itself. It was simply a matter of successive approximations to more desirable and constructive solutions to problems, both academic and emotional-social. The general guidelines referring to "increasing or firming-up structure" were held to; the specific solutions to problems fell under this general aim and it was often necessary to shift and maneuver, to roll with the punches to keep the structure both firm and flexible.

EXPERIMENTAL DESIGN

Some mention should be made of the selection of cases. After the request went out to principals about the activation of these classes, eighty-five referrals were received for processing. Since the size of the two classes was to be limited to eight each, a total study population of 30–32 children was anticipated—i.e., 15 or 16 in the two experimental classes and the same number as controls.

The children in the experimental and control groups were compared on the basis of group means and standard deviations as to intelligence, achievement and grade placement. The judged seriousness of the child's behavior was a qualitative problem, but effort was made to distribute this variable evenly between the control and experimental populations. The dependent variables, then, became the educational progress and behavioral improvement shown over time. While the teacher was an important variable in this process, there was no possibility of studying the teacher's role experimentally as to its influence on the child's progress. In a theoretical sense, the role of the teacher was included in the overall aim of increasing structure in the classroom; had there been a failure on the part of any teacher to perform this function, the teacher would simply have been replaced and one put in who could function in the structure-increasing role required by the design of the study. The assumption, then, is that the teacher performed a "standard role" of increasing structure, and that is the extent to which the analysis of this role goes in the present findings.

A second, peripheral control group was also available in one class in another elementary school. This peripheral control group had eight boys and seven girls, not as severely disturbed emotionally but having been described as a group of behavior and achievement problems, and about 1½ years older on the average than the main experimental populations. This group was far from perfect in serving as a control group since the size of the group was twice that of the experimental classes and the severity of the problem was less. This second control group existed under a mostly permissive and non-structured classroom atmosphere, and serves more as a contrast in this respect than in any other.

The teachers of all children in the study were given a rating scale for "before" and "after" ratings. Each child was rated on 26 behavioral items in each of three circumstances: in the classroom during formal, educational pursuits; in the classroom in free, socially oriented group situations; and on the playground in non-academic free play, but inter-personally related circumstances.

RESULTS

Testing the hypothesis that the socially and educationally structured classroom atmosphere, as opposed to a relatively free and permissive one, would be beneficial, was not subject to easy, clear test in this study. The limitation is owed mainly to the inability to control class size; other relevant variables seemed to have been much better controlled. Within the limits of this condition, the qualitative and quantitative results follow:

The children in the two experimental (structured) classrooms showed a total educational gain on the California Achievement Test (reading, arithmetic, language) of 1.9 grade levels. They moved from an initial status of 2.30 grade level to 4.20 grade level. This progress was based on a mean IQ level (Stanford-Binet) of 104.52 ($\pm$15.90), which was a pretest. The control group of 15 controls, remaining in a less ordered classroom

environment, showed a gain of 1.02 grade levels (from 3.03 to 4.05 grade levels), over a full academic year. The experimental group had a mean exposure time to the structured classrooms of about six months, since the two experimental groups were not fully constituted at the outset of the study. Parallel to this result the children in the second or peripheral control group moved from grade level 5.25 to 6.06, on the same achievement test. The gain of the experimental group over either of the control groups was statistically significant: $p < .05$.

As to behavioral or social-emotional development, the experimental children showed statistically reliable progress in comparison to the two control groups. With each of the three broad variables (each with 26 items rated on a pre- and post-test basis), the experimental group in the structured classrooms gained an average of 1.76 points, compared to a gain of only .05 points for the matched controls, and a gain of 0.936 points by the second, peripheral control group. These ratings were made on a 7-point scale varying from "1" (lowest) to "7." A gain of one unit (1.00) probably represents an average gain toward maturity over one year.

This result shows the experimental groups to have about twice as much gain as the second control group and about 35 times as much gain as the compared controls. A conservative conclusion, even taking differences in class size into consideration, suggests some superiority for the structured classroom on the rated variables. In addition to these findings, other qualitative results are reported. One of the 15 children from the experimental population progressed so well that he was allowed to return to his "home" school after seven months. A two-months follow-up on his adjustment showed him to continue to make excellent academic gains and moderately good social-emotional gains. On the other hand, three of the matched control children had either to be removed to private schools or to go into individual psychotherapy due to a continuance of their adjustment problems. The teachers of these children did not know of the fact that the children were serving as controls, or even that they were in any study. The three children had three different teachers; they were not from the same school, hence there was no cumulative effect on the teachers, or the principal from any combined pressures by the three children.

Other qualitative indices emerged frequently from conferences with parents and from the parent discussion meetings. Most of the parents in the experimental group felt that this experience was the first truly constructive one that their children had experienced. The children, too, expressed their satisfaction with remarks like the following: "We like it here." "We like a strict teacher." "We know what we're supposed to do." Their complaints were more like those of the normal child in the classroom, not the continuous, strong opposition to teachers and to school authority which had characterized their behavior prior to admission to the special class.

INTERPRETATION

The advantages of a structured type of classroom environment for meeting the needs of emotionally disturbed children exceed those reported upon here. The average teacher can probably improve the conduct and achievement of her children by looking for the "firming up" instances of unclear structure. The average teacher can probably handle a class of the type of youngsters studied herein provided she has some direction and support from more experienced psychologists, special education experts, and principals. Good teaching supervenes; good teaching consists in knowing each child well and in having the ability and perseverance to give the specific direction to the child which is necessary for his growth and progress. A structured classroom is one in which clear direction, firm expectations and consistent follow-through are paramount; this is a healthy state of

affairs for normal children as well as seemingly necessary for emotionally disturbed children.

BEHAVIOR PROGRESSIONS

While the results of the Arlington County study were extremely encouraging, further refinement of certain procedures and measures have increased the efficiency of behavior modifications. The convergence in this paper is upon the improvement of this position to a more circumspect observation of the behavior of children over an eighteen month period. This observation has revealed several continuous stages through which children develop in the order and the nature of their responses. We have found ourselves modifying our expectations as the responses of the children become more organized. The need for reinforcement was reduced and the nature of the reinforcement changed, as the child progressed through the treatment. Specific examples of the behavior of children are given to demonstrate the observations raised above.

INITIAL PATTERNING OF TASKS AND BEHAVIOR

The primary consideration in the program for emotionally disturbed children is to bring about behavior that is controlled, constructive, predictive, and has order. This has been accomplished in the Arlington County study, the Montgomery County study, the classes at the Children's Rehabilitation Unit, and a host of classes in various schools over the country. This is no longer a remarkable accomplishment. The pattern of organized behavior is brought about simply by providing a prosthetic environment, presenting a clear behavior model for the child and reinforcing all behavior that approximates the model.

As the children are admitted to the class, each moment of the school day is planned and great importance is placed upon actually engaging each child in tasks.

This includes school tasks, arts and crafts, physical activities, classroom chores and responsibilities. Usually more than half of the children in a class will settle into the expected pattern early by clearly presenting the pattern or behavioral model and providing rewards. The few that remain, usually about three or four out of ten, will require constant reinforcement for a slightly longer period of time to bring about appropriate behavior. Even with this more stubborn group, however, it is reasonable to expect their behavior to conform within two or three months. If no remarkable changes have occurred in the behavior after the third month, we must assume that the stimulus, reinforcement, or reinforcement scheduling, is not having, and probably will not have, a controlling influence on the child's behavior. For the one or two in a given class who have resisted all attempts to initiate controlled, patterned behavior, further inspection and modification of the variables mentioned above will be necessary.

Positive reinforcement, i.e., objects, food or activities that the child enjoys, provide the most potent influence upon behavior. It has been reported by Michael (1962) that punishment can bring about a repetition of the very behavior that one is attempting to extinguish. "Punishers sometimes show a greater disposition to provide positive reinforcement shortly after they have administered punishment. This results in a temporary increase in some kinds of behavior, and under proper conditions, even a future increase in the punished behavior" (Michael, 1962, p. 394). In addition, for some children punishment is the most frequent response they receive from the individuals in their environment. These children may perceive this as their main source of attention. In such cases, any response, negative or positive, could be linked with gaining attention. While agreeing with Michael (1962) that punishment may be inadequate for shaping behavior, we have discovered that emphasizing alternatives of behavior, i.e., consequences, is quite effec-

tive in reducing unacceptable responses. Correct behavior responses are reinforced; incorrect ones are followed by withholding positive reinforcers. The important aspect of this situation is that the child is cognizant of the consequences, negative and positive, of the behavior alternatives available to him.

The preceding formulations are particularly true when the consequences are presented in the form of rather natural effects that follow the behavior, i.e., if the child fails to complete a reasonable assignment of tasks, he must work through a part of his free-time activity, until these tasks are finished. We emphasize the actual consequences of the child's behavior. This is done because we want to promote an awareness among these children that their behavior is consequential, and that it is important for them to increase discrimination among the stimuli as well as to extend their response repertoire.

STAGES

These stages we refer to do not actually exist. We have arbitrarily grouped behavior into discrete stages in spite of the fact that the actual phenomenon is quite obviously continuous. These stages in the reorganization of behavior through a reinforcement model serves only as a gross measure of progress.

Orientation. This is the period when the children get accustomed to the routines of the classroom. It has been described by many teachers as the "honeymoon," essentially because during this period the children are at their best. They are somewhat reluctant to test the limits and usually follow directions willingly. In preparation for the children being admitted to class, the teacher has studied all the information that has been sent from the school or referring agency. He has completed an educational evaluation of the child which may include the Illinois Test of Psycholinguistic Abilities, the Wepman Test of Auditory Discrimination, the Detroit Learning Aptitude Test, the Wide Range Achievement

Test, an informal test of reading, and an informal test of visual perception. The teacher, being well acquainted with the child's academic ability and developmental status, begins to plan the child's program.

As the orientation period begins, all tasks are assigned so that the child will achieve a 95 per cent success experience. The reinforcement sessions are introduced also during this period. Reinforcement is provided to each child after each task has been completed correctly. Depending upon the child's level of academic and motor development, tasks are assigned in the following areas: visual perceptual activities, eye-hand motor activities, reading readiness activities and reading activities, activities involving concepts of quantity, numbers and arithmetic, gross motor activities including training in laterality, balance and coordination. Reinforcement periods follow the completion of a series of tasks in each of the areas mentioned above throughout the day.

The tasks assigned in series will include six to ten tasks. Each child indicates when he has completed the task and the teacher places a check in the righthand corner of the child's answer sheet. The child then goes on to the next task. When the series of tasks has been completed, the child is then ready for a reinforcement period. Ten minutes of each hour is allocated for reinforcement.

These reinforcement sessions include: a juice break, arts and crafts activities, free play time, gross motor training and science activities, all of which are closely supervised.

We have mentioned that children usually fit into the pattern set forth by the teacher during the first two or three weeks. This includes hyperactive, aggressive and withdrawn children alike. Some children with very severe behavior disorganization, however, do require what we refer to as response building. In these cases, we show the child exactly what is expected, even if this means picking up his hand and helping him complete the task. With a child who has severe emotional disorders, the teacher will often need to work closely with him in order to construct the required responses. When the first correct responses are obtained from the child, he receives immediate reinforcement. After this initial process, more complex behavior patterns are built by reinforcing acceptable behavior.

Shaping. The term "shaping" is used here to describe a longer process which involves presenting a behavioral model repeatedly, obtaining a response, reinforcing, or failing to reinforce the response, depending upon whether or not it approximates the model of behavior that is expected. After this so-called orientation period is over, we observe that the child begins to test limits, and in effect becomes assertive about his demands. This is true even with the child who has been described as withdrawn. He seems to come out of his shell. Some of our teachers have remarked that for the first time the child who has been previously withdrawn will assert himself, will express his demands. This behavior is often referred to as a healthy sign, an indication of "real progress" when it occurs in traditional individual psychotherapeutic session. Traditionally, the withdrawn child's "acting out" behavior is reinforced even though it may be inappropriate. In behavioral or educational group management, however, a careful discrimination is made between appropriate and inappropriate behavior, and reinforcements are not given to any child unless his behavior has been appropriate.

The most remarkable difference between the hyperactive, aggressive and the withdrawn child is that the aggressive child extends his limit testing somewhat further. The hyperactive is more likely to refuse to do his tasks, to get up from his desk, roam around the room, strike out at other children, become destructive, tear up his work and sometimes the work of the other children. It is here that the consequences of each child's behavior are clarified and acted upon by the teacher.

The reinforcement, or consequences,

are associated as closely as possible with the child's behavior. When he has neglected completing the task because of wasting time, the reinforcement is simply withheld. Rather than his taking part in the reinforcement session, he is asked to complete the task which he had neglected during his work period.

Since we are discussing a special class situation involving eight to ten children, we must deal with the differences that arise in the management of groups as contrasted with the one-to-one treatment procedure. With individual treatment, the teacher can permit a wider latitude of behavior; thus we can ignore a reasonable amount of disorderly conduct providing reinforcement only for appropriate conduct and academic performance. Group management is not that simple. Disorderly behavior among these children is dynamic and contagious. When permitted to occur in a free environment, the combined behavior repertory of these children can exceed one's imagination.

It is here that we have found withholding positive reinforcement (consequences) is of value in the shaping process. The teacher must establish bounds and hold firm. In the face of these behavioral limits established by the teacher, certain children may become vehement, have tantrums and fight out. We ignore these displays and remain, at least outwardly, unshaken and composed. If it becomes necessary, and it certainly may, the child is removed from the classroom and placed in isolation. When this happens, the tasks or expectations which preceded the outburst follow him to the isolation area, where he is expected to complete the assigned work.

Blowups of this amplitude do not usually occur more than two or three times during the shaping process with any one child. The withdrawn child and the phobic child may tend to become fearful and anxious as we continue our realistic expectations for performance which approximate the behavioral model. It is not necessary

or perhaps even wise to isolate this child. Our experiences have been that this child does condition rather easily and usually missing a few reinforcement sessions is sufficient to continue him on his course. During the shaping period, reinforcement follows each time a task has been completed correctly. As has been mentioned earlier, this is considered the *acquisition* stage and reinforcement seems to be more influential when given each time the desired response has been elicited.

This shaping period can take as long as two months, but after that usually only a few regressions back to an earlier stage are observed. This regressive behavior is usually given up quickly and without much objection on the part of the child.

Cognition. By cognition we mean that the child is developing an understanding of the relationship between his behavior and its consequences. When we see this understanding taking place, we can decrease the continuous reinforcement scheduling and maintain constructive behavior with intermittent reinforcement. Our interest now turns to promoting an attitude by the child toward completing projects and concern for quality and efficiency. We now reinforce a more generalized behavior that indicates, when observed in the child, that he feels productivity and high quality of work is important. Several additional activities are added to the list of reinforcers.

During the juice break the child is seated at a circular table and is engaged in discussion about how and why his behavior shows improvement. Several small group activities are planned by the children. Teams of two children are assigned vocabulary words to look up and report. Science activities are assigned involving two children working together and their results are prepared in a report.

The idea that each child has to do his share of the work on cooperative projects is brought out. When cooperative and social constructive responses are noted, they are reinforced. Whenever a team's cooperation breaks down for any reason, their collective activities are halted, and they return to individual tasks. Children who require more time adjusting to group participation are introduced slowly to these planned group activities. A great deal of status is connected with being able to work cooperatively. Those children who experience successful group activities may continue. It is even possible to add two or more children on certain projects. Science activities are particularly good for involving groups of children. These groups can be referred to as research teams and are assigned various problems to investigate. The important thing to remember here is that every possible effort should be made to expand the activities and to reinforce group participation and cooperation.

Integration. By integration we mean that the child's behavior is being maintained well within the limits of the level of expectation set for him. He now understands why it is important to face up to tasks and assigned responsibilities. Reinforcement is considered more or less a bonus but not necessary. He begins to make his own decisions about how to schedule himself, the importance of neatness and the importance of cooperative work with other children. He is provided an opportunity for making more decisions from a larger number of choices.

We are attempting to expand and reinforce a larger repertory of appropriate responses. By this time we have converted almost completely to social reinforcements. A pat on the back and an acknowledgment of work well done is sufficient to keep the child on his course toward constructive behavior.

Throughout each of the stages, from time to time, the child regresses to earlier stages. It is not at all unusual to find a child doing well in the final stage to regress back to behavior that was commonly displayed at the beginning of his placement. It is soon evident that this is not satisfying to him, and as a result, these regression periods do not last long.

Again it is important for the reader to remember that these stages are continuous and overlapping. We are discussing behavior stages here arbitrarily to show the course of growth as the child begins to take hold and perform appropriately in the classroom.

Space will not permit a multi-presentation of cases to document the preceding formulations. However, one typical case summary will suffice as an explanation of the processes involved in planning educational, behavioral, growth experience for emotionally disturbed children. In this descriptive case history analysis, particular attention is devoted to the continuous positive growth phases through which the child progressed as he experienced day-to-day interaction with the special class program.

CASE HISTORY

K., a male, was referred for evaluation and placement in a special class for children with learning disabilities and emotional problems. The historical background of the case is as follows:

MEDICAL HISTORY

K. was born in a hospital on May 11, 1952. At age two months he was adopted by the present foster parents. K. suffered asthmatic bronchitis during the first two years of life, and was hospitalized frequently because of the condition. A physical examination given at the time of referral revealed a normal male except for some obesity.

FAMILY CONSTELLATION

K. is the older of two adoptive children of a middle-aged couple. Father is a successful professional man; mother confines her activities to the household. The other child in the family is an adopted girl who was brought into the family when K. was approximately two years old. The parents were married thirteen years before adopting K. During K's early years, father had to travel a good deal, and mother was absent once because of an operation which required hospitalization. The parents feel that because of their periodic absences from the home, K. developed the behavioral difficulties that have arisen subsequently.

Mother comes from a family of five children whose father died when she was two years of age. Her mother remarried but died when mother was eight years old. Mother's stepfather then remarried and there were several stepbrothers and sisters born. Despite mother's unusual childhood, she feels that it was happy and that the entire family is quite close and fond of one another.

In contrast, father was an only child born to a close-knit German immigrant family. His childhood was happy, secure, and his family still remains quite close.

SCHOOL HISTORY

K. attended the same school until referral for placement in the special class. His behavior in kindergarten exhibited lack of self-discipline and general immaturity. K's school work was inadequate, far below indicated capacity level. He was described by his teachers as a mentally alert child with a vivid imagination, but his relationships with peers and adults were inappropriate. A summary of behavioral patterns observed is as follows: lacks social maturity; completely uninhibited; verbalizes incessantly; erratic work habits; disrupts the class with antics which other children don't appreciate; minimal scholastic production, and then only on his terms; disorganized, fluid thinking; illegible handwriting; sloppiness in everything he does; periods of talking to himself.

PSYCHOLOGICAL EVALUATION

Psychological testing indicated WISC scores of 120 on the verbal scale, 104 on performance, and 114 on the full scale. The psychologist reported that K. experienced difficulty sitting quietly in his chair; his attention would unpredictably wander to various details of the room, and often he could not refrain from getting up from his chair and wander to distant corners of the room in order to inspect some object. He verbalized copiously, often interrupting the process of the examination in order to ask a question or make a comment quite unrelated to the context of the tests. Further examples of K's poorly organized relationship to the structure of the situation was his hyperalertness to normally overlooked sounds from outside the testing room.

K. exhibited disturbance in identification, fluidity of ego boundaries, extreme anxieties, inconsistent functioning, poor reality testing, helplessness in the face of impulse, and tenuous defenses. This parsimonious review was selected from the psychiatric and psychological data accumulated by the department of Pediatric Psychiatry at the Kansas University Medical Center. Based upon K's accumulated examination data, a diagnosis of "childhood schizophrenia" was formulated with a recommendation that he be placed in a residential treatment center.

EDUCATIONAL EVALUATION

Individual assessment of K's educational status revealed a reading score at the 4.5 grade level, and an arithmetic score at 3.0 grade level. In general, the educational testing replicated observational data made available through K's teachers at the public school. However, in addition, it was observed that K. displayed definite gross and fine motor difficulties. K's intellectual prowess was not available to him when he was confronted with tasks requiring immediate effort, and sustained attention or concentration. In tasks such as arithmetic problem solving, where K. could not verbalize an elaborate solution, he achieved below capacity level. In coping with superficial tasks, K. could function adequately, but his integration and organization broke down rapidly when confronted with tasks which required concentration, and association processes. Anxiety and tension became intertwined with intellectual functioning which served to hinder K's ability to focus upon the reality requirements of school experiences.

IMPLEMENTATION OF CLASSROOM PROCEDURE

Based upon diagnostic information, the availability of the Children's Rehabilitation Unit special education program, and a decision to initiate therapeutic intervention in the home environment rather than residential treatment, K. was placed into a class for boys with learning disabilities and emotional problems. K. was a member of the class for two years and is now enrolled in a public junior high school at his appropriate age-grade level. K. represented one of the two major types of children we have witnessed over the years of experience in this area of special education, the withdrawn, bizarre behaving, covertly aggressive, fantasizing youngster. As indicated in the case history, K. had many fears, bizarre mannerisms, flights into fantasy, and in new situations would withdraw into an unreal world of his own construction. For these reasons, and for purposes of illustrating the behavioral stages, a brief historical review of K's progress in the class will be presented.

During the *orientation* stage, K. presented a picture of a somewhat anxious, timid boy who tried very hard to please the teacher by accepting assignments and following through to completion. The over-controlling, constricted aspect of K's functioning was readily apparent to the teacher; however, to a casual observer, K. appeared to be a conscientious, productive student. Knowing that K. was utilizing a great deal of "psychic energy" in making an initial adjustment to the class, the teacher programmed his academic and social activities at a level where success was virtually assured 95 per cent of the time. K. became accustomed to reinforcements scheduled periodically during the school day, and presented a behavioral pattern far different from that obtained during the evaluation period.

However, after approximately three weeks, K. became more comfortable in the special class. He soon discovered that the teacher was not going to physically or magically destroy him if he displayed symptoms, and behavioral deviations. K. gradually entered in continuous rather than discrete progressions, the *shaping stage* of the therapeutic-educational process. He began to "stall," produce sloppy work, verbalize bizarre words, draw pictures of Nazis, grotesque pre-historic animals, and often jumped out of his seat to flap his arms. He often said that the tasks did not interest him so he wasn't going to do them. This rather unilateral, unproductive behavior did not lead to closure or completion of assigned tasks. When the natural consequences for such behavior, lack of reinforcement, were applied, K. immediately tested the teacher to discover if the class structure would be realistically maintained. After many exposures to this sort of patterning model, K. would return to his tasks until he had completed them. During his earned free periods, K. returned to drawing pictures of war, Nazis, and dinosaurs. At this phase of the total process, the reinforcement of the actual task completion, i.e., the OK placed upon the tasks, was not sufficiently strong to counteract a return to earlier patterns of behavior.

After approximately three months, K. exhibited behavior which signified his progression into the *cognition* stage of the program. Indicators of this were apparent in terms of K. experiencing more consecutive days of productive work and behavior. His testing of the structure became more perfunctory, as if he had to make sure that the teacher was "on his toes." At times, he would take advantage of any real or imagined "chinks" in the program, but he was easily brought back to his responsibilities of the moment. Attempted power struggles with the teacher over assigned tasks, or behavioral expectations, became quite short in duration, and without the desperate aspect of completely controlling the situation. During this period, K. began to verbalize his use of the structure as an aid in helping him attend to the expectations of the day. For example, K. said the following: "I really know how to do these problems; I was just trying to get out of doing them." At other times he said, in effect, that he truly wanted to do his work, but when left to his own devices he could not follow through. During this phase of development, K. often said: "I feel good when I get my work done." Further evidence of overall gain was noted in that even while K. was protesting about his tasks, saying that he wasn't going to do them, etc., he was busily engaged in completing them and receiving the reinforcements for completion. K's drawings became more realistic and pictures of Nazis, war, etc. disappeared. Bizarre behavioral patterns diminished as he became more interested and productive in day-to-day completion of tasks.

In summary for this stage, K. became more tractable, and was able to recognize and verbalize the relationship between his behavior and its consequences. He still relied upon the external pattern or model for support, but was gradually assuming and integrating more behavioral controls of his own.

This slow, but gradual transition enabled K. to progress into the *integration* stage of the program. Consecutive days of productive work became the rule rather than the exception. He entered the room and eagerly went to work without reminders from the teacher. He received much satisfaction from accomplishing his tasks correctly and neatly. He became quite proud of his OK on each piece of work and would promptly remind the teacher if he forgot to place the mark on the task. He became more cooperative about accepting difficult assignments; rather than give up, or struggle with the teacher over the work, he asked for assistance and was able to follow through to completion. His use of free time became quite productive. Instead of drawing, he chose to read books of interest to him. He was able to budget his time, and when a new assignment had to be initiated, he could leave his reading until

the next free period. His growing independence from the external reinforcement was noted in that he often passed up the juice break in order to pursue a particular problem. He became able to work cooperatively in small groups, assuming his portion of the requirements in order to get group closure on the task. While K. still maintained an interest in dinosaurs, it took on the aspect of a hobby. He delved into historical, and anthropological studies; his interest and information in this area became more organized and less associated with his prior fantasy life. As he experienced achievement, success, he turned his attention away from himself and focused it upon the world of people and things about him. Whereas before, K. evaluated most everything in terms of its direct effect upon him, he became aware of how other people and events were involved too.

Social, verbal reinforcements became effective. K. became adept in discussing outcomes of behavior and in most instances could choose the correct alternative without prompting.

Concrete examples of K's continued growth can be discerned from the following discussion: The teacher kept all of K's old drawings, past work, etc. in a place where K. could go over them if he desired. When he looked at his earlier drawings, he would often say: "Did I draw those silly, crazy pictures? They sure are dumb, aren't they?" He could easily identify his progressions in the actual work. When he compared his first academic efforts with later ones he often remarked how much neater and organized his later work was. Also, when observing the quite large collection of work, he expressed much pleasure at having accomplished so much. K. became able to observe the behavior of newer children who entered the class. Comments such as "Doesn't he know that that kind of behavior is silly, and won't get him anyplace," were expressed periodically.

K. has now returned to a public school program. Separation from the class was relatively "painless" for K. He initiated a discussion with the teacher about returning to public school, and they arrived mutually at the decision that returning to a regular class was reasonable. In the meantime, K. eagerly "tidied up his school affairs" with the assistance and support of the teacher. Several weeks before the end of the spring session, he reverted back to some of his earlier demands. This behavior occurred on a Monday and lasted for a short period on that school day. This approach was almost one of "tongue in cheek." K's behavior seemed to indicate that he had to try these demands once more. When they weren't reinforced, and after a brief private discussion with the teacher, K. realized that these inefficient, unproductive patterns had no satisfaction at all, and he readily gave them up. K. took some of his more productive, positive projects home with him, but he showed no desire to keep his earlier bizarre drawings. He returned to the special class for the summer. Throughout that session his behavior was free of symptoms; he was well organized and quite productive.

K's experiences in public school will be followed and scrutinized by the special class teacher, the regular class teachers, and counselors at the junior high school. If K. needs short term supportive assistance, it will be available to him, and also to his parents. K. will experience the same frustrations and pleasures as his peers, but now that he has gained strength, he should be able to solve daily dilemmas with a reasonable amount of success and a minimum of anxiety. He is a more productive, socially outgoing boy able to meet daily responsibilities, and yet retain his own individuality. He possesses the strength to tolerate stress from peers, teachers, and parents without retreating into fantasy, autistic-like realms.

DISCUSSION

We have observed cases of continuous behavioral progressions analogous to K's experiences in our ongoing program for educating emotionally disturbed children.

The other type of clinical diagnostic category seen most frequently in classes for emotionally disturbed children, the acting out, overly assertive, aggressive child, proceeds through similar patterns of progressive growth and reorganization. However, for each individual child the period of time spent in each stage, and regression to a lower stage, is quite unique and can be compared only in a gross, descriptive, fashion to the process experienced by other children.

From the cognition stage to when they are ready to leave the special class program, the children often provide verbal feedback which enables the teacher to modify the nature of daily tasks, gradually shift reinforcement schedules, and initiate social verbal consequences to shape positive, acceptable behavior. External reinforcers, such as juice, free time, crafts, and so forth, lose some of their significance to the children as they become able to reflect upon behavioral choices and their associated consequences.

Examples of these verbal clues which indicate cognitive, insightful and purposeful processes are as follows:

1. "I like to be in your class because I know what's going to happen from one minute to the next." (This statement was made by a boy who had been previously a pupil in a special class program which emphasized a "permissive, acting out of conflictual psychic material." After experiencing success in tasks, and behavioral expectations in a structured special class, the boy related the statement to his teacher.)

2. "I believe what I see, not what I hear." (This pupil made this comment after the teacher moved into a complete social, verbal reinforcement paradigm before the child was able to assimilate enough control from the environment into his own behavior repertoire.)

3. "They sure catch on to your tricks fast around here." (A withdrawn boy made this comment when the teacher remained consistent in his expectation that a task

had to be completed before the boy became involved with the pleasurable reinforcement. To test the teacher, the boy had withdrawn into a nonverbal, catatonic state. After observing that his efforts to unilaterally control the teacher and the situation were not effective, he made the statement to the teacher, started to work on the assigned tasks, and went on to experience a successful, gratifying school day.)

4. "I am sick and tired of being so happy." (After several consecutive, rewarding days of productive task completion and behavior at school, an aggressive, hostile, defiant boy, with an impish grin on his face, made this statement to the teacher.)

5. "That behavior is really crazy." (This comment was made by a pupil who was in the cognition stage of the program, when he observed the testing behavior of a newer pupil who was attempting to manipulate the teacher into becoming punitive and inconsistent.)

6. "Never underestimate the power of a teacher." (A boy related this to his teacher after she remained firm in expecting the child to complete his assigned task. After making the comment, he initiated contact with the task and followed through to completion.)

7. "Boy, am I glad my day's work is done!" (With a facial expression of obvious contentment, satisfaction, pride and pleasure, a formerly severely disturbed child made this statement to the teacher. The boy could now look forward to engaging in after school play without feeling guilty about non-productive, disorganized, unsatisfactory school experiences.)

Behavioral, educational progress emanating from our program for emotionally disturbed children and reported in this article offers realistic encouragement for future planning. However, we firmly believe that research pertinent to the education and management of emotionally disturbed children must be continued. For example, research efforts should concentrate on a problem that is obtrusively evident, the objective measurement of be-

havior. In our program, we have used measures such as quality and amount of work completed, recording duration of time for each child to complete tasks, totaling the number of times each child is involved in destructive and constructive behavior encounters, and computing each child's total activity in the classroom. Modern learning theory, which utilizes a reinforcement model for acquiring and maintaining behavior, can provide the techniques for measuring behavior in the natural setting of the classroom. Refinement and sophistication of measurements, within the boundaries of such a model, present experimental problems for further study. Application of modern learning theory to solving complex problems associated with emotional disturbance should suggest techniques for objective measurement of behavior, and implementation of specific remedial methods which could obviate the debilitating effects of disorganized, ineffective behavioral responses.

References

Birnbrauer, J. S., S. W. Bijou, M. M. Wolf, J. D. Kidder, and C. Tague. "A Programmed Instruction Classroom for Educable Retardates." Paper read at American Association of Mental Deficiency Convention, Portland, May 1963.

Eysenck, H. J. (Ed.). *Behavior Therapy and the Neuroses.* New York: Pergamon Press, 1960.

Ferster, C. B., and M. K. DeMeyer. "A Method for the Experimental Analysis of the Behavior of Autistic Children." *American Journal of Orthopsychiatry,* 1962, **32,** 89–98.

Ferster, C. B., and B. F. Skinner. *Schedules of Reinforcement.* New York: Appleton-Century-Crofts, 1957.

Haring, N. G., and E. L. Phillips. *Educating Emotionally Disturbed Children.* New York: McGraw-Hill, 1962.

Levin, G. R., and J. J. Simmons. "Response to Food and Praise by Emotionally Disturbed Boys." *Psychological Reports,* 1962, **11,** 539–546.

Lindsley, O. R. "Experimental Analysis of Social Reinforcement." *American Journal of Orthopsychiatry,* 1963, **33,** 624–633.

Lindsley, O. R. "Direct Measurement and Prosthesis of Retarded Behavior." *Journal of Education*, 1964.

Michael, J., and L. Meyerson. "A Behavioral Approach to Counseling and Guidance." *Harvard Educational Review*, 1962, **32**, 382–402.

Phillips, E. L., and N. G. Haring. "Results from Special Techniques for Teaching Emotionally Disturbed Children." *Exceptional Children*, 1959, **26**, 64–67.

Wolf, M., H. Mees, and T. Risley. "Application of Operant Conditioning Procedures to the Behavior of an Autistic Child." Paper read at Western Psychological Association, 1963.

A third approach to the education of emotionally disturbed children, proposed by Rhodes, lies somewhere between the psychoeducational approach and the interference method. Rhodes' premise is that the teacher should focus on the positive forces of health and well-being in the child, rather than on the pathological forces. In psychodynamic language, this would be termed "building on the child's ego strengths." Rhodes' curriculum consists of carefully planned experiences to help the child recognize his own potentials, capabilities, and resources within a "life space" similar to the one that initially contributed to his maladjustment. Since the curriculum is not restricted to the school, but includes the use of all appropriate reality lessons even ones originating on a street corner, the teacher must be highly skilled in selecting experiences for the individual and the group. This is a thoughtful article that should lead to some interesting experimentation in the future.

Curriculum and Disordered Behavior
William C. Rhodes

Education can add an important dimension to the existing approaches to emotionally and socially maladjusted children. Its basic human concerns and major human goals differ quite radically from those of the clinically oriented professions. It is not concerned with cure or eradication of pathology and disease. It has no pills, no chemicals, no tranquilizers to be administered to sick organisms. Its methods all address themselves to positive drives—drives toward knowing, learning, discovering, exploring. It is concerned with liberating and catalyzing positive energies, potentials and capacities within the human being.

Education implies a ready to be born

Abridged from William C. Rhodes, "Curriculum and Disordered Behavior," *Exceptional Children* (October 1963), pp. 61–66. Reprinted with permission.

The author is Professor of Psychology, George Peabody College for Teachers, Nashville, Tenn.

capacity in man which can be addressed or stimulated from the outside. It is a process which mediates between nature and nurture, exciting the interaction of one upon the other to bring forth new ways of being and reacting. It is a way of reconciling and transcending the claims of the individual and the claims of the culture.

Jacques Maritain has said that, "To liberate the good energies is the best way of repressing the bad ones. . . ." and in this statement suggests the way in which education can provide a different dimension to approaches traditionally used with the socially, educationally and emotionally maladjusted child. The real art of education, he says, "is to make the child heedful of his own resources and potentialities for the beauty of well being."

To repress bad energies by liberating good ones, to make the child heedful of his own resources and potentialities has nothing to do with the art of positive thinking. The teacher expects to encounter resistance in the emotionally disturbed or socially maladjusted child. There is tension and resistance in all teaching-learning transactions. Learning demands change and the human organism resists change. Part of the teaching function involves resolution and transformation of resistance to change.

Despite the reality of strong resistance within the emotionally or socially maladjusted child, we can make the same assumption about him that we do for the average child. There are forces for growth, for exploration, for discovery within him. These motivations are every bit as real as basic tissue drives associated with thirst, hunger, sex, etc. We must prepare the lessons we direct toward this child in such a way that we engage such motivation. We must handle our human encounter with the child in such a way that avoidance behavior gives way to approach behavior and the child reaches out for the lesson presented him.

What are the lessons that the teacher offers the emotionally and socially maladjusted child? A lesson is a preparation for a particular kind of experience which the child needs in order to make him aware of and use his own resources and potentialities; an experience which releases positive energies and behaviors to replace destructive or discordant energies and behaviors. The lessons concern themselves with all aspects of behavior needed for living—particularly those behaviors crucial to living in the home, the school, the group, the community. We know that there are substantive skill deficits in the school behavior of the socially and emotionally maladjusted child. However, these are not the only areas in which he is in need of lessons. We must capture him in subject matter, but we must also transform relationships with authority, communication with other people, concepts of self, into constructive and positive new experiences for him.

We must concentrate upon existing disjunctions between the child and cul-

turally cherished social organizations such as home, school, and community play units. We must locate, specify and recreate the site and conditions of his disjunction with the culture of these social organizations. The child is part of a social microcosm, with various acculturation media constantly harmonizing his demands with the demands of the culture. Within the organizational independence of each of these media are myriad opportunities for disjunctions between the demands of the child and those of the culture. If the particular disjunction occurs between the child and subculture of more than one of these organizations, we usually speak of emotional maladjustment. If it occurs outstandingly in the school, we usually speak of educational deficiency or educational maladjustment; and, if it is localized more particularly in the community, we talk about social maladjustment or juvenile delinquency.

The preparations for experiences at the site of the child's disjunctions form the crucial nucleus for the educational approach to the problems of emotional disturbance and juvenile delinquency. We should be guided by all we know about ways to prepare vital new experiences and ways to stabilize these in behavior. The form in which we plan the preparation and the patterning of the forms can be called the curriculum. The crux of the educational approach to emotional disturbance and juvenile delinquency, then, is contained in the preparations we make for the child to have constructive new experiences which will make him aware of and use his own resources, capacities and potentialities and which liberate positive motivations and behaviors within him. It is the experience— something actually happening to the child, within the child, in an important life episode—that is the heart of the educational task. In order to accomplish this task we must develop preparations which provide as ideal a medium as possible for the experience. We should have a set of guides or criteria against which to measure our preparation. These can be distilled, derived or evolved from the composite of educational principles and crucial "learning" experimentation of great educational theorists and psychological theorists concerned with educational problems. A series of these developed and tried by the author are offered below as a tentative statement of guidance. Concrete examples and brilliant application of one guide or the other were found in Froebel (1909), Itard (1932), Montessori (1912), Seguin (1907), James (1939), Wolpe (1958), Eysenck (1960), and Jones (1958).

The author's current position holds that in order for the preparation to have maximum power and efficiency in insuring the intended experience, all of the guides are important for a single preparation or a series of preparations.

GUIDES TO PREPARATION FOR EXPERIENCES

1. We should prepare surroundings, circumstances, situations and events so that they excite new experiences in the child in relationship to old problems. We cannot act as though the child has had such an experience. We must conduct our preparations in ways that insure the experience. His responses will provide the cues to the quality and intensity of the experience and will provide suggestions to the teacher for additional preparation.

2. The preparations must continue to surround the child with opportunities for new experiences which would strongly engage such excitatory motives as adventure, conquest, achievement, exploration, and discovery. The preparations might also associate the experience with positive satisfaction of tissue drives such as hunger, thirst and sex.

3. New experiences and newly developed abilities should ultimately be imbedded in events and settings very similar to those in which the child's responses have previously been a problem to himself and to others. The teacher can gauge the extent of success in approximating problem set-tings by the extent of transfer of qualitatively new behaviors to old problem situations.

4. If the child strongly rejects or avoids an approximate replica of the site and conditions of his disjunction, the teacher should decrease the similarity of the replica to the life setting until the child begins to respond positively to the replica. The aspects of the replica can then be prepared gradually to simulate the problem setting. The rate of approximation can be adjusted to the reactions of the child. As long as there is approach and intensity in the child's responses, the degree of similarity can be increased. When there is avoidance or when there is rejection by the child, the degree of similarity should be decreased until avoidance and rejection disappear.

5. Learning should be an active process in which the child has to do something with materials, conditions and surroundings. The more activity and manipulation required, the better the opportunity for a meaningful experience.

6. To increase the probability of excitation of new experiences in the child, the preparation should involve the engagement of as many sensory channels as possible. As long as the child is responding favorably, the teacher may assume that the more sensory channels which can be engaged, the better the conditions for learning.

7. Learning requires repetition of experiences until new abilities and positive behaviors begin to stabilize. The repetitions should be pleasurable to the child and should involve constant new discovery. Preparation for repetition should be guided by the child's reactions. Rejection or rebellion would be a signal for caution. Continued rejection or avoidance would signal the need for change or termination. Approach and eagerness from the child would be a signal for the teacher to continue.

8. Preparations should include the child's control over those parts of the surroundings, circumstances or events which concern him most, or which he most wants

to control. This control should be reduced only gradually as the child seems willing to relinquish it.

9. Preparations for experiences and development of new abilities should be channeled toward goals which the child cherishes and which can be culturally tolerated; and should always include elements which the child prizes.

10. The preparation for experiences should include natural and immediate consequences for the child's activity. The consequences should grow out of the lesson and should occur as soon as possible after the child performs in the lesson. It is very important that consequences early in the learning sequence should be satisfying and stimulating to the child. The child's behavior will inform the teacher of the quality of the consequences.

11. The preparations should require only performances which are in line with the child's present level of ability and accomplishment. In stimulating new experiences in the child, the teacher should nudge the child slowly up the gradient of achievement as increased mastery and challenge is apparent in the child's functioning.

12. It is important that the preparation for an experience should attempt to stimulate the child's awareness of the experience as it relates to his resources and abilities. The teacher should find ways to help the child reflect back upon the experience and its meaning for him so that it is bound as a permanent record within him. The teacher must test this out in many ways to be sure that there has been cognitive assimilation of the experience.

LESSON FORMS

There are many forms which the above preparations might take, and many patternings for the forms selected. I will discuss five forms which I have experimented with in curricula for socially, emotionally, and/or educationally maladjusted children.

The Unit. The unit is a special form of preparation to induce specific experiences in a child. The unit is built around a theme which has dramatic appeal to a boy or girl in a particular age range. It should be a theme which has endless possibility for exciting positive motivations such as adventure, conquest, achievement, mastery, or exploration. It should be a theme broad enough to incorporate many methods, activities, situations, etc. It should also be able to touch intimately upon the problem area of each individual. The theme can either be a substantive one such as "The Pioneers," or a psychological one, such as "Fantasy." In either case we should weave together both substantive areas and psychological areas. Psychological areas would embrace hostility, family interactions, sex, love, triumph, etc.

The important orientation to keep in mind is that we are attempting to produce experiences in the child which will release and develop positive energies in place of negative ones and make him aware of and use his own resources and abilities in his future behavior. We are particularly interested in producing new positive experiences at the very site of his disjunctions with the culture. All of the preparations which have been discussed should go into the unit. You will remember that these include simulating circumstances in which the child has had difficulty, leading step by step, making the child very active, engaging many senses, repetition, giving the child a measure of control, utilizing goals and elements cherished by the child, providing for natural consequences, and beginning where the child is at the particular moment of the lesson. The purpose of the theme of the unit is to provide coherence, organization, and intrinsic relationship of experiences for the child.

Behavior Training. This is a very old form which can best be exemplified in the methods used by Itard (1962) to retrain the wild boy of Aveyron to wear clothes, to eat "properly," to show affection for his guardian, to distinguish sounds, and to sense temperature differences.

This form can be much more effective if it will make use of experimental findings in psychology. This approach to behavior problems is not new, but it fell into disrepute during the period of extensive development of psychotherapy as the only way to deal with disjunctions between the child and his settings. It is beginning to emerge again as a useful method for modification of behavior.

An old example of this form is the conditioning procedure used by M. C. Jones (1924). She worked with a child who feared a white rabbit and had generalized this fear to all white, furry objects. The fear was "unconditioned" by presenting the rabbit in the corner of the room while the child was eating, and slowly, over a period of days, moving the rabbit closer and closer. The child was gradually desensitized and the pleasure of eating seemed to have been associated with the rabbit.

A new example is the method used by Wolpe (1958). He evokes a response antagonistic to anxiety in a situation which is disturbing for a particular individual. The person is placed in the problem situation and Wolpe adds elements which produce anxiety-inhibiting responses such as anger, sexual excitement, relaxation, competing motor activity, and pleasure.

The method of behavioral retraining requires a careful specification of the problem setting or situation, the particular disjunctive behaviors involved, and the behaviors which would be more successful for the individual in that setting or situation. One then recreates crucial elements of the setting or situation; and establishes procedures which will extinguish disjunctive behaviors, substitute new behaviors in their place, or accomplish both behavioral goals at the same time.

In this form, the teacher is concerned with behaviors of crucial importance to the child's functioning in important life settings such as home, school and community. The preparation must be thought through carefully, structured economically, focused clearly, and aimed toward more specific goals than any other form. More detailed examples of this form are briefly reviewed in Rhodes (1962).

Skill Training. Another form, and one which teachers know very well, is skill training. It concentrates on basic subject matter skills, play skills and skills in human interaction which we call "manners." All of the preparations for experiences are important in the skill areas. The only emphasis that is crucial here is that there be special effort to appeal to the excitatory motives such as adventure, discovery, exploration, achievement, etc.

Discussion Sessions. Discussion is a supplement to experience and a cognitive replica of experience. It can be accomplished in a group situation or a person-to-person situation. Discussion is experience-dependent and age related. The child needs to have reached a certain developmental level and accumulated sufficient experience before the discussion can be useful to him. Therefore, it appears to be more effective for children over nine or ten years of age than for younger children. It provides a stimulus to reflection and rumination which binds the experience within the child and makes it available to future behaviors.

Discussion cannot substitute for experience, but it can add new interpretations and reflections. It can provide a form for release of motivations toward knowing, learning, discovery, and exploring. It can help make the child "heedful of his own resources and potentialities for well-being."

Group Interaction. This involves teacher utilization of the flexible dynamics of functioning groups. Such group interaction cuts across all settings of the child's life. It offers a natural laboratory within which the child is constantly having to respond and interact, and in which he receives constant and immediate feedback on his behavior. The group presents ideal conditions for new experiences and new learnings. All the excitation, cues, responses and rewards which he needs for new learnings are recurrently present. The sensitive problem areas in his functioning are constantly being stirred.

In the group the teacher has a succession of conditions and surroundings which require little structuring effort and a series of concrete behaviors which might be reflected back to the child. Having analyzed the necessary areas for release of the child's positive motivations and for creating an awareness of his own resources and abilities, the teacher can utilize the natural flow of events in the group to provide the appropriate lessons.

Now that I have talked about one kind of curriculum for socially, emotionally and educationally maladjusted children, let me raise an important issue for educators to consider.

THE ISSUE OF THE SETTING

While I believe that education has a unique contribution to make in this area, the contribution should not be bound to the stereotyped pattern of classroom or school. Teaching can and should occur in many settings. The more flexible the teacher is in being able to use many settings, the more influential the proposed curriculum could be. For instance, a truly effective teacher should be able to capture the junior gang member on the streets and offer needed lessons on street corners, in community centers, settlement houses, camps, or parks. Teaching should be able, when necessary, to environ lessons with real life circumstances and should be able to make use of any setting or situation which would most likely engage and liberate positive motivations, potentials and capacities within the

child at the very site of his disjunctions with the culture.

The only important criteria for the setting are: (a) how close is it to that in which the performance of the child will be crucial in the future; and (b) how effective is it in providing the right kind of nurture to catalyze the nature and resources of the child? . . .

References

Eysenck, H. J. (Ed.) *Behavior Therapy and the Neuroses.* New York, Oxford, London, Paris: Pergamon Press, 1960.

Frobel, F. *The Education of Man.* (Translated by W. N. Hailman.) New York: D. Appleton & Co., 1909.

Itard, J. M. G. *The Wild Boy of Aveyron.* New York: Appleton-Century-Crofts, Meredith Publishing Co., 1962.

James, W. *Talks to Teachers on Psychology.* New York: Henry Holt & Co., 1939.

Jones, H. G. "Neurosis and Experimental Psychology." *Journal of Mental Science,* 1958, **104,** 55–62.

Jones, M. C. "A Laboratory Study of Fear— The case of Peter." *Pedagogical Seminary (Journal of Genetic Psychology),* 1924, **31,** 308–315.

Maritain, J. *Education at the Crossroads.* New Haven: Yale University Press, 1943.

Montessori, Maria. *The Montessori Method* (Translated by Anne E. George.) London: William Heinemann, 1912.

Rhodes, W. C. "Psychological Techniques and Theory Applied to Behavior Modifications." *Exceptional Children,* 1962, **28,** 333–338.

Seguin, E. *Idiocy and Its Treatment.* New York: Columbia University, Teachers College Foundational Reprint, 1907.

Wolpe, J. *Psychotherapy by Reciprocal Inhibition.* Stanford, Cal.: Stanford University Press, 1958.

Special education teachers report that the initial adjustment from home to school during the first fifteen minutes of class is extremely important and can set the atmosphere for the entire morning. Louis Hay and his staff have systematically reviewed the multiple problems that occurred during this brief period in their Junior Guidance classes in New York City.

Their report, which follows, reflects the cooperative efforts of more than 200 teachers of emotionally disturbed children, and offers the beginning teacher specific methods that have been proved by practical use.

Good Morning, Boys and Girls
Louis Hay and Gloria Lee

WHO ARE OUR CHILDREN?

John enters the room like a bomb. He flings the door open and crosses the room in two or three leaps, vaulting over a desk or two on the way. He proclaims to the group that he has had several fights on the way to school and has beaten one or two boys. He seems wound up like a coiled spring. . . .

Vanessa comes into the room dragging her feet. She pulls her books along the floor behind her. She goes directly to her desk and sits in a forlorn fashion, slumped in her seat. . . .

Henry is late. He slips furtively into the room. He hides his books in the closet, gathers together some art materials, and begins working—yet fully dressed in his outer clothing. . . .

Harold is late every morning. He does not come into the classroom but stands by the side of the door. His shirt is unbuttoned, his shoes unlaced, he wears one sock. His hands are in his pockets holding up his pants because he has no belt. Sporadically, he kicks the wall. . . .

Each morning the emotional bridge from the world of the home to the world of the school must be built anew by each child with the help of the teacher. She

An unpublished paper by Louis Hay and Gloria Lee, with the assistance of Shirley Cohen, Hellie Jones, Lottie Ranig, and Judy Schmidt, Board of Education of the City of New York, Divisions of Child Welfare and Elementary Schools.

Louis Hay is Clinical Coordinator and Gloria Lee is Educational Coordinator for the New York City Junior Guidance Classes Program.

helps the child view himself as an accepted individual. For children in Junior Guidance Classes this marks the most significant transition of the day, calling for a rallying and redirecting of psychic energies from the focus of the home to that of the school.

In schools where classes line up in the yard, children of Junior Guidance Classes should proceed directly, singly or with classmates, to their rooms. Each child of this population of troubled children has his own physiological and psychological tolerance for non-mobility. Lining them up invites inevitable disturbances.

WHERE HAVE THEY BEEN?

At the close of each school day a disturbed child returns home, often reluctantly, to the source of his major conflict. Here the drama that fostered his patterns of maladjustment is re-enacted. This may be a parent-child or a parental conflict or sibling rivalry in which the child becomes a pawn. Peer pressure may also augment dissension. Meal time and bed time are crucial periods with nighttime bringing nightmares instead of tranquility.. There may be simple neglect with no breakfast, or little nurturing provisions or over-insistence upon eating. The morning views another occasion for a new round of conflicts at breakfast. For most of our children the home represents an arena of painful experiences in which anxiety and anger mount and aggression or withdrawal is used as a defense. In either case, the price is a loss of self-confidence as well as a loss of trust of the adults. It is left to the teacher each morning to help recreate an atmosphere of security.

The morning period should be a quiet one in both tempo and substance. Problems can emanate from the class structure as well as the materials which lead to a high level of activity or stimulation. Competitiveness should be avoided. This should be a time in which children can be alone if they need to be; can move freely; can obtain needed nourishment; can find constructive release opportunities and can test wholesome social relationships. This kind of atmosphere helps children to move into the day's activities gradually.

HOW CAN THE TEACHER HELP?

The opening period of the day is a time when the teacher is vitally needed by her pupils. She must be available and active. She reveals her *respect* for the children by providing the materials and the opportunities for activities which are fitted to the needs and interests of the children.

The teacher also sets the stage and defines this time by the materials which she makes available and by the activities she allows, encourages and suggests. She is faced with the problems of how and when to help the child who needs adult direction in getting started; how and when to involve the child who flits about interrupting the activities of other children and how and when to introduce new materials.

The teacher is active in the following ways:

1. She observes carefully each child as he enters the room. She uses this morning observation as a comparative basis for noting daily differences in clothing, tempo, mobility, physical well being, etc. She participates most actively during the first period by observing "inner movement" through non-verbal communication.

2. She gives each child some sign of welcome and continued interest.

3. She looks at each child individually to sense which children will need that little bit of extra support this day.

4. She is available to answer questions and mediate controversies.

5. She moves in temporarily to support a faltering group activity.

6. She listens to accounts of experiences from individual children.

7. She interests a child who is at "loose ends" in an activity.

The art of encouraging a child toward initiative without making him dependent on the continued presence of the starter is invaluable in a Junior Guidance classroom. It is therefore extremely important that this period be set within a carefully planned but flexible framework. It must not be a haphazard one.

WHAT KINDS OF ACTIVITIES CAN BE PLANNED?

Early morning projects should be nonthreatening and gratifying. They should not depend upon teacher direction. It may be possible to have an ongoing activity that is carried on only during the first period. The last period of the day can serve as a link with the first period of the next day.

Suggested activities for younger children:

1. Individual scrapbooks (These pupil-made scrapbooks may be no more than three or four pages.)
2. Personal story books, written and illustrated by the children
3. Water painting on blackboard (mop should be available)
4. Surprise box (a large box, decorated, containing enough activities for the whole class)
5. Listening to phonograph or radio (child may be able to assume responsibility for operation of machine)
6. Salt, coarse (for pouring)
7. Writing on blackboard
8. Sorting materials (arithmetic chips for color, kinds of beans, kinds of beads, etc.)
9. Table blocks

10. Small finger puppets
11. Dominoes
12. Trays of different materials
    a. Two or three toy cars and a box for a garage
    b. A little bath tub and small plastic doll and water (in limited amount) for bathing doll
    c. Pieces of very small furniture
    d. Science materials
13. Easel painting
14. Sewing and knitting (horse reins, etc.)
15. Special art materials (felt pens, colored pencils)
16. Looking at magazines
17. Puzzles
18. Housekeeping activities
    a. Watering plants
    b. Straightening block shelf
19. Stringing (beads, cut-up straws, macaroni, buttons)
20. A shelf of special books available only during the first period. This supply of books should be changed periodically.

Older children can be helped to a positive carryover from the previous day through helpful classroom discussion.

Suggested activities for older children:

1. Special interests (scrapbooks, collections)
2. Science materials and projects (dry cells, magnets, old clocks or radio to take apart and put together, microscope)
3. Knitting, weaving and sewing, particularly for girls
4. Class projects (class newspaper with use of typewriter, writing letters)
5. Mailbox (for communication among children in class and teacher)
6. Small scale construction (e.g., models)
7. Listening to phonograph or radio, with child or children assuming responsibility for operation of machine
8. Making articles for a younger class (Word Lotto game, Go Fish cards)
9. Special jobs for the teacher or for the class
10. Sorting (making picture files, collating rexographed worksheets for the class)

11. Notes on the bulletin board to the class or to individual children telling them about something special available that day or suggesting a particular activity
12. Brousing through newspapers and magazines

Suggested activities for individual children who pose special problems:

1. Finger painting
2. Surprise bag for an individual child (two or three small toys)
3. Care of a doll
4. Printing set
5. Miniature slide viewer
6. Easily assembled construction games such as "Mr. Potato Head"
7. Follow-the-dot books

Some of the activities mentioned previously, such as stringing, sorting, or using the phonograph for quiet records, prove soothing to distraught children.

ADDITIONAL GUIDELINES

1. Seasonal changes should be considered.

2. This is not a work period with floor blocks, wood working, etc. Activities that require a long period of time and self-investment should be bypassed.

3. One cannot talk of meeting the needs of children in Junior Guidance Classes at the beginning of the day without planning for the availability of food at this time. Children who are hungry cannot turn their attention to the world around them except in anger. A tray of sandwiches saved from the previous day, a few boxes of dry cereal, some slices of bread and jelly or some cookies are signs of welcome which these children cannot mistake.

4. The sharing of food is also a natural way for bringing the class together at the close of the morning period. How much easier it is to look ahead to the rest of the day while sipping from a container of milk, or a cup of hot cocoa, and feeling good about being in this place.

5. This is a time for children to renew their relationships, to talk and play together, to exchange experiences and feelings.

6. At all times opportunities for individual differences should be respected. One child may enter, sit down and not participate in any activities. Whether he is accessible for some direction from the teacher may vary from child to child and at different times with the same child. Doing "nothing" may be doing much.

The therapeutic meaning of school games has recently come under experimental evaluation in the search for answers to such questions as: How does a particular game or activity influence the expressions of children's feelings? What difference does it make whether a group plays dodge-ball, in which the group is against the child, or tag, in which one child is against the group? Is it more frustrating for a group to play volley ball or Red Rover, Red Rover?

Some of the specific variables to consider in a game are: the amount of body contact (football), body mobility (Statue vs. Tag), the complexity of rules and the skill requirements (chess, monopoly, checkers), the degree of luck (dice and spinner games), the use of space, the duration of the game (War), the use of props (balls, rackets, etc., role-taking factors (quarterback, pitcher, It), and the degree of horse-playing the game can tolerate (Mother, May I vs. darts).

In their article "Therapeutic Play Techniques," Gump and Sutton-Smith describe the types of social interaction among emotionally disturbed children during two camp activities, swimming and crafts. Ultimately, this type of research should lead to a systematic evaluation of all school games to determine their effects on behavior. With this knowledge, the teacher could select games and activities for their value in developing group cohesion and helping shy children become more aggressive and aggressive children more controlled.

Therapeutic Play Techniques

Paul Gump and Brian Sutton-Smith

When the relationship between children and their activities is investigated, interest usually centers upon the question of how children select and use various activities to express their personal and social needs. The present study, and the larger research project from which it derives, attempts to reverse the direction of this interest and ask the question: How do

From "Activity Setting and Social Interaction: A Field Study," by Paul Gump and Brian Sutton-Smith, *American Journal of Orthopsychiatry*, XXV, No. 4, 755–760. Copyright, 1955, the American Orthopsychiatric Association, Inc. Reprinted by permission.

The authors are Research Associates, School of Social Work, Wayne University, Detroit.

activities limit, provoke, or coerce the expression of children's needs and problems? This form of consideration is based upon the general hypothesis that activities have a reality and a behavior-influencing power in their own right. An activity, once entered, will exclude some potential behaviors, necessitate other behaviors, and, finally, encourage or discourage still other behaviors. This coercive and provocative power of an activity rests upon two sub-aspects: the behavioral limitations and possibilities in the *physical* setting and its objects, and in the "standard patterns of performance" which constitute the activity. Thus, the activity-setting identified as "making a boat in craft shop" includes the physical objects of shop, wood, saws, etc., and the performances of hammering, sawing, attending to materials, etc. Beyond the performances which are standard in boat making, are behaviors which may become more or less *likely* because a child has entered this particular activity-setting. For example, if the setting should provide one saw and the standard performance should require sawing, conflict interaction may be more likely in such an activity-setting than in one in which tools are plentiful or in which boys are not pressed to use the same tool at the same time.

Those behaviors which are made more likely, although not required, by the physical setting and its standard performances may be labeled *respondent behaviors*. In the present study, the respondent behaviors under investigation were social interactions. The hypothesis tested was that the amount and kind of social interaction are significantly affected by variation of activity-settings. In all, four usual camp activity-settings were investigated: cook-outs, boating, swims, and crafts. Only material from swims and crafts is offered here. The following report, then, deals with a comparison of the amount and kind of social interaction which occurred in the craft and swim activity-settings.

METHOD

The subjects were 23 boys, aged 9½ to 11½ years, who were campers at the University of Michigan Fresh Air Camp. Most of these boys were referred to camp because of some adjustment difficulties.

Boys went to each activity as members of a cabin group. Therefore, both participants and directly responsible adults (counselors) were similar from activity to activity. This established a natural control over personality, sociometric, and leadership variables which otherwise might have accounted for differences in social interaction between the swim and the craft activity-settings.

TABLE 1.   RELEVANT SECTIONS OF INTERACTION ANALYSIS CODE

CATEGORY	DEFINITION AND EXAMPLE
Sharing	The subject either makes or receives an interaction with the quality of mutuality. Neither the subject nor his associate asks or is asked to serve the purposes of the other but to share an experience or an activity. E.g.: "Hey, look at the boat coming in." "Let's make a submarine."
Helping	The subject asks, or is asked for help (material, information, effort). The subject gives or receives assistance. The interaction is not one of mutuality as in sharing. E.g.: "How do you make this lanyard?" The counselor gives swimming or craft instruction, etc.
Asserting	The subject is involved in an interaction attempt, the intent of which is to gain admiration or interested attention. E.g.: "Hey, look at me! I'm a drunk!" "I know how to do that—that's easy!"
Blocking	The subject is involved in a deliberate "stopping" interaction. The blocker may refuse, ignore, etc. E.g.: "I will not!"
Demanding	The subject makes or receives a forceful request. No autonomy implied to the associate. E.g.: "You give me that!" "Get outa here!"
Attacking	The subject is involved in an interaction attempt, the purpose of which is to "hurt" the recipient—to reduce him, or beat him. E.g.: "You s.o.b.!" One boy physically attacks another or takes something from him.

Observers took full, on-the-spot recordings of ten minutes of each boy's behavior in each setting. The project director divided the resulting protocols into units so that each interaction of each subject could be coded. (Reliabilities of observation and of coding were checked and were satisfactory; there was 86% agreement on 11 code possibilities.) The code was so designed that the number and kind of interactions and the persons (counselor or boys) involved could be tallied. Categories in the code were defined in terms of the *intent* of the *source* of the interaction toward the *target* of the interaction. Categories were abstract enough to be applicable to any setting. The six most relevant of the 11 code categories are briefly defined and illustrated in Table 1.

RESULTS

The effect of activity-setting upon respondent social behavior can be ascertained by checking the amount of over-all interaction, the amount of specific kinds of interactions, and the persons involved in these kinds of interactions. Figure 1 indicates results with regard to amount and kind of interaction.

The difference in amount of interaction in favor of swim is indicated by the higher columns for swim interaction in each category except help. The over-all difference is as follows:

Average *swim* interactions	38.8
Average *craft* interactions	26.4
Average difference in favor of swim	12.4

This difference is significant at the .01 level. Other significant differences are indicated by arrows in Figure 1. These differences indicate that the help interaction is more frequent in crafts but that the more "robust interactions" (assertion and attack) are more frequent in swim. Sharing and docking tend to be more frequent in swim but differences are significant at only the .10 level.

To determine if the kind of interaction differs between settings, one may compare the percentages of interaction falling in the various categories. In this way the predominant mode or modes of interaction are indicated for each setting. When such a conversion is made, the following results are obtained:

1. One of the most predominant types of interactions in both settings is sharing—about 30 per cent in each.
2. The most predominant nonsharing interaction in crafts is helping—29 per cent (opposed to 8% in swim).
3. The most predominant nonsharing interaction in swim is the aggressive combination of assertion and attacking—33 per cent (opposed to 8% in crafts).

It is also instructive to note which setting generated the greatest per cent of interaction between boys and their counselors (and, necessarily, the least per cent of interaction among the boys themselves):

Amount of total *craft* interaction which is counselor-involved	46%
Amount of total *swim* interaction which is counselor-involved	26%

The predominant kinds of interaction in which the counselors are involved are shown by the following percentages:

1. The predominant counselor-involved interaction in crafts is help—41 per cent (17% in swim).
2. The predominant counselor-involved interaction in swim, aside from sharing, is conflict combination of demand, block and attack—34 per cent (17% in crafts).

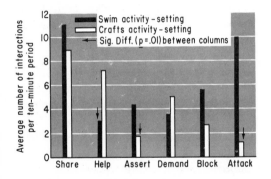

FIG. 1. AMOUNT AND KIND OF
SOCIAL INTERACTIONS BY
PARTICIPANTS IN SWIM AND CRAFTS
ACTIVITY-SETTINGS

DISCUSSION

The preceding data demonstrate that activity-settings determine more than the specific activity engaged in by a child. The properties of the activity-setting produce significant and general effects upon the respondent social behavior of its participants. In the settings investigated, these effects were noticeable in the amount and kind of interaction, in the type of person (boy or counselor) involved, and in the types of interaction sought from or offered by these different persons. The results do not seem explicable on the basis of differences in groups or in adult personnel involved— these were similar in each setting.

The general implication for recreational and therapeutic work with children is that choice of activities per se is very important; this choice will markedly affect the children's relations to one another and to the leader or therapist. Specifically, the above results indicate that in the swim setting, the counselor often will be called upon to admire and recognize assertive actions and to settle or supervise conflict interactions; he will be involved in relatively few helping interactions. In crafts, the opposite tends to be true; here the counselor's role involves less admiration and conflict supervision and more helping. Related to setting-produced variations in counselor's role, are

the variations in kinds of peer social experiences of the child participants. The counselor learns from such data that a "prescription" of swimming will send a child to a "robust" social climate in which total interaction is high and in which assertion and attacking are highly likely. A crafts "prescription," on the other hand, will place a child in a "mild" social climate in which total interaction is low, assertive and conflict interaction minimal, and dependency (helping—being helped) interaction high.

Findings for this particular camp setting and population cannot be freely generalized to all swim and craft settings. However, a review of the protocols permits one to hypothesize that certain characteristics, *intrinsic* to the physical setting and to the standard pattern of performance of crafts and swims in general, are responsible for the obtained results. These hypothesized intrinsic characteristics are our next concern.

With crafts as a base line, some of the hypothesized characteristics of the two settings may be compared and contrasted.

1. The materials and the standard performances of crafts involve "difficult" goals.

In crafts, one is supposed to "make something." This has several subsidiary effects. Interest and effort tend to go from the child to his project; he is "too busy" to seek interaction. This tends to reduce interaction in crafts. In swim, on the other hand, most of the standard performances are easily accomplished and one has freedom to seek and to respond to interaction. A second effect of the difficult goal is that it leads to need for technical assistance and to need for validation of one's efforts. The latter need is more subtle but important. Boys often ask counselors to approve (not just admire) their progress, although no "real" help is necessary. Thus, the predominance of the help type of interaction in crafts. In swim, the boys need little help or validation for the simple motor acts they accomplish.

2. The materials and the standard performances of crafts are restrictive of the

gross motor actions and of "bodily expansiveness."

In crafts, boys have to be careful; running, falling, jumping, etc., are, of course, not a part of the usual craft activity. Swims, however, provide a physical setting with elevations (docks and diving boards) and water (which can break a fall); these, together with standard performances of leaping and diving, lead to novel and "gravity-defying" acts. Cries of "Look at me!" are a likely part of such acts. As one experienced counselor puts it: "They want you to watch the darnedest things—little silly things that wouldn't be possible on land." Protocol material shows that this freedom of bodily action apparently leads to the display reflected by the high incidence of assertive interaction in the swim activity-setting. For some boys, the freedom of bodily actions also seems to lead to a need to test one's physical prowess in competitive or combative interaction; this would account for the high number of conflict interactions in swim.

In the final analysis, the basic characteristics of the activity-setting—not the activity-settings as such—determine the impact upon participants. The problem for research is the delineation of these characteristics and the discovery of their relationship to the participant's respondent behavior and experience. This problem may be approached by determining what are the major behavioral limitations and opportunities presented by typical settings and by their standard patterns of performances. Then one is in a position to ask what respondent behaviors become more or less likely because children engage in activity-settings with these characteristics.

From here on, the problem may be followed up in two ways: the modal or average effects of certain characteristics can be investigated (as was attempted in the discussion of this study); or, the particular effects upon participants with known personality needs and organizations can be assessed. The first approach is merely a step toward the second; as the second is developed, it becomes feasible to prescribe strategically activities for specific children and groups; it becomes possible to make activity-settings congruent with diagnostic knowledge and with therapeutic aims.

Reading presents a prime learning problem for emotionally disturbed children, one that holds acute implications for their future adjustment. Studies have shown that approximately 50 percent of disturbed children are in critical need of remedial reading. In our next article Margolin explores the problem, suggesting possible causes and remedies. First, he describes the general dynamics of reading. Second, he presents some interesting data on the relationship between middle-class children and reading disability. Third, he describes an experimental project for hard-to-help delinquent children from the lower socio-economic class, pointing up the relative futility of conventional treatment and methods for this group. Finally Margolin proposes a new approach to re-educating these children.

His keen observations and his knowledge of the total educational problem with so-called delinquents, deprived children, and neurotics make his contribution to this chapter a most important one.

An Experimental Approach to Reading Therapy

Joseph B. Margolin

This paper on reading retardation is less concerned with the reading processes than with a number of factors determining the development of the reading skill. In an effort to demonstrate the relatedness of education to the body of behavioral science, the subject is approached from the point of view of Social and Clinical Psychology, Public Health and Group Therapy. It is characteristic of the new nature of educational research that all of these skills and others are being directed to understanding and to seeking solutions for many of the problems of the field. Herein lies the primary purpose of this discussion—the development from the many fields of behavioral science and education of programs for the prevention and treatment of reading difficulties.

For the past six months or so, I have learned much about reading by what is probably the most empirical of all means. I have been watching my five year old daughter learning to read. This has proven a fascinating experience. She is drawn to it magnetically, filled with curiosity, yet also with anxiety at the wonder of this essential and inevitable, yet terribly complex process. Her movements toward and away from learning have brought new meaning to my understanding of the process and to our influence on it as adults. For some children, reading is fraught only with terror and for others it is lightly considered if at all. In either case the outcome is not inevitable. Many of our children with intact potential capacities are unable to master this essential skill which opens to each of us the past, present and more important, the future. Even we, the educators and clinicians, do not understand well enough the nature of this learning operation which includes so

An original article by Joseph Margolin, Expert Consultant on education of deprived children, U.S. Office of Education, Washington, D.C.

many intellectual, emotional and interpersonal aspects. So involved and interrelated are these factors that the concept of cause and cure are threatened with loss of meaning. Yet despite the complexity, most children learn and many who demonstrate initial difficulty are helped. "Why" they have difficulty and "how" they are helped must be approached. From many years of research, one fact has become clear. There is no single pattern of reading disability. It is a different phenomenon in different places and in different social groups and subcultures. The same case can also look different to observers with different approaches or vantage points. There is less similarity among the reading difficulties than there is among "the fevers." Thus we are faced with a problem in demography and eventually in epidemiology, and it should be the demography and epidemiology of reading success as well as reading failure. The reading disabilities as we know them now constitute a group of syndromes, some totally unrelated to others except that the child affected develops into later childhood and sometimes into adulthood without adequate skill in the basic tool of reading with the technical and psychological limitations that are associated with that limitation. It is possible that successful reading can be achieved via a number of pathways.

Early in 1954, a survey of mental health needs in Prince Georges County, Maryland, by Miller and Margolin of the research staff of NIMH located there, suggested that one of the most pressing mental health concerns for pupil personnel and special education people as well as for the clinical and court staffs was the "epidemic" of learning problems, especially reading difficulties, that seemed to be developing. In trying to find out the extent of the problem, Mental Health clinic records which

NUMBER AND PERCENTAGE OF BOYS AND GIRLS WITH RETARDED READING IN THE THIRD AND FIFTH GRADES, 1955–56

GRADE	SEX	TOTAL NO.	AMOUNT OF RETARDATION (YRS.)	NUMBER RETARDED	PERCENT RETARDED
3rd	Boys	3,077	1.3	826	26.8
	Girls	2,982	1.3	372	12.4
5th	Boys	2,103	2.3	451	21.4
	Girls	1,850	2.3	184	9.9

were immediately available were examined. Of the 536 children (age 7–17) seen at the Mental Health Study Center,[1] 13 percent had been diagnosed as mentally defective and 7 percent had been referred directly for reading difficulties. Of the remaining 427 children, 30 percent of the boys and 22 percent of the girls had been reported to be poor readers by the person providing their history despite the fact that the staff had not been alerted to this problem and the question is not asked directly. These figures can, therefore, be considered minimal estimates of the extent of the problem in the clinic population. Even so, they are higher, by far, than the distribution of reading difficulties in the general county school population. In examining the literature, we discovered that Gates (1936) found an incidence of emotional disturbances as high as 75 percent in groups of deficient readers. Gates has always associated reading difficulty with emotional states and personality disturbances which interfere with the learning process. . . . Without doubt organicity, social and educational deprivation and poor teaching are also major causes of reading disability. However, in the face of the social and personal pressures to which a child is subjected even these etiological factors lead to an overlay of disturbance and excessive anxiety. In this context, Gates' generalization begins to assume perspective.

This relationship between learning problems and mental health problems ob-

tained at the Study Center led us first to a crude and then to a more careful examination of the distribution of reading disability in Prince Georges County and finally into a full-fledged epidemiological study. The extent of the problem in a general population is evidenced by the findings for two grades in the first year of this study.

The data for this study was derived from a mutually helpful collaboration between the psychology staff of the Mental Health Study Center and the school examiner, that is the person responsible for selection and administration of group tests in the school system. The Study Center psychologist provided consultation on test selection and collaborated with the school psychologist in the interpretation of findings for educational purposes. The research mission of the Study Center was in this way provided with large amounts of "available data" describing the educational characteristics of the total school population without any unusual or distracting interruption of school procedures.

Analysis by school districts revealed that reading disability was not distributed randomly throughout the county. Fairly well defined clusters of high rated schools emerged as well as comparably well defined clusters of low rated schools. Further, these clusters were not randomly located, but approximated meaningful geographic entities, communities or land utilization patterns.

This introduced a host of issues, including the fundamental question of what accounts for the reading level in each clus-

---

[1] A research community mental health facility of the NIMH located in Prince Georges County, Maryland.

ter? The school itself is an important factor. Yet it must be remembered that all of the schools were administered by a single board of education with a common standard and philosophy of education as well as supervision and test criteria. Also reading materials are comparable. From a then recent (1956–57) study of neighborhoods we had data on quality of housing, population density, rate of social assistance, Juvenile Court cases and available community facilities and neighborhood file. Employing these as criteria of social and economic level, school districts with high reading levels were rated at least one quartile higher and usually more than those with low reading levels, on quality of housing, population density, social assistance, and Juvenile Court cases. This served to highlight and support what we already had surmised from earlier experience, i.e. the socio-economic dimensions of the problem. The urban-suburban-rural continuum also showed some consistent relationship with reading ability, with suburban, individual dwelling, housing areas showing best results; crowded urban areas and poor single dwelling units lower and rural areas faring least well. The correlation between the suburban-urban-rural spectrum and socio-economic factors was, of course, quite high.

Some elaboration of the meaning of the social class difference can be derived from a look backward to 1951 when a very useful research sequence was begun at the Manhattan Children's Court in New York City. In 1951–52 while developing a treatment program for delinquent youth in the Court Clinic, we encountered several problems.

A. Large numbers, 76 percent, of our population showed marked and disabling reading difficulty. One-half of this 76 percent manifested a disability of five or more years. (Compare this with national averages of 10 percent by Traxler and even the 30 percent of clinic population obtained in the MHSC study.) This population did not include the so-called "school part," i.e. Board of Education referrals in which reading problems probably occurred even more frequently.

B. Conventional treatment methods both educational and psychological were relatively ineffective and often seemed inappropriate to this population. The individual children comprising the population present a tediously repetitive pattern. Let us examine one youngster who is by no means atypical.

When Johnny entered school he had a more difficult job adjusting to his surroundings than most children do. This was a new world, different from his own. The tasks and the language were strange. The demands were somehow different, more difficult to satisfy, yet not supported by an open show of force. A thoroughly unfamiliar set of rewards and punishments prevailed. Worst of all he was expected to sit still and work and wait for rewards that were slow in coming or that never arrived. This whole strange environment, with its middle class values and especially the demand for the delay of gratification, was alien to Johnny's different socio-economic background. It differed as well from the image of middle class behavior that he obtained from television. Before long Johnny was labeled "unmotivated" and "unsocialized," a "problem child." In slum schools Johnnies compose much of each class.

Margolin, Roman and Harari have called attention to some of the barriers to effective learning inherent in many of the lower socio-economic subcultures or derived from their interaction with middle class institutions.

To the teacher the burden of oversized classes, inadequate and inappropriate materials, arriving too late in the child's life, as well as her own lack of professional preparation for such a setting, may be coupled with a real difficulty in understanding or identifying with the low socio-economic child. Such situations lead to frustration, clinging to those children closest to the teacher's middle class values and the de facto if not intended rejection of the "Johnnies." "She doesn't like me, she just wants me to sit and be quiet." These words are heard in a dozen regional accents on a hundred occasions. The teacher is like Johnny's parents, frequently overwhelmed with their own needs and unable to meet his requirements. Faced with the imposition of an unwanted, unappreciated and meaningless task by a hostile authority Johnny is likely to react accordingly. The easiest and most benign way is by direct resistance to learning. As this proves less than satisfactory, behavior problems may develop.

At home Johnny is faced by quite a different environment but with the same final effect on him. His parents tend to project responsibility, and probably care little about the value of school to the child, until some undesired attention summons them to school or court. Then the response is to the inconvenience or embarrassment of the situation, not to the absence of success for the child. There is little real valuation of learning and very little example of it. In some of the more extreme families in our population upward mobility in a child is regarded as "thinking he's too good for us." Some groups (i.e. Jewish, Greek) despite low socio-economic status have a traditionally high valuation of learning and characteristically show few reading problems. Indeed the crucial variable is not social class but more closely approximates "relative direction or pace of social mobility."

Other personal tendencies that are favored include concern with "what it is and how to use it," rather concrete levels of thought. Symbolic and "casual" thinking, both essential to advanced reading and learning, are not favored. In many of these homes the mother works to supplement income or is the only source of income. This absence of the mother and of any interested and stimulating adult usually impoverishes the environment still further and achievement scores go down with it. It should be noted that it is not the absence of stimulation but of *school relevant stimulation* that produces these effects. It is not the working mother per se that is a source of concern, but the mother too ill equipped or harassed or preoccupied to provide proper stimulation in the form of experience and the use of tools. Neither does she guide them directly or indirectly toward productive attitudes and behavior.

When analyzed, the youngsters' lack of readiness has several closely related components: (a) low motivation for school-centered tasks and goals; (b) little exposure to relevant and necessary ideas, experiences and things; (c) low capacity for delay of impulse gratification—in total a rather discouraging picture by the time the disability is "discovered" in the second and third grade.

One of the syndromes that appeared in the research with a middle class population in Prince Georges County superficially presents quite a different picture.

In addition to the demographic work there was a need for more case material and content if true epidemiological insights were to be gained. Therefore we became much more attentive to reading problems referred by schools and other agencies and set up several treatment groups composed of 5–7 boys ages 10 to 12. Parallel to these groups, groups of their parents were set up, in one case mothers only—in the other cases fathers and mothers. The treatment staff operated in teams with one therapist treating the boys' group and the other the parents with each therapist observing the other's sessions through a one-way screen. Later as some youngsters improved part of the population was seen in "family group" treatment—an unusual and at that time radical method, but fruitful of family dynamics.

These methods brought to light a good deal of family conflict, more than usually encountered in comparable samples of reading youngsters seen by ourselves and other researchers.

However, there was far more than conflict—there was a surprisingly consistent family structure and relationship in which the mother had in one way or another rejected the role of homemaker. Very frequently she had gone out to work. It is important to observe that it is a psychological rejection of the maternal and often the female role that is crucial, not the act of employment outside of the home. Many women in our society work away from home and continue to be effective wives and mothers.

These mothers seemed to be aggressively in search of status and recognition, not that it was always obtained. Almost inevitably they belittled and despised their more passive or remote husbands. Sometimes they presented a picture of such a father to the children even if he was not this kind of person. One of these women regarded any man with ego-strength, as arrogant. Yet she despised those "without starch" or courage.

These insights into the family relationships of many of our cases led to a series of interesting speculations some of which we were able to support, others that have been supported by Irving Harris in *Emotional Blocks to Learning*.

The significance of this perception of the father is evident when we consider the meaning of the father's role as a model for the young male. In our society perception of the father's "adequacy" emerges as a vote of confidence to the son's masculinity and a model for his productive achievement.

The fathers were men who had failed to meet their own expectations, a failing easy to find in a world characterized by an ever present and accelerating need for success. Sometimes they were jealous and competitive with the son or were so portrayed by the mother.

The mother's direct relationship with the child also affects his desire and willingness to achieve. In some cases, the mothers were ambitious beyond the boys' ability. Both Harris and the NIMH researchers found two different sequelae to this situation. In some cases when pressure encountered resistance from the child, some relaxation of the mother's pressure followed and a fair prognosis ensued. In other cases the youngster's resistance led to increased pressure from the mother and a very poor prognosis. The ambitious mothers could be viewed along another dimension when the child's success or failure is seen by the child to be instrumental in mother's goals—the prognosis is poor. When the child's failure leads to concern over self (mother) rather than over the child's non-achievement—the prognosis is poor. When the mother is able to derive satisfaction and reflected glory from the child's success then likelihood of learning is better. As Harris put it— mothers of non-learners seem to lack the ability to or have not "integrated their ambitiousness into the larger scheme of the family goals." Their needs are personal, not familial or cooperative. The one group of mothers whose children have a better prognosis are simply ambitious—the others are ambitious, narcissistic and competitive with the males.

Thus research at the Study Center and by Harris supports related dynamic bases for non-achievement.

1. To express hostility by thwarting mother or mother substitute.
2. To preserve autonomy and independence. This was also demonstrated by a tendency to select odd and exotic hobbies.
3. To avoid accepting the mother's standard which might lead to being measured and found wanting "the way Dad was." This is usually associated with a low estimate of father.

A summary of interrelated factors affecting the middle class child with reading disability would include:

1. Primarily there is the absence or destruction of a stable model for goal orientation and attainment.
2. Conflict and insecurity in the family resulting in insufficient energy to meet the requirements of school.
3. The absence of real constructive ego-building communication with parents.

Let us pause for a moment and compare Johnny, our boy from the slums, and

Edward, our boy from middle class suburbia. Neither is learning to read and yet here the resemblance stops—or does it? The nature of learning must be considered and here the argument becomes somewhat tenuous. As a working formulation, Weir's concept of "the self incorporation of learning," may be useful. It is a process of personal, though not necessarily conscious, choice making in which the learner, out of his experience and motivations, decides what he is to believe and whether and how he is to use and arrange the materials that are set forth for him. In short the individual learns only what he chooses to learn. He may choose among many configurations offered or he can create new ones—once he has "learned" that this is possible. Thus he is not a passive lump of clay, subject to circumstance—he is a significant part of his own circumstance. A person cannot be made to learn by simply exposing him to stimuli and demanding learning with a periodic report of his success. He will learn only to the degree that he thinks it important, appropriate and meaningful. He may even go through the motions in acquiescence to pressure but effective learning has not taken place. The crucial events take place at the point where decision, unconscious decision, but nonetheless a choice, takes place. If learning is desired it is important that a receptive structure exists. This involves more than motivation. It is the existence in the individual of an ego structure that provides goal direction, a feeling of strength or ability to achieve the goal, and, most significantly, a model of sufficient emotional importance to make the favored goals central to the life of the individual. If we are to develop effective learning patterns in otherwise normal boys, the means must exist to transmit to these boys the models, the strength and the support for successful goal achievement as well as the materials and experiences with which to build. At the core Johnny and Edward are not very different. Both lack the model that will guide the choice and give it force. Both have low energy levels

to devote to school. Both are denied constructive communication with their parents. The only difference between them is that Edward was exposed to reading readiness material early in life and is better prepared for middle class oriented school experience. Nevertheless, when we set about doing something about it through a program, the means will probably have to be different, for the available agents are different and the boys' states of readiness are somewhat different. For both boys we must provide a physical and psychological setting conducive to learning.

The development of reading skills produces and is dependent on development of certain intellectual processes involving such ego operations as abstraction, differentiation, integration, etc. There is a pattern to the development of the higher cognitive processes. It may be described as movement through a number of levels—labeling, relating, conceptualizing, etc. It moves from mass action (diffuse) to more differentiated and integrated processes. The effect of deprivation on intellectual development can parallel the effects of deprivation on physical growth and development.

Margolin, Roman and Harari point out that

the configuration of forces affecting the child of low socioeconomic level is not conducive to learning in a school system with a middle-class orientation. Specifically, the child of low socioeconomic status is handicapped by several factors in his efforts to learn to read:

He is deficient in preschool readiness experience. Attitudinally he is unprepared for school living and learning. His use of oral English is poor, and in view of the subcultural de-emphasis of verbal communication, his interest in language skills is minimal. The books and materials used in the school system are essentially geared to the middle-class child and have little meaning to the child from an underprivileged background.

The processes we have described point to a set of conditions, relationships, pressures and rewards which induce certain characteristics, attitudes, and role expectations in the child from the lowest socio-economic group.

These processes are being explored at the University of Chicago, the New York Medical College, and other research centers. One of these research operations has resulted in the development of a program which may be described as preventive or therapeutic depending on the point of intervention. It is a complex program, yet simple compared to the task of meeting the child's needs later in life.

At the New York Medical College, in the East Harlem area of New York, children aged 3 to 5 are being helped through Day Care Centers, and through a program of cooperation between school system and research staff. Teachers are being trained to provide experiences not available in the child's home. They are trying to bring the mothers of these children into the centers to help with the pre-school program and simultaneously to have them learn about it. Optimal social distance and relationship is sought between teachers and children. Materials and ideas hitherto unavailable are being offered to these young minds and hands and in a carefully predetermined sequence and context designed to maximize the development of school relevant skills. Uncertain of the extent to which classroom teachers can provide adequate stimulation in the primary grades, they are starting earlier. Ages 3–5 are made into exciting adventures in living rather than dull waiting with increasing fear for the advent of a poorly understood school experience for which the child is not prepared intellectually, socially or psychologically. Simultaneously primary grade teachers are being instructed in improved methods for assessing the child's needs and providing help. Such a program is more than school or school mental health; ideally it should involve education, housing, community organization, social agencies and mental health groups.

For some of those children to whom essentially preventive programs arrive too late, a pattern of treatment has emerged which may provide some benefit. Arising from the work with delinquents at the Children's Court in New York City, it is a technique combining some features of group psychotherapy and others of remedial reading in a manner which provides those ego supportive and developmental processes so necessary to the acceptance of the learning experience.

At about the same time Fisher was engaged in studying the relative effectiveness of group psychotherapy, remedial reading, and group therapy *plus* remedial reading. In this research "pure group therapy" resulted in greater improvement than either remedial reading or the combination of the two. Fisher concluded that the remedial-therapeutic procedure was relatively unsuccessful because the negative attitudes toward remedial reading instruction were not dealt with in the treatment program.

Dreikurs suggests:

Corrective measures should not be limited to the area of deficiency, but should be applied to the larger issues and the psychological dynamics underlying this deficiency. The teacher cannot ignore the faulty values of the child, his mistaken self-concepts and erroneous approaches. Efforts to change them should become the essence of remedial teaching. Individual, and particularly group discussions, can successfully influence children in changing their values and concepts.

Redl and Wineman also feel that

there is no way out of the dilemma but the invention of a new design, which offers us opportunities of strategy in a different dimension than either good education or thorough psychiatric treatment seem to grant.

Margolin, Roman and Harari stated:

Our clinical experiences had shown that with emotionally disturbed delinquent children, academic tutoring in reading was essentially unproductive. Likewise, psychotherapy in its 'pure' form often found the disability a rather persistent symptom and one found clinicians recommending remedial work after the child had undergone an intensive therapeutic experience. In view of this it was our conviction that we could not consider the reading problem of the delinquent child apart from his total functioning as an individual. Effective treatment, as we saw it, involved a modified psychotherapeutic approach incorporating treatment techniques designed to deal with the child's unproductive attitudes and emotional conflicts, and remedial techniques designed to yield those positive educational experiences leading to a more satisfactory orientation toward reading, school, and other areas of maladjustment.

Toward this end an intensive experimental treatment program was undertaken to explore the effectiveness of a new therapeutic approach, "tutorial group therapy."

Matched groups of "Remedial Reading" and "Group Therapy" and "Tutorial Therapy" groups were set up. The subjects were told that they had been referred to the clinic by the probation officers. In the remedial and tutorial therapy groups the referral was attributed to "reading difficulties," in the "pure therapy" group to "difficulties in the community." In the tutorial therapy group

They were then told . . . that the therapist was not going to teach them to read, but would try to help them discover what could have interfered with their ability to learn to read. In essence, while they were encouraged to speak about early school experiences, attitudes toward teachers and toward reading, they were free to discuss any other matter. The therapist also indicated that they were free to make use of the reading material located in the room. The group was told that they could use the meetings as they saw fit—they could "talk" or "read." If the group chose to "talk" the meeting was conducted along formal therapeutic lines. If, on the other hand, they decided to "read," the therapist utilized remedial techniques appropriate to their reading needs. The emphasis, however, was always on the emotional con-

comitants of the reading process. For example, if a child blocked while reading something to the group, he was asked to describe how he felt at that particular moment; to try to recall similar situations in school; and to try to relate past experiences to present performance. On such occasions, the other members of the group were encouraged to relate some of their own experiences and difficulties specific to the reading problem under discussion. Thus, the therapist, while providing remedial assistance, used the reading process as a means of stimulating discussion.

The percentages of group improvement in reading based on group means were 39 percent for the Remedial Group, 26 percent for the Pure Therapy Group, and 74 percent for the Tutorial Therapy Group, a rather significant difference by any standards. Improvement in home adjustment were 71 percent, 71 percent, and 81 percent respectively.

Margolin, Roman and Harari went on to observe:

There are several formulations which appear basic to tutorial group therapy:
1. Therapy is anchored in an area where the delinquent child is aware of, or can be made aware of, his inadequacy and can 'see' the possibility of concrete help.
2. The therapy group is reality-oriented in that it resembles the classroom situation. The members consistently referred to the therapist as teacher, and Tony commented, "It's like school, but better." The therapist, however, is perceived as a different type of teacher in that he is not interested in achievement *per se,* but is more interested in the adolescent as a person. . . .
3. The dual orientation of the group —namely, that they can read or talk—permits easy movement from one task to another and thereby highlights reactions to stress and patterns of resistance. This provides the therapist with the opportunity to maintain therapeutically optimal levels of tension and to utilize resistance constructively. . . .
4. The group develops its own reading material based on the interests and life

experiences of the members. This material is used for both remedial and therapeutic purposes. . . .

5. As identification with the therapist is developed, there is an increasing adoption of his attitudes, values and goals. The peer group, which we have observed to be of fundamental importance in the development of attitudes, facilitates this process through its subtle pressures to conformity.

The development of this treatment technique represents a first step. It has been and can be further refined. In addition, it offers convincing proof of the interrelatedness of emotional and intellectual aspects of the etiology, the treatment and the prevention of the learning-behavior problem syndromes.

From these small beginnings and as the larger problem is perceived, even more imaginative solutions can be anticipated and improved programs derived therefrom.

In the case of reading problems in the middle class family, another major social trend may be involved. We have many indications of the subordination of the paternal role; however, there is also evidence of a resurgence of the position of the father. With this group higher educational levels may increase the potential effectiveness of mental health education, but there is also the potential for greater resistance. These people frequently attend PTA meetings but may not be psychologically available once they are there. At least the child is closer and more available to middle class teacher population.

The experience with youngsters from middle class background in tutorial group therapy suggests that this is a useful method in this setting as well. However, as with the court population, considerable flexibility is required in allowing the youngsters to program their own materials. Collaborative group therapy, in which both the parents and children meet in treatment groups, offers a very promising treatment medium and is further strengthened by close teamwork between the two therapists. Family group treatment is effective in many cases; however, it is difficult to conceive of "making a real dent" in this problem through treatment alone. As with the lower S-E population the development of effective program depends on what we can do in the classroom. . . .

The child's approach to life, his way of perceiving and being perceived, affect and are affected by his early educational experience. In short, a child's learning experience and his experience in learning are inextricably interwoven with his personality development and his mental health. In this context mental health cannot be considered irrelevant to the goals of education. The major burden for all of our school population becomes one of primary prevention, of developing methods of intervention that are a part of and do not interfere with the normal educational process. Through such programs we may avoid or minimize the need for clumsy and sometimes ineffective treatment programs that are costly to society, the family and the child.

References

Dreikurs. "Emotional Predispositions to Reading Difficulties." *N.A.T. News*, II, No. 4 (October 1952), 1–4.

Fisher. *An Investigation of the Effectiveness of Group Therapy for the Remediation of Reading Disabilities.* Doct. Thesis, School of Education New York University, 1953.

Gates. "Failure in Reading and Social Maladjustment." *Journal of the National Education Association*, **25**, 1936, 205–206.

Margolin, Roman and Harari. "Reading Disability in the Delinquent Child." *American Journal of Orthopsychiatry.* **25**, No 1 (January 1955).

Redl and Wineman. *The Aggressive Child,* 2 Vol. Chicago: The Free Press, 1952.

SUMMARY

Of the three different approaches to educating emotionally disturbed children discussed in this chapter, our personal bias of working with children on a self-concept level leads us to prefer the psychoeducational approach. However, experimental evidence supporting any of the approaches either does not exist, or is questionable. As we examine more specific teaching methods and diagnostic techniques, we are impressed by the many new, though fundamental, ideas they offer this field of teaching. As each of these concepts and methods is studied more completely in many different educational settings under controlled conditions, we predict that patterns of instruction will emerge based on firm empirical foundations.

7

How Do We Measure
Improvement and Interpret
Failure?

As a group, teachers are a living example of academic success. They have graduated from accredited colleges, selected realistic vocations, and are contributing to the welfare of the community. Psychologically, success strengthens the ego in many ways by providing it with feelings of pride, responsibility, accomplishment, and self-assurance. The feeling of success is comforting; it encourages a person to try new activities and to look into new relationships that were once too frightening to explore.

The opposite of success, failure, causes feelings of anger, embarrassment, and inadequacy. Many teachers, as children, never experienced the feeling of failure that comes from receiving a flunking grade; however, many of them learned to fear failure. Often, parental standards of achievement were so high that an "A" grade in a course was expected, a "B" grade was tolerated, and a "C" grade was totally unacceptable. For these children, achievement was motivated not by an inner desire to explore and explain the expanding world around them, but by the dread of failure. Since the fear of failure was effective for them, we can understand why some teachers use the threat of failure as their most powerful and natural method of motivating under-achieving children. While this technique may be appropriate for some children, the threat of failure throws emotionally disturbed children into a state of panic, or else triggers counteraggressive feelings and activities.

We are not implying that children should never receive a failing or unsatisfactory grade. We are implying only that the use of failure as a motivating technique is unsuccessful and usually creates many secondary problems for emotionally disturbed children.

Teachers in special education face another hazard in the unrealistic expectations voiced by uninformed people—those who believe that smaller classes are the total answer and will provide teachers with the necessary time to remedy all of a child's educational and behavioral problems. The following comments, often heard by special teachers, are typical: "Doesn't it make you feel wonderful knowing that you are helping these children improve and return to the community?" "Is it true you have only ten children in your class and all of them are average or above average intelligence?" "How long will it take you before these children can return to a regular class?"

It is extremely difficult to convince these people that disturbed children have a low frustration level, that regression is frequent, and improvement is not only hard to see and judge but also slow in coming; that, furthermore, a certain number of children will continue to fail regardless of our efforts; and that the improvement of some other children can in no way be attributed to the educational process directly. In other words, teaching emotionally disturbed children is challenging, but not so exciting nor so gratifying as others picture it. Teaching these children is complex, frustrating work, in which the teacher must be willing to give of himself emotionally, knowing his children will seldom return any continued warmth. For when a child does, it is an indication that he is ready to leave the setting and enter into new educational relationships.

Four articles have been selected to demonstrate the various considerations in measuring improvement—or accepting failure. First, Nandeen Miller describes her unsuccessful attempts to teach an emotionally disturbed girl to read. After three years of intensive tutoring, plus one year of psychiatric treatment, this girl showed little or no improvement. An experienced, capable teacher, Miller explains how one can learn from failure as well as from success. She describes her feelings of frustration when her pupil was unable to retain material and how the cycle of failure continued until the girl's parents stopped the tutoring sessions.

Learning Difficulties in a Brain-Injured Child
Nandeen Miller

This paper reports a teaching-learning experience with a child who failed to learn to read. The hope is that newcomers in the field of remedial reading may be more realistic if they appreciate the fact that experienced teachers face failure in some of their cases. We may learn as much from failure as from success.

It is important to establish a criterion for interpretation of the phrase "learn to read." In this study success or failure to learn to read connotes the acquisition and integration of skills adequate for obtaining meaning from the printed page. Such skills should be acquired within a period of time reasonably comparable to that of the customary grade level as we know it in the public schools. For example, a child might through remediation overcome a retardation of two or three years during the intermediate school period. However, if a child's

skills are at primary level when. he is chronologically ready for high school, and if this inadequacy has persisted through a period of remedial instruction, this constitutes failure to learn to read. For such a child, learning to read has been so long delayed that the use of reading as a tool for gaining information is very unlikely.

The study covers a period of five years, including: three years of individual reading therapy, one year of psychiatric treatment, one year of observation in public school without individual attention, and a recall period of three months for individual instruction and observation during the fifth year. During this entire period the child lived in her own home and attended public school. Except for repetition of third grade she was "socially" promoted each year.

DESCRIPTION

Jane was admitted to the educational clinic for remedial instruction at age eight years. She was the youngest of five siblings in a privileged home with cultural advantages providing an adequate background

From Nandeen Miller, "Learning Difficulties Confronted in Teaching an Emotionally Disturbed, Brain-Injured Child," with revisions by the author, from *The Reading Teacher*, March 1963.

Nandeen Miller is Reading Supervisor, Children's Psychiatric Hospital, Ann Arbor, Mich.

for school success. She had acquired a fund of information on many subjects through travel, living on a farm, and from her older siblings. Her appearance to the casual observer was normal. She was friendly and cheerful, and usually cooperative during testings and instructional effort. Her parents must have seen her as within normal range for they did not become anxious about her until she failed to learn in school.

This failure was then explained to Jane as being the (possible) result of an early illness, accompanied by high fever. To this explanation Jane added her own: "I was sick once, and I think I damaged my reading thing."

Psychological tests given at age eight indicated intelligence in the low average range, with marked discrepancy between the verbal and performance areas. She obtained a verbal score of 74 and a performance score of 90, with an overall Intelligence Quotient of 80. Both attention span and concentration seemed impaired. Drawings showed emotional immaturity and perceptual distortion. Organic impairment seemed a possibility since there appeared to be a diffuse and general involvement in the integration of all areas of communication. Behavioral symptoms which might support the suggestion of brain injury were: physical awkwardness, disorganized and impulsive behavior, drooling, and poor directional orientation. Symptoms indicative of some emotional disturbance were present throughout the study such as: inappropriate hitting out, clinging, make-believe allergies characterized by sneezing and coughing. Later, in the reading situation, blocking in word recall was accompanied by involuntary tongue and throat movements.

On the surface level Jane appeared cheerful and showed little concern about her inappropriate behavior and learning difficulty. In general, her behavior was that of an emotionally immature child, who was very dependent upon and over-protected by her mother. Jane was pampered by her family to the point that she had never been required to perform any duties in her home. Jane demanded that her mother lie down beside her every night until she went to sleep. This continued until age nine when the reading therapist pointed out to the mother that such manipulation in family relationships was the antithesis of helping Jane separate from mother and grow up.

THE READING PROGRAM

The program began with an exploratory period of several weeks to evaluate instructional needs. Since reading readiness skills had not been mastered, the program began at this level. Two goals were set for the first year of instruction: to support behavioral control, especially in the area of attention span and impulse control; and to improve discriminatory skills which would be a basis for reading.

Activities were planned for the development of visual perception, auditory perception and motor proficiency. Those pertaining to visual perception include: detection of similarities and differences, matching games, drill in memory recall through numerous activities specific to the child's own interests and spontaneous demands. Auditory perception improved with the use of singing and listening games, music records suitable for dramatization, clapping or marching. Coordination and motor proficiency were not greatly improved, though such techniques as the use of scissors, making and remaking puzzles, tracing dot pictures, sewing cards and playing jacks—all aimed toward the goals of readiness.

Symbol imagery was presented in conjunction with phonetic sounds. Jane had learned to sing the alphabet at home, but was unable to discriminate between the letters. A tracing block was made for kinesthetic re-inforcement of visual perception. This block was particularly effective for letters b and d, h and n. Matching pictures with beginning letter sounds was done in a variety of activities which later proved successful.

COGNITIVE AND PERCEPTUAL PROBLEMS

Cognitive problems were confronted immediately upon attempts to read from the printed page. Though well grounded in beginning consonant sounds by this time, and skilled in reading readiness activities, Jane was unable to retain words, and her concepts were not adequate to take advantage of context clues. By using the process of word calling, several primers were read, but this resulted in no measurable achievement.

The pressure of extensive remedial work built up tension in Jane which resulted in regression in other areas. Symptoms such as sulking, manipulation, drooling and "allergies" became more intense and frequent.

As Jane became older, what had first appeared to be minor discrepancies in speech began to look more like disorders in language, cognitive integration, and visual perception. Examples of some specific responses are interesting. These were recorded during the third year of remedial instruction.

1. After a demonstration that the letter *W* is really double-U, she replied, "Yes, I know, S has two U's in it, too."
2. When reading, "The flag is red, white, and blue," she read, "The flag is red, ——." Question: What color is the flag? Answer: Red, white, and blue. Question: Then what is the word after red? Answer: That's what I don't know!
3. When drawing the picture of a farmer, she began with the feet, proceeding upward toward the head. When the picture was finished, she exclaimed, "Oh, I forgot the fork-pitch."

These examples indicate certain learning and perceptual problems such as:

1. Inability to associate the symbol representation to her own oral response.
2. Inability to carry thought; visual perceptual errors distort reception of thought from printed words.
3. Inability to apply phonetic skills when reading. This skill was functional on vocabulary tests; however, when reading continuous context this skill was not applied.
4. Inability to transfer learning. She had ample knowledge and experience for reading but did not bring this to the printed page.
5. Inability to associate ideas, resulting in inability to benefit from any kind of context clues.

THREE-YEAR EVALUATION

At the end of three years of remedial instruction, neurological, psychological and educational examinations were repeated. An electro-encephalogram was added at this time. The diagnostic findings were inconclusive: some indications of irregularities similar to brain injury, with some emotional disturbance. Psychiatric treatment was prescribed at this time, and remedial instruction was discontinued to await results of treatment.

Because of parental indifference the treatment was terminated in about a year. The psychiatrist's report indicated that this termination was premature, and little progress was made that would relate to the reading problems.

FINAL STAGE

Jane continued in public school during the year of psychotherapy, and continued another year without remediation or therapy. She was able to participate and gain information in the social and physical sciences through oral presentations in the classroom. She was recalled to the reading clinic at the age of thirteen, for further reading therapy. At this time she showed no overt symptoms of anxiety about her learning problems, but appeared eager to learn. Her attention span was adequate and responses to the tutor and to reading activities were positive.

The tutor began by using the experience story technique and later added the

Fernald Method. These techniques were decided upon since they would make her reading attempts more meaningful. Jane conversed easily and was always glad to tell of her experiences. A vacation trip with her parents to California furnished ample material for the study technique.

Though she related her experiences clearly, her disorientation in time was evident in her confusion about the order of events. Her speaking vocabulary was adequate to tell of thrilling experiences in Disneyland, but connecting words and verbs were not available for a fluent narrative. However, the total vocabulary from her stories was on a much higher level than she could be expected to read.

Stories were printed on newsprint in large letters. Each word was also printed on a card for flash card use. Study of this vocabulary was carried on in several ways:

Match the word with the same word in the newsprint story.
Sound it out phonetically, if possible.
Print it.
Type it.

Matching the word in the story did not increase recall. Phonetic blending was often productive, but all words were not adaptable to this method. Typing seemed to be most helpful. On one occasion after trying a very long time to recall a word, she turned to the typewriter and recalled it when she had typed the last letter. This suggested that a kinesthetic technique was of value to her which reinforced the use of the Fernald Method. Jane however, continued to "read" with hesitation and with word-by-word monotonous delivery. Even in "reading" her own ideas, she often blocked, and could not use context clues. During these times she showed evidence of extreme effort with false movements of the lips, throat and tongue, and drooling. Even when words from one story were used in another, concepts were not adequate to suggest clues for recall.

Results obtained by use of the Fernald technique were similar to those of the story method. Jane chose to trace and learn to read the Gettysburg Address which her classmates were studying.

The results once again were very disappointing. The reading substitution errors were very unusual and different from those often found such as: *was* for *saw*, *went* for *want*. Jane made these common errors too, but produced other bizarre combinations of substitutions and reversals:

Word	*Substitution*
animals	summer
went	there
tropical	through
real	very
flew	four, hours

Analysis of a few of these errors is attempted in the light of what we know of the learning process.

Summer is substituted for *animals*. We see here a directional confusion as well as vertical and lateral reversals. The final consonant of one word becomes the initial consonant of the other. The letters *n* and *u* are vertically reversed.

Real and *very* indicate inaccurate visual response, the letter *r* furnishing the stimulus. Reversal of the two letters *re* and *er* follows the previous pattern.

Through and *tropical* seem to be more logical substitutions, in that word contour calls for a similar visual response and beginning consonants are the same. Here recall constitutes the major effort, and meaningful concepts are absent.

SUMMARY

We have observed that Jane was able to learn a limited vocabulary by rote, but used words only in parrot fashion, without concepts necessary for functional reading. This vocabulary could not be retained, for no associations came to her aid for this purpose. Her errors were similar to those made by mildly retarded readers, but they increased in number and complexity. Errors tended to become so numerous and persistent that reading became impossible, and only word finding and word calling resulted, at best. Frustration in these two attempts contributed to the cycle of failure.

There was absent in this child the ability to integrate or synthesize segregated skills which result in "reading." There was a gap between phonetic skills, mimicry, word naming—and the intellectual process of taking intended meaning from the printed page.

Returning to our initial concept of "learning to read" we must conclude that Jane failed to learn, even under favorable educational circumstances, and in spite of investment of abnormal amounts of time and effort in a remedial program. It seems pertinent to point out this fact in order to refute a general impression that failure need not occur under favorable climate. The "gap" must be filled by the learner.

From Miller's experience one could hypothesize that somewhere during her treatment, Jane decided to give up and accept failure. In the next article, Bettelheim discusses the complexity of failure and describes how the decision to fail is sometimes more difficult to attain than the decision to succeed. Bettelheim says that certain children seem to develop learning problems as a way of being consistent in their own way of life. Their incompetence becomes the positive force that leads them to the "successful" solution of failure. Under this category he includes five types: (1) the child who wishes not to make his parents feel inferior by exceeding them academically even though his parents encourage him to learn; (2) the child who identifies with a negative parent-attitude toward school out of a sense of loyalty; (3) the child who feels that competition is wrong and refuses to compete; (4) the child who wishes not to be separated from his mother because it would mean giving up infantile pleasures and finding appropriate substitutes; (5) the child who believes that the only way to obtain status is to be different from his peers, because he discovers that a huge failure attracts more attention than a minor achievement. The last one initially wins admiration and acceptance from his peers as the class clown, but his feeling of acceptance is short-lived. By the time the class enters high school the reaction has changed from admiration to pity, and finally to detestation.

The sources of nonlearning also include such classifications as inappropriate curriculum, unrealistic teacher behavior, physical and emotional exhaustion, and an unconscious wish by the child to defy and punish his parents. Bettelheim illustrates that this last reaction is more common among middle-class subservient children who are unable to express their aggressive feelings toward their parents. In such cases learning also symbolizes an internal conflict that is too threatening and too painful for the child to tolerate at this stage of development. For example, inability to read may serve as a defense against learning about forbidden sexual secrets which the child fears. Bettelheim's article has stirred up considerable debate, particularly over the reasons he believes underlie the decision to fail.

The Decision to Fail

Bruno Bettelheim

. . . A child's determination not to learn can often spring from wishes as positive, and at least as strong (though different), as those that motivate the good learner. Both learner and non-learner, often with equally strong desires, seek the same goal: success. Only what constitutes success in their eyes may lie at opposite ends of the continuum stretching from total failure to unusual achievement.

Sometimes this determination grows out of the parents' attitudes or social position. The child does not wish to do better than his parents because he does not want to make them seem inferior. Typical for this source of learning difficulties is the wish of most children to look up to their parents. Out of the need to rely on them, they anxiously protect the image of their parents as the best of all parents. Because our dominant creed is that every new generation will do better than the last, it often overshadows the fact that many children have reason to wish the opposite. This emotional block to learning has a very strong, positive motivation.

It is not as simple as if these parents might resent superiority in their children. On the contrary, most of them tell the child he must acquire a better education than they themselves were able to. Nevertheless the parent who, with the very best of intentions, tries to encourage his child in this way may still make him feel guilty about his better opportunities. In order to avoid feeling guilty, he may quit learning at exactly the point where the education of one of his parents stopped. I have observed dropouts, or the sudden appearance of severe learning blocks, in many high-school and college students, terminating a young person's education at exactly the

point where that of a parent once ended.

A teacher does not need to express openly critical attitudes about the child's parents or their way of life to make him feel he must side with his parents against teacher and school. Sometimes the teacher, wishing the child to achieve middle-class standards, asks him to adopt principles of behavior that are above those of one or both of his parents. Such a child may, unbeknown to parent and teacher, express his deep loyalty to the parent by rejecting all that school (and with it, learning) stand for, because it seems to belittle his parents or their way of life or both.

Often severe blocks to learning are due to efforts at taking one parent's side against the other or a parent's side against the school. This happens, typically, when two parents have differing levels of education and one disparages the other. But here, as when the child protects both parents against the school, the block can be readily overcome once the underlying cause is recognized. What is needed is for both parents, or parents and school, to truly agree about what is desirable, and to make this clear to the child.

Two further steps are usually necessary to erase these learning inhibitions. First, we must show our appreciation of the child's wish to protect the pride of one or both parents by not doing better than they were able to; and, second, we must convince him that he can do much more for his parents, and at the same time for himself, by satisfying their justified wish to be proud of his achievements.

The wish, by not learning, to protect a parent's pride or the validity of the parents' living conditions, does not begin to cover the variety of positive reasons for unconscious, though deliberate, failures in class. Realizing that these failures are due to laudable motives is the most important step in removing them. For this reason,

Abridged from Bruno Bettelheim, "The Decision to Fail," *The School Review*, LXIX, No. 4 (1961), 389–412. Copyright © 1961 by The University of Chicago. Reprinted by permission.

and also because adults do not usually see anything positive in a child's determination not to learn, I should like to add a few more illustrations.

Some children are poor learners because they do not wish to compete, feeling that competition is wrong. Such thoughts in a school child are easy to understand if we consider how often they have been admonished not to take advantage of a brother or sister, to let others take a turn first, to be considerate of others' feelings, and so on. Other children feel so guilty or worthless that they do not dare to add to their faults by getting ahead of children they think are much worthier. In order to protect the other child (a positive desire) and not to add to their guilt, they stop learning so that others will more readily succeed. While the particular reasons may vary, the feeling that a child has no "right" to succeed is by no means rare.

Probably the commonest positive reason for not achieving academically is the wish to retain closeness to the beloved mother. To learn means to grow up. Therefore many children see it as giving up the mother, or certainly mothering, and this they are unwilling to do.

Equally positive, as an underlying motive for failure, is the desire we all have to be special, different, unique. If the need for status and self-respect is accepted as a positive motivation, then we must count the wish to be first among the lowly, rather than second among the best, with the group of learning inhibitions based on positive wishes.

The good learner who believes he can go to the top of the class is spurred by this conviction to work harder. As long as a child can believe that if he tries he will do well, he usually applies himself to gain status and self-respect. Even if his best efforts land him only in the mediocre group, he may still settle for that, as many children do, but only if he can be satisfied with being one of the gang.

If this moderate station is not enough for his self-respect, if he cannot give up the need to be special, or is frustrated in wanting to be one of the gang because the others reject him, then the wish to be unique is reinforced powerfully. He may then arrive at the conviction that he can gain status only by being the worst. In this way he attracts attention to himself; true, in a negative way, but attention nevertheless.

The learner who does poorly, on the other hand, is convinced he can never make the grade. He is impelled to stop learning by his wish to maintain his self-respect. Believing that he will fail even if he makes his best efforts, he protects himself by deciding not to learn. Then he will be able to tell himself that his failure is not due to inability, but to a deliberate act of will. Hence it is not rare for such a child to feel he can gain more status or self-respect through not learning than through diligent application.

When we wish to help such children, we must begin by realizing that almost never can a child recognize on his own that he chose failure because he was afraid he could never do best, or average, or was unacceptable to the gang. He may be only a little readier to accept the idea that he chose to be a huge failure rather than risk being a small failure or an insignificant success. The reason is that any such acknowledgment would destroy his chance of achieving self-respect through not learning. Instead, a child in such a predicament usually tells himself and others that he could do very well, could be tops if he wished. Only with such claims can he gain the attention accorded those who are genuinely different and still tell himself that his uniqueness is not a matter of inability, about which he thinks he can do nothing, but the result of a freely made decision. Only in this way can he protect the image of himself as an adequate person, the image he sought by defying schoolwork in the first place.

A child's need to protect his self-respect in this way is among the most dangerous blocks to learning. Once he has fallen into such a pattern, he honestly believes that his greatest desire is not to be special but to defy school and adults by deliberately not learning.

For other reasons, too, this is an insidious process. Because the further he falls behind, the more his pretense of adequacy is threatened and the more drastic the steps he must take to protect it. That is why a fourth-grader can be satisfied that he is a big shot when he defies the teacher by not learning, while the seventh-grader must, in addition, defy police and society by delinquent acts. The fourth-grader who acts "dumb" is the easily admired clown. A few years later the same behavior makes him look stupid, and instead of being admired he is despised. By then it is usually too late to regain status by academic success, so the child tries to get it by delinquency.

When a child fails for such reasons, it is of little avail to encourage him to try harder so that he can string along within the middle group, because the decision not to learn was made to quiet the fear that his work would never get him much higher than that group of low achievers. A much better approach is to boost the child's self-esteem, since the lack of it drove him to find it by defiance. This can be done, for example, by showing him how ingenious he was in protecting himself and by giving him credit for his determination, without agreeing that its goals are desirable. Only much later, after he is convinced that we recognize his competence, can he be helped to see that he behaved like the fox with the sour grapes. At the same time we must help him to truly achieve in academic skills. Through many such efforts on our part he may eventually recognize that defiance of learning is not the only way to gain personal distinction.

To summarize, we must never forget that many learning inhibitions can come from a child's desire for inner honesty and truth, and from his trying to succeed in terms of his own life experience and of clear-cut desires and values.

As a matter of fact, given similar natural endowment, and with the whole pressure of school, parents, educational system, and society at large favoring success in learning, it often takes a great deal more determination on the part of the non-learner to fail than for the good learner to do well in school. This is so because all the breaks, all the encouragement and rewards, are in favor of the learner. If, despite this powerful system of rewards, a child fails, then we must assume that his motives for not learning, as likely as not, are stronger than are those of the child who is successful in class.

After devoting so much space to those learning inhibitions that have positive motives, I come now to those caused by negativism. Some children may be set against the school, not because they wish to protect a parent's pride or be loyal to his way of life, but simply because they do not wish to acquire a different set of values.

Others do not learn because learning was not made attractive enough or because the teacher has hurt their feelings and they want to hurt hers in retaliation. A child may also be so tired, physically or emotionally, that to exert himself intellectually seems expecting too much of him, and he will not even do the little he could. All this is so well known that I mention it here only in passing.

Behind other learning inhibitions may lie the wish or the need to defy adults, to punish a parent, or to do both at the same time. A child often opposes his parent with "my teacher said so." This tempts us to overlook the fact that quite often the same child cannot accept what the freely quoted teacher says or stands for. Because he needs to defy authority and cannot do it without adult support, he claims the teacher's backing when he speaks up against his parent. The wise parent will not object, because to be able to use the teacher against the parent makes the teacher, school, and learning very attractive to the child. But if a child cannot so use the teacher to achieve some independence from his parents, he will have to defy the teacher instead, to gain independence from at least some adult.

Some children are quite overwhelmed at home, less frequently today by being pushed around or beaten down and more often by being nagged to desperation or driven to achieve beyond their ability. Their need to defy is so great that they will defy adult authority whenever they see a chance to do so without fatal hazards. Because our teachers are much more lenient than their nagging or driving parents, the child who does not dare to oppose an overpowering parent, defies the teacher instead by not learning. This is usually reinforced by a secondary gain; by not learning he can effectively punish the parents to whom he is otherwise subservient. Not learning in class has become the commonest whip that the middle-class child can hold over a parent whose pride is deeply hurt by the child's academic failure.

Similarly, intellectual superiority was, and sometimes still is, the whip that many a lower-class child, or the child of new immigrants, holds over his parents. Since this is an emotional motive for higher achievement, and often a powerful one, it does not concern us here. But as a negative motivation for academic success, it may round out our discussion of the negative motivations for academic failure.

So far I have spoken of learning inhibitions that extend, more or less, over the totality: school. Equally frequent are emotional blocks to learning that spring from the avoidance of a specific learning task or a specific subject matter, for a particular reason.

Contrary to widespread belief, a child with intelligence that is average or better will more often have trouble because he understands the content of a subject matter all too well than because he is inattentive or finds the task beyond his mental capacity. Mere inability to comprehend what is taught may lead to indifference to a subject matter. It is only if we do understand what the subject matter is about, but resist it out

of moral scruples or because it scares us, that we actively reject it. Then a child cannot understand because he does not wish to understand.

Usually he has one of two reasons. Either the essential principles underlying a learning task would throw him into inner turmoil when applied to himself, or the particular content reminds him of experiences much too painful or threatening to think about. To ward off such pain, he convinces himself as well as others that he cannot understand how to apply what he dreads to apply to a personal problem; that he cannot grasp what (if he did grasp it) would remind him of an unbearably unpleasant experience.

Children whose own history is forbidden territory, or who cannot make sense of it, or only painfully so, protect themselves from finding any meaning in their personal history. One solution is to be totally uninterested in all history. Or else they deny there is any sense to the historical sequence of events. To insist that they should understand and accept as meaningful any sequence of events in the history of men or of nations means acquiring perceptions that would cause unmanageable anxiety if applied to themselves. They may therefore prefer not to understand the meaning of history. Otherwise they might have to realize, for example, that certain bad experiences of their past or present which, for emotional reasons, they wish to chalk up as random chance, really sprang out of basic and permanent attitudes in themselves or their parents.

That one's deep suffering was and is due to chance one can accept and still continue to live and to strive. Eventually the wheel of fortune turns, and what was due to bad luck may suddenly change for the better. But if we must accept our misfortunes as the result of consistent and irreversible attitudes, or the design of our parents, we can no longer hold on to the hope that things will change for the better very soon or at some time in the future.

Because the study of history normally

means learning to make sense of a sequence of events, it is an enriching experience; merely recognizing this fact makes learning history possible and rewarding. (This is not true, of course, if for one reason or another a child cannot study the subject without direct application to himself.) But if the cost of this advantage is having to realize that one's own life is devoid of inner meaning, then the pain of the realization seems too high a price to pay. Thus in the case of history it is not an inability to comprehend, but rather a true understanding of its essence, that may block a student from learning.

To illustrate, though with a different subject matter, one adopted girl had severe difficulties at home though she maintained herself fairly adequately in her classes until high school, where she had to take a general science course. In this class she created continual disturbances and was in such severe conflict with her science teacher that most of the time she was sent from the room and spent her time in the office of the dean of students. The criticism at home and at school was so severe that within a few months her difficulties extended to other subjects as well. What had started as a resistance to attending only the science class became a head-on clash with all of school.

The reason this girl had to protect herself from attending the science class was that general biology and heredity were part of the subject matter. She did not want to learn about the beginning of life, since it reminded her too painfully of how badly her own had begun: her real mother had given her up, and her adoptive parents had no use for her. Up to then she had maintained herself by making herself believe that these were her true parents, despite their rejection. Now, even the teacher became her enemy, since she expected the child to remember how life really begins, which only increased her violent anger against her home. To this was added the reminder that the beginning of her life had

been so different from that of her schoolmates; and with the study of heredity came the realization that she did not even share a common heredity with her adoptive parents. Since she was too intelligent not to understand what all this meant to her personally, her only way out was to misbehave. Then she would be sent from the class and not have to hear about matters that only created a dangerous rage in her. Had all this been recognized in time, the rejection of one subject matter might not have extended to the rejection of school in general.

In this example, all of school learning became unacceptable because of a single subject matter. But it happened rather late in the girl's educational career. Things are even more serious when this occurs early and around such basic subject matter as reading or arithmetic.

For example, one boy committed a crime at an early age, probably not quite knowing what he did. His parents impressed him with how severely he would have been punished had he not been an ignorant child. Realizing his inner destructive wishes, the only protection he knew of was not learning to read. If he could read (he thought), he could no longer claim ignorance of the law. But the pretended inability to read soon extended to all learning.

When we taught him that ignorance is no excuse before the law, he was able to recognize the protection and advantages of reading: if he could read, he could find out which actions are punishable and which are not.

It is well known that many children develop learning inhibitions because of the parental command not to know. Sometimes a child extends a parent's order not to explore his own body or what goes on in the parental bedroom, to mean that all curiosity is wrong. But without curiosity one cannot learn. Teachers can get a child to repeat what he is told, but without the child's own spontaneous wish to know, it is not learning but parroting. And a child can remain fixated at this level if he thinks it is bad to be curious or to wish to learn secrets.

Other children develop the notion that, while it is all right to look, they are not supposed to understand the meaning of what they see. This happens typically when a child observes his parents behaving in a way they either disapprove of (as in marital discord) or where they do not wish the child to understand their actions or motives. If such experiences are repeated, the child may get the idea that while his parents do not object to his observing details correctly, they severely disapprove his understanding what it all means. Such children may learn to recognize letters and words but, in obedience to what they consider a parental command, remain unable to understand sentences or the meaning of paragraphs. But reading without understanding is frustrating, not rewarding; if they are further criticized by their teachers for not understanding sentence meaning, they may give up learning altogether.

Nor is it always the parents who inhibit the child's ability to see and comprehend. The child himself may do so for what he considers valid reasons. One child claimed he could not see the words in his book clearly, and his behavior was such that there was reason to believe his vision was actually defective. Seeing the letters only vaguely, he could not read.

Eventually this boy was able to remember the first time his vision suddenly blurred; it was when he first saw his mother attending to his newborn brother. Seeing another child getting the attention he wanted was more than he could stand. So to blot out the experience, he became unable to see what went on.

The wish not to see what is painful to see is a relatively simple defense. Sometimes a more complex mechanism is at work, such as the one called *undoing*. An obvious and well-known form of undoing is what is technically called a *washing compulsion*. Lady Macbeth, deeply perturbed by the blood that once stained her hands,

continued to clean them with such intensity that little time or energy was left for anything else in her life.

The need to undo, to reverse a too painful situation, may also find expression in reversal. This is an exchanging of letters in reading which can so distort the meaning that no progress in learning takes place. Often the deeper purpose of such behavior can be overlooked or explained away by pointing to the similarity in the appearance of the letters. But such simple explanations may only deprive the child of the help he needs, which alone will clear up his learning problem.

Other reversals may affect not letters, but words. One child who witnessed a terrifying scene early in life was so preoccupied with what he had seen that everything else that had happened in the past reminded him only of what he once saw. Thus he read the word *was* as *saw*.

Another child wished so intensely to be a boy that for time periods she delusionally believed she was one. She also resented her brothers' luck in belonging to the envied sex. So she went about correcting it. Whenever she encountered the words *boy* or *man* in her reading, she read *girl* and *lady*; if the printed page read *girl* or *woman*, she read it *boy* or *man*. Similarly, she read all *he's* for *she's* and the other way around.

While some reversals can be traced back to specific events, wishes, or anxieties, sometimes any reversal will do, if the child wishes to undo, or reverse, not a specific event, but the totality of his life situation. The shattering event in one boy's life was his mother's sudden desertion. Without any warning she took off with her lover and was never heard from again. The wish to undo this event was so overwhelmingly important to this boy that he reversed letters in every word he tried to read.

All learning is based on the manipulation of symbols and concerns itself with abstractions. Learning is a process of intellectualization, a process in which thought is freed of its personal emotional content and achieves a higher "objective" meaning for the symbols used in verbal or thought exchange. To the infant, the peculiar smell of his baby blanket, its color, texture, the strange way it was worn down by him, make it unique, entirely different from all other blankets produced in the same factory. His chair is unique to the infant, although it is identical with all other chairs in the dining room. The family's kitchen table is entirely different from all other tables that look like it and serve the same purpose.

As long as the child has not acquired sufficient identity in himself, he is interested only in the unique, not the general, aspects of objects. Not any blanket, but only his blanket, can give him security, though all blankets may make him feel warm. As long as he cannot afford to be covered by any other than his own blanket, he is not yet able to abstract from the unique meaning objects have for him, and he is not really ready to learn to deal with general, abstract concepts and their symbolic representations, such as words and numbers.

Some psychologists differentiate, therefore, between a perception of the world that is autocentric and one that is allocentric: "In the autocentric mode there is little or no objectification; the emphasis is on how and what the person feels; there is a close relation, amounting to fusion, between sensory quality and pleasure or unpleasure feelings, and the perceiver reacts primarily to something impinging on him. In the allocentric mode there is objectification; the emphasis is on what the object is like; there is either no relation or a less pronounced or less direct relation between perceived sensory qualities and pleasure-unpleasure feelings." When for the child "my blanket" changes into "the blanket I used to need to be able to fall asleep," he has made (in respect to blankets) the crucial step from an autocentric to an allocentric perception of the world.

Many steps are necessary in this development. Another important one is acquiring the conviction that objects remain the same; because if they did not, no generalization would be possible about them. (Thus the central problem of early Greek philosophy: how can we have secure knowledge about an ever changing world?) That is why the small child wishes to hear the same story over and over again, engages in the same game over and over again. Or as Schachtel puts it: "A change in the story is about as upsetting to the child as it might be to an adult to discover that overnight the table in the living room had changed its shape. The idea that one can make a story, hence also change it, dawns much later on the child than the earlier implicit conviction that a story is a piece of reality on which we can rely, so that any change interferes drastically with the important task of getting thoroughly acquainted with this particular piece of reality."

Or to put it differently: the story must first be recognized as a piece of reality and hence remain unchanging. Only then can it be comprehended as a symbol that merely represents a reality and hence is changeable, since at different times it represents different aspects of reality. For the greater part of man's history, and in nonliterate societies, the same stories were repeated over and over again. In this way one did not "tell a story"; it remained a significant part of reality, as the Scriptures were when read over and over without variation.

Learning to manipulate abstract symbols such as printed words or numbers thus presupposes at least a three-step development. First, the object has only a unique meaning, is little else but part and parcel of the perceiving person, receives its meaning only from the meaning it has for this person. Second, the object acquires an independent reality of its own. To do so it has to be perceived as unchanging, always one and the same. And finally, once it is fully grasped, its unchanging and independent existence becomes less important, while its generic qualities acquire ever greater importance. Only then can a symbol represent different examples of the same object.

Obviously, learning in school can take

place only when the mental development of the child has by and large reached this third stage. Our reading readiness tests, for example, measure this when they require the child to connect a unique object as drawn, with its symbolic representation by a printed word.

Unfortunately, the child does not reach this third level all at once. For some experiences he may remain fixated on the first or second level, but for other experiences he may have reached the third level. If this is the case, serious learning difficulties may result when the child is expected to understand and manipulate the symbolic process but is still fixated on one of the two earlier levels. The learning difficulty will be most serious when he has not yet freed himself of the autocentric way of experiencing reality.

Such inability to abstract and go beyond the personal and emotional meaning is behind many reading difficulties, though it need not always interfere with learning to read altogether. Because if everything goes well, the child who learns to read can invest words with his unique meaning and it need not interfere with his ability to read. The dog, the cat, the table, the book about which the child reads in his primer can be the unique dog, cat, table, or book to which he is closely attached. He may insist, and rightly so, that one dog is entirely different from all other dogs; and, if the teacher agrees, she permits him to learn to read and spell *dog* without having to give up the deep personal meaning his dog has for him.

The symbol of the printed word refers to a particular object, such as a home; and, while the letters *h-o-m-e* must stand for all homes, in learning to read the child is not forced to accept this, if he does not wish to. He may think of this or that particular home. He may think that what he learns through reading about a home need not apply to his home. Thus despite the general nature of the printed word, nothing prevents the reader from giving it only a particular meaning in his mind.

Now it should be easy to see how to

some children, one or another word in their readers is emotionally unacceptable. Sometimes a child will spontaneously find his own remedy. The pressure of his emotions will force him, in his reading, to express not the thoughts presented in the book, but those predominant in his mind.

Fortunately such "misreadings"—or one should say correct readings in terms of the child's interests and emotional needs, but incorrect in terms of the printed letters —are usually restricted to one word or a few emotionally loaded words. While bothersome, they need not interfere with the child's learning to read or his over-all academic progress, provided the particular obnoxious words are not too crucial for getting the meaning of what he reads. But in order to remain narrowly circumscribed, it is often necessary that an understanding teacher (or, given the reality of our school situation, probably a careless one) does not focus her criticism on the child's few errors. If too much is made of them, the emotions connected with them may force the child to protect himself from recognizing what bothers him. This he may do by extending his misreadings to many other words, so that nobody, including himself, can guess what lay behind them in the first place.

One such child was the daughter of an albino. The mother's pale blond hair was less of an emotional problem to her daughter than the near blindness. That put the girl under a tremendous burden and also made her afraid she might have inherited her mother's disabilities. Whenever she saw the word *blond* in her reading, she misread it *blind*. These two words meant the same thing to the girl: "my mother's disabilities." For this emotional reason they were identical to her, and she reacted to what she saw as their common essential meaning: "blindness."

In this case the teacher was aware of the mother's condition and ignored the misreading. The result was that it remained restricted to these rather insignificant words, with no other effect on the girl's academic progress. Here, a deliberate and selective inattention to the reading difficulty was the best course of action. But inattentiveness is by no means suggested as the wisest procedure in all cases.

For example, one boy who spent his first years in an institution and was then in many foster homes, consistently read *house* for *home*. Never having known a home, he admitted he had at least lived in houses. When the teacher insisted that he read *home*, he changed his reading from *house* to *hole*. The teacher showed him that she could not view a house as an acceptable substitute for a home, though he had been forced to be satisfied with it. So he retired even further, into a hole, where he buried himself emotionally. For similar reasons he was unable to read or spell *love*, for which he regularly substituted *life*. Never having known love, he tried to comfort himself with the life that still lay ahead of him.

Up to then his difficulties were restricted to a simple substitution for a few offensive words; the new words were relatively appropriate, started with the same letter, and had as many syllables as the rejected word. But his second substitution, of *life* for *love*, was again not accepted by the teacher. Soon he misread all words, not just the few unacceptable ones that started with *h* (*home*), *l* (*love*), *m* (*mother*), and so on. Misreading so many words, he was constantly being corrected and criticized, until eventually he gave up reading altogether. It took years of hard work and deliberate encouragement for him to again substitute words starting with the same letter for unacceptable words, and more years before the boy could again learn to read easily and well.

Another child, a girl with a very low opinion of herself, refused to capitalize her own name or *I*. To do either would have run counter to her inner honesty, because she felt that nothing about her was, or deserved to be, big. Though she felt very competitive toward her classmates, her feelings of worthlessness kept her from openly competing. The only way she knew of not to fall further behind was to keep the others

from progressing. She was most ingenious in pursuing her goal, diverting the children's attention, occupying the teacher's time. Only after she was given ample recognition for her ingenuity was she able to relent, since the recognition reduced her inferiority feelings considerably.

Although most of my examples are from the area of reading and spelling, the same psychological problems may lead to learning inhibitions in any or all subject matter. I have concentrated on reading because it is basic to all other learning experiences. Without the ability to learn arithmetic a child can still progress up to a certain level in class, while without the ability to read, he cannot. Still, it may be of interest to note briefly how arithmetic lends itself better than reading to express certain crippling emotional preoccupations.

I have said that while in reading the symbol of the printed word *home* must stand for all homes, the child may have a particular home in mind and still learn to read. Not so in mathematics. There the very essence is that the printed number symbolizes not unique or vaguely incomparable situations. On the contrary, what holds true for one mathematical operation must hold equally true for all others. If seven minus two leaves five, this is true not only for apples, or any other unique set of objects or events, but equally true for when two people are subtracted from seven so that only five are left.

This may be one of the reasons why numbers have had a magical meaning from the earliest days of mankind. Whatever the reason, we do not have to understand it to understand some of the difficulties of learning arithmetic. Arithmetic is based on the principle that units are like each other, otherwise they could not be added. Children to whom numbers have retained their autocentric meaning—so that *one* stands for the father, *two* for the mother, and *three* for the child—may meet insurmountable difficulties when we ask them to add up to four or five.

One such child was adopted before

the parents had a child of their own. He could readily add up to three but not beyond that, because, as he put it, to count to four was not the same as to count to three. In his life experience it was indeed not the same. The fourth addition to the family entailed an entirely different emotional experience than the condition of Three before a fourth member was added. Contrary to what the teacher wanted him to learn (that four is more than three), he knew he had had much more when there were only three and that four was much less than three. Moreover, four, to him, was not one added to three, but rather that Three (himself) was pushed out by Four, since the arrival of the fourth member meant there was no longer any place for him in the life of his parents.

Or again, a family of five children lost both their parents under very traumatic circumstances. The oldest boy was particularly hard hit by the loss and the changes it entailed in his position within the family. He had a hard time with all arithmetic operations where the number *five* (the number of the children) was involved, with one exception: he had no difficulty in adding two to five, since that seemed to restore the original family constellation. But when asked to subtract two from seven, it threw him into a panic that extended for a considerable time during which he was unable to function at all. He was fascinated by the number *eight* (his age when the deaths occurred) and introduced it in all kinds of anxious contexts. Whenever anything went wrong, he was convinced it was connected with eight. If somebody was late, he was eight minutes late; it would rain in eight minutes, and so on. Any arithmetic operation that involved numbers beyond eight was beyond his ken. All things had stopped for him with eight.

Other children find fractions extremely hard because in their homes it is not true that a pie is divided into six equal parts. In their emotional experience, and often in reality, the six pieces into which pies are divided in their families are never

alike. Therefore they cannot accept as true and correct what the teacher tries to teach: that one sixth is exactly like the other five sixths.

Another child who could not master fractions suffered from the fact that he formed only an insignificant part of the whole family; he could bear neither the thought that a whole could be split, nor the thought that something could be only a fraction. Both ideas ran counter to his all-pervasive wish to be an integral part of a well-integrated whole.

As long as the child is not able to separate certain numbers from the emotional meaning they have for him, he cannot master mathematical processes involving them. The same is true not only for specific numbers but also for entire processes. Therefore many children find subtraction much more difficult than addition. This is so not only because it is the reverse of the process just learned, but also because most children are emotionally more in favor of adding something to their lives, but cannot afford to see anything subtracted from it. For similar reasons multiplication usually presents fewer emotional problems than division.

Conversely, there are children who have less trouble learning the more complicated processes such as division than the simpler process of multiplying. Multiplication involves a fast increase in numbers. But this they may fear more than anything else if they are afraid, for example, of the arrival of new siblings in the same sense that the Scriptures speak of multiplying. For similar reasons some children can learn to subtract but have great difficulties with addition.

One child, for example, had no difficulties with any multiplication tables except the table of fours. There were four in his family, and he feared nothing more than a fast increase in their number. Fast increases in the numbers *three, five,* or *seven* he did not fear and therefore mastered quite easily.

There are, of course, innumerable

ways in which children can express one and the same emotional problem that perturbs them. Sibling rivalry, and the wish to do away with a hated newcomer, can therefore be expressed in a variety of ways. One bright youngster could perform rather difficult mathematical problems in addition, subtraction, multiplication, and division, but only if one allowance was made: the answer was always incorrect by one. She always deducted the one who she felt was one too many in her family: her younger sister.

As if to show that this was not a case of poor learning, she occasionally found another way to do away with one. Sometimes when several rows of problems were given to her, she would solve the top row of problems perfectly well; after all, she was the first to arrive in her family, and her arrival was perfectly correct. But the second row, representing her younger sister, was full of errors; it was all wrong just as the sister's arrival in this world was "all wrong."

Thus the common emotional difficulties that find expression in the failure to learn arithmetic remain those that relate to simple numbers and their relations. Much as the most serious emotional problems originate in the very simple experiences of childhood and only much later grow more intricate, so too, contrary to what one might expect, it is not the advanced and very complex mathematical processes that often stymie the child, but the very simplest steps in addition or subtraction. Trigonometry, or complex algebraic problems or formulas, may present difficulties of an intellectual nature, but they rarely lead to learning inhibitions. The reason is that they are too far removed from the direct and tangible nature of those life experiences that arouse emotions deep enough to block the child's ability to learn them.

It does not come naturally to the child to express the family constellations that upset him in such elusive formulations as algebraic equations. But simple addition or plane geometry can present insurmountable difficulties, as they do, for example, to the child who cannot understand the properties of triangles because he cannot understand the triangular relations within his family. Here it is only rarely the love triangle that is so baffling to the child, though this is sometimes the case. Much more often it is the fact that the two parents and the child form a triangle of such complex emotional relations that the child cannot understand the first thing about its form or inherent characteristics.

The unsolvable emotional problems that a triangle may present to the only child may be expressed by another child through a quadrangle or by his inability to grasp the relation of these two geometric forms to each other. This may be the case if he cannot accept the fact that what was once a family consisting of three elements suddenly changed, to his bewilderment, into a unit consisting of four elements.

At the same time, what may make one subject matter particularly difficult for one child, may, for other reasons, make it very attractive for others. The very abstract nature of mathematics can make it serve opposite emotions. A child who feels desperately unlike the other children in his home may throw himself into arithmetic because it teaches that all numbers are basically equal in their meaning. He may make his own, as if with a vengeance, that one fourth is like all other fourths, just to deny that he, one of the fourths of his family, is treated so differently from the other three fourths.

Thus if one wants to understand what may be emotionally implied in the learning of arithmetic, one has to start with the realization that each child is unique. To some, arithmetic is very difficult because they cannot separate the abstract processes of mathematical reasoning from their emotional involvement with numbers and their manipulation. By the same token mathematics is eminently attractive to those who can use it defensively to separate themselves from all related emotions. Basically both groups are equally unready to study mathematics, though the first may do very poorly, the second very well. Only those who have gained enough distance or control of their emotions not to let them interfere positively or negatively are really ready for the study of mathematics. . . .

A child who is successful in his decision to fail has built an elaborate fortress of defense against standard educational procedures. To re-educate him, the teacher should delay initiating new instructional techniques while focusing on removing some of the barriers that protect him from learning. In other words, before any learning can take place a significant amount of unlearning must occur.

In the next article, Newman describes her experimental work at the Child Research Branch of the National Institute of Mental Health with six hyperaggressive educational misfits. The primary goal of her experiment was to change the children's perception of their environment and the people around them. This was accomplished by accepting a child's infantile needs whenever possible and by replacing deprivation with gratification, hostility with affection, and neglect and exploitation with reliability. It is important to remember that these six boys were extremely disturbed and that the first phase of Newman's re-education process, in which the patients' symptoms were accepted and tolerated, took place within a locked psychiatric ward. After three years, a significant amount of improvement was noticed and measured in the following five categories: (1) the child's self-picture, (2) the child's ability to handle and control his inner drives, fantasies, and fears, (3) the child's ability to deal with his infantile needs and frustration, (4) the child's ability to perceive the adult (teacher) as benevolent, and (5) the child's ability to relate to his peers in a more positive way. Here is a realistic picture of the chronic problems that face a teacher who combines psychodynamic theory with remedial education.

Changes in Learning Patterns of Hyperaggressive Children
Ruth G. Newman

The severely disturbed hyperaggressive child without perceptible brain damage and with adequate intelligence is a challenge to the school, society and the learning theorist. If he can be maintained in school at all, he appears unable to assimilate school subjects, incapable, on the one hand of attending to any task for more than a moment, or, on the other of tearing himself away from a task in which he is engrossed. He cannot share the teacher or the spotlight: he must be the first and get the most. He demands immediate and constant attention. He cannot bear to be wrong or to fail, yet he cannot ask for help or follow directions. No school routines, methods, material or subject matter seem to suit him. No teacher recipes from educational psychology courses designed to make him feel wanted or acceptable work for more than a day. If he is placed in a lower grade or a class with mentally retarded, or physically damaged children, matters deteriorate rather than improve. Wherever he is placed within an ordinary school set-up, he disrupts classes with violent, alarming, unpredictable outbursts. He is without controls and driven to act out any impulse which floods his awareness no matter how inappropriate the circumstances or how disastrous the outcome.

Given such a child, is he capable of

An original article by Ruth G. Newman.

learning at all? If so, under what conditions can he learn and to what extent can he be taught? If not, since there appears to be no physiological detriment and no want of average intellectual capacity, what is the nature of the barriers to learning? How can they be removed?

Under the direction of Dr. Fritz Redl, The Child Research Branch of the National Institute of Mental Health has devoted six years to the study of the hyperaggressive child in order to help answer these questions and many others. Along with a series of short term groups of hyperaggressive boys who have been studied at various times in the history of the project, a long term, residential group of six severely disturbed hyperaggressive boys have been hospitalized for a period of five years. On admission, the boys were eight to ten years old. None of them had perceptible organic damage. All had at least average intelligence and all had been in serious difficulties with school and courts because of their pathological behavior. Though their social, racial and economic backgrounds differed, they had all suffered severe traumatic experiences and deep affectional deprivation. In addition to intensive psychotherapy they were offered a school program especially designed to meet their needs as an intrinsic part of the total therapeutic treatment program.

The school became the laboratory for the research on cognitive and behavioral disturbances affecting the learning process. After three years on a confined ward, the boys moved to a freer, cottage-type residence on the hospital grounds. Here they continued to have individual psychotherapy, group treatment and supplementary educational help, but they were placed in ordinary, though extremely carefully selected public school classes. Here again, their school learning and adjustment processes were studied. This report is based on the data that has been gathered and analyzed on the learning experiences of these boys both while in the specifically designed hospital school and in the community school.

If learning is considered an adaptation to a given environment, a study of the severely disturbed hyperaggressive child's case history soon demonstrates that he is assuredly capable of learning. Regardless of differences in socio-economic background, from infancy and early childhood these children have shared the common experiences of a noxious environment. They are presented with a hostile, precarious world, peopled by unreliable, violent, immature adults, incapable of providing dependable affection or adequate care. Because of the adults' own circumstances or illness, the children are offered a mercurial life pattern in which the child is pushed and pulled in all directions at once, in which he is used according to the needs of the adults to the exclusion of his own needs. He learns only too well to adapt to this unyielding soil and toxic climate. He learns to distrust the untrustworthy; hate the hostile, careless, undependable people he is forced to depend on. He fights off seductive advances as well as threatening gestures having learned to perceive both as exploitative techniques. He learns rage and with it a momentary sense of power that for a second blots out the helpless, inadequate despair. By means of a frantic expression of rage, adults quail and other children flee. In a frenzy of destruction, the paraphernalia of the hated object world is torn down and for a moment the face of things is changed. Since the hyperaggressive lives in the moment and has not yet learned a future, even though it be but a second away, the disastrous consequences of his acts are beyond his knowledge or his caring. He has learned that words are unsatisfactory as a means of conveying the turmoil and despair he feels. Moreover, from past experiences with adults, he has learned that words rarely mean what they say. Thus, forsaking verbal communication, save for invective, as a means of conveying feelings, he learns to communicate by living out a charade. He walks about with his basic needs and frantic despair, naked to any eye who will look. In this way, he communicates both the helpless, unlovable, torn-apart mess he feels himself to be and his fury at the world which has not taught him to feel differently and yet expects him to conform to its standards and values. Indeed, his responses show that he is capable of learning: he has already taken an intensive life course in hate and distrust and has graduated with a battery of methods and means to enrage adults and render them as helpless to deal with him as he is to deal with the deprivation he has experienced.

The teaching task, then, becomes the more difficult one of re-education, of unlearning. In order that the hyperaggressive child may learn what society wishes him to learn, he must be taught to forget and then to adapt to a less hostile environment. Clearly this cannot be done, unless, in truth, he is given a more trustworthy, rewarding environment where he can, in time, distinguish between what is and what was.

Let us take another approach for a moment. Add to the premise that learning is an adaptation to the environment, the fact that it is a process of development. There are things a human must learn first in order to accomplish the next stage. What is good learning for a two-year-old is inadequate for a twelve-year-old. On the basis of a developmental scale, a disturbed hyperaggressive child has proceeded in physiological development along with his peers. In psychological development, having been deprived of positive environmental stimuli, he has been arrested. His learning needs are those of infancy or extreme early childhood. He has not been sufficiently nurtured to proceed. Thus, to ask him to concentrate on subject matter or complicated directions for a class period, let alone a school day is as futile as demanding such a task of a year old baby. When an infant is hungry or in pain, his demands are overwhelming and urgent. He cannot postpone or wait; for him the future does not exist and may never come. Similarly, the hyperaggressive child has no conceptual tools to deal with delay. It must be now. There is no tomorrow. The school by its structure

and program must teach him not only that he can wait but there is something worth waiting for. When a two-year-old bumps himself against a chair, he is infuriated and kicks the offending furniture. When a hyperaggressive child bumps against the fact that nine and five do not make twelve and he is wrong, he tears the paper, attacks the teacher and blames arithmetic, pencil, teacher, anyone but himself. To have been wrong, becomes a total picture of wrongness and ineptitude. If he accepts responsibility for one flaw, he perceives himself as one big flaw much as a three-year-old cries out to a mother who has scolded him, "You don't love me. You hate me. You think I'm awful." A teacher will show him that a mistake is only a mistake and one can survive a multitude of errors without loss of love or loss of identity. Simply because he looks big and acts tough, we cannot overlook his baby needs and even his baby speech, baby mannerisms, baby methods. He cannot be expected to take the third, fourth, and fifth steps to learning when he has not been offered the essential first and second steps on which our teaching expectations are based. Step one: you are worthy of help and worthy of love. Step two: you can feel adequate when you postpone immediate gratification for a future goal. All phases of his treatment life will offer him these two basic experiences. The school by its goals of adequacy through learning will convey this message differently from therapy or ward life but no less surely.

Putting the statement that learning is an adaptation to environment together with the statement that learning is a process in development, we arrive at the understanding that to teach the disturbed hyperaggressive child we must radically alter his living environment in order that he may unlearn old learnings and we must take him at his present psychological moment of development, going back to the point where deprivation became the structure for his learning. In order to motivate him to learn what society wishes him to learn his basic life needs must be met. Only then, will he be able to graduate to those steps of learning which require a self-image of potential adequacy and an ability to postpone immediate gratification for a future goal.

The greater the degree of disturbance, the more necessary it becomes to alter the entire environment of the disturbed hyperaggressive child in the direction of a more gratifying, more therapeutically oriented total experience. How much can be done in the school situation alone is an untested question. But assuming a change in pathogenic living conditions, what must be done in the school life of the child to re-educate him? Obviously, the teacher must begin work with a hyperaggressive child at the level where he is and not where his age expectancy or size would place him. The atmosphere of the classroom and the teacher's attitude must be different from everything he has come to expect from unreliable, contradictory and exploitative adults in his past. The teacher must be accepting, dependable and consistent. Where possible, stimuli to old patterns of response must be avoided, anxiety provoking situations placed at a minimum. It is not possible, nor even advisable for a ten-year-old to be treated like a one-year-old, yet his program should include as many opportunities as possible for the infantlike need for quick success and deserved approval. He should be offered a surplus of reassurance, attention and affection for a period of time. It will take him time to recognize the surplus. The recognition that these indeed are a different kind of people will cause him anxiety and temporary outbursts. In time, he will begin to learn that these adults are not depriving or exploitative and the atmosphere is not one which seeks to defeat him or make him feel more helpless, but instead one which seeks to help him and make him more adequate. Such a revolution in perception carries with it a need to give up old defenses. Even if they were not workable defenses, they were the only thing the child had. To give them up will cause him pain and difficulty and may look to the naive teacher as if nothing had been

accomplished. Therefore, the teacher needs to be able to wait without despair for long, trying, testing periods. At first the teacher must accept the unacceptable symptoms much as a mother accepts the vomiting of a sick child. Later the symptom must be tolerated, not accepted, and the difference between toleration and acceptance must be conveyed to a child, much as a mother tolerates the thumb sucking of a child past the point where it usually disappears, knowing that it is at the moment necessary, but soon may be given up. Later, when the symptom is not necessary to the developmental stage of the child, the teacher will firmly set a limit and no longer permit behavior which was permissible in the early days of re-education. For example, the swear words of a hyperaggressive child may go purposely unnoticed in the classroom at first, if such behavior does not disrupt the rest of the class. Later, the teacher will point out that these words are not appropriate in school. Finally, when the child no longer needs them as an outlet or a crutch, and when he has come to be able to hear and accept the teacher's authority, he will be asked to leave the class temporarily if he needs to swear.

To teach a disturbed hyperaggressive child with average intelligence or above, a person must be stable, flexible, skilled in the use of a variety of methods, materials and subject matter at a range of levels going from pre-school to high school. He must be sufficiently confident of his professional competency so that he will not need to demand accomplishment and productions from the child beyond his immediate ability. The moment such a child becomes aware that he is used for the teacher's personal goals, he will defeat the teacher, even though the expectation may meet his own healthier desires. The teacher must be able to respond to the child's behavior without personal threat: to take him back in the classroom after personal attack, to maintain simultaneously warmth and distance. The hyperaggressive child cries out for a monopoly of individual attention, but is often totally incapable of using it when he gets it. He is desperately afraid of closeness. He considers it a snare that will end in further demands, disappointments or expectation that he change before he is ready. An arm around a shoulder may be right one day and may cause a violent disruption the next. A chair placed close, may be a source of comfort or may lead to a devastating scene. To tolerate the implied rejection and the conflicting demands made by the child with his insatiable needs and his panicky withdrawal, a teacher must have a basic security. He must be sufficiently aware of his own problems and in control of them so that he does not become involved in those of his hyperaggressive pupils. Otherwise, he will, without knowing it, either induce the child to act out his own resentments and defiance or take an unfruitful dislike to the child. In either case, he will have lined up with the child's pathology rather than his health. In order to survive and usefully teach the deeply, disturbing, anxiety provoking hyperaggressive child, a teacher himself needs insightful and sympathetic supervision and support.

At first when a failure is equivalent to total inadequacy and helplessness, the hyperaggressive child needs to avoid experiences of failure. Frequently it is wise to use safe, old, learned material so that his shaky self-structure will not be threatened by frustration. New material needs to be presented virtually complete with only one step missing so that the process is done before the child is fully aware that he has done anything. A subtraction problem, for example (always a symbolic horror for a child from whom so much has been subtracted in life) can be switched about and put in terms of the more comfortable addition process. A required map or drawing can have only one small area to complete with much of the outline already done. Simple completion reading exercises go better than open-ended questions. Directions for any activity, be it shop, science or bringing milk in at recess must be clear and simple and require only one act. The time neces-

sary to do a task must be limited at first and still must be great enough for a task to be fully completed. A read story must be brief. A song must be literally short and sweet. A question must require an unambiguous one word answer. Results, though unvalued and destroyed by the child must be valued by the teacher and kept. Even if the child will not permit the work to be displayed, it means something to him to know the teacher kept and respected the effort that went into it. Later, gradually, higher standards and expectations can be intensified so that the child never has genuine cause to feel belittled and incompetent because of the easiness of the task.

Overstimulation needs to be avoided. Similar in some ways to the methods used with the organically damaged child, the classroom, though attractive, should not be full of seductive objects. A normal child can use, and needs stimulation. A hyperaggressive becomes disorganized and pulled in all directions by the appeal or distractibility of objects. Only those tools immediately necessary should be on hand; even these should be brought forth with careful timing. To a skillful teacher's dismay and disappointment, the hyperaggressive child cannot for a long while, if ever, use the creative, open-ended approach to subject matter. He requires limits, boundaries and confinement in materials as well as behavior. The known gives him security. The unknown floods him with fantasy or anxiety. A corollary to this fact is that the hyperaggressive child cannot use a gestalt method of approach. The whole idea is either too frightening or too overwhelming. He is able to deal with one item at a time if it is concretely presented. The less verbal, the more concrete the approach, the greater the chance of success. Manual tasks are more useful for basic teaching of the hyperaggressive than verbal. Communication is clearer and more effective. For a hyperaggressive youngster, the daily routine of the child should be sufficiently clear and stable that a child knows what to expect at different periods in his school day.

Materials and subject matter need to be carefully chosen for the individual needs of the hyperaggressive child. In trying to avoid overstimulating material and subject matter, it is often difficult to find out what precisely will turn out to be overstimulating, what, in other words, will evoke old responses or ulcerous memories. A tone of voice, an odor, a particular expression can do it where a gangster television script arouses a bland response. Familiarity becomes the best guide. But generally speaking, the average reader which tells of happy family excursions and merry, naughty pranks are poisonous. Much to be preferred are short, neutral, nature and science readers. Tender stories such as Bambi or the Christmas tale evoke such longing and feelings of denial that they lead to violent disintegration or depression. Neutral material should be sought and used for a long time. Sensory or motor stimulating events such as creative dancing, free, interpretive drama, use of drums, too messy clay, finger paints, large selections of bright colors need to be avoided or introduced with care and timing.

Although the structure of a group of children (no matter how small the group) is an essential part of the learning experience, expectations for group activities as such come late in the re-education program. Like infants, these children operate in a self-involved universe. Later they use parallel activity much as nursery school children play in a parallel manner. At length they are ready for group goal directed projects and finally for carefully defined, short group discussions and planning.

Time and space concepts, so necessary to our learning, are difficult for the hyperaggressive child. It has been noted above that the future is a concept that does not exist and can only be built in when a basic amount of need fulfillment has occurred in the total environment. Time, itself, has been experienced as unreliable. The present is threatening: the past, painful. In school when such a child can understand and accept "Tomorrow, you can take your ship model with you when you leave class," he has made an enormous step forward. Telling time, even for intellectually competent hyperaggressive youngsters comes slowly. Space is often even more confusing than time. The question "Where am I?" after all, is so inextricably woven into the fabric of "Who am I?" An eight-year-old child with a ten-year-old reading level may still get lost in one floor of a locked ward in which he has lived for two years. To locate an object, let alone an abstraction such as a country, is utterly unfeasible. Only after a good bit of personality re-education has permitted the child to feel more safe and more certain can he look around him to discover where he is and where other things are in relation to him. The boundaries of space are as frightening and fantasy provoking as those of time. Slowly, one needs to build up a consciousness of personal geography, then proceed to local and finally general geography.

The Child Research Branch has found that given time, patience, skill and a total therapeutic attack, this re-education process can be set in movement. After three years of residential treatment with a school designed to meet the needs of the six severely disturbed hyperaggressive children, a study was made which demonstrated, statistically as well as clinically, that these boys had changed in the direction of greater school learning and adjustment. The observed changes were categorized in terms of (a) each child's self picture, i.e., his ability to perceive himself as worthy of and able to be helped; (b) his increased ability to handle and control his inner drives, fantasies and fears; (c) his increased ability to deal with his infantile needs and frustration tolerance; (d) his greater ability to perceive the adult (teacher) as benevolent and to relate more appropriately to him; (e) his greater ability to relate to his peers, i.e., to share the time and attention with a peer and to work with a peer without choosing a scapegoat or a bully role. In a further study of these boys' adjustment to the specially selected public school classes in which they were placed, it was learned that while varying degrees of gaps in areas of control, stamina, attention span, frustration tolerance and academics exist, five of the six boys were able to adjust to the demands of public school and to proceed with expected school learning in ways unlike those they used when they failed in school previous to hospitalization. The sixth boy has had more difficulty, but has changed in the direction of greater school adjustment and school learning.

It should be said that the observed success of these children in their re-education and school learning is a relative matter. They are unquestionably doing better than they did. Their ability to survive in a community school in itself gives proof of the fact that they are more able to maintain control of themselves and more able to bear frustration and postpone immediate gratification. Though academic lacks are severe, they have made great strides in many academic areas as judged by standard school tests. Nonetheless, all, except one boy, is a year to two years behind his expected grade level. Moreover, their school adjustment has been facilitated by careful planning, and selection of schools and teachers. Many contacts have been established between the institution and the school and special programming has been planned, all of which allows a child to get out of a situation when it becomes too stressful for him, his classmates or the teachers. In addition, though their learning and school behavior may be better controlled, in their carefully supervised treatment life at the residence before and after school, they frequently exhibit the explosive, disintegrative, uncontrollable pathology for which they were hospitalized. They are not "cured," in other words. However, it can be said that they have learned to better handle areas where social expectations are greatest for set periods of time. They have learned containment, which again can be seen as a developmental step in learning. The four-year-old who has tantrums at home but is able to contain himself in school, is considered healthier than the child whose behavior spills over to all areas of his life.

In summarizing, then, it is possible to alter the environment of the severely disturbed, hyperaggressive boys sufficiently so that a re-education program can be set in motion and take effect. In order that re-learning may take place, the child's environment must provide areas where his basic infantile needs are accepted and where possible, met. Thus, the primary goal of teaching is to alter his perception of the environment and the people in it and finally, his perception of himself. By a total therapeutic attack and by a school program with specific educative techniques and teaching relationships, progress can be made and the child can change in terms of his self-picture, the handling of his inner drives and pressures, the handling of his infantile needs and frustration tolerance. He can change too in his relation to adults and to peers and in his adjustment to school methods and routines as well as in academic skills.

It is unlikely that a total unlearning of past experiences and past responses can take place, no matter how intensive the treatment or how radical the change in his environment. Old wounds can be reopened easily and underneath the layer of new learning, there exists a damaged foundation. When provoked, or made anxious, he will respond in the old disintegrative, violent manner. However, with adequate treatment he is not so easily provoked, nor do so many things make him so anxious that his new found controls give way. Moreover, he can learn to contain himself in certain, socially demanding areas while he exhibits pathology in areas where it is safer for him and less destructive to him to do so. It would seem that this much progress is a great deal, granted that it is by no means ideal.

In returning then, to the questions posed at the outset of this report: The severely disturbed, hyperaggressive child without perceptible organic damage and with an average intelligence not only can learn, he has learned. The problem is to re-educate him, to help him unlearn his past depriving, damaging experiences and responses. To do this his total environment must be radically changed and it must be recognized that in order to proceed with his learning, his basic, infantile needs must be accepted and met. There must be areas where gratification replaces deprivation, benevolence replaces malevolence, affection replaces hostility, and reliability replaces inconsistency, neglect, and exploitation. After a sufficient amount

of un-learning has occurred along with a sufficient amount of fulfillment, new learning can begin to take place. When this happens, the child's basic feeling of inadequacy and helplessness is diminished and he becomes more able to cope with the demands of the newly perceived environment. The school with its structure, teaching methods and relationships is an important part of re-education process. It is a long, tedious, forward two steps, back one step procedure requiring great understanding, skill and concerted effort. Yet, despite its difficulties and imperfections substantial progress can be made.

Newman described how her pupils in the experimental program improved by taking two steps forward, and one step backwards. What effect did this see-saw type of improvement have on the teachers? How could they determine whether the improvement was real or temporary? If it were real, what side effects did it have on the child and the other members in the group who observed this change? These are some of the questions discussed in Redl's paper on the concept of improvement. Redl refutes any naive conviction that improvement can be measured completely by tests or on the basis of new educational skills, lowered anxiety, reduced symptoms, or a more lovable affect.

Clinical Speculations on the Concept of Improvement
Fritz Redl

. . . Long ago, Freud made the casual remark that, if an especially brilliant patient uses obviously especially stupid arguments for his defense, then it is a sure sign that there is more to the resistance involved in this than meets the eye. If some people on our level of clinical endurance are thrown into frenzy by a process of "improvement"—the very thing we are actually working and living for day and night—then there must be angles to this that might well stand exploration beyond what we are aware of right now. . . .

Abridged from Fritz Redl, "Clinical Speculations on the Concept of Improvement," presented at the American Orthopsychiatric Association Meetings, 1959.

IMPROVEMENT—WHAT DO WE REALLY MEAN?

If anything became clear to us . . . when we tried to come to grips with our collective improvement panic, it was the fact of multiple meanings with which this term is bandied about in discussion. This isn't much of a discovery, of course, but since the hesitation—or resistance—against coming to grips with this multiplicity of meaning seems to be very strong, it might help future discussants if we laid bare the major traps in concept formulation right here and now. When people argued about improvements the following four meanings seemed to be involved—and confused:

Meaning A. Improvement—meaning a specific function in mid-air. Thus, one would hear claims that children can read better now than before, that they are able to stick to an assignment, to fulfillment of a task, that they can participate in a competitive game without being thrown by failure or success, or that they can now "allow themselves to learn" how to swim, paint, spell, or what have you. Such claims by the various disciplines involved in the cultivation of such skills would frequently be met by the therapists with an uneasy frown, a polite nod in the direction of the sister-discipline, followed by a hot debate as to whether this "really" constitutes improvement—but that one we shall come back to soon.

Meaning B. Improvement in overall mental health. In this respect, staff would argue whether a given child is getting "better"—usually referring to a rather specific part of his well known pathology. Most frequently though this type of statement ends up in a list of "symptoms dropped," or in more hard to formulate statements about desirable attributes customarily described in our American Culture as signs of well being: less tense, more relaxed, freer to react to reality as it is, less "driven" by irrational impulse, etc. etc. etc.

Meaning C. Improvement from the vantage point of the consumer. By this I mean all the adjustment demands which are made on a child by the surrounding universe, many of which have primarily to do with the comfort and taste buds of those who are on the receiving end of the line of child behavior. Thus one would find statements such as these: He is less rough on trips outside, sticks within rules better, is much quieter, has fewer tantrums and then they aren't quite so hard to live through; when in a sulk it doesn't take quite as long to get him out of it, etc. etc. etc.

Meaning D. Improvement as a "human being." Into this category fall a variety of statements which do not seem to be quite founded in either psychiatric theory nor in any special educational creed, and frequently mark themselves quite clearly as different from strictly clinical statements. People get easily embarrassed while making them in the course of a case discussion, and frequently also apologize for them with the type of pride one usually displays when apologizing for something one really deems more important than what happens to be on the official agenda. Thus staff would refer to our children as "more lovable" than before, would insist that Bobby is more of a "Mensch" right now, and he seems to be a more "decent" human being, more responsive to overall expectations or just in terms of plain human charm.

Needless to emphasize—any one of these four different meanings may actually be contained in a given statement in mixture with the other three. . . .

The moral of the story that we want to lead up to today lies in the impact of the above described multiple connotations on staff discussion in an interdisciplinary team. The following chance observations may be of interest:

1. Individual staff members lose, under the impact of improvement panic, whatever level of *conceptual astuteness* they really possess, at least for the duration of a case conference. Thus you may find a therapist who knows very well that a given teacher who said that Bobby has improved in reading, does *not* for a moment delude herself that this might mean he is cured—you may find a therapist going, in spite of this knowledge, into a long harangue about "improvements" often really being in "the service of resistance" and so forth, which then in turn leads to a somewhat angered insistence by the teacher that skills do count also, after all.

2. Members of disciplines which have a reputation for being "clinically more sophisticated" than some others (Psychiatry versus Teaching, art therapy versus nursing, etc., as the case may be) have a tendency to get irritated beyond reason by even modest statements of improvement of part

functions or skills, and on the whole pride themselves in a somewhat over-ostentatious pessimism—as though even the mention of improvements would throw them back into a lower status field. The representatives of more part-skill oriented disciplines have a tendency to hide their improvement observations, for fear of being deemed unpsychiatric or clinically too naive for words. The debate thus avoided usually breaks out in displaced areas of clinical or technical issues.

3. On a good team, members of the same discipline who meet the children in their daily life in different roles or at different times, have a tendency to hide their observations of improvements if their revelation might seem as though they took undue credit for them. Thus, in our case, a lot of quite clearcut improvements remained unmentioned for a while simply because a given counsellor was afraid his teammates might interpret his statements about Bobby's new relationship of trust as though it was meant to tell the others on the team how skillful the speaker was. Such is the price of good battle-morale after return to civilian life.

4. A frank discussion of these issues and an encouragement to record observed improvements, and never mind what they might *imply* brought about an increase in recording and observations offered, but the effect of such "medication" never lasts very long, it needs to be repeated more often than one might assume.

IMPROVEMENT—HOW DO WE KNOW IT IS "REAL"?

What people are most afraid and ashamed of on a high-level interdisciplinary clinical team, is to appear overconfident, overoptimistic, too naive in one's expectation about human change, rash in one's claims, and "too easily fooled." Working with child patients whose very pathology seems to lay traps for such weaknesses with special wile and skill, this "countersus-

piciousness" of the adults in battle with the suspectness of child motivations, seems to assume an even higher force.

In discussions, this theme usually comes up under the guise of questions, whether a given claim of improvement is "real" or not. Some of this way of putting it is actually only a concession to the amenities of middle class conduct—for you can't very well tell a teammate that he is a fool who doesn't know what he is talking about and sees improvements where there are none. Rather, one can concede the appearance of improved behavior claimed, as long as one shifts one's incredulity to the question of the substance it might hold.

In actuality, the question "but is it real" seemed, in our struggles at least, to cover six rather discrete issues that should be carefully kept apart:

1. Is it "real"—or is this only improved behavior, produced as a *defense* against treatment or change?

Example: the tough kid who becomes quite "goody-goody" after arrival for a few weeks, because he wants to stall for time to "size up the joint."

The originally obstreperous youngster who suddenly becomes more amenable to adults because he has changed tactics: he takes revenge on them now by manipulating the behavior of his peers into anti-adult escapades behind the scenes.

2. Is it "real"—meaning, *is it ready for transfer?* In this respect, we do not doubt the appearance of improvement where it is claimed, but question whether it would stand up if situations were even slightly changed.

Example: Youngster suddenly opening up in a real friendship for one counsellor—does this mean he is reducing his hostile warfare against the adult world, or does he simply reserve this attitude to this one person alone, thus even re-inforcing his warfare against the rest of the world.

Bobby shows more interest in activities on the Ward, gets involved in much more complex art projects there—does this mean now he is ready for prolonged interest spans in his work in school?

3. Is it "real"—meaning, *is it re-traumatization-proof?* What we really question in that case is not the clarity of improvement, but just how much of the old bad stuff could the youngster take without a relapse. It should be noted, by the way, that I have found many clinicians fall into the trap of General Public Opinion on this score. I find therapists blushing at the thought that somebody might come around a year—or two foster home placements— away from now and say: "see, I told you it wouldn't last"—irrespective of the questions whether the new breakdown wasn't perhaps due to totally unacceptable traumatization of the child. In no other field of medicine do I find people that trust less in their own domain. A cured pneumonia remains cured as far as the physician goes, and nobody expects re-traumatization proofness for the rest of the patient's life.

Example: Bobby has made tremendous strides in trust, is capable of accepting reprimands or even punishment if handled wisely and with proper care. But what will happen if he runs into a sadist of a teacher, a drunken fool of a foster-home parent, a stupid prediluvian practice of rule enforcement in a next institution?

4. Is it "real"—or rather, is the basis on which behavior rests *"genuine"?* In this frame of reference we do not really doubt the factualness of an improvement claim. What we wonder, however, is how much improved behavior or attitude flows out of real "personality change from within" or how far it is actually maintained only through unusual pressure from without.

Example: Some children suddenly get scared we might "abandon them" if they are too bad. Under the impact of that separation panic, their surface behavior seems to "improve." However, does that mean that the "real problem" has been solved?

Under the impact of a momentary enthusiasm for a special project or a newly found adult friend, we find youngsters acting and promising way above their means. The way they act and feel during that phase is quite visibly an improvement over what we saw before—how solid, though, is the *basis* on which such improvements are erected?

5. Is it "real"—meaning: is this improvement worthwhile as measured against the *price we may pay?* This is especially true where our ambition may lead us to squeeze out of youngsters levels of operation which are developmentally premature, thus cramping the style of life they ought to have in order to complete their developmental phase at ease.

Example: A pre-adolescent who is trapped into displaying a lot of "Emily Post" adaptation to adult taste patterns as to how a little lady or a little gentleman should act, thus missing the leeway for rough and tumble play which this age phase ought to have a large dose of.

An adolescent who is trapped into premature job or vocational ambitions, thus becomes a much more "serious" youngster, while he is actually postponing an important shift in adolescent psychosexual growth into a much later phase, or forces himself into a compulsion-neurosis-like state of pseudo maturity.

6. Is it "real"—or are we just *having luck for a while?* Often our improvement statements are obviously well rooted, and we are sure we haven't done anything to force the children into a higher level of operation. Only—we soon discover that all that happened was that we had a special piece of luck. Sometimes, it just so happens we hit a day of unusual relaxedness for the program we had in mind, or one of those situations where a "positive mood" simply is in the air from the first waking hour on, or where a lucky surprise, and unusual event, sets the tone so well that even disturbed children, with that much supportive luck, can really *live above their means* for a while. Only, it would be premature to ex-

pect their continued function on that level, or to forget what price in regressive interludes we may have to be taxed for after a while.

Example: A skillfully designed school or play hour would often turn out unexpectedly well. Seduced by such luck, the adults may try to make such planning part of the regular and prolonged diet of the group. If premature, the result is a throwback or regression to, or beyond the original level, and the insight that the experience of such happily "improved reactions" was just a piece of unusual good luck.

By the way, this element of "living above their means" should not be ignored entirely. The ability to do so for certain stretches seems to be one of the safest signals of imminent ego change.

In summary—all those 6 interpretations of the question whether a given phenomenon of "improvements" is "real" or not, are valid issues in their own right. They need to be viewed separately, though, and confusion between them is among the most dreaded pitfalls in staff debate.

Observations from our own "Improvement Panic phase" as to these issues:

1. In interdisciplinary team discussions, *disappointments* along the line of meaning No. 6 (is it "real," or did we just have luck for a while) and No. 2 (is it ready for transfer) seem hardest for the staff to take with grace. They frequently lead to "I told you so" debates rather than time spent on realistic re-appraisal of the scope of improvement exploitability, or they lead staff members to withdraw all their previous improvement statements, rather than to modify their degree of transferability at the time.

2. *Irrespective of realities* in the picture, *therapy staff* in the stricter sense of the term, is inclined to suspect all program and school staff of overexploiting mild improvement cues beyond what the treatment traffic can bear, child care and teaching staff has a tendency to suspect and accuse therapy staff of being "overfussy" and hold-

ing the kids back from experiences for which they would be quite ready.

3. Faced with *predictions* as forerunners of a widening scope of community contact of the child patients—partial, as before changing room, hospital school to community school, or total, as in the case of impending home, foster home, or after care placement, *all staff* tends to become panicky and ends up with predictions much more negative than they really thought the improvements themselves amount to. In short, trust in transfer power of improvement goes down, panic about retraumatization vulnerability goes up. In fact, sometimes it even looks as though we *hoped* or at least *expected* that the subsequent handling of the child will have to be traumatic in nature, for only then could we have an alibi for having thought him ready for discharge to begin with, in case it didn't work out.

IMPROVEMENT—AT WHAT COST?

In the preceding discussion we mentioned the case where we feel that improvements can be obtained at "too high" a price in terms of other areas of the child's life. Of course, such mistakes will have to be avoided. However—let's face it, all improvements give us a rough time, at least for a while. Of course we somehow know this, and in specific case discussions this problem is invariably raised. Yet, I do not find that literature has given enough emphasis to the very specific problem it constitutes for the child to run around with an improved personality in the same old stable, for the adult to live with a child who has improved program readinesses, and for the institution which has to maintain a disease-protective atmosphere for some of its patients while others need to be put on the path to the way out.

In the following I shall try to list just a few of the thoughts that forced themselves upon us during those months of improvement panic.

JUST WHAT DOES IT IMPLY FOR THE CHILD?

The Ego of a child who allowed himself to "improve" while under our treatment and care—and let's forget for a moment just which of the aspects of "improvement" we may be talking about, the problem is there in all of them to some degree—has the following added complications to face, and will need a lot of resilience to bear the burden of improvement with courage:

1. *Extra elation and depression load.* Children of the type we are talking about remain, for a long time, quite incapable of dealing with even normal quantities of feelings of elation or depression, excitement or emptiness. Both throw them into frantic gesticulation of their ego instead of eliciting the usual coping mechanisms children have available for such events. Therefore, for a long stretch of time, the therapeutic team needs to avoid any planning that contains too much of a chance for either, and the adult has to substitute for coping mechanisms his controls from without, if either experience should hit the child too hard. Under the grip of improvements occurring within—even of partial ones, such a state of protectedness from elation or depression can no longer be maintained. Widening the scope of their experiences in areas where they are ready for it also implies the exposure to elation and triumph, of sudden insight into the distance between where they think they are as to where they really are, and a sudden onslaught of depression. For all practical purposes then, an ego that is exposed to the right diet of challenging enough experiences to feel elations will also have to take in its stride accompanying accidents of depressions, and will have to be ready for both. Only—often enough the movement in skill or personality area where improved functioning can occur is not necessarily well timed with the development of such coping mechanisms. Result: the children's ego experiences more failures with coping with either than before, which makes life for and with those children more tumultuous than it had been while they were still in the grip of their old pathology.

2. *Increased problems in dealing with failure and success, criticism and praise, punishment and rewards.* For years we had to learn to avoid exposing our child patients to either of those, since the incapacity of their egos to cope with such experiences or educational techniques is among their primary characteristics. Astounding ingenuity had to be developed by staff to find a way of life in which to spare the children's ego the necessity for such coping, to find forms of child handling and child care which would substitute for the challenge such experiences and techniques involve.

With the emergence of new improvement potentials, this state of affairs, too, can no longer be maintained. Expanded exposure to life of more complexity makes use of such techniques unavoidable. Growing into normal life makes the learning of how to deal with such experiences paramount. Thus, hardly freed from the onslaught of their old pathological impulsivity, these children now have to practice new ego techniques in coping with the consequences of their widened area of potential functioning.

3. *Increase in newness panic and additional fear of loss of control.* More newness brings with it also an increase of the anxiety that goes with exposure to new situations—a liability from which we had to protect these children for quite a while. Exposure to trying themselves in situations of increased scope also implies their increased fear of loss of control, of being overridden by an onslaught of impulsivity. In fact, since these children along with the improved functioning also usually develop some level of increased insight into their selves, their own awareness that they *might* be suffering loss of self-control in a new situation also goes up. It seems paradoxical but is an important fact of clinical life, that with improved movement toward mental health the self-perception of these children's actual weakness of internal controls becomes more *realistic*, which increase in internal realism, so to say, has in its wake

a new wave of anxieties about loss of control. A chain reaction which probably poses one of the most delicate clinical policy problems of all.

4. *Fear of commitment, nostalgia for old pathology fun.* This phase of the improvement curve has been better documented in reports on individual therapy with children and adults than the others. It nevertheless introduces new challenges to meet in the children's daily lives. What we are referring to is the well documented fact that the emerging awareness of the healthier ego and what life in health implies, also brings with it the dawning idea of the price one pays for freedom and health, and the demands society—and oneself—is likely to make once one has left the dreary but relatively safe refuge of mental disease. Also—newly tasted gratifications are still wobbly, the secondary gain extorted from old pathology-geared gratification, while spurious is, at least safely predictable and well known. Thus, the "improvement prone" child travels a road more challenging, but also much emptier of the known, and much more unpredictable in terms of the nature of the gratifications to be expected as a reward.

5. *The diversion of improvements as bargaining tools with the world of adults.* Of all the pitfalls, this is probably the worst one, at least in therapy with the type of children we have in mind today. For, once improvement on several levels has been tasted, these children are not slow in detecting its terrific bargaining power over the adults on the behavioral scene. And once a given piece of improvement becomes a bargaining tool in the battle with the surrounding universe, its *value, clinically speaking, has been nullified.* In fact, the improvement we produced, once it is in the service of such a battle against change, is but an additional weapon in the child's hand. We shall talk about the problem of keeping staff from playing into the hands of this vicious and perverse process in a minute. At the moment what we are referring to is the tendency and skill of children

on the way to health to bribe and blackmail their surroundings with that very issue of health itself. Only after they have improved enough, can they use regression as an efficient weapon for punishing their therapist or themselves. Only after they have shown considerable gains on several levels, can they successfully trap us into confusing surface improvements with real change, or taking their coins of more pleasing behavior as a sign of advancement rather than of the resistance it really is. The "promise" to be good—by word or deed, the "threat" to regress—by deed or word, are a new piece of agenda on the strategy discussion table during those phases in the children's clinical life.

6. *Estrangement from peer group and peer culture with all that this implies.* This phenomenon is most visible, of course, when some of the children move "faster" than others in the same subgroup, or if an individual's move out from under pathology happens more rapidly than the behavioral code of the peer group can keep step with. Since this is the more frequent situation anyway, we might list shortly what the problems of the "improving" child will be under those conditions:

a. Behavior which is rated as "improved" in the world of the therapy-success eager adult, may have the opposite rating on the peer code scale, which still has strong natural power in their lives, and needs to retain such for quite a while to come. Thus, for instance, the ability "to ask for help rather than to lash out in wild destructive despair" is a clearcut improvement item on anybody's scale. For the kid who produces such behavior it easily contains the flavor of "sissiness," of "giving in" or "playing up to" the adults, of acting like a "teacher's pet."

b. Improvements in basic health issues invariably also are accompanied by changes in *taste.* Accepting sublimated gratifications for more primitive ones obviously creates a gap between the child now and the child before, and therefore between him and his less advanced playmates. Thus, we will find two phenomena in the wake of such moves: our improved youngster may become *contemptuous* of, or hostile to, those who still linger in their old rough, obviously crazy and uncomfortable pleasures and behavior, or he may become envious of them, developing nostalgic yearnings for the more simple life of yore. Experiences, by the way, which our youngsters may not yet be able to cope with, even at the time when their improvement in sublimation of their taste-buds already has taken place.

c. *Exposure to additional dare and group-loyalty tests. Ambivalence also toward this new image of the self.* Groups don't like to let people go. In the organized adult crime gang, the punishment for estrangement is death. In kid groups it is ostracism or an endless chain of "loyalty tests." Thus, the changing child in the not yet changing group will find himself suspect of being a fifth columnist in the battle against adults, for the very "improvements" he has not yet learned how to savor. He will be exposed to a constant flow of "dares" to show that he is still O.K. in spite of that suddenly discovered eagerness to hold up his hand in class for contributions, to finish products adults are proud of, or his obviously gratifying use of his relationship to a therapist. Thus, our changing individual undergoes a new phase of group conflict at the very time when his first improvements need a chance to emerge.

7. *The turmoil of choice.* Improved personalities need a wider scope to operate in. The nourishment of improvement potentials invariably implies the increase of free choice. Thus, the very children who, during their sickness had to be protected by the adult from being exposed to too exciting choice making, because their egos could never bear such a load, will now have to emerge into choice making on a stepped-up scale. Rather than have an adult stand behind them who can hold them when they make the wrong decision, they will have to be kept in a program that gives them a chance to be on their own, to make their own decision whether to behave or to mis-

behave, so that the consequences of such decisions can then be picked up in therapy or life-space interview work. No matter how closely supervised their overall life frame may remain, this withdrawing of the adult in tactful awe of the importance of an autonomous decision making process, is the core of all treatment into health.

The result of this for the internal household of our children is obvious: wrong decisions have to be made. The ego will then be tempted to use its old alibi and projection techniques to ward off the insight-consequences that might have to be drawn from them. Our "Life Space Interview" records are bursting with colorful illustrations of just this very sort of thing. It is the clinical exploitation of life events—life events which are allowed to occur—that marks this phase of therapy, as against the protection from stress that marked the previous one. While this is the only safe way back into health, it isn't an easy one, and the casualties on this path are not less numerous than those on the previous treatment stretches.

All in all it should be clear by now that we are deeply impressed with the fact that real improvements—on any one of the counts we mentioned above—make additional demands on the child. This is especially true for settings in which the children under treatment live in a group with other child patients, while in part branching out into widened areas of school and community life. While the "group" may, under circumstances, support the way to health, it is also quite likely to try to block it. In either case, the "improving child" will be faced with frustrations and failures which are the result of the widened horizon of his experiential life and to which he would not have been exposed to begin with, had he not improved. Thus, the child's ego assumes with each "improvement" step, also the challenge of managing more complex life situations, and a new batch of frustrations, anxieties, confusions and fears. Quite a job to perform until, finally, digested experiences of this sort can be turned, by the child, into a renewed concept of his self.

IMPROVEMENT—WHAT IS THE COST FOR THE CLINICAL OR EDUCATIONAL ADULT?

To lump both of them together isn't really quite fair; for, obviously the problems we have to face vis-à-vis the improvement issue will vary considerably in terms of the specific function we are expected to fulfill in the youngster's overall treatment scheme, and the specific role we have to play in his daily life. However—time is costly at this point, so let us oversimplify and abbreviate without too much apology and guilt:

1. *Coping with the temptation to over-expect and exploit.* Frankly, not all of the resistance of youngsters against our therapeutic wiles to bring about a change, is just a function of their pathology. Even without its distorting influence, I can't blame some of them for being leery of being free to improve, for there is one instinct most powerful in all adults in this professional game—a terrific drive to hang onto whatever changes we finally seem to notice; and, while they hardly show us a finger of improvement, to grab the whole hand and try hard to pull them into a level of health they are far from ready for.

We all know that, but we haven't spent as much time learning to recognize our secret wishes in that direction, as we have spent learning to know when we are liable to get angry and mad, frustrated or hostile, so we can take professional action against such feelings flooding our clinical gates.

The more skill-oriented professions have a natural tendency in that direction by the very nature of their job. But the therapist, in the stricter meaning of the term, isn't free of it either. It only shows in different ways. In fact, I have seen Bobby's therapist mad at his group worker for expecting the child to enjoy games or experiences still much too frightening to him, just because he had improved some,

and yet would find the same therapist disappointed an hour later that a youngster who had been so capable of insight style therapy by now, should suddenly return to a phase of non-verbal resistance against any and all interview work, and wondering what mistakes we had made. In short—one of the greatest internal problems of staff is that once they have smelled the flavor of a few moments of success, felt the relief in seeing irrational kids respond with normal reactions, they are liable to forget all they have learned through the years of severe pathology onslaught—or rather, to throw it out of the window as though the millennium had arrived.

2. *Bargain basement deals with the pseudo-normal child.* Worse than the temptation to over-expect and exploit improvement potentials, is the temptation to fall into the trap of using their promises and "good behavior" or their verbal threats of regression for bargain deals which are clinically as destructive as anything could be. To make this point, which I consider the most important of all, safe against misinterpretation, a slight detour back into our pre-improvement policies seems justified.

The specific type of child patient on whose backs, so to say, we discuss the whole improvement issue today, require, during the first years of therapy, an avoidance of all *punishment* in the usual sense of the term. I cannot re-argue the reasons for this here.

The appearance of marked "improvements" seemed to confront us with the need to plan as carefully about our anxieties about optimism and hope as we had needed to plan about our dangers of hostility and despair. It is my impression that there was no automatic transfer from the principles that had guided us against the wrong reactions to the youngster's "bad" behavior into the avoidance of the wrong handling of their promises to be "good." In the struggle with all this, the following directives resulted as a side piece to our original batch of training policies:

Whenever we are confronted with it,

we cannot afford to make them feel our widening of their leeway for autonomy and expressional scope, is *"reward"* or *"privilege."*

a. If we did, this would only stir up their "make-a-deal" philosophy of life and seduce them into exploitational pseudo-promises and adjustments, and they would *escape the real issue* again.

b. They would not tie up the experience of Reward and Promise with either their own past behavior nor with the future predicament anyway, so those rewards and privileges would only be considered a premium for symptom-disguise.

c. However—we must not be considered as being *indifferent* to their improved behavior and attitude. It is important to show them that we are happy about it, but not to the degree that the loss of such recognition would become something to be *constantly afraid of.*

d. Whenever we have to terminate temporarily a new scope in their autonomy and mobility, we must make sure they do not experience this as *punishment*. This must be interpreted quite similarly to our previous intervention policy; we just think you can't make it yet, that's all there is to it. Not whether they were good or bad, but *whether we know they are ready* for an experience is the criterion for them to have it. Thus, we must also protect them from their own *illusionary need to produce phoney or rash promises*. We have to protect them against unrealistic self-expectation just as we used to protect them against unrealistic feelings of defeat.

e. The attitude to be conveyed is: "We love you anyway, we shall do everything to help you 'make it,' whenever you enter a new area of widened autonomous decision making, or experiential tryout of new situations. However, we shall also protect you from trying more than we know you can handle, even if you get mad at us at the time. We are happy about every step forward you can make, but we don't want you to feel you have to produce improved behavior as a prize. We shall help you

move at your own rate. On the other hand, the production of improved behavior as a coin for special privileges is out, in this outfit, too. It isn't necessary. What you get, you get because you need it, it is good for you and you are ready for it."

These are the only basic criteria on which the granting of special extensions in autonomy of decision making, and of experiential expansion depends. To convey such an attitude in the turmoil of daily events is not an easy task, but neither was the handling of negatively experienced interventions mentioned above. Only, staff is usually caught unawares for the latter, and the very fact these kids begin to look and act in many moments of their lives so much like plain ordinary normal kids, easily fools us into the same type of bargain deals, or of institutionalized punishments or rewards that, with normal children, are known to work so well. In fact, the healthier these kids get, the harder it is to remain aware of the amount of clinical caution and clinical tact that still has to remain part and parcel of our treatment policy. In all those cases where we made bad mistakes along that line, and tried to rely on promises, threats, rewards, punishments, no matter how mild and wise, we were soon forced to regret it. And even then it was hard for us to realize that the only people we can afford to get mad at for such mistakes is ourselves, rather than at the kids who "disappointed" our fond hopes.

3. *Improvement muteness because of a repressed desire to grow.* After so many months and years of hard labor without any reliable signs of success that could be trusted, it is hard to avoid a strong wish to brag about a real improvement, or to overtalk it in case conference or in luncheon gossip with the rest of the clinical crowd. Afraid that we might do so, and realizing that this would be misinterpreted by the rest of the gang as a rather prima-donnish and conceited act, we often defended ourselves against our own narcissistic hopes by not admitting or noting actual improvements to begin with. Thus,

one often sees children handled with much too little improvement leeway, thereby slowing up the possible clinical pace. And recordings, just when improvements of all sorts actually set in, become quite unreliable, a not inconsiderable deficit for an operation that is geared toward research.

4. *Renewed competitiveness among team members and distorted relationships to "the other field."* With the first "improvements" finally becoming undeniable, a new wave of competitiveness is likely to hit an otherwise already quite team-oriented staff. It seemed easier to love each other and to respect the other guy's discipline, as long as we were all in the same boat of struggling with little visible success against overwhelming odds. Once improvement happens, our narcissistic investments are re-inflamed. This may happen on a personal level—why should Bobby do this (showing reliable behavior when trusted with keys) for counsellor X when I know he would never have done that much for me? It may also happen on the level of displacement into interdisciplinary issues: sure that teacher thinks she got Bobby to read. Little does she know that he would never have allowed himself to want to do so, unless I had opened it all up for him in that therapy hour the other day. To bring this new wave of potential staff conflict under control seems to be a more arduous task for all involved, than to become aware of and cope with our feelings of frustration, aggression, and fear.

In summary—there seems to be a considerable implication of all this for the task of pre-service and in-service training of staff, and for the ongoing supervisory process on all levels. Without going into any of these details today, it may suffice to state that the clinical morale and astuteness of a given residential staff well developed for the original onslaught of pathology in the raw, may need considerable re-structuring, in order to be equally foolproof against the terrific onslaught of the first improvement wave.

IMPROVEMENT—WHAT IS THE COST TO THE INSTITUTION?

When child patients are treated in an institutional setting of any kind—and some of this even holds for the less enduring settings, such as outpatient therapy clubs—the phenomenon of improvement creates new tasks and new problems, which seem to me to deserve much more recognition than they have gained in the past. All too often do we design our institutional framework primarily for the "treatment" of a given disease entity or disturbance of some kind. Somehow we hope that within all this the patient will "get better" and finally be ready for discharge. Not enough do we often realize, how the step by step impact of improvements which have already taken place may change the whole treatment need of individual or group, to the point where co-existence with the originally clinically correct pathology service design becomes a problem of first order. To mention but a few of the most obvious observations to the point:

1. *Danger to a real "treatment atmosphere" in favor of a system of institutionalized penalties and rewards, or of assessments of part achievements.* In a place where most kids have shed their worst primitiveness, it is quite possible to make demands, set standards, which give a smooth image of a well run place, with the kids on the health-proximity end of the line more or less setting the tone and representing the place to the world outside. As soon as this happens, regression becomes a luxury hard to afford, conformity to some standardized expectations becomes a real issue with the group of kids, even if the adults would retain clinical flexibility in their thoughts. Individualization, respect for special anxieties, oddities, and pathological blow-ups become something the institution is increasingly ashamed of. They blush if it happens, instead of taking pride in how wisely they handled it when it occurs. Even a clinically highly sophisticated setting may temporarily suffer such a *relapse*

into pre-clinical naivete just at the very moment when their first successes become clear to all. In our own experience, for instance, I had little trouble convincing even clinically not very sophisticated or highly trained staff, of the impossibility of using punishments on kids who have obviously no sense of future or of past. When the children began to improve, I found myself forced to write long essays to reassure even the treatment staff of the difference between intervention and punishment, between normal children at home and child patients on a still closed or just opened ward. . . .

2. *The emergence of a system of "caste" and "outcast."* The adults may "understand" why Bobby is now ready for more leeway and less tight supervision, more trust with gadgets and less fussiness, and even Bobby may. But how will this affect the other children? For *them,* what I and the child know is simply a concession to his greater self-control, looks like rank favoritism of the worst kind. Also, if the group "improves" in too uneven rates, it is unavoidable that some consider themselves quite excluded from "privileges" which the others seem to enjoy, and the concept of the "privileged character" can be as destructive in a treatment setting as in detention homes. Also, under the pressure of such a system of "privileges one enjoys after one has improved" and "absence of rights one is doomed to because one isn't trusted enough" becomes more or less institutionalized, it develops a suction power of its own with disastrous effects all around.

Only the constant vigilance of staff about their own motives, and the careful interpretation—by word or deed—of all events that might give rise to such suspicions to all children involved—including the group of "onlookers"—can safeguard an institution against this trap.

3. *Program distortion for the rest of the group.* Aside from these interpretational pitfalls, it also easily happens that the program diet which the less improved children get *actually* changes way beyond what is

clinically wise. This change may occur in two directions: it may lead to a *pauperization* of the program for those who don't quite seem to be up to it yet. Staff may betray their annoyance with the level of operation of the less improved, and too openly display their understandable gratification with the program for those who are more advanced and therefore more gratifying to work with. Or the change may lead to *stepped up demands* for all, with disastrous results for those who just cannot yet make it. In both cases an institution would lose its clinical value for some of the children, while increasing its fitness for those on top.

4. *Differentiation between "regression" and legitimate "improvement mess."* One of the hardest issues to interpret to outsiders, and occasionally to oneself, is the fact that improvement, in growing kids, of course does not mean the termination of problems or even of problem behavior. An adolescent, for instance, who spent his pre-adolescent years on a closed ward with a small group of also disturbed peers, and who is really "coming along well," will be *expected* to have to live through all the usual turmoil of adolescent awakening sexuality, of concern about peer status, of battle with home personnel about his newly discovered status of emancipated young man. Life with teenagers alone, no matter how normal, can be full of problems, and of problem behavior of considerable proportions. Why should "our kids" be an exception to this? And yet, we were very tempted to interpret their first steps into adolescent rebellion as just "regression to their old ways," to react to their normal adolescent overestimation of anything outside and devaluation of what they have at home, as though it simply meant "we never got anywhere, they are as hostile and hard to please as they were when they came." In fact, if your youngsters enter their adolescent phase just at the time when improvements set in and when their scope of activities is branching out into the community more and more, staff is likely to

develop some sort of envy toward people outside, who seem to have an easier time with them, than the home base personnel. Yet any parent of any normal child is quite used to just that. The real problem, however, lies in the difficulty to *assess* correctly even in our own domain, just what we have before us: regression or problem behavior which accompanies their coping with a new part of life. Research in this direction is practically nonexistent; its expansion way beyond its present state devoutly to be wished.

5. *Accepting the challenge of the calculated risk—and the public hatred in its wake.* It is hard but safe to run a place for the extremely sick. Nobody expects any better from you, as long as you keep them out of their hair. You, yourself, have a constant alibi in your vest pocket—in view of the enormous pathology that stares you in the face, even superhuman effort can't well be blamed for failing.

Once the children "improve," doubt rises, whether we couldn't do "more" for them, and indeed, ever more seems to be needed. To cater to the needs of an "improved" personality on the way back to health, however, is quite a different task from treating a bunch of incurables humanely and with some clinical hope. It involves an increased demand for *calculated risk*. For some institutions, such as mental hospitals for instance, this even constitutes a legal and administrative problem of considerable scope.

To use just one illustration for many: at a certain state in his development, Bobby could be trusted with the ward keys for a short trip down to the coke machine. In fact, he *needed* such trust experiences when halfway ready for them, for how can anybody develop autonomy on a leash? On the other hand, in a mental hospital such practice is strictly against the rule, lower status staff can well be fired for such a breach of rules. Or: Johnny and Max are now in need of partial independence from the group, and of an experience of behaving well, out of decency to the counselor who is "on." Result: this said counselor will of course give in to their requests to "go on up the creek a little for some more crabs while you are packing up, we will be back in five minutes, honest." If the counselor knows his children and their mood, and the clinical phase they are in, such a permission is a clinical *must*. Yet, he better not record the incident, for it is against all laws of the land. And of course, we don't even insist that this judgment was entirely right. We even hope the risk will misfire from time to time, for only such misfiring gives us the chance for the "clinical exploitation of a dramatic life event," which may shorten the child's treatment by months.

In the transition from a closed unit to open life in the community, the cost of the improvement of our children became even more painfully visible. For the public in general has little tolerance for a risk that misfires, no matter how well it was calculated, or how wisely exploited for the therapy of the child. In fact, this may well be one of the reasons why we still have so many closed wards or highly restrictive institutions, and so many fewer places where the "last stretch from sickness to health" could be taken. For, as our societal hatred of those who deal with the dangerous and the mentally sick is what it is known to be—who could take the risk of supporting that last stretch toward mental health, without losing his own?

SUMMARY

The readings in this chapter reflect the diversity of our concepts of improvement and failure, still in their theoretical stages of development. In trying to explain Jane's failure in remedial reading, Miller suggests we need more precise methods of translating diagnostic information into specific teaching procedures. Bettelheim offers both positive and negative reasons that could explain Jane's decision to fail. Newman tells how the fusion of psychodynamic theory and remedial methods can bring significant change. She would hypothesize that Jane probably needed a comprehensive approach to her reading difficulty, which alternated individual psychotherapy and individual tutoring. Finally, Redl re-opens the entire question of improvement, emphasizing its complexity and the necessity of translating the dynamics of observed improvement into useful ways of helping children.

8

How Is Research Helping?

The very term "research" defies precise definition and cannot be circumscribed by a given set of methods. Educational research, defined broadly, is "any systematic striving for understanding actuated by a need or sensed difficulty directed toward some complex phenomenon of more than immediate personal concern stated in problematic form."[1] Some specialists working with the emotionally disturbed speak of "research" when they record their observations following a classroom visitation. Others speak of "hard" research—meaning the application of rigorous statistical tests to given data. But, even here, statistically significant findings may have very low power of determination and little predictive value. Although you may know that group A differs significantly from group B, you still cannot always tell how any single member of either group will behave.

The clinical and educational fields overlap in the research we are concerned with here—in the broad area between mental health as seen in the normal child and the sickness of the purely psychiatric cases. There is as yet no encyclopedia of research on the nature and education of the disturbed child. However, the *Annual Review of Psychology,* the *Handbook of Psychiatry,* and, more specifically, periodic issues of *The Review of Educational Research* cover material in this area. Still the topic remains to a considerable degree amorphous.

One profound limitation in this area of research is the great difficulty of asking the right questions. We are still in the crude stage of formulating rational generalizations. We treat polyglot groups of children as if each member were of the same composition. We can't compare the results of one study with another because we can't identify the nature of the various samples studied. Then, when we do ask a reasonable question, we frequently find ourselves without adequate scales for measuring the conditions or attitudes we wish to assess. Ancillary conditions we once thought unimportant sometimes turn out to be more powerful than the controlled variables we set out to study. For example, we try to find out whether disturbed children learn more effectively in the regular class or in a special class, but we do not know the pupil attitudes toward being integrated or segregated. These attitudes may prove to be more important than teaching procedures.

Given this state of affairs, what can be accomplished by this chapter? Our goal is simply to present several prevalent styles of research and expose the complexities involved.

It should be emphasized that our comments do not constitute a negative

[1] C. W. Harris, ed., *Encyclopedia of Educational Research,* 3rd ed. (New York: Macmillan Co., 1960). The reader interested in an extensive discussion of the many meanings of research, kinds of research and "good" research should consult this source.

evaluation of the work under review. Only the uninitiated have the naiveté to belittle what painstaking research is now available. Carefully read and thoughtfully digested, this scientific knowledge is the key to professional growth.

Since we are interested only in examining representative researches and not in devising a systematic classification scheme, we are using a simplified organization in this chapter, examining several types of work without any implication of hierarchy: (1) the anecdotal style, (2) analytic examination, (3) systematic recording, and (4) controlled experimental work.

ANECDOTAL

This is the most common style of research. Information exchange between teachers tends to be *anecdotal*. In staff discussions, example follows example. The advantage is that the material is *specific*, frequently *vivid*, and carries its own insight, like a clear vignette. However, anecdotal material depends upon the adequacy of recall and is subject to the distortion of the agent. Since each instance is particular, generalization is limited. Life and reality take precedence over universality. As a matter of fact, one of the difficulties in applying this type of information is deciding whether or not our intended use is appropriate, torn as it is from the totality which gave it honesty. The idiosyncratic nature of events and the vast "unconscious" which constitute unspoken determinants are often ignored. Real "look alikes" or "be alikes" are rare indeed.

Anecdotal recall is only one step away from dramatic recall, or fictionalized experience, where the highlights are higher and the etching is unmistakable. Frequently compounded of many anecdotes and distilled through the sensitivities of the gifted writer, fictionalized experiences may be more real than reality in the power of what they can convey. Many selections in this book of readings contain illustrative anecdotes, sometimes used to build up concrete meaning for statistical findings. But the major reflection of the anecdotal type is found in Chapter 1, How Does It Feel to Be Emotionally Disturbed? We see what each writer-researcher has taken great pains to present. Emphatic identification is provided in a way that we sense reality where we might miss it in a sterile case history. It is one thing to say that twenty percent of a given number of the cases are anxious, as indicated by their scores on a projective test. It is another matter to communicate the essence of anxiety, not as a statistic, but as a person's state of being.

How bitter is the hostile delinquent? How does it feel to be culturally deprived? What is the feeling of dissonance and strangeness? These examples from literature illustrate what has been sometimes called the "Law of the Case." With all its limitations and possible misuses, anecdotal research deserves our attention. It conveys truth and is a source of knowledge. We are not illustrating this again since this volume already contains many examples.

ANALYTIC EXAMINATION

A second division of research consists of reports embodying an analysis-in-depth of a given situation. While the *analytic examination* system is built from a series of anecdotal observations, it is more than a mere compilation of observations. The research element so important here is the keen intellectual analysis, which often takes unconventional and arresting directions, rather than the use of statistical tests on the significance of differences and so on.

We are not so likely to receive edification from the data alone as we are from the penetrating analysis of the implications and the iconoclastic revelations that result. After reading a research of this type we sometimes find ourselves saying, "Of course." "Simple." "I knew it all the time." This only means that the power of the analysis has made the conclusion appear obvious, even simple. But it took unusual creativity to uncover the concept in the first place.

Redl's articles in previous chapters illustrate the evolution of theory from the application of a creative approach to the observation of data. In his material on milieu (Chapter 3), research was focused on an undefined but often used concept, noted both for its importance and vagueness at one and the same time. Redl first points out that this concept of milieu needs specificity and proceeds to tell us what it is not. Then he proceeds to clarify the various meanings. By taking the Gestalt (the whole) apart and turning to one element after the other, he enables us to understand how the therapeutic-milieu approach functions. In his speculations on improvement (Chapter 7), Redl again points up the need for specific definitions. Actually improvement is one of the most vexing and yet essential concepts in all of our work. By what token are we to say the patient has improved, he asks. We have all realized that we differ, but the systematic examination of the elements has been needed.

The selection reprinted here, by Rabinovitch and Ingram, is notable for the clinical insight displayed in its observations of a series of cases seen in a psychiatric setting. It would be misleading to think this was all the result of *ad hoc* appraisal. It is but part of a series of studies leading to the development of a new instrument through the examination of test data and the "sensing" of interview and case-history material. This is typical of the way first-run hunches are re-examined and then refined to the point that they can be tried on a new population.

Three major diagnostic groupings are formulated. We do not know in what percentages these types are found but we do see clearly what they are. Then the syndrome of "primary retardation" is developed in detail with concrete examples. The generalizations drawn from the cases and the etiology are woven into the practical implications for treatment.

Neuropsychiatric Considerations in Reading Retardation

Ralph D. Rabinovitch and Winifred Ingram

A close, interdependent relationship between our schools and our psychiatric clinics and hospitals is generally recognized as essential for effective work with school age children. Two relatively new developments have further highlighted the need

From Ralph D. Rabinovitch and Winifred Ingram, "Neuropsychiatric Considerations in Reading Retardation," *Reading Teacher*, XV (May 1962), 433–439. Reprinted with permission of the International Reading Association and the authors.

Ralph D. Rabinovitch, formerly Director of the Children's Psychiatric Hospital, University of Michigan Medical School, is Director of Hawthorn Center in Northville, Mich. Winifred Ingram heads the Center's Department of Clinical Psychology.

for this integration of effort. On the one hand there is the rapid growth of special education classes for the emotionally disturbed in the public schools, and on the other hand expansion of specialized classroom programs in psychiatric day-care and in-patient centers (6).

In our work in both public school and psychiatric settings we have been impressed with the high incidence of reading and language problems among the total referrals. We have been particularly interested to note that in those schools that have developed special psychiatric or social adjustment rooms, the regular classroom teachers have tended to recommend children with both personality and gross reading problems. Even severe disturbance tends to be found tolerable in the classroom if the child is making adequate academic progress. This was not anticipated when some of these programs were established and we now find teachers trained to work with the emotionally disturbed faced with virtually illiterate children whose special remedial needs they do not feel competent to meet. Similarly, through bitter experience, we have learned that for a significant percentage of the *boys* admitted to Hawthorn Center's day-care or in-patient units, psychotherapy and milieu therapy alone are insufficient for rehabilitation; intensive specific remedial reading therapy must be added. Of necessity, then, our multidiscipline group has been forced to give major research and clinical attention to reading problems.

A severe burden imposed on child, family and clinic worker alike, is the tendency of many school people and pediatricians to refer the child with the assumption that the psychiatric clinic will find the learning problem to be due to an "emotional block" and that through the magic of psychotherapy, perhaps limited to a few interviews, the child will be "released" to learn adequately. Unfortunately some of us in child psychiatry and clinical psychology have fostered this attitude in the past, overgeneralizing dynamic formulations. The problem is much more complex and there is a need for careful differential diagnosis in each case studied.

Two broad factors in the child's reading functioning must be assessed: (1) The mastery of specific techniques and skills necessary for reading; (2) The application of skills in the learning situation.

In recent years there has been a valid emphasis by educators on content in learning, on the social meaningfulness of what is taught, and this has led to many positive changes in curriculum. Repetitive drill work has been reduced in both language and arithmetic, much to the benefit of the victims of schooling. In the large majority of children, reading skills tend to evolve spontaneously, stimulated and directed by good teachers. With these children content becomes the major concern. But, unfortunately, there are some for whom written material remains meaningless and for whom there can be no content because the *technique* of reading itself is lacking. Despite the highest level of motivation and effort, they have difficulty learning to translate letter symbols into concepts. The *process of symbolization* is impaired and learning through "normal" teaching methods cannot be expected.

In some of these cases history indicates brain injury (encephalopathy) as the probable cause of the disability. In other cases no such history is found and the disability is felt to be due to a developmental neurological deficit.

Using the broad term "reading retardation" to describe all cases in which there is a significant discrepancy between mental age on performance tests and level of reading achievement, we can, then, define three major diagnostic groupings (7, 8):

1. Capacity to learn to read is impaired without definite brain damage suggested in history or on neurologic examination. The defect is in the ability to deal with letters and words as symbols, with resultant diminished ability to integrate the meaningfulness of written material. The problem ap-

pears to reflect a basic disturbed pattern of neurologic organization. Because the cause is biologic or endogenous, these cases are diagnosed as *primary reading retardation.*

2. Capacity to learn to read is impaired by frank brain damage manifested by clear-cut neurologic deficits. The picture is similar to the early-described adult dyslexic syndromes. Other definite aphasic difficulties are generally present. History usually reveals the cause of the brain injury, common agents being prenatal toxicity, birth trauma or anoxia, encephalitis, and head injury. These cases are diagnosed as *brain injury with resultant reading retardation.*

3. Capacity to learn to read is intact but is utilized insufficiently for the child to achieve a reading level appropriate to his mental age. The causative factors is exogenous, the child having a normal reading potential that has been impaired by negativism, anxiety, depression, emotional blocking, psychosis, limited schooling opportunity or other external influence. We diagnose these as *secondary reading retardation.*

Unfortunately the criteria for definite differential diagnosis are still uncertain and the problem is complicated by much overlap in etiology in individual cases. It is difficult to be certain in the cases of suspected secondary reading retardation, the problem being to rule out a basic developmental deficiency mild in degree. Through the years our research group has come to view the incidence of secondary retardation as lower than we had at first anticipated. While the meaningfulness to the child of what he reads will be strongly conditioned by his life experience and personality, and while the rapidity of his progress in learning will be much influenced by his social opportunities, his basic mastery of symbolization is probably much more neurologically determined than we had once thought. Detailed studies of the reading skills of severely disturbed inpatients, presenting a wide range of psychopathology and attending school in residence, should prove helpful in assessing the effects of specific rela-

tionship and life experience distortions on the reading process and its application. Such studies are now in progress at Hawthorn Center.

Of all the children with reading problems those with primary retardation present the greatest challenge. In our research we have devoted major attention to this group. Beginning with the surface symptom we can define the syndrome in terms of the following levels of process disturbance:

1. *Reading Retardation:* The level of disability is usually severe and apart from a small sight vocabulary, learned by rote, and sporadic simple phonic skills there may be almost no functional reading ability. Arithmetic competence is usually also low although it may be somewhat higher than the reading level. Greatest impairment may be in spelling, reflected in the child's attempts at writing to dictation.

2. *Reading Process Disturbance:* Analysis of the child's reading performance indicates difficulties in both visual and auditory areas and directionality also tends to be impaired. Visual recognition and discrimination on a perceptual level are intact but letter forms and combinations cannot be translated into meaningful concepts. In a similar way, in the auditory sphere, differences in vowel sounds are appreciated when presented orally, but the sounds cannot be translated into their letter symbols. For example, when a series of short vowel sounds "i, i, e, i" are presented orally, the "e" is readily recognized as different from the "i's" but the crucial step required for reading and spelling, the translation of the sound into its appropriate letter symbol, is impaired. The difficulty then is in symbolization in both visual and auditory fields. Complicating the problem may be left-right directional confusion with or without mixed laterality. Some typical illustrative examples of writing to dictation by children with a severe primary syndrome follow (5):

Paul is aged twelve, referred for psychiatric study because of severe depression. He is in the fifth grade, having repeated both the third and fourth grades. On the Wechsler Test performance I.Q. is 114, verbal I.Q. 82. Tested reading level is pre-primer despite a performance mental age of fourteen years. Diagnosis is severe primary retardation. Paul produces the following when asked to write to dictation "The boy came home":

ICiᵇ ɟIL Lıet GꟻLe

Paul's production reveals total confabulation with no capacity to deal with letters as symbols. Both visual and auditory skills are grossly deficient.

Bill, aged nine, was referred because of school truancy and acting-out behavior in the classroom. Originally considered mentally retarded because of inability to learn at school, psychometric testing indicates that Bill is of normal intellectual potential, performance I.Q. being 94; verbal I.Q. is 72. Reading level is low first grade. Bill writes "The boy came home" as follows:

The doy nor house

This child depends totally on his visual memory and has virtually no phonic skills. He recalls "nor" as a word and just hopes that by chance it will turn out to be "came." He struggles with "boy," but cannot differentiate from "dog" and the contamination "doy" emerges.

Tom is diagnosed as having primary reading retardation at age seven, midway through the first grade, which he had repeated. At that time he wrote "The boy came home" as follows:

TꝈꟻ T LoıꞰ

An intensive remedial program was instituted and at age nine he has progressed to this point:

the doy cane home

Tom still reverses "b's" and "d's" but he is well on the road to reading competence.

3. *Broader Language Deficits:* While in everyday conversation the child may ap-

pear to manage relatively well, careful attention to the language pattern reveals frequent difficulties in specific name finding, imprecise articulation and primitive syntax. Typical examples drawn from the responses by severe primary cases to test questioning follow:

Why is it better to build a house of brick than of wood? "Well just in case a hurricane the house can break down, but you put the brick on, it can just hit it but not break nothing down." (Age nine years)

What must you do to make water boil? "You should put it under a fire." (Age ten years)

How did he get hurt? "He sprang a thing, a arm when he felled out of that tree." (Age eleven years)

Is it night-time or day-time now? "Day-time. It's, well, clouds are out and stuff. It's white the clouds, it's lightsen up, the clouds and stuff." (Age nine years)

Is it morning or afternoon? "It's in the noon-time. Noon. In the noon." (Age nine years)

These tend to represent extreme examples, but we look for similar disturbances in expressive language in all cases of the primary syndrome.

4. *Specific Concept-Symbolization Deficiency in Orientation:* The symbolization defect is not limited to the reading processes alone, but is found to be more basic. There is difficulty in translating orientational concepts into symbols. Thus while the child has no trouble appreciating which of two people is taller, he cannot define their height in feet. Similarly, while he knows clearly that he wakes up in the morning, he may be unable to express this knowledge in terms of a specific hour. To explore further this orientational factor we have devised the Hawthorn Center Concept-Symbolization Test with questions relating to personal information, time, quantity and dimension, number, directionality and laterality. Drs. Ingram, Katz, Kauffman, Langman and Lynn of our group are now completing standardization of the test which we hope may prove helpful as a diagnostic and prog-

nostic instrument, especially with young children, and as a partial key to therapy need (4).

5. *Body Image Problems:* Even more basic, there may be disturbances in personal-orientation or body image but these have been much less clearly demonstrated. Now we are using Benton's Laterality and Finger Localization Test and other approaches to study further this aspect of the pathology (1).

All of us working with children with severe reading problems recognize the need for more precise differential diagnostic criteria. We are approaching this problem in two ways. First, a longitudinal study of reading progress of classes of children in public schools is under way. A large battery of tests has been given, starting with first grade, and two groups have been isolated for detailed comparative investigation, those at the highest and at the lowest end of the scale of reading competence; from this study, now in its fourth year, we hope to isolate prognostic indices. Second, our psychologists are attempting to refine differential diagnostic criteria through detailed analysis of psychologic test data, obtained from children presenting a wide range of psychopathology, including language and reading disabilities. Tests used are the Wechsler, the Stanford-Binet LM, Bender-Gestalt, Draw-A-Family, Hawthorn Center Concept-Symbolization Scale and Benton Laterality and Finger Localization Battery. Thus far all data point at least in one direction: the problem is not one in perception per se, but rather in the translation of perceptions and concepts into meaningful symbols that can be used in reading and related language functions.

The total symptom complex of the primary reading retardation syndrome gives, we feel, a clue to the etiology: a neurological deficit, often familial in origin, and expressing parietal cerebral dysfunction (2, 3).

No discussion of neuropsychiatric considerations in reading problems can avoid mention of the inordinate suffering experienced by otherwise normal children, cut off from communication channels, increasingly vital for survival today. With limited resources to meet their specific needs we are obliged all too often to limit our involvement with them to documenting their successive psychological reactions from initial anger to guilt feelings, depression and ultimate resignation and compromise with their aspirations. Work in clinics throughout the country has encouraged us to hope that early intervention by well trained language therapists may permit many children with primary reading retardation to develop at least functional reading competence. Major needs are for early diagnosis and the provision of intensive remedial programs in the public schools. In addition, an adjusted curriculum throughout the school years, relying minimally on literacy, must be devised for some students. It is interesting, if disconcerting, to note how much further advanced our speech correction programs are, in comparison with those for reading therapy. It may be that the speech correction workers have been more aggressive in presenting their reasonable demands and have in the past had more clear-cut programs to offer. But now, as reading diagnostic issues are becoming clarified and as specific remedial techniques are evolving, the time is ripe for implementation of large-scale special education reading services in our public schools. Such programs, financed by special reimbursements available in many States, must take their place alongside those already established for children with speech, visual, hearing, orthopedic and other handicaps. In view of the fact that no responsibility of the public school is greater than to teach all children to read, the inclusion of remedial reading as a recognized branch of special education would seem as logical as it is essential.

References

1. Benton, A. L. *Right-Left Discrimination and Finger Localization: Development and Pathology.* New York: Hoeber, 1959.

2. Critchley, M. *The Parietal Lobes.* Baltimore: Williams and Wilkins, 1953.

3. Drew, A. L. "A Neurological Appraisal of Familial Congenital Word-Blindness." *Brain,* **79**:440, 1956.

4. Langman, M. P. "The Reading Process: a Descriptive Interdisciplinary Approach." *Genetic Psychol. Monographs,* **62**:3, 1960.

5. Missildine, H., and L. Eisenberg. "Physician's Role in Management of Retarded Reader." *Feelings,* **3**, No. 9, October 1961.

6. Morse, W. C. "Education of the Socially Maladjusted and Emotionally Disturbed Children." W. M. Cruickshank and G. O. Johnson, eds., *Education and Exceptional Children and Youth.* New York: Prentice-Hall, 1958.

7. Rabinovitch, R. D. Learning and Reading Disabilities, in S. Arieti, ed., *Handbook of Psychiatry.* New York: Basic Books, 1959.

8. Rabinovitch, R. D., A. L. Drew, R. N. DeJong, W. Ingram, and L. Withey. "A Research Approach to Reading Retardation," in R. McIntosh, ed., *Neurology and Psychiatry in Childhood.* Baltimore: Williams and Wilkins, 1956.

SYSTEMATIC RECORDING

The major research format in special education is *systematic recording* of the status of events or a sequence of events. Surveys, which constitute a significant body of evidence, do not attempt to control an event but rather, examine what occurs. Many studies in this volume are of this type, in which the incidence of one or another condition is the focal point. These may be with or without prejudice. For example, reports may include without comment the percentage of neurotic versus psychopathic children in a population; or evaluation of the information may suggest that the true state of affairs differs from the reported state of affairs.

In the raw state, such data are frequently unwieldy and almost meaningless. The research effort comes in ordering and interrelating information to gain insight from it. At the present time even definitions are so loose and confused that the ordering and classifying of them becomes a research task in itself. The taxonomic process is thus systematically used to give a base line for further research, such as we saw in Hollister and Goldston's paper in Chapter 2.

No one would experiment with children by placing groups of youngsters under the care of presumed pathological parents in order to see what differences in their school achievement might result. But often when such conditions occur naturally we are helpless to interfere, and, properly assessed, these cases provide the researcher with experimental equivalents.

Quasi-experimental research of this nature is very difficult because we have no control over the variables. For instance, we may have a group of children whose mothers are rejecting, only to find that in half of the cases the fathers are living in the home, while in the other half they are not. Thus, the purity of the "experimental" condition is weakened, and only through complicated statistical procedures can the group be used to test certain hypotheses. The researcher, therefore, may concentrate on the variables he can modulate or those he is interested in, ignoring the others.

Even in laboratory studies, similar difficulties are often present. Ignored or presumed nonrelevant conditions may actually confound the interpretations. For example, it is known that the desire of willing subjects to do what experimenters want makes for very suggestible subjects. Or the unconscious feelings of children may be more potent than the effect of a special method we are investigating. For instance, the reliability of an achievement score may be affected by whether or not the pupil puts forth the same effort on the two days he takes an achievement test.

The following research, exemplifying the systematic recording method, is the summary chapter from a book by Irving Harris. He takes advantage of an *in situ* condition to study the kinds of family situations which might make a difference in pupil achievement. For his research, he selects one hundred emotionally disturbed boys *without* learning problems and one hundred emotionally disturbed boys *with* learning problems. What home conditions can account for these behavior differences? As nearly as possible, the groups are equal in disturbance but unequal in achievement. Harris investigates certain conditions that might account for the differences.

Emotional Blocks to Learning
Irving D. Harris

In reviewing the highlights of the previous sections, we will recall that the study began with an inquiry into those psychological factors which are specific to learning difficulties. One hundred emotionally disturbed boys with learning problems were compared with 100 emotionally disturbed boys without learning problems. We hoped, for example, to find why a boy with an I.Q. of 110 would be failing in all subjects whereas another emotionally disturbed boy with the same I.Q. would have no trouble in school. Our task was complicated by the fact that learning difficulties did not take one particular form. Thus, among the non-learner boys we saw such different symptoms as lack of motivation, low-average intelligence, difficulties in concentrating, repeating of grades, resistance to the educator, specific difficulty in reading, etc. We turned our attention, then, to finding which emotional or psychological factors are related to the several symptoms of learning difficulties.

In general, the factors are: socio-economic status; family disorganization; ambitiousness of parents (especially of the

mother); expectations of maturity; and aggression and submission.

Socio-economic Status. A significantly greater proportion of boys from lower-middle-class or lower-class families were present in the non-learner group than in the learner group. The particular manifestations seen in the non-learner boys from low status homes were: (a) low average intelligence; (b) teachers' descriptions of "dull but working to capacity"; (c) the repeating of grades. These manifestations were explained by lack of motivation in the lower-class family to learn for the sake of learning, by lack of stimulation of the boy's intellect, and by the family's low anxiety about the boy's repeating a grade.

Family Disorganization. The disorganization of the family was measured by two factors—the incompatibility of the marriage and the employment of the mother outside the home. The non-learners differed from the learners significantly in that many more of the former were from homes in which both factors were present. This was especially true of boys under the age of ten. The particular manifestations seen in the non-learners which appeared to result from this factor were: (a) difficulties in concentrating; (b) reading problems; (c) the repeating of grades. These manifestations were attributed to a chronic feeling of anxious insecurity in the boy as to whether his home would stay intact or come apart. This feeling, in turn, was traced to the personality of the mother who was unable to function as a homemaker or rejected that role.

Parental Ambitiousness. The effects of this factor were more complicated than were those of the previous factors. In the non-learner group, the mothers were ambitious for the boys with low average intelligence; whereas in the learner group, the mothers were ambitious for the boys with superior intelligence. Thus, the most pronounced learning difficulties were seen in the non-learner boys who apparently did not have the intellectual capacity to gratify their mothers' need for achievement and status. The particular manifestation seen was resistance to the teacher, a resistance which frequently took the form of dawdling or procrastination. Several explanations of this were offered: (1) the boy can punish his pressuring mother by thwarting her; (2) he resists the educator in order to preserve his autonomy; (3) he is afraid of being measured and found wanting; (4) he is afraid of being measured and found to be successful—since his success is a threat to his rivalrous mother or father.

Birth Order and Expectations of Maturity. The non-learner group had significantly more last-born and fewer first-born sons than the learner group. To explain this, evidence was presented that indicated that the last-born tended to be less serious and responsible than the first-born; consequently, the former are less prone to apply themselves arduously to the task of learning. Further, it appeared that parents usually have lower expectation of maturity of last-born children than of first-born children.

Aggression and Submission. In this part of the study, two aspects of the problem of aggressive behavior were investigated. First, it was found that parents who did not take responsibility for their own mistakes, but rather projected the blame onto scapegoats such as their spouses or the schools, tended to have sons who emulated them in not taking any responsibility for their own aggressive behavior. On the other hand, parents who guiltily took on too much self-blame tended to have sons who were overly co-operative, submissive, or anxious to please.

The other aspect of the topic dealt with learning itself. The non-learner group, in comparison to the learner group, more often showed extremes in the area of aggression; they were aggressively hostile or extremely submissive. In the non-learner group, both of these extremes were associated with difficulties in reading. The explanation appeared to be that extremes of rage (or anxiety over expressing rage) interfered with learning in general and with the delicate mechanism involved in reading in particular. That the intelligence scores of the openly aggressive boys were higher than those of the submissive ones suggested that the energy of free aggressiveness is necessary for intellectual vigor and alertness. . . .

These, in terse form, are the essential points of the previous chapters. One conclusion is easily evident: namely, that since learning problems have several causes rather than just one, each case has to be understood in its own terms. Understanding why a lower-class boy does not learn will not necessarily help one to comprehend why an upper-class boy fails. Even upper-class boys have different reasons for learning problems—worry about a disorganized family in one case, resistance to an unusually ambitious mother in another. Any one of the factors discussed *may* predispose a boy to some difficulty in learning. The greater the number of factors existing simultaneously in one case, the greater is the likelihood that a learning problem will be present.

Another, and very common, type of systematic-recording research is the follow-up study. This involves studying, after a time lapse, children who at one time exhibited common behavior. Or the study may be done in reverse—that is, it may go into the individual childhoods of adults who exhibit common symptoms, to discover the similarities or differences that existed in their earlier years. Often we do not know why given changes have taken place or, more particularly, why they happened to one child and not another. In some instances, the reasons for differential change can be studied through contrasts of subgroups. These works can be classified generally as follow-up studies, and in the examples presented are samples of the wide variety of findings that can come from this most common methodology.

In the first follow-up study, Bower and his co-workers include both a status survey and follow-up data. The group studied was identified after its members had developed a recognized deviancy, schizophrenia. Next, a random control group was located. Then the researchers examined the previous behavior of both groups when the members were in school. Here the interest is in comparing known schizophrenics with known normals, and the authors do not imply anything more. The study does not enable us to know how other students, perhaps with high school behavior similar to those of the schizophrenic group, turn out in later life. When reading research, one must avoid the pitfall of going far beyond the intent of the scientist himself and improperly extrapolating his findings. The explicit discussion of the many difficulties encountered in doing a tight examination of the problem under study gives this article particular value as an example of systematic recording.

Characteristics Observed in Preschizophrenic Adolescents

Eli M. Bower, Thomas A. Shellhamer, and John M. Daily

There are significant gaps in our present knowledge of the personality antecedents of schizophrenics which are most visible by scrutinizing the research methods and procedures which have been used to date. Most researchers have aimed their energies at follow-up studies of known groups of children. One of the difficulties in research of this type lies in the disappearance of the more mobile members of the group who in some studies constitute a sizable number. For example, a follow-up study of persons seen as children in a municipal psychiatric clinic and a control

From Eli M. Bower, Thomas A. Shellhamer, and John M. Daily, "School Characteristics of Male Adolescents Who Later Became Schizophrenic," *American Journal of Orthopsychiatry*, XXX (October 1960), 712–729.

group 30 years later showed that the geographic mobility of the patient group significantly exceeded that of the control group. Not only did persons seen in the clinic move more often from town to town but they tended to change their address more often within a city. The investigators concluded that children who are sufficiently disturbed to be referred to a child guidance clinic grow up into adults who are highly mobile. Another limitation of this type of research study is that the status of the follow-up group is often evaluated on the basis of a single criterion such as difficulty with the law.

Age and circumstances may play a large part in defining how the vulnerability of the individual to emotional problems is expressed. Those studies which attempted to assess the total psychiatric health of the follow-up group have had to do this in short time periods with limited staff. In some cases such as in the Kasanin and Veo study (2), the respondents knew that the persons about whom they were reporting had been or were patients in a mental hospital. Indeed it is difficult to mask the intent or nature of retrospective or follow-up studies. One can only surmise the extent to which a person's perception of another is altered by knowing that the person has been or is mentally ill. In the present study much effort went into disguising the purpose of the study; only in two cases did respondents indicate that they knew one of the boys had been hospitalized. Much effort also went into concealing the identity of the hospitalized boys from the interviewer to minimize his perceptual biases.

Another major difficulty in this type of longitudinal follow-up and evaluative research lies in the control or comparison group. This was mentioned by Bowman (1) 25 years ago with the admonition that "there are almost insurmountable difficulties in obtaining suitable control material. Ideally, one would wish for a group showing the same distribution of sex, age, race, intelligence, social status, etc., as found in the group of psychotic cases. The same method of obtaining material, i.e., interviewing relatives, friends, employers and others . . . should be utilized. Such a study might, theoretically, be made by picking persons at random on the streets, in stores, in the subway and similar places and securing their consent to such an investigation. Practically, it would seem impossible to carry out." . . .

Many studies do not include any relevant comparison group. Such a group may add little in some cases; in others it may prove to be of major importance. For example, in their evaluation, Witmer and Tufts (5) concluded as follows: "The chief importance of the Cambridge-Somerville Youth Study, so far as evaluation is concerned, is its use of a control group for checking results. Had this been lacking,

much greater claims for the effectiveness of the program . . . might have been made" (p. 30). With the exception of the O'Neal and Robins study (3, 4), control groups, where present, have been drawn from children who were referred to a child guidance clinic. This is of inestimable help in understanding differences among the various groups of children referred to a clinic but may be of minimal assistance in locating the significant differences in the history of the child or his follow-up adult counterpart from that of the average, randomly selected individual.

RESEARCH PLAN

The present investigation has attempted to resolve some of the problems inherent in this type of research by identifying the follow-up group first and working backwards. It was considered best, for example, to begin with a group with as much commonality in degree and kind of illness as could be psychiatrically ascertained. For this group, a group of hospitalized mental patients was selected all of whom had been studied by the staff and diagnosed as schizophrenic. The idea of getting everything and anything about the lives of these patients (and a control group) was abandoned; instead a good, clear-cut slice at some relevant point in the person's life was sought. For this cross-sectional slice the high school and the high school adolescent were chosen—his record, grades, extracurricular interests, and his perception by teachers and counselors. The final choice of this period for retrospective viewing was made after preliminary investigation demonstrated that most of the faculty of the average high school could well remember students who had attended within the past five years. Another reason for choosing the high school period is that demonstrable differences at this point in the life of the preschizophrenic and other youth could perhaps be more effectively used in any preventive effort by the school. The question the research project hoped to answer was: To what extent are the high school records and staff perception of an adolescent who later becomes schizophrenic significantly different from those of other high school students?

As the research plan developed it was acknowledged by all that to get valid information on students, one should not divulge the exact nature of the study to the respondents and that the results might be less biased if the interviewer did not know which of the boys was hospitalized. To accomplish this, the study procedure needed to combine the subtlety of the OSS with the guile of a con man. Fortunately, the two agencies undertaking the research project could accomplish this without disproportionate effort or time. One had access to patients; the other to high school records and staff.

RESEARCH PROCESS AS SEEN BY THE SCHOOL

The process of the research might best be recounted by permitting the reader to don a cloak of invisibility and accompany two investigators from the staff of the California State Department of Education as they visit a high school. The two investigators have staff positions with research responsibilities and are no strangers to most of the schools or administrators in the state. They are first observed ascending the stairs of a high school and entering the principal's office. After the customary greeting, the principal, referring to a letter on his desk, says, "Your letter mentions that you are trying to find out something about the characteristics of high school students and how they are related to their later occupational success. We are very interested in this problem, too. I often wonder about some of our graduates and how they're getting along. We hear about some, but most we never see again. But tell me, how are you going to do this?" The investigators then explain that this high school and the others in the study are selected at random from the high schools in the state. After the high school is

selected the students to be studied are randomly selected from a class yearbook. All available information is then sought on each student from faculty and other staff who might have known both students. Copies of transcripts, cumulative records, grades, extracurricular activities and standardized test scores are also obtained. Other agencies are then responsible for the follow-up work.

After this explanation the investigators select a year at random from a group of possible years and obtain the appropriate class yearbook from the principal. Investigator A selects two boys at random from the yearbook. With the help of the principal and other administrative staff, interviews are scheduled with faculty or counselors who have known both boys. Such interviews are conducted by Investigator B. Meanwhile, Investigator A records all information in the files or cumulative records about each boy. The interviews and record compilation are usually completed within a few hours. From September 1956 to October 1958, approximately 50 such visits were made and information obtained on 88 students.

RESEARCH PROCESS AS IT REALLY OPERATED

To understand fully what went on in the afore-mentioned scene, one would need a little help from a time machine. This would take one back to the time when the California State Department of Education and the Veterans Administration Hospital, Palo Alto, had planned to gather information to confirm or reject the following hypotheses:

1. High school students who later become schizophrenic will be significantly different from a control group in the manner in which they are perceived by school staffs and in certain phases of their school records.

2. The school staff and school records contain sufficient relevant data on students who have left school within five or less

years to adequately assess their school mental health.

3. The developing schizophrenic is readily recognizable during his high school years and is perceived as having more emotional problems by the school staff.

The research task of the hospital staff was to identify white patients in the hospital population who had attended high school in California at least one full year, who were born after January 1, 1933, and who had been diagnosed as schizophrenic. The names of these patients and information as to the high school attended and the year or years of attendance were mailed to a research consultant in the State Department of Education. Each name was then placed in a sealed envelope upon which was written the name of the high school and the years of attendance. The State Department of Education then sent a letter to the principal of the high school to make arrangements for a visit of research staff who were doing a study on Relationship of the Characteristics of High School Students to Their Later Occupational Success." One of the two research investigators who visited the school memorized the name of the patient and the date of his last year of attendance. Under the guise of selecting two students at random he selected the patient and a control, usually the next name in the yearbook or class list unless the photograph in the yearbook indicated a difference of race, or the name indicated a possibility of family relationships. The other investigator then did the interviewing of high school staff without knowing which was the control or experimental subject. The final list of controls was later checked by relevant state agencies to rule out the possibility of mental illness in members of the control group.

The interviews of the school staffs were structured in large part by a rating sheet developed by the staff of the VA hospital and the State Department of Education, which contained 18 descriptive statements of behavior including such behavior as *degree to which liked by other students, appearance, ability for*
leadership, participation in group activities, interest in girls, apathetic-energetic, depressed-cheerful, careless-perfectionistic. There were two items, *over-all school adjustment* and *mental health,* which were presented at the end of the interview, with the interviewee defining in his own way the meaning of the terms. All statements were rated on a 5-point scale consistent with the item. For example, *degree to which liked by other students* had the following rating categories: (1) tends to irritate and be disliked by most people who come in contact with him; (2) in general, not too well liked by others; (3) liked as well as most; (4) tends to be liked somewhat more than most; (5) liked by almost all that know him. The last two items, *over-all school adjustment* and *mental health,* were rated on a 5-point scale from exceedingly poor to excellent.

In almost all cases the interview was begun by showing the interviewee the pictures of both students and asking, "What is the first thing that comes to your mind about each of these boys?" The interviewee was then encouraged to continue in his free association responses until he ran out of memories. Some direct questions were then asked to complete the gaps on the Interview Rating Scale. Faculty members who had known both boys were given priority as interviewees. In almost all cases staff were available who remembered the boys in class, as counselees, or as members of athletic teams. In some cases, boys made little impression on staff but were remembered as such.

RESULTS

The results indicate that the school staff perception of the preschizophrenic boy is essentially one of general passivity toward others and toward the school environment (Table 1). This includes specifically lack of interest in girls, group activities, and sports. The preschizophrenic boy was also rated as more apathetic, careless, dependent, irresponsible, depressed and sub-

TABLE 1. COMPARISON OF STAFF PERCEPTIONS ON
INTERVIEW RATING SCALE OF PRESCHIZOPHRENIC
AND CONTROL GROUPS

ITEM	CHI SQUARE	P
1. Degree to which liked by others	12.00	.020
2. Conformity to rules and regulations	3.98	—
3. Appearance	7.76	—
4. Interest in environment	16.40	.010
5. Leadership	19.60	.001
6. Participation in group activities	20.26	.001
7. Participation in athletics	16.48	.010
8. Interest in opposite sex	28.60	.001
9. Overt expression of hostility	1.86	—
10. Submissive–aggressive	9.60	.050
11. Apathetic–energetic	15.72	.010
12. Cautious–impulsive	8.40	.050
13. Manifest anxiety	13.48	.010
14. Depressed–cheerful	10.34	.050
15. Complaining–noncomplaining	7.60	—
16. Dependent–independent	13.40	.010
17. Irresponsible–dependable	11.08	.020
18. Careless–perfectionistic	14.12	.010
19. Over-all school adjustment	22.40	.001
20. Mental health	32.62	.001

missive than his control. In addition, he was perceived as possessing more overt anxiety and was less well liked by his peers.

Comparing the preschizophrenics and controls on the basis of the classification devised by Kasanin and Veo (Table 2), it is noted that the present group of schizophrenics are behaviorally different from the control group in high school and are also different from the group of patients studied by Kasanin and Veo. The difference between the preschizophrenics in the Kasanin and Veo study and the present study is undoubtedly the result of a combination of differences in research plan and technique. The Kasanin and Veo group of schizophrenics were culled largely from elementary school records as opposed to high school records in the present study. One might argue that the group of schizophrenics in the present study were a healthier group with more personality strength and resilience, since many were able to survive the academic regimen of high school and all were able to pass the psychiatric screening test for military service. Other differences in the two studies consisted of the inclusion of 31 females in the 45 schizophrenics studied by Kasanin and Veo as compared to no females in the present study. In addition, about one-third of the Kasanin and Veo group were undiagnosed or had a nonschizophrenic diagnosis. Also, the persons reporting on the Kasanin and Veo group were aware that the individual had become mentally ill and had been hospitalized. Nevertheless, to obtain an adequate descriptive comparison it is interesting to compare the numbers of pre-schizophrenics and controls who fell into the five categories devised by Kasanin and Veo (Table 2). The following brief histories are case examples of adolescents who later became schizophrenic, as classified on the basis of the descriptions of Kasanin and Veo.

Category I. Children of unusually striking personality. Children noted by others to be odd . . . peculiar. Teacher noted something wrong with child's development. . . .

TABLE 2. DISTRIBUTION AND COMPARISON OF KASANIN AND
VEO (1932) PRESCHIZOPHRENIC GROUP AND PRESENT
PRESCHIZOPHRENIC AND CONTROL GROUPS ON THE
BASIS OF KASANIN AND VEO'S CLASSIFICATION

| | DISTRIBUTION | | | | | |
CLASSIFICATION	PRESCHIZOPHRENIC GROUP (1932) KASANIN AND VEO N = 54		PRESENT STUDY PRESCHIZOPHRENIC GROUP N = 44		PRESENT STUDY CONTROL GROUP N = 44	
	NUMBER	PER CENT	NUMBER	PER CENT	NUMBER	PER CENT
I. Children of unusually striking personality. Children noted by others to be odd, peculiar, queer and at times crazy. Teachers noted something wrong with child's development.	12	22.2	9	20.5	2	4.5
II. Children with slight personality problems, somewhat different but not markedly so. Shy, dreamy, lacked concentration, temperamental and stubborn. Teachers' opinions mixed.	16	29.6	19	43.2	3	6.8
III. Children who are well liked by some teachers. Appear to be well adjusted, well integrated, moderately popular, sociable with no apparent difficulty in school.	5	9.3	9	20.5	31	70.5
IV. Children with qualities of leadership in athletics or scholarship, "pride of the school," eager for success, perhaps a little too eager at times.	6	11.1	3	6.8	8	18.2
V. Children who were no problem, seldom noticed, seclusive and quiet. They are often hazily remembered as sensitive, shy, passive and colorless.	15	27.8	4	9.0	0	0.0
Total	54	100.0	44	100.0	44	100.0

	COMPARISON	
	CHI SQUARE	P
Kasanin and Veo (1932) Preschizophrenic group (present study)	9.4	.05
Preschizophrenic group (present study) Control group (present study)	23.6	.001

Category II. Children with slight personality problems, somewhat different but not markedly so. . . .

Category III. Children who are well liked by some teachers, appear to be well adjusted, well integrated, moderately popular, sociable, with no apparent difficulty in school. . . .

Category IV. Children with qualities of leadership in athletics or scholarship, "pride of the school," eager for success, perhaps a little too eager at times. . . .

Category V. Children who were no problem seldom noticed, seclusive and quiet. They are often hazily remembered as sensitive, shy, passive, and colorless. . . .

SCHOOL RECORDS

Comparisons of the preschizophrenic and control groups on various aspects of

TABLE 3. SIGNIFICANT COMPARISON OF PRESCHIZOPHRENIC
AND CONTROL GROUPS ON SELECTED ITEMS
IN THEIR SCHOOL RECORDS

ITEM	MAJOR DIFFERENCE OF PRESCHIZOPHRENIC GROUP FROM CONTROL GROUP	STATISTICAL TEST	P
1. Graduation	Fewer graduated	$X^2 = 9.2$	.01
2. Course of study followed (College preparatory or general)	Enrolled in general course of study	$X^2 = 6.6$	.01
3. Best subjects	Did best in foreign languages. Did poorest in physical education and mathematics	$X^2 = 28.5$	.001
4. Subjects failed	English, social studies, and mathematics	$X^2 = 20.6$	.02
5. Over-all grade pattern	Declining	$X^2 = 10.2$	.02
6. Grade average	One grade below control	$CR = 3.67$	.001
7. Attendance	Poorer	$X^2 = 6.2$	.02
8. Extracurricular activities	Less interest in sports and dramatics	$X^2 = 16.8$	.05
9. IQ score	Preschizophrenic: M = 99.3 Control: M = 106.3	$CR = 2.1$	.05

school records are shown in Table 3. The school records showed that 65 per cent of the preschizophrenic group and 90 per cent of the controls graduated from high school. While in school 38 per cent of the preschizophrenic group and 62 per cent of the control group followed a college preparatory program. The preschizophrenic group tended to achieve their highest grades in foreign languages. The control group achieved significantly better than the preschizophrenic group in vocational courses, physical education, and mathematics. A larger percentage of the preschizophrenic group failed English, social studies, and mathematics than did the control group, which is understandable since these are largely required courses for all. The over-all grade patterns of both groups were analyzed to determine whether the student's achievement in his high school career followed a declining, inclining, or erratic trend. Six per cent of the control group showed a declining grade pattern as compared to 25 per cent for the preschizophrenic group.

On a grade point distribution of A = 4, B = 3, C = 2, D = 1, F = 0, the preschizophrenic group achieved a grade average of 2.04 as compared to 2.48 for the control group. The preschizophrenic group had significantly poorer school attendance records compared to the controls.

In none of the extracurricular activities such as interscholastic sports, dramatics, school clubs, and student government activities did the preschizophrenic group show a higher degree of participation than did the control group. The control group showed particularly high participation when compared to the preschizophrenic group in interscholastic sports and drama. The IQ's derived from the last group test taken by the student in high school showed the mean score of the controls to be significantly higher than the mean score of the preschizophrenic group.

CONCLUSION

High school students who later become schizophrenic were found to be significantly different from a randomly selected control group of their peers in the manner in which they are perceived by their school staffs and in certain phases of their school records. The school staff and school records were found to contain sufficient relevant data on students to adequately assess the predisposition of the preschizophrenic group.

The developing schizophrenic boys tended to have less interest in girls, group activities, and athletics. They showed less leadership skills and were more submissive, anxious, dependent and careless than the average boy. Although they were less well liked by their peers and teachers and did less well in school, they were not usually perceived as major problems or as being emotionally disturbed. However, in almost all cases their over-all mental health and school adjustment was rated significantly poorer than the control group. With a few exceptions most of the preschizophrenics could be characterized as tending toward the shut-in, withdrawing kind of personality.

References

1. Bowman, K. M. "A Study of the Prepsychotic Personality in Certain Psychoses." *American Journal of Orthopsychiatry*, **4**, 473–48, 1934.
2. Kasanin, J., and L. Veo. "A Study of the School Adjustments of Children Who Later in Life Became Psychotic," *American Journal of Orthopsychiatry*, **2**, 212–227, 1932.
3. O'Neal, Patricia, and Lee N. Robins. "The Relation of Childhood Behavior Problems to Adult Psychiatric Status: A 30-Year Follow-up Study of 150 Subjects." *American Journal of Psychiatry*, **114**, 961–969, 1958.
4. ———————. "Childhood Patterns Predictive of Adult Schizophrenia: A Follow-up Study." *American Journal of Psychiatry*, **115**, 385–391, 1959.
5. Witmer, Helen, and Edith Tufts. *The Effectiveness of Delinquency Prevention Programs*. Washington, D.C.: Children's Bureau, 1954.

In a sense, the follow-up just reported might be called a follow-back. Brown's study, in the next example, starts with the known population at an early age and traces what takes place with them over a long period of time. One of the great problems in this type of research is the number of "lost" cases. Also, frequently the follow-up periods are so short that one questions the significance of changes observed. Therefore, it is notable here that a high percentage of the cases were subsequently located and that the time span is considerable. The manner in which the survey study can be converted to an experimental type-analysis is also well demonstrated.

Follow-Up of Children with Atypical Development

Janet L. Brown

In our long-term study at the Putnam Children's Center of preschool children with atypical development, we have realized that careful history-taking during the diagnostic or treatment period, and repeated follow-ups after treatment termina-

From Janet L. Brown, "Follow-Up of Children with Atypical Development (Infantile Psychosis)," *American Journal of Orthopsychiatry*, XXXIII (October 1963), 855–861. Reprinted by permission.

Janet L. Brown is Psychologist for the James Jackson Putnam Children's Center, Boston, Mass.

tion, help immeasurably to illuminate our understanding of the etiology of the psychotic process and the multifold adaptive and defensive functions employed by a child in his struggle toward psychological equilibrium. . . .

PROCEDURE

In the follow-up study reported here, information is summarized on the 105 boys and 31 girls who were at least nine years old on January 1, 1962, and who had been diagnosed at the Children's Center during their preschool years as having atypical development (infantile psychosis). Most of these children received psychiatric treatment, either at the Children's Center or elsewhere after diagnosis, but the follow-up also included those with no treatment.

Diagnostic evaluation at the time of original referral usually included two individual play sessions with a psychiatrist, two nursery school sessions, and psychological and neurological examination of the child, as well as interviews with both parents. The diagnosis was made during an intake conference that pooled the diagnostic impressions of the various team members, and was periodically re-evaluated for those cases that continued in treatment.

The optimal follow-up method was that of psychiatric evaluation of the child, either at the Children's Center or through a report from a therapist if one was currently working with the child. An evaluation at the Children's Center usually included both a psychiatric session and psychological testing of the child, as well as interviews with the parents. When distance, institutionalization or parental reluctance made a Center visit impossible, information was obtained in other ways. Forms were sent to schools and institutions requesting information on diagnosis, academic status and IQ, areas of special competence, capacity for self-care, quality of interpersonal relationships, special areas of disturbance and prognosis. Some information was also obtained from telephone calls or letters from parents and, in two cases, from telephone conversations with the children themselves.

RESULTS

Type of follow-up information. Table 1 indicates the type of information obtained on the follow-up of these 136 children. If more than one type was obtained, the case was listed under the more complete category, for example, psychiatric evaluation rather than parental report. Information

TABLE 1

TYPE OF FOLLOW-UP INFORMATION	NUMBER	PERCENTAGE
Psychiatric evaluation	61	47
School or institution report	39	30
Conversation with parent	21	16
Letter from parent	6	5
Phone conversation with child	2	2
	129	100
No information	7	5
	136	

was obtained on all but 5 per cent of the children; for almost one-half (47 per cent), the data was in the form of psychiatric assessment.

Age of the children at most recent follow-up. Table 2 presents the age of the

TABLE 2

AGE AT MOST RECENT REPORT	NUMBER	PERCENTAGE
7–10	32	25
10–13	34	26
13–16	30	23
16–19	23	18
19–22	10	8
	129	100

children during our most recent follow-up, before January 1, 1962, when they were at least nine years old. Because the services of the Center have expanded in recent years, there are more younger children. In addition, increasing sophistication on the part of pediatricians, nursery school teachers and parents has also contributed to an earlier referral of children for psychiatric evaluation, so the Center now evaluates many children of preschool age who formerly either were considered retarded or did not become problems to society until school age. With the exception of one boy in the Armed Services at the time of follow-up, all children were in a school or institution setting. None were working full time or married.

Type of school. Schools were divided

into six groups: (1) regular schools, both public and private, not specifically for emotionally disturbed or retarded children; (2) special classes in the public school system for retarded children; (3) private schools for retarded children; (4) private schools for emotionally disturbed children; (5) custodial institutions for retarded children; and (6) custodial institutions for mentally disturbed children. Table 3 presents the

TABLE 3

TYPE OF SCHOOL	NUMBER	PERCENTAGE
Regular schools	46	36
Special class, public school	14	11
Schools for retarded	17	13
Schools for disturbed	10	8
Institutions for retarded	22	17
Institutions for disturbed	12	9
At home, no school	7	6
	128	100

distribution of cases in this breakdown. It also includes a few children who were living at home but not attending any school.

More than one-third of the children (36 per cent) were receiving their schooling through normal educational channels. The low figure for the number of children in a therapeutic residential setting (8 per cent) probably is influenced by the high cost of such treatment, rather than accurately reflecting the percentage of children for whom this would have been the program of choice. (At the time of this follow-up, special classes for emotionally disturbed children in the public school system had not yet been initiated in Massachusetts.) Nevertheless, it is striking that, of the 41 children who were not in regular school, 31 or 76 per cent were in programs for retarded children. Even of those requiring custodial care, almost twice as many were in institutions for the retarded as were in state hospitals for the mentally disturbed, which implies, at the least, that they were relatively free of gross behavior disturbances.

Level of formal learning. The children were rated on four levels of formal learning: (1) up to, or close to, their age level; (2) somewhat retarded; (3) very retarded; and (4) no formal learning, that is, no ability to deal with letters and numbers in a conventional way. Table 4 presents the results of this grouping.

TABLE 4

LEVEL OF FORMAL LEARNING	NUMBER	PERCENTAGE
Up to, or close to age	47	37
Somewhat retarded	28	22
Markedly retarded	18	14
No formal learning	34	27
	127	100

It can be seen that about three-fifths (59 per cent) of the children seemed to be absorbing enough formal learning to function as adults in our society.

Psychological adjustment. Six categories were used to rate emotional adjustment:

1. The child appears within normal limits to an untrained observer. Although these children might be assessed in psychiatric interviews as somewhat disturbed, they were accepted by parents and peers as being "like other children."

2. The child appears neurotic, with apparent limitations such as obvious obsessive-compulsive defenses, but relates in a nonbizarre way.

3. The child is poorly related to people and appears schizoid, but otherwise functions fairly well, especially in relation to formal learning and the physical environment.

4. The child functions on a limited level in a protected environment, but socialized behavior such as toilet training is stable and speech is present.

5. The child functions on a preschool level, but with some socialized behavior.

6. The child is completely uneducable, and has no object discrimination, socialized behavior or speech.

Groups 1 through 3 included those children who, on the whole, were not institutionalized, and who might be expected to maintain themselves within society, while groups 4 through 6 would need custodial or semicustodial care. Such assessment, of course, was not stable for any one child. Children in therapy or in a benign environment might develop increasing integration and ego skills, passing from a 3 to a 2 or even a 1 rating. Occasionally, children in custodial care would respond to the special devotion of an attendant and, after years of stagnation, begin to acquire socialized behavior and the rudiments of formal learning. On the other hand, the stresses of puberty and adolescence, or the uncertainty of the future after completion of high school, precipitated such crises in some children that protective care was suddenly mandatory. These ratings, then, merely catch a moment in a dynamic process. In addition, they were obviously more subjective than those for type of school or amount of formal learning, especially if they were made on the basis of school reports or information from parents, who often tended to minimize or maximize progress. Table 5 presents the results of this gross assessment of level of functioning.

TABLE 5

PSYCHOLOGICAL ADJUSTMENT	NUMBER	PERCENTAGE
1. Appears "normal"	7	5
2. Appears "neurotic"	30	23
3. Appears "schizoid"	34	26
4. Protected environment, but object relation	25	20
5. Minimal, but stable, socialized behavior	24	19
6. No socialized behavior, no object relation	9	7
	129	100

It is thus apparent that well over half the children (54 per cent) functioned within society, though few of them appeared symptom-free, even to the casual observer.

Factors affecting outcome. As already mentioned, detailed analysis of factors contributing to favorable or unfavorable outcomes has barely begun. In an earlier paper I demonstrated that severity of illness at the time of original diagnosis, as measured symptomatically, was of utmost importance in predicting outcome statistically. Individual exceptions do occur of course. Other variables considered, some of statistical significance, are discussed below.

a. *Treatment vs. no treatment.* For the purpose of this paper, "treatment" was defined as six or more months of individual psychiatric sessions, or one year or more of participation in a small group setting with specially trained, psychiatrically oriented personnel. Medication was seldom used as part of the therapeutic strategy at the Children's Center, and shock or insulin treatment was totally absent. A legitimate comparison between the outcomes for the treated and untreated children cannot really be made from our sample to date, since the number in the untreated group is quite small. In the early days of the Children's Center, nonacceptance for treatment was usually on the basis of age or geographic location. Such children often found treatment elsewhere. More recently, the Center has been more selective in accepting for treatment only those children who are felt to have a reasonably good prognosis. This, of course, immediately creates a bias in favor of a better outcome for the treated cases. Briefly, of the 129 cases for whom follow-up information was available, 94 had been treated at the Children's Center, 15 had been treated elsewhere and 20 were untreated. Five of these had not been accepted for treatment because of poor prognosis, and all five were currently in custodial care. Of the remaining 15 children, none achieved a "normal" or 1 rating, though four were assessed as "neurotic" and five as "schizoid," thus showing ability to maintain themselves to some degree without treatment.

b. *Effect of additional internal or external handicaps.* A number of the children with atypical development also had other

TABLE 6

COMPARISON OF OUTCOME OF "PURE" CASES
WITH THOSE WITH HANDICAPS

	"PURE" CASES		HANDICAPPED	
ADJUSTMENT RATING	NUMBER	PERCENTAGE	NUMBER	PERCENTAGE
1. Appears "normal"	5	5	2	7
2. Appears "neurotic"	26	25	4	15
3. Appears "schizoid"	26	25	8	30
4. Protected environment	21	21	4	15
5. Some socialization	18	18	6	22
6. No socialization	6	6	3	11
	102	100	27	100

handicaps. These included (and, of course, may have contributed to the atypical development) the presence of an overtly psychotic parent (12 cases), evidence of neurological abnormality, other than abnormal EEG, (6 cases) or a physical handicap such as poor eyesight or hearing (5 cases). In addition, four children had multiple handicaps. Adjustment ratings of these children, as compared with the remaining "pure" cases, are given in Table 6, which suggests that the presence of additional handicaps does mitigate against a positive outcome (30 vs. 22 per cent in "1" and "2" and 24 vs. 34 per cent in "5" and "6"), although the difference in outcome between the pure and handicapped cases is not statistically significant.

 c. *EEG data*. EEG records were available for 68 of the 129 children; 36 of these had been read as abnormal, though many deviations were considered of minor im-

TABLE 7

PSYCHOLOGICAL ADJUSTMENT
AS A FUNCTION OF EEG
RECORDS*

	ABNORMAL EEG	NORMAL EEG
In society, rating 1, 2 or 3	10	16
Out of society, rating 4, 5 or 6	26	16

* $X^2 = 3.61$. One-tailed $p = <.05$.

portance. Grossly, 14 showed spike waves, 7 showed asymmetry, 5 showed abnormal slowing, 4 were dysrhythmic and, for the remaining 6, records were unspecific as to type. The outcome for the children with abnormal EEG records is compared to that of those with normal EEGs in Table 7. The difference is significant. With one exception, all children with grossly abnormal records (spike waves) were in custodial care.

DISCUSSION

 The current status of a group of children who were diagnosed during their preschool years as having atypical development (infantile psychosis) has been summarized. Our group probably includes a majority of the children so diagnosed in preschool years in the Greater Boston area since 1945. Our concern is to keep in touch with the total group and eventually to obtain a "natural history" of the process of atypical development. This static statistical summary is only the beginning of a series of the snapshots required for an understanding of the dynamic process.

 The essential characteristic of atypical development was . . . "ego fragmentation," in that the ego of the developing child fails to integrate and synthesize experience in a harmonious way due to a particular combination of fusion and detachment in the parent-child relationship. The focus on the specific parent-child interaction and the specific emotional disorder it produces distinguishes atypical development from other deviant developmental conditions. . . .

Although every effort was made to use the diagnostic label of "atypical development" with specificity, it is possible that our group contains some children who might have been congenitally retarded or brain-damaged. Nevertheless, all of them presented severe disturbances in object relations during the preschool years. Much continuing research is needed to determine whether the varieties in the presenting picture, which have previously been shown to correlate highly with later status, reflect variations in the child's vulnerability as well as parental capacity. The problem is further complicated by the fact that recent research has suggested that autonomic and EEG functioning reflect not only current changes in the external environment but previous experience with pathological environments.

Our results do indicate a wide range of functioning in later years. We feel moderate optimism regarding the ability of some of the children to find defensive and adaptive means for coping with their illness, particularly the "pure cases" not complicated by obvious neurological or physical handicaps or grossly abnormal EEGs. On the other hand, some children made little or no progress even after years of devoted therapeutic endeavor, and therefore seemed essentially unresponsive to current outpatient treatment techniques. Much more microscopic research is necessary to illuminate the factors in individual cases that seemed to influence outcome, and especially to trace those children for whom the outcome was markedly different, either positively or negatively, from what might have been expected during our early contacts in the preschool period.

The latter pair of researches in this subsection on systematic recording illustrate both the overall and the specific follow-up examinations into the consequences of school and treatment. You will note that the so-called experimental variable—what was done with the children—is neither specific nor differential. It is an experience presumed to have happened to all of the children, although the impact was not identical. Since most teachers work with an assortment of children with various pathologies, the differential expectations for various types is a matter of great interest.

From Rubin's report, we next learn many things about the children in the overall programs—ages, lengths of stay, abilities, etc. Both educational and psychiatric diagnostic information is given. We know where the children were placed. The year-by-year material (Table 4) enables us to see that although disposition varies with time, most children were returned to their homes. Rubin's tables, each a complete unit in itself, do not tell us the relationship between diagnosis and outcome. However, Rubin explains something about it in his discussion, which ends with the need for more research.

The pattern involved in Rubin's work is typical of many researches. Although collection and tabulation of base-line information is necessary in all fields, special education is still too new to contain an adequate amount of even this fundamental type of information.

Special Education in a Psychiatric Hospital

Eli Z. Rubin

The majority of young emotionally disturbed children who come into residential settings for treatment have shown a history of maladjustment in school. These children have demonstrated their inability to adjust behaviorally or to learn under the usual circumstances of the public school. The majority are educationally retarded. They have failed to benefit from the ordinary methods of instruction and show either specific or general deficiencies in one or more significant areas of learning. This finding is even more startling when one considers that these children are generally of average or better than average intelligence. More often than not their achievement is uneven. Some children may show adequate progress in arithmetic, with an ability to handle simpler number combinations and concepts, but show an inability to read beyond the primary level. Others may show specific deficits, such as inability to grasp concepts for number work and similar difficulty in gaining meaning from their reading work or in understanding fundamental concepts involved in language skills.

There are other children whose academic achievement is consistent with their age expectancy, but who have failed to adjust to the social situation of the school setting. These are the children with behavior problems, who manifest poor attentiveness, short spans of concentration, excessive motor restlessness, day-dreaming, withdrawal, fear, impulsive aggressive behavior, temper outbursts, or other forms of immature reactions. These youngsters, because of their behavior disturbance, eventually become disturbed in their learning

From Eli Z. Rubin, "Special Education in a Psychiatric Hospital," *Exceptional Children*, XIX (December 1962), 184–190. Reprinted with permission of *Exceptional Children* and the author.

Eli Z. Rubin is Director of Rehabilitation, Lafayette Clinic, Detroit, Michigan.

progress. In addition, they are often considered detrimental to the other youngsters in the classroom and there is the desire on the part of teachers and administrators to exclude or segregate them. While segregation is often beneficial to the other members of the class, it does not contribute to social improvement or learning progress of the disturbed child without the addition of some special program. . . .

A residential treatment setting incorporating a special school program within its own institution has much to contribute toward the formulation of rationale and guidelines in the establishment of educational programs that may prove beneficial to emotionally disturbed children. The interrelationship between the emotional problem and learning difficulties indicates the need for modifications of the school situation and the approach to learning if educational progress is to be furthered. The experience of many of these centers, including the Lafayette Clinic school department, suggests that even with little time for school per day, children with previous histories of educational failure alter their attitudes toward school and can make considerable progress. This is often achieved by children having one or two hours of academic schooling per day. There is a need to demonstrate this observed occurrence through careful measurement. However, it is equally important to formulate a rationale to account for these clinically observed results. By making explicit a rationale for the operation of a school department within a clinical setting and observing the progress of children in this department, we may develop a clearer understanding of the dynamics of school failure and the relation of schooling to treatment of emotional disturbances in children. It is hoped that this will lead to the development of special education classes for the emotionally disturbed child based on assumptions and principles which stem from an understanding of his problems.

PROBLEMS OF EDUCATIONAL PLANNING

Impairment of ego functioning by overwhelming anxiety is a consistent finding in severely disturbed children who require hospitalization. These children are unable to sustain attention on tasks for any appreciable length of time. They are easily distracted by ideas, fantasies, or feelings from within. They are quick to respond to stimulating events or unusual happenings around them. They are quick to anticipate failure, and through their fantasies and fears tend to misinterpret the attitudes of teachers and others, expecting undue pressure or rejection for not achieving at some expected level. Motivation to learn and interest in school are markedly low. Those children whose anxiety has been kept at a high level have chronically failed to develop and practice cognitive functions important in perceptual discrimination, thus creating reading problems and interference with comprehension of meaningful material. In some children, motor control is impaired, showing up in poor handwriting, writing reversals, or in impulsive and restless motor movements. In some cases there is a fundamental lack of basic skills in academic areas, making adequate adjustment or progress in a regular class exceedingly difficult. Detailed analysis of the child's functional assets and limitations must be undertaken early for proper educational planning. Any assessment of value must point to an appropriate remedial program. Clinical psychiatric diagnoses do not provide sufficient precision to allow for adequate school planning. Investigations are being undertaken to provide a classification that will be more meaningful for educational planning.

One of the first goals of the institutional setting is to provide an atmosphere that is supportive to the child's impaired ego functioning, weakened by excessive stress placed upon him by frustrations within his prior environment. Reduction of overstimulating situations by removal from home and community is the initial step in this direction. The child is then provided substitute parental figures who are more neutral and objective in their response to his behavior, reducing the reinforcement of maladaptive patterns of response. Another ego-supportive technique within the total milieu is the provision of planned daily routines which are consistently followed and predictable. The child can begin to rely upon certain events and happenings from one day to the next which are unaltered by his own behavior and allow him to form a relationship to the unit, thus providing the first step toward relating to individual members of the staff. Opportunities for pleasure through tension release in games and play contribute to the security the child feels within the institution. Careful planning of peer group interactions further protects the child from being overwhelmed by those superior to him in size, strength, or ability, and from opportunities to lose control over his aggressive feelings directed at those less strong or capable than he. Finally, when the child is given an opportunity to learn whatever basic skills he lacks, and to practice at whatever level he happens to be, he can begin to alter his self-picture of unacceptability to others or feeling of helplessness at being unable to master frustrations of everyday life. The development of those skills which are necessary in participating with other children in play and school achievement is a significant contribution to increased emotional stability.

A child's inability to adjust to the public school environment is often a major factor determining the need for hospitalization. In many instances the school failure is symptomatic of the child's impaired ability to cope with reality situations in an open environment demanding independent functioning. In some instances failure at school can be seen as leading to further ego decline, resulting in secondary symptoms that tend to fix the disturbance and preclude improvement, even with treatment on an out-patient basis.

For other children the regular school situation with its social complexities and achievement requirements overtaxes the intellectual, conceptual or discriminative abilities to such a degree as to constitute an overwhelming stress situation. The child cannot find satisfactions for basic needs for acceptance, status, reward, or identity through school achievement and so may take on those methods of achieving his ends which are available to his characterological makeup. For some children, the situation is completely overwhelming and they can only avoid the stress through daydreaming, inattentiveness, withdrawal, or even autistic behavior. Others may attempt to seek their satisfactions through attention-getting devices, such as clowning, teasing, or provocative behavior. For others, the only solution lies in avoiding the demand for more independent behavior and retreating to immature methods of response, including negativism, stubbornness, clinging, or temper outbursts.

THE LAFAYETTE CLINIC SCHOOL

The Lafayette Clinic is a 146-bed psychiatric hospital, the research and training unit of the State Department of Mental Health affiliated with Wayne State University. It provides diagnostic and short-term intensive inpatient treatment services for children, adolescents, and adults who show a wide variety of psychiatric conditions. Outpatient diagnostic and treatment services are also provided. One of the primary aims of this unit is to conduct research in the field of mental health that will contribute to the understanding of mental illness and to attempt to develop more effective methods of treatment. Through its service to patients, the clinic provides training for students in a variety of disciplines, including adult and child psychiatry, clinical psychology, psychiatric social work, special education, nursing, occupational therapy and vocational rehabilitation.

The school department is under the Division of Rehabilitation and provides separate but coordinated educational programs for adolescents and for children of elementary school age. Schooling is considered one aspect of the total treatment plan. Special education programs are devised in order to (a) prevent the child from losing ground in his schoolwork; (b) provide those skills that will enhance the opportunity for progress in learning by involving the child in successful academic accomplishment and gratification; (c) contribute to a total therapeutic milieu that is supportive to the individual treatment of the child by supplying satisfactions of the normal emotional and social needs, including the need for achievement and success, for structure, stable relationships and healthy identification; (d) effect a beneficial school placement following discharge through a follow-up program involving close liaison with the staff of the school to which the child returns.

This school department within the clinical setting recognizes and accepts the need for education goals upon which to establish its programs. The Lafayette Clinic school program is designed, in general, to provide an atmosphere that will reduce those conditions which put the child under undue stress and which further contribute to the maintenance of his anxiety at a high level. While in the hospital, the child undergoes many other experiences that help to reduce the effects of externally induced anxiety, such as removal from home, dilution of parental authority, and provision of a planned day.

The school's contribution to the total treatment of the youngster is to provide an atmosphere which is adapted to the capacities and needs of the disturbed child so that he may show progress in learning and gain satisfaction from his progress. In contrast to those goals of the clinical approach, which are aimed at the resolution of the emotional conflict, the educational team orients its techniques and attitudes toward promoting improved attitudes toward school and achievement in learning. Techniques and attitudes applied to each child are planned and directed in accordance with an understanding of his current efficiency level of ego functioning. The teaching staff learns about the child's functioning in a classroom situation as well as from contributions from educational, psychological, and psychiatric examinations.

They recognize that this child comes to the school situation with poor motivation for learning and an accumulation of negative attitudes toward school and school personnel. They are ready to recognize the role of anxiety in disturbing the individual's capacity to take advantage of learning opportunities which, although consistent for his age and intellectual level, may be beyond his capacity to integrate and incorporate. Thus, a school program for each child is planned to provide basic skills where indicated or to give opportunity for successful practice of acquired skills. There is a major emphasis on school conditioning experience for all the children. In graduated steps, the child is exposed to classroom conditions, attitudes and procedures that will allow him to increase his tolerance for the demands made on him by a school situation.

Our children's unit is a short-term intensive treatment unit, providing inpatient clinical services for 22 youngsters between the ages of six and 12. The school department is a major component of the milieu therapy program and is closely coordinated in its planning with the occupational therapy and recreational therapy departments, all of which are within the division of rehabilitation.

Tables 1, 2, 3, and 4 provide some basic descriptive data on 97 youngsters who have been in our school program and have been discharged since the opening of this unit in 1956. These tables reveal that an overwhelming majority (87 percent) of our patients had experienced serious difficulties in school. Twenty-one percent (20 children) had been excluded from school. These results support the concept that rehabilitation must include schooling experience. Table 3 indicates that a wide variety of clinical types are provided treatment. Differences in diagnosis do not appear to preclude grouping together.

Our experiences with those children who have participated in the school department over the past five years have led to the formulations reported here. Educational experience has always played a significant role in the treatment program for the children. The specific programs offered have varied, depending upon the population on hand. However, the current program has evolved over the years. The pattern of groups is determined primarily by the level of educational achievement or readiness for school functioning. Every effort is made to put youngsters together

TABLE 1. PATIENTS DISCHARGED FROM LAFAYETTE CLINIC
1956–60

YEAR	NUMBER	FEMALE	MALE	AVERAGE LOS* (MONTHS)	AVERAGE AGE AT ADMISSION	AVERAGE IQ	IQ RANGE
1956	10	3	7	4.2	10.3	93.3	62–109
1957	26	5	21	7.6	9.1	89.0	68–117
1958	26	10	16	8.0	9.2	88.9	56–115
1959	20	3	17	7.3	9.2	94.0	55–125
1960	15	6	9	10.5	9.2	97.3	56–125
Totals	97	27	70	7.5	9.4	92.5	55–125

* Length of stay

in groups so that (a) the size of the class allows for individualized attention; (b) the grade achievement span is narrow; (c) children's readiness for school is essentially similar; and (d) the group composition will tend to reduce symptomatic behavioral difficulties. This means that children are not grouped by age or psychiatric diagnosis, but rather according to their readiness for school and classroom conditions.

Thus, at the present time the school department offers the following classes which provide educational experience for all but two of our 21 patients:

1. *School Adjustment Group.* This is designed as a small group. Children needing help in getting adjusted or readjusted to the routines of going to school are placed in this group. Educational diagnosis is carried out and each child is continually reviewed for reassignment to other groups. This class also serves as a temporary placement for a youngster whose adjustment in one of the other groups is showing deterioration.

2. *Pre-primary Group.* This is also designed as a small group. The children placed here are those who are beginning first grade work and are ready to learn fundamental skills in reading, numbers, etc. Individualized instruction is provided.

3. *Primary Group.* This is a structured class situation for children with academic skills above the first grade level, but within the primary grades. These are children who are able to read and who show a capacity

TABLE 2. SCHOOL ADJUSTMENT PRIOR TO ADMISSION

Behavior Disturbance	28
Behavior Disturbance and Academic Difficulty	45
Academic Difficulty	11
No School Problem	13
Excluded from School	20
	97

TABLE 3. DISTRIBUTION OF PSYCHIATRIC DIAGNOSES

Adjustment Reaction of Childhood with Behavior Disorder	15
Adjustment Reaction of Childhood with Neurotic Traits	3
Psychoneurotic Conditions	16
Personality Disorder	21
Chronic Brain Syndrome with Psychosis	15
Chronic Brain Syndrome with Behavior Disorder	15
Schizophrenic Reaction	7
Psychotic Reaction	5
	97

to adjust to this kind of school situation. There is a concentration on basic school subjects, although considerable attention is paid to helping the child adjust to the classroom conditions. This group currently has six members, but probably could contain up to 10.

4. *Elementary Group.* This is essen-

TABLE 4. DISPOSITION UPON DISCHARGE

	1956	1957	1958	1959	1960	TOTAL
Home	6	22*	14	11	10	63†
Foster Home	2	1	1	1	0	5
Group Placement	1	0	2	3	4	10
Institutional Care	1	3	9	5	1	19
Totals	10	26	26	20	15	97

* 3 to await placement at Institution
† 1 to await Group Placement

tially the same as the Primary Group, but is geared to those youngsters whose academic skills are at the fourth grade level or above. The setting is structured like regular school and more opportunity for independent functioning is afforded. This group, too, can accommodate a larger number, and at one time did serve 10 youngsters with a variety of psychiatric disturbances.

The results of our total program are promising. A majority (67 percent) of these seriously disturbed and disorganized children have been returned to the community to live in a family type setting, either in their own home or in a foster home. These results are in general agreement with figures reported by other similar hospital units as well as by long term residential treatment centers. The ultimate criterion is, of course, the subsequent adjustment of these children over several years. As yet, the long range results of our school program have not been carefully ascertained. Such a study through follow-up evaluation of post-discharge school adjustment is in progress. Through this we hope to gain considerable knowledge about the impact of our total treatment program upon subsequent school adjustment.

CONTROLLED EXPERIMENTAL WORK

All of the dimensions which characterize research occur in varying degrees. We speak of *controlled experimental work,* but we have already seen that control may be a matter of data selection rather than laboratory type-management. The word *experimental* implies the application of known specifics to given populations. Yet life experiences themselves may occur in a nonrandom fashion that, in essence, makes an experiment. All is relative. However the task of developing painstaking procedures with selected measurement devices is an aspect of research that deserves increasing attention. The precision with which we would like to speak may evade us for many years, and the science of education for the disturbed child requires much more precision than we now have.

The three studies selected as examples here cover different matters. The first by Peterson, Quay and Cameron is an involved research on a complicated subject; the second, by Kitano, is on a very specific element; finally Libaw, Berres, and Coleman contribute one of the few examples in the literature concerned with the methodological problems we face.

Peterson and his associates at the University of Illinois demonstrate the value of a series of related researches with sophisticated statistical methodologies, all contributing to a common goal. Their goal is the investigation of personality adjustment and family background using new approaches to distill out factors from a welter of symptomatic data. Rather than *a priori* decisions, they prefer empirically determined decisions about the nature of maladjustment and family behavior that generates a given pattern.

Their research printed here followed a study[1] that revealed two distinct patterns underlying child-behavior problems. The acting-out syndrome was found to be associated with maladjusted parents who did not control their own emo-

[1] W. C. Becker, D. R. Peterson, L. A. Hellmen, D. J. Shoemaker, and H. C. Quay, "Factors in Parental Behavior and Personality, as Related to Problem Behavior in Children," *Journal of Consulting Psychology,* XXIII, No. 2 (1959), 107–118.

tional life. The second pattern concerned the child with personality difficulties of inferior feelings, sensitivity, and shyness: this was found to result from mal-adjusted-father behavior of thwarting the child. Among other things, the authors point out, this shows the need to give attention to fathers as well as mothers in studying children.

In the study given here, groups of delinquents and nondelinquents were selected for study. Confusion in interpretation, which could have resulted from differences in race, age, and place of residence between the groups, was eliminated by matching. Most factor analytic studies are written in such a manner as to defy understanding by a classroom teacher who has not taken several courses in statistics. Therefore, some aspects of this article may be beyond the general practitioner; but one can grasp the purpose from the opening statement. The statistical procedures are subservient to the problem at hand, and do not dominate the results. One thing to keep in mind with a study of this sort—we can receive from a factor analysis an understanding only as complete as the data put into the computer.

Personality and Background Factors in Juvenile Delinquency

Donald R. Peterson, Herbert C. Quay, and Gordon R. Cameron

Most investigations of personality factors in crime and delinquency have begun with a legally defined sample of offenders, proceeded with various comparisons between that group and a more or less carefully matched group of nonoffenders, and ended with ambiguous results. After reviewing 113 such comparisons, Scheussler and Cressey (1950) stated that "The doubtful validity of many of the obtained differences, as well as the lack of consistency in the combined results, makes it impossible to conclude from these data that criminality and personality elements are associated" (p. 476). Like all negative findings, however, these can be interpreted in at least two ways, viz., as evidence for essential identity between offenders and nonoffenders in respect to personality, or as consequences of methodological failure. We believe the latter interpretation to be more plausible than the first, and submit that the most glaring defects in many previous investigations lie in the gross behavioral heteroge-

From Donald R. Peterson, Herbert C. Quay, and Gordon R. Cameron, "Personality and Background Factors in Juvenile Delinquency as Inferred from Questionnaire Responses," *Journal of Consulting Psychology*, XXIII, No. 5 (1959), 395–399.

neity of legal offenders and inadequacies in the instruments used to examine them. The first condition is likely to lead to serious attenuation of all observed relationships, and to eventuate in a most unimpressive array of low correlations and small differences. The second condition is likely to obscure true relationships beyond all recognition.

As correctives, we propose that greater care be exercised in defining and measuring certain personality traits of empirically demonstrated importance in the predisposition to delinquent activity, and that subsequent research be concentrated upon the origins and consequences of these tendencies, rather than in the direct but premature search for the causes and outcomes of delinquency itself. The response-based inference of constructs which relate to delinquency, the development of progressively more adequate measures of these constructs, and the patient delay of the search for causal antecedents until such steps are taken, is slower and more restrictive than most of the earlier approaches, but it promises a degree of explanatory depth and precision which the older methods can never afford.

The present study is an attempt to define such constructs through the factor analysis of two sets of questionnaire items previously shown to differentiate between delinquents and nondelinquents (Gough & Peterson, 1954; Quay & Peterson, 1958). The initial mode of item selection has guaranteed that these response tendencies have *something* to do with delinquency and, in fact, one of the item sets, comprising the Socialization Scale of the California Psychological Inventory, has displayed a degree of construct validity truly unusual among personality tests (Gough, 1957; Gough & Peterson, 1954; Peterson, Quay, & Anderson, 1959). Inspection of the items, however, reveals a diversity of content and meaning nearly as great as for delinquency itself, and this analysis was undertaken in the belief that factor analysis could lead to the education of a set of reasonably unitary, independent, possibly meaningful constructs that would offer more powerful hypotheses for further research than is provided by the original more heterogeneous measures.

SUBJECTS AND PROCEDURE

In an effort to maximize variance along dimensions of primary concern, both delinquents ($N = 116$) and nondelinquents ($N = 115$) were included in the sample. To minimize variance along at least one irrelevant dimension, the analysis was restricted to data from white subjects (Ss). Delinquents and nondelinquents had been matched in respect to age and place of residence for the purposes of another study (Peterson et al., 1959), the report of which contains more information about the selection of Ss than this one can.

All Ss were given a combined form of two previously developed "delinquency" scales (Gough & Peterson, 1954; Quay & Peterson, 1958), phi coefficients were obtained for all item pairs, and 15 factors extracted by the complete centroid method. Judgments based on Tucker's function and contributions to total variance led to the exclusion of 10 of the factors. The remaining five provide a highly efficient, if not exhaustively sufficient, accommodation of the relationships in the phi matrix.

Rotations were pursued in two ways. First, an orthogonal analytic solution was reached by means of the quartimax routine for the electronic computer (Neuhaus & Wrigley, 1954). This yielded an acceptable but not strikingly impressive solution, in terms of the usual criteria of simple structure. All hyperplanes were significant at the .05 level by Bargmann's (1954) test, but visual inspection of the plots suggested that the solution might be improved somewhat by further shifts. The centroid factors were then rotated to an oblique analytic solution by means of the oblimax routine for the computer, and this was followed by a series of visually directed rotations until a virtually unimprovable solution had been found. All hyperplanes defined by these latter operations were significant far beyond the .001 level. Intercorrelation of loadings, however, demonstrated that the two independent solutions were very closely similar (r's for analogous factors ranged from .89 to .99), and the simplicity and objectivity of the orthogonal quartimax solution led to its choice for presentation here. The factors given below are utterly free of contamination by interpretative bias, offer the simplicity of an orthogonal space, and are, for all practical purposes, equivalent to an oblique solution which is unassailable on the grounds of simple structure.

RESULTS

The combined questionnaire as it was actually administered, the centroid factor matrix, and the rotated factor matrix are reported elsewhere. The factors will be defined here, in order of descending variance, by statement of the items which have loadings of .30 or more. A positive sign for any loading[1] implies that the response "true" is associated with the positive pole of the factor; a negative sign indicates that a "false" response is associated with the positive pole of the factor. Item numbers refer to the variables as they appeared in the

---

[1] [The relative contribution of each component factor—Eds.]

questionnaire as used herein and as deposited with the American Documentation Institute.

Tough, amoral, rebellious qualities are obviously implied by the variables given in Table 1, and these meanings, together with those of impulsiveness, a con-

ysis of the Psychopathic Deviate (*Pd*) scale of the MMPI.

Tendencies toward impulsive action again appear in Factor 2, but the intrapsychic concomitants, and perhaps the dynamic bases, of the behavior are decidedly not psychopathic. Remorse, tension, guilt,

TABLE 1. FACTOR 1: PSYCHOPATHY

NO.	LOAD-ING		NO.	LOAD-ING	
18	64	The only way to settle anything is to lick the guy.	33	43	If somebody does something to me, I always get them back.
31	62	Winning a fight is more fun than anything.	30	42	Most brothers and sisters are more trouble than they are worth.
17	62	The people that run things are usually against me.	32	40	I don't mind lying if I am in bad trouble.
12	61	Cops usually treat you dirty.	70	40	I go out of my way to meet trouble rather than try to escape it.
27	60	If you don't have enough to live on, it's OK to steal.	40	39	I do what I want to, whether anybody likes it or not.
24	54	A lot of times it's fun to be in jail.	14	−38	I would rather be at home when things go wrong.
35	53	The only way to make big money is to steal it.	20	35	I got (or used to get) into a lot of fights in school.
47	52	A person is better off if he doesn't trust anyone.	98	34	I never cared much for school.
34	51	If the cops don't like you, they will get you for anything.	84	33	I have never done any heavy drinking.
46	48	Life usually hands me a pretty raw deal.	19	33	I have run away from home because my folks treated me bad.
22	46	Cops and judges will tell you one thing and do another.	10	32	I'm really too tough a guy to get along with most kids.
21	43	A guy like me hits first and asks questions later.			
6	43	It's dumb to trust older people.			
51	43	I would do almost anything on a dare.			

spicuous distrust of legal and other authority, and an apparent freedom from family ties, led to our designation. Factor meaning seems very close to that of "Unsocialized Aggression," as identified in the work of Jenkins and his colleagues (Hewitt & Jenkins, 1946; Jenkins & Glickman, 1947), and strongly involves the same disregard for public opinion so prominent in the "Psychopathic Personality" dimension which emerged from Comrey's (1958) factor anal-

depression, discouragement—in short, neurotic responses—covary with antisocial activity. The factor bears strong resemblance to a factor labeled "Disturbed Delinquency" by Jenkins and Glickman (1947), and to the "Neuroticism" factor isolated by Comrey (1958).

This is clearly a family background factor. The items are so uniform in meaning that no further discussion is necessary.

Unlike the previous dimensions, Fac-

TABLE 2. FACTOR 2: NEUROTICISM

NO.	LOAD-ING		NO.	LOAD-ING	
58	68	I often feel that I am not getting anywhere in life.	41	39	I get nervous when I have to ask someone for a job.
49	56	Sometimes I used to feel that I would like to leave home.	3	39	Sometimes I feel (or used to feel) that if I could just get away from home, everything would be all right.
67	56	I seem to do things that I regret more often than other people do.			
83	55	I have often gone against my parent's wishes.	22	38	Cops and judges will tell you one thing and do another.
64	54	My parents often disapproved of my friends.	75	37	In school I was sometimes sent to the principal for cutting up.
100	52	I sometimes wanted to run away from home.	4	36	My folks usually blame bad company for the trouble I get into.
94	52	I often feel as though I have done something wrong or wicked.	87	−35	Most of the time I feel happy.
95	51	I don't think I'm quite as happy as others seem to be.	69	34	I have more than my share of things to worry about.
93	48	People often talk about me behind my back.	81	33	It is hard for me to act natural when I am with new people.
101	47	With things going as they are, it's pretty hard to keep up hope of amounting to something.	11	32	It isn't their fault that most guys get into trouble.
68	44	I would rather go without something than ask for a favor.	7	32	My folks have sometimes been in trouble with the law.
42	43	I sometimes feel that I made the wrong choice in my occupation.	28	32	When I was a little kid, I was always doing things my folks told me not to.
63	42	I have very strong likes and dislikes.	96	32	I used to steal sometimes when I was a youngster.
66	40	I often act on the spur of the moment without stopping to think.	74	−30	I have never been in trouble with the law.

tor 4 is difficult to interpret. It was principally the pervasive sense of incompetence and failure which suggested "Inadequacy" as an interpretative label, and the general impression is indeed that of an inability to cope with the problems of a complex world. The meaning of the factor, however, is obscure and our interpretation tentative.

This factor [5] is no easier to interpret than Factor 4. Only three of the items, however, attained very high loadings, and these

all stand in some relationship to a history of conflict with school authority. The title we have tentatively attached implies such a history.

SUMMARY

Research on personality factors in delinquency has long been impeded by the gross behavioral heterogeneity of delinquents, and various inadequacies in the measures used to study them. A factor

TABLE 3.   FACTOR 3: FAMILY DISSENSION

NO.	LOAD-ING		NO.	LOAD-ING	
39	61	My mother and father argue a lot.	65	−39	My home life was always happy.
36	60	My step-father (or step-mother) treats me badly.	56	38	My home life as a child was less peaceful than those of most other people.
104	−49	My home life was always very pleasant.	19	36	I have run away from home because my folks treated me bad.
103	49	I was often punished unfairly as a child.	29	36	I have lived in an orphans' home or a foster home at some time.
99	−46	The members of my family were always very close to each other.			
37	41	My folks yell at us kids a lot.			
13	39	My mother and father have never really been friends of mine.			

TABLE 4.   FACTOR 4: INADEQUACY

NO.	LOAD-ING		NO.	LOAD-ING	
74	−43	I have never been in trouble with the law.	62	34	I hardly ever get excited or thrilled.
2	41	I am behind at least a year in school.	80	31	I enjoy work as much as play.
38	39	I'd quit school now if they would let me.	25	30	My folks move (or used to move) from place to place a lot.
92	38	When I was going to school I played hooky quite often.	44	30	I would have been more successful if people had given me a fair chance.
82	35	When something goes wrong I usually blame myself rather than the other fellow.			

TABLE 5.   FACTOR 5: SCHOLASTIC MALADJUSTMENT

NO.	LOAD-ING		NO.	LOAD-ING	
92	48	When I was going to school I played hooky quite often.	98	33	I never cared much for school.
75	47	In school I was sometimes sent to the principal for cutting up.	96	33	I used to steal sometimes when I was a youngster.
52	47	As a youngster in school I used to give the teachers lots of trouble.	57	−31	I think I am stricter about right and wrong than most people.
76	−34	I keep out of trouble at all costs.	91	30	I have used alcohol excessively.
32	34	I don't mind lying if I am in bad trouble.	83	30	I have often gone against my parents' wishes.

analysis of two questionnaire scales of dem- onstrated effectiveness in differentiating delinquents from nondelinquents was con- ducted in the belief that future research on the origins and consequences of mediating personality tendencies thus defined would lead to greater scientific progress than di- rect investigation of legally defined delin- quency itself. Three personality dimensions and two background factors emerged. The first was characterized by a number of psy- chopathic qualities and was named accord- ingly. In the second factor, impulsive anti- social behavior covaried with expressions of regret, depression, and other negative af- fect. It was interpreted as a neurotic dimen- sion. The third putative personality factor implied a general sense of incompetence and was regarded as an expression of in- adequacy. Of the two background factors, one clearly related to family dissension, and the other seemed, much less clearly, to re- late to a history of difficulty in school.

References

Bargmann, R. "Signifikanzuntersuchungen der einfachen Struktur in der Faktoren- analyse." *Mitteilungsblatt f. math. Statist.*, 1954, Nov., 1–24.

Comrey, A. L. "A Factor Analysis of Items on the MMPI Psychopathic Deviate Scale." *Educ. psychol. Measmt*, 1958, 18, 91–98.

Gough, H. G. *Manual for the California Psy- chological Inventory.* Palo Alto: Consult. Psychologists Press, 1957.

Gough, H. G., and D. R. Peterson. "The Iden- tification and Measurement of Predispo- sitional Factors in Crime and Delin- quency. *J. consult. Psychol.*, 1954, 16, 207–212.

Hewitt, L. E., and R. L. Jenkins. *Fundamental Patterns of Maladjustment: The Dynam- ics of their Origin.* Springfield, Ill.: Green, 1946.

Jenkins, R. L., and Sylvia Glickman. "Patterns of Personality Organization among Delin- quents." *Nerv. Child*, 1947, 6, 329–339.

Neuhaus, J. O., and C. F. Wrigley. "The Quartimax Method: An Analytic Ap- proach to Orthogonal Simple Structure. *Brit. J. statist. Psychol.*, 1954, 7, 81–91.

Peterson, D. R., H. C. Quay, and A. C. Ander- son. "Extending the Construct Validity of a Socialization Scale." *J. consult. Psy- chol.*, 1959, 23, 182.

Quay, H. C., and D. R. Peterson. "A Brief Scale for Juvenile Delinquency." *J. clin. Psy- chol.*, 1958, 14, 139–142.

Scheussler, K. E., and D. R. Cressey. "Personal- ity Characteristics of Criminals." *Amer. J. Sociol.*, 1950, 55, 476–484.

This volume of readings contains several studies in which groups given different treatments are equated; and the resulting differences in performance are attributed to the treatment. For example, Margolin reported (Chapter 6) differ- ential effects from various methods in teaching delinquent boys to read. With such preplanning, it is necessary to equate the groups and carefully control the experimental variable which, in this case, consisted of methods of teaching reading.

It is far more common in the study of disturbed children to examine group differences. For instance, one group may be disturbed and the other normal, or two groups with different types of disturbance may be contrasted. Usually the method is not seen as a variant even though details of the method are not delineated. For example, on the average, disturbed children read less well than normal children and it is presumed, with significant sized groups, that an exami- nation of the methods of teaching reading to each would show them to be alike. But the accuracy of this assumption has not been proved during the years the children have been exposed to special help with reading.

Kitano also makes some assumptions, but he has a rough control for other factors which might make a difference between his groups, such as intelligence and socioeconomic background. Our main interest in using his research as an example is to see what can be learned by very specific attention to a very particular aspect of a large problem—by scrutinizing the types of spelling errors found in the papers of maladjusted children. Such specificity is unusual in our field of total-achievement changes, where large-scale generalizations are the order of the day.

Spelling Errors of Maladjusted Children
Harry H. L. Kitano

Disability in subject matter areas, such as reading and spelling, have been a major target for research. For example, Gates and Russell (1940) have attempted to hypothesize emotional difficulties as possible causes for reading and spelling failures. Bower (1958) has shown that adjustment-class children (also known as emotionally disturbed and behavior-problem children) score significantly lower than regular-class children in reading, arithmetic, and other subject matter areas. The purpose of this paper is to study the quantitative and qualitative errors in spelling between regular- and adjustment-class children.

Logically, it appears that adjustment-class children should make more errors and different types of errors than their regular-class counterparts. Their overall poor adjustment in school (Bower, 1958), lower reading ability (Bower, 1958), and other related factors indicate poorer spelling achievement. These, plus their higher anxiety and rigidity (Kitano, 1958) and poorer ego controls (Kitano, 1958) suggest the following hypotheses: (a) that adjustment-class children will be poorer spellers than regular-class children; (b) that adjustment-class children will make different types of errors than regular-class children.

DEFINITIONS, SAMPLE, AND DELIMITATIONS

Adjustment classes are set up for behavior-problem children in the San Francisco Unified School District. The children

are often referred to as the "emotionally disturbed"; the common underlying symptom is the inability to get along in a regular class assignment. The classes are set up for children who have normal intellectual potential.

The regular-class children in the study were drawn from one school in a lower-middle class area. This roughly corresponds to the socioeconomic status of the adjustment-class group as reported in a previous study (Kitano, 1958). The principal of this school describes her children as being from "fair to poor" in spelling achievement and reports the mean IQ to be around 95. This again roughly corresponds to the IQ level of the adjustment-class group (Kitano, 1958). Therefore, an attempt was made to match the groups in regard to socioeconomic status and IQ through this selection procedure.

The sample consisted of all the fourth, fifth, and sixth grade children from the regular-class group of one school and all the fourth, fifth, and sixth grade children in the adjustment classes. The number in each group was 88; the sample consisted of 176 children.

The spelling words were chosen from Gates' A List of Spelling Difficulties in 3876 Words (1937). Twenty words classified by Gates as being between the 4.6 and 4.9 grade levels were chosen as it was believed that these words would be familiar, yet difficult enough for fourth, fifth, and sixth grade children.

In a paper devoted to spelling errors, the delimitation of the method of classification of such errors is of utmost importance. Spache (1940) reviews the various classifications and suggests various criteria which must be met in order to analyze spelling

From Harry H. L. Kitano, "Refusals and Illegibilities in the Spelling Errors of Maladjusted Children," Journal of Educational Psychology, L, No. 3 (1959), 129–131.

errors. The method of classification used in this research is a combination of the Spache (1940) and Gates and Russell (1940) classifications, modified for the exploration of the hypotheses under investigation. The six types of errors and classifications are listed below:

> Additions and insertions, such as sticke for stick
> Omissions, such as fether for feather
> Phonetic errors, such as wate for wait
> Substitutions and reversals
> Words refused or not completed
> Unrecognizable

All testing was done in December of 1957. The writer gave the spelling test to

class children made significantly more errors through refusals and unrecognizable spelling. There was no significant difference between the groups in omissions.

The regular-class children scored significantly higher on the number of words correct. Of the total number of attempted and legible words, the adjustment-class children missed 52.7%; the regular-class children 17.6%.

DISCUSSION

Causes of spelling errors have been classified into three broad categories by Cole (1936), and Gates and Russell (1940).

TABLE 1. COMPARISON AND SIGNIFICANCE OF TOTAL ERRORS BY GROUPS

	ADJUST-MENT-CLASS ERRORS	REGULAR-CLASS ERRORS	CHI SQUARE	P
Additions	70	110	8.8	.02
Omissions	80	110	4.7	.10
Phonics	70	114	11.5	.01*
Substitutions	161	342	65.0	.01*
Words Refused	616	155	2756.4	.01*
Unrecognizable	312	155	52.9	.01*
Cases	88	88		
Spelling Words	20	20		

* Significant at .01 level.

the regular-class children; the individual adjustment-class teachers gave the test to their own classes.

Coding of the spelling errors was done by the experimenter.

A comparison of the type of errors was made by group, and statistical significance was tested through chi square.

RESULTS

The summary of findings is presented in Table 1. The regular-class children made significantly more errors in additions, phonetics, and substitutions. The adjustment-

The errors include (a) deficiencies within the pupil, (b) difficulties inherent in the English language, and (c) inappropriate methods of teaching.

The errors under the first two categories were explored in the present study. There was no attempt to control or analyze teaching methods.

It is possible to think of errors in additions, omissions, phonetics, and substitutions as being errors primarily due to the difficulty of the English language, or external errors. It is of interest to note that the regular-class children made more external errors than adjustment-class children.

The type *a* errors, or difficulties within the pupil, manifest themselves in errors due to "refusals" and "unrecognizable spelling." Something within the child makes it impossible for the child to try writing the word or to come up with something completely unrecognizable when he does write. It is suggested that the higher anxiety of the adjustment-class child (Kitano, 1958) is one reason for the "refusals" and the unrecognizable spelling. The findings appear to confirm an earlier study by the author (Kitano, 1958) in which adjustment-class children were found to have significantly higher anxiety and rigidity scores than regular-class children. Higher anxious and higher rigid children should be characterized by a refusal to try something new—in this case spelling words—while children with less anxiety and rigidity should feel relatively free to try.

In effect, the high anxiety blocks learning, the high rigidity channels the anxiety into a refusal to attempt or try words, and the rigidity and the refusal to try evidently creates more anxiety. This vicious circle in one specific subject matter area is no doubt repeated over and over again in school and is one probable cause for much of the discharge of anxiety by adjustment-class children through extremely hostile, aggressive behavior.

It is evident that the role of a teacher in an adjustment class is to somehow alleviate some of the excessive anxiety, perhaps by giving praise to those who try, no matter what the result, and to minimize the competitiveness of the normal spelling lesson. Success at a lower level, such as reduced spelling load, longer time intervals for learning, and the minimization of the formalized spelling test can be of possible value towards alleviating some of the anxiety producing situations.

References

Bower, E. M. *A Process for Early Identification of Emotionally Disturbed Children*. Sacramento, Calif.: California State Department of Education, 1958.

Cole, L. *The Elementary School Subjects*. New York: Rinehart, 1936.

Gates, A. I. *The Psychology of Reading and Spelling with Special Reference to Disability*. New York: Columbia Univer. Teachers Coll., 1922.

Gates, A. I. *A List of Spelling Difficulties in 3876 Words*. New York: Columbia Univer. Teachers Coll., 1937.

Gates, A. I., and D. Russell. *Diagnostic and Remedial Spelling Manual*. New York: Columbia Univer. Teachers Coll., 1940.

Kitano, H. *Anxiety and Rigidity in Adjustment-Class Children*. Unpublished doctoral dissertation, Univer. of California, Berkeley, 1958.

Spache, G. "A Critical Analysis of Various Methods of Classifying Spelling Errors." *J. Educ. Psychol.*, 1940, 31, 111–134.

As a final example, Libaw, Berres, and Coleman have given attention to one of the major problems of educational research with disturbed children. They have introduced the concept of using the group as its own control by using each individual case as its own control. Certain shortcomings of the method are admitted. Others might be mentioned, such as the general unevenness of individual growth patterns of children, which makes the accuracy of straight-line prediction doubtful. Also the inadequacy of the instruments used to get the points for the line embody a potential error. However, the procedure offers a technique which many teachers might find worth using to assess the effects of special schooling on pupil progress. The authors also indicate that this procedure holds promise for research on change in other areas, such as the consequences of therapeutic efforts.

Evaluating the Treatment of Learning Difficulties

Frieda Libaw, Frances Berres, and James C. Coleman

Any psychology clinic which offers special treatment services is faced with the problem of evaluating the effectiveness of these services. The staff of the UCLA Psychology Clinic School has felt this responsibility keenly. In this school, special techniques are used in a remedial program designed to help pupils of average or superior intelligence overcome serious learning difficulties—difficulties which have resulted in severe retardation in basic school skills.

Investigators who have attempted to evaluate the success of other programs with similar goals have typically used one of three conventional methods of appraisal: (a) the follow-up type of study in which the attempt is made to ascertain pupil competence in a regular school placement at some specified time after treatment, (b) the control-experimental group comparison type of study in which the improvement made by a treatment group is compared with that of a matched group of non-treated subjects, and (c) the achievement method in which achievement scores before treatment are compared with achievement scores after treatment.

None of these methods has proven entirely satisfactory. The first method suffers from the practical difficulty of keeping track of numbers of subjects over sustained time periods and of determining the influence of experiences intervening between time of termination of treatment and time at which follow-up is undertaken. The second method denies needed services to children in order that they may serve as control subjects; the third method does not take into account individual differences in the severity of initial disability, e.g., the

From Frieda Libaw, Frances Berres, and James C. Coleman, "A New Method for Evaluating the Effectiveness of Treatment of Learning Difficulties," *Journal of Educational Research*, LV (August 1962), 582–584.

relative gain made by a subject suffering from severe learning disability may be much greater than the gain made by a less handicapped subject, even though each of them makes the same objective gain in achievement test scores. The method proposed in this paper avoids these difficulties while at the same time it yields a more meaningful measure of individual achievement.

THE METHOD

The method itself may be considered to consist of six basic steps. These are:

1. Obtaining measures of achievement prior to treatment.

2. Computation of the individual's rate of learning before the start of treatment.

3. Extrapolation, on the basis of this computed rate, to predict achievement after a given time interval.

4. Obtaining a measure of achievement after treatment has been underway for this given interval.

5. Comparison of the predicted measure with the actual measure obtained at a period during or after treatment.

6. Computation of a sign test of the significance of the difference between the predicted and the obtained measures of achievement.

In the application of the method at the Clinic School, these steps take the following form:

1. The measures of achievement prior to the onset of treatment are taken from the scores obtained either on the Stanford Achievement Tests or from the California Achievement Tests administered at the time the pupil enters the Clinic School. Alternate forms of a single test are used throughout.

2. Since selection procedures insure that all Clinic School pupils are of average or superior intelligence, the computation of

the rate of learning is based on the expectation that the pupil should have made normal school progress and that he should be at a grade level commensurate with his chronological age—had it not been for emotional or other factors which interfered with normal learning. Therefore, the rate of learning is computed by dividing the pupil's test score, expressed as a grade-equivalent, by the expected grade-placement for his chronological age. For example, the normally intelligent child of nine should be at the fourth grade level. If his test scores place him at second grade, his rate of learning would be 2 divided by 4, giving a rate of learning of 0.5.

3. An extrapolation is made on the basis of this computed rate to predict achievement after a given time interval. The pupil's expected score after a specified time interval is obtained simply by multiplying rate by time. Thus our hypothetical pupil with the 0.5 learning rate would be expected, after a two-year period, to have increased his achievement score by one year. He could, in other words, be expected to test at the third grade level even if no special treatment had been instituted.

4. The actual grade placement at the end of the specified time interval is obtained by administering an alternate form of the same standardized achievement test that had been given before treatment.

5. The actual scores made by the pupil on these tests are then compared with the scores that could be expected if the learning rate had remained constant. A simple subtraction of the predicted score from the actual score gives the amount of gain or loss in achievement. If, for example, at the end of two years, the student actually scores at the fifth grade level, even though at that time he would still be below expected grade level for his age, he would have made a gain of two years beyond the year's progress that would have been predicted on the basis of his past performance. Moreover, for the two-year period of treatment, his rate of learning would have been 1.5. The ratio of the rate of learning during

treatment to the rate of learning prior to treatment constitutes a measure of the change of rate of learning, presumably contributed by the treatment process. In this instance, the ratio of rates would be equal of 1.5 over 0.5, indicating that the pupil had learned three times as fast during treatment as he had prior to its onset. Obviously, the ratio may also be expressed as a percentage increase in rate. Any ratio greater than 1.0 indicates an increase in rate. Any ratio below 1.0 indicates a decrease. We thus have two obtainable measures for the appraisal of the individual pupil's progress. First is the gain (or loss) in grade-equivalents from predicted to actual measures of achievement. Second is the measure of rate of increase or rate of decrease in learning.

6. The sixth step, the computation of a sign test for determining the significance of differences of predicted to actual achievement, provides a simple and convenient means for appraising the effectiveness of the remedial program as a whole rather than its effect on the individual.

DISCUSSION

The present method permits the assessment of an individual pupil's progress by giving a comparison of his present to his past rate of learning. Since increase in rate of learning is essential if the individual is to overcome his retardation, this comparison provides a meaningful picture of the student's response to treatment and of the specific progress which he, as an individual, is making. It also provides a basis for prognosis in relation to the probable amount and duration of treatment that will be required.

The use of the sign test makes it possible to determine whether an entire group's performance is significantly better after a specified treatment interval. While it is less powerful than parametric tests, it is considered more valid in a clinic setting because it does not rest on any assumptions of normality of distribution or homogeneity of variance in the population, nor does it require that treatment be the same for all members of a group—all of which are required for the legitimate use of t-tests and F-ratios (1, 2). The sign test only requires that both members of a single pair, each assigned to one of the two groups, be directly comparable. Since the proposed method directly compares the scores of the same pupil before and after treatment, each pupil effectively serves as his own control. The matching pairs in each group is maximally accurate for such usually uncontrolled variables as motivation and anxiety, and any distortion due to uncontrolled differential treatment of matched pairs is eliminated.

The proposed method, however, rests on two assumptions which should be explicitly examined. The first of these is that the learning has proceeded at a uniform rate prior to the onset of treatment. Most psychologists would question this assumption, pointing to the evidence of spurts and plateaus in learning curves. However, it should be remembered that the rate of learning used by the present method is computed on the basis of scores made on standardized achievement tests and that these scores represent the operational definition of learning in the present method. Standardization procedures in well-constructed tests adjust grade-level equivalents so that a uniform rate of learning equal to 1.0 will be obtained empirically by the majority of school pupils. They will make one grade-level gain for each year spent in school. Also from another point of view, the assumption of a uniform rate of learning is justified since it represents, in effect, a mean of the learning rates over time and the mean of past performance would appear to be the best single predictive index for performance in the future.

Moreover, there is indication that in pupils with learning disabilities who do not receive treatment, there tends to be a continual decline in the rate of learning when achievement test scores are used as the basis for computation. If this is so, and both logic and inspection of our data indicate

that it is, then the assumption of a uniform rate of learning by the present method will give an underestimate of the pupil's actual progress during or after treatment. If the uniform rate is used in evaluative research, it is legitimate for the researcher to bias results against his hypothesis and for practical purposes, when progress is indicated by the present method, it can be viewed as genuine.

The second assumption underlying the proposed method is not unique to it but is basic to nearly all evaluative research which uses achievement test scores as measures of pupil progress. There is an implicit assumption that the various levels and alternate forms of a standardized achievement test are equated and that no significant practice effects occur in a test-retest program using different forms of the same test. The fact is that the correlations between scores obtained on various forms are not perfect, that practice effects are unknown and unaccounted for and that no scientifically based means exist for appraising the reliability of a test for an individual. There is even less evidence of comparability among various types of achievement tests standardized on different populations and using different types of items to arrive at scores for similarly labeled achievement categories. Careful consideration, therefore, should be given to the reliability and validity of tests of achievement and caution should be exercised in drawing conclusions from the use of this or any method of evaluation which uses test scores as its fundamental data. No method can be better than the measures it employs. However, all methods of evaluation are dependent on some measure of achievement, and the present method is under no greater handicap in this respect than are other methods which use standardized achievement tests for assessing improvement.

The present method recommends itself for use not only for evaluating the effectiveness of remedial treatment in learning difficulties, but also as a research tool in relating personality, task, and procedure variables. It can also be used as a method for assessing the effectiveness of psycho-

therapy or other procedures which are adjunctive to the remedial treatment proper.

SUMMARY

The sophisticated reader learns that research is as much noted for what it does not say as for what it does say. And frequently the implications interest us more than the proven hypotheses.

This chapter has illustrated the methods by which knowledge in our field of special education has advanced. The categorization of research into the four divisions used is, of course, arbitrary. A serious study of any type of research will be of value to the teacher. But he should first learn to distinguish types of evidence in accordance with their particular values.

We repeat that the examples of research you have read here (or in other books of the field) cannot be considered ultimate perfection. Nor are they to be considered as "straw men" for criticism of their all too obvious limitations. They are important as representatives of various research styles and of the progress that has been made in the field to date. As such, they hold intrinsic value for teachers of disturbed children.

There is a time in the professional growth of any teacher when sufficient general theory has been accumulated. Then the paths to professional improvement are two: the intensive supervised study of individual cases; or the study of research and participation in it. It is significant that more and more teachers are becoming involved in research similar to the studies presented in this chapter.

BIBLIOGRAPHY

Alpert, Augusta. "The Treatment of Emotionally Disturbed Children in a Therapeutic Nursery," *American Journal of Orthopsychiatry*, XXV (October 1955), 828–834.

Andrew, Gwen H., and Hilda Lockweek. "Teachers' Evaluations of the Mental Health Status of Their Pupils," *Journal of Educational Research*, XLVII (April 1954), 631–635.

American Council on Education. *Helping Teachers Understand Children*. Washington, D.C.: American Council on Education, 1945. 468 pp.

American Educational Research Association. "The Education of Exceptional Children," *Review of Educational Research*, XXIX, No. 5 (December 1959).

Axline, Virginia Mae. *Play Therapy*. Boston: Houghton Mifflin Company, 1947. 379 pp.

Barbe, Walter B. "Locating Children with Emotional Problems," *Childhood Education*, XXX (November 1953), 127–130.

Beck, Bertram M. "Delinquents in the Classroom," *N.E.A. Journal*, XLV (November 1956), 485–487.

Bender, Lauretta. "Childhood Schizophrenia," *Psychiatric Quarterly*, XXVII (October 1953), 663–681.

Berkowitz, Pearl. "Some Psychophysical Aspects of Mental Illness in Children," *Genetic Psychology Monographs*, LXIII (February 1961), 103–148.

_____, and Esther Rothman. *The Disturbed Child: Recognition and Psychoeducational Theory in the Classroom*. New York: New York University Press, 1960. 198 pp.

_____. "Art Work for the Emotionally Disturbed," *Clearing House*, XXVI (December 1951), 232–234.

_____. "The Dynamics of Need-Acceptance Relationships for the Emotionally Disturbed Child," *Nervous Child*, X (1954) 387–390.

_____. "Language Arts as Personality Projection," *Understand the Child*, XXII (January 27, 1953), 11–15.

_____. "Music for Life Adjustment," *Clearing House*, XXIX (October 1955), 108–111.

Bettelheim, Bruno. *Truants from Life*. Glencoe, Ill.: The Free Press, 1955. 511 pp.

_____. *Love Is Not Enough*. Glencoe, Ill.: The Free Press, 1950. 386 pp.

_____. "The Special School for Emotionally Disturbed Children," 47th Yearbook, *National Society for the Study of Education*, Part I, Chicago, 1948, pp. 145–171.

_____, and Emmy Sylvester. "Milieu Therapy—Indications and Illustrations," *The Psychoanalytic Review*, XXXVI (1949), 54–68.

_____. "A Therapeutic Milieu," *American Journal of Orthopsychiatry*, XVIII (April 1948), 191–206.

_____. "Therapeutic Influence of the Group on the Individual," *American Journal of Psychiatry*, XVII (1947), 684–692.

Billig, Albert L. "Serving the Emotionally Handicapped," *Phi Delta Kappan*, XXXVI (May 1955), 303–304, 308.

Birch, Jack W. "Special Classes and Schools for Maladjusted Children," *Exceptional Children*, XXII (May 1956), 332–337.

Bloomberg, Claire, and Ann Salzman. *Training of Teachers in Application of Mental Health Principles: A Study of Teachers' Classroom Problems and Needs*. Washington, D.C.: School of Psychiatry, 1957.

Board of Education of the City of New York. *Guidance of Children in Elementary Schools*. New York: New York City Board of Education, 1960. Curriculum Bulletin 1955.1956 Series, No. 13. 271 pp.

Bower, Eli M. "Early Identification of Maladjusted School Children," *California Schools,* XXVI (May 5, 1955).

—————. "Emotionally Handicapped Child and the School." *Exceptional Child,* XXVI (January 1960), 232–242.

—————, and J. A. Holmes. "Emotional Factors and Academic Achievement," *Review of Educational Research,* XXIX (December 1959), 529–544.

Bowman, Paul H. "Effects of a Revised School Program on Potential Delinquents," *Annals of the American Academy of Political and Social Sciences,* CCCXXII (March 1959), 53–61.

Buell, Bradley, Paul T. Beisser, and John M. Wedmeyer. "Reorganization to Prevent and Control Disordered Behavior," *Mental Hygiene,* XLII (April 1958), 155–194.

Buswell, Margaret. "The Relationship between the Social Structure of the Classroom and the Academic Success of the Pupils," *Journal of Experimental Education,* XXII (September 1953), 37–52.

Caplan, Gerald. "Mental Health Consultation in Schools," *The Elements of a Community Mental Health Program.* New York: Milbank Memorial Fund, 1956, pp. 77–85.

Chansky, Norman M. "Threat, Anxiety, and Reading Behavior," *Journal of Educational Research,* LI (January 1958), 333–340.

Charny, Israel W. "Communication between Psychotherapist and Teacher in Treatment of the Severely Disturbed Child," *Mental Hygiene,* XLIII (January 1959), 40–47.

Clawson, Arleen. "The Bender Visual Motor Gestalt Test as an Index of Emotional Disturbance in Children," *Journal of Projective Techniques,* XXIII (June 1959), 198–206.

Committee of Public Education of the Group for the Advancement of Psychiatry. *The Psychiatrist in Mental Health Education.* New York: Group for the Advancement of Psychiatry, October 1954. Report No. 35.

Cox, Katherine. "Permissive Atmosphere in an Adjustment School," *Clearing House,* XXX (September 1955), 44–45.

Cruickshank, William M., Frances A. Bentzen, Frederick H. Ratzeburg, and Miriam T. Tannhauser. *A Teaching Method for Brain-Injured and Hyperactive Children.* Syracuse, New York: Syracuse University Press, 1961.

Cunningham, Ruth, and Associates. *Understanding Group Behavior of Boys and Girls.* New York: Teachers College, Columbia University, 1951.   446 pp.

Cutts, Norma E., and Nicholas Moseley. *Teaching the Disorderly Pupil.* New York: Longmans, Green and Co., 1957. 164 pp.

—————. *Practical School Discipline and Mental Hygiene.* Cambridge, Mass: Houghton Mifflin Company, 1941.   324 pp.

—————. "Classroom Teachers Can Help Maladjusted Children," *Exceptional Children,* XV (January 1949), 71–74.

Davis, Allison. *Social Class Influence upon Learning.* Cambridge, Mass.: Harvard University Press, 1958.   100 pp.

Deese, James E., Richard S. Lazarus, and James Keenan. "Anxiety, Anxiety Reduction and Stress in Learning," *Journal of Experimental Psychology,* XLVI (July 1953), 55–61.

Dettelbach, Miriam H. "Criteria for Agency Referral of a Child to a Residential Treatment Center," *American Journal of Orthopsychiatry,* XXV (October 1955), 669–674.

Devereux, George. *Therapeutic Education.* New York: Harper & Brothers, 1956. 435 pp.

Dollard, John, and Neal E. Miller. *Personality and Psychotherapy.* New York: McGraw-Hill Company, 1956.   488 pp.

Driscoll, Gertrude P. *Child Guidance in the Classroom.* New York: Teachers College, Columbia University, 1955.   91 pp.

Dunnett, Ruth. *Art and Child Personality.* London: Methuen, 1948.

Dupont, Henry J. "Emotional Maladjustment and Special Education," *Exceptional Children,* XXIV (April 1957), 10–15.

Eickoff, Louise F. W. "Treatment of Childhood Schizophrenia," *Journal of Mental Sciences,* CI (1955), 399–403.

Ewald, M. O. "Emotionally Disturbed Child in the Classroom." *Education,* LXXVI (October 1955), 69–73.

Felix, Robert V. "Evolution of Community Mental Health Concepts," *The American Journal of Psychiatry,* CXIII (February 1957), 673–690.

Frampton, Merle E., and Elena D. Gall, eds. *Mental and Emotional Deviates and Special Problems.* Vol. III in *Special Education for the Exceptional.* Boston: Porter-Sargent, 1956.

Gallagher, J. Roswell, and Herbert I. Harris. *Emotional Problems of Adolescents.* New York: Oxford University Press, 1958. 174 pp.

Gardner, George E. *Case Studies in Childhood Emotional Disabilities,* Vol. I. New York: American Orthopsychiatric Association, 1953. 368 pp.

Garrison, I. K. "Developing the Potential of Exceptional Children," *Exceptional Children,* XXVI (May 1960), 510.

Gerard, Margaret Wilson. *The Emotionally Disturbed Child.* New York: The Child Welfare League of America, 1955. 168 pp.

Glueck, Sheldon and Eleanor. *Predicting Delinquency and Crime.* Cambridge, Mass.: Harvard University Press, 1959.

Goldberg, Ilsa. "Tutoring as a Method of Psychotherapy in Schizophrenic Children with Reading Disabilities," *Quarterly Journal of Child Behavior,* IV (1952), 273–280.

Goodlad, John I. "Some Effects of Promotion and Nonpromotion upon the Social and Personal Adjustment of Children," *Journal of Exceptional Education,* XXII (June 1954), 301–327.

Graver, Palmer A. "Facilitating the Results of Therapy," *Elementary School Journal,* LVIII (December 1957), 166–169.

Gronlung, Norman E. "Personality Characteristics of Socially Accepted, Socially Neglected and Socially Rejected Junior High School Pupils," *Educational Administration and Supervision,* XLIII (October 1957), 329–338.

——————. "The Relative Ability of Homeroom Teachers and Special-Subject Teachers to Judge the Social Acceptability of Pre-Adolescent Pupils," *Journal of Educational Research,* XLVIII (January 1955).

Gutheil, Emil, et al. *Music and Your Emotions.* New York: Liveright, 1952.

Hannig, Paul B. "Therapy through Control," *Education,* LXXX (December 1959), 201–205.

——————, and Ilse Judas. "Education for the Emotionally Disturbed," *Elementary School Journal,* LIX (November 1958), 90–96.

Harbert, W. K. "Some Results from Specific Techniques in the Use of Music with Exceptional Children," *Music Therapy.* Washington, D.C.: Music Educators National Conference, 1952, Vol. 2, pp. 147–151.

Harper, Louis E., and Benjamin Wright. "Dealing with Emotional Problems in the Classroom," *Elementary School Journal,* LVIII (March 1958), 316–325.

Havighurst, Robert J. "The Hard-to-Reach Adolescent," *School Review,* 66 (1958), 125–134.

——————, and Lindley J. Stiles. "National Policy for Alienated Youth," *Phi Delta Kappan,* XLII (April 1961), 283–291.

Hay, Louis. "A New Guidance Approach to Troubled Children," in *New Steps to Mental Health.* Brooklyn, New York: Brooklyn Council for Social Planning, 1953.

Heck, Arch O. *The Education of Exceptional Children.* New York: McGraw-Hill Book Company, Inc., 1953, pp. 29–43.

Hirschberg, C. "The Role of Education in the Treatment of Emotionally Disturbed Children through Planned Ego Development," *American Journal of Orthopsychiatry*, XXIII (October 1953), 684–690.

Holmes, Jack A. "Emotional Factors and Reading Disabilities," *Reading Teacher*, IX (October 1955), 11–18.

——————. "Personality and Spelling Ability." *University of California Publications in Education*, Vol. 12, No. 4. Berkeley: University of California Press, 1959. 88 pp.

Hunter, Elwood C. "Changes in Teachers' Attitudes towards Children's Behavior over the Last Thirty Years," *Mental Hygiene*, XLI (January 1957), 3–11.

Hymes, James L. *Behavior and Misbehavior*. Englewood Cliffs, New Jersey: Prentice-Hall, 1955.   140 pp.

Jacobson, Stanley, and Christopher Faegre. "Neutralization: A Tool for the Teacher of Disturbed Children," *Exceptional Children*, XXV (February 1959), 243–246.

Jahoda, Marie, *Current Concepts of Positive Mental Health*. New York: Basic Books, Inc., 1958.   136 pp.

Johnson, Orval G. "The Teacher and the Withdrawn Child," *Mental Hygiene*, XL (October 1956), 529–534.

Johnson, Paul E. "Juvenile Delinquency," *Education*, LXXXI (March 1961).   395 pp.

Knapp, Robert H. *Guidance in the Elementary School*. Boston: Allyn and Bacon, Inc., 1959.   394 pp.

Konopka, Giselda. "The Role of the Group in Residential Treatment," *American Journal of Orthopsychiatry*, XXV (October 1955), 679–685.

Kornberg, Leonard. *A Class for Disturbed Children*. New York: Columbia University Press, 1955.   157 pp.

Kramer, E. "Art Therapy at Wiltwyck School," *School Arts*, LVIII (May 1959), 5–8.

Krugman, Morris, ed. *Orthopsychiatry and the School*. New York: American Orthopsychiatric Association, 1958.   264 pp.

Kvaraceus, William C. *Prediction of Maladjustive Behavior*. Proceedings of the 1958 Invitational Conference on Testing Problems. Princeton, New Jersey: Educational Testing Service, 1959, pp. 26–34.

Layne, William S. "Techniques for Handling the Atypical Behavior Problem," *California Journal of Secondary Education*, LI (May 1956), 295–297.

Landy, Edward, "Working with Parents of Troubled Children," *National Education Association Journal*, XLIX (September 1960), 29–31.

Licht, Sidney. *Music in Medicine*. Boston: New England Conservatory of Music, 1946. 132 pp.

Lippman, Hyman S. *Treatment of the Child in Emotional Conflict*. New York: McGraw-Hill Book Company, 1956.   298 pp.

Liss, Edward. *Motivations in Learning, Psychoanalytical Study of the Child*, Vol. X. New York: International Universities Press, 1955, pp. 100–116.

Long, Nicholas, and William C. Morse. "Special Classes for Children with Social and Emotional Problems in Public School," in *Social Maladjustment*, ed. William Wattenberg. Chicago: National Society for the Study of Education, 1965. Chapter 12.

Lunden, Robert W. *An Objective Psychology of Music*. New York: Ronald Press Company, 1953.   303 pp.

Mackie, Romaine, and others. "Teachers of Children Who Are Socially and Emotionally Maladjusted," *Bulletin No. 11*, Washington, D.C., Government Printing Office, 1957.   92 pp.

Mase, Darpel J. "Emotionally Insecure and Disturbed Children," *Childhood Education*, XXXII (January 1956), 218–220.

Mayer, Morris F., and Charlotte M. Wolfenstein. "Diagnostic Criteria for Intramural and Extramural Schooling of Disturbed Children in a Residential Treatment Center," *American Journal of Orthopsychiatry*, XXIV (April 1954), 351–367.

Mayer, Morris. "The Role of Residential Treatment for Children," *American Journal of Orthopsychiatry*, XXV (October 1955), 667–668.

McCandless, Boyd R., and Alfred Castaneda. "Anxiety in Children, School Achievement, and Intelligence," *Child Development*, XXVII (September 1956).

McCorkle, Lloyd W., Albert Elias, and F. Lovell Bixby. *The Highfields Story: An Experimental Treatment Project for Youthful Offenders.* New York: Henry Holt and Co., 1958.

Miller, Walter B. "Juvenile Delinquency," *Education*, LXXXI (March 1961), 389–391.

Mitchell, Lucy Sprague. *Our Children and Our Schools.* New York: Simon and Schuster, Inc., 1950, pp. 3–319.

Moustakis, Clark. *Children in Play Therapy: A Key to Understanding Normal and Disturbed Emotions.* New York: McGraw-Hill Book Co., 1953. 218 pp.

Muuss, Rolf E. "Mental Health Implications of a Preventive Psychiatry Program in the Light of Research Findings," *Marriage and Family*, XXII (May 1960), 150–156.

National Elementary School Principals Association. "Those First School Years Helping Children Develop Emotionally," by Laura K. Eads, *National Elementary Principals Yearbook*, XL (September 1960), 126–135.

National Society for the Study of Education. *Mental Health in Modern Education*, 54th Yearbook, Part II. Chicago: University of Chicago Press, 1955. 397 pp.

Newman, Ruth G. "Acting-Out Boy," *Exceptional Children*, XXII (February 1956), 186–190.

—————. "The Way Back, A Transitional Treatment Phase Where Institutionalized Children Are Placed in Community Schools While Still in Treatment," *American Journal of Orthopsychiatry*, XXX (July 1960), 588–598.

—————. "The Assessment of Progress in the Treatment of Hyper-Aggressive Children with Learning Disturbance Within a School Setting," *American Journal of Orthopsychiatry*, XXIX (July 1959), 633.643.

Pearson, Gerald H. J. *Psychoanalysis and the Education of the Child.* New York: W. W. Norton and Co., 1954. 357 pp.

—————. "A Survey of the Learning Difficulties in Children," *Psychoanalytic Study of the Child*, Vol. VII. New York: International Universities Press, 1952, pp. 322–386.

Pflieger, Elmer F., and Grace L. Weston. *Emotional Adjustment: A Key to Good Citizenship.* Detroit: Wayne University Press, 1953. 152 pp.

Phillips, E. L., and N. G. Haring. "Results from Special Techniques for Teaching Emotionally Disturbed Children," *Exceptional Children*, XXVI (October 1959), 64–67.

Piper, Bertha J., and Dorothy Le Grow. "Tutoring for Behavioral Delinquents," *American Journal of Occupational Therapy*, X (July–August 1956), 147–149.

Plank, Emma N., and Robert Plank. "Emotional Components in Arithmetical Learning as Seen through Autobiographies." *Psychoanalytic Study of the Child*, Vol. IX. New York: International Universities Press, 1964, pp. 274–293.

Price, Claude C., and Ben Strongin. "The Emotionally Disturbed Child in a Residential Treatment Center," *Exceptional Children*, XXIV (December 1957), 160–168.

Punke, Harold H. "Exclusion of Pupils from Public Schools," *Bulletin of the National Association of Secondary School Principals*, XLII (September 1958), 41–59.

Rabinow, Barney. "The Role of the School in Residential Treatment," *American Journal of Orthopsychiatry*, XXV (October 1955), 685–691.

Rabinowitz, Clara. "Socially Deprived Children: I. Therapeutic Work," *Children*, III (January–February 1956), 3–8.

Rashkis, L. L. "Meeting the Reading Needs of Emotionally Disturbed Pupils," *Exceptional Children,* XXIII (March 1957), 272–279.

Redl, Fritz. "Research Needs in the Delinquency Field," *Children,* IV (January 1957), 15–19.

—————, and Stanley Jacobson. "The Emotionally Disturbed," *National Education Association Journal,* XLVII (December 1958), 609–611.

—————, and George Sheviakov. *Discipline for Today's Children.* Washington, D.C.: Association for Supervision and Curriculum Development, National Education Association, 1956.   64 pp.

—————, and David Wineman. *The Aggressive Child.* 2 vol.: *Children Who Hate* and *Controls from Within.* Chicago: The Free Press, 1952.

Resnick, J. "Teacher-Counselor's Role," *Education.* LXXX (December 1959), 206–209.

Rinaldi, James N. "The Important Years: Early Identification and Prevention Programs," *Pathways in Child Guidance,* II (April 1960), 7–8.

Rosenberger, Homer I. "Education for the Emotionally Unstable," *Bulletin of the National Association of Secondary School Principals,* XL (February 1956), 136–148.

Ruzicka, William J. "Effectiveness of Short-Term Group Therapy for High School Students," *American Psychologist,* XIV (July 1959), 343.

Schachter, Norman. "In Lieu of a Special School," *Bulletin of National Association of Secondary School Principals,* XLI (November 1957), 53–60.

Settlage, Calvin F. "The Values of Limits in Child Rearing," *Children,* V (September–October 1958), 175–178.

Shoemaker, Rowena M. *All in Play.* New York: Play School Association, 1958.   97 pp.

Shoobs, Nahum E. and George Goldberg. *Corrective Treatment for Unadjusted Children.* New York: Harper & Brothers, 1952.   240 pp.

Silver, Archie A. "Management of Children with Schizophrenia," *American Journal of Psychotherapy,* IX (April 1955) 196–215.

Smith, Carol C. "Using Films in Group Guidance with Emotionally Disturbed Maladjusted Boys," *Exceptional Children,* XXIV (January 1958), 205–209.

Smith, Louis M. "The Concurrent Validity of Six Personality and Adjustment Tests for Children," *Psychological Monographs: General and Applied,* LXXII, No. 457, 1958.   30 pp.

Smith, D. W. "Schools and the Emotionally Disturbed," *Education,* LXXX (December 1959), 195–200.

Stavsky, W. H. "Using the Insights of Psychotherapy in Teaching," *Elementary School Journal,* LVIII (October 1957), 28–35.

Stiles, Frances Smythe. "A Study of Materials and Programs for Developing and Understanding of Behavior at the Elementary School Level," Unpublished Doctoral Dissertation, University of Iowa, 1947.   216 pp.

Stiles, Grace E. "Unmet Needs of Accident-Prone Children," *Safety Education,* XXXVII (March 1958), 19.

Stouffer, George A. W. "Behavior Problems of Children as Identified by Today's Teachers and Compared with those Reported by E. K. Wickman," *Journal of Educational Research,* XLVIII (January 1955), 321–331.

Stullken, E. H. "Chicago's Special School for Special Adjustment," *Federal Probation,* XX (1956), 30–36.

Suttenfield, Virginia. "School Phobia: A Study of Five Cases," *American Journal of Orthopsychiatry,* XXIV (1954), 369–380.

Talbot, Mira. "Panic in School Phobia," *American Journal of Orthopsychiatry,* XXVII (1957), 286–298.

Tallman, I., and S. Levine, "Emotionally Disturbed Children in the Classroom Situation," *Exceptional Children,* XXVII (October 1960), 114–116.

Tamkin, A. S. "Survey of Educational Disability in Emotionally Disturbed Children," *Journal of Educational Research,* LIV (October 1960), 67–69.

Terhune, William B. "Physiological Psychiatry," *American Journal of Psychiatry,* CVI (October 1949).

Tierney, Thomas E. "Psychotherapy and Reading Tutoring: Effect of Psycho-Therapy and Social Adjustment and Reading Instruction on Reading Ability and Personal Adjustment" (Doctor's Thesis). New York University, 1956. 56 pp. Abstract: *Dissertation Abstracts,* XVII (April 1957), 811–812.

Wachstein, Sonia, and Alice Walter. "Troubled Children in a Junior Guidance Class," *Pathways in Child Guidance,* III (October 1960), 6–7.

Waite, D. "Winning a Victory for Emotionally Disturbed Children," *Children,* VII (September 1960), 190–195.

Wall, William D. *Education and Mental Health.* New York: Columbia University Press, 1955.   347 pp.

Washburn, Ruth Wendell. *Children Have Their Reasons.* New York: Appleton Century Crofts, Inc., 1942.   257 pp.

Wattenberg, William W. "Mental Health and Illness," *National Education Association Journal,* XLVIX (September 1960), 17–19.

Whiles, W. H. "Treatment of Maladjusted Children in Hostels," *Journal of Mental Science,* CI (April 1955), 404–412.

Withall, John, and A. Rittenhouse. "Child Therapy—A Frame of Reference," *Exceptional Children,* XXI (January, 1955), 122–126.

Witmer, Helen, ed. "Prevention of Juvenile Delinquency," *The Annals of the American Academy of Political and Social Science,* Vol. 322, March 1959, Philadelphia.

_____, and Ruth Kotinsky. *Personality in the Making.* New York: Harper & Brothers, 1952, pp. 230–272.

Wright, Betty Atwell. "Helping Children Understand Why They Feel as They Do," *National Education Association Journal,* XLVIII (September 1960), 24.

Wyatt, Gertrude L. "The Mental Health Approach to Learning Disorders in Children with Normal or Superior Ability, Treated within a School System." Paper read at the 38th Annual Meeting of the American Orthopsychiatric Association, New York City, 1961.

Zuckerman, George, and Pearl Berkowitz. "Creative Arts with Emotionally Handicapped Children," *Creative Arts for Exceptional Children,* Kansas City, Mo.: 36th Annual Convention of the International Council for Exceptional Children, 1958.